The Making of Assisi

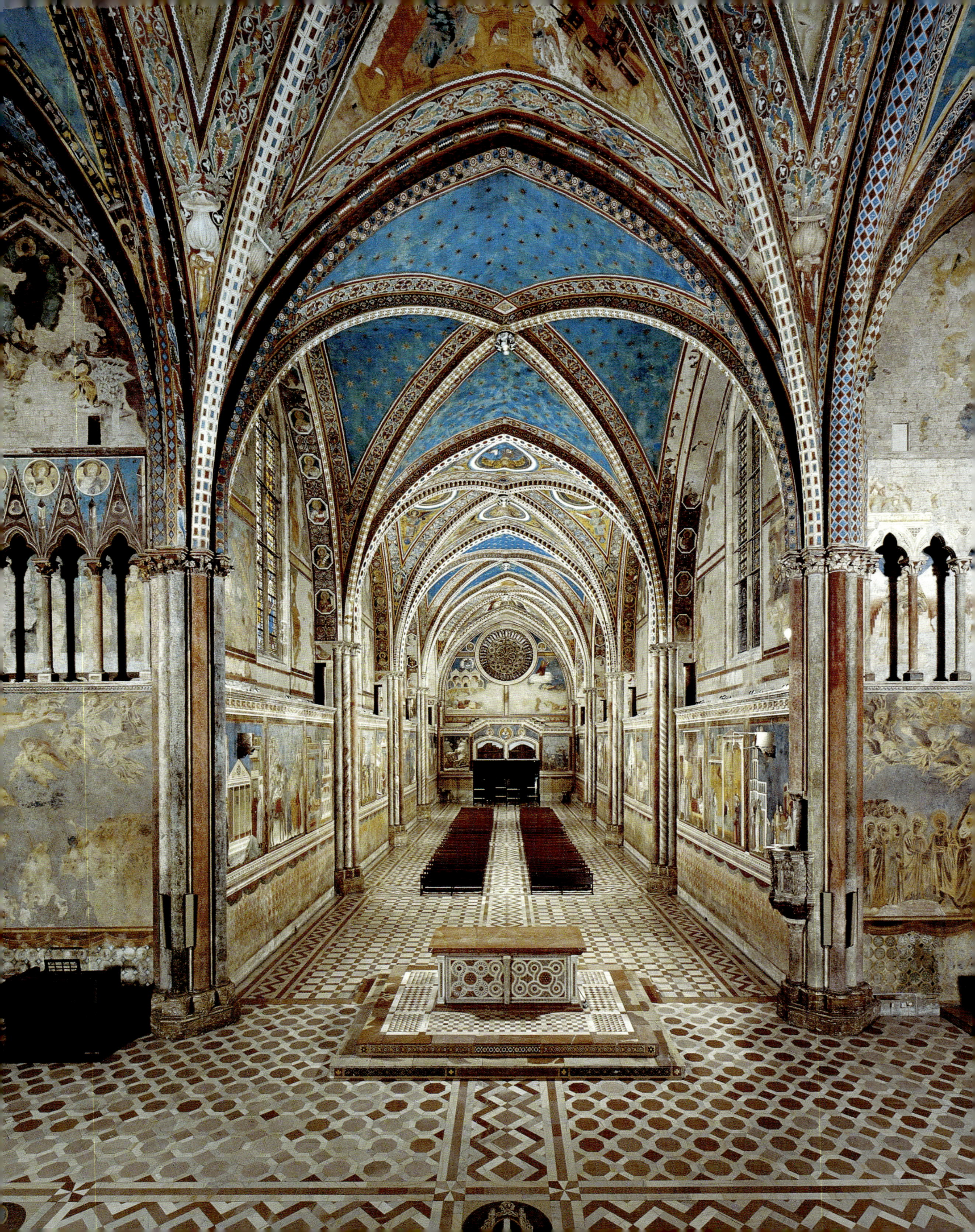

The Making of Assisi

THE POPE, THE FRANCISCANS AND THE PAINTING OF THE BASILICA

Donal Cooper and Janet Robson

YALE UNIVERSITY PRESS ✶ NEW HAVEN AND LONDON

PUBLISHED WITH THE ASSISTANCE OF THE LILA ACHESON WALLACE –
READER'S DIGEST PUBLICATIONS SUBSIDY AT VILLA I TATTI

Designed by Emily Lees
Printed in China

Library of Congress Cataloging-in-Publication Data

Cooper, Donal.
The Making of Assisi : The Pope, the Franciscans and the Painting of the Basilica / Donal Cooper and Janet Robson.
pages cm
Includes bibliographical references and index.
ISBN 978–0–300–19571–2 (cl : alk. paper)
1. Franciscan mural painting and decoration–Italy–Assisi–History–To 1500. 2. Art patronage–Italy–Assisi–History–To 1500.
3. San Francesco (Church : Assisi, Italy) 4. Francis, of Assisi, Saint, 1182–1226–Art. I. Robson, Janet, 1959– II. Title.
ND621.A87C66 2013
751.7'30945651–dc23
2013007069

A catalogue record for this book is available from the British Library

frontispiece Basilica of San Francesco, transepts and nave of the Upper Church (detail of fig. 5).

Contents

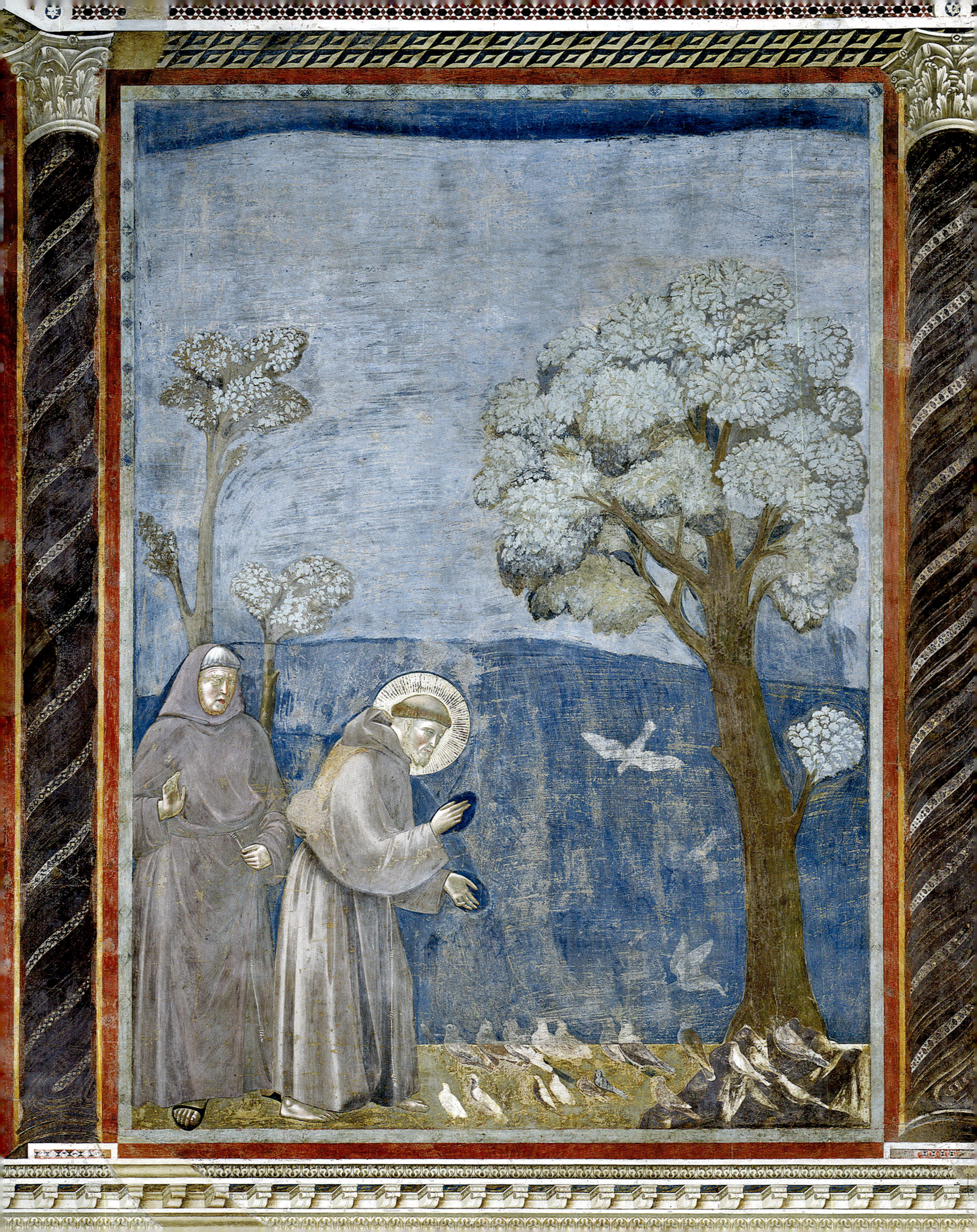

Acknowledgements

This book has been many years in the making and we have accumulated many scholarly debts along the way. The most fundamental is to Joanna Cannon. Her inspiring teaching at the Courtauld Institute of Art shaped us both as art historians, and it was in the cooperative spirit she fostered amongst her doctoral students that our collaboration on Assisi began. The constructive feedback of the wider research community at the Courtauld, in particular the members of Giotto's Circle and professors John Lowden, Paul Hills and Paul Crossley, has refined our ideas and saved us from many errors. Our interdisciplinary approach reflects the scope of the Warburg Institute's peerless library, which has provided the natural London base for our research.

Sections of this book have been presented in draft form at seminars and conferences in the United Kingdom, United States, Italy and Croatia. We are grateful to all the attendees, who always listened attentively, often responded enthusiastically, and sometimes corrected tactfully our mistakes. We have benefited greatly from the generosity of scholars who have shared with us their wisdom, expertise and time: our particular thanks are due to Paul Binski, Sible de Blaauw, Caroline Bruzelius, Andrea De Marchi, Anne Derbes, Dillian Gordon, Amy Neff, Linda Pisani, Mark Sandona, Dominique Thiébaut and Thomas de Wesselow. We owe a special debt to Chiara Frugoni, who kindly read and commented on the complete manuscript prior to publication. Our thinking on Assisi has been enriched by discussion with colleagues at Birkbeck, University of London and the University of Warwick, including Francis Ames-Lewis, Laura Jacobus, Jenny Alexander, Vicky Avery, Louise Campbell, Rosie Dias, Michael Hatt, Karen Lang and Paul Smith. This project has formed the basis for a number of BA, MA and summer school courses that we have taught jointly and independently over the past decade, and we thank all our students at the Courtauld, Warwick and Birkbeck for engaging so wholeheartedly with the Basilica and its art, and for contributing (much more than they perhaps realized) to this book. We thank in turn those who first introduced us as students to the late Middle Ages and the Franciscan Order: David d'Avray at UCL, Gervase Rosser and Miri Rubin at Oxford University.

On many occasions we have benefited from the learning of present-day sons of Saint Francis. Like all scholars of Assisi, we owe a significant debt to the late Padre Gerhard Ruf, who warmly welcomed us on our initial visits to the Sacro Convento; in addition to the numerous citations to his publications, our book is enhanced by images from the

facing page *Preaching to the Birds* (see fig. 169).

photographic archive that Padre Ruf was instrumental in establishing. That archive is now in the able hands of Stefan Diller, who supplied more than half of our photographs with unfailing efficiency and good humour, especially when faced with our eleventh-hour requests for images. The librarians of the Sacro Convento's marvellous Biblioteca, Padre Pasquale Magro and his successor Fra Carlo Bottero, granted essential access to the convent's archives and allowed us to photograph in the Basilica when it was closed to the public. We are grateful to them and to their colleagues, in particular Stefano Cannelli and Francesca Silvestri. The Basilica's chief conservator, Sergio Fusetti, facilitated our research visits to many parts of the Sacro Convento complex, as well as to his *cantiere*. In Rome, Padre Servus Gieben of the Istituto Storico dei Capuccini generously shared his unparalleled knowledge of Franciscan iconography and legend.

Both of us have been extremely lucky in being able to spend extended periods of time in Italy while researching this book. Scholarships at the British School at Rome and the Istituto Universitario Olandese di Storia dell'Arte in Florence were fundamental in the early stages. The Leverhulme Trust has been especially generous in supporting Donal's research in Italy, first via a Study Abroad Studentship and more recently through a Philip Leverhulme Prize. We are grateful to our friends in central Italy for encouragement as this project has edged towards completion: Jim and Maureen Banker in Sansepolcro; Francesco Nevola and DeAnna Maganias in Cortona. La Capriola has always afforded a retreat for meditative contemplation in the Umbrian countryside. In Assisi itself, Elvio Lunghi provided invaluable assistance on the ground (especially with regard to photographs) and shared with us his latest research on the Basilica. In nearby Perugia, Alberto Sartore and Rita Silvestrelli supported Donal's research in many ways and sustained him with memorable cooking, while Lorenzo Donati – with characteristic generosity – provided a tranquil research base in Via degli Olivi. Many of our ideas have been (literally) chewed over during lunches in and around Assisi, and we offer our appreciation to our favourite Umbrian restaurateurs for enhancing the creative process.

Much of this book was written in the serene setting of the Harvard University Center for Italian Renaissance Studies at Villa I Tatti where, thanks to the sponsorship of Hanna Kiel and Deborah Loeb Brice, we held fellowships in successive years (Donal 2009–10 and Janet 2010–11). We are grateful to the Villa's Directors, Joe Connors and Lino Pertile, and to their staff for creating such a conducive scholarly environment. The community and friendships fostered by I Tatti provided both sounding boards and support as our project took shape. In particular, we thank Frances Andrews, Claudia Bolgia, Eve Borsook, Louise Bourdua, Lorenzo Calvelli, Claudia Chierichini, Anne Dunlop, Lisa Kaborycha, Elizabeth Mellyn and Andrea Rizzi. Meanwhile, Andrea Cornia and Jeannie Liu provided Janet with a wonderful place to live and work in Fiesole. Harvard's support did not end with our fellowships: without the generous subvention from the Lila Acheson Wallace – Reader's Digest Publications Subsidy at Villa I Tatti, our illustrations would be more meagre and far less colourful. Additional support for images has come from the Humanities Research Fund at the University of Warwick.

We are especially fortunate in our editor at Yale University Press, Gillian Malpass, without whose commitment and energy this book would simply never have been published in its current form. We are grateful to the three anonymous readers of our manuscript for their perceptive comments and enthusiasm for the project. Daniel Hadas kindly translated Pope Nicholas's bulls and inscriptions into English for the first time. At Warwick, Julia Brown, Claire Nicholls and Maureen Bourne helped with the preparation of proofs and illustrations. The meticulous and perceptive copy-editing of Rosemary Roberts improved the text in countless ways. Martin Brown created the map and diagrams. Over the years we often wondered what this book might eventually look like. Thanks to our designer, Emily Lees, the final volume has surpassed all our expectations and hopefully does some justice to the visual experience of the Upper Church itself.

Finally, although this is a joint project, there are some acknowledgements which can only be made individually.

✳

I owe an immeasurable debt to my wife, Annette, for indulging my obsession with all things Franciscan and for unflagging encouragement throughout the many ups and downs this book has taken. Writing a book on the Upper Church has sometimes felt like an impossible task: without her faith and support, it certainly would have been. My parents, Mary and Jim, have always encouraged my studies, and to them

I owe my interest in art and the past. My final thanks go to little Serena, who arrived in time to see this book appear, but just late enough to allow her father to finish his share of writing it. DC

I consider myself very blessed that both my parents were teachers. My father, Kenneth, taught me to love history and the joy of sharing it, and my mother, Eileen, how to communicate that love to others in the classroom. My deepest regret is that they are no longer around to see this book published, but their boundless faith in me endures. In 1986, when my partner Peter suggested we go on holiday to Assisi, little did he know what a life-changing idea that would turn out to be. He was beside me the first time I stepped inside the Upper Church, and has since accompanied me on every stage of my Assisi adventure. Without him, *lux non esset.* JR

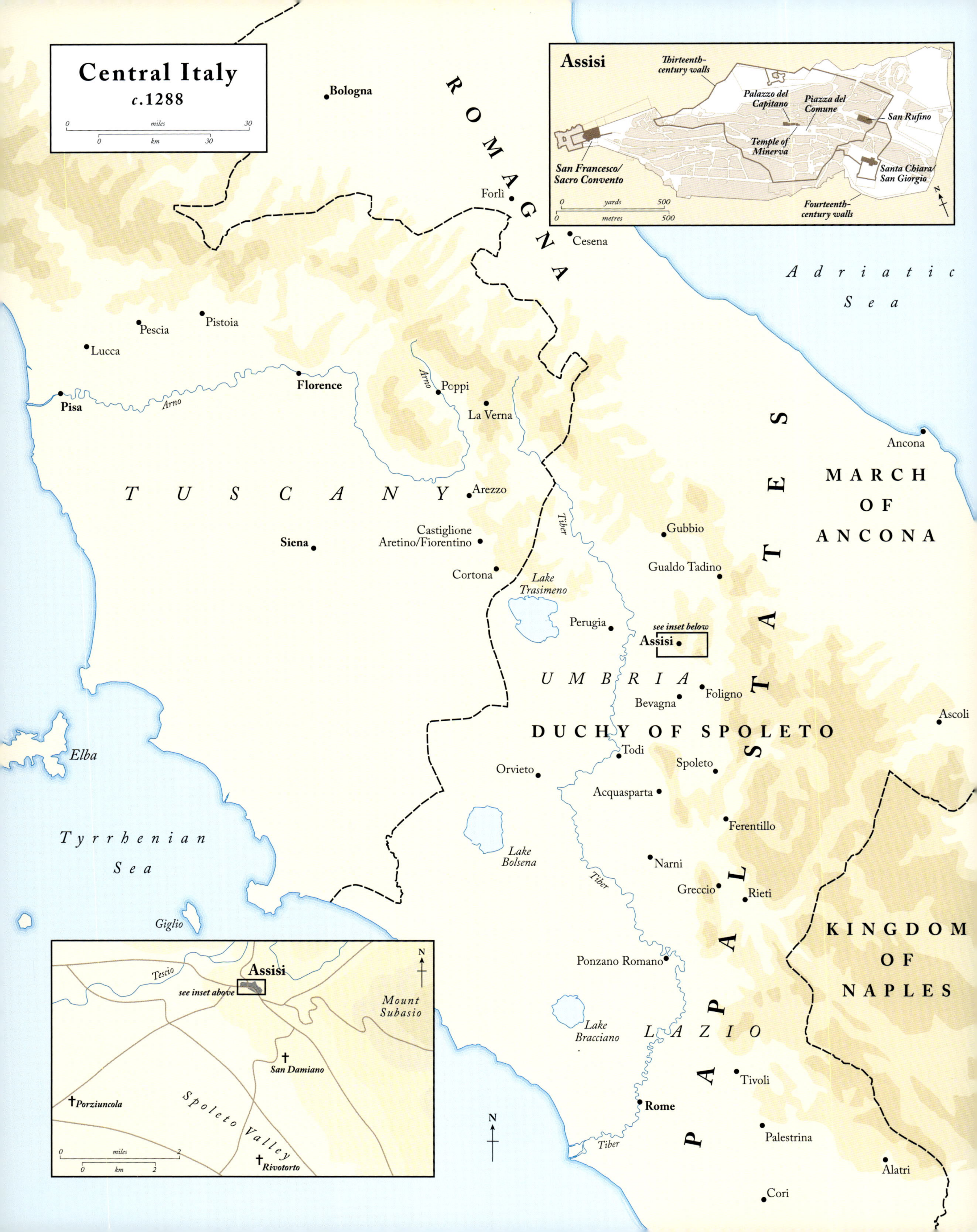

Central Italy
c.1288
0 miles 30
0 km 30
Assisi
Thirteenth-century walls
Palazzo del Capitano
Piazza del Comune
San Rufino
Temple of Minerva
San Francesco/ Sacro Convento
Santa Chiara/ San Giorgio
Fourteenth-century walls
0 yards 500
0 metres 500
N
ROMAGNA
Bologna
Forlì
Cesena
Adriatic Sea
Pescia
Pistoia
Lucca
Florence
Pisa
Arno
Poppi
La Verna
PAPAL STATES
Ancona
MARCH OF ANCONA
TUSCANY
Arezzo
Tiber
Gubbio
Castiglione Aretino/Fiorentino
Siena
Gualdo Tadino
Cortona
Lake Trasimeno
Perugia
see inset below
Assisi
UMBRIA
Foligno
Bevagna
Ascoli
DUCHY OF SPOLETO
Elba
Todi
Spoleto
Orvieto
Acquasparta
Ferentillo
Tyrrhenian Sea
Lake Bolsena
Narni
Greccio
Rieti
Giglio
KINGDOM OF NAPLES
Ponzano Romano
Tescio
see inset above
Mount Subasio
Lake Bracciano
LAZIO
San Damiano
Tivoli
Porziuncola
Spoleto Valley
Rome
Palestrina
0 miles 2
0 km 2
Rivotorto
Alatri
Cori

Note to the Reader

Ground Plan of the Basilica

The orientation of the Basilica of San Francesco is unusual in that its apsidal end points west rather than east. Indeed, in liturgical terms it can be said to be 'occidented' rather than orientated. This may, in part, have been a pragmatic solution to the Basilica's awkward site, on falling ground beyond the city wall at the western end of Assisi. But it also expressed the Basilica's status as a papal foundation, the Upper Church having been designed to accommodate the specific demands of the papal liturgy. The Basilica of San Francesco shares this distinctive reverse alignment with the major papal basilicas in Rome, notably Saint Peter's, Santa Maria Maggiore and Saint John Lateran. In the papal liturgy the priest celebrated Mass standing on the far side of the altar, looking across the *mensa* to face the congregation (*versus populum*). This differed from general liturgical practice during the later Middle Ages, according to which the priest celebrated on the near side of the altar, facing east (*ad orientem*), with his back turned to the congregation. In the Upper Church at Assisi the high altar was sited at the head of the nave with the papal liturgy in mind. The two side altars in the transepts were intended for the ordinary liturgy of the Franciscan community. They were orientated accordingly, set up against the eastern walls of their respective bays, even though this means they face away from the apse.

For clarity, we use the magnetic compass when describing the Basilica's architecture: the façade to the east, the apse and high altar to the west, etc. So the north wall of the nave is the right-hand wall as the viewer faces the high altar and the south wall of the nave is the left-hand wall. Most of the existing literature on Assisi applies the same coordinates.

We number the bays in the nave of the Upper Church from one to four, proceeding from the altar end towards the counter-façade. For a ground plan of the Upper Church, see fig. 47. For a plan of the fresco cycles in the nave of the Upper Church, see fig. 90.

Biblical Texts

Latin texts are taken from the *Biblia sacra vulgata* (Vulgate Bible) and English texts from the Douay–Rheims Catholic Bible, Challoner Revision (DRB), which is a revised, literal translation from the Vulgate. Names of biblical books are anglicized versions of the Latin names used in the Vulgate. Where book names in the Vulgate and DRB substantially differ, both names are given. Psalms are numbered according to the Vulgate and DRB (which differ from Protestant Bibles). Parallel texts of the Vulgate and DRB can be consulted at www.drbo.org.

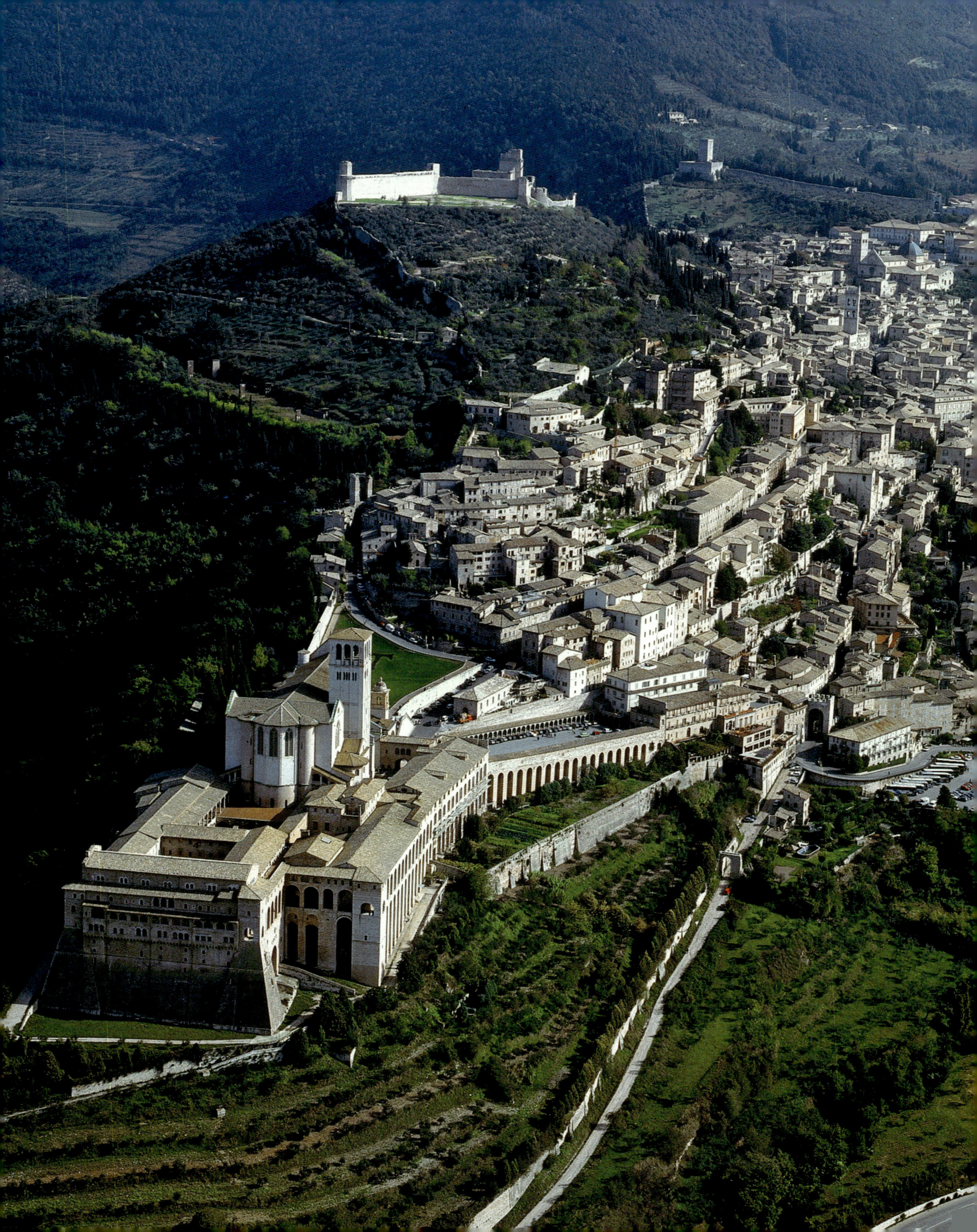

Introduction

In the second half of May 1288 a set of documents arrived at Assisi that would transform the Basilica of San Francesco (figs 1 and 2) and ultimately alter the course of Western art. Even before opening them, the friars of the Sacro Convento (the Franciscan monastery adjoining the Basilica) would have felt the weight of the leaden seals, sewn with hemp to the bottom of the parchments, and recognized their sender. These were papal bulls, dispatched from the curia at Rieti some fifty miles to the south, where they had been composed on 14 and 15 May.[1] There were two different letters, and the friars at Assisi received two copies of each – the four parchments are still preserved in the Sacro Convento's archive.[2] Although their texts differed, the two epistles repeated the same incipit – *Reducentes ad sedulae* – and are known jointly by that name. The bulls were addressed to senior Franciscan officials: the provincial minister of Umbria, the custodian of the Sacro Convento and the minister general of the whole Order. Their lead seals bore the stylized heads of the apostles Peter and Paul on the front (fig. 3), and on the back the inscription 'Nicolaus PP. IIII' (fig. 4): Pope Nicholas IV, born Jerome of Ascoli, elected only three months before and the first Franciscan friar to sit on the throne of Saint Peter.

facing page 1 Aerial view of Assisi from the west, with the Basilica of San Francesco and the Sacro Convento in the foreground.

The Pope's 'Remedy' for Assisi

Nicholas's letters were the catalyst for one of the most ambitious artistic projects of the later Middle Ages, the frescoing of the nave of the Upper Church of San Francesco (fig. 5). As well as narratives from the Old and New Testaments, the decorative scheme would include the most famous set of images in the whole Basilica: the life and miracles of the Order's founder, Saint Francis of Assisi (1182–1226), set out in twenty-eight scenes and known today simply as the 'Saint Francis cycle'. Given that the *Reducentes* bulls are often identified as key documents for the renewal of the Basilica's fabric and architecture at the end of the thirteenth century, it is surprising how rarely they are quoted in the original, and stranger still that they have never before – to our knowledge – been translated into English. Since the two

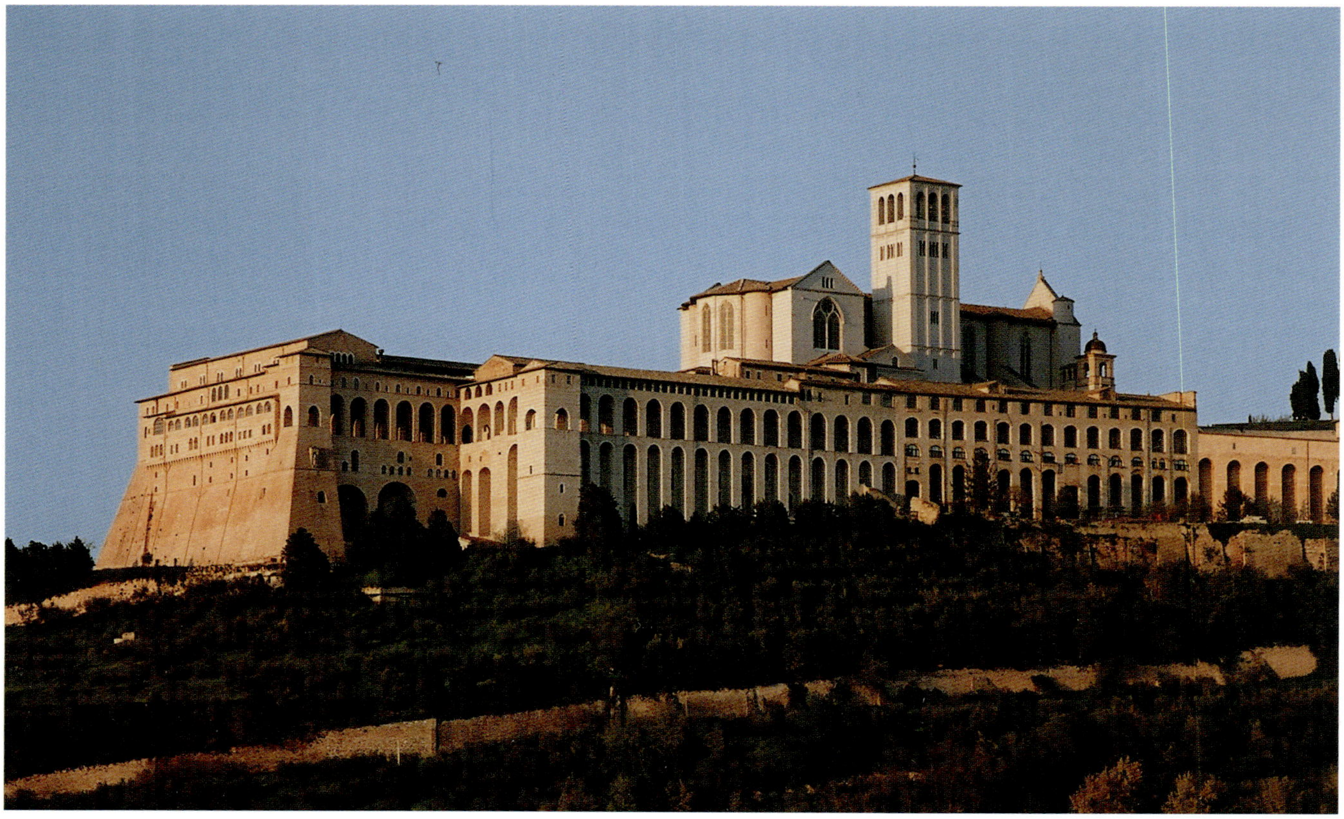

2 View of the Basilica of San Francesco and the Sacro Convento from the south.

letters will run like a thread through this book, Nicholas's words are worth reproducing here in full. His first, shorter, epistle of 14 May addressed the minister of the Order's Umbrian province (which encompassed Assisi) and the custodian of the Sacro Convento:

> To our beloved sons the minister of the province and the custodian of Saint Francis, greetings and apostolic benediction. Noting, with the scrutiny of our diligent consideration, that the ongoing maintenance of the church of the blessed Francis of Assisi is known to be more than a little expensive, and that a countless multitude of brothers of your Order gathers there, where the most glorious body of the saint himself reposes, and also at the church of Santa Maria of the Porziuncola, for reverence of the same saint, and that the city of Assisi is confined in a small space, and is therefore unable to supply the needs of the same brothers, we are led by the eagerness of our paternal care to provide a remedy, to make suitable provision for these things. Since, then, it is our intention that whatever is offered, by way of any money or coin in the churches or in the same places by the Christian faithful, be used for this conservation of the same church of Saint Francis, and the support of the brothers gathering at the aforesaid churches and also of those who dwell there, by [these] apostolic letters we order your discretion to have a care to appoint one or several suitable and faithful persons, which person or persons will seem appropriate to you, and who are not from your Order, in the name of the Roman Church, and acting for her, when and as you will think expedient, and [we also order you to] appoint as deputies in their place another person or persons, not of that same Order, as and when you will see fit, who will carefully collect, and diligently guard and conserve whatever is offered in money or coins, in the churches or aforesaid convents by the Christian faithful, as mentioned above. Given at Rieti, on the second Ides of May, in the first year of our pontificate.[3]

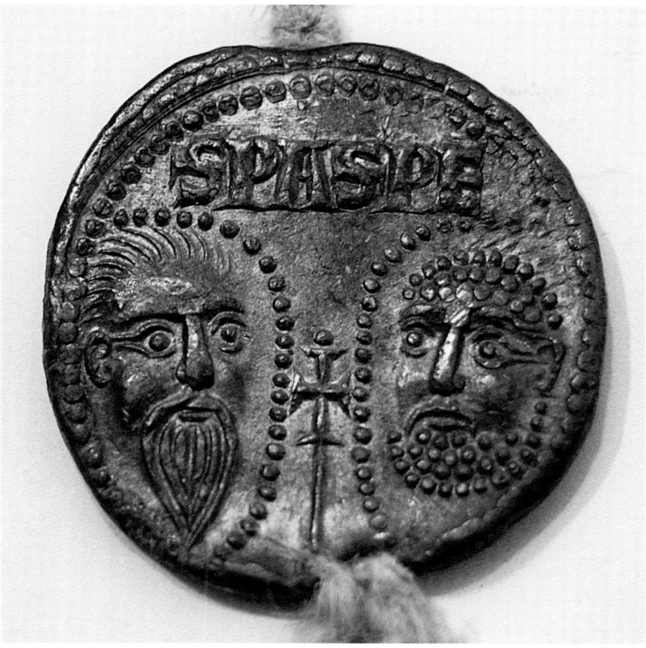

3 Lead seal of Nicholas IV, recto, Assisi, Archivio del Sacro Convento, Bollario VII/220, dated 1288.

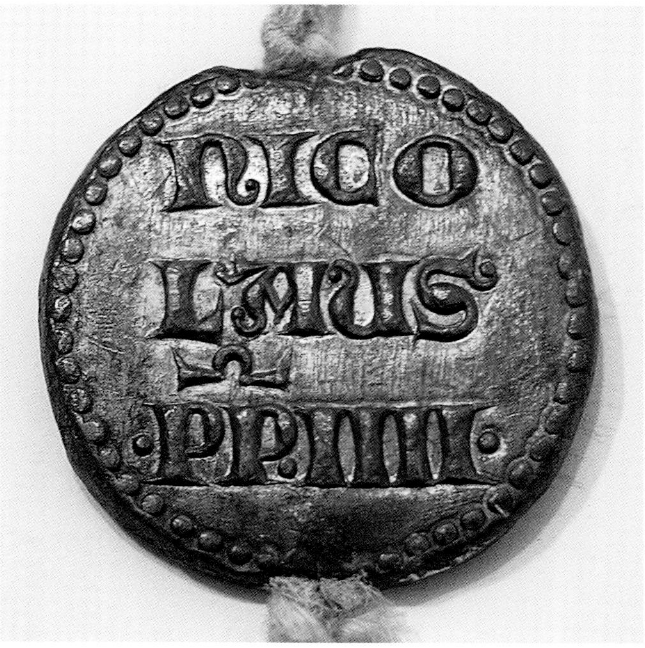

4 Lead seal of Nicholas IV, verso, Assisi, Archivio del Sacro Convento, Bollario VII/220, dated 1288.

The second letter (fig. 6), composed the following day, was addressed to 'our beloved sons the [minister] general of the Order of Friars Minor and the ministers of the province of Saint Francis'.[4] The opening sections repeated verbatim the text of Nicholas's first missive. Again, the pope's instructions were directed to the Umbrian friars, notwithstanding the initial greeting to the minister general of the whole Order. Nicholas ordered 'you, minister of the [Umbrian] province, and also our beloved son the custodian of Saint Francis, through other letters of ours' (evidently referring back to the copies of the first bull) to appoint 'suitable and faithful persons' to collect the alms of the faithful.[5] But in addition to the text of the first bull, the following lines were appended to the bottom of the second, spelling out in greater detail how Nicholas wished the money to be spent:

> Therefore, as we have, in the Lord, particular confidence in your prudence, by the authority of this [letter], we permit you, our sons the ministers, each of you, both in common and separately, *to have the aforesaid churches and their convents maintained, repaired, built, modified, enlarged, furnished and decorated* [our emphasis], from the aforesaid offerings or alms, by the counsel of wise brothers of the same church of Saint Francis, when and as your discretion will see fit. And if something is left over from the above-mentioned offerings and alms, it may be used with integrity for the needs of the brothers gathering at the aforesaid churches and convents, and also of those who dwell there, until something else should be arranged by us, or by our successors, the Roman popes, by their letters patent and sealed with the apostolic bull. Given at Rieti, on the Ides of May, in the first year of our pontificate.[6]

Nicholas's call to 'maintain, repair, build, modify, enlarge, furnish and decorate' the Basilica of San Francesco must be read against the context of a building that was architecturally complete and already extensively embellished with images in fresco and glass. Work on the Basilica had begun six decades before *Reducentes*, Pope Gregory IX having laid the foundation stone as early as 1228, less than two years after Francis's death. Construction seems to have progressed with remarkable speed over the next quarter-century. The building was conceived from the outset as a great double basilica, comprising two superimposed structures known simply as the Upper Church and Lower Church (fig. 7). The Lower was intended as the shrine church for Saint Francis, whose

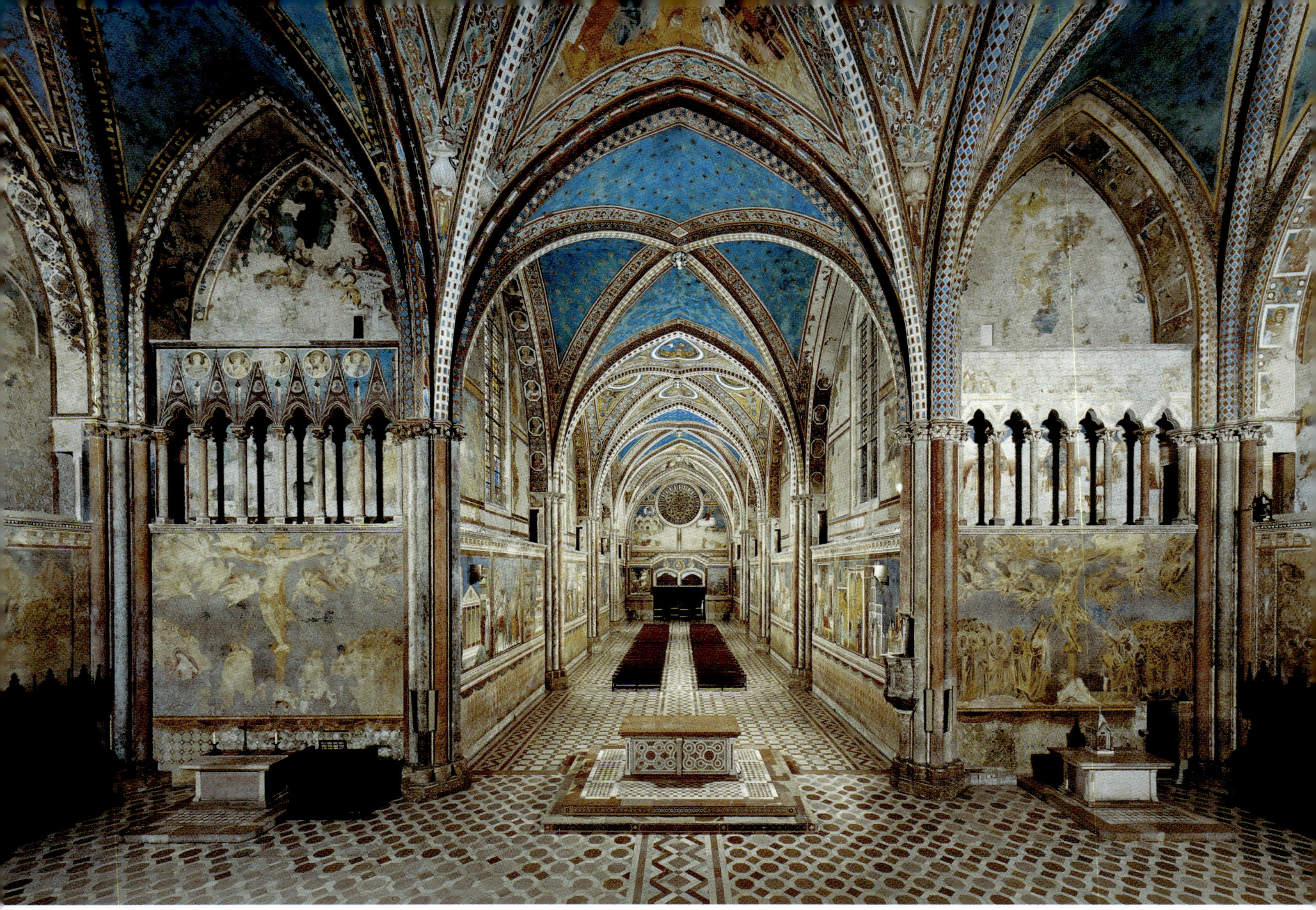

5 Basilica of San Francesco, transepts and nave of the Upper Church, looking towards the counter-façade.

remains were translated there in May 1230 and buried below the high altar at the centre of the crossing.[7] The Upper was to be a papal throne church, equipped to accommodate the papal liturgy should the curia descend on Assisi – a reasonable expectation given the papal practice of using the central Italian hill towns as seasonal retreats from Rome's political violence and summer heat. The divide between the two churches also represented an architectural watershed, as the shallow Romanesque arches of the Lower (fig. 8) gave way to the soaring Gothic vaults of the Upper (fig. 9). The string course between the two superimposed apses both marks and masks the transition from a hemispherical to a polygonal plan (fig. 10), and the Upper Church is commonly regarded as the first truly Gothic building in Italy. The principal elements of the Basilica's superstructure must have been standing by 1253, when a visiting Polish Dominican described candelabra suspended from the vaults of the Upper Church.[8] A range of decorative interventions in both the Upper and Lower Churches continued through the next three decades, concentrating on stained glass (another novelty in Italy) and mural painting, but momentum seems to have slowed by the early 1280s.

Sixty years after the Basilica's foundation and at least thirty-five after its completion, Nicholas's bulls now called for a comprehensive renewal of San Francesco's fabric and ornament. They set in motion a radical reconfiguration and expansion of the Basilica complex that far exceeded the ambitions of the original architects or the parameters of the initial design. What is more, *Reducentes* authorized the collection of funds to achieve these goals: the friars were to use

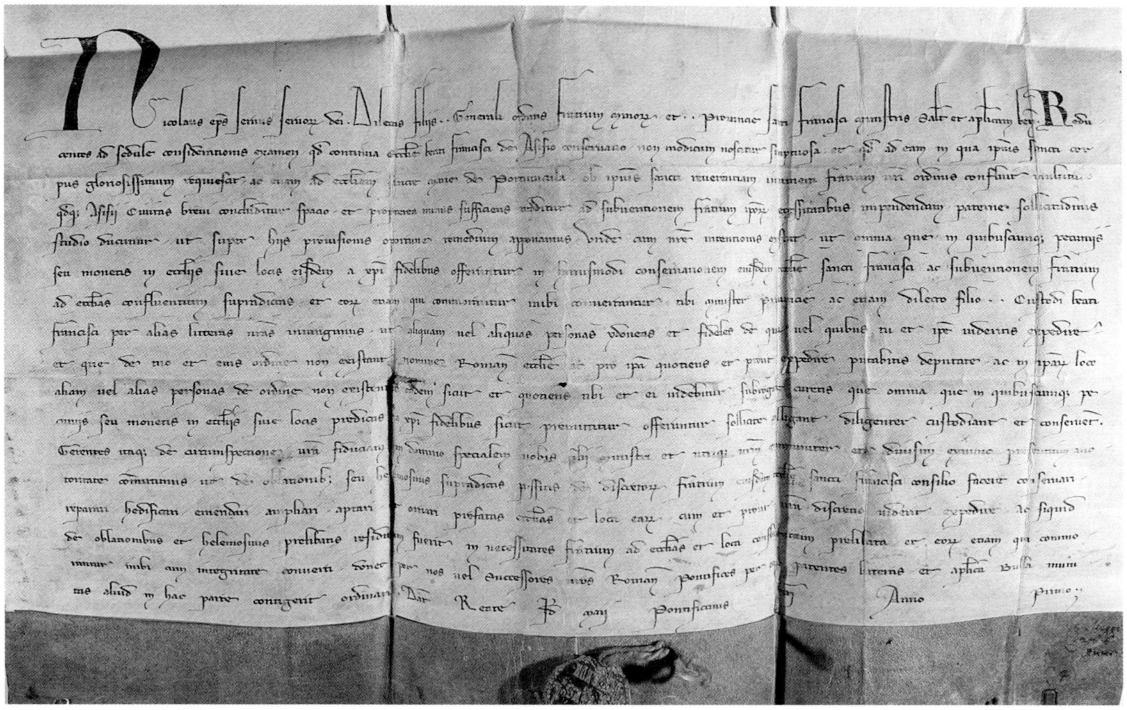

6 *Reducentes ad sedulae*, Assisi, Archivio del Sacro Convento, Bollario VIII/225, dated 1288.

7 Giovanni Battista Mariani, cross section of the Upper and Lower Churches, *c.*1830, lithograph, Österreichische Nationalbibliothek, Vienna.

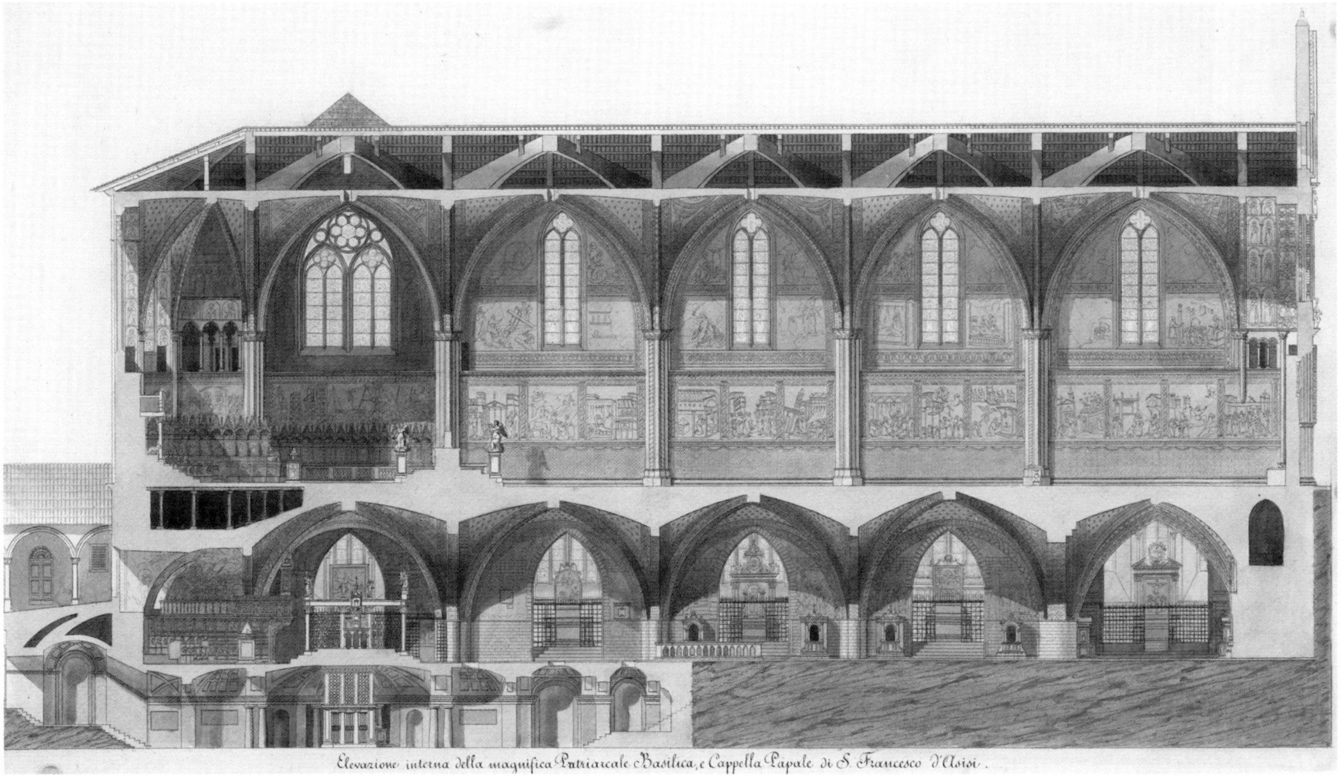

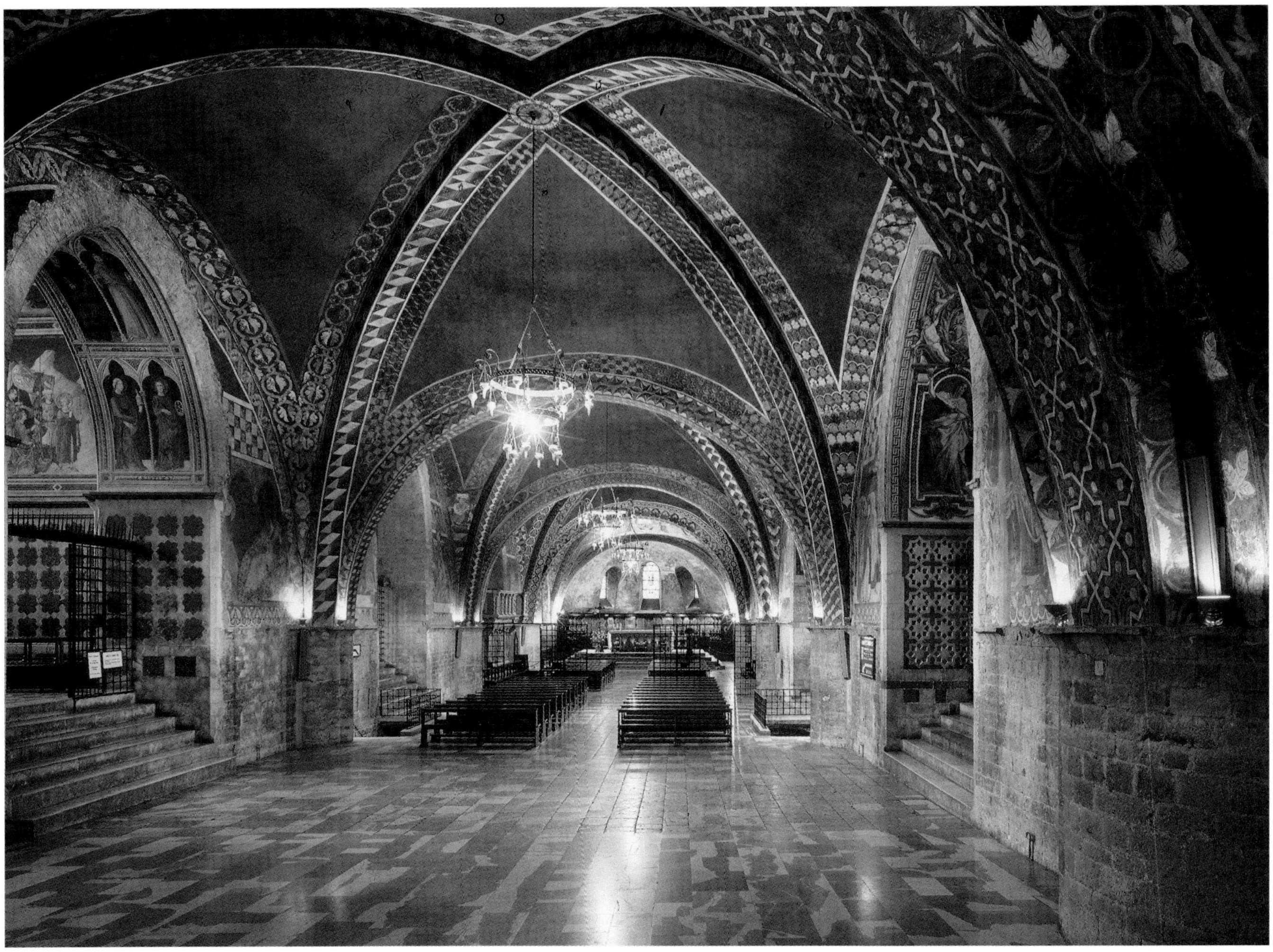

8 Basilica of San Francesco, nave of the Lower Church, looking towards the high altar.

the alms left by the faithful in the Basilica and at the Porziuncola (the chapel on the plain below Assisi, where Saint Francis died), appointing 'suitable and faithful' laymen to administer the money on their behalf. Franciscans were forbidden by their Rule from handling money directly, reflecting the vow of poverty that every friar swore on entering the Order. Even if the arrangements specified by *Reducentes* remained within the letter of the Rule, Nicholas's bulls would in time be castigated for mocking the Franciscan ideal of poverty at Assisi, the very birthplace of the Order.

We cannot tell from the succinct wording of *Reducentes* exactly what Nicholas and his circle envisaged in terms of architecture and imagery, but we do know that the friars at Assisi responded by inaugurating two decades of intensive work on their mother church. From the mid-1290s, the Lower Church would become a construction site as its walls were pierced to build a circuit of new side chapels around the nave and transepts. The aggressive enlargement of the Lower Church created new spaces for the tombs of private donors and eased the flow of pilgrims towards the tomb of Saint Francis below the high altar. Such extensive structural work took time, and a comprehensive fresco scheme for these new spaces would be attempted only in the first two decades of the fourteenth century. By then patrons and poli-

facing page 9 Basilica of San Francesco, nave of the Upper Church, looking towards the high altar.

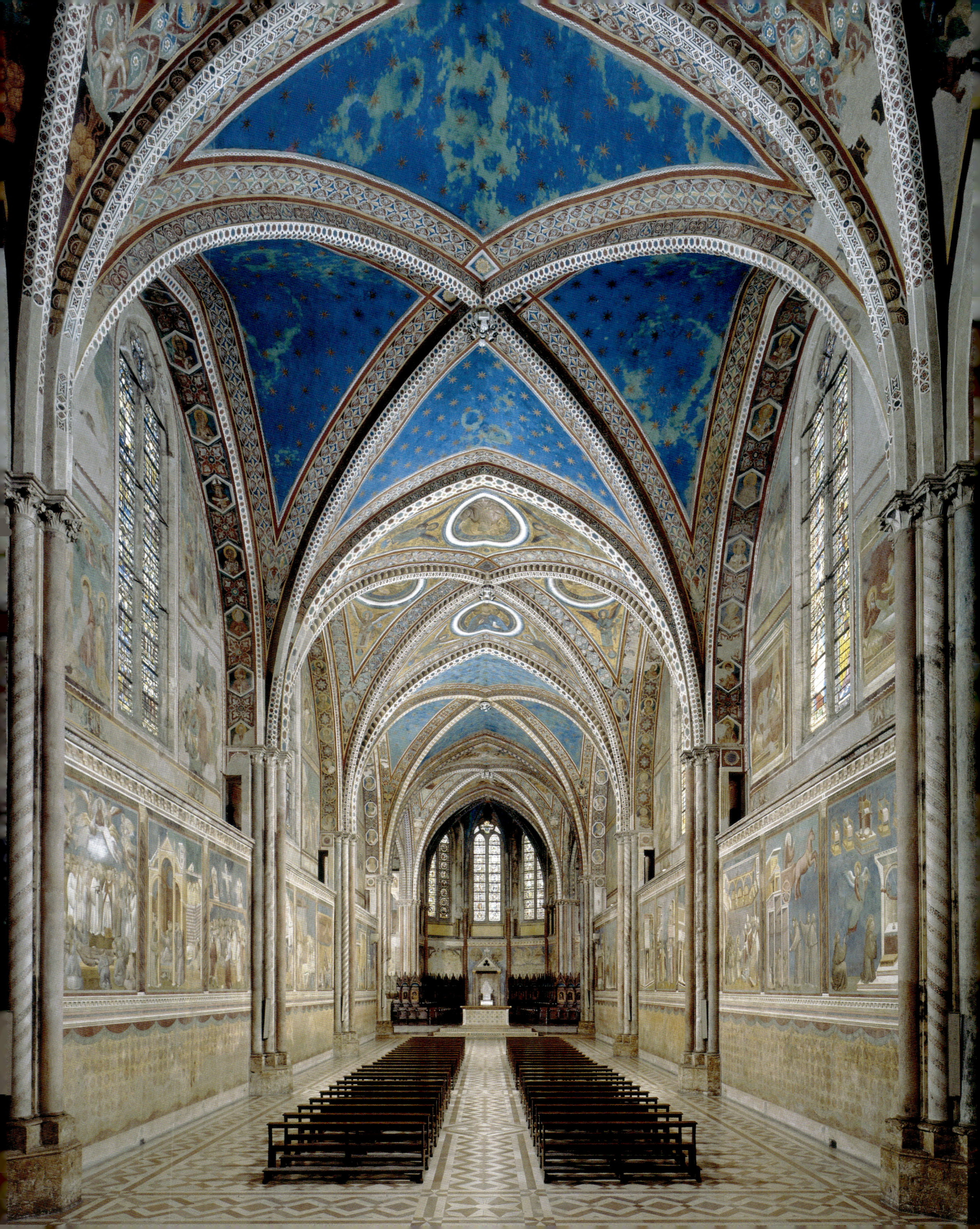

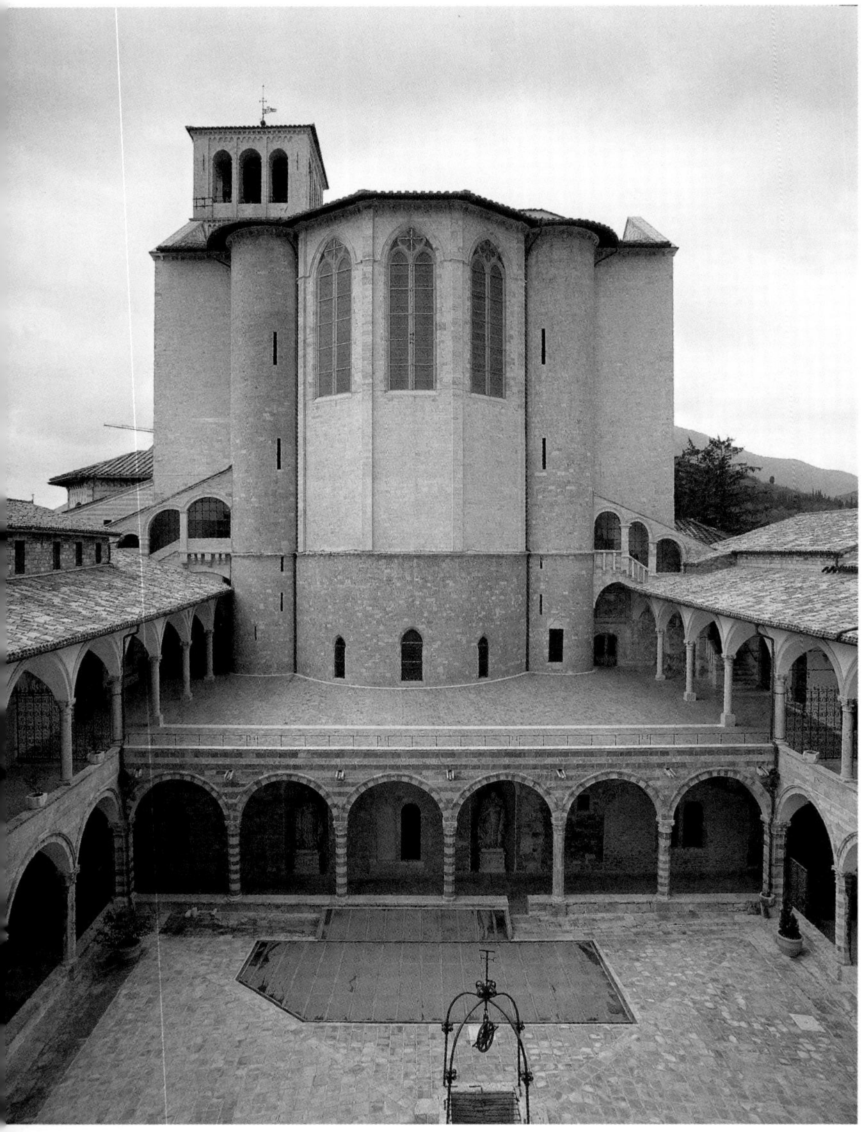

10 Basilica of San Francesco, exterior view of the apses of the Upper and Lower Churches from the Sacro Convento.

tics had moved on, the papacy itself had migrated from Rome to Avignon, and Nicholas IV's original agenda for Assisi had been overtaken by renewed fissures within the Order over the observance of poverty and the interpretation of the Rule.[9]

In the Upper Church the artistic impact of *Reducentes* was more immediate. Within several months, perhaps a year at most, work had begun on the mural decoration of the nave, the subject of this book. Earlier fresco campaigns in the Upper Church had concentrated on the sanctuary area (located, most unusually, at the building's western end), and almost a decade had passed since Cimabue had painted the cycles of the Last Judgment and the Apostles in the two transepts (fig. 11) and the vault of the Evangelists over the high altar (fig. 12).[10] The nave remained unfrescoed and in 1288 must have represented an obvious lacuna in the Basilica's decoration. *Reducentes* provided the impetus and the means to revive the Upper Church *cantiere* and remedy this glaring void in the mural scheme.

The result was a fresco programme of outstanding visual ambition and intellectual scope. Two of the nave vaults were frescoed to complement Cimabue's four Evangelists over the crossing: one bears the four Doctors of the Church (damaged in the 1997 earthquake), the other an idiosyncratic *Deesis* scheme where Saint Francis joins the canonical trio of Christ, the Virgin and Saint John the Baptist (fig. 13). On the upper walls, biblical scenes stacked in two registers face each other across the nave: Old Testament to the north, New Testament to the south. Below them, the best-known and most contentious images at Assisi – the twenty-eight scenes of the Saint Francis cycle – are wrapped in a single clockwise band around all three walls of the nave. It is the greatest surviving spectacle of medieval mural painting and it was almost certainly unprecedented at the time.

Twenty-four years after *Reducentes* a group of learned Franciscans, trying to defend the observance of poverty across the Order, acknowledged the impact of Nicholas's bulls on the Basilica's mural decoration: 'nor have we seen a great sumptuousness of paintings in the churches of the friars except in the church at Assisi, and these paintings were ordered by Lord Nicholas IV out of reverence to Saint Francis, whose relics are buried there'.[11] This passage from the polemical tract *Contra quasdam* was written in 1312, in the midst of fierce debates over poverty and the Franciscan Rule, but the reference back to Nicholas and Assisi sheds further light on the *Reducentes* initiative of 1288. The 'great sumptuousness of paintings' must refer principally to the nave of the Upper Church. By 1312 this space would have presented the viewer with the expansive, all-enveloping mural decoration that still confronts visitors today, but with its saturated blues and radiant gold leaf undiminished by time.[12] The *Contra quasdam* text, written by senior Franciscan theologians who would have remembered the Franciscan pope, confirms that the commissioning of the fresco scheme was associated at the time with Nicholas IV. This is important, as *Reducentes* had not specified images or murals in its list of commands (although frescoes could have been understood within the call to decorate – 'ornare' – the Basilica). Equally significant is the fact that the authors of the 1312 tract regarded the mural decoration at Assisi as something utterly exceptional in its scale and sophistication, its 'sumptuositatem magnam'.

Assisi Problems

This book offers a new and innovative account of how the terse instructions in the *Reducentes* bulls led to the extraordinary visual statement of the Upper Church nave. It is concerned with the intellectual and ideological agendas that shaped the nave programme, and with the historical moment in which the frescoes were designed and executed. It does not add extra ink to the obsessive attribution debates over the authorship of the murals: this is emphatically not another book on Giotto and Assisi.

Whether Giotto did or did not paint the twenty-eight scenes of the Saint Francis cycle has been the central preoccupation of research on the Basilica for over a century. The so-called 'Assisi Problem' continues to dominate the historiography on the Upper Church to the exclusion of other, more contextual (and historically sound) approaches. This scholarly myopia has, we would suggest, been detrimental to an understanding of the Basilica complex. Anyone exploring the bibliography on Assisi has to negotiate dense thickets of debate surrounding the relative contributions of Giotto, Pietro Cavallini and the many anonymous painters created by art historians to staff their connoisseurial conjecture. The 'Isaac Master', the 'Saint Cecilia Master', the 'Master of the Betrayal' and numerous others jostle for space on these fantasy scaffolds. Equally unhelpful is the blanket attribution of the Saint Francis cycle to Giotto, first advanced by Giorgio Vasari in the sixteenth century. This book is perhaps the first volume dedicated to the nave frescoes that will not discuss Giotto *per se*, and in general the painters of the frescoes are not our primary object of interest. This bias does not imply a disregard for the importance of artists at Assisi, rather it reflects our view that it is time to apply some fresh thinking, focusing on historical and intellectual contexts. These can offer alternative and productive avenues for explaining the creation and meaning of the Upper Church frescoes. Furthermore, there is little prospect of the attribution issues

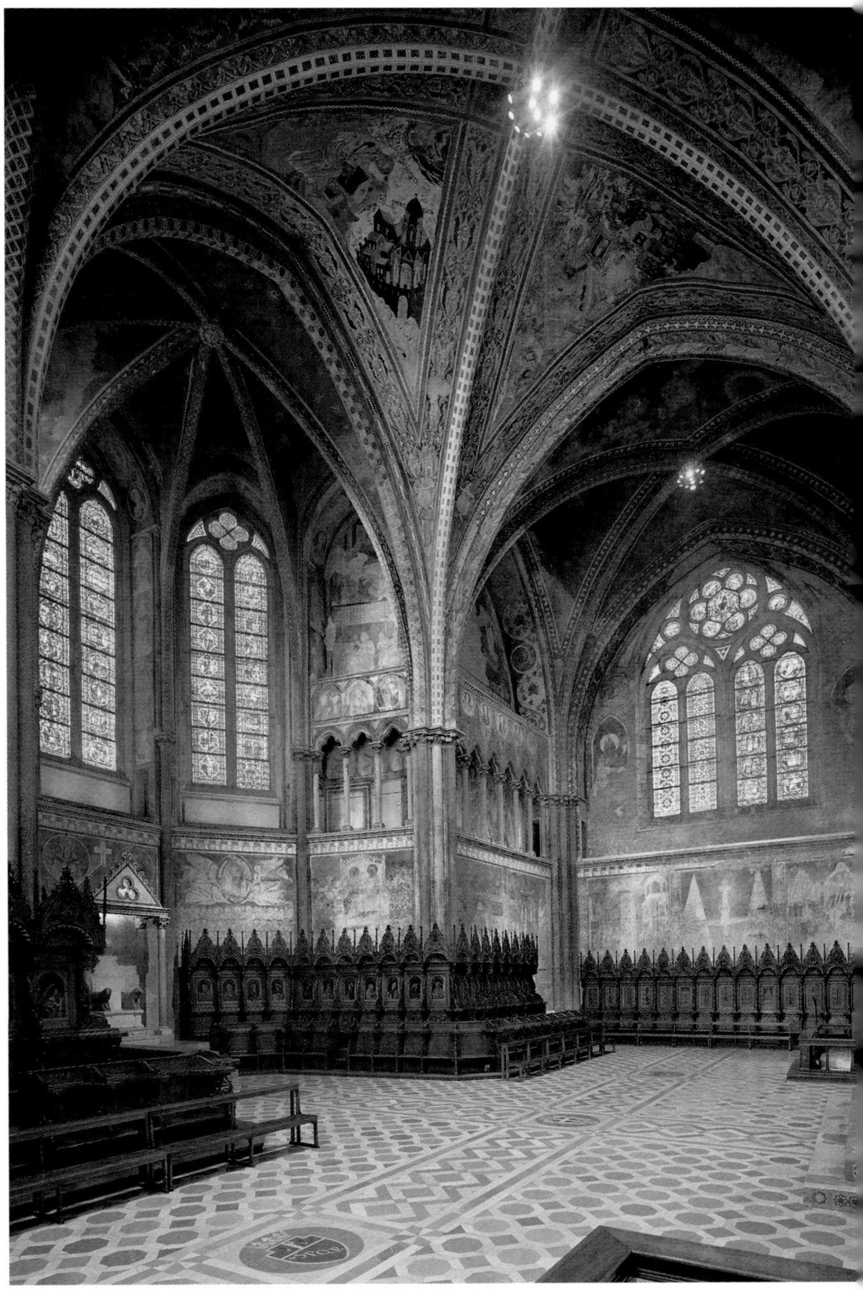

11 Basilica of San Francesco, apse, crossing and north transept of the Upper Church.

following spread (left) 12 Cimabue, vault of the Evangelists (crossing vault), *c.*1277–80, fresco, Upper Church, Basilica of San Francesco.

following spread (right) 13 Jacopo Torriti, *Deesis* vault (second bay of the nave), *c.*1288–90, fresco, Upper Church, Basilica of San Francesco.

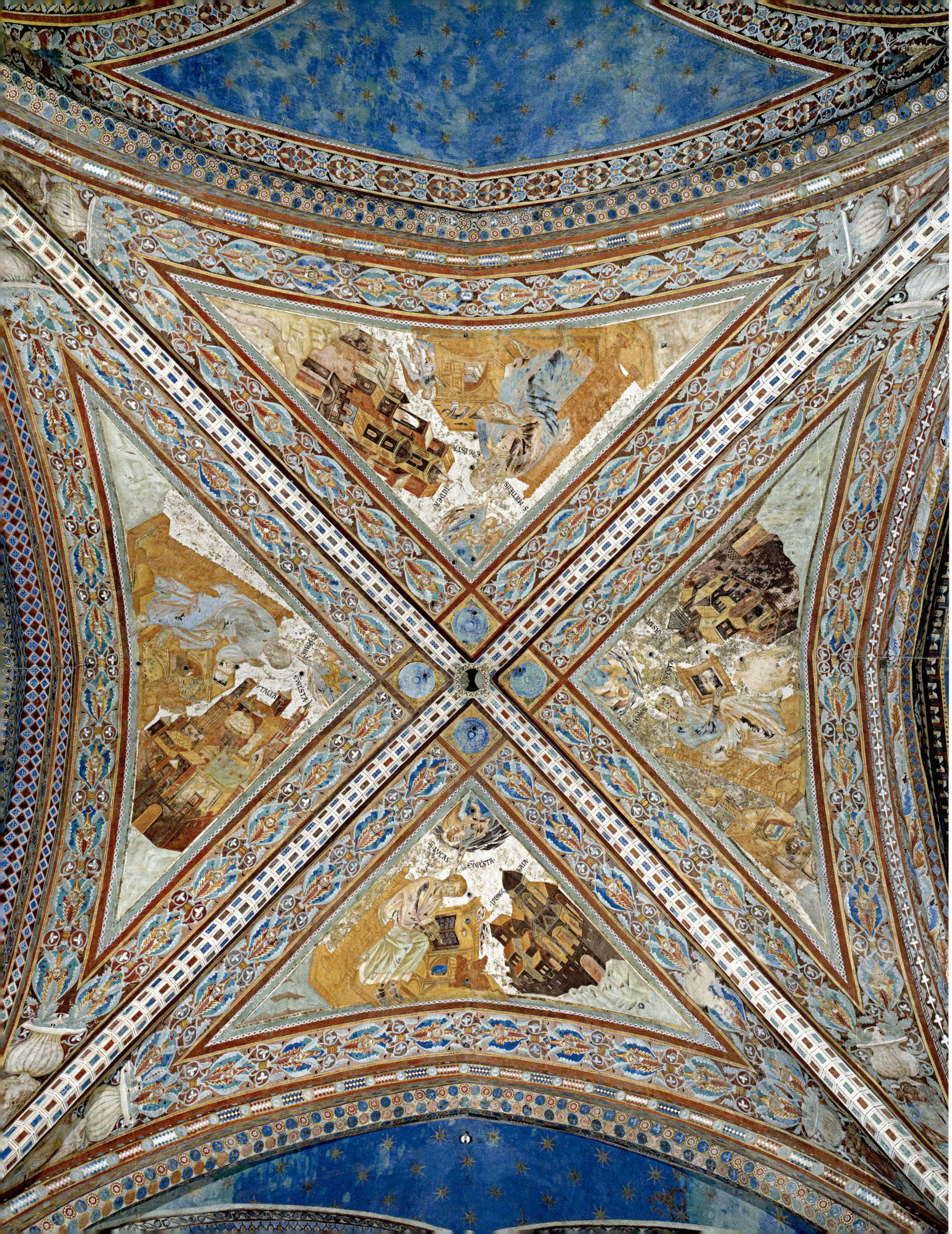

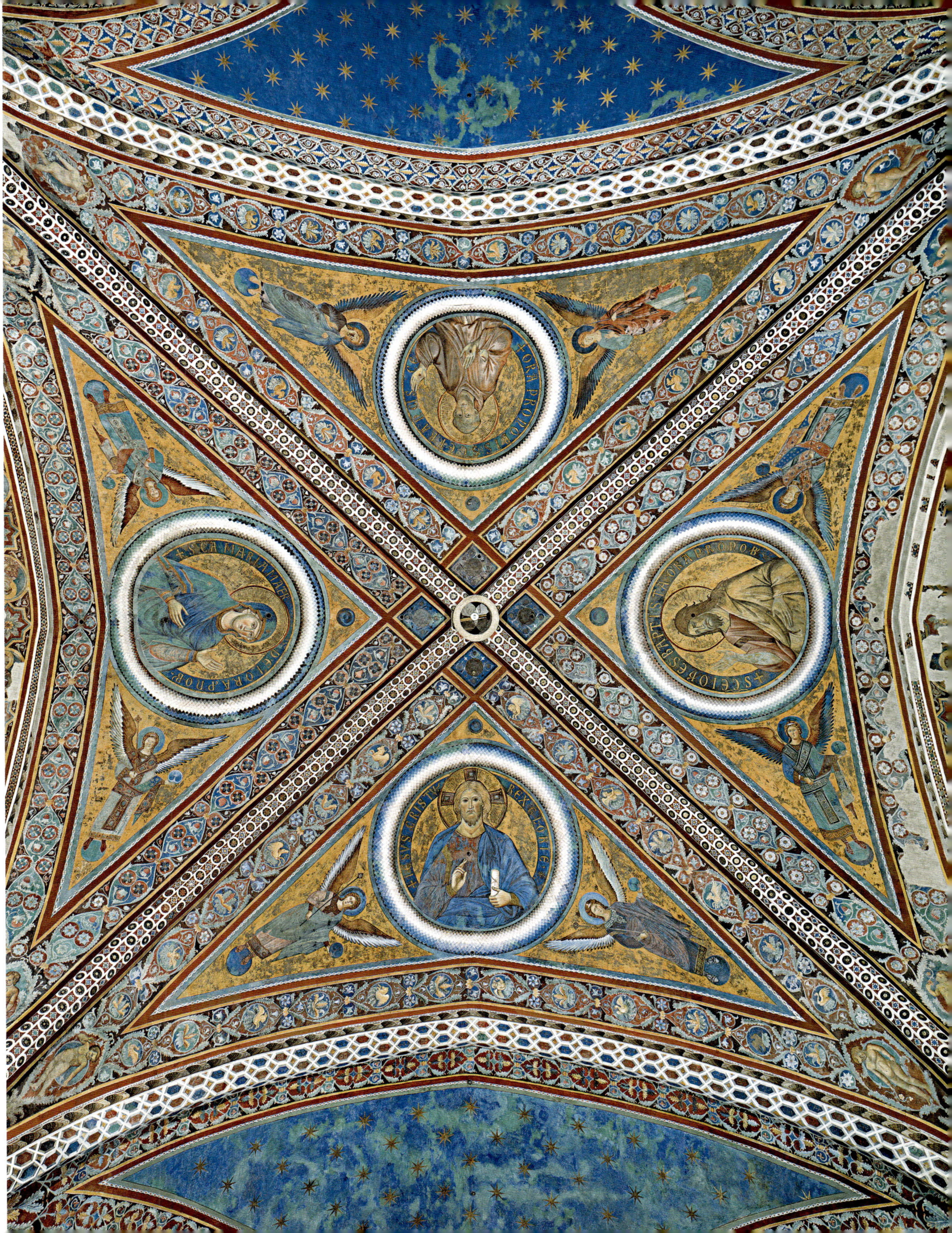

surrounding the nave cycles being resolved, given the evidence currently available. While we have our own views on the authorship of the frescoes, in this book we deliberately set these interminable debates to one side.

If the stormy attribution debates seem destined to rumble on, the dating of the Upper Church frescoes has at least become rather clearer of late. Recent discoveries have established May 1288 to May 1297 as the maximum chronological range for the execution of the nave cycles.[13] The entire nave of the Upper Church – from the vaults of the *Deesis* and the Doctors, through the Old and New Testament cycles on the upper registers, to the Saint Francis cycle wrapped around the lowest – must have been painted within this nine-year window. The reduced timeframe undoubtedly simplifies matters, but even this abbreviated period was eventful, encompassing not only the four years of Nicholas's papacy, but also the two-year vacancy and protracted conclave following his death in 1292, the brief pontificate of Celestine V in 1294, and the early years of Boniface VIII's reign up to his clash with the Colonna family in 1297. Complexities persist, but at least we may now discount one of the most disruptive readings of the nave frescoes (one that has retained a residual following in the Anglophone and German literatures), that the Saint Francis cycle was painted only after Giotto had completed the Arena Chapel in Padua in 1305.[14] Finally excluding this awkward post-dating has profound consequences for all treatments of the Upper Church frescoes, and confirms the fundamentally innovative nature of the Saint Francis cycle.

One other salient point about the execution of the frescoes constitutes a fundamental premise for this book. Recent technical examination of the Saint Francis cycle has established what more perceptive critics had long suspected: the cycle was executed in several phases by a sequence of workshops comprising many different painters.[15] So even within a single narrative cycle we need to acknowledge multiple artistic contributions, and to the Saint Francis scenes we must add the Old and New Testament cycles above, with their own questions of attribution.[16] It would be wrong to characterize the painters of the nave murals as mere executors of preconceived compositions. The artists undoubtedly contributed a great deal, and their distinctively visual imagination underpins many of the specific iconographic and spatial effects within the nave frescoes that we identify and discuss in this book. The finished murals are surely the result of intense collaboration. However, it is highly unlikely that the painters were responsible for the scope of the programme or the messages it sought to communicate. Given the turnover of artistic personnel on the scaffolds, the remarkable coherence of the nave murals must have resulted from the guidance of the patrons. This is what one would expect: such a significant statement of corporate identity and historical mission in the mother church of the most dynamic religious order of the age would hardly have been left to a succession of different artists to design.[17]

In Search of a Patron

While the issue of patronage has generally played an ancillary role to attribution in the literature on the Upper Church, a number of likely patrons have been proposed. The tendency has been for scholars to champion prominent ecclesiastics at the Roman curia: Nicholas IV himself is now one of the most popular candidates, especially since we first drew attention in 2003 to the *Contra quasdam* text that cited his name in connection with the frescoes.[18] Other contenders include the cardinals Matthew of Acquasparta and Matteo Rosso Orsini. The interests of the noble Colonna family, led by Cardinal Giacomo Colonna, have also been perceived behind the decoration of the Upper Church.

In the first two chapters of this book, we subject these hypotheses to greater scrutiny, tracking the movements of key individuals between Rome and Umbria and assessing their influence in and around Assisi in this period. While the Rome–Assisi axis is emphasized throughout, it is never taken for granted. In truth, it is debatable whether any of the major players at the curia could have been responsible for designing the scheme in all its details. The pope and his cardinals had numerous demands on their time and when not in Rome their itinerant retinues criss-crossed central Italy. It is instructive to note that the curia never came to Assisi while Nicholas was pope, despite lengthy papal sojourns in Rieti and Orvieto.

Indeed, it is questionable whether the design can be attributed to any single individual. Conceiving the complex, intricate scheme for the Upper Church would have entailed considerable attention to detail. The programme was highly site-specific, drawing on the spatial dynamics and juxtapositions offered by the architecture of the Upper Church.

Moreover, the scheme undoubtedly evolved to some extent once work was under way, and the increasing proficiency of the painters opened new iconographic possibilities as they progressed down the nave walls. These factors imply substantial contributions from figures present at Assisi, and this assumption forms the basis of our analysis of the likely patronage of the nave cycles.

Distinctions may be drawn between those who facilitated the initiative in general terms – Nicholas IV and his allies at the curia – and those who elaborated the detail of the programme on site. The opening pair of chapters form a diptych around the hinge of *Reducentes*, the first considering the project's genesis at the papal curia, the second its execution at Assisi. Chapter 1 sets *Reducentes* within the context of Nicholas IV's pontificate and examines his broader artistic patronage and cultural experience. It also investigates the projects that Nicholas initiated in Rome. The Franciscan pope's interventions at the Lateran and Santa Maria Maggiore illuminate his strategy of using art and architecture to reposition the Friars Minor at the heart of the Church. The Roman campaigns also reveal how Nicholas's close alliance with the Colonna created a powerful patronage dynamic, which endured for several years after the pope's death in 1292.

Chapter 2 returns to Assisi and to the recipients of Nicholas's bulls. Although the minister general, Matthew of Acquasparta, has been considered before in the scholarship on the Assisi frescoes, the provincial ministers of Umbria and the custodians of the Basilica have not. These offices were frequently held by friars with impressive academic backgrounds, significant social status and extensive political connections: we piece together their biographies, their intellectual capabilities and interests. Assisi was no intellectual backwater in the late thirteenth century: the Sacro Convento numbered university-trained masters of theology among its community and housed an extensive and up-to-date library. Assisi-based Franciscans, with these resources to hand, were more than capable of devising and directing the nave scheme. The reference in *Reducentes* to the 'wise brothers' of the Sacro Convento may well allude to friars of such calibre.

An emphasis on the Umbrian context does not render the Franciscan pope and his cardinals redundant for our reading of the frescoes, however. Nicholas's bulls had set the bar of ambition and provided the funds for the renewal of the Basilica. Furthermore, the friars of the Sacro Convento must have expected the pope, together with the curia (including the powerful Colonna cardinals), to visit the Basilica and inspect their work. In this sense, the frescoes of the Upper Church could be said to have been painted *for* Nicholas IV as much as having been commissioned *by* him.

Constructing Meaning in the Upper Church

To understand how the Franciscans at Assisi set about designing the nave scheme, we need to know what confronted them in the Upper Church as they contemplated Nicholas IV's command to renew their Basilica. The interior was not a blank canvas. Chapter 3 assesses the state of the Upper Church in May 1288, surveying the panel, glass and wall painting that had been commissioned during the previous half-century, much of which was to be conserved and integrated within the new scheme. Some earlier features, notably the great painted crucifix by Giunta Pisano and its accompanying panels, are considered for the first time in relation to the post-1288 mural decoration. Now long gone, Giunta's ensemble of images, set over a beam at the head of the nave, would have dominated the interior of the Upper Church in the Duecento.

Chapter 4 reflects on the practical challenges facing the friars in planning such a complex yet coherent programme. By comparing the Old and New Testament cycles to their Roman basilical prototypes, we gauge the extent to which the choice of biblical scenes at Assisi was unusual, and designed specifically to relate to the Saint Francis cycle below. Drawing on the work of Padre Gerhard Ruf, we argue that the planners of the Upper Church nave must have begun by deciding the key points where the separate narratives would interlock.[19] Once these initial coordinates were fixed, other scenes could be chosen and planned around them.

This book is concerned with the meaning of the frescoes in the Upper Church rather than their authorship. Chapters 5 to 7 represent the most sustained effort so far to describe the Franciscan systems of thought manifested in the nave frescoes and the messages they would have communicated to their late thirteenth-century audiences. Each chapter focuses on particular sets of ideas that were prioritized within different sections of the iconographic programme. This thematic approach means that the chapters do not proceed through the Saint Francis cycle in narrative sequence, nor do they give equal treatment to every scene. In offering our interpretation of the nave programme, we go well beyond the confines of Bonaventure's *Legenda maior*, the official life of the saint, to investigate a broad range of Franciscan writings in various genres, including biblical glosses, devotional texts, theological tracts, sermons and papal bulls. By setting these familiar images within the context of sacred space and Franciscan exegesis, we advance a new reading of the Saint Francis cycle and the central concerns that motivated the selection, arrangement and composition of its scenes. Placing Saint Francis in the context of Old Testament patriarchs gave his life story prophetic weight, and stressed his salvific role as the renewer of the Roman Church. In the Franciscan scenes below the Passion cycle, an unprecedented degree of emphasis on the stigmata – the wounds of the Crucifixion, miraculously impressed on Francis's body two years before he died – advanced the saint's unique claim to be another Christ (or *alter Christus*).

The application of Franciscan exegesis to the nave programme is innovative but not unprecedented in the Assisi literature. In terms of approach, our principal debts are to a brace of books published as long ago as the early 1970s. The first is Alastair Smart's *The Assisi Problem and the Art of Giotto* of 1971, a misleading title given that the great majority of the text is dedicated to a thorough iconographic analysis of the Saint Francis cycle in the light of contemporary Franciscan politics and theology, with little mention of Giotto.[20] The second volume is Padre Gerhard Ruf's *San Francesco e San Bonaventura* of 1974, which offered an integrated analysis of the entire nave for the first time, incorporating not only the Saint Francis cycle but also the Old and New Testament scenes above.[21] Ruf's book can now be seen to have been decisively ahead of its time and has strongly influenced our thinking on the nave programme.

Beyond Smart's and Ruf's work specifically on Assisi, Chiara Frugoni's many publications on Franciscan imagery and hagiography have transformed our understanding of the thirteenth-century painted lives of Saint Francis.[22] Similarly, Rosalind Brooke's 2006 volume *The Image of Saint Francis* has set Franciscan texts and iconography on the same plane.[23] Amy Neff's recent research on the Upper Church has convincingly established the dependence of sections of the mural scheme on particular works of Franciscan devotional and mystical literature.[24] Neff's findings are especially important for our analysis of the nave frescoes, as her research demonstrates the depth of reading that lies behind the programme, extending far beyond core works like the *Legenda maior* to include biblical commentaries, mystical tracts and sermons. These contributions, however, represent only a sliver of the scholarly output on Assisi, the vast bulk of which continues to concentrate on formal issues of style, dating and attribution.

Any straightforward concept of 'meaning' is, of course, hardly appropriate to a monument as complex and layered as the Basilica of San Francesco. We would never claim that the themes on which we have chosen to focus represent the totality of intended significance in the nave programme. But we do suggest that certain aspects of the mural scheme are so eye-catching, unusual and carefully wrought that they must have been meaningful to medieval viewers, or were at least intended to be so. While the multi-tiered programme of the Upper Church offers myriad opportunities for identifying theological, political and ideological connections, our analysis focuses on those we regard as the strongest, which would require special pleading to deny. In forging these key correspondences, the designers and artists of the programme deployed sophisticated compositional strategies to articulate some of the most prominent themes in contemporary Franciscan thought and legend.

'The sun and the moon clothed in our habit'

If there is one aspect of the Upper Church on which all scholars have implicitly agreed, it is the overwhelming success of the nave frescoes. With their dating to the decade following 1288 now secure, there is no question that the murals inaugurated a new kind of narrative art. The twenty-eight scenes of the Saint Francis cycle immediately achieved a canonical status as the definitive visual account of Francis's life and works.

Comprehending the historical moment and intellectual milieu of their execution helps to explain the extraordinary pictorial achievement of the nave murals as much as any debate on attribution. Many of the most innovative visual solutions in the frescoes were responses to the challenges posed by the programme's iconographic ambition. Today, the wealth of imagery in the Upper Church is often viewed as a contradiction of the Franciscan ideals of simplicity and poverty. Visitors to the Basilica still sense the same tension that the authors of *Contra quasdam* sought to dispel as far back as 1312. 'What would Saint Francis have made of all this?' remains one of the most common responses before the frescoes. To understand this apparent disjunction, we need to examine the preoccupations and priorities of the Order at the end of the thirteenth century, rather than the ideals of Francis and his early followers at its beginning. The scheme's scope reflects a distinctively Franciscan agenda which can be recovered only by immersing oneself in the intellectual world of the Order in the final years of the Duecento. That is what this book sets out to do.

Whatever the precise mechanics of patronage between Rome and Assisi, Nicholas IV's papacy provides the crucial historical context for the *Reducentes* initiative and the mural programme it inspired. Sixty years after the canonization of Saint Francis in 1228, his Order had grown to be the most dynamic religious movement in the Latin Church. The four years of Nicholas's pontificate arguably represent the zenith of the Order's influence: under his reign the friars could boast that 'we have the sun and the moon clothed in our habit'.[25] The momentary Franciscan grip on the papacy galvanized the bonds of shared interest between Rome and Assisi. These years also marked one of the final phases of unity within the Order itself, before the simmering tensions between friars with differing views on the observance of poverty spilled over into open factionalism. By the time *Contra quasdam* was composed in 1312 the ascetic minority – later known as the Spirituals – was in open conflict with the Conventual majority, and the Order's internal differences were high on the agenda of the great council of the Church convened at Vienne by Pope Clement V.[26]

In the Franciscan spring of 1288, however, these troubles lay far in the future. The friars charged that May with realizing Nicholas's plans for the Basilica must have approached their task in a mood of exceptional confidence. Only in this frame of mind could they have conceived such an ambitious and far-reaching pictorial programme for the Upper Church, which made such lofty claims for their Order's founder. The friars responsible for the frescoes had not been born during Saint Francis's lifetime. As living memory of the son of an Assisi cloth merchant faded from the Order, a new generation of Franciscans moved beyond the historical portrait towards a more mystical and allegorical vision of their founder. In so doing, they created a work of art that would redefine the terms of narrative painting at the dawn of the Renaissance and fix an image of Francis that endures to the present day.

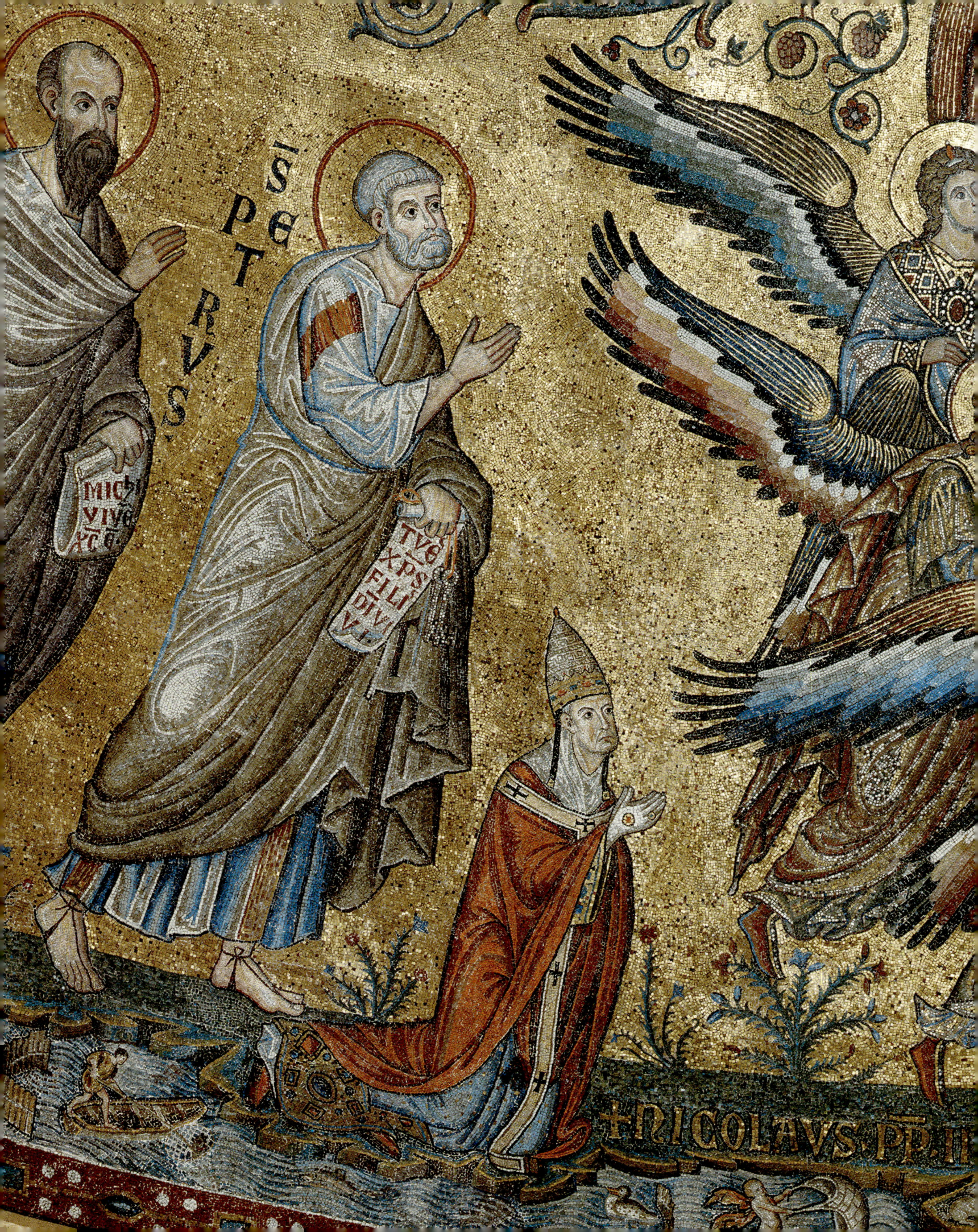

S PETRVS
TVE XPS FILI DIVI VI
NICOLAVS PP II

I

Nicholas IV: A Franciscan Pope

To gauge the significance of the *Reducentes* bulls we must first place them in the context of Nicholas IV's papacy (1288–92). The new pope's intervention at Assisi was no isolated or impulsive gesture. What we know of his biography indicates a lifetime's engagement with Francis's legend and its historic significance. A man of unusually wide visual experience, who had spent substantial periods in both Paris and Constantinople, Nicholas was an active patron of the arts.[1] His name can be connected with mosaics, panel paintings, goldsmiths' work, embroideries and frescoes. As pope he moved quickly to insert Saint Francis into the heart of the sacred and artistic topography of Rome. Moreover, his principal supporter at the curia, Cardinal Giacomo Colonna, undoubtedly shared his vision for the Franciscan movement. Nicholas quickly promoted another Colonna, Giacomo's young nephew Pietro, to the purple, together with the minister general of his own Order, Matthew of Acquasparta, a learned theologian from Umbria.

The letters that arrived in Assisi in the spring of 1288 therefore reflected the wishes and priorities of a group of powerful friars and ecclesiastics at the apex of the Church, who had invested heavily in the Order and its ideals. The Franciscans and the Basilica had enjoyed whole-hearted backing from earlier popes, some of whom had known or met Saint Francis. Nicholas's generation could claim no such direct link, but this distance arguably allowed them to form a more ambitious interpretation of the Order's historic mission, a project of renewal that had crossed a new threshold with the election of the first Franciscan pope.

We should be cautious, however, in assuming that Nicholas IV himself played any part in the detailed planning that must have preceded the redecoration of the Basilica. The new pope had many demands on his time and attention, from subduing the papacy's enemies in central Italy to the dire situation in the Holy Land (where the last Crusader stronghold, Acre, would fall in 1291). It is instructive that Nicholas never visited Assisi during his four-year pontificate, although he must have longed to sit on the papal throne in the apse of his Order's mother church. The *Reducentes ad sedulae* bulls are better read as documents of delegation, and for their implementation we should look to their recipients, the senior friars of the Sacro Convento and the Umbrian province. As we shall see, these were significant figures in their own right, with one of the Order's principal libraries at their backs.

Before turning to consider the situation on the ground in Assisi, however, it is essential to understand the context of

facing page 14 Jacopo Torriti, apse mosaic (detail of fig. 25).

the new Franciscan papacy, especially its impact in Rome. This chapter examines the ecclesiastics at the papal curia associated with launching the *Reducentes* initiative. It reassesses Nicholas's better-documented Roman projects at Saint John Lateran and Santa Maria Maggiore to shed new light on the intellectual and political agendas that drove his artistic patronage. Furthermore, it introduces the pope's powerful Colonna allies, exploring how they worked with Nicholas to realize his artistic commissions and then completed them after his death. Contemporary developments in Rome helped to shape the physical renewal of the Assisi Basilica, in terms both of political backing and artistic templates. For this reason, our story begins three months before the arrival of the papal bulls at Assisi, in Rome with the election of Nicholas IV.

Jerome of Ascoli and the Colonna

On 22 February 1288, after a week of reflection, Jerome of Ascoli, cardinal bishop of Palestrina and Friar Minor, finally accepted the papacy, taking the name Nicholas IV.[2] He was the first Franciscan to wear the tiara and could be forgiven for believing that providence had delivered the papacy to a son of Saint Francis. The conclave following the death of Honorius IV the year before had been the most arduous in recent history. The college of cardinals, gathered on the Aventine hill, struggled to reach a decision during the punishing summer of 1287. Five cardinals died from malarial fever; the others fled Rome. Jerome alone remained in the torrid heat of the Savelli palace at Santa Sabina, surrounded by braziers to keep the mosquitoes at bay, while striving to keep the wheels of papal diplomacy turning as best he could.[3] His dedication and endurance attracted the praise of contemporary chroniclers.[4] When the college gathered again in conclave the following winter, the nine surviving cardinals voted unanimously for Jerome.[5]

Jerome of Ascoli was an unlikely candidate for the papacy. He had no claim to noble origin, and does not seem to have possessed a coat of arms.[6] His rise depended on two factors. The first was the Franciscan Order, which he had joined in his youth, and which gave him opportunities to demonstrate his talents as an administrator and a diplomat.[7] The second was the backing of the powerful Colonna, the 'first family of thirteenth-century Rome', and especially his friend and fellow cardinal Giacomo Colonna.[8]

Biographical details for Jerome's life before 1288 are scarce. Probably born in Ascoli or nearby *c.*1225–30, he first appears in the historical record as late as 1272–4, as a senior member of a papal embassy to Constantinople seeking to achieve the union of the Byzantine and Latin Churches.[9] At this time he seems to have held the post of provincial minister of the Franciscan province of Sclavonia, comprising Dalmatia and adjacent regions.[10] On the return voyage from Constantinople, the boat carrying Jerome and his fellow ambassadors narrowly escaped shipwreck off the Peloponnese (the sister vessel, bearing gifts from the Byzantine court, was lost with all hands).[11] As he made his way back to the Church council sitting at Lyon, Jerome would have learnt that he had been elected, *in absentia*, minister general of the Franciscan Order by the general chapter held in May 1274, succeeding Bonaventure of Bagnoregio.[12] While Jerome seems to have been an active minister general, he was also in demand as a papal ambassador, travelling in this capacity to Spain and France.[13] As minister, Jerome used the great Pentecost seal of the Order, which dated back at least to the early 1250s and depicted the Virgin seated among the apostles, with a friar raising his hands in prayer below their feet (fig. 15).[14] The image signalled the authority of the minister, elected by the Franciscan general chapter (which traditionally convened at Pentecost). It also implied the identification of the Friars Minor with the apostles. As we shall see, similar Pentecostal imagery and apostolic claims would recur in Jerome's own artistic patronage in Rome, and also, we shall argue, in Assisi.

In March 1278 the newly elected Orsini pope, Nicholas III, raised Jerome to the purple, with the title of cardinal priest of Santa Pudenziana.[15] Jerome was in Paris at the time, and journeyed back to Italy only in the spring of the following year. His return is significant for our purposes, for it was timed to allow Jerome to preside over the Franciscan general chapter held in Assisi at Pentecost (21 May 1279).[16] Jerome's familiarity with Assisi is implied by the texts of his later bulls and he almost certainly spent extended periods at the Sacro Convento, but the 1279 general chapter represents his only documented presence there. In the summer of 1279 Jerome also played an active part in the discussions leading to Nicholas III's gloss on the Franciscan Rule, published as the bull *Exiit qui seminat* on 14 August.[17] According to a later Franciscan source, Jerome, in his new position as a cardinal, spent a considerable sum of money to have copies of *Exiit* made and distributed to all of the provinces of the Order.[18]

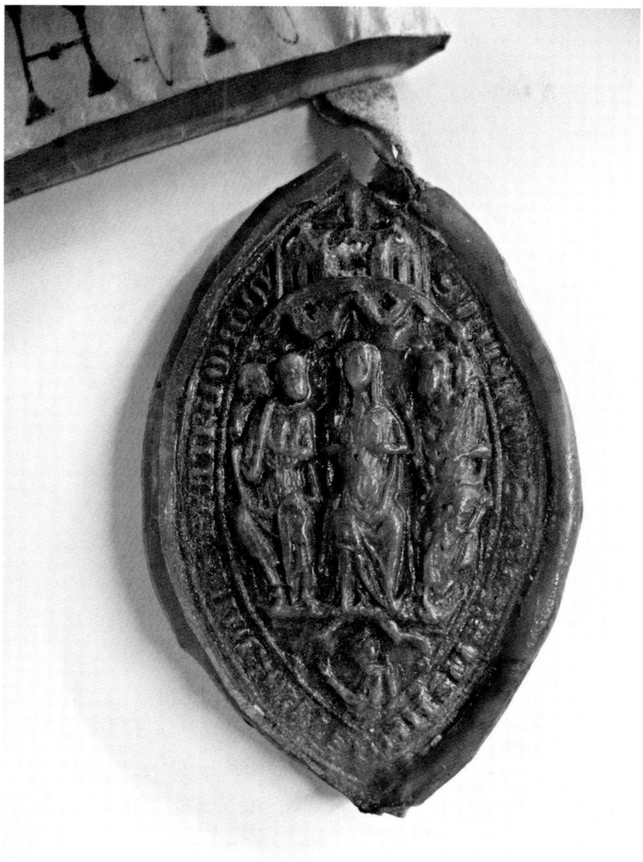

15 Wax impression of the Franciscan minister general's Pentecost seal, Gent, Rijksarchief, fonds Sint-Pietersabdij, charter nr 644, 1254.

Evidently Jerome continued to interest himself in Franciscan affairs. The friar and chronicler Salimbene of Parma claimed that the Order petitioned Nicholas III to have Jerome appointed as their cardinal protector, but, in the event, the pope preferred to choose his kinsman Matteo Rosso Orsini for this office.[19]

Jerome's involvement in the *Exiit* discussions raises the question of his education. Bernard of Besse, Bonaventure's secretary, classed Jerome as a 'lector of no small learning'.[20] Franciscan historians would later attribute to Jerome a series of writings, including a commentary on the *Sentences* of Peter Lombard.[21] From this list, only a single volume of sermons survives, and their derivative nature has led their modern editor, Cesare Cenci, to speculate that during the 1260s Jerome was lector in a large Franciscan convent, possibly Santa Maria in Aracoeli in Rome, rather than a master at one of the Order's leading university schools like Paris or Bologna.[22] As minister general, he was certainly interested in Franciscan hagiography, commissioning John Pecham to write a new legend of Saint Anthony of Padua and adding fresh miracles to Bonaventure's *Legenda maior*.[23] One of these was a highly impressive curing of blindness that occurred in the Assisi Basilica before the altar of Saint Francis.[24]

Jerome was made a cardinal at the same time as Giacomo Colonna, and his Roman titular church of Santa Pudenziana was close by the Colonna-dominated basilica of Santa Maria Maggiore. His ties with the Colonna must have intensified when Pope Martin IV elevated him to the cardinal bishopric of Palestrina on Easter Saturday, 12 April 1281.[25] This promotion was surely favoured by the Colonna, for Palestrina was the family's principal stronghold outside Rome.[26] Jerome's new cathedral church of Sant'Agapito nestled below the imposing fortress of the Colonna at the summit of the town. Their lordship of Palestrina was reflected in its *duomo*: the cosmati decoration of Sant'Agapito's high-altar frontal incorporated the family's column device and perhaps their coat of arms as well (fig. 16).[27] In 1283 Jerome and Giacomo

16 Cosmati altar frontal, second half of the thirteenth century with seventeenth-century additions, chapel of Saint Lawrence, cathedral of Sant'Agapito, Palestrina.

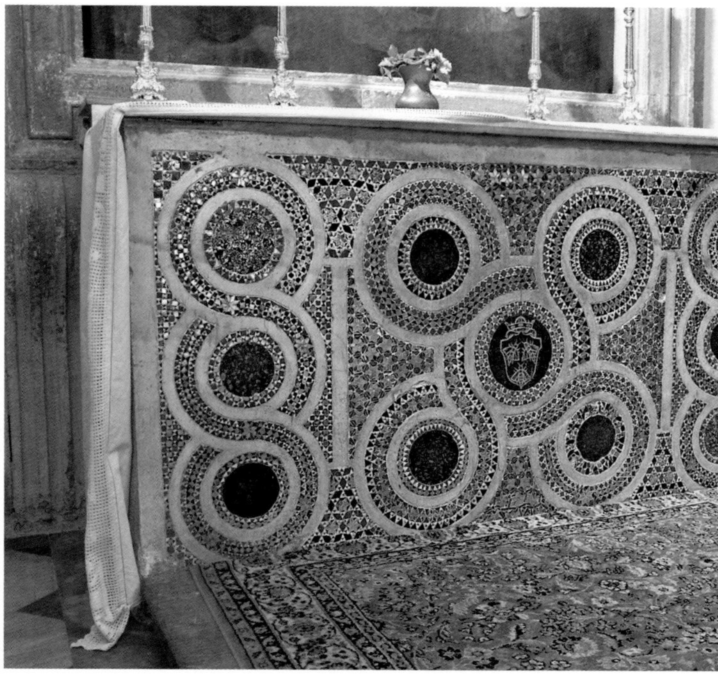

travelled together to the Romagna on behalf of Pope Martin to try to pacify local factions and remove hostile fortifications around Forlì and Cesena.[28] More significantly, Jerome was entrusted by Pope Honorius IV Savelli in 1285 with the foundation of a new monastery for the followers of Blessed Margherita Colonna (†1280), Giacomo's sister, securing the prestigious abbey complex of San Silvestro in Capite as the community's new base in Rome.[29]

Our first firm indication of Jerome as a patron of art and architecture dates from the same year. Claudia Bolgia and Julian Gardner have recently drawn attention to a lengthy marble inscription of 9 November 1285 from the small Roman church of San Salvatore in Pensilis, which proclaimed the concession of an indulgence of two years and forty days by Pope Honorius.[30] In addition, the text commemorated the recent restoration of the church by 'our brother Jerome bishop of Palestrina', who had commissioned a bell tower, wall paintings ('muri pictura'), throne, vaults, a rose window ('rosa') and probably a chancel screen.[31] Gardner speculated that San Salvatore, now enveloped by later construction, may have been the *intra muros* seat of the bishop of Palestrina within Rome itself, which would explain the otherwise unexpected reference to a throne ('sedile') in such a small church. As Gardner observed, the use of the term 'rose' to refer to a window is especially precocious. Rose windows were a novelty in Rome, but Jerome must have seen impressive examples during his Parisian sojourn of 1276–9 and he would also have known the great oculus on the façade of the Upper Church at Assisi.[32] As for the inclusion of wall painting within this comprehensive litany of renovation, Gardner rightly highlighted the implications of the 1285 inscription for our reading of *Reducentes ad sedulae*, Jerome's intervention at Assisi as pope less than three years later. The more specific wording of the San Salvatore text further supports the assumption that the terms of *Reducentes* must have envisaged fresco decoration as part of a comprehensive plan of renewal for the Basilica of San Francesco. In Gardner's words: 'He knew exactly what he was encouraging. Nicholas IV had form.'[33] Jerome's extensive restoration of San Salvatore in Pensilis in the early 1280s has multiple ramifications for our understanding of his later artistic patronage. For one thing, it is probably no coincidence that San Salvatore was in a Colonna neighbourhood. For another, the 1285 inscription very unusually comments on the speed of Jerome's restoration: it was done quickly ('tempore submodico').

Jerome's earlier ties came into sharp focus once he became pope; Colonna support, we may assume, had been instrumental in securing the papacy. As Nicholas IV, he swiftly elevated Giacomo's young nephew Pietro to the cardinalate, balanced by the promotion of Napoleone Orsini. They and four others were raised to the purple at Pentecost 1288, a date that would have held Franciscan connotations for the new pope.[34] Nicholas's choice of residences also betrays his deep alliance with the Colonna. He spent the first two months following his election in Rome between Saint Peter's and the Lateran.[35] In a recent study of curial itineraries, Pierre-Yves Le Pogam has suggested that by the late thirteenth century an initial residency at the Vatican was advisable, serving to validate a newly elected pontiff.[36] Nicholas's coronation in the Petrine basilica was certainly laden with apostolic symbolism, celebrated on the feast of the Enthronement of Saint Peter with the new pope seated on the *Cathedra Sancti Petri*.[37] But after this early Vatican sojourn, Nicholas returned there only once and showed no interest in patronizing Orsini-dominated Old Saint Peter's.[38] Nicholas stopped using the Lateran too, but for a very different reason: he had initiated a far-reaching renewal of the basilica that probably rendered its interior unusable for the duration of his pontificate. Instead, the Franciscan pope adopted Santa Maria Maggiore as his permanent base in Rome, utilizing the adjoining residence of the Marian basilica's archpriest, Giacomo Colonna.[39] A calendar of papal audiences from these years tells us that Nicholas usually resided at Santa Maria Maggiore and convened his audiences nearby in his old titular church of Santa Pudenziana.[40]

Nicholas's debt to the Colonna was a matter of common knowledge: a contemporary lampoon portrayed the Franciscan pope trapped inside a column, flanked by two further columns standing for his two Colonna cardinals.[41] Their alliance brought mutual political benefits, but it also drew on the genuine friendship between Nicholas and Giacomo Colonna, and their shared devotion to the Franciscan movement. Giacomo oversaw Nicholas's eventual burial in Santa Maria Maggiore, where he then endowed an altar in the pope's memory, providing for priests to celebrate daily masses for Nicholas's soul there.[42] Giacomo had been extremely close to his sister Margherita, a Clarissan nun who by the early 1290s was a prime candidate for Franciscan sanctity. According to the legend composed by their brother Giovanni, the cardinal himself had experienced miraculous

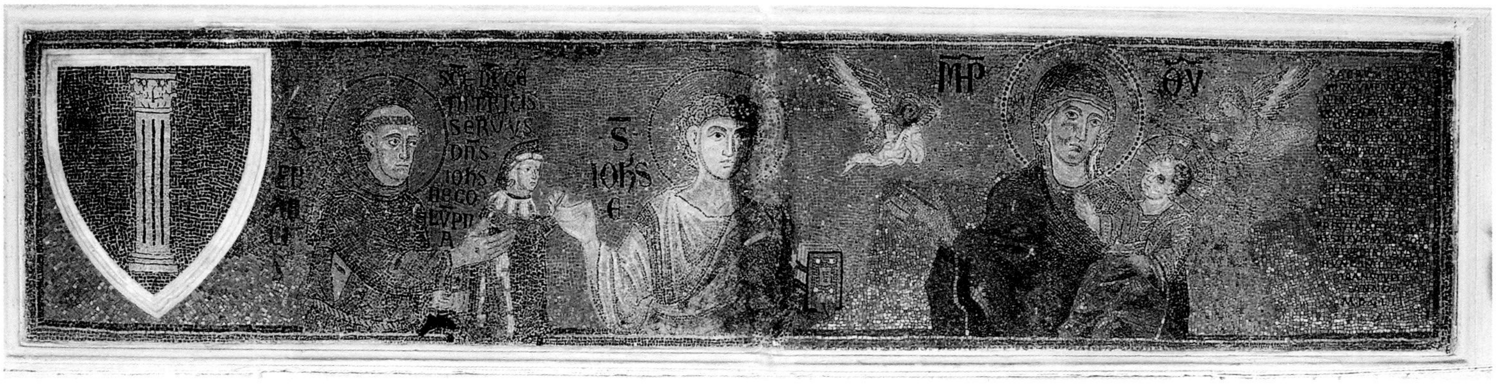

17 Virgin and Child with Saint John the Evangelist, Saint Francis and Giovanni Colonna, *c.*1294, mosaic panel, Palazzo Colonna, Rome (originally Santa Maria in Aracoeli, Rome).

visions of Margherita's conversion.[43] Giacomo's sincere devotion to Saint Francis and his Order was encapsulated in the judgement of Salimbene of Parma: 'lord Giacomo Colonna, who is a wholehearted friend of the Order of Friars Minor'.[44] This affiliation was shared by other leading members of the family, doubtless cemented by the example of Margherita's saintly life. The same Giovanni Colonna who had acted as his sister's hagiographer chose to be buried in the main Franciscan church in Rome, Santa Maria in Aracoeli. Giovanni was commemorated in the church by an elaborate mosaic retable, in which the donor was presented to the Virgin and Child by Saint Francis and by his name-saint John the Evangelist (fig. 17).[45]

The Lateran Rebuilt: A Prophecy Fulfilled

In Rome, Nicholas IV's vision of the Franciscan Order at the centre of the Church shaped the pope's ambitious campaigns of renewal at Saint John Lateran and Santa Maria Maggiore, two of the city's three principal papal basilicas (the third being Saint Peter's). In both cases, powerful iconographic statements were glossed by donor inscriptions, which give us some sense of the rhetoric that accompanied the Franciscan pope's artistic projects. Nicholas's Roman schemes therefore provide essential points of reference for Assisi.

Pope Innocent III's dream of Saint Francis saving the Lateran basilica from collapse was a key moment in the Franciscan Order's foundation story. The legend was associated with the journey Saint Francis made from Assisi to Rome in 1209 or 1210 with a band of his followers to seek approval of their Rule from the pope of the day, Innocent III. According to the story, Innocent was struck by Francis's humility and eloquence, but what persuaded the pope to grant Francis's request was the connection he made between the saint and a vision that had recently come to him in a dream of a 'little poor man' sustaining the weight of the Lateran on his back and preventing its fall. The earliest account of Innocent's dream appeared in Thomas of Celano's second life of Saint Francis (composed *c.*1245–7) and it quickly became a canonical episode in Franciscan hagiography. Innocent's words, as reported by Celano and Bonaventure, underlined the symbolic reading of the Lateran basilica as standing for the Church at large: 'I am sure that he [that is, Francis] is the one who will hold up Christ's Church by what he does and what he teaches.'[46] The identification of the 'poor man' with Saint Francis was, however, contested by the Dominicans, who were convinced that the figure in Innocent's dream was really their own founder, Saint Dominic.[47] Both Orders promoted their rival versions vigorously through texts and images from the 1240s onwards, neither ceding ground to the other.

From a Franciscan point of view, Pope Innocent's vision had not only led directly to the approval of the Order's Rule, it also offered a powerful visual allegory for the pre-eminent role that the Friars Minor perceived for themselves in the reform of the Church. The Lateran legend now provided an ideological template for Nicholas IV's ambitions to position his Order at the heart of the Eternal City's sacred topography. It was probably during his pontificate that a monumen-

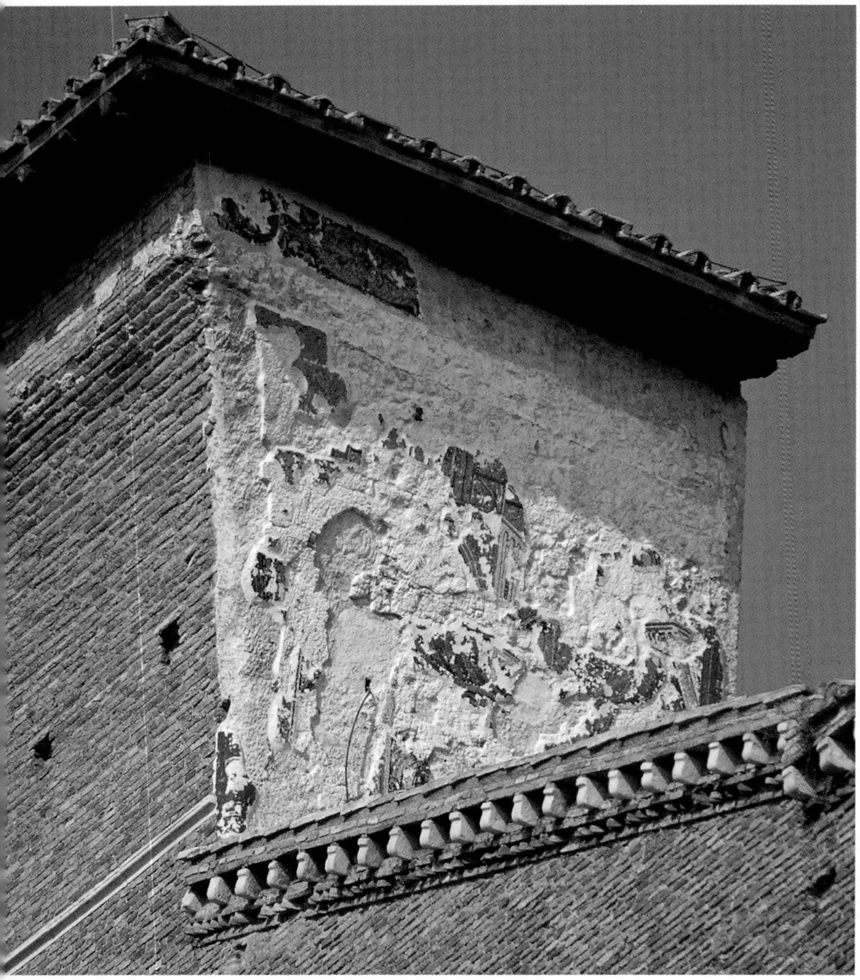

18 *Dream of Pope Innocent III*, *c*.1288–92, façade mosaic, Santa Maria in Aracoeli, Rome.

tal mosaic of the subject, some 3.65 metres in height, was added to the façade of the Order's newly completed church of Santa Maria in Aracoeli (fig. 18).[48] The image was placed high up on the coving at the very top of the façade. But it was on the right-hand return of the façade wall, and so invisible from the front of the church. Instead, the mosaic overlooked the Capitol, site of the senatorial palace and the principal centre of civic authority in Rome. In addition, the Aracoeli mosaic – as Maria Andaloro observed – surveyed the city towards the Lateran to the south-east.[49] Although early sources describe fragments of tesserae on the front of the church, the *Dream of Innocent III* was unlikely to have been part of a larger narrative sequence.[50] The subject of the mosaic was more likely deliberately chosen as an isolated scene, with the Lateran basilica standing for *Ecclesia*, thereby signalling Innocent III's prophecy of Francis holding up 'Christ's Church'. Hardly more than a pale blemish on the Aracoeli's smart brickwork in its present, ruined condition, the mosaic would originally have been a vivid flash of colour, easily legible from below given its generous scale. The real-life overhang of the façade coving would have added to the sense of Francis supporting the leaning Lateran basilica.

The same themes of destiny and renewal were pushed even further at the Lateran itself, where Nicholas IV's direct patronage was proclaimed by commemorative inscriptions and a donor image. His renovation of the Lateran involved the demolition of the basilica's Constantinian apse and its replacement by a loftier hemispherical vault on the same foundations.[51] The conch of the rebuilt apse was then entirely mosaiced by Jacopo Torriti (fig. 19), who signed his name in the lower left corner of the semi-dome: JACOPUS TORRITI PICT[OR] OHOP [that is, HOC OPUS] FECCIT.[52] Elements of Torriti's mosaic reprised the iconography of its palaeo-christian predecessor, but the donor inscription along its lower border was wholly new and broadcast the good works of the Franciscan pope in emphatic terms: 'Pope Nicholas IV, son of Blessed Francis, had the ruined back and front parts of this holy temple rebuilt from the foundations and adorned with mosaic work, and he had the Holy Face of the Saviour put back as it was in the place where it first miraculously appeared to the Roman people, when this church was consecrated. In the year of the Lord 1291.'[53] With this statement, Nicholas presented his interventions at the Lateran as a continuation of the basilica's venerable early Christian heritage, calling the viewer's attention to the bust of the Saviour at the apex of the new apse, which had been physically salvaged from the earlier mosaic. This was believed to be an image not made by human hands, or an *acheiropoieta*, which had miraculously appeared on the apse when the basilica was consecrated.[54] But Nicholas's inscription mixed old and new, for it was also a powerful assertion of his Franciscan identity, declaring the pope to be a 'son of Blessed Francis'.

Unfortunately, Torriti's mosaic was lost when Nicholas's apse was in turn demolished in the early 1880s during a recklessly destructive project to expand the sanctuary area. What we see today is a copy executed in 1886 after drawings taken from the original before its destruction.[55] The present facsimile at least seems to be an iconographically reliable (if

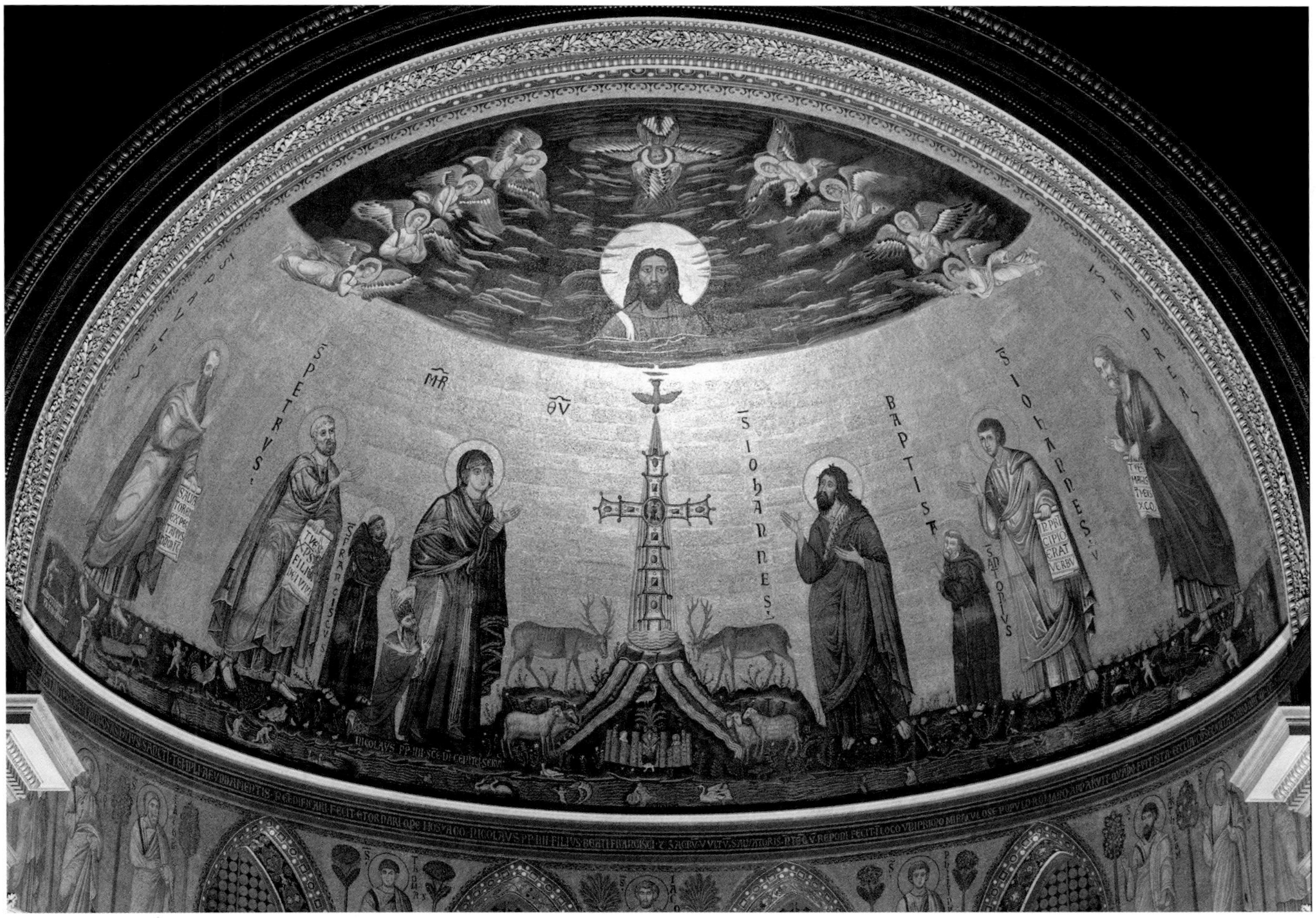

19 Jacopo Torriti, apse mosaic, dated 1291, with later additions to *c.*1294 (reconstructed 1886), Saint John Lateran, Rome.

aesthetically much inferior) record of Torriti's original. When the medieval mosaic was being torn down in the 1880s, the Saviour's head was discovered to be on a separate and much older block of travertine stone, which had been embedded in the surface of the thirteenth-century vault and secured by iron clamps, confirming the substance of Nicholas's donor inscription.[56]

Like that inscription, the iconography of Torriti's mosaic combined early Christian tradition with messages specific to the late thirteenth century. The jewelled cross at the centre was probably copied from the earlier palaeochristian apse mosaic (fig. 20).[57] The dove of the Holy Spirit descends to the cross, with water spraying from its beak.[58] This Pentecostal shower bathes the cross, which is embossed with a medallion of the Baptism of Christ, before collecting into the four rivers of paradise below. These streams quench the thirst of four sheep and two deer, the latter a reference to Psalm 41: 'As the hart panteth after the fountains of water; so my soul panteth after thee, O God.'[59] The rivers also shelter a miniature depiction of the heavenly Jerusalem, inhabited by the apostles Peter and Paul and guarded by Saint Michael, before converging to form a single body of water, identified in the mosaic as the river Jordan (IORDANES), that flows out to left and right along the bottom edge of the apse. The aquatic imagery in the Lateran apse is worth noting, for similar ideas and symbols would find their way into the mural decoration of the Upper Church at Assisi.[60]

Torriti arranged six large-scale saints on the apse's main register, three to either side of the central dove and cross. The innermost figures of the Virgin to the left and Saint John the Baptist to the right combine with the bust of the Saviour above to form a central *Deesis* group. The reference

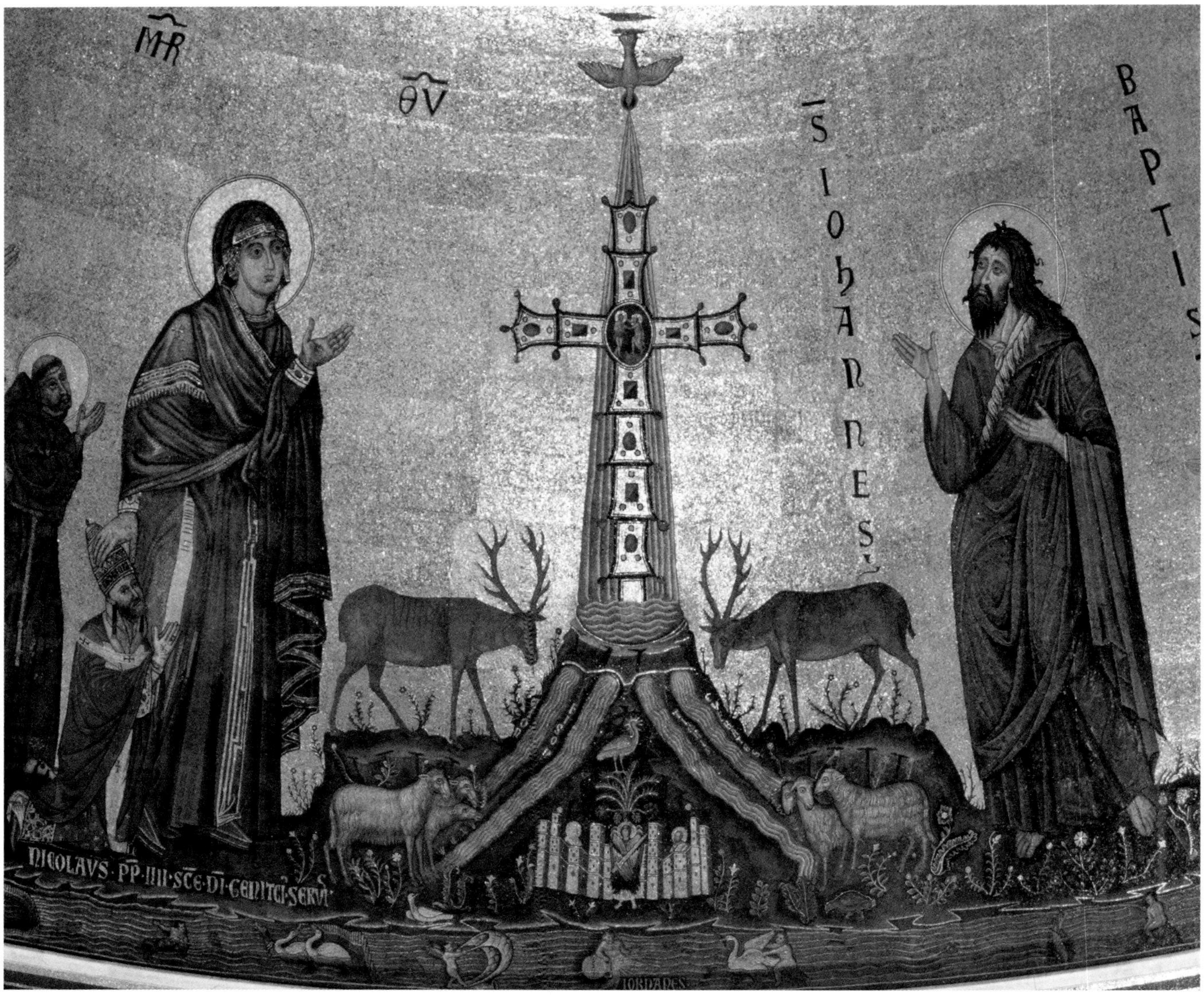

20 Jacopo Torriti, apse mosaic, dated 1291, with later additions to *c.*1294, detail of the central cross and rivers of paradise, Saint John Lateran, Rome.

to the *Deesis* may have been a departure from the earlier apse (which probably privileged Saints Peter and Paul), and echoed the *Deesis* vault that Torriti had just painted in the Upper Church at Assisi (see fig. 13).[61] At the Lateran, the Virgin shelters the kneeling donor figure of Nicholas IV, touching his tiara with her right hand. She is accompanied on the left-hand side of the semi-dome by Saints Peter and Paul, while Saints John the Evangelist and Andrew line up behind the Baptist to the right. Where Torriti broke radically from established conventions of apse design in Rome was in adding two extra saints, on a smaller scale, behind the Virgin and the Baptist. They were Francis and the other canonized Franciscan, Anthony of Padua. It was an unprecedented iconographic gesture. The saints of a specific religious order had never before been so favoured in the major papal basilicas of Rome.

The intention was clear: Nicholas's mosaic announced Saints Francis and Anthony as new apostles, uniquely privileged to accompany the Virgin, the Baptist and Saints Peter, Paul, Andrew and John the Evangelist. The nine remaining biblical apostles appear on the register below, split between the four windows of the apsidal drum. At their feet kneel

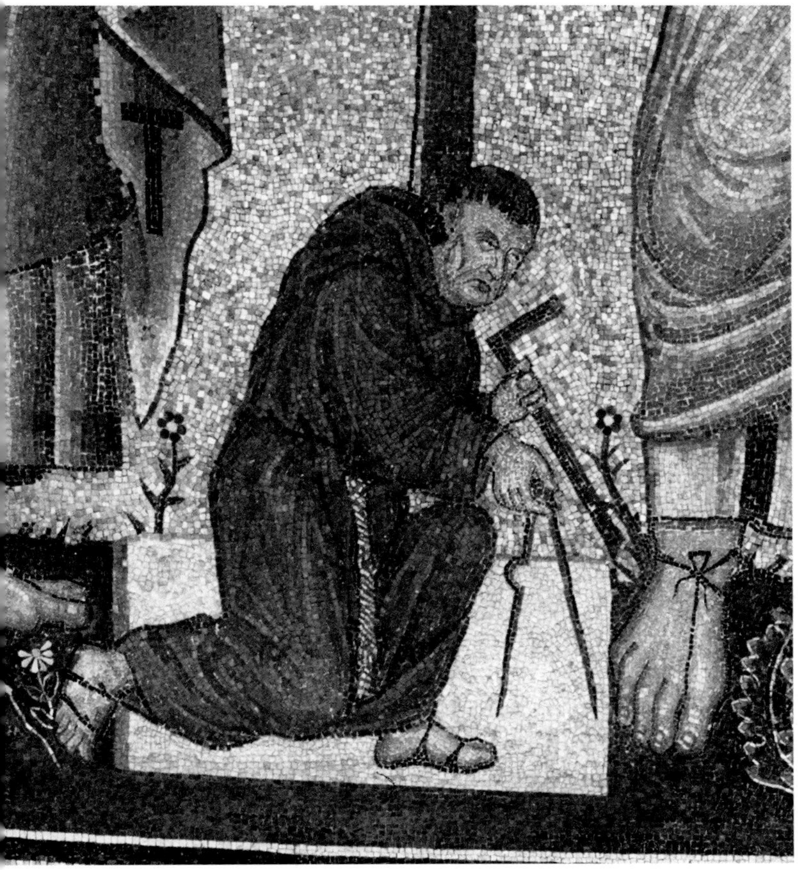

21 Jacopo Torriti, apse mosaic, *c.*1291–4, detail of Jacopo Torriti, Saint John Lateran, Rome.

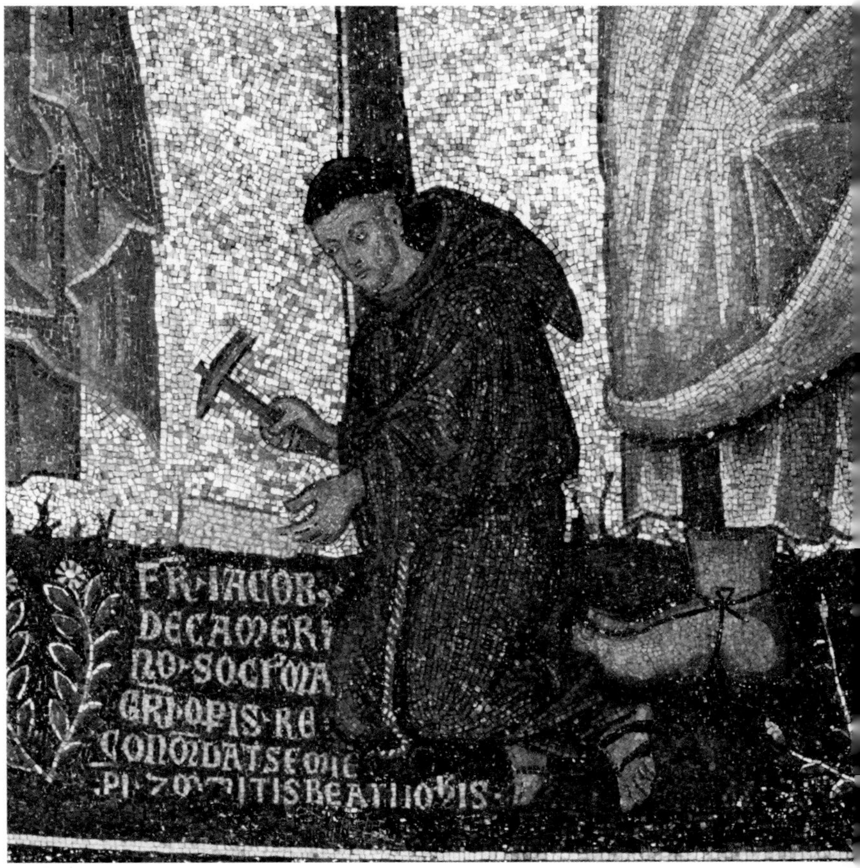

22 Jacopo Torriti, apse mosaic, *c.*1291–4, detail of Jacopo of Camerino, Saint John Lateran, Rome.

the diminutive figures of two Franciscan friars. The miniature friar to the right works a piece of stone with a hammer and is identified by an inscription: 'Brother Jacopo of Camerino, assistant to the master of the work' (fig. 22).[62] The friar to the left is shown with a set-square and compass, kneeling over and poised to incise a white rectangle, perhaps intended for a slab of stone (fig. 21).[63] This must have been the designer of the work, Jacopo Torriti, who had already signed his name above in the lower left corner of the apse.[64] Torriti's portrait in the lower register lacks an inscription, but his instruments leave little doubt as to his identity as the 'master of the work'; furthermore, as Valentino Pace observed, Torriti portrayed himself kneeling at the foot of his name-saint, the apostle James.[65] The Lateran apse was therefore not only commissioned by a Franciscan pope, it was executed by artists who were themselves Friars Minor. In particular, it is immensely significant that Jacopo Torriti can be identified as a Franciscan. Not only was Jacopo Nicholas IV's favoured artist in Rome, he was also – as we shall see – the leading painter during the initial phase of decorating the nave of the Upper Church at Assisi.[66] At the Lateran, the two Jacopos are pictured hard at work. As Brooke perceptively remarked, 'they are engaged, literally, in the rebuilding and embellishment of the Lateran . . . the embodiment of the ordinary Friars Minor, the rank and file of the Order, whose task it is, as followers of Saint Francis, to renew the Church'.[67]

The sheer audacity of the Franciscan imagery on the Lateran apse must have been obvious at the time. Contemporary hostility to such a partisan statement is suggested by a miracle appended to the *Legenda prima* of Saint Anthony of Padua in the early years of the Trecento.[68] This story records the anger of Pope Boniface VIII Caetani (1294–1303) when he heard how two Franciscan mosaicists working in the Lateran (evidently to be identified with the kneeling

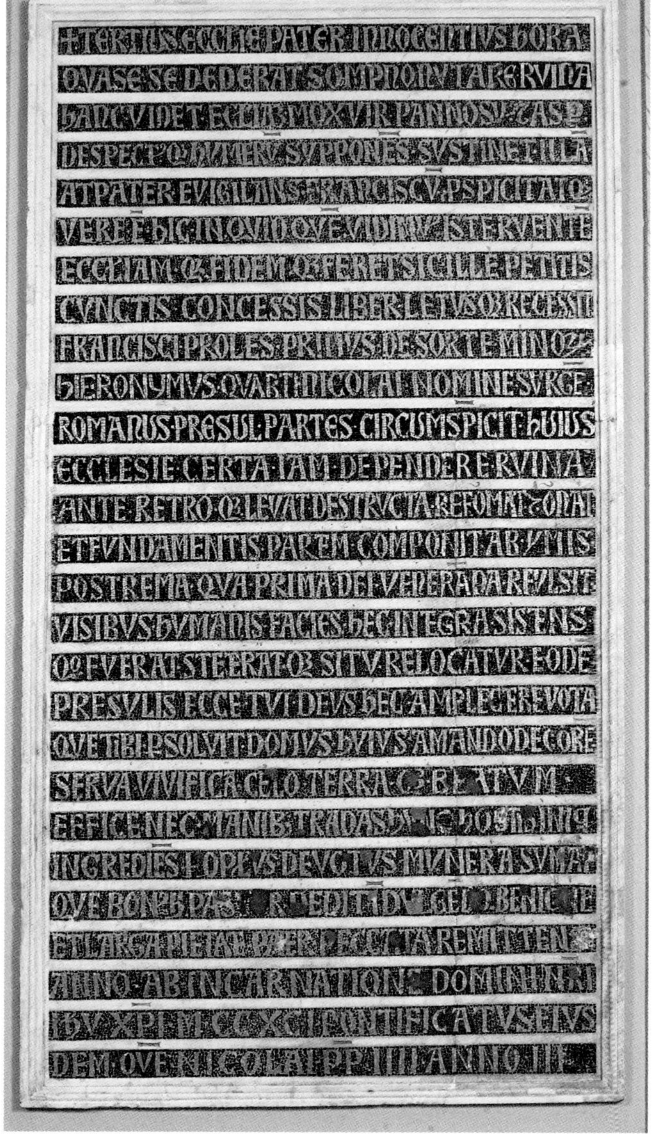

23 Pope Nicholas IV's donor inscription, dated 1291, mosaic panel, Saint John Lateran, Rome.

friars portrayed in the lower register) had inserted, on their own initiative, the figures of Francis and Anthony into the apsidal mosaic.[69] Boniface was willing to tolerate the presence of Saint Francis but ordered the image of Saint Anthony to be removed, only for the Paduan saint to intervene, thwarting the workmen who were sent to destroy his image. On hearing this news, the Caetani pope is said to have relented, concluding that 'we have more to lose than gain' from such iconoclasm.[70]

If the Antonine story has any basis in reality, it has consequences for the completion date of the Lateran apsidal mosaic.[71] Benedetto Caetani had been elected pope in Naples in December 1294, and returned immediately to Rome in the new year of 1295. Most likely the episode should be dated to the first months of 1295, when Boniface is known to have resided at the Lateran.[72] This would imply that work on the mosaic was still ongoing in the years 1292–4, notwithstanding the 1291 date inscribed at the bottom of the main apsidal field. There are some reasons to think that this extended chronology may be correct. Nicholas had completely rebuilt the ambulatory around the back of the Lateran apse, and this could have delayed work on the lower sections of the mosaic.[73] Perhaps the lower register with the nine apostles was completed after the pope's death. Such a caesura could explain why Torriti's signature is separated from his portrait. Similarly, the two Franciscan saints may have been inserted into the main apse field in this second moment.[74] As far as we can tell from the existing nineteenth-century palimpsest of the original, Saints Francis and Anthony do seem to be awkwardly scaled and positioned between their larger and more monumental companions. Francesco Gandolfo went so far as to suggest that the Franciscan saints were not necessarily part of Nicholas IV's original scheme.

In the absence of the original mosaic or better documentation it is not possible to establish such a detailed chronology for Torriti's apse, but Nicholas IV's specifically Franciscan vision for the renewal of the Lateran should not be doubted. It received its most articulate formulation in a lengthy mosaic inscription, now located by the door to the basilica's sacristy, but originally set either on the wall of the main apse or beside the entrance to Nicholas's new ambulatory (fig. 23).[75] Dated, like the main field of the apse mosaic, to 1291, the inscription openly associated Nicholas's rebuilding of the Lateran with Innocent III's dream of Saint Francis supporting the basilica:

> Innocent the third, father of the Church, at the time when he gave himself over to sleep, saw this church toppling into ruin. Soon a rough, despised man in rags held it up by leaning his shoulder against it. But the father, awaking, recognized Francis, and said: 'Truly it is he whom we see. This man will bear the collapsing Church and faith.' Thus he departed freely and joyously, all his prayers having been granted. A child of Francis, Jerome, arising under the name

of Nicholas the fourth, as Roman bishop, the first among those whose lot is that of the Minors, saw that parts of this church were already falling into certain ruin. He raised it up at the front and the back. He remade and adorned what had been destroyed, and built up part of it from its lowest foundations. Finally, where the venerable face of God first shone for human eyes – this he made whole: it was relocated in the place where it had been and stood before. Come, God, embrace these vows of your bishop, which he has fulfilled by loving the beauty of your house [Psalm 25:8]. Save him, give him life, make him blessed in heaven and on earth, and do not hand him over to the hands of the evil enemy. May the devout people who enter take up the gifts which this good shepherd and father gave by kind indulgence, and generous piety, forgiving sins. In the year 1291 from the Incarnation of Our Lord Jesus Christ, the third year of the pontificate of that same Pope Nicholas IV.[76]

This text, probably composed under Nicholas's close supervision, is the most substantial record we have of the Franciscan pope's personal sense of historical mission. It also reveals the significance he attached to images and architecture, already evident in the commemorative inscription from San Salvatore in Pensilis discussed above. Nicholas's prayer for salvation is weighed against his renovation of the church and his conservation of the miraculous face of the Saviour, good works which are in turn explained by the example of Saint Francis. The Lateran inscription is categorical in identifying the poor man of Pope Innocent's dream as Francis, ignoring the widespread counter-claims for Saint Dominic. The mosaic text follows this assertion immediately with the fact of Nicholas's election to the papacy. The implication is unavoidable: his pontificate should be understood as the historical consummation of Innocent's vision. Moreover, Nicholas is referred to not only as pope, but also by his secular name Jerome and as the first Franciscan pontiff ('primus de sorte Minorum').[77] By stressing his Franciscan identity in such prominent terms, Nicholas cemented the central rhetorical message of his renovation of the Lateran: that he personally, by virtue of his Franciscan past and his elevation to the papacy, was the living fulfilment of Innocent's prophecy.

Nicholas's campaign of works at the Lateran was extensive and multifaceted. Not only were the apse and ambulatory wholly renewed, the main façade was rebuilt, and it may have been at this date that the basilica acquired its transept.[78] The resetting of the Holy Face was sufficiently important for commemorations in both the apse and ambulatory inscriptions. By emphasizing this miraculous image, Nicholas doubtless sought to bolster the Lateran's status vis-à-vis Saint Peter's, which possessed an even more prestigious Holy Face, the relic of the Veronica. The rivalry with the Vatican also informed another inscription commissioned by Nicholas, which originally ran below the windows of the apse, and proclaimed the primacy of the papal throne below, taunting a similar apsidal legend in Old Saint Peter's.[79] A further mosaic inscription catalogued the numerous relics within the basilica's high altar, from Christ's robes to the Ark of the Covenant with the tablets of the law.[80] This panel formed a pair with Nicholas's lengthy donor legend connecting his renovation with Pope Innocent's dream. These matching mosaic inscriptions, identical in size and materials, were almost certainly mounted symmetrically to either side of the main apse or by the entrances to the new ambulatory.

Nicholas IV's interventions at the Lateran amounted to a rewriting of church history. The Franciscan pope reasserted the basilica's centuries-old claims to primacy over Saint Peter's. But these claims were now refracted through a thirteenth-century prism, gaining additional strength from the Lateran's pivotal role in the Franciscan story. The Lateran in turn provided Nicholas with a vehicle for positioning the Franciscan Order at the heart of the Roman Church. By turning Innocent's dream into a physical reality of marble and golden mosaic, Nicholas obliged Rome to gaze on the Friars Minor as the chosen apostles of a new age.

Santa Maria Maggiore: Working with the Colonna

The rebuilding of the Lateran must have absorbed an enormous quantity of papal resources. But it represented only one half of Nicholas's broader effort to renew and redefine the sacred topography of Rome. He lavished at least as much attention on the basilica of Santa Maria Maggiore, the city's principal shrine to the Virgin, on the Esquiline hill.[81] Many aspects of the new decorative programme at Santa Maria Maggiore paralleled Nicholas's interventions at the Lateran. If anything, his plans for the Esquiline basilica were even more extensive. Nicholas had the old apse demolished and a new one built some six and a half metres further to the west, inserting a transept into the resulting gap.[82] Once again Nicholas commissioned an apsidal mosaic, this time entirely new, from his chosen artist and fellow friar, Jacopo Torriti.[83] While the early Christian mosaics in the nave were left undisturbed, Nicholas rebuilt the façade, which would be frescoed within and mosaiced without.[84]

The relative chronologies of the Lateran and Santa Maria Maggiore campaigns are difficult to disentangle. A generous indulgence granted on 27 September 1288 to those faithful who gave alms for the Marian basilica's repair suggests that the pope began plotting far-reaching changes on the Esquiline soon after his election.[85] But it seems, broadly speaking, that the renewal of the Lateran was pushed forward with greater urgency.[86] As we have seen, the main apse there and Nicholas's mosaic inscriptions were already in place by early 1291, while it is clear that the pope's projects at Santa Maria Maggiore were largely unfinished at his death on 4 April 1292. Torriti signed his mosaic at the bottom left of the semi-dome, as at the Lateran, but added the date 1296 in the opposite corner.[87] Even more than the miracle worked by Saint Anthony against Boniface VIII at the Lateran, the completion of the decorative programme at Santa Maria Maggiore forces us to consider the fate of Nicholas's projects after his death. This progression is also crucial for understanding contemporary events at Assisi, given that the frescoing of the Upper Church, initiated under the authority of Nicholas's bulls in 1288, must have extended well into the 1290s, and certainly beyond the pope's demise in 1292.

At Santa Maria Maggiore, the continuation of Nicholas's projects can be explained by the dominant role of the Colonna. The Esquiline basilica was undoubtedly their church. Giacomo Colonna was its archpriest, and Nicholas's indulgences to Santa Maria Maggiore were addressed directly to the cardinal.[88] The Colonna seem to have possessed as many as four chapels in the basilica.[89] As we have seen, Nicholas's friendship with the Colonna and his political dependence upon them were clearly displayed at Santa Maria Maggiore. When in Rome, he based the curia at the basilica or in his old titular church of Santa Pudenziana not far away. The Franciscan pope also asked to be buried in Santa Maria Maggiore, and Cardinal Giacomo saw to his tomb and its altar.[90] Nicholas's own attachment to the Marian basilica was evidently sincere. He wished the new cathedral at Orvieto, his favoured base outside Rome, to be built as a copy of 'Sanctae Mariae maioris de Urbe'.[91] Perhaps he was attracted by the relics of his name-saint, Jerome, held on the Esquiline.[92] But this was likely to have been a secondary consideration after Nicholas's deep devotion to the Virgin.

Torriti's apse at Santa Maria Maggiore, unlike its twin at the Lateran, has endured the centuries of decay and renovation and can still be appreciated in its full splendour. It is the Franciscan artist's surviving masterpiece (fig. 24).[93] At its centre, Torriti set the *Coronation of the Virgin* within an enormous, starred roundel of brilliant blue tesserae. Freed from the constraints of an early Christian predecessor, the Santa Maria Maggiore mosaics were iconographically more adventurous than the Lateran's, reflecting both Roman tradition and up-to-date northern European models. Below the main apsidal field Torriti arranged five Marian narratives predella-style along the bottom of the conch. The *Dormition of the Virgin*, lifted out of sequence, was placed at the centre of this cycle, directly below the *Coronation*.[94] This served to underline the Coronation as the culmination of the Virgin's death and Assumption into heaven. An inscription below the main clipeus, moved there for greater legibility as the mosaic was being executed, further emphasized the Virgin's Assumption.[95] As Alessandro Tomei has shown, Torriti's Coronation iconography took a firm lead from the texts of Nicholas IV's indulgences to Santa Maria Maggiore, which identified the Virgin as the woman of Apocalypse 12:1, clothed by the sun with the moon beneath her feet, in the same breath as describing her elevation to heaven above choirs of angels – both details that found their way into the apse mosaic.[96]

But Torriti's Esquiline mosaic also repeated several notable features of the Lateran apse. The four rivers of paradise, although much less prominent at Santa Maria Maggiore, do issue forth below the central Coronation clipeus, filling the semi-dome's lower border with a riverscape where Torriti displays his extensive knowledge of ancient and early Christian mosaics.[97] Two deer drink at the river's bank and at the very centre the waters part to reveal a miniature walled Jerusalem, guarded by a seraphic angel brandishing a sword, while the haloed busts of Saints Peter and Paul emerge over the battlements. Moreover, Saints Francis and Anthony were again incorporated into the main register of the apse conch. This time they occupy the furthest positions from the centre: Saint Francis behind Saints Peter and Paul on the left, Saint Anthony behind the Baptist and Saint John the Evangelist on the right. But the Franciscans are now only marginally smaller than their biblical companions. As at the Lateran,

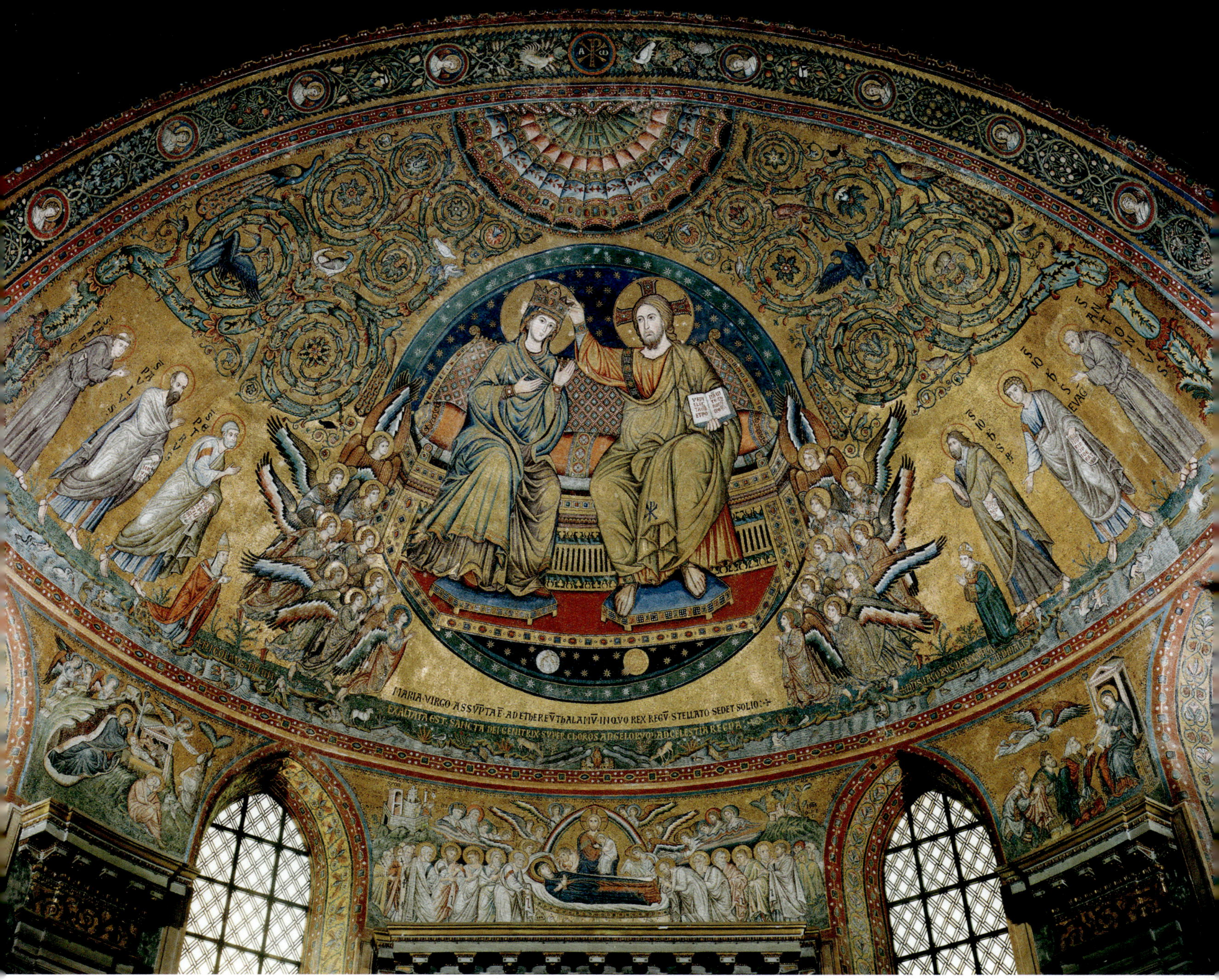

24 Jacopo Torriti, apse mosaic, signed and dated 1296, Santa Maria Maggiore, Rome.

Nicholas as donor kneels to the left of the central field, and this version at Santa Maria Maggiore constitutes the most credible portrait we have of the Franciscan pope (fig. 25). Nicholas's patronage was also commemorated by an inscription that originally ran along the conch's lower border: 'The pope was the fourth Nicholas. He restored this ruined temple of the Virgin, and what was old becomes new. May father Francis preserve his apostolic pupil. At the request of His mother, may the Almighty protect and bless him.'[98] Once again, Nicholas's Franciscan identity was woven into his prayer for salvation. The pope is a son – or an 'alumnus' – of Saint Francis, invoking the protection of his spiritual father as well as the prayers of the Virgin.

However, Nicholas did not take sole credit for the apsidal mosaic at Santa Maria Maggiore, as he had at the Lateran. His donor effigy was balanced by a matching figure of Cardinal Giacomo Colonna on the other side of the apse (fig. 26). Indeed, it is likely that much, if not all, of Torriti's mosaic was executed after Nicholas's death. In one of his final bulls, issued on 21 March 1292 (only two weeks before his death),

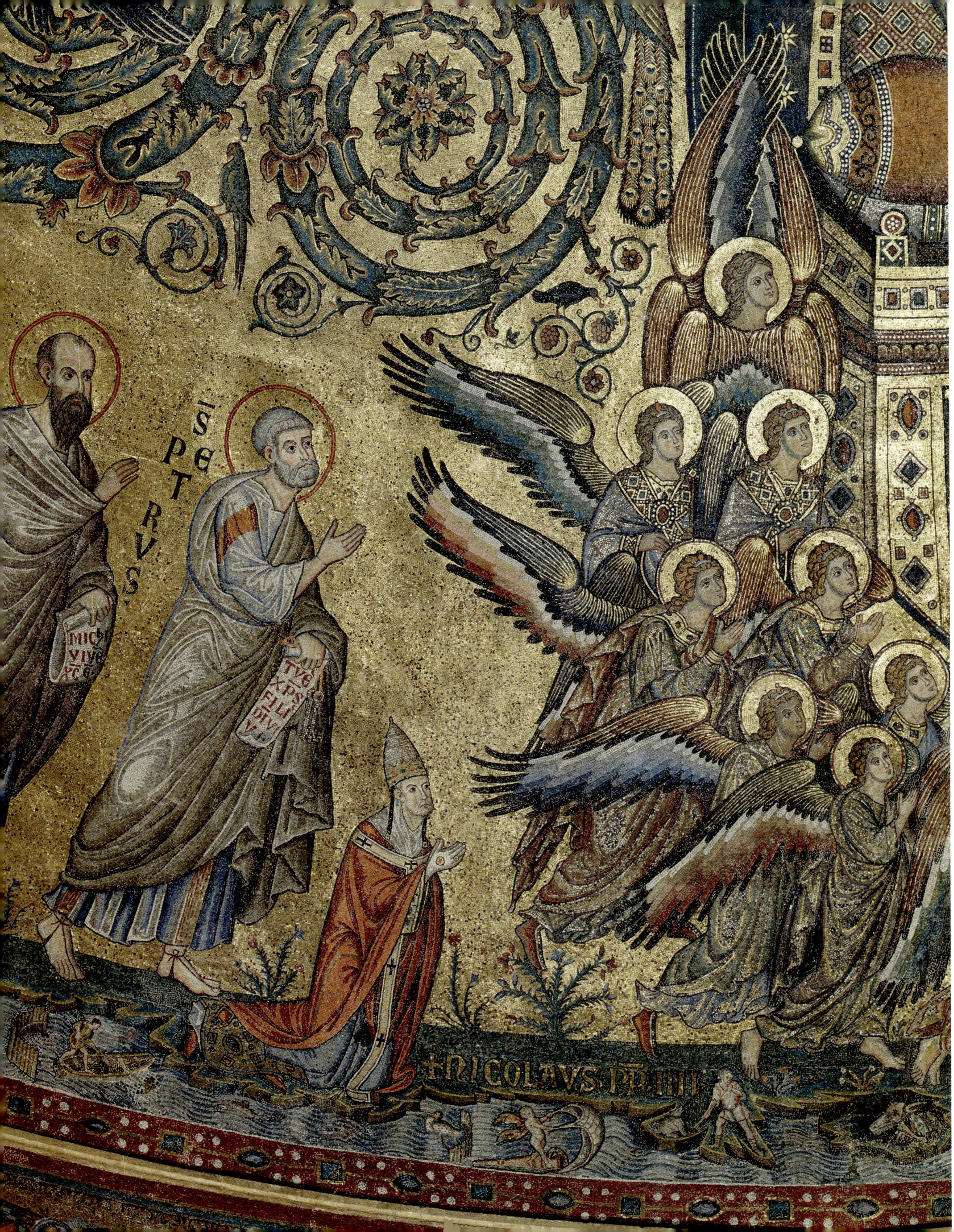
S̄ PETRVS
+NICOLAVS PP IIII

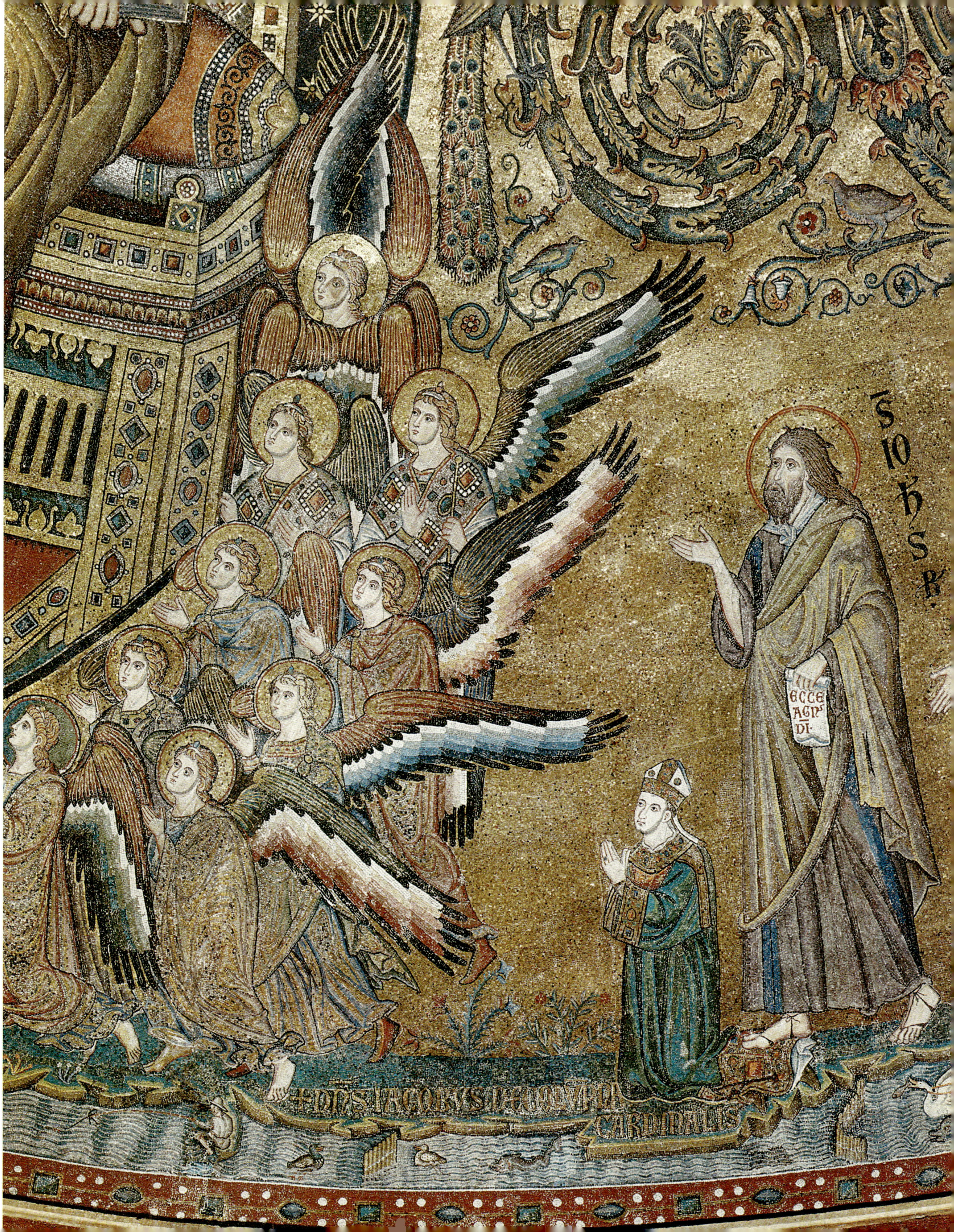
ECCE AGN' DI
CARDINALIS

the ailing pontiff sought to safeguard his vision for the Esquiline basilica. He fined the wealthy Chiarenti firm of bankers from Pistoia 1,000 gold ounces as atonement for their usury, and this enormous sum was to be reserved 'for the repair of the walls of Santa Maria Maggiore in Rome'.[99] Evidently much remained to be done. The Colonna must have been instrumental in conceiving the basilica's renovation and the family now pushed the project towards completion. The years after Nicholas's death offered the Colonna cardinals ample opportunity to promote their familial patronage at Santa Maria Maggiore. Deadlock in the college of cardinals led to a twenty-seven-month papal vacancy, resolved only by the desperate election of the hermit Peter of Morrone as Pope Celestine V in July 1294. Celestine's chaotic papacy lasted little more than five months before his infamous abdication. It was only with the election of Cardinal Benedetto Caetani as Pope Boniface VIII in December 1294 and his arrival in Rome the following January that papal authority was reasserted in the city.

The power vacuum created by this period of instability marked a high point in the Colonna's artistic patronage in Rome. As we have seen, it may have been in these years that the original programme at the Lateran was 'radicalized' by the insertion of the Franciscan saints into the recently mosaiced apse. At the Esquiline, Saints Francis and Anthony clearly formed part of Torriti's initial design, rather than being added as an afterthought. But the Santa Maria Maggiore apse was not finished until 1296, and was probably begun only after Nicholas's death. The two pairs of Franciscan saints, at the Lateran and Santa Maria Maggiore, may therefore have been executed at virtually the same moment. We cannot know if their inclusion deviated from Nicholas's intentions, but it is tempting to see the hand of the Colonna behind the initiative.[100] At Santa Maria Maggiore the Colonna's role in the design of Torriti's apse is also suggested by the donor inscription that ran along the lower border of the conch. It repeated, almost word for word, the second half of the epitaph that decorated Nicholas's original floor-tomb. This modest sepulchre no longer survives – the pope's remains were moved to a far more ornate marble tomb in the Cinquecento – but the original inscription has come down to us through Roman antiquarian sources: 'This grave buries a humble man who, adorned with the *fasces*, decided when dying that his bones were to lie in this way. Francis fostered him to be a cardinal, and the kind seat of Peter made him great, the grace of God blesses him. He was Pope Nicholas the Fourth. He restored this ruined temple of the Virgin, and what was old becomes new. May Peter the apostle protect his companion, Francis his pupil. May the Almighty protect him, at His mother's request.'[101] Giacomo Colonna had been responsible for Nicholas's burial and chantry, and it would be logical to assume that the cardinal also supervised his friend's epitaph. The text then provided the basis for Nicholas's posthumous donor legend on Torriti's apse, which was being completed under Colonna auspices in the years following the pope's death.

The Colonna cardinals also went to unprecedented lengths to display their own patronage at Santa Maria Maggiore. The façade mosaics, signed by Filippo Rusuti, incorporated multiple Colonna coats of arms around the main rose window, as well as kneeling figures of Cardinals Giacomo and Pietro to either side of the central Christ Enthroned.[102] These donor figures were destroyed with the addition of Ferdinando Fuga's loggia in the 1740s, but are recorded in a seventeenth-century drawing of Rusuti's façade mosaics, now in Edinburgh and identified by Julian Gardner (fig. 27).[103] Most of all, the inclusion of Cardinal Giacomo in Torriti's apse mosaic, at exactly the same level as Nicholas IV and on an identical scale, was unprecedented. Serena Romano judged the gesture 'sensational'.[104]

The Colonna's moment did not last long. Simmering rivalries within the family and tensions with Boniface VIII exploded into open rebellion against the Caetani pope in 1297.[105] On 3 May Cardinal Giacomo's nephew Stefano ambushed the papal treasure as it travelled from Anagni to Rome, making off with 200,000 gold florins. The consequences for the Colonna cardinals were devastating. On 10 May an enraged Boniface issued the incendiary bull *In excelso trono*, by which he excommunicated Giacomo and Pietro and stripped them of all property and benefices. In December the pope proclaimed a crusade against the rebel cardinals, and the Colonna fortresses in Lazio were taken by force of arms. Even Palestrina, the family's final stronghold, capitulated after a lengthy siege and was razed to the ground.

previous spread (left) 25 Jacopo Torriti, apse mosaic, signed and dated 1296, detail of Pope Nicholas IV, Santa Maria Maggiore, Rome.

previous spread (right) 26 Jacopo Torriti, apse mosaic, signed and dated 1296, detail of Cardinal Giacomo Colonna, Santa Maria Maggiore, Rome.

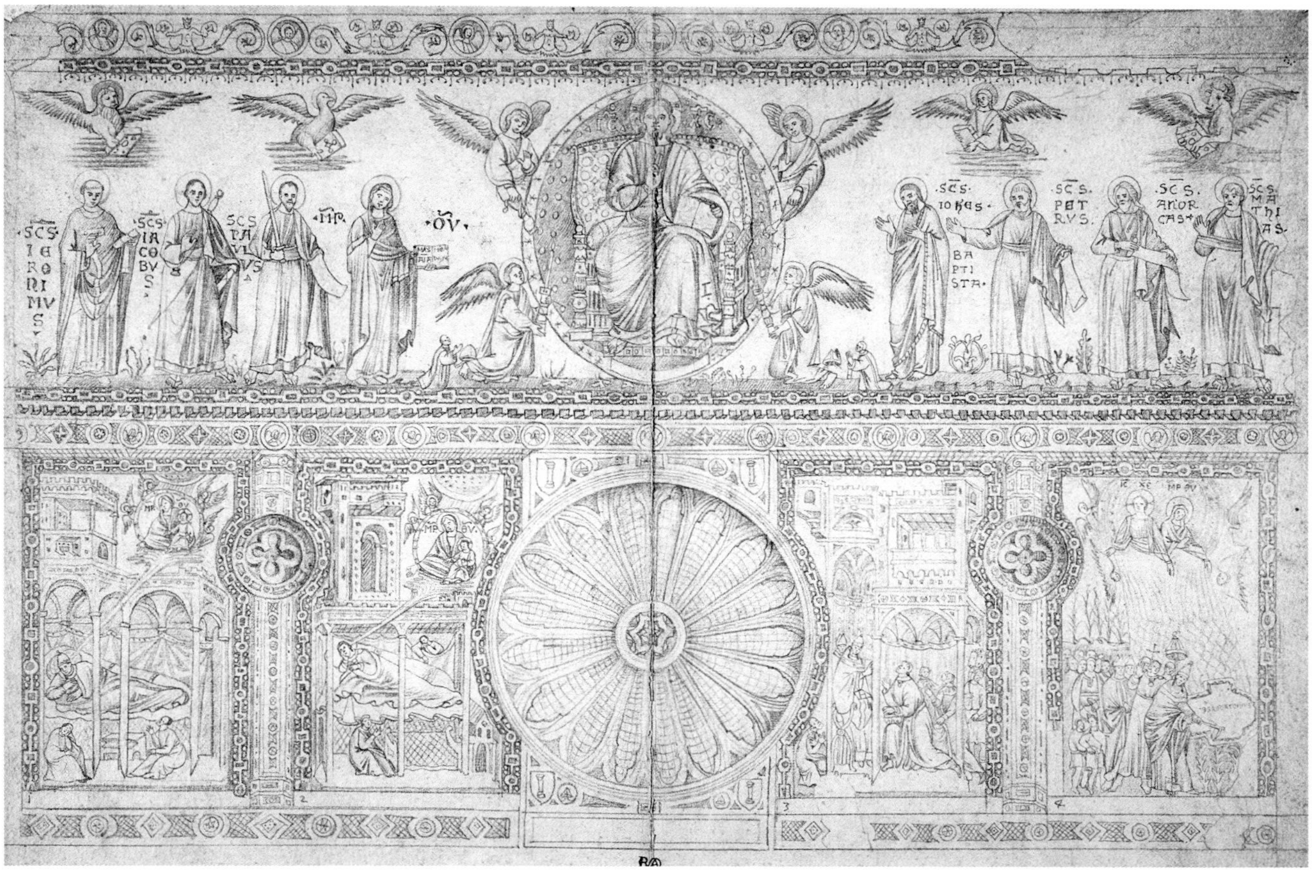

27 Roman school, copy of the thirteenth-century façade mosaics by Filippo Rusuti for Santa Maria Maggiore, seventeenth century, red chalk on paper, Edinburgh, National Gallery of Scotland, D1051.

The disgrace of the Colonna cardinals was complete. Fugitives from papal authority, they would be rehabilitated only by Pope Clement V, nearly a decade later. For good reason the fall of the Colonna in 1297 is generally accepted as a secure *terminus ante quem* for dating artistic projects linked to the family in the closing years of the thirteenth century.

✳

Nicholas IV's interventions at the Lateran and Santa Maria Maggiore demonstrate both the Franciscan pope's principal ideological concerns and his predilection for using architecture and imagery to promote them. Nicholas's vision identified Saint Francis as an epochal figure in Church history, and privileged the Friars Minor as the most significant movement of reform since the apostolic era. The renewal of the two Roman basilicas also reveals a formidable patronage dynamic, with papal authority reinforced by the influence and wealth of the Colonna family, whose leading members shared the pope's devotion to the Franciscan cause. At Santa Maria Maggiore, and perhaps also at the Lateran, the Colonna ensured the completion of Nicholas's projects after his death. Thus, the relatively brief patronage window of Nicholas's papacy (22 February 1288 to 4 April 1292) was extended for several years, at least until Boniface VIII's arrival in Rome at the start of 1295. It closed definitively with the fall of the Colonna in 1297.

These were also decisive years at Assisi. The *Reducentes* bulls of May 1288 carried Nicholas's command to 'maintain, repair, build, modify, enlarge, furnish and decorate' the Basilica of San Francesco. Bearing in mind the Franciscan pope's explicit patronage in Rome, declared through donor portraits and multiple inscriptions, should we envision him wielding similar influence at Assisi?

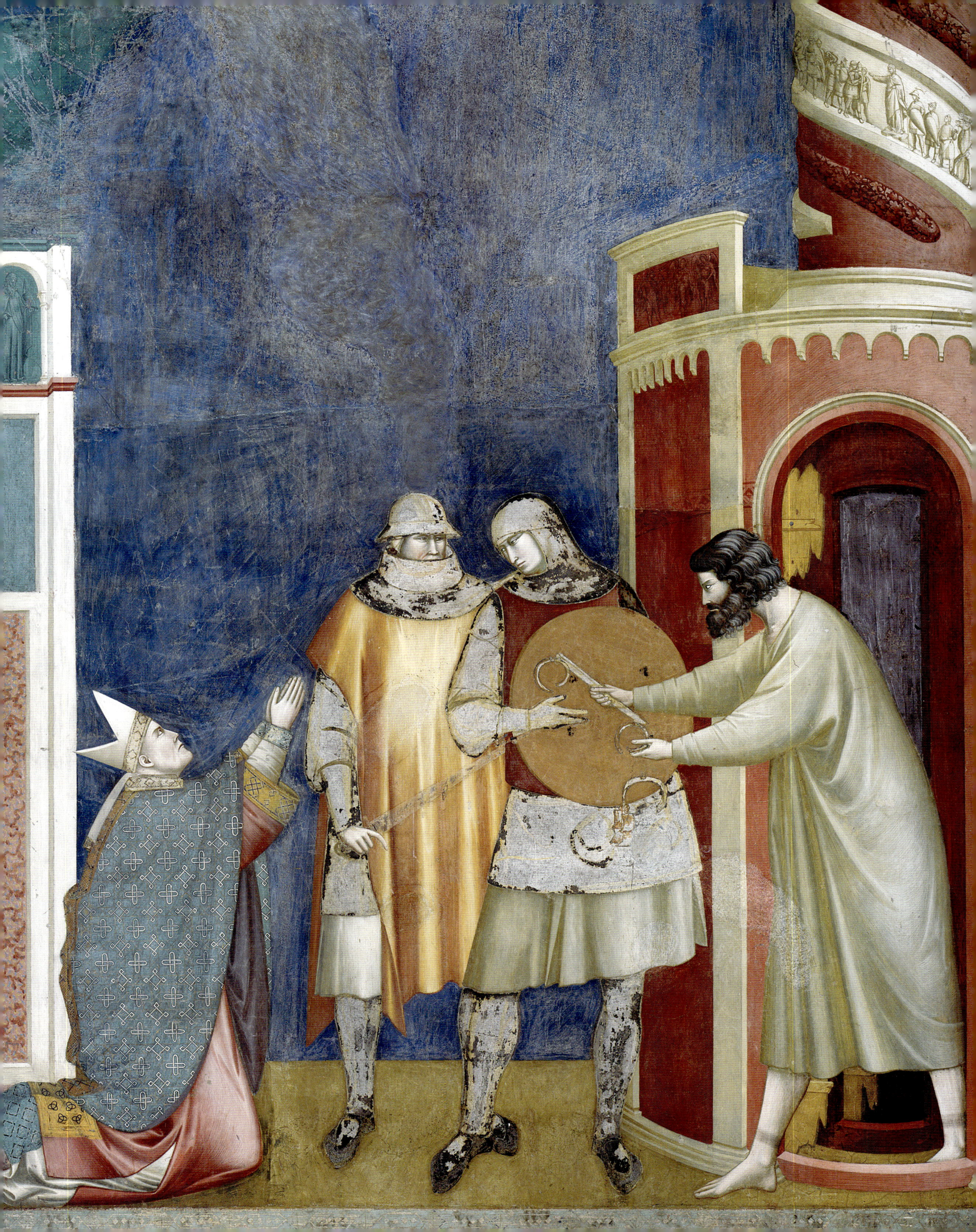

2

Power and Patronage at Assisi

Turning from Rome back to Assisi, should we view the Upper Church programme as another result of papal–Colonna patronage? As we saw in the Introduction, the fresco decoration of the Basilica was associated with Nicholas IV within living memory of its execution: in the words of the authors of the *Contra quasdam* tract, the Franciscan pope had 'ordered' these images.[1] This chapter investigates how a patronage mechanism fashioned in Rome could have functioned within an Umbrian context, scrutinizing the direct contacts between Nicholas's circle and Assisi. It also highlights the figures who probably were directly involved on the ground, particularly the senior Franciscans of the Sacro Convento, to whom the *Reducentes* letters were addressed.

At the outset, it is important to acknowledge that, in theory if not always in practice, the pope exercised both temporal and spiritual dominion over Assisi. The Papal States, roughly equating to the modern regions of Lazio, Umbria, the Marches and much of Emilia-Romagna, were by this date a political reality but notoriously difficult to govern.[2] The principal agents of metropolitan authority in these provinces were rectors, who exercised extensive powers and were direct papal appointments. To fill these key positions, Nicholas more often than not turned to the relatives of his trusted Colonna cardinals. Through these appointments Nicholas's alliance with the Colonna extended beyond Rome across central Italy. The pope assigned Giovanni Colonna, Cardinal Giacomo's elder brother, to the rectorship of the March of Ancona, where he was succeeded by his son Agapito.[3] Another of Giovanni's sons, Stefano, was given the rectorship of the Romagna.[4] More significantly for Assisi, Nicholas dispatched Giovanni's and Giacomo's brother, Landolfo, to govern the Duchy of Spoleto, an area approximating to present-day Umbria. This must have been one of the pope's very first actions, as Landolfo held the rectorship of the duchy as early as 1 March 1288.[5] Nicholas's chief political aim in Umbria was to bolster the city of Foligno in its ongoing struggle with Perugia, a conflict that caught Assisi in the middle.[6] On 13 April Landolfo was in Bevagna, scarcely ten miles from Assisi.[7] Given the peripatetic nature of the rector's court, it is all but certain that Landolfo visited Assisi around this time.[8] Indeed, Nicholas wrote to the *podestà* of Assisi on 26 April, ordering him to support the Colonna rector against the Perugians or face dismissal and a fine of a thousand silver marks.[9] We do not know how long Landolfo stayed in Umbria, but he was still rector of the

facing page 28 *Liberation of Peter of Alife* (detail of fig. 34).

duchy in 1289.[10] By March 1291 he had been succeeded by the papal notary Rainerius of Pisa, who held the rectorship for the remainder of Nicholas's pontificate.[11] Landolfo later sided with Boniface VIII against his brother Giacomo, but his testament of 1300 reveals his own close connections with the Franciscan Order.[12]

Had the communal archives of Assisi survived from the medieval period, it is highly likely that we would have further notices connecting Nicholas IV and the Colonna with the city in these years.[13] As it is, we have to turn to sources from other Umbrian centres for traces of the family's influence in the region. Mario Sensi has highlighted the close ties binding the Colonna to the city of Foligno and the counts of Antignano, one of the most powerful noble families in the Spoletan valley.[14] Cardinal Pietro Colonna was elected *podestà* of Foligno for ten months in 1290, although he appointed a vicar to serve in his stead.[15] These connections bring us no closer to the patronage of the Assisi frescoes, but they do demonstrate that the family's authority was a concrete reality in Umbria in the final years of the thirteenth century.

Notwithstanding the absence of unequivocal documentary evidence, both Nicholas IV and the Colonna have been advanced as direct patrons of the nave cycles. As we shall see, the case for Colonna involvement with the Upper Church programme has recently been made on iconographic grounds. These arguments will be supplemented by new evidence here, but their validity will also be reviewed. Meanwhile the combination of *Reducentes* and *Contra quasdam* raises the question of Nicholas IV's direct involvement at Assisi. Since we first introduced the *Contra quasdam* tract into the debates surrounding the dating of the Upper Church cycles, a number of scholars have argued that the passage categorically proves Nicholas IV's role as patron – and even planner – of the nave murals.[16] Is this an accurate characterization of curial micro-management, or a clumsy simplification of a much more complex and stratified design process?

Nicholas IV and the Basilica

The link between Nicholas and Assisi grows stronger still if one considers that the frescoing of the Upper Church nave was begun by Jacopo Torriti. Rare consensus surrounds Torriti's authorship of the majestic *Deesis* vault in the Upper Church, which must have been one of the first frescoes executed under the authority of the *Reducentes* letters (see fig. 13).[17] The Franciscan artist also frescoed the first scenes of the Genesis cycle on the north wall of the nave before vanishing from the Upper Church *cantiere*.[18] There is an obvious explanation for his disappearance: Pope Nicholas, who had probably been instrumental in sending Torriti to Assisi in the first place, had recalled his favoured artist and fellow friar to Rome and set him to work on the Lateran apse, perhaps as early as 1289.[19]

The Franciscan pope's personal munificence towards his Order's mother church is well documented. Only days after his coronation, Nicholas sent a range of gifts to the Basilica, including silver vessels, silk vestments and a sum of money. These were named in the bull *Suscepimus nuper* of 25 February 1288, to which a list of further donations was appended.[20] This supplementary list (or *cedula*) has not survived, but a number of objects given by Nicholas IV are described in the inventories of the Basilica's sacristy, compiled in 1338, 1370 and 1473. Items linked to the pope in 1338 included an ivory pyx, two silver-gilt candlesticks, four textile altar frontals, a cope embroidered with images of the apostles and a number of silk chasubles and dalmatics.[21] Two of his gifts are still preserved in the Basilica's Treasury: a silver-gilt reliquary casket topped by a cross, containing a fragment of the True Cross, one of Saint Andrew's fingers and numerous other relics (fig. 29);[22] and a magnificent silver-gilt chalice signed by the Sienese goldsmith Guccio di Mannaia and encrusted with eighty jewel-like basse-taille enamels (fig. 31).[23] One of the translucent enamel plaques on the chalice's base depicts Nicholas himself, wearing both the papal tiara and cope on top of the Franciscan habit (fig. 30).

But the most impressive of Nicholas's gifts to the Basilica must have been the embroidered orphrey (or *aurifrisium*), which was sent from Rieti on 7 August 1289, accompanied by its own dedicated bull of donation, *Excitamur ab intimis*.[24] This was an ornate textile hanging, sewn with gold and silver thread and laden with pearls, intended for display on the front face of an altar. Nicholas expressly forbade the orphrey's future alienation, perhaps because he was conscious that Franciscan statutes specifically prohibited the use of this kind of luxurious altar textile.[25] While the objects dispatched to Assisi immediately after Nicholas's coronation could hardly have been bespoke commissions for the Basilica, the altar orphrey almost certainly was.[26] The patient stitching of its embroidered imagery can explain the eighteen-month time-

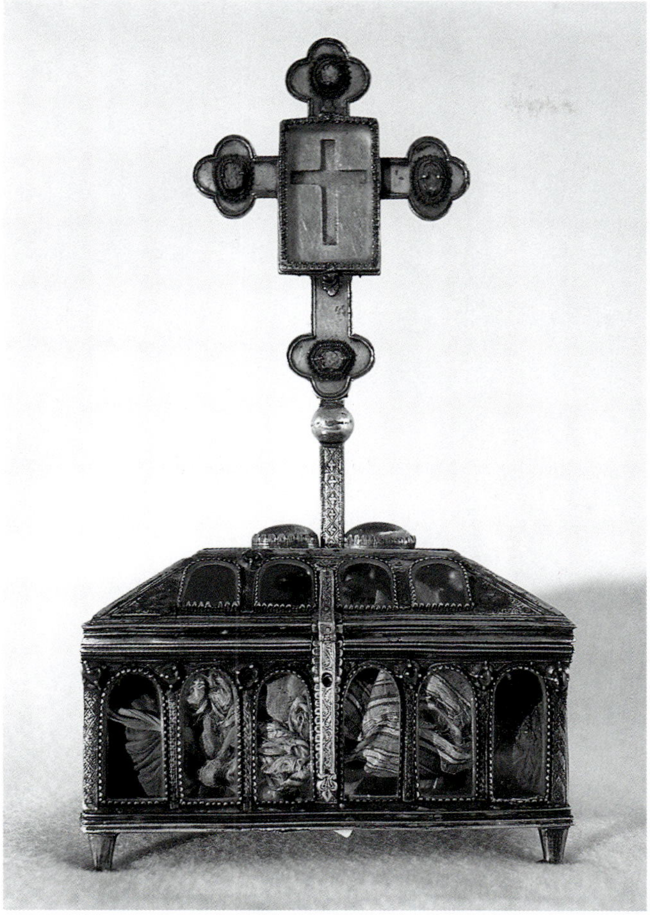

29 Roman goldsmith, reliquary casket containing Saint Andrew's finger and other relics, *c.*1278–81, silver gilt with rock crystal and rubies (39.2 cm × 21.5 cm × 12.6 cm), Treasury Museum, Sacro Convento, Assisi.

lag between the two donations. Indeed, the text of Nicholas's bull confirms that the orphrey had been newly woven.[27] It was surely made to measure, for the Basilica's high altars were unusually wide.[28] The orphrey was destroyed or lost by the end of the seventeenth century, but earlier inventories praised its 'noble and precious' decoration.[29] The inventories are consistent in specifying the subject matter of its embroideries as a legend of Saint Francis. Two engravings made in the mid-seventeenth century are the only visual evidence we have for what must have been an extensive narrative cycle.[30] The copies are frustratingly imprecise and somewhat abstracted, the artist being more concerned to record the original form of the Franciscan habit than the overall composition, but one print clearly records figures from a *Death of Saint Francis* (fig. 32). Chiara Frugoni has now identified a scene of the *Apparition at Arles* as the source for the second engraving (fig. 33).[31] Given its likely breadth, the orphrey could easily have incorporated over a dozen scenes.[32] If this was the case, it was probably more extensive than any of the earlier cycles of the saint's life in the Basilica.[33] The orphrey's iconographic relationship to the twenty-eight-scene Saint Francis cycle, painted shortly after the embroideries arrived in Assisi, is a tantalizing imponderable.[34]

Nicholas matched these material gifts with administrative privileges and spiritual indulgences.[35] The pope's steady generosity must have intensified the Sacro Convento's determination to meet the challenge posed by *Reducentes*, and it is tempting to link Nicholas's gifts with facets of the Basilica's renewal. Did the narratives on the pope's orphrey influence the decision to paint such a lengthy cycle of Saint Francis's life in the Upper Church and inform specific aspects of its iconography? We can assume that Nicholas knew the Basilica extremely well, and Rosalind Brooke has speculated that as minister general he may have been involved in earlier phases of its decoration during the 1270s.[36] All the same, we should

30 Guccio di Mannaia, base of the chalice of Pope Nicholas IV, translucent enamel plaque showing Nicholas IV wearing a Franciscan habit, Treasury Museum, Sacro Convento, Assisi.

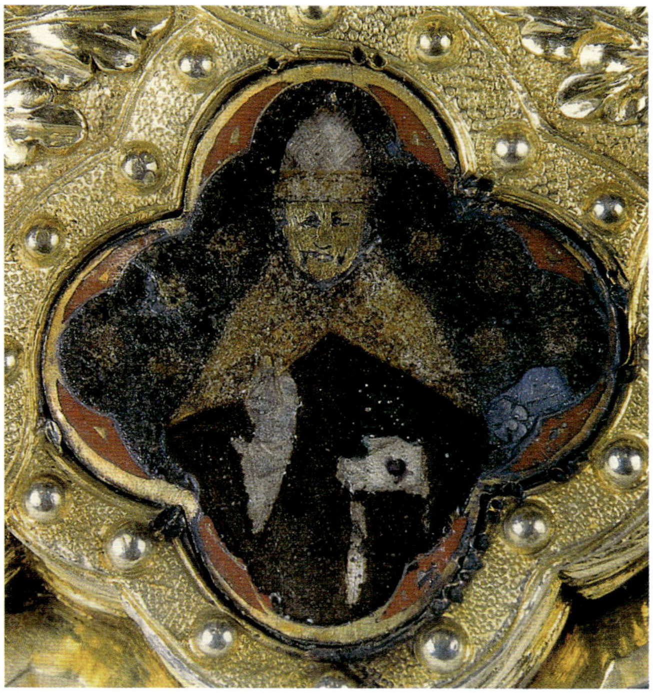

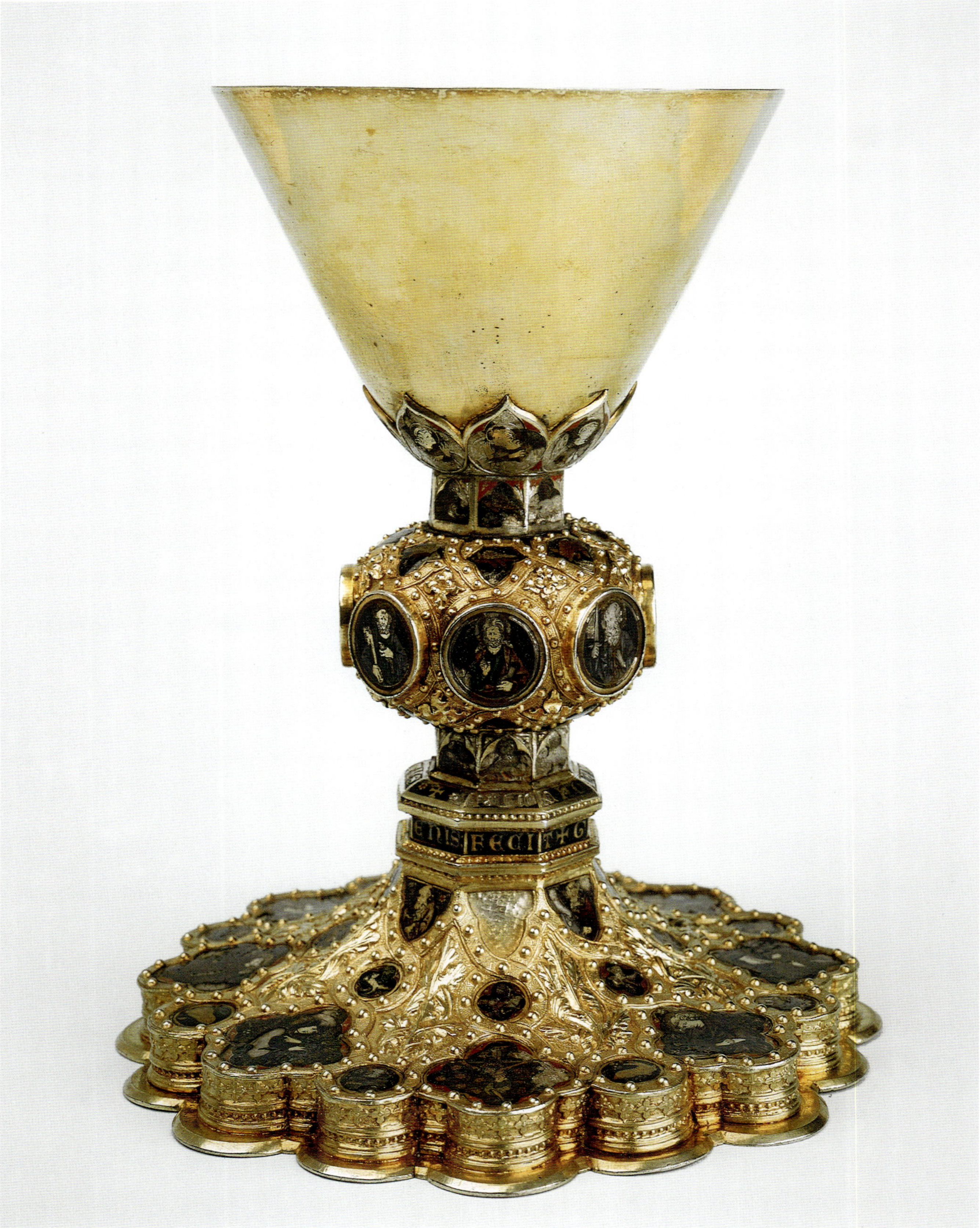

31 Guccio di Mannaia, chalice of Pope Nicholas IV, *c.*1288–90, signed, silver gilt with translucent enamel (22.4 cm × 18 cm), Treasury Museum, Sacro Convento, Assisi.

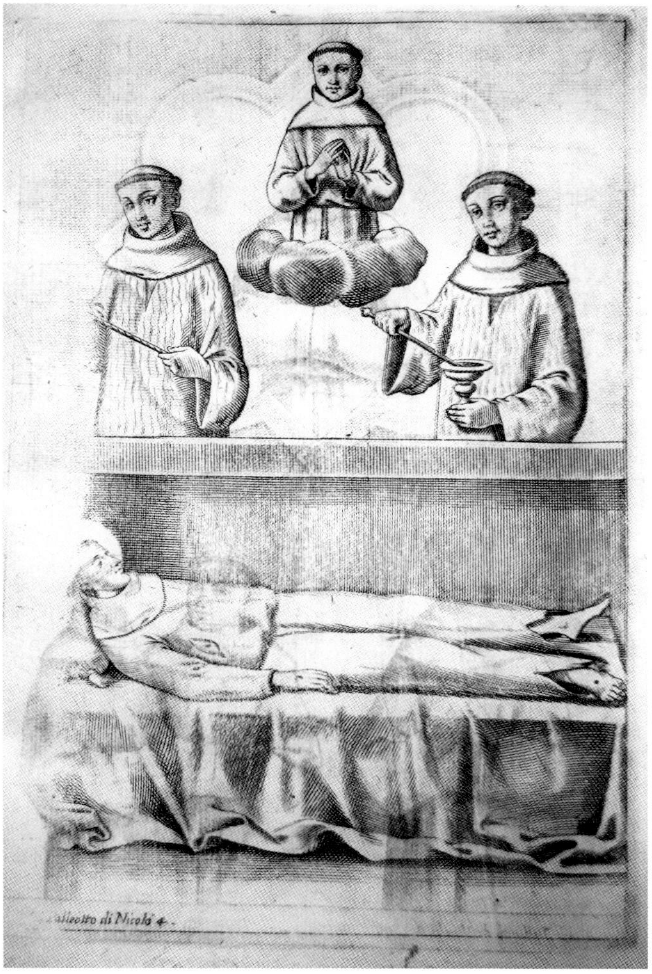

32 'Paliotto di Niccolò 4', engraving after Giampaolo Zampa, in Niccolò Catalano, *Fiume del terrestre paradiso diviso in quattro capi, o discorsi* (Florence, 1652), p. 319.

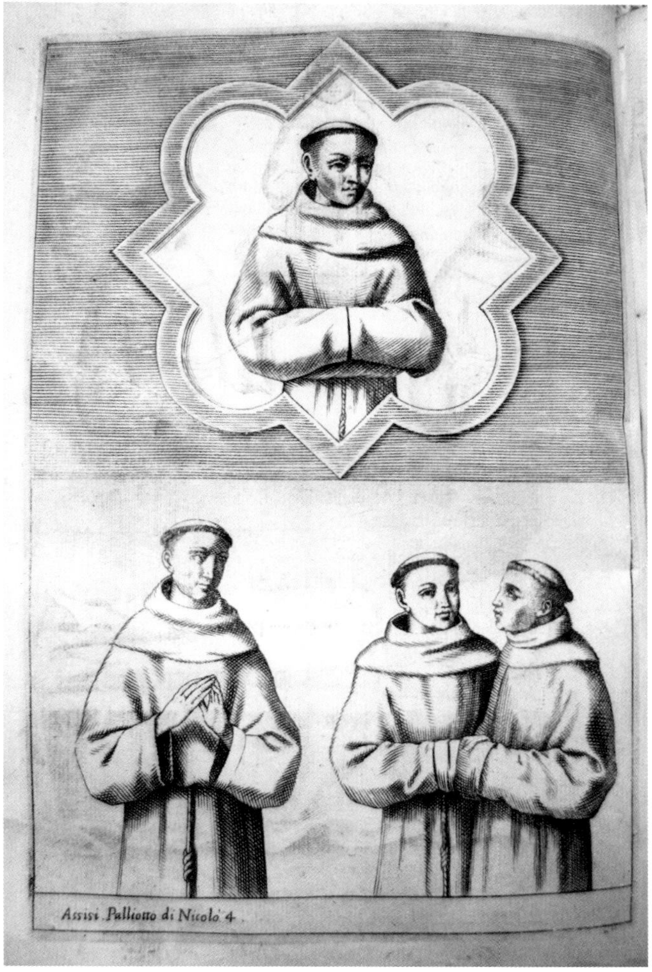

33 'Paliotto di Niccolò 4', engraving after Giampaolo Zampa, in Niccolò Catalano, *Fiume del terrestre paradiso diviso in quattro capi, o discorsi* (Florence, 1652), p. 320.

be cautious when naming the pope as the patron of the Basilica's post-1288 rebuilding, and especially of its mural decoration. *Reducentes* confirms Nicholas's overarching role, while *Contra quasdam* associates him with frescoes. In addition, Jacopo Torriti's movements indicate that the pope could determine the availability of key personnel. But the terms of *Reducentes* were broad and Nicholas never visited Assisi after his coronation. In particular, it is difficult to see how much he could have contributed to the planning of fresco cycles that, as we shall see, relied for much of their impact on the latest pictorial innovations and on site-specific juxtapositions. We should distinguish Assisi from Nicholas's interventions at the Lateran and Santa Maria Maggiore, which he would have been able to follow closely during his residencies in Rome. The prominent donor portraits and highly original commemorative inscriptions commissioned for the Roman basilicas imply Nicholas's personal engagement with those projects. It is instructive that donor figures and inscriptions are entirely absent from the nave of the Upper Church.[37]

The Shadow of the Colonna

If Nicholas was a powerful but distant patron at Assisi, what of his Colonna allies? As we have seen, the family exercised considerable influence in Umbria during Nicholas's papacy

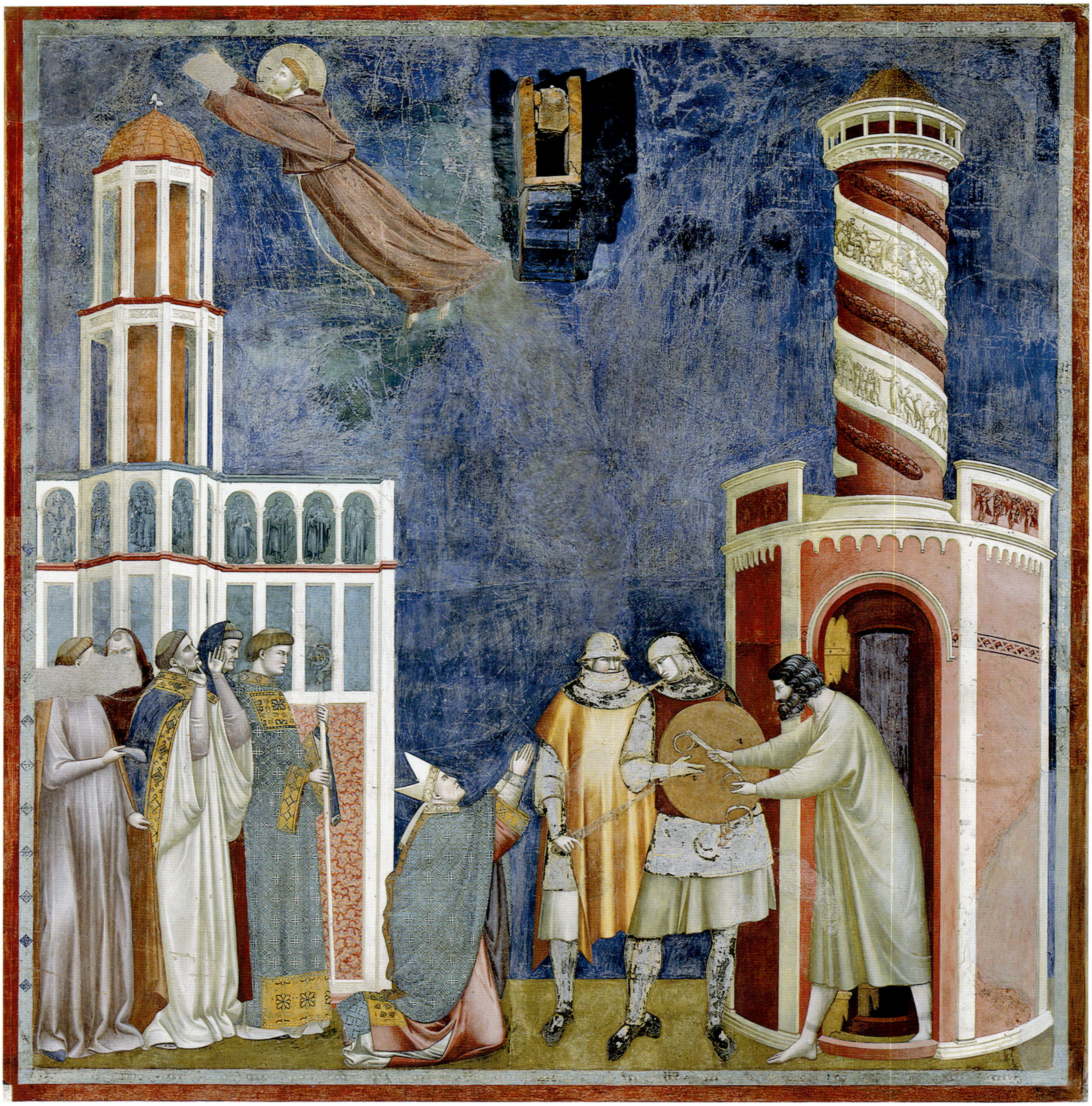

34 *Liberation of Peter of Alife*, Scene 28 of the Saint Francis cycle, *c.*1290–96, fresco, south wall of the nave, Upper Church, Basilica of San Francesco.

through the rectorship of the Duchy of Spoleto. Jacopo Torriti has recently been categorized as a Colonna artist, although he would later work for Boniface VIII after their fall.[38] The question of the family's patronage in the Basilica has taken on greater importance since Colonna allusions were identified in the concluding scene of the Saint Francis cycle, the *Liberation of Peter of Alife* (fig. 34). This was also one of the final scenes to be painted, and it completed the mural decoration of the Upper Church.[39] The subject was an unexpected choice. Indeed, as far as we know, it had never been illustrated before it was selected as the closing scene of the Upper Church cycle.[40] The story focused on one Peter of Alife, arrested in Rome on suspicion of heresy by Pope Gregory IX (1227–41).[41] Gregory handed over the accused to the bishop of Tivoli for safekeeping, threatening the bishop with the loss of his see should Peter escape. In prison Peter renounced any heretical beliefs and prayed to Saint Francis. The saint answered his prayer, appearing on the eve of his feast day to break Peter's chains and smash down the prison door from the inside. Peter was so astonished that once outside he did not try to escape. On hearing the news, the bishop of Tivoli hurried to the prison. Realizing that a miracle had occurred, he worshipped God on the spot before sending the chains to Gregory and his cardinals, who were similarly astounded.

The Assisi fresco captures the moment of the bishop's comprehension, as he kneels in prayer before the prison. Peter of Alife emerges from within, presenting his manacles, while, far above, Saint Francis flies away to the upper left. Chiara Frugoni was the first to observe that the historical bishop of Tivoli in the story must have been Giacomo Antonio Colonna, who held the office from 1209 to 1248. He was mentioned by name in another miracle, which had been appended to Bonaventure's *Legenda maior* by Jerome of Ascoli in 1276.[42] Frugoni concluded that the Peter of Alife miracle must have been chosen as a calculated compliment to the bishop's descendant and namesake Cardinal Giacomo Colonna. This inflection, she noted, helps to explain the emphasis placed on the prelate in the fresco: he kneels at the centre of the composition and is named as the bishop of Tivoli by the summary inscription below the scene. Frugoni also observed that the historiated, spiral column rising over the prison in the fresco referenced the traditional link between the Colonna name and Trajan's column.[43] Rosalind Brooke and Serena Romano subsequently followed Frugoni's lead in identifying a Colonna subtext to the scene.[44] Paul Binski then took the argument further, proposing that the column was an overt Colonna rebus, its spiral form and colour scheme of white marble reliefs against a red ochre ground providing further allusions to the family's coat of arms.[45] The Colonna blazon could take several forms, with either a straight or twisted column: a good example of the latter device set on a red mosaic ground, dating from the late thirteenth century, is preserved in the family's chapel at San Silvestro in Capite, Rome (fig. 35).[46] Binski argued convincingly that the Assisi fresco, with its multiple Colonna references, must have been painted before Cardinals Giacomo and Pietro broke with Pope Boniface in May 1297.[47] He also speculated that the Colonna may have sponsored the whole mural decoration of the nave of the Upper Church.[48]

In fact, the corkscrew column in the *Liberation of Peter of Alife* is not the only Colonna allusion in the Upper Church. There is at least one more, which has hitherto been overlooked by all contributors to the Assisi debates. It is to be found in the gallery of standing saints painted on the broad archivolt that abuts the counter-façade wall. There are sixteen saints in all, paired in four registers that climb either side of

35 Colonna coat of arms, late thirteenth century (before 1297), marble with mosaic inlay, San Silvestro in Capite, Rome.

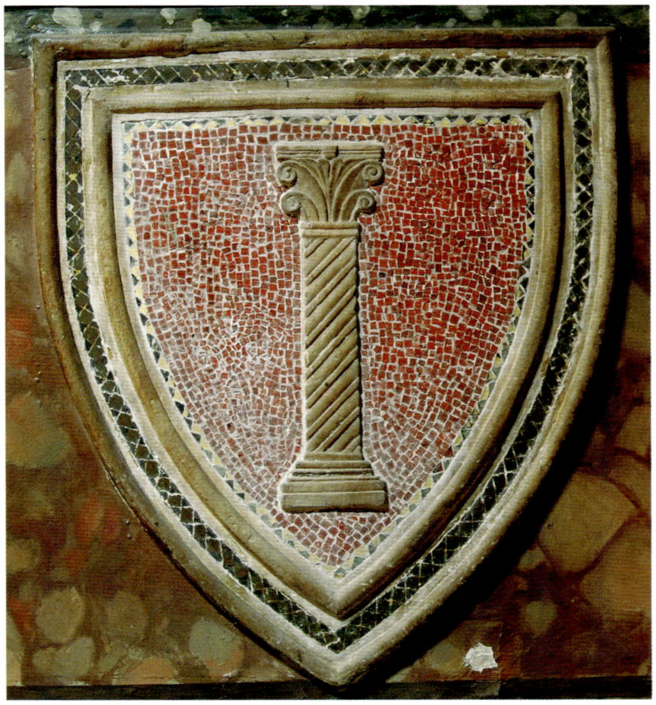

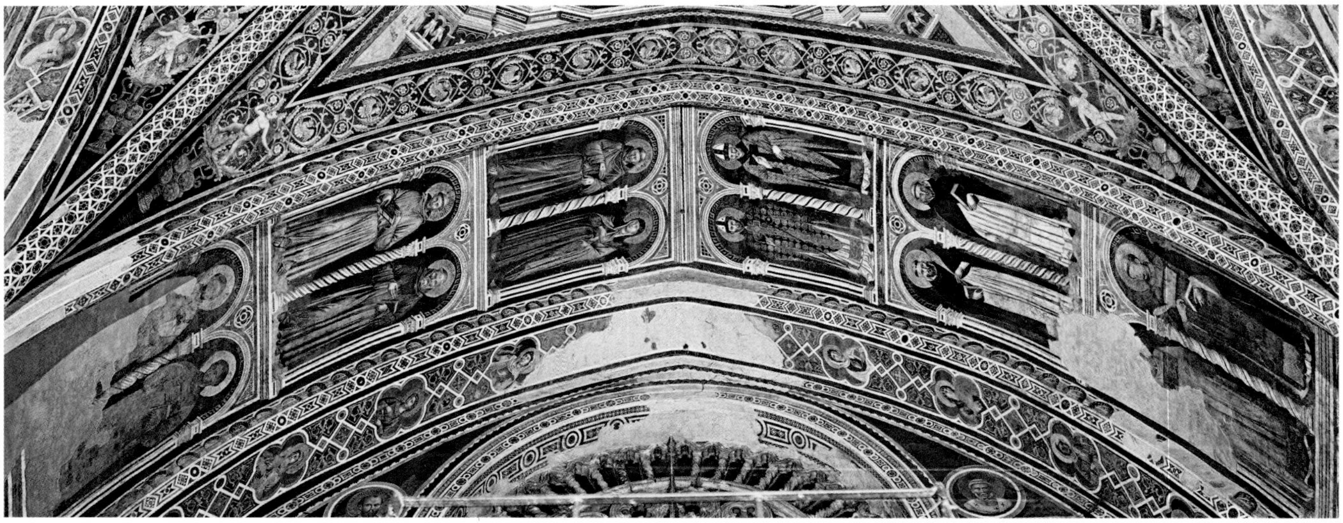

36 Standing saints, *c.*1288–91, fresco, archivolt of the counter-façade, Upper Church, Basilica of San Francesco.

the arch (fig. 36). They were painted at the same time as the nave vaults and are usually dated to *c.*1288–91. Some are predictable choices: the Order's two Assisi saints, Francis and Clare, are paired opposite the city's episcopal patrons, Saints Rufinus and Victorinus, at the apex of the archivolt. The next register down emphasizes links between the Franciscans and other religious orders: Saint Anthony of Padua is paired with Saint Benedict on the north side of the arch, and they face the two canonized Dominicans, Dominic and Peter Martyr, on the south. These eight saints in the two uppermost registers were largely destroyed in the September 1997 earthquake, but thankfully had been extensively photographed before their collapse.[49] Each of the figures was named by an inscription bracketed around their shoulders and in any case their habits and vestments were easily recognizable.

Distinguishing the eight saints in the lower two registers is more problematic. While they escaped the destruction of 1997, the majority had already suffered from centuries of water seepage from the façade. Their inscriptions have gradually flaked away, some almost entirely. The bottom register is dedicated to a quartet of female saints. The pair on the south side can be identified as Saints Agnes and Catherine of Alexandria from fragmentary inscriptions that were still visible in nineteenth-century photographs (fig. 38).[50] The pair to the north is more severely damaged, but one of the female saints is clearly crowned (fig. 37).[51] The next register up depicts four deacon saints. The two figures on the southern side have lost their inscriptions (fig. 40), but the legends on the north are still legible and identify the pair as Saint Lawrence and Saint Agapitus (fig. 39). Lawrence is a conventional choice for a quartet of deacons, but Agapitus is an obscure figure, whose cult was unknown in Umbria.[52]

The appearance of Saint Agapitus in the Upper Church can be explained only as a reference to Nicholas IV and the Colonna (fig. 41). He was patron saint of Palestrina and, as we have already seen, the titular of the town's cathedral.[53] The inclusion of Agapitus at Assisi would have appealed to Nicholas, cardinal bishop of Palestrina before his election to the papacy. A relic of Saint Agapitus was among the holy remains contained in the reliquary casket that Nicholas had donated to the Basilica (see fig. 29).[54] Equally, the inclusion of Saint Agapitus honoured the Colonna, secular lords of Palestrina. Their column motif was emblazoned on the high altar of the town's cathedral dedicated to the saint (see fig. 16). Moreover, Agapito was an important family name among the Palestrina branch of the Colonna, to which Cardinal Giacomo belonged. The eldest son of Giacomo's eldest brother, Giovanni, was named Agapito, and he served Nicholas IV as Giovanni's vicar in the March of Ancona.[55] Pope Boniface VIII evidently believed that the saint was associated with the family. After the rebellion of the Colonna and the capitulation of Palestrina, the pope decreed that a new altar dedicated to his own name-saint, Saint Boniface, be erected in the town's cathedral of Sant'Agapito.[56]

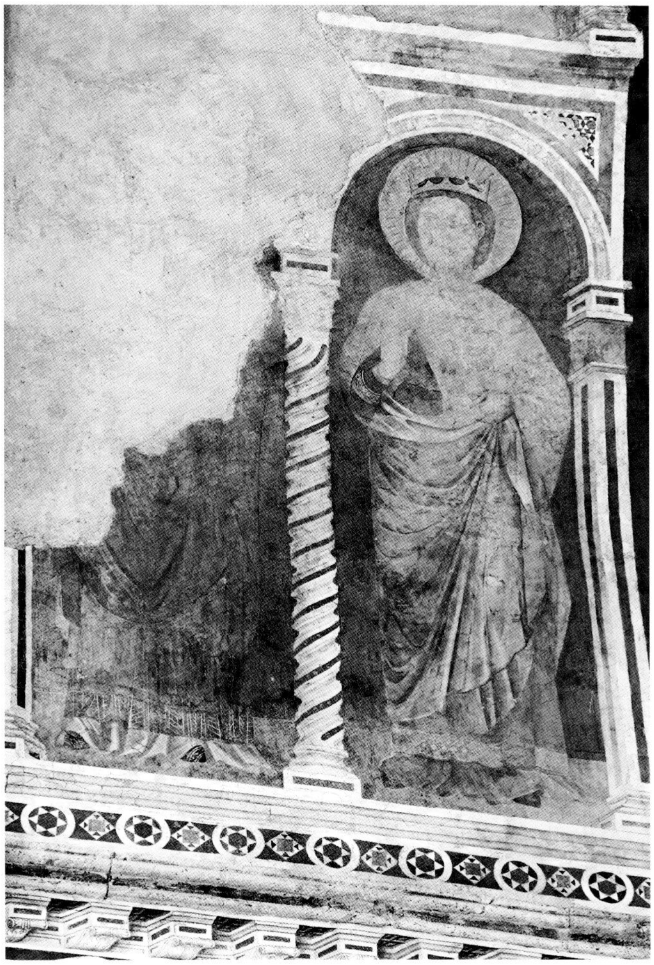

37 Unidentified female saints, *c.*1288–91, fresco, archivolt of the counter-façade, Upper Church, Basilica of San Francesco.

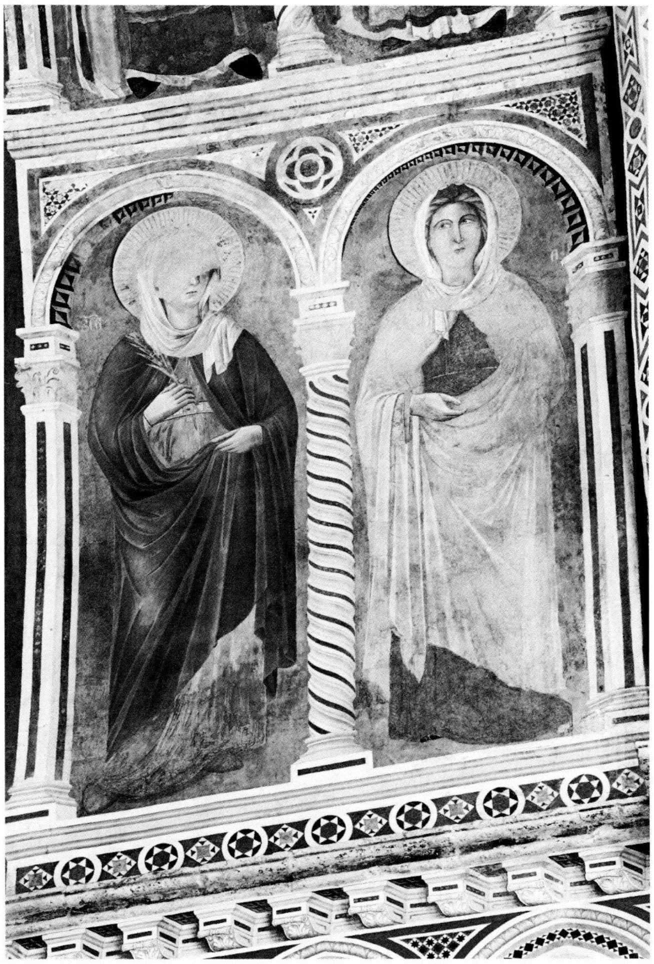

38 Saints Agnes and Catherine of Alexandria, *c.*1288–91, fresco, archivolt of the counter-façade, Upper Church, Basilica of San Francesco.

The inclusions of Saint Agapitus towards the start of the mural programme and the corkscrew column in the *Liberation of Peter of Alife* at the very end demonstrate a desire to please a philo-Colonna audience, and they fix the decoration of the nave more firmly than ever within the date range 1288–97. But should we consider the Colonna as possible patrons of the Assisi frescoes? We have already seen that the family wielded significant influence in Umbria under Nicholas IV. The retinues of the two Colonna cardinals also hint at numerous personal connections in the region.[57] Moreover, their interest in Assisi and the surrounding area intensified after Nicholas's death. After more than a year of deadlock and growing unrest in Rome, the cardinals reconvened in Perugia in October 1293, where they remained until the election of Celestine V on 5 July 1294. For these nine months the Umbrian city effectively became the epicentre of the Roman Church. Charles II of Naples visited Perugia in March 1294 to address the cardinals, and by a charter of 26 March bestowed fiefs in his kingdom to the nephews of Cardinal Giacomo: Stefano, Agapito and Giovanni Colonna.[58] The deed was composed in Perugia, suggesting a strong family presence in the city at the time. Although the papal election was not conducted in strict conclave (it was the last not to be), the Colonna cardinals, Giacomo and Pietro, must have resided in Perugia or the surrounding district for most of this period. This lengthy stay in Umbria helps to explain Giacomo's familiarity with the local Franciscan mystic Angela of Foligno, whose *Memoriale* he approved *c.*1296.[59] In 1294

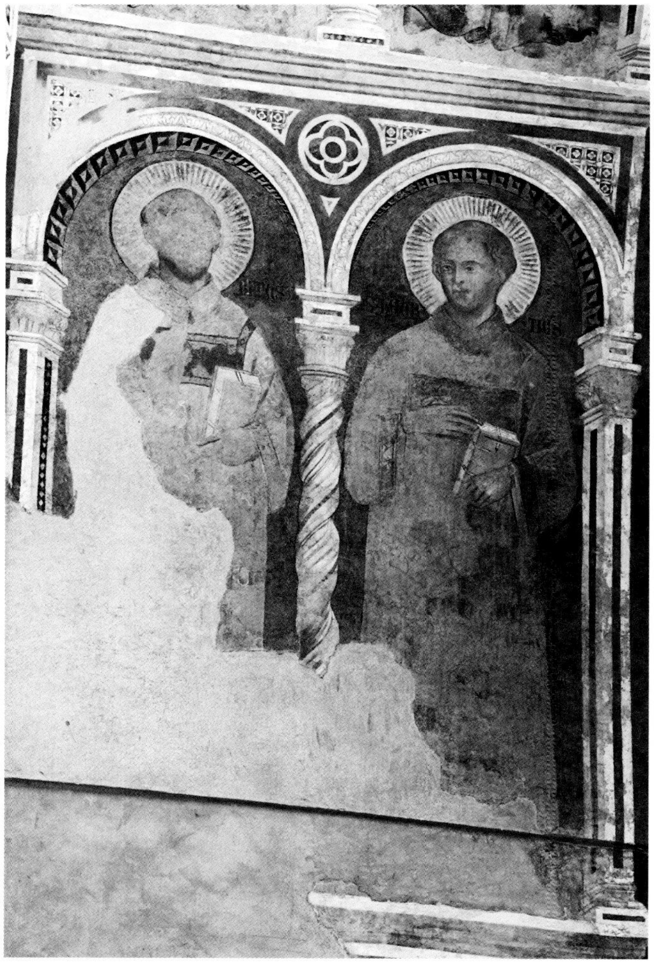

39 Saints Agapitus and Lawrence, *c.*1288–91, fresco, archivolt of the counter-façade, Upper Church, Basilica of San Francesco.

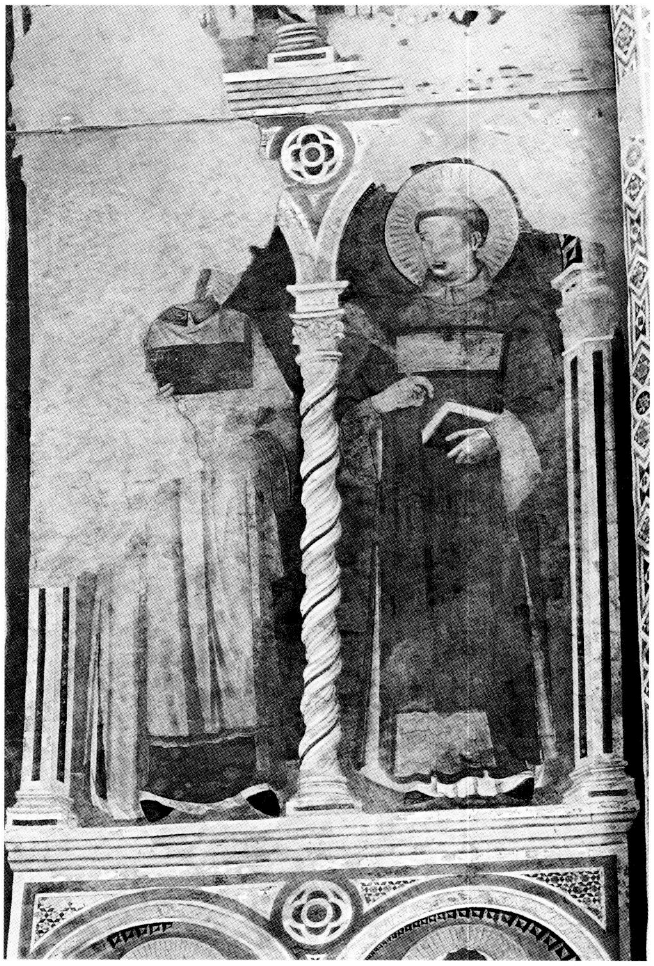

40 Unidentified deacon saints, *c.*1288–91, fresco, archivolt of the counter-façade, Upper Church, Basilica of San Francesco.

Giacomo was named alongside four of his fellow cardinals as executors for Count Rinaldo of Antignano's will, rogated in Foligno on 11 May, while the college was still based in Perugia.[60] At this juncture, having cardinals as executors made sense: based close by, they were the most powerful figures in the region. We should expect that the Colonna cardinals, especially Giacomo, given his long-standing devotion to the Franciscan movement, would have visited Assisi during their prolonged Umbrian sojourn. The nine months between October 1293 and July 1294 lie plumb in the middle of the chronological parameters that have now been established for the painting of the Upper Church nave.[61]

There is additional evidence for individual patronage at the Basilica on the part of Giacomo Colonna. The fourteenth-century inventories record a silver-gilt crucifix with a fragment of the True Cross and a castellated silver-gilt censer, both sent by 'dominus Iacobus de Columpna'.[62] It is, however, unclear when Giacomo donated these objects (the earliest descriptions come in the 1338 inventory). They may have post-dated the family's rebellion and subsequent rehabilitation at the start of the fourteenth century. It is possible that other gifts were destroyed or altered in the wake of 1297. One might have expected hangings or vestments with Colonna heraldry to have featured in the lists of liturgical textiles, alongside those emblazoned with the Orsini escutcheon.[63] Although Boniface VIII is not traditionally considered a significant patron at Assisi, he ensured that his Caetani heraldry would be prominently displayed in the Basilica

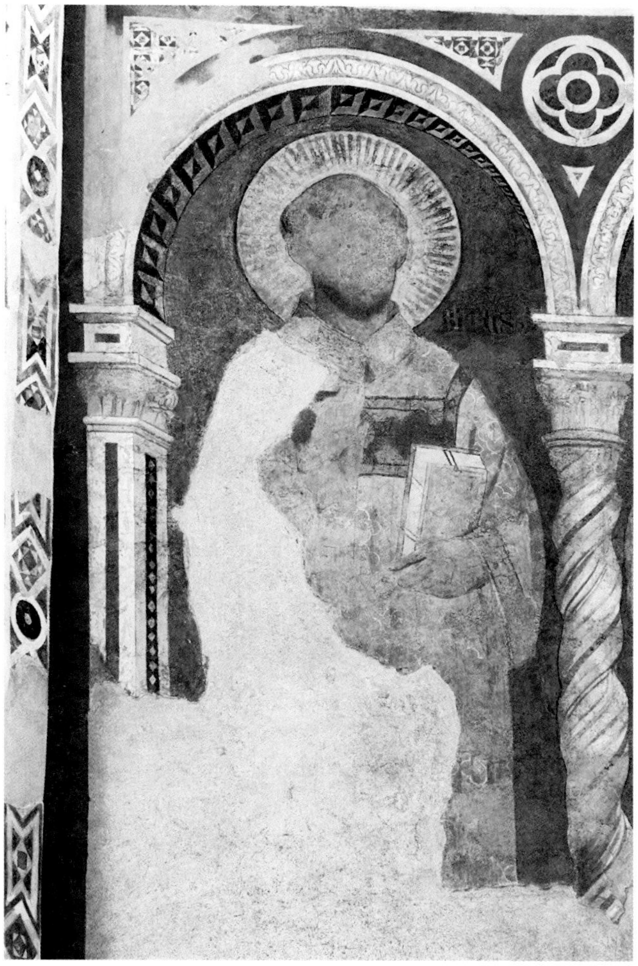

41 Saint Agapitus, *c.*1288–91, fresco, archivolt of the counter-façade, Upper Church, Basilica of San Francesco.

through the donation of a fine cope and altar hangings, decorated with his coat of arms.[64] These statements of patronage, although movable and impermanent, would have been at least as colourful and visible as coats of arms in the fresco decoration. Perhaps the friars conveniently disposed of similar Colonna altar cloths after 1297: we simply cannot know. Boniface's pursuit of the Colonna certainly extended to Umbria and Assisi; the Caetani pope wrote to the city's *podestà* and council in March 1298 thanking them for their actions 'against the Colonna, schismatics and rebels against us and the Church'.[65]

We can be confident that the Colonna cardinals, unlike Nicholas IV, visited Assisi after 1288, especially once the college decamped to Perugia in 1293. But the problem with advancing the Colonna as leading patrons of the Basilica's regeneration, and of the mural decoration of the Upper Church nave in particular, is the same: the absence of any donor portraits, commemorative inscriptions or open display of family heraldry. The Colonna inflections identified in the Upper Church frescoes – Saint Agapitus and the column in the *Liberation of Peter of Alife* – cannot compare with the copious repetition of the Colonna arms in the projects sponsored by the family in Rome. One way to address this gap is to recalibrate the question, to view the making of the Basilica as larger than any one patron and to ask who would have been responsible for pushing the project forward on the ground.

Matthew of Acquasparta

All the arguments attributing the considerable labour of designing the fresco programme of the Upper Church nave to individual ecclesiastics at the papal curia share a common weakness. Nicholas's bulls were not addressed to the Colonna, or to the cardinal protector of the Order, Matteo Rosso Orsini (another candidate recently advanced as a presiding intelligence behind the mural decoration).[66] Instead the *Reducentes* letters were sent to the three Franciscan friars with direct administrative responsibility for the Basilica: the minister general, the provincial minister of Umbria and the custodian of the Sacro Convento.

Of the three recipients, one can be easily identified: the minister general, Matthew of Acquasparta. The *Reducentes* bulls were composed on 14 and 15 May 1288, on the eve of Matthew's elevation to the college of cardinals at Pentecost (16 May). He had been head of the Order for less than a year, having been elected by the general chapter at Montpellier on 25 May 1287. It was perhaps for this reason that Matthew chose, presumably with Nicholas IV's approval, to combine the office of minister general with his new duties as a cardinal for a further year, until the next general chapter convened at Rieti for Pentecost (29 May) in 1289.

By the 1280s, Matthew was the Order's pre-eminent intellectual in Italy. Born in the small town of Acquasparta in southern Umbria around 1240, he took the Franciscan habit at the convent of San Fortunato in nearby Todi, probably in 1254.[67] Around 1268 Matthew was sent to study at the Order's *studium generale* at the University of Paris, the most

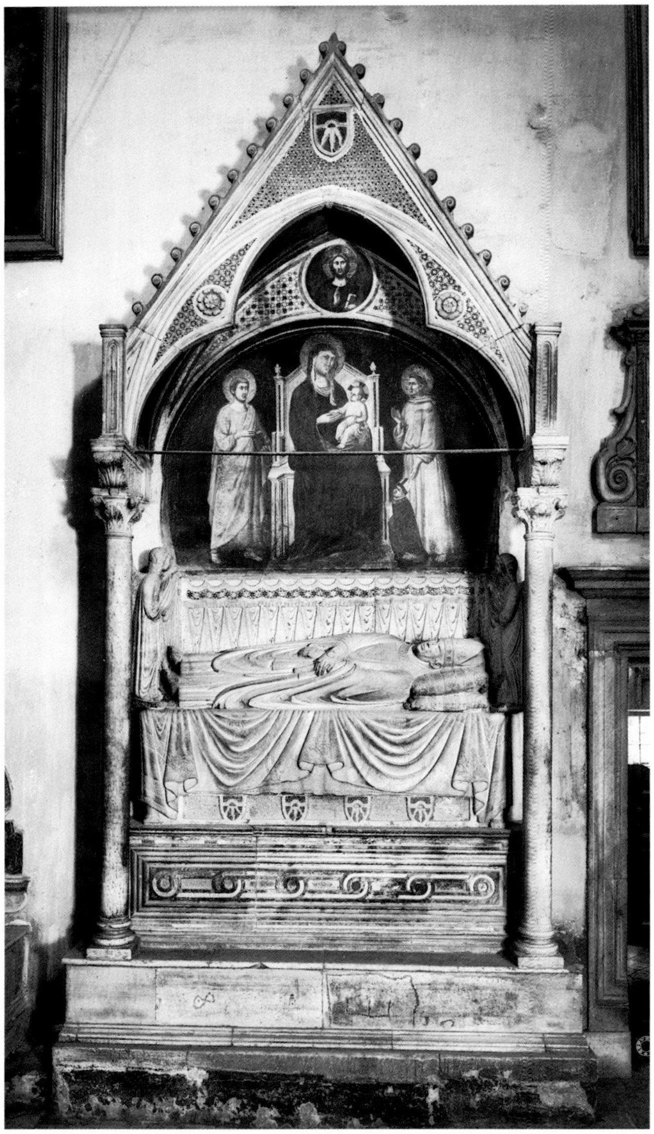

42 Tomb monument of Cardinal Matthew of Acquasparta, *c.*1302, white marble, cosmati inlay and fresco, Santa Maria in Aracoeli, Rome.

demanding academic environment in Europe at the time.[68] It was the beginning of a brilliant career as a theologian, first in Paris, where by 1278 he was regent master of the Franciscan *studium*, and then in Rome, where he was appointed lector of the papal curia in 1279, a post he retained until he became minister general in 1287.[69] Shortly before his election, in the early months of that year, Matthew donated his magnificent scholarly library, accumulated over twenty years, to the Sacro Convento at Assisi and to his old convent at Todi.[70] Matthew must have known that he was the Montpellier chapter's likely choice as the Order's next minister general; presenting his books to Assisi and Todi was a signal that his years of theological study were drawing to a close.[71]

Matthew's affection for Assisi and Todi is also evident from his gifts of liturgical objects to both convents. At Assisi, the fourteenth-century sacristy inventories record a coral crucifix with a silver corpus and a range of ecclesiastical vestments, all given by 'Frater Matheus de Aquasparta cardinalis'.[72] Matthew did not die until 1302 and the objects are documented only from 1338, but it seems likely that some were donated around the same time as his books in 1287.[73] Neither the crucifix nor the textiles have survived, but many of Matthew's books are still in the Sacro Convento library. They can be identified from the inventory appended to his donation and by the invocation to the Holy Spirit with which he signed the volumes of his personal library.[74] For evidence of Matthew's artistic patronage and taste, we do have impressions of his cardinal's seal. This must have been an especially fine matrix, and its design has been associated with Guccio di Mannaia, the same Sienese goldsmith responsible for Nicholas IV's Assisi chalice.[75] At his death on 29 October 1302, Matthew was buried in a canopied tomb monument in the left transept of Santa Maria in Aracoeli (fig. 42). Above Matthew's marble tomb effigy, Pietro Cavallini frescoed the kneeling cardinal being presented by Saint Francis to the Virgin and Child and his name-saint Matthew (fig. 43).[76]

Matthew of Acquasparta is in many ways an ideal candidate for impresario of the mural decoration of the Upper Church. His writings – above all his sermons on Saint Francis – will be referenced repeatedly in our discussions of the frescoes and their iconography. Famously cited by Dante as the personification of moderate, even lax, Franciscanism, Matthew undoubtedly had the learning and intellectual capacity to devise such a sophisticated scheme.[77] However, granting him a leading role as patron and/or designer is problematic. Matthew would have known the Basilica very well, but it is difficult to place him in Assisi during the key years of Nicholas's pontificate. By July 1289 at the latest, Nicholas had appointed Matthew as papal penitentiary, an office the Franciscan cardinal would hold until his death.[78] Matthew's academic background must have been well suited to the work of the penitentiary tribunal, but we can assume that the demands of the office precluded lengthy absences

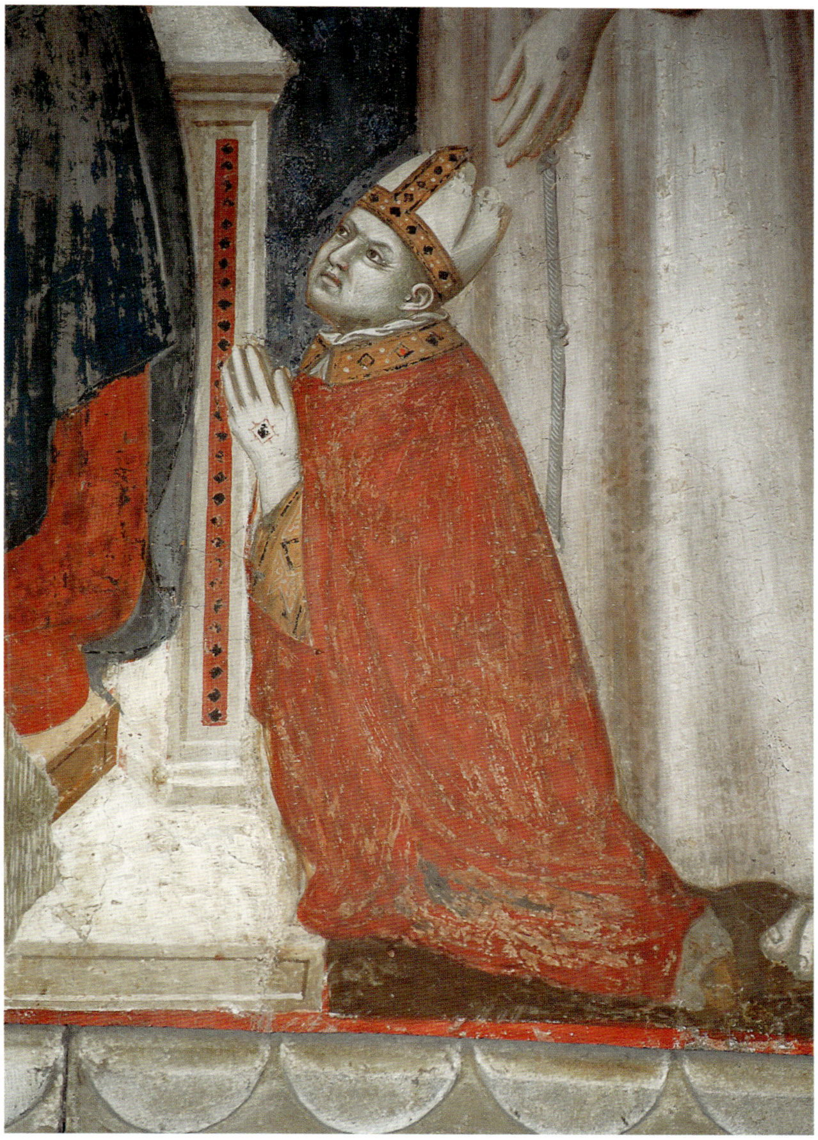

43 Pietro Cavallini, Matthew of Acquasparta being presented to the Virgin and Child by Saint Francis, detail from lunette on Acquasparta's tomb, *c.*1302, fresco, Santa Maria in Aracoeli, Rome.

from the curia.[79] Moreover, by the mid-1290s Matthew's political outlook would have sat uneasily with the Colonna rebus that has been identified in the final scene of the Saint Francis cycle. Nicholas IV's circle gradually fragmented after the pope's death in 1292, and the Franciscan sympathies of the Colonna cardinals did not prevent them from targeting Matthew once he proved an obstacle to their ambitions during the long Perugian conclave.[80] When the Colonna rebelled in 1297 Matthew emerged as a loyal and able lieutenant to Boniface VIII, whom he had probably known as a young man in Todi in the late 1250s or early 1260s.[81]

One last detail may be more than incidental: Matthew was not named in the *Reducentes* bulls. This was a practical consideration: the privileges they articulated accrued to the office not the individual, and the arrangements they established were designed to endure over a substantial period of time, sufficient to realize major renovation and rebuilding works and likely to span several different ministerships. The *Redu-*

centes bulls empowered not only Matthew but also his successors, reflecting the administrative hierarchy of the Order at the close of the thirteenth century, when the minister general was given special responsibility for the Sacro Convento.[82] The letters were also issued on the eve of Matthew's elevation to cardinal at Pentecost 1288. We do not know whether the minister general was at Assisi or with the curia at Rieti that spring, but both Matthew and Nicholas knew that, within the year, their Order would need a new leader.

The Franciscan Community

What of the other two officials addressed by the *Reducentes* letters: the provincial minister of Umbria and the custodian of the Sacro Convento? This emphasis on local authority suggests an alternative source for the extraordinary iconographic achievement of the Upper Church nave frescoes, within the Franciscan community at Assisi. These figures have never before been considered in the debates surrounding the genesis of the Upper Church programme, despite their prominence in Nicholas's bulls. In part this reflects the paucity of surviving documentation: there are certainly gaps in the lists of provincial and local office-holders for this early period.[83] But the names we do have suggest that these posts were often held by friars possessing impressive academic backgrounds, significant social status and extensive political connections.

There was no fixed term of service for either the custodian or the provincial minister and both positions rotated with higher frequency than did that of minister general. So again it is no surprise that neither incumbent was named by *Reducentes*. To begin with the more junior office, in 1287 the custodianship of the Sacro Convento was occupied by Jacopo of Assisi, cited as a witness to the donation of Matthew of Acquasparta's library (a document composed in the Sacro Convento in the early months of that year).[84] By August 1288 Jacopo had been succeeded as custodian by Galgano of Gubbio, who had already accumulated considerable administrative experience in the Umbrian province.[85] Galgano had been guardian of the Perugian house in 1282 and was inquisitor general for the Duchy of Spoleto between 1285 and 1287 (the source for the latter date is, once again, the charter recording the gift of Matthew's library).[86] We do not know how long Galgano served as custodian of the Sacro Convento, but by July 1293 the office had passed to Bonaventura of Montedoglio (also known as Schiatteschi).[87] By 1294 the custodian was Monaldo of Orvieto, a friar who is documented at Assisi from 1280 onwards, serving as the Basilica's sacristan *c.*1282–4.[88]

Moving up to the ministry of the Umbrian province, the 1287 library donation records that the post was held that year by a certain Bartolo. It is tempting to identify this friar with the Bartolo of Perugia who had already been named as provincial minister in 1280 and 1284.[89] If these Bartolos are indeed one and the same, his periods of office were interrupted by Matthew of Chieti, cited as provincial minister in 1286. Matthew of Chieti was still at Assisi in 1287, when the library charter names him among the lectors of the Sacro Convento.[90] A later Franciscan source judged Matthew a 'vir eminens', who went on to be papal envoy to Armenia before returning to Umbria as an inquisitor in 1294.[91] A parchment now in Perugia places him at the papal curia in Orvieto on 7 May 1291, serving as vice-chancellor and lobbying Nicholas IV and Matthew of Acquasparta for indulgences for Franciscan houses in Umbria.[92]

In 1289 the provincial minister was Angelo of Todi, who had earlier succeeded Galgano of Gubbio as inquisitor for Umbria.[93] By 1292 at the latest the ministership had passed to Matthias (or Matthew) of the noble Sant'Eustachio family from Rome.[94] Matthias of Sant'Eustachio moved on to become provincial minister of the Roman province, probably in 1295, and at his death was buried in Santa Maria in Aracoeli. His fine marble tomb slab (fig. 44) still survives in the Aracoeli and its original location in the left transept, close to the legendary altar of Augustus, occupied the most holy point in the church.[95] The same area was later chosen for the burial of Cardinal Matthew of Acquasparta and at least one member of the Colonna family.[96] Matthias's successor as provincial of Umbria was Bonaventura of Montedoglio, who had already served as custodian of the Sacro Convento and who would remain minister for nine years until 1304.[97]

The donation deed for Matthew of Acquasparta's library, referred to several times above and composed in the Sacro Convento ('Actum Assisi in loco sancti Francisci'), provides an effective snapshot of the leadership of the Umbrian province in 1287.[98] Eleven friars are named among the witnesses, including the provincial minister Bartolo, the custodian of the Sacro Convento Jacopo of Assisi, and the custodian of the neighbouring Spoleto custody, one Andrea of Bevagna. There then follows a list of no fewer than six lectors: Angelo of

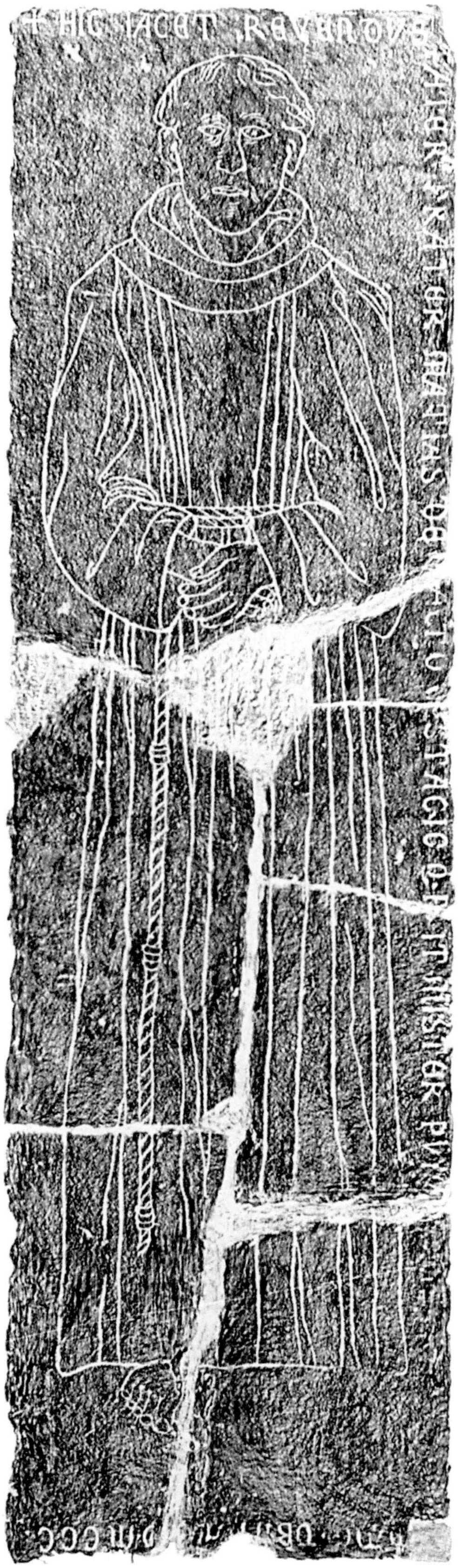

Perugia, William of Foligno, Matthew of Chieti (the former provincial minister), Philip of Perugia, Jacopo of Todi (just possibly the friar-poet Jacopone of Todi) and Rainaldo of Todi.[99] Angelo of Perugia can be identified as the friar of that name documented as the 'minister administrationis' for the Sacro Convento in 1278 and 1279, and he was certainly a lector at Assisi by 1284.[100] Philip of Perugia was a friar of some stature. During his term as provincial of Tuscany from 1279 to 1282 he had investigated the circumstances of Saint Francis's stigmatization, composing a short treatise from the findings. Before moving to Tuscany, Philip had served as chaplain to Cardinal Giovanni Gaetano Orsini, who would later become Pope Nicholas III, and was evidently well connected in both conventual and curial circles.[101] In his old age Philip recalled being a member of the commission of friars and ecclesiastics that had drafted Nicholas III's new commentary on the Franciscan Rule, published as the bull *Exiit qui seminat* on 14 August 1279.[102] The two lectors from Todi, Jacopo and Rainaldo, probably represented the interests of that town's Franciscan convent of San Fortunato, which was to receive half of Matthew of Acquasparta's library. After the lectors, the final two witnesses to Matthew's library donation were the inquisitor Galgano of Gubbio, who would be appointed custodian of the Sacro Convento the following year, and Henry of Siola, about whom we know little except that he gave a large piece of coral to the Basilica's sacristy.[103]

The presence of so many lectors is especially significant: these were friars with at least four years of theological training at one of the Order's *studia generalia*, and some of them would have been students at Paris.[104] Their number reflects the existence of a *studium generale* at the Sacro Convento, which can be documented from at least 1285 (it may have been established much earlier; there is already evidence of schooling at Assisi from *c.*1225–7).[105] The Assisi *studium* could not compete with Paris in prestige. For one thing, it was not attached to a university and so could not confer theology degrees (the so-called 'magisterium theologiae').[106] But Assisi was certainly one of the principal Franciscan schools in Italy, and friars from many other provinces of the Order came to study there.[107] The Sacro Convento *studium* could also draw on one of the most impressive of all Franciscan libraries,

left 44 Tomb slab of Matthias of Sant'Eustachio, *c.*1310–12, marble (218.5 cm × 63 cm), Santa Maria in Aracoeli, Rome.

which Matthew of Acquasparta's donation had just embellished further.[108]

This necessarily brief survey of office-holders has uncovered a network of distinguished friars based at the Sacro Convento in the years around 1288. Most of the custodians and provincials had extensive administrative experience; several had also served as inquisitors, suggesting a significant level of theological expertise. We may safely assume that a friar like Matthias of Sant'Eustachio, given his high noble status, possessed impressive social connections in Rome.[109] What is notable is the frequent combination of administrative responsibility and theological training. The university-trained lector Matthew of Chieti moved quickly from the Sacro Convento to the papal curia at the accession of Nicholas IV. From an older generation, Philip of Perugia had been a member of Nicholas III's household and provincial minister of Tuscany, as well as teaching at Assisi and composing a treatise on the stigmata. None of these names has been cited before in the vast literature on the renewal of the Basilica's fabric in the wake of *Reducentes*, but these friars and their peers are far more likely than any cardinal to have been present on the ground to give Nicholas's ambitions concrete form.[110]

Rome and Assisi

In examining the precise historical circumstances of the *Reducentes* bulls, we have so far explored opposing but complementary perspectives. Looking at *Reducentes* from the stance of its authors, we asked: What factors motivated and sustained Nicholas's initiative for Assisi? Then, adopting the viewpoint of its recipients, charged with putting *Reducentes* into action, we have investigated how and by whom the Franciscan pope's ambitions were to be interpreted and realized. Only by considering both questions together can we understand how the mural decoration of the Upper Church came to be.

The answers to the first question lie in Rome as much as Assisi, in the artistic and ideological milieu surrounding Nicholas's election. The decision to reconfigure the Basilica so boldly was deeply informed by the contemporary understanding of this first Franciscan papacy. Nicholas's own interpretation of his pontificate can be gauged from his commissions in Rome for the new apse mosaics at the Lateran and Santa Maria Maggiore, where Francis and Anthony of Padua now stood among the apostles. If the unprecedented inclusion of the Franciscan saints were not explicit enough, Nicholas proclaimed through monumental inscriptions how his rebuilding of the Lateran was a literal realization of Innocent III's vision of Francis supporting the basilica, and by extension the entire Roman Church. This powerful sense of historical significance and destiny fulfilled must have been shared by many Franciscans, as well as Nicholas's principal backers in the curia, the Colonna cardinals. Through *Reducentes,* Nicholas and his circle wished to make a similar mark at Assisi by – *inter alia* – completing the mural decoration of the Upper Church left unfinished by the Franciscan pope's mentor, Nicholas III Orsini.

The second question has taken us back to Assisi, to the Franciscan community of the Sacro Convento and the issue of who was directly responsible for overseeing the decoration of the Upper Church. Until now scholars have addressed the execution of the frescoes overwhelmingly in terms of artists, whether through old-style attribution or more nuanced treatments of medieval workshop practice. But can we attribute the design of the Upper Church solely to painters? Our analysis of the frescoes (see chapters 5–7) demonstrates the programme's iconographic sophistication, and its engagement with theological concerns specific to the Franciscan Order. Even the most educated painters of the day would have required guidance from clerics with theological training to execute it. The nave programme was begun by the friar-painter Jacopo Torriti, and it is tempting to allot him an important role in devising the broad outline of the mural scheme (given that the basic disposition of the cycles was already implicit in the Genesis scenes and *Deesis* vault he frescoed before departing for Rome). But, with few exceptions, the painters who worked on the Upper Church would not have been friars, nor would they have possessed any theological education. Moreover, the multiple discontinuities between workshops, which probably changed with every season of work, argue for a substantial contribution from the friars themselves to realize such a complex but ultimately coherent programme.

Could the decorative programme of the Upper Church have been devised elsewhere – at the papal curia in Rome or Rieti?[111] External stimuli were certainly important, especially the examples of Nicholas's renovations at the Lateran and Santa Maria Maggiore in Rome. Chiara Frugoni's new analysis of the lost altar embroideries that Nicholas sent to Assisi establishes another important and more direct channel of iconographic influence for the Saint Francis cycle. But several factors militate against design at a distance. First: our treatment in this book of the nave frescoes will reveal how the success of the programme depends at pivotal moments on the interaction between imagery and the specific spatial context of the Upper Church. Many details which appeared, as far as we know, for the first time at Assisi were responses to the demands of this unique setting.[112] Furthermore, there is an appreciable development in the compositional and narrative complexity of the murals from the beginning of the nave programme to the end. The innovative solutions devised for some of the scenes in the Saint Francis cycle were far in advance of anything attempted in the Old and New Testament cycles. The enhanced visual possibilities that emerged as work progressed could hardly have been foreseen. While the broad disposition of the nave cycles and certain key juxtapositions must have been mapped out in advance, the detail of the programme evidently evolved to a significant degree once work was under way. This surely precludes remote supervision of the fresco campaign and suggests a great deal of input on site from the friars of the Sacro Convento, working closely with the various painters and workshops to forge the interlocking iconography of the three nave cycles. Our analysis of the custodians, provincial ministers and lectors based at Assisi during this period has confirmed that the Sacro Convento possessed the necessary intellectual capital to make this contribution. It was this community that Nicholas empowered through the *Reducentes* letters.

Reading *Reducentes* as an act of delegation as well as a command for action is key to understanding the decoration of the Upper Church that followed. Nicholas wished both to complete and to expand the Basilica complex. The bare walls of the Upper Church nave were an obvious place to start and the fundamental decision to combine a quintessentially Roman disposition of Old and New Testament cycles with the most extensive narrative of Saint Francis's life yet attempted in monumental art could well have been taken by Nicholas himself, or someone close to him, like Matthew of Acquasparta or Giacomo Colonna. The painting of the nave had probably been debated for many years – perhaps as far back as Nicholas's own time as minister general. Now, as pope, Nicholas would finally provide the impetus and resources to complete the work.

But the painting of the nave of the Upper Church was not a project like Nicholas's interventions in the papal basilicas in Rome. At Assisi, as we have already observed, there are no coats of arms, no donor portraits, no inscriptions, nor any other overt sign of private patronage. The commemoration of personal interests was evidently regarded as inappropriate within such an important conventual space for the Franciscan Order. Instead, the programme of the Upper Church makes a largely timeless claim for the central place of Saint Francis's life within the historical scheme of salvation. Assisi also differed from Nicholas's other artistic projects in being physically distant from Rome and the other centres he used as a base for the curia, Rieti and Orvieto. Nicholas would have seen his rebuilding of the Lateran take shape with his own eyes, but he was never able to visit Assisi as pope.

The renewal of the Basilica, including the completion of the Upper Church's mural decoration, was therefore left to the Order. But the Franciscans at Assisi did not work in a vacuum. They would have been aware of Nicholas's projects in Rome (to which they quickly lost their star artist, Jacopo Torriti) and would have been familiar with the pope's intellectual interests and artistic tastes. Nicholas had joined the Order as a boy and had served as minister general for six years in the 1270s. He must have been well known to many Franciscans of the older generation, including the senior friars at Assisi. While to the community at Assisi in the spring of 1288 the pope in Rieti might have seemed a distant patron, the Basilica's renewal must have been carried forward in the hope of meeting his approval. This is especially true of the first interventions to be begun during his brief pontificate, namely the frescoes of the nave of the Upper Church. As they pondered their response to *Reducentes*, the friars of the Sacro Convento could not have known that their fellow friar would never return to Assisi; they must have assumed that Nicholas would come to survey their efforts from the papal throne in the apse of the Upper Church.

A critical distinction must be made here. In very general terms, Nicholas can be considered as a patron at Assisi. His bulls authorized and financed the works; his Roman projects set the ideological agenda and raised the bar of ambition. But in its specifics, the mural decoration of the Upper Church nave was commissioned *for* the pope, not *by* the pope. We would characterize this as the context in which to

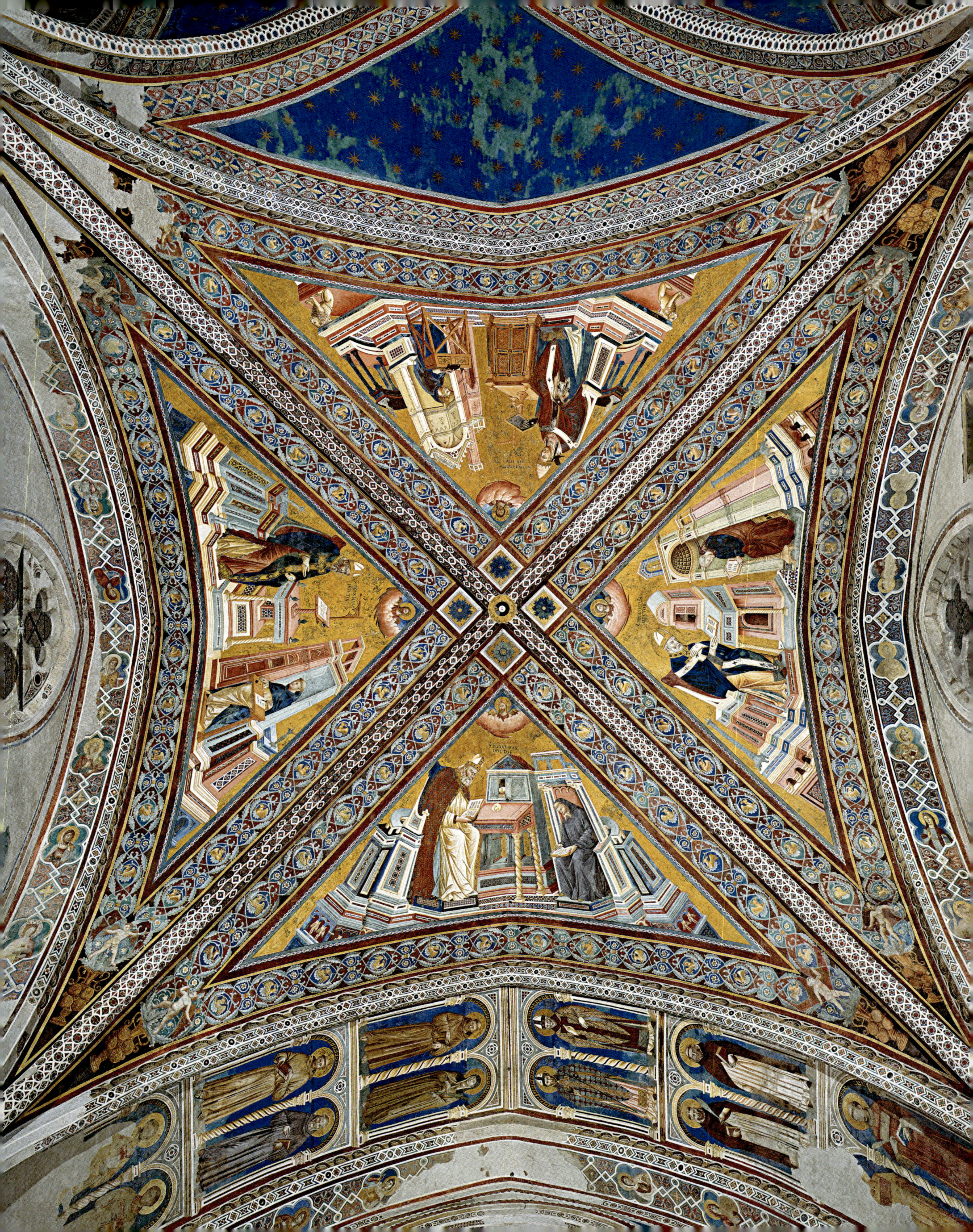

understand details like the inclusion of Saint Agapitus amid the gallery of saints on the arch of the counter-façade. The relationship between the Franciscans and their pope finds its most eloquent expression in the adjacent vault of the Doctors (fig. 45). It can be no coincidence that the eastern web of the vault, the field that was visible down the length of the nave, was given to Saint Jerome. Had he ever sat on the papal throne, Nicholas would have faced his patron saint at the opposite end of the Upper Church, commemorating the name that he had probably taken on joining the Franciscan Order in his youth and which he continued to treasure after his elevation to the papacy.

facing page 45 Vault of the Doctors of the Church (fourth bay of the nave), *c.*1288–91, fresco, Upper Church, Basilica of San Francesco.

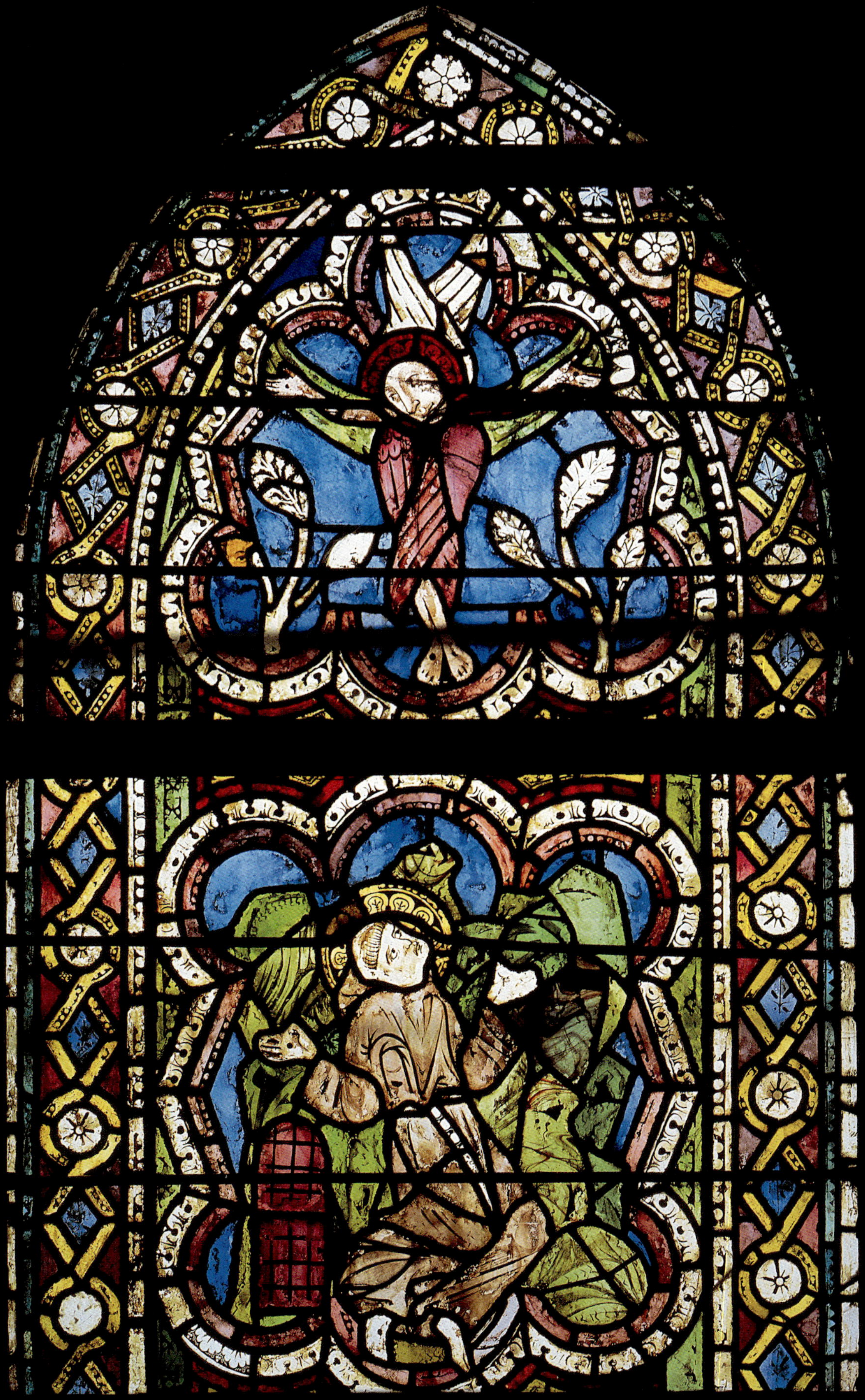

3

The Upper Church in 1288

By 1288 the architectural superstructure of the Upper Church had been standing for at least thirty-five years. The eye-witness account of the canonization of Saint Stanislas in the Upper Church on 8 September 1253, discovered by Silvestro Nessi, confirms that the vaults had been finished by that date, for lamps were described as hanging from them.[1] As we shall see, panel paintings had already been commissioned for the Upper Church in the 1230s, and must have been *in situ* for the Polish bishop's canonization in 1253. But, even so, that summer Pope Innocent IV had found the appearance of the Basilica wanting. His bull *Decet et expedit*, issued on 10 July 1253, ordered San Francesco to 'be completed with a noble structure and decorated with the peak of splendid workmanship', for which he released the pilgrim offerings at the Basilica's altars for the next twenty-five years.[2]

Over the subsequent quarter-century a series of decorative campaigns was launched in the Upper Church, first in glass and then in fresco. The mural scheme was concentrated in the apse and transepts, at the sanctuary end of the church, leaving the nave walls bare. The programme of stained glass, however, encompassed the entire fenestration of the Upper Church, including the lancet windows in the nave. Clement IV added an extra three years to Innocent's initial grant of twenty-five, extending the flow of funds up to 1281.[3] After that, progress seems to have petered out and the project probably lay dormant for several years before 1288.

The nave programme initiated under the authority of *Reducentes* was not a straightforward continuation of these earlier interventions. Ideologically it was much more ambitious than anything that had gone before and was rooted in the specific milieu of Nicholas IV's Franciscan papacy. But it did not neglect the images that were already there. The scope of the new decorative scheme is laid out in Chapter 4, but first we need to understand what confronted the planners, patrons and artists in 1288. The Upper Church was an idiosyncratic building, imitating the major Roman basilicas by facing west rather than east. The new frescoes exploited the Basilica's unusual architecture and picked up iconographic details from some of the earlier imagery in the stained glass and on the sanctuary walls. Most importantly of all, later alterations have stripped the Upper Church of some of its oldest images, in particular a set of monumental painted panels that guided some of the fundamental organizational choices behind the new nave programme. These Romanesque pictures have never been considered before in relation to the post-1288 nave frescoes, but their impact on

facing page 46 Maestro di San Francesco, *Stigmatization* (see fig. 80).

the Nicholine programme was profound. This chapter surveys the state of the Upper Church on the eve of *Reducentes*, establishing the context within which the new scheme would take shape.

The Space of the Upper Church

By the time Innocent IV consecrated the Basilica on 25 May 1253 the basic elements of the Upper Church's liturgical furniture must have been usable, in particular the three altar *mensae*: the high altar, dedicated to the Virgin (probably originally sited at the centre of the crossing bay), and a side altar in each of the transepts.[4] These side altars were orientated, facing east despite the westward disposition of the Basilica as a whole (fig. 47). All of the original altar blocks and tables survive, although the high altar has been reconstructed following the 1997 earthquake, when it was smashed by the falling masonry from the vault above. The high-altar block was faced on all sides with marble panels inlaid with cosmati work, which have now been restored several times (fig. 48).[5] In its original position, the high altar was raised on a stepped platform, the step faces of which were decorated with glazed terracotta tiles.[6]

The side altars stood clear of the transept walls. They did not compete with the cosmati work on the high altar, but were plain except for the dedication inscription to Saint Michael on the front of the south transept block (fig. 49).[7] The feast of Saint Michael was raised to the status of a double feast at the general chapter at Assisi in 1269, along with the major Marian feasts, which would have been celebrated at the high altar.[8] It is unclear why a matching inscription was not carved on the altar in the north transept, but we know from later sources that this was dedicated either to Saints Peter and Paul or to the twelve apostles.[9] The latter alternative is suggested by the analogy of San Francesco in Gualdo Tadino, a church modelled on the Upper Church, where one of the two principal side altars was dedicated to the twelve apostles in the early fourteenth century (fig. 50).[10] Both dedications would have made sense to the early Franciscans: their founder's devotion to Saint Michael was renowned, and the friars were often compared to the apostles. The choice of the second dedication was probably informed by the Order's practice of holding its general chapters at Pentecost.

47 Plan of the Upper Church, showing the positions of the altars and papal throne. A: Apostles altar; H: High altar; M: Saint Michael altar; P: Pulpit; T: Throne.

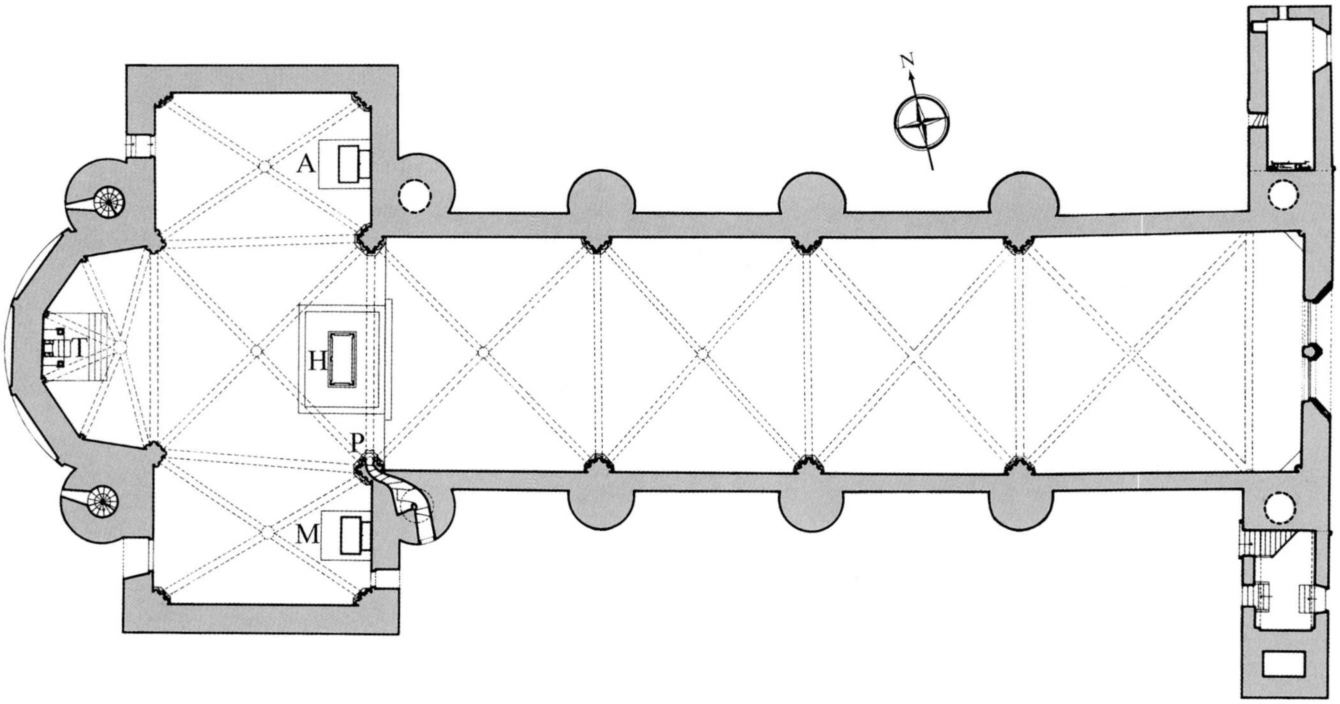

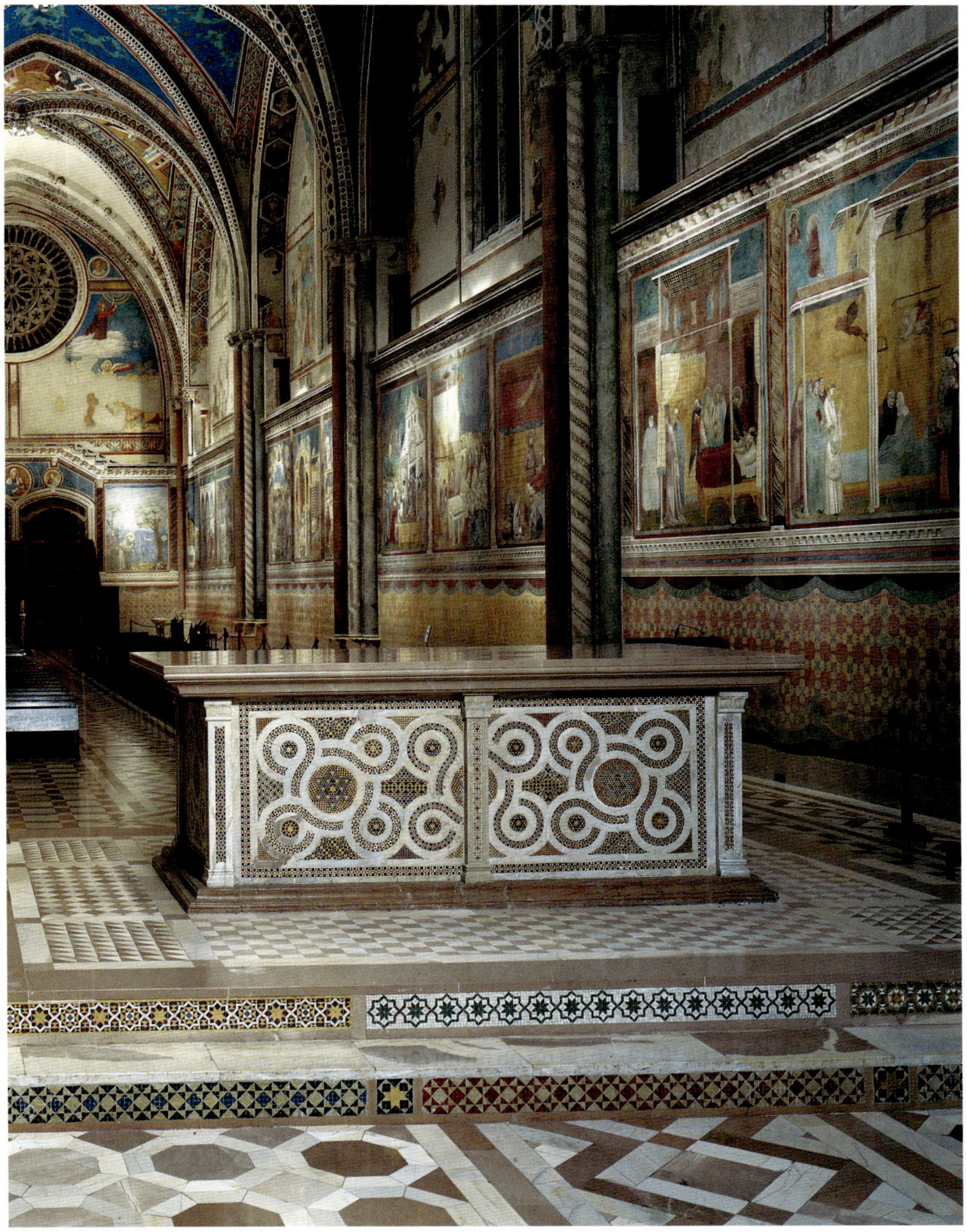

48 High altar, consecrated 1253, marble with cosmati inlay, Upper Church, Basilica of San Francesco (reconstructed several times, most recently after the earthquake of September 1997).

Besides the three altars, the most significant element of furniture in the Upper Church was the papal throne, at the centre of the apse (fig. 52).[11] This proclaimed the status of the Upper Basilica as a papal chapel, the liturgical equal of the major Roman basilicas and other papal-throne churches in central Italy, such as Anagni cathedral. Various suggestions have been made for the date of the throne and its canopy: some commentators believe that the throne itself was erected for the 1253 consecration or perhaps when Clement renewed the Basilica's privileges in 1266;[12] others prefer to date it to the late 1270s.[13] It is possible that the throne arrangement was realized in several stages, with the gabled baldachin and

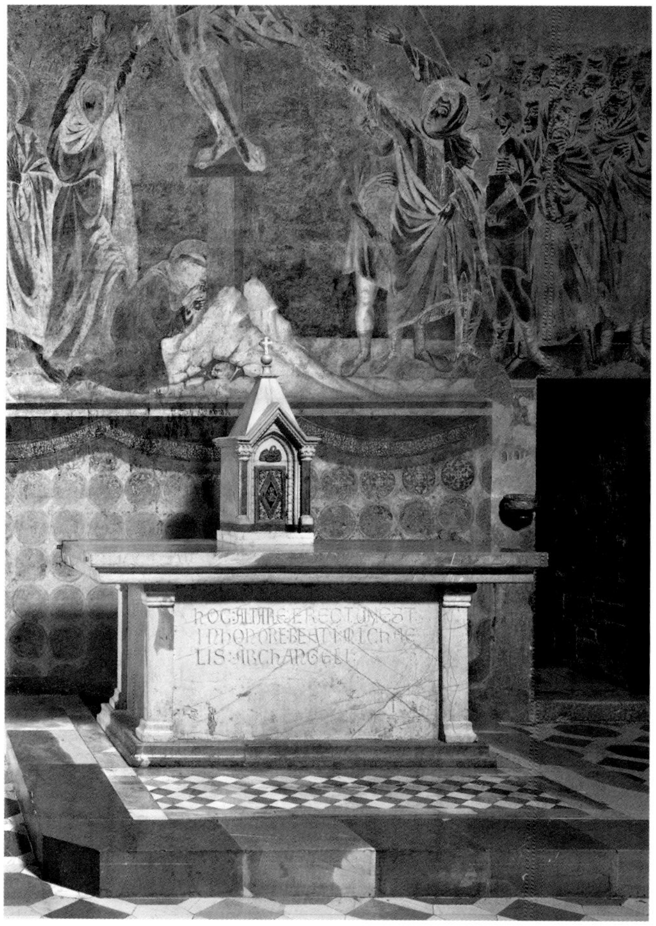

49 Saint Michael altar, mid-thirteenth century, Subasio limestone, south transept, Upper Church, Basilica of San Francesco.

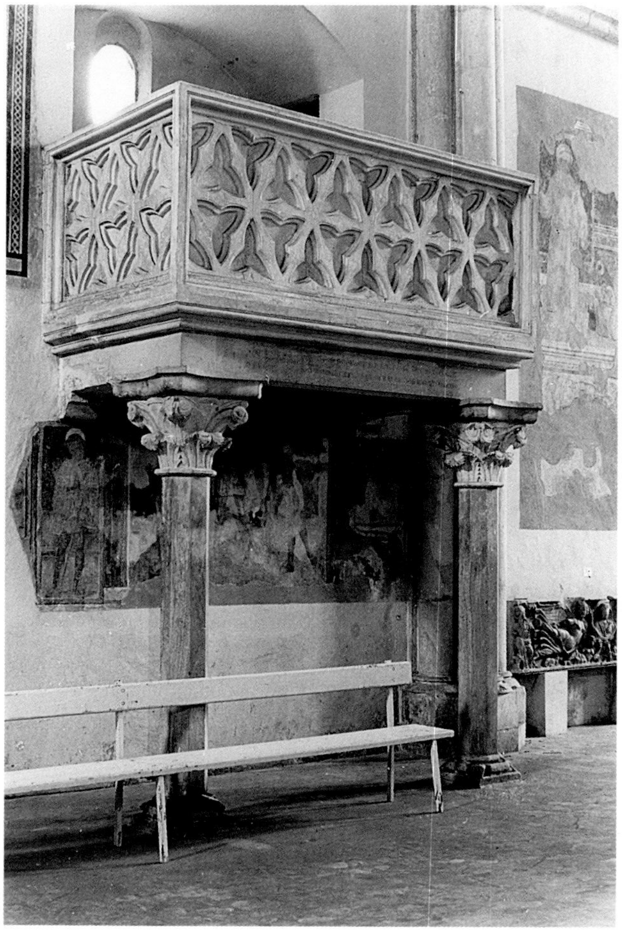

50 Pulpit incorporating fragments and inscription from an altar dedicated to the twelve apostles, early fourteenth century, San Francesco, Gualdo Tadino.

flanking columns being added some years after the cathedra was first installed; but the entire ensemble was certainly in place before Cimabue frescoed the walls around it *c.*1280 (for this dating, see below).[14] The arms of the throne are formed of two lions, each mauling a stricken calf. The foot-rest bore an inscription, now largely worn away, from Psalm 90:13: 'Thou shalt walk upon the asp and the basilisk: and thou shalt trample under foot the lion and the dragon.'[15] These four demonic animals are depicted in a relief frieze immediately below (fig. 51). The throne thereby adapted the venerable iconographic tradition of the victorious Christ trampling the creatures described by the psalmist to show the pope as Christ's vicar doing the same.

Comparisons are often made between the throne at Assisi and the now fragmentary papal cathedra that was formerly in the apse of Saint John Lateran in Rome.[16] Both incorporated reliefs of the asp, basilisk, lion and dragon below the sitter's feet. The Lateran throne was installed around 1290 as part of Nicholas IV's extensive programme of renovations,

51 Relief of the lion, asp, basilisk and dragon, with inscription from Psalm 90:13, on a step of the papal throne, apse, Upper Church, Basilica of San Francesco.

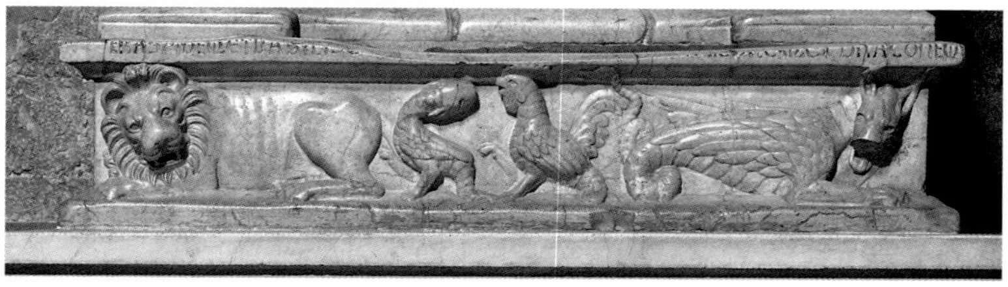

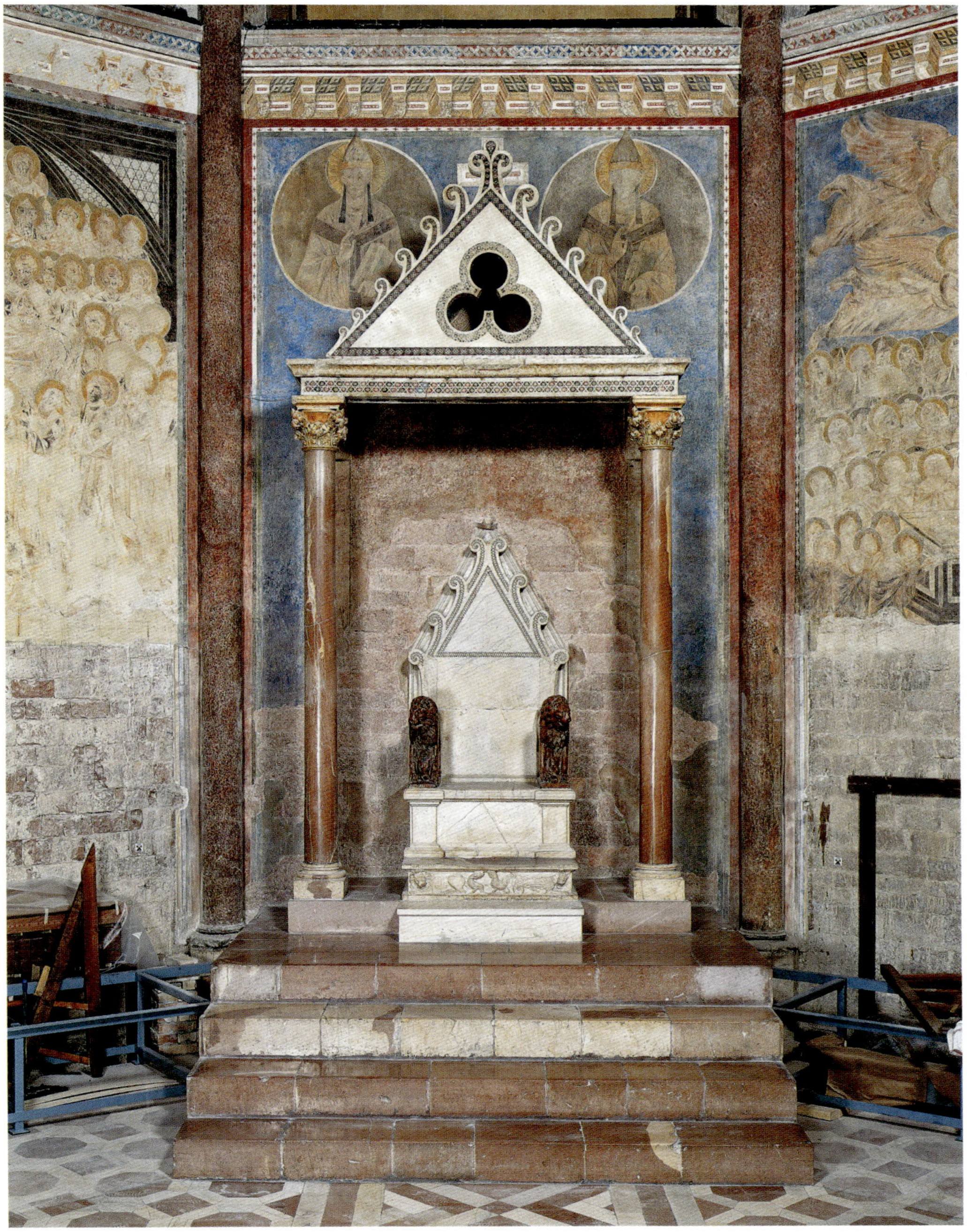

52 Papal throne, *c.*1253 (canopy added *c.*1280), apse, Upper Church, Basilica of San Francesco.

discussed in Chapter 1. So the influence in this case probably flowed from Assisi to Rome rather than the other way round. The similarities between the two thrones reflected the analogous institutional roles of the two churches. The Basilica of San Francesco had been founded as the 'head and mother' ('caput et mater') of all the churches of the Order, a title that consciously aped the Lateran, 'head and mother of all churches' ('caput et mater omnium ecclesiarum').[17]

Although the thirteenth-century altars and throne have survived in a relatively undisturbed state (at least until 1997), other aspects of the Upper Church's original furniture are much more difficult to reconstruct. The biggest point of

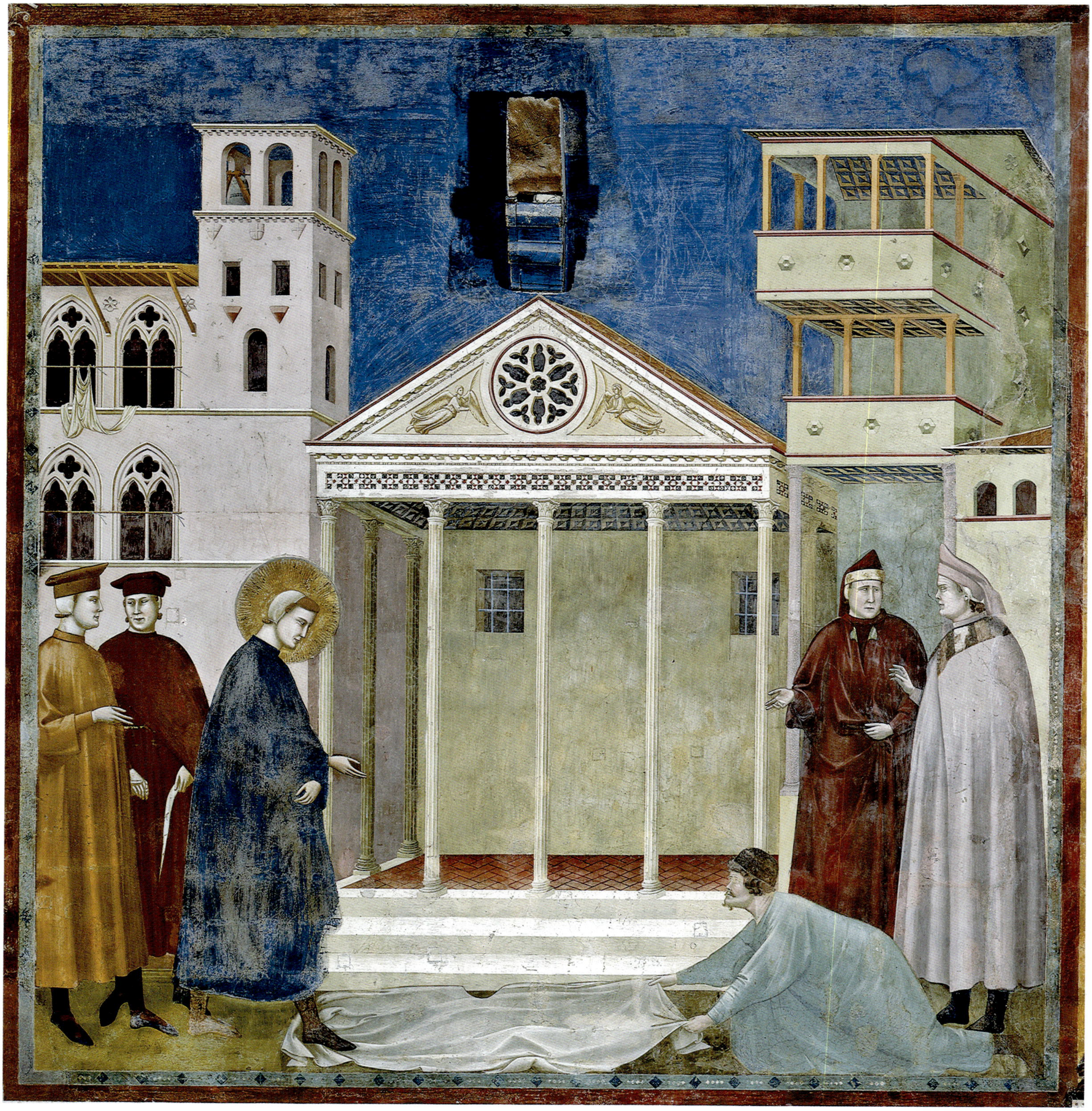

53 *Homage of a Simple Man*, Scene 1 of the Saint Francis cycle, *c.*1290–96, fresco, north wall of the nave, Upper Church, Basilica of San Francesco.

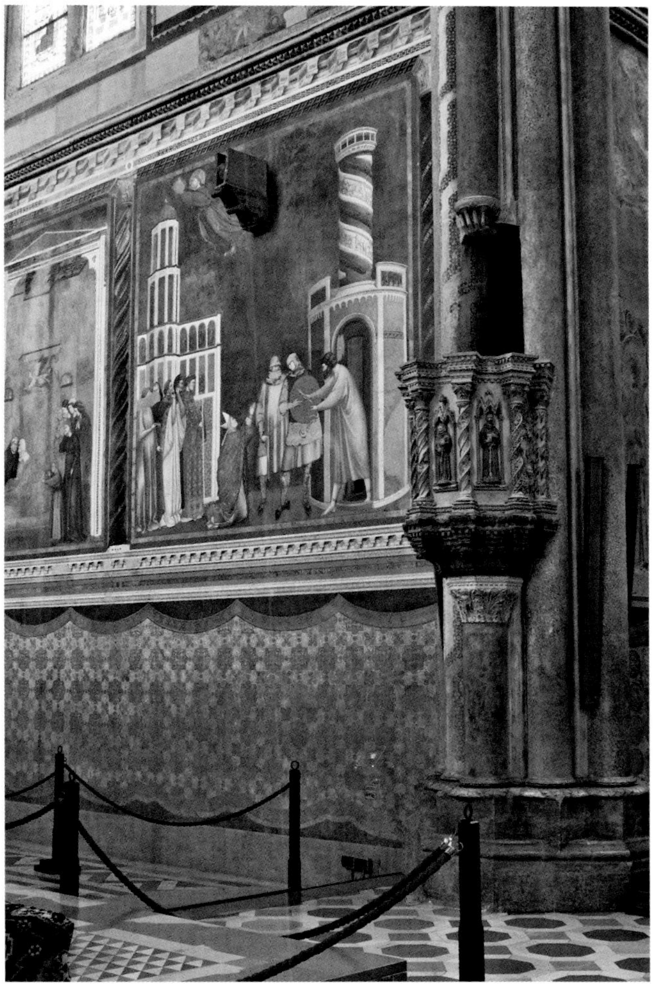

54 Pulpit, *c.*1347, south-eastern pier of the crossing, Upper Church, Basilica of San Francesco.

uncertainty is the possible existence of a physical division between the transept and the nave. Irene Hueck has proposed that the initial Duecento arrangement incorporated a screen at this point in the church, perhaps an open colonnade similar to the barrier that still divides nave and sanctuary in San Marco, Venice.[18] Under-floor foundations have been identified that could have supported a masonry screen running across the head of the nave, and the profiles of the adjacent pier bases seem to be shaped to engage such a structure. But any monumental barrier was demolished in the wake of *Reducentes*, sacrificed to allow the frescoing of the lower parts of the nave walls in the 1290s. At the same time, the prior existence of a screen at this point may explain one of the most curious features of the Saint Francis cycle: that the first scene, the *Homage of a Simple Man* (fig. 53), was painted last, following the final scene, the *Liberation of Peter of Alife* (see fig. 34) on the opposite wall.[19] The need to dismantle a screen structure at the head of the nave could account for the need to leave the execution of the two westernmost scenes of the Saint Francis cycle until the very end.

The sculpted pulpit now set into the south-eastern pier of the crossing is a much later addition (fig. 54). On stylistic and documentary grounds, it is usually dated to the mid-fourteenth century.[20] The internal staircase behind the pulpit has been roughly hewn out of the solid mass of the Basilica's corner buttress (fig. 55), a firm indication that it was not initially planned during the construction of the Upper Church. On the other hand, the painted surfaces of the sur-

55 Passageway within the south-eastern pier of the crossing, excavated *c.*1290, Upper Church, Basilica of San Francesco.

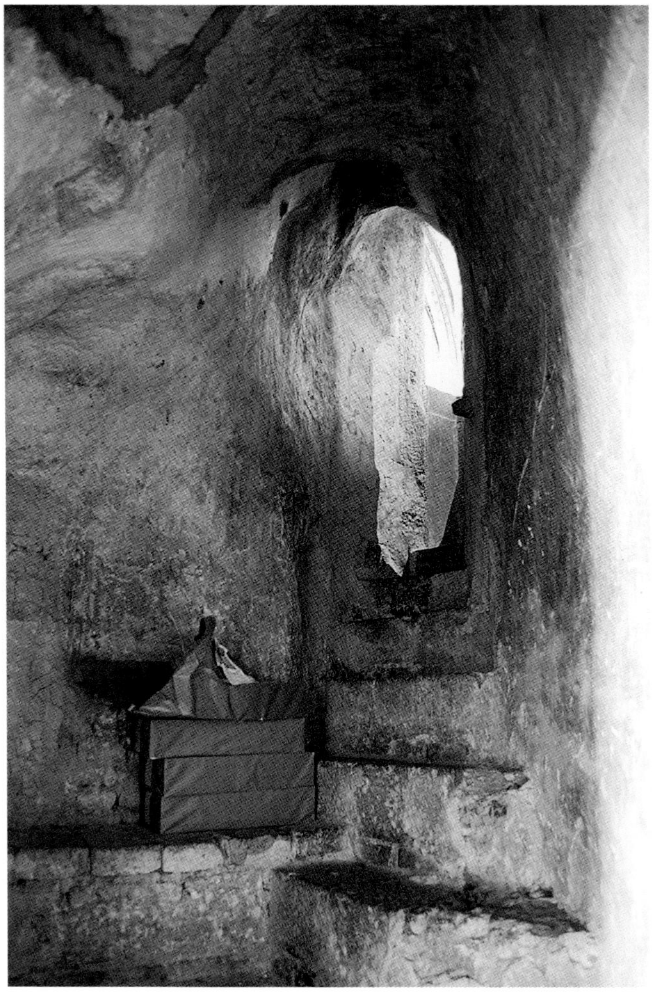

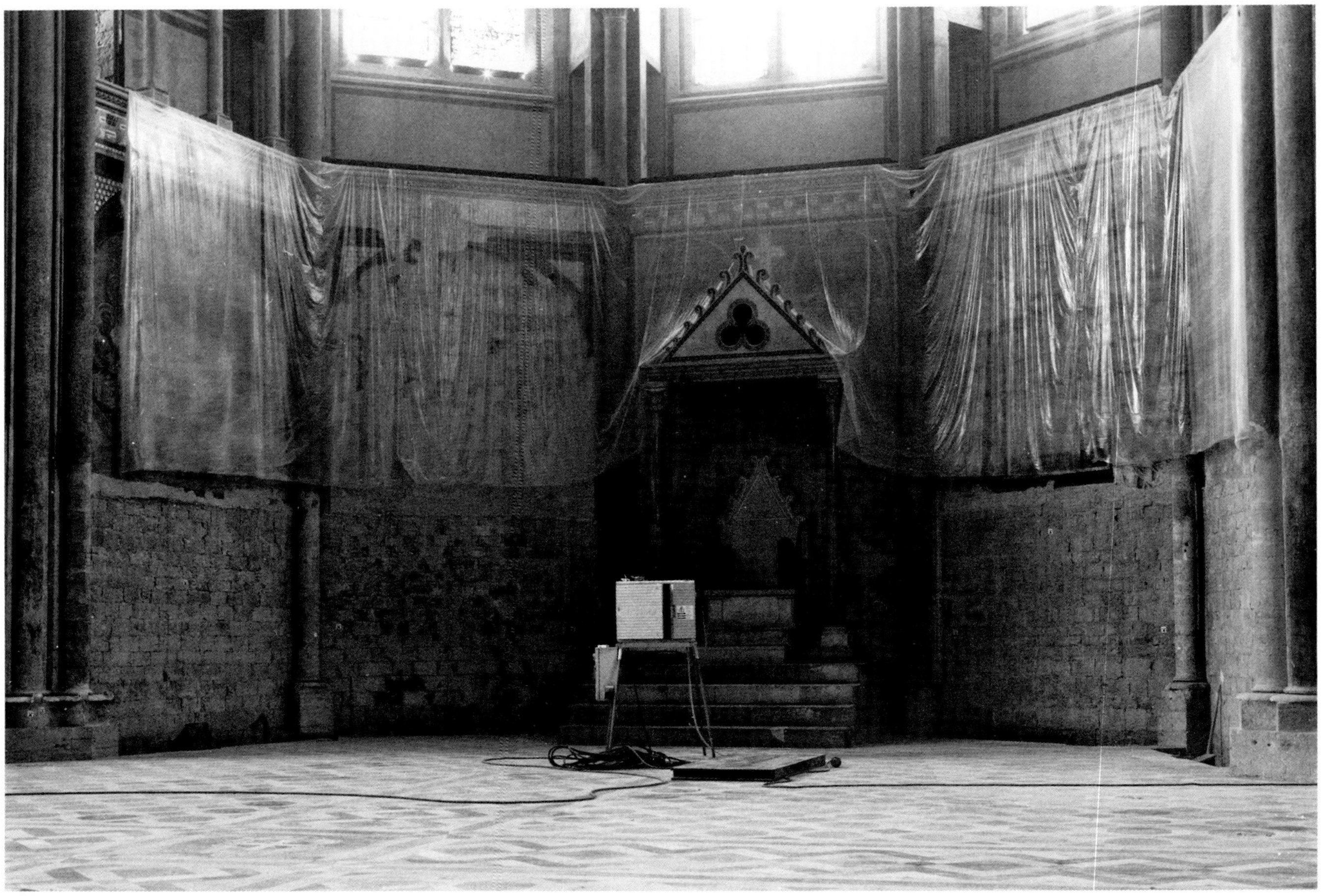

56 View of the apse, photographed with the sixteenth-century choir stalls removed following the earthquake of September 1997, Upper Church, Basilica of San Francesco.

rounding transept piers establish that the passageway had been opened before the Saint Francis cycle was painted, indicating that the present Trecento pulpit must have replaced an earlier one.[21] A pulpit is referred to in the description of the canonization of Saint Stanislas in 1253, but this could have been a movable wooden structure, similar perhaps to the raised wooden balcony depicted in the scene of the *Canonization* in the Saint Francis cycle (see fig. 95).[22] Alternatively, a masonry screen at the head of the nave may have incorporated a lectern for preaching and reading the lessons. In either case, the 1253 account is unlikely to refer to a pulpit in the present location. More likely is that the friars decided to insert a pulpit and access passage into the crossing pier around 1290, shortly before the painting of the Saint Francis cycle, a move that would only have been possible once the screen was removed.

The original seating provisions in the Upper Church are not known, but the curtailed lower borders of Cimabue's frescoes in the apse indicate that there were stalls to either side of the papal throne by *c.*1280 at the latest (fig. 56).[23] These stalls would have been wooden and must have been of high quality: they were sufficiently impressive to serve as a model for the local cathedral of San Rufino some decades later. In 1349, via a *modo et forma* contractual clause, the cathedral canons expressed their desire for new choir stalls of the same size and workmanship as those in the Upper Church.[24] The Upper Church choir was eventually replaced in the 1490s by the present intarsia stalls by Domenico Indivini da Sanseverino (see fig. 11).[25] The 1491 contract instructed Domenico to replicate the extent of the previous choir but also to add new ranks of stalls in the transepts, so the earlier arrangement should probably be assumed to have

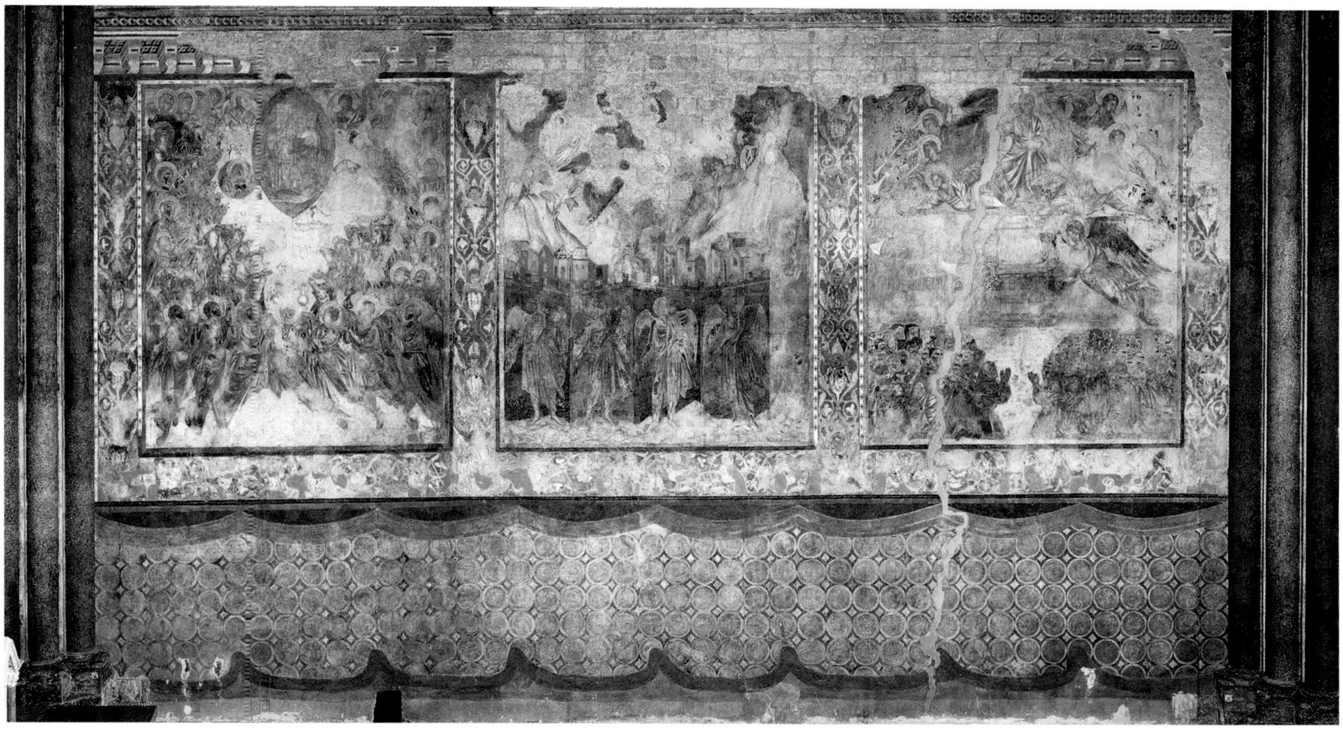

57 Cimabue, scenes from the Apocalypse with fictive textile hangings below, *c.*1279–82, fresco, south transept, Upper Church, Basilica of San Francesco.

been confined to the apse.[26] Cimabue had frescoed the lower sections of the walls in the transepts with fictive textiles, suggesting that seating was not envisaged in these areas (fig. 57). Pia Theis proposed the existence of a marble *schola cantorum* precinct at the head of the nave in the Upper Church, but the evidence for this remains circumstantial.[27] She identified various marble and cosmati-work fragments in the Lower Church as elements from the hypothetical *schola* in the Upper Church.[28] Their subsequent re-use downstairs would imply that the *schola*, if it ever existed, must have been dismantled towards the end of the thirteenth century.[29]

Giunta Pisano's Cross for Brother Elias

When Innocent IV consecrated the Basilica's altars in May 1253 the freshly built Upper Church would have been almost devoid of pictorial decoration. But one image that must have been there already was a mighty crucifix, painted by Giunta Pisano in 1236 for the then minister general, Elias of Cortona.[30] This painted panel cross dominated the nave of the Upper Church until 1622, when it was taken down to clear the view of a temporary elevated stage erected in front of the high altar.[31] Until then, Giunta's crucifix had been supported by a wooden beam that spanned the nave close to the mouth of the transepts. The stubs of this beam, together with the supporting consoles, still mark the first and last scenes of the Saint Francis cycle (figs 58 and 59). The cross itself is now irretrievably lost. In the seventeenth century, after the friars of the Sacro Convento had dismantled the beam arrangement, the panel was hung on the counter-façade, directly below the great rose window.[32] This sealed the crucifix's fate, for here it was exposed to the moisture entering the church through breaks in the lower section of the oculus. In 1683 Padre Francesco Maria Angeli noted the deteriorating condition of Giunta's cross over the façade door.[33] At some point in the eighteenth century the crucifix seems to have fallen to the floor and broken into several pieces.[34] By 1785 no trace could be found of it.[35]

While the 1236 cross pre-dated Nicholas IV's interventions at Assisi by over half a century, acknowledging its dominant position in the Upper Church is crucial for understanding

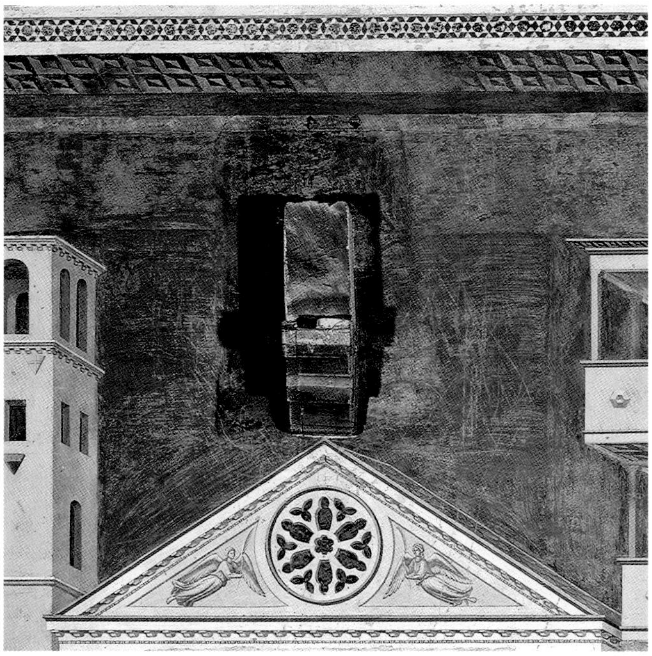

58 Stub of the beam that spanned the nave, with supporting console, embedded in the *Homage of a Simple Man*, Scene 1 of the Saint Francis cycle, *c.*1290–96, fresco, north wall of the nave, Upper Church, Basilica of San Francesco.

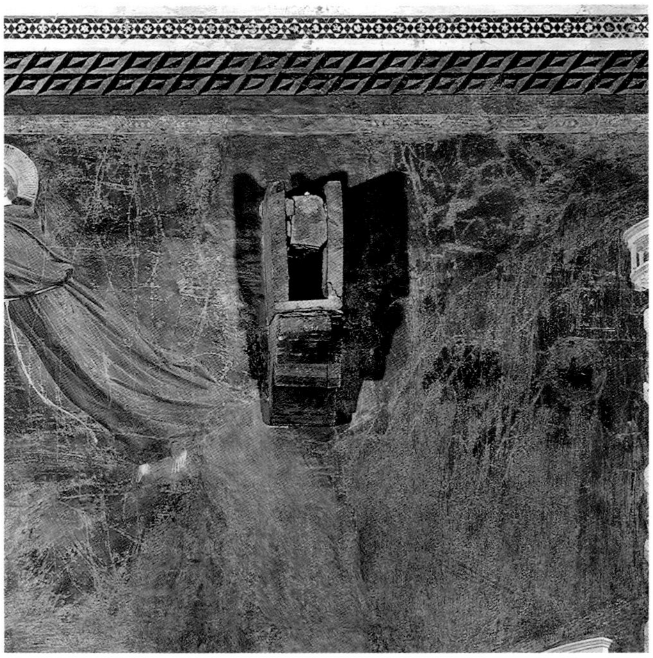

59 Stub of the beam that spanned the nave, with supporting console, embedded in the *Liberation of Peter of Alife*, Scene 28 of the Saint Francis cycle, *c.*1290–96, fresco, south wall of the nave, Upper Church, Basilica of San Francesco.

the decorative programme devised for the nave at the end of the Duecento. The murals took account of Giunta's great rood and, as we shall see in later chapters, certain compositional choices responded specifically to its presence. In significant respects, the cross and its beam arrangement constituted a fourth side for the nave programme. For these reasons, it is important to reconstruct the lost crucifix and its beam as far as possible, to clarify what the planners of the later fresco cycles had to accommodate and incorporate within the new scheme.

Fortunately the appearance of Giunta's cross can be recovered from textual descriptions and through comparisons with works that imitated its form, iconography and scale. In the 1560s Giorgio Vasari saw the crucifix over a beam that traversed the Upper Church and judged it to be a work 'alla greca' by his thirteenth-century compatriot Margaritone d'Arezzo.[36] The attribution, date and patronage of the cross were clarified only when the beam was dismantled in 1622. Able to examine the crucifix at close quarters for the first time, the friars discovered an inscription at the panel's base, which revealed that the image had been painted in 1236 by Giunta Pisano for Brother Elias of Cortona, sometime minister general of the Order, Franciscan apostate and reputed architect of the Basilica:

FRATER ELIAS FECIT FIERI
JESU CHRISTE PIE
MISERERE PRECANTIS ELIAE.
JUNCTA PISANUS ME PINXIT
ANNO DOMINI M.CC.XXXVI.
INDICTIONE NONA.[37]

Which may be translated as: 'Brother Elias had this made; merciful Jesus Christ have mercy on the praying Elias; Giunta Pisano painted me in the year of our Lord 1236, in the ninth Indiction.' The inscription accompanied a donor figure of Elias that was painted by Christ's feet on the panel's *suppedaneum*. The discovery soon excited the interest of a number of Franciscan historians and Giunta's likeness of the minister general was preserved through a number of paintings and prints (fig. 61).[38] One of the closest copies was conserved in the Capuchin church of Santa Maria della Concezione in Rome until it was stolen in 1999 (fig. 60).[39]

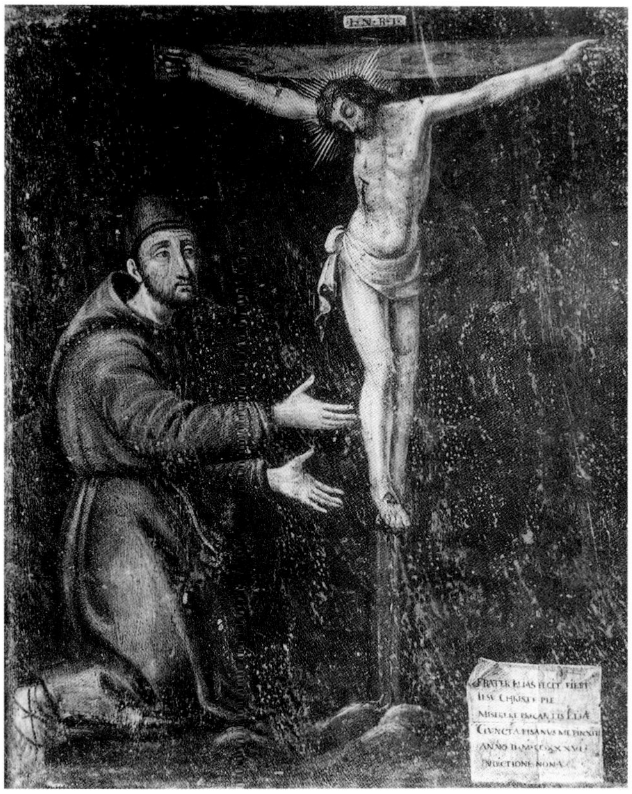

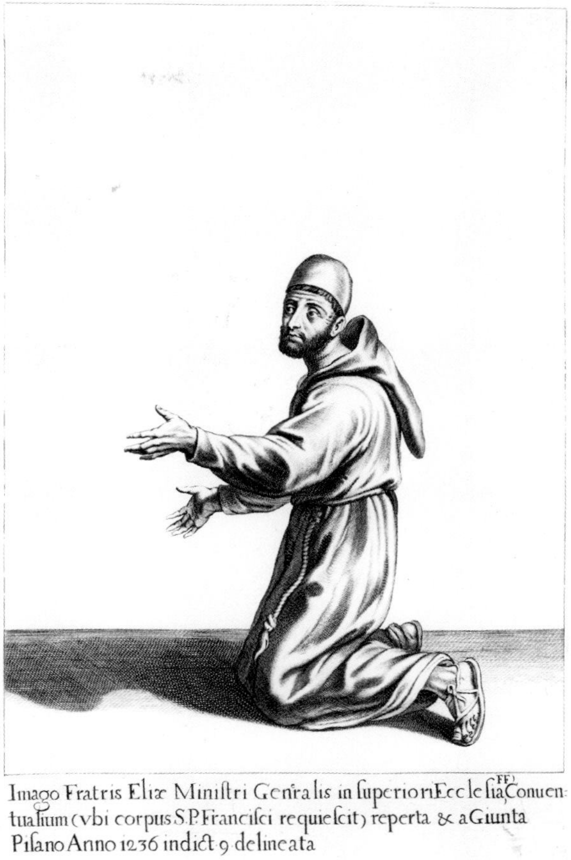

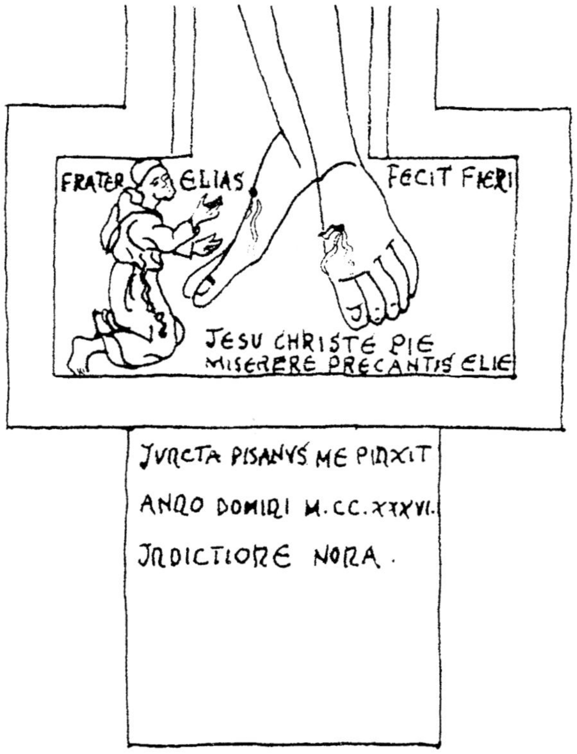

top left 60 Francesco Providoni, *Brother Elias of Cortona and the Crucifixion*, late seventeenth century, oil on panel, after donor portrait by Giunta Pisano (formerly Santa Maria della Concezione, Rome, stolen 1999).

top right 61 Flemish printmaker, *Brother Elias of Cortona*, 1666, copperplate engraving after donor portrait by Giunta Pisano, Rome, Collegio di San Lorenzo da Brindisi, Museo Francescano, Stampe II-B-27.

bottom 62 Reconstruction by Silvestro Nessi of the *suppedaneum* of Giunta Pisano's crucifix for the Upper Church, Basilica of San Francesco (Nessi (1994), p. 204, fig. 86).

From this and other sources, Silvestro Nessi has deduced a convincing reconstruction of the lower zone of Giunta's crucifix (fig. 62).[40]

Several seventeenth-century writers used the same emphatic phrase to signal the panel's impressive dimensions: 'the enormous/gigantic crucifix'.[41] Dominating the nave, the 1236 cross was the likely stimulus for Angela of Foligno's vision of Christ Crucified in the Upper Church in August 1300.[42] Giunta's panel also served as the prototype for a number of large crucifixes in Umbria, Tuscany and Emilia-

Romagna.[43] Some of these surviving examples are nearly six metres in height, and must have imitated the Elias cross in size as well as design (fig. 63).[44] The visual impact of a panel on this scale on the nave of the Upper Church can be gauged from photographs taken following Giovanni Battista Cavalcaselle's historicist restoration campaign of the 1870s, which included a speculative reconstruction of the 1236 crucifix arrangement (fig. 64).[45] Vasari's designation 'alla greca' suggests that the Upper Church crucifix established the byzantinizing iconography of the suffering Christ, or *Christus Patiens*, that then became standard for Franciscan crosses until the end of the century.[46] A much smaller crucifix in Assisi, signed by Giunta and now at Santa Maria degli

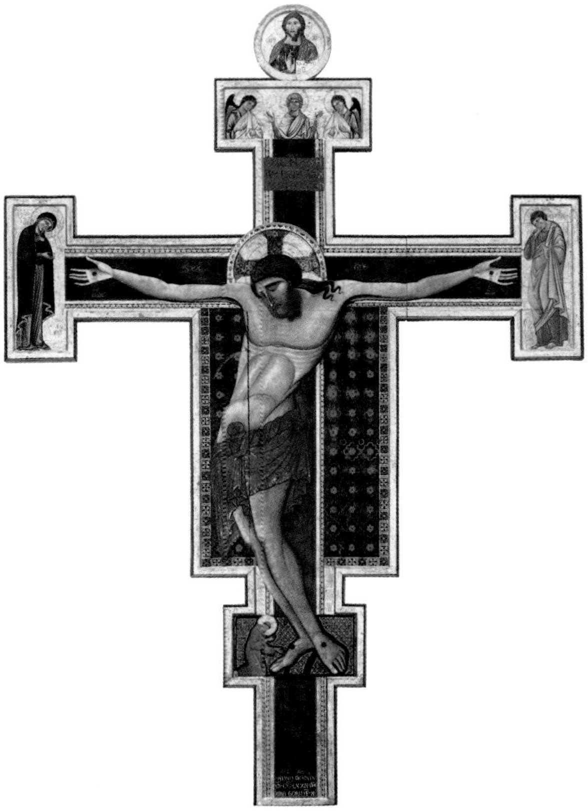

top 63 Maestro di San Francesco, crucifix, dated 1272, tempera and gold on wood (486 cm × 352 cm), Galleria Nazionale dell'Umbria, Perugia (originally San Francesco al Prato, Perugia).

bottom 64 View of the nave, Upper Church, Basilica of San Francesco, *c.*1874–1900, showing the reconstruction by Giovanni Battista Cavalcaselle of the beam spanning the nave and the installation of Giunta Pisano's crucifix.

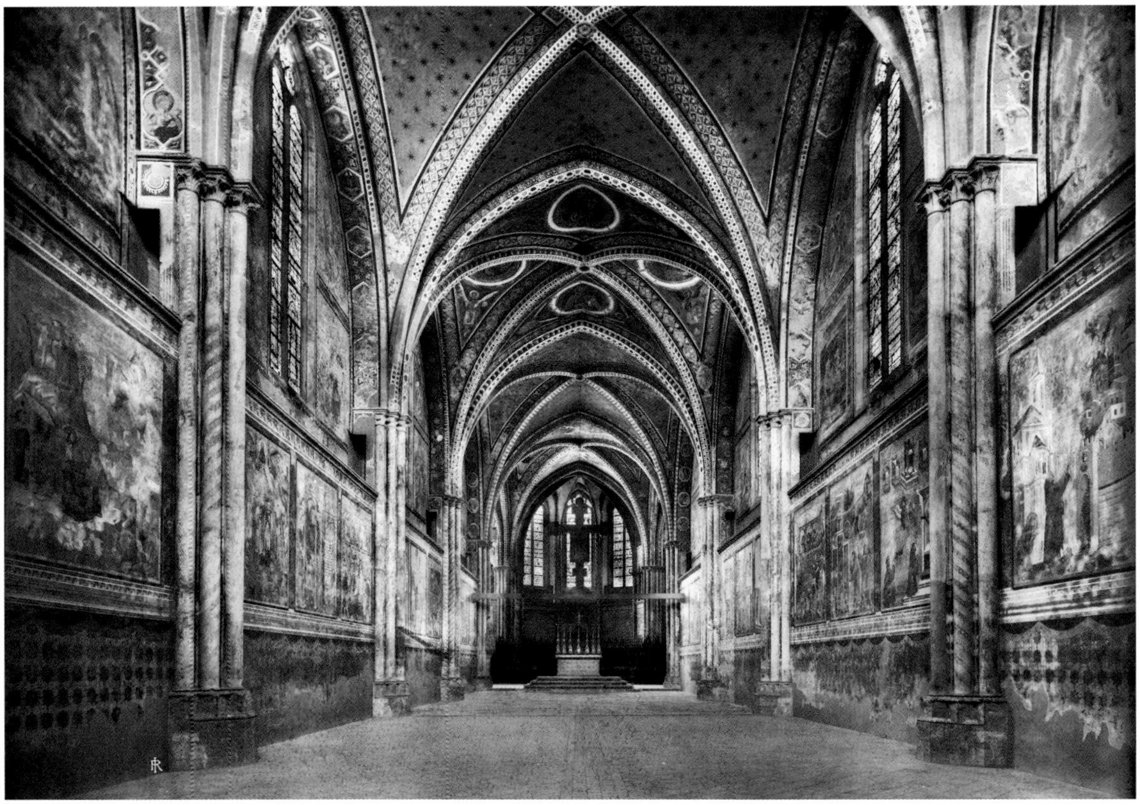

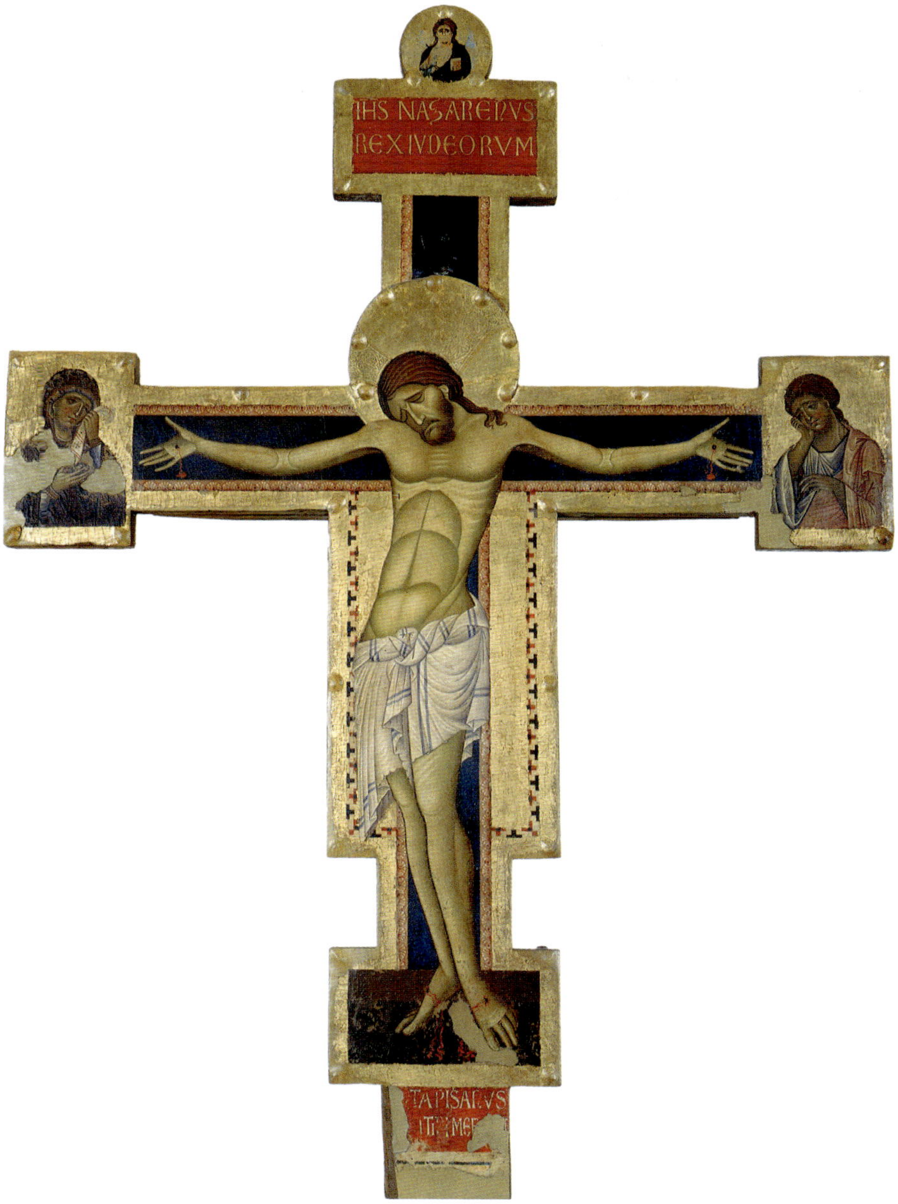

65 Giunta Pisano, crucifix, *c.*1236, signed, tempera and gold on wood (174 cm × 131 cm), Museum, Santa Maria degli Angeli, Assisi.

Angeli, used the same imagery and is our most reliable guide for the style of the much larger cross for Brother Elias (fig. 65).[47] It is highly likely that Giunta painted both the Santa Maria degli Angeli and Elias crosses during the same Assisi sojourn in 1236.[48] The Conventual friar Niccolò Catalano, who saw the Elias cross before it was destroyed, compared it to another panel crucifix in Assisi, the large surviving cross in Santa Chiara (fig. 66).[49] The Clarissan rood also took Giunta's panel as the prototype for its own *suppedaneum* arrangement, with the kneeling figure of Abbess Benedicta (†1260), the first abbess of Santa Chiara after Saint Clare herself, supplanting Elias in the donor role (fig. 67).[50]

The early date of the Elias cross has led some specialists to question whether it was really painted for the Upper Church, whose construction (as we have seen) is unlikely to have been completed by 1236. Several contributors to the

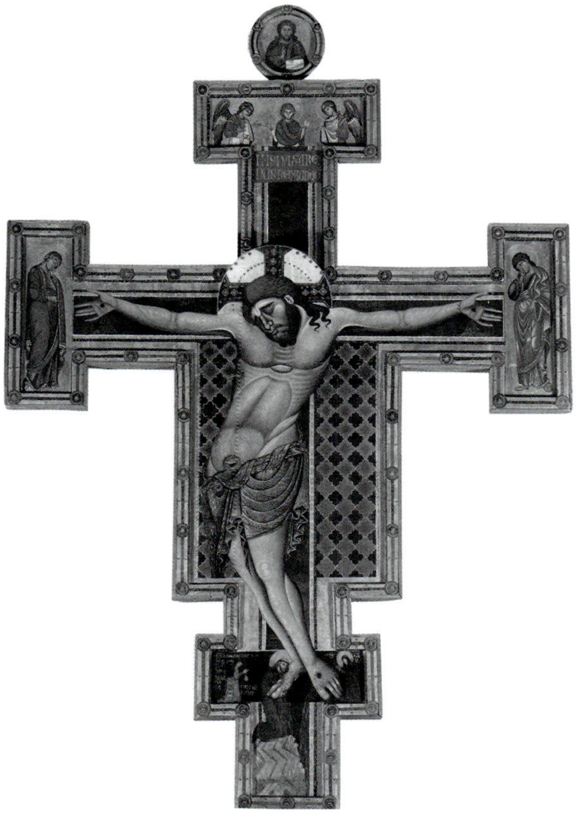

debate have speculated that the cross was originally painted for the Lower Church and only subsequently relocated to the Upper in the 1510s.[51] A related theory posits the existence of a crucifix by Giotto (presumably painted at the same time as the Saint Francis cycle) on the beam of the Upper Church before the Elias cross was moved upstairs.[52] But numerous factors weigh against these hypotheses. Firstly, the 1236 cross, which may have been over five metres tall, would have been disproportionately large for the relatively shallow vaults of the Lower Basilica, which at their highest points are only about ten metres clear of the floor, compared to approximately nineteen metres for the Upper Church.[53] Secondly, there is no convincing evidence for the re-installation of the cross in the Upper Church at any date before 1622.[54] Thirdly, the manner in which the designers of the Saint Francis cycle in the early 1290s accommodated the crucifix's

top 66 Umbrian school, crucifix, *c.*1255–80, tempera and gold on wood (415 cm × 300 cm), Santa Chiara, Assisi.

bottom 67 The *suppedaneum* of the Santa Chiara crucifix, *c.*1255–80, tempera and gold on wood, Santa Chiara, Assisi.

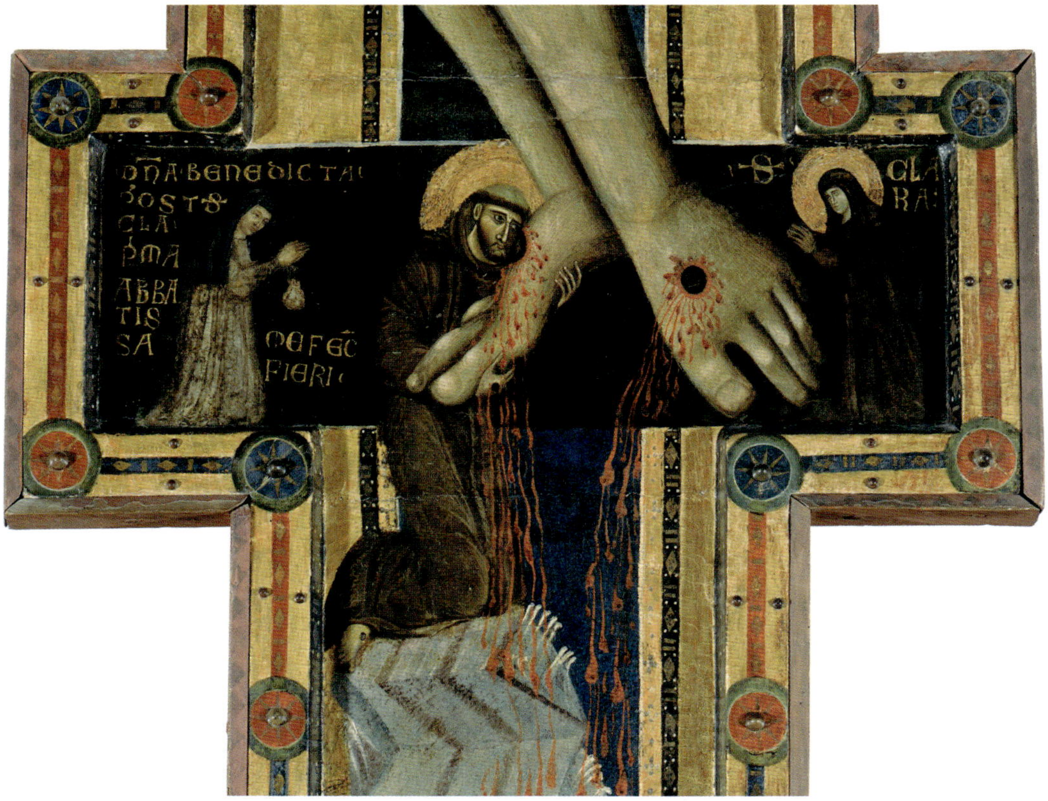

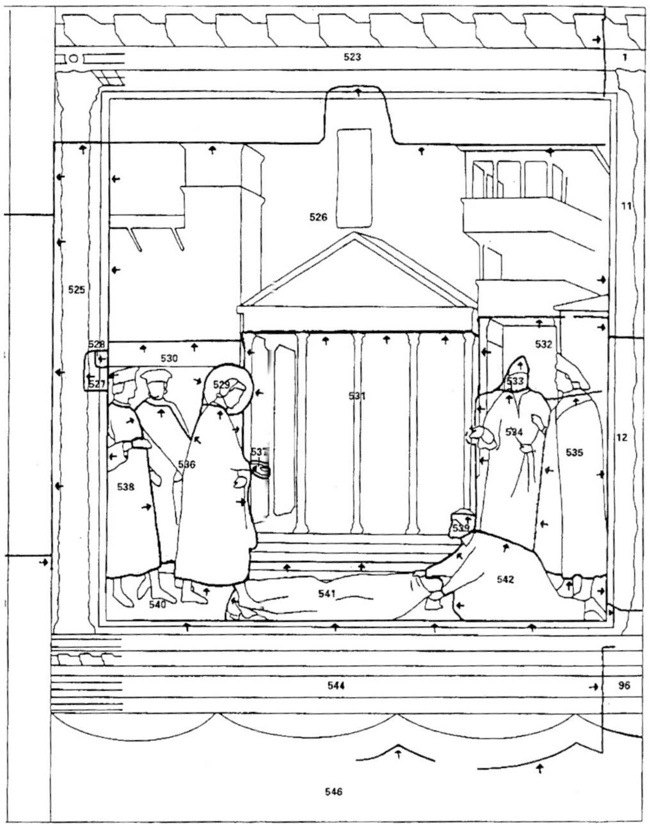

68 Plan by Bruno Zanardi of the *giornata* patches in the *Homage of a Simple Man*, Scene 1 of the Saint Francis cycle, *c.*1290–96, fresco, north wall of the nave, Upper Church, Basilica of San Francesco (Zanardi, Frugoni and Zeri (1996), p. 69).

beam was evidently a pragmatic solution to a pre-existing problem (see figs 58 and 59). The *giornate* maps for the first and last scenes of the cycle, as well as the blue pigment on the consoles themselves, confirm that the beam was already there before the frescoes were painted: the map for the opening scene of the cycle, the *Homage of a Simple Man* (fig. 68), shows clearly how the plaster spread over the sky area (*giornata* nr 526) took account of the console.[55] Most important of all, we should remember how difficult the cross would have been to move. Like Cavalcaselle's copy, Giunta's original would have been held in place not only by a bracket on the beam, but also by a chain attached to the vault of the church. In this way, the cross was integrated into the architectural superstructure of the Basilica, braced between the beam below and the vault above. This interdependence between image and architecture can help to explain why large crosses of this kind were sometimes commissioned while their intended settings were still under construction. A comparable example from the end of the Duecento is Giotto's crucifix for the Dominican church of Santa Maria Novella in Florence (fig. 69).[56] Giotto's panel is generally dated to around 1288–9 and was almost certainly intended for display above the *tramezzo* screen in the middle of the church.[57] However, it is debatable whether the nave of Santa Maria Novella would have been ready to receive the panel when it was first painted. The foundation stone for the present church of Santa Maria Novella had been laid as recently as 1279 and building work on the nave extended well into the fourteenth century.[58] Such majestic panels may have served as statements of architectural ambition, painted in advance so as to be ready when the time for their installation came. So the 1236 date for the Assisi cross does not necessarily mean that the Upper Church was complete by that date. Nor, conversely, does it exclude the Upper Basilica as the panel's intended destination.

The most likely scenario is that Giunta painted the cross in 1236 for the as yet unfinished Upper Church, and that it was mounted on the beam at the head of the nave at some point between then and 1253, when we know that the Upper Church was sufficiently complete to be consecrated and serve as the setting for the canonization of Saint Stanislas. Elias directed work at the Basilica until he was deposed as minister general in 1239.[59] In May that year he was still addressed as 'lord and custodian of the church of San Francesco in Assisi' and – still in 1239 – two of the Basilica's bells were cast with inscriptions recording Elias's patronage.[60] Even after Elias's departure from Assisi towards the end of 1239, his break with the papacy the following year and his final excommunication in 1244, his former confrères in the Sacro Convento may not have found his donor figure as contentious as later generations of Franciscan writers would have us believe. In any case, it seems that Elias's donor portrait and inscription on Giunta's crucifix were too small to be easily visible once the cross was raised onto its beam.[61]

The 1236 crucifix is an early sign of artistic eclecticism at Assisi. Vasari's description of its 'alla greca' style reminds us how effectively Giunta was able to imitate and adapt Byzantine prototypes. Elias may well have chosen the Pisan artist for just this reason. As provincial minister of the Holy Land, Elias had travelled widely in the eastern Mediterranean in the 1210s, and his appreciation of Orthodox art is evident

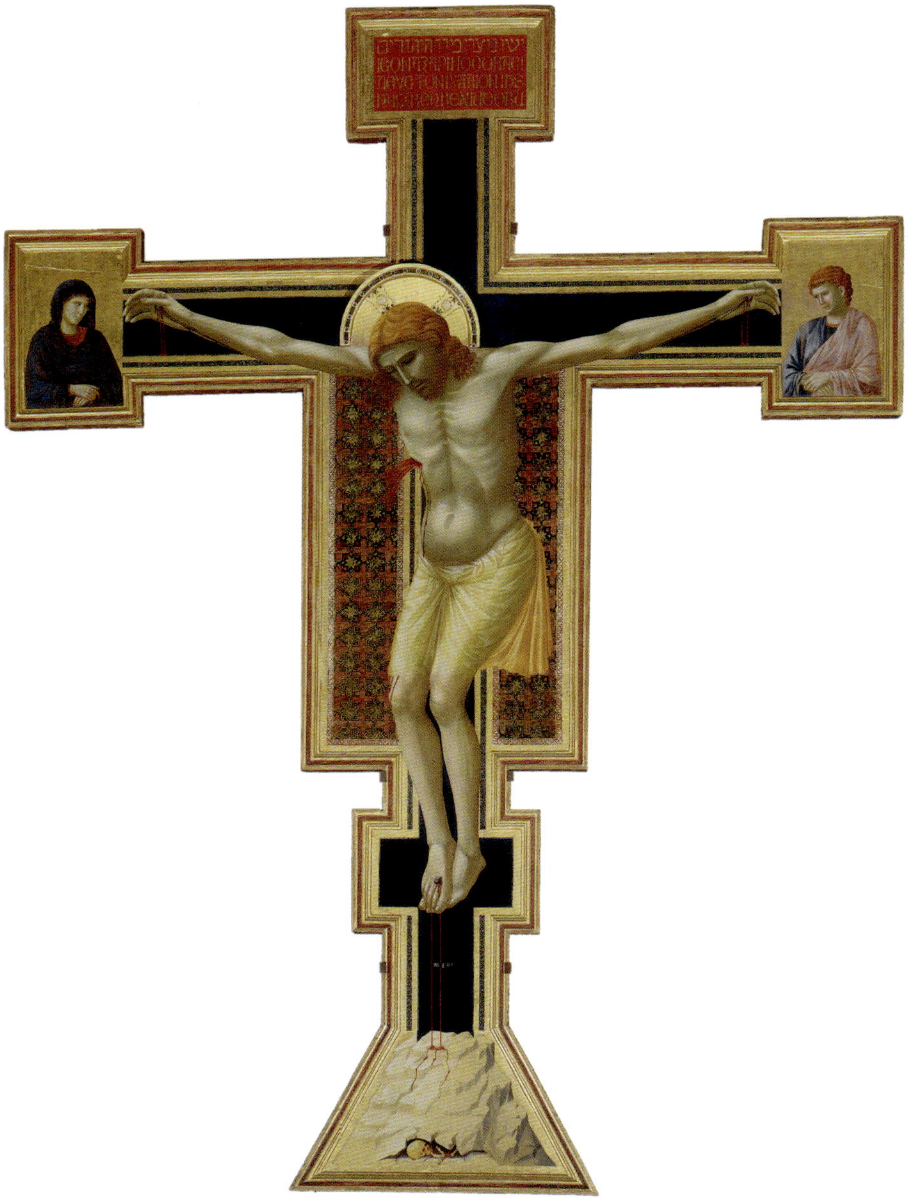

69 Giotto, crucifix, *c.*1288–9, tempera and gold on wood (530 cm × 400 cm), Santa Maria Novella, Florence.

from his later gift to the Franciscans of Cortona of a relic of the True Cross encased within a refined tenth-century imperial Byzantine ivory.[62] Only the exceptionally broad cultural horizons of the early Franciscan movement can account for the combination of Gothic architecture and Byzantine-style panel painting at Assisi in the 1230s.

But Giunta's crucifix was itself arguably a mixture of Latin and Byzantine traditions. The resonance of the donor figure was specific to its setting within the Basilica. By placing his image at the foot of the most prominent image on the central axis of the Upper Church, Elias was appropriating an established convention in Latin iconography for depicting church and abbey founders. One twelfth-century Benedictine precedent that may just have been familiar to Elias was Abbot Suger at Saint-Denis. Suger had donor figures of himself inserted at multiple points on the central axis of his

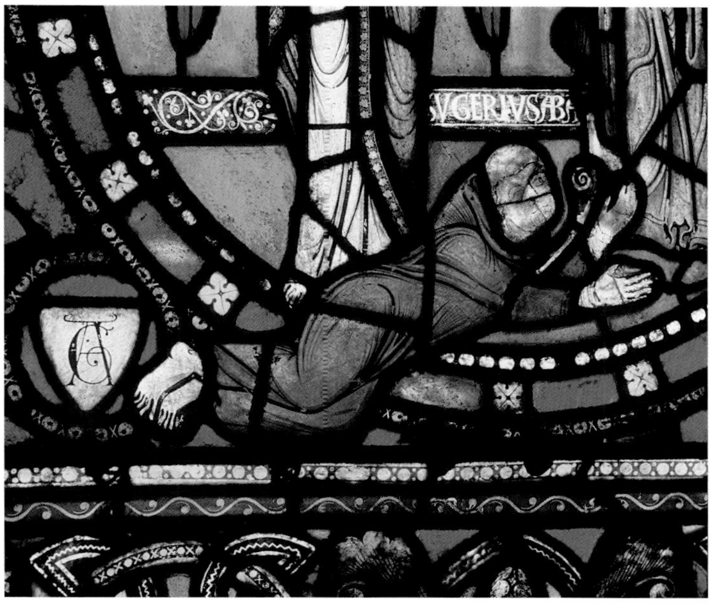

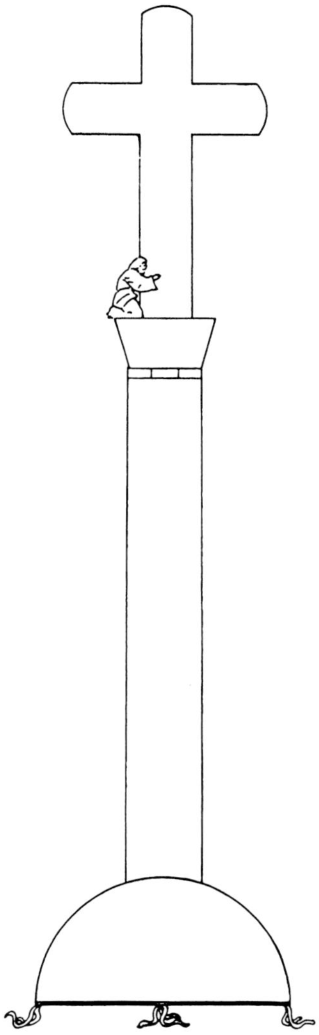

left 70 Donor figure of Abbot Suger, *c.*1144, stained glass, ambulatory chapel, basilica of Saint-Denis, Paris.

right 71 Hypothetical reconstruction by Paula Gerson of Abbot Suger's great cross, consecrated 1147, in the basilica of Saint-Denis, Paris (Gerson (1986), p. 192, fig. 10).

new abbey church (fig. 70).[63] One figurine was placed among the resurrected souls below Christ in the Last Judgment tympanum on the central façade portal. More pertinently, another effigy was positioned at the foot of the crucified Christ on the great cross, now lost, which Suger erected in front of the new chevet (fig. 71).[64] This cross, over twenty feet tall, was consecrated by Pope Eugenius III on Easter Day 1147. In the accompanying inscription, Suger appealed for Christ's mercy in terms strikingly similar to Elias's dedicatory prayer on Giunta's crucifix at Assisi.[65] Comparisons can also be drawn between their respective donor figures. At Saint-Denis, Clark Maines has interpreted the lack of a gift, the portrayal of the donor in prayer and the explicit request for mercy as distinctive features of Suger's donor imagery.[66] At Assisi, Elias held out his hands in an *orans* gesture of prayer, again with no attempt to include a miniature church. On balance, it is unlikely that Elias knew directly of Suger's cross but, in terms of setting, wording and donor imagery, Giunta's great cross for the Upper Church finds a suggestive parallel with the cross erected at Saint-Denis some eighty-nine years earlier.[67]

Appealing as the Suger analogy may be, there is no need to force a direct dependence between Assisi and Saint-Denis, as the portrayal of church founders at the feet of crucifixes was also widespread in Italy. Elvio Lunghi has compared Giunta's lost crucifix with the metal bas-relief cross commissioned by Ariberto, archbishop of Milan, for the basilica of San Dionigi in that city around 1040.[68] It is more likely that Elias was aware of the artistic patronage of the great eleventh-century Benedictine abbot Desiderius, whose name was recorded in rhyming inscriptions in his new basilica at Montecassino, consecrated in 1071, and whose donor image can still be seen in the apse of Sant'Angelo in Formis.[69] Was Elias at Assisi seeking to align himself with the legacy of Desiderius and other Benedictine founders of great abbey and pilgrimage complexes? In this light, we should acknowl-

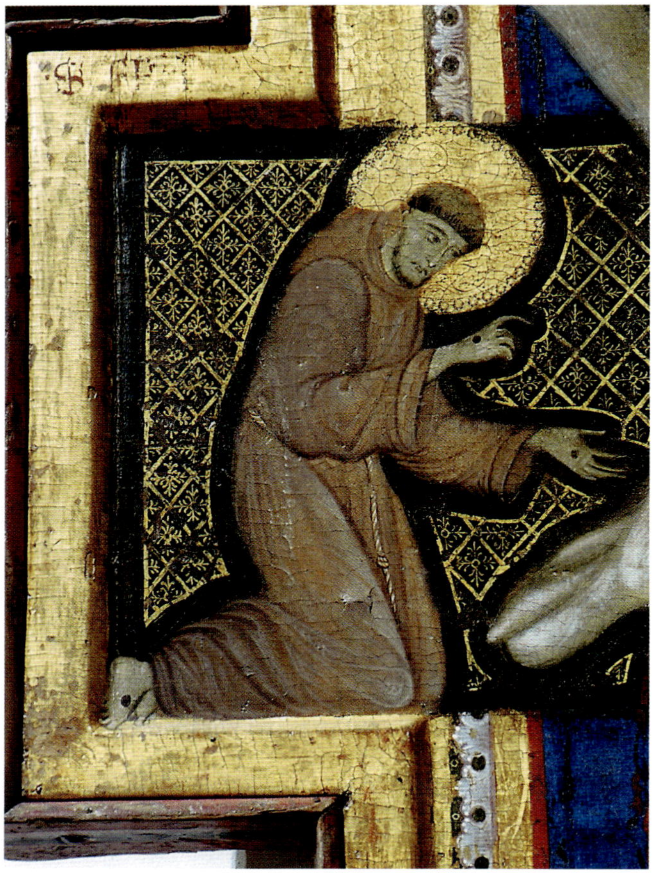

72 Maestro di San Francesco, Saint Francis on the *suppedaneum* of the Perugia crucifix, dated 1272, tempera and gold on wood, Galleria Nazionale dell'Umbria, Perugia (originally San Francesco al Prato, Perugia).

edge the tradition, first recorded by Mariano of Florence in the early sixteenth century, of Elias as an able architect who personally presided over much of the Basilica's construction.[70] The claim is borne out by the evidence of the 1239 campanile bells, Elias's title of 'lord and custodian' of the Basilica and his later role in founding (and, it seems, building) the Franciscan convent in his native Cortona.[71] The active part Elias played in the temporal affairs of the empire and the papacy suggests further comparisons with powerful monastic figures like Suger or Desiderius.[72]

The figure of Elias at the foot of Giunta's crucifix, the first significant image commissioned for the Upper Basilica and set on the central axis of the church, placed the minister general of the Franciscans at the head of a long sequence of major monastic church builders, commemorated through inscriptions and donor figures.[73] The organization of the Order was still evolving during Elias's period of office, and in 1236 he could not have foreseen that there would ultimately be no accepted place for comparable figures among the Friars Minor. The precedent of his donor figure was never repeated. Its place was taken by supplicant figures of Saint Francis on the *suppedanea* of later crucifixes painted for the Order's churches (fig. 72).[74] Even Benedicta's cross for Santa Chiara, which provides the closest parallel to Elias's 1236 rood, carefully subordinated the abbess to first Saint Francis and then Saint Clare (see fig. 67).

The Images on the Rood Beam

The Elias cross may not have been the only panel image that Giunta painted for the Upper Church. In his monograph on the Basilica, the *Collis paradisi amoenitas* (published posthumously in 1704), Father Francesco Maria Angeli linked two other panel paintings in the Upper Church to Giunta, in addition to the Elias cross. Probably writing around 1683, Angeli described the 1236 crucifix, by then 'quasi corrosam', before noting two further 'icones', which he also attributed to Giunta: one representing the Holy Spirit descending upon the Virgin and the apostles and the other Saint Michael crushing Lucifer.[75] The same two images are also described in a separate source: a small, unpublished seventeenth-century notebook of *memorie* in the Sacro Convento archive.[76] Once again, they are given to Giunta Pisano and recorded in the same breath as the large crucifix. By the 1600s commentators on Assisi were already concerned to attribute correctly the various paintings and murals in the church. Angeli and the anonymous author of the notice in the Sacro Convento archive were no exceptions. We can therefore assume that this pair of images, even if they were not painted by Giunta, dated from the thirteenth century, and struck their seventeenth-century observers as markedly earlier than the Saint Francis cycle.

Like the Elias cross, these panels are long since lost, but their recorded iconography – Pentecost (a quintessentially apostolic subject) and Saint Michael – immediately suggests a relationship with the dedications of the side altars in the north and south transepts. Neither subject was included in the relevant transept cycles, perhaps because Cimabue saw no need to repeat images that were already represented by

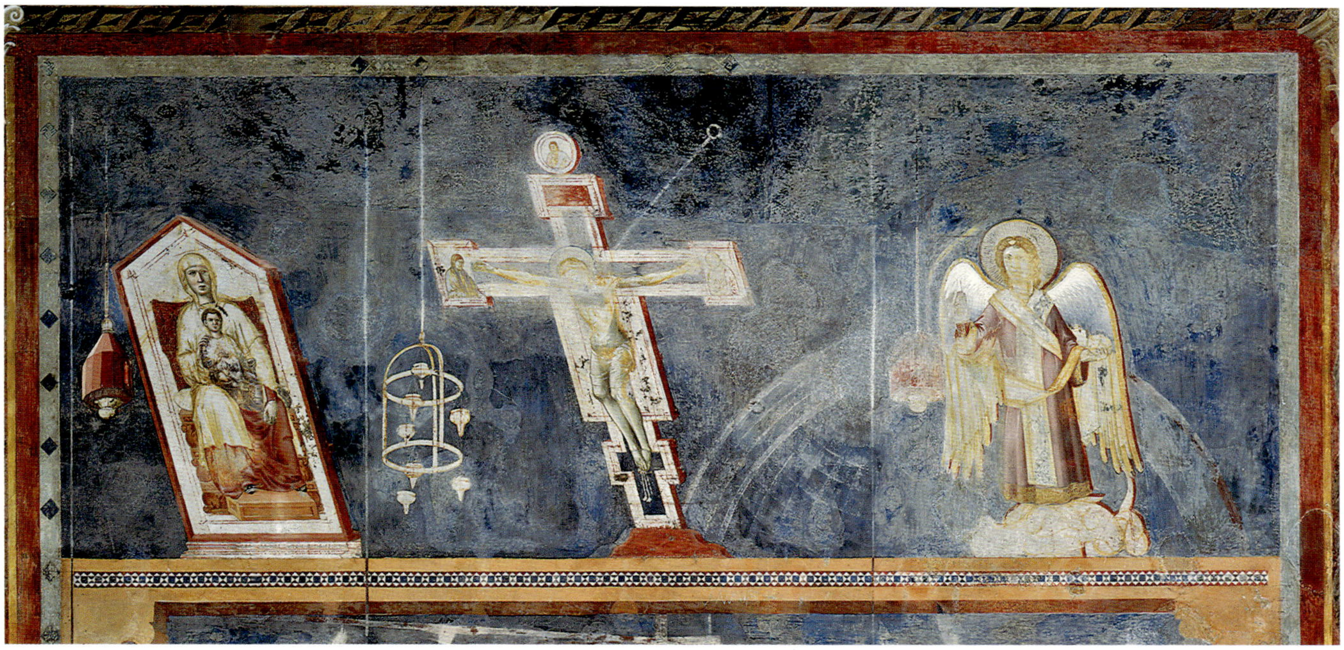

73 Rood beam with painted panels, detail from the *Verification of the Stigmata*, Scene 22 of the Saint Francis cycle, *c.*1290–96, fresco, south wall of the nave, Upper Church, Basilica of San Francesco.

existing panels. One possibility is that the two 'icones' served as altarpieces for the transept altars, and that the surrounding frescoes were intended to complement them. But it is hard to envisage panel paintings of any shape or size serving as altarpieces for the two altar tables without obscuring Cimabue's great *Crucifixion* frescoes on the eastern walls of the transepts. Indeed, Cimabue's murals themselves seem to have been intended as altarpieces for these two altar blocks.

Another possibility, and one that we favour, is that the Pentecost and Saint Michael images were painted as companion panels for Giunta's crucifix on the beam at the head of the nave.[77] A triple ensemble of beam images was later depicted in the *Verification of the Stigmata* scene in the Saint Francis cycle (fig. 73) and a similar arrangement has been reconstructed around the Abbess Benedicta crucifix in Santa Chiara, a church that in many ways was conceived as a pendant to the Basilica of San Francesco (fig. 74).[78] An important study by Andrea De Marchi has established the prevalence across central Italy during the thirteenth century of beam or screen arrangements that incorporated trios of large-scale panel paintings.[79] In addition to Santa Chiara, it is possible to reconstruct other Franciscan arrangements at Santa Croce in Florence and at San Francesco in Pisa, the

74 Reconstruction by Donal Cooper of the thirteenth-century beam arrangement that supported the Abbess Benedicta crucifix in Santa Chiara, Assisi (adapted from Cooper (2000), fig. 5.32).

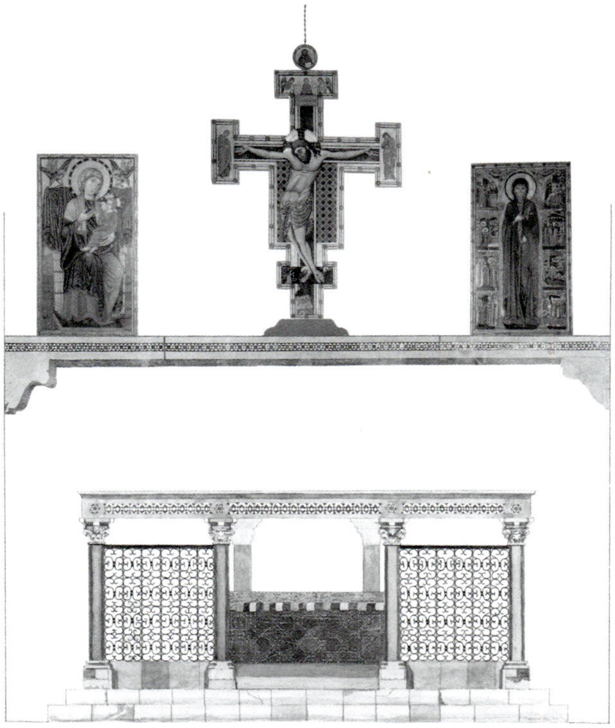

latter incorporating Giotto's gabled panel of the *Stigmatization of Saint Francis* now in the Louvre.[80]

The ensemble of painted panels in the *Verification of the Stigmata* fresco was certainly no literal record of an extant arrangement in the Upper Church.[81] Indeed, given that here the fictive and real beams would have inhabited the same space, what could be more banal than simply copying what was already there? The fictive panels in the fresco combine archaic elements with some of the most innovative features of the late Duecento. One of the lateral images in the fresco depicts Saint Michael (a peculiar cut-out panel) but the other is a *Virgin and Child Enthroned* (frontally posed in similar style to the Virgin and Child in the so-called 'Angel Window' in the fourth bay of the south nave wall).[82] The choice was informed by the setting of the *Verification* episode in the chapel of the Porziuncola, dedicated to the Virgin of the Angels (Santa Maria degli Angeli). The beam in the fresco therefore advertises the titular dedication of the space where the narrative unfolds.[83] Real-life images of Pentecost and Saint Michael set to either side of Giunta's crucifix would have served a similar purpose in the Upper Church, projecting the altar dedications of the transept down the length of the church. As we shall see in Chapter 7, a similar concern with the Upper Church's altar dedications would later inform the design of the counter-façade frescoes that faced the crucifix beam down the length of the nave.

Stained Glass

Giunta's monumental crucifix and its companion panels would have exerted a powerful physical presence, but the decoration of the Upper Church seems to have disappointed Pope Innocent IV when he arrived in Assisi in 1253. This year is of great importance in the history of the Basilica. Not only was the church consecrated in May, but Innocent's six-month stay over the spring and summer represents the only sustained residence of the papal curia at Assisi.[84] Innocent IV had fled to France in 1244 to escape the Holy Roman Emperor Frederick II and returned to Italy only after the emperor's death in 1250. The pope resided at Perugia from November 1251, before moving on in April 1253 to Assisi, where he remained until 6 October, when the curia finally returned to Rome after nearly a decade of exile.[85] During the summer of 1253, Innocent would have lodged in the papal apartments built for Gregory IX in the 1230s in the northern wing of the Sacro Convento, and to judge from surviving documents it was the Upper Church that was commonly used for the business of the curia.[86]

It is in the context of this papal residency at Assisi that we should consider Innocent's extraordinary bull *Decet et expedit*, issued on 10 July 1253. This is one of the key texts for the decoration of the Basilica, establishing the ideological justification for its pictorial embellishment at the same time as earmarking the funding required to realize it. *Decet et expedit* is thus the most meaningful precedent for the *Reducentes* bulls issued thirty-five years later. In 1253 Innocent wrote in these terms:

> To his dear son Philip of Campello, Friar Minor, master and *praepositus* of the works of the church of Saint Francis at Assisi, greetings and apostolic benediction. It is fitting and expedient to build splendid basilicas for those who have – glorious in their merits – attained the loftiest habitation of the heavenly palace. Thus those who have been held worthy of the honour of being lifted up in the world above, should be in every way revered on earth by Christ's faithful people with a worthy devotion; and famous churches may be made for them by the faithful, in which the Almighty may be fittingly worshipped, and the memory of [the saints] be publicly honoured – so that while thus the beauty of God's house is loved, and the tabernacle of his praise carefully set forth, his mercy may be more readily and fruitfully obtained by the intercessions of the saints themselves. Hence – because the venerable church of Saint Francis of Assisi is not yet completed with fitting workmanship, as is proper – we, desiring for the reverence of the same saint, a sedulous patron of the Christian people before God, that the said church be both completed with a noble structure and decorated with the peak of splendid workmanship, grant by apostolic authority that you, and other *praepositi* of the works of the same church who may be from time to time, may receive offerings in money at the altars of the same church and elsewhere also, to be wholly and faithfully spent for the same works, as our venerable brother the bishop of Ostia and Velletri, or another cardinal of the Roman Church, who may be protector of the Order of Friars Minor, shall think fit to ordain and dispose – any statutes to the contrary of the same Order or prohibitions of the general or provin-

cial ministers or the custodian or the guardian of the house or any other brothers of the same Order not at all withstanding . . . These present instructions will cease to be valid after the twenty-fifth year.[87]

Resident in the Sacro Convento, the pope had already used the Basilica for two months before the composition of *Decet et expedit*, so this bull was no distant papal edict, but a direct, on-site demand. What 'splendid workmanship' did Innocent have in mind? Some scholars have read the bull to mean that the architecture of the Upper Basilica was still incomplete, but this ignores the description of the lamps hanging from the vaults during the canonization of Saint Stanislas of Poland in September of the same year. Innocent is known to have left significant gifts to the Basilica – a silver cross and a portable altar are connected to the pope in later inventories – but the 'noble structure' specified by *Decet et expedit* clearly refers to work on a monumental scale. Recently, it has been suggested that Innocent was concerned about the lack of suitable liturgical furniture for the papal liturgy, and that *Decet et expedit* provoked the construction of an elaborate marble *schola cantorum* complex for the Upper Church.[88] But on balance this seems unlikely.

Instead, the primary result of Innocent's bull was the commencement of the stained-glass decoration of the Upper Church, beginning with the three apse windows.[89] The decision to start with stained glass, a medium almost unheard of in Italy at this date, may have reflected the pope's own preferences. Innocent had been based in Lyon during almost seven years of exile north of the Alps, and had convened an ecumenical council of the Church in the city's cathedral of Saint-Jean in the summer of 1245. He would have been familiar with the ongoing construction work on Saint-Jean in the 1240s, and may have been personally involved. At any rate, Innocent could hardly have failed to appreciate the two impressive rose windows installed in the cathedral's transept during this decade.[90]

At Assisi, it is unlikely that much had been achieved by the time Innocent died in Naples at the end of 1254, but *Decet et expedit* ensured a steady flow of revenue for the following twenty-five years and entrusted progress to the cardinal protector, Rinaldo di Jenne, bishop of Ostia. Rinaldo in turn succeeded Innocent to the throne of Saint Peter as Alexander IV. Like his predecessor, the new pope consistently promoted the interests of the Franciscans.[91] Work on the windows continued apace, and the attempt to regulate stained glass at the Order's general chapter at Narbonne in 1260 may, in part, have been a response to the new windows at Assisi.[92] Once the apse and transept windows were complete, the eight double lancets in the nave were glazed. Various chronological schemes have been suggested for the Upper Church windows, which were clearly executed by a series of different workshops: the glaziers of the apse windows may have been Austrian, those in the south transept probably French.[93] Gradually an Italian workshop, led by the Maestro di San Francesco, took over the programme, realizing the north transept glass and the majority of windows in the nave.[94] The last of the glass may have been inserted only in the 1280s.[95]

A detailed treatment of the glass in the Upper Church lies beyond the scope of this book. All the windows had certainly been completed by the time Nicholas IV turned his attention to the Basilica in 1288. But the designers of the Nicholine programme in the Upper Church took account of some of the earlier glazed images in the nave windows. A number of iconographic ideas in the transept glass are also prescient of the subsequent mural decoration. For these reasons it is important to consider several aspects of the glazed programme.

It seems unlikely that the glass in the Upper Church was planned as a single coherent scheme. Instead, it appears to be the result of several staged interventions, executed by different workshops.[96] Perhaps most significantly, the nave windows function as an independent programme from the apse and transepts, a spatial and conceptual division that would be repeated in the later mural decoration. The three apse windows, each formed from two lancets, were glazed first and may have been conceived as an independent group. Each window pairs New Testament scenes in its right lancet against Old Testament scenes in its left to form a single unified programme. Many of these parallels repeat well-worn typologies: Christ bearing the cross and the sacrifice of Isaac, for example, or the Ascension and Elijah in the fiery chariot. As Martin and Ruf observed, the conventional pairing of Old and New Testament cycles was a safe choice in the mid-1250s, a difficult moment, when the Order's minister general, John of Parma, was compromised by the heresy of the Eternal Gospel.[97]

The transept windows present more difficulties of interpretation, in part because several lights do not survive. The window in the south transept depicts a Genesis cycle across

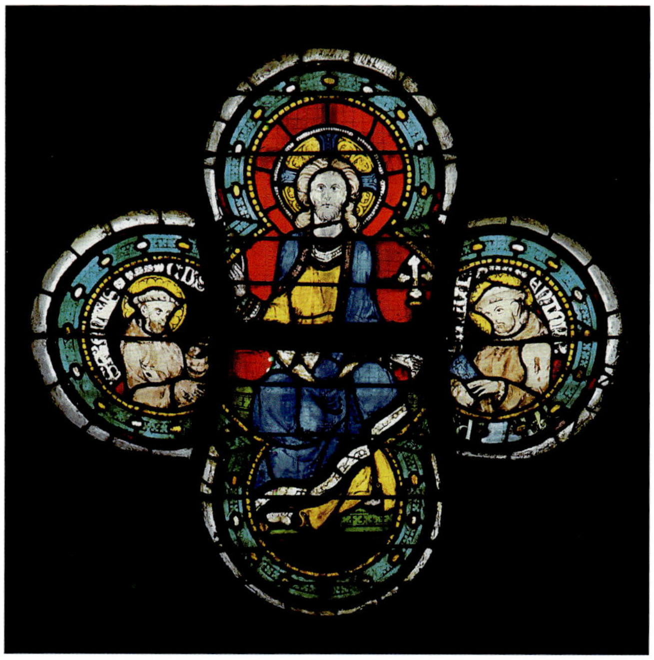

75 Gothic workshop, *Christ in Glory with Saints Francis and Anthony*, *c.*1275, stained glass, south transept, Upper Church, Basilica of San Francesco.

two lancets, perhaps to complement the Old Testament scenes in the apse. The other two lancets contain enthroned female saints, with Saint Clare set amid seven virgin martyrs. This group makes little sense when considered in relation to the other windows, but may have been an attempt to commemorate Saint Clare, canonized in 1255, within the Basilica. Two quatrefoil lights surmount the lancet windows. That on the left above the Genesis cycle depicts *Christ in Glory* with Saint Francis to the left (Christ's right) and Saint Anthony to the right.[98] So far as we can tell, this is the first time that the two Franciscans appear in the decoration of the Upper Church and both are identified by inscriptions (fig. 75). In addition, as Brooke noted, Francis's side wound is prominently included. The matching quatrefoil to the right displays a Virgin and Child enthroned, flanked by the prophets Isaiah and Jeremiah bearing texts foretelling the Incarnation.[99]

Only two of the four lancets in the north transept window contain figurative glass. The light on the far right is filled with six post-Resurrection scenes, possibly intended as a continuation of the New Testament scenes in the apse. Its companion lancet on the left depicts six angelic visitations from the Old and New Testaments. In contrast to the south transept, the rose in the north still contains its original figurative glass, a large *Ascension*, which is clearly legible from the church below (fig. 76).[100] Christ is seated on a throne borne by angels, while the apostles and the Virgin, accompanied by two angels, gather in awe beneath. Here the Maestro di San Francesco made intelligent use of the six medallions around the central field, reserving four for attendant angels and the lowest two for the apostles. These last two overlap the central hexagon of the *Ascension*, and Brooke noted how they are provided with fictive lids, which appear to open, allowing the apostles to apprehend the vision of Christ enthroned above.[101] Christ himself is dressed in a striking red mantle, which accords with the scroll held by the prophet Isaiah in one of the lateral medallions: 'Who is this that cometh from Edom, with dyed garments . . .?' (Isaiah 63:1; the following verse clarifies that the garment is red: 'Why then is thy apparel red . . .?')[102] The use of the red mantle to signify a transfigured state would later be taken up again in the mural decoration of the nave.[103]

The eight double lancets in the nave form a relatively coherent iconographic scheme. Five of the windows contain large-scale standing figures of the apostles, surmounted by scenes from their respective lives.[104] A sixth window, on the north side of the fourth bay, contains figures of Saints Francis and Anthony, with narrative scenes from their legends above, following the same format used for the apostle windows.[105] An explicit claim is therefore made here that the two Franciscan saints are new apostles, worthy of representation on the same scale as their biblical prototypes. This is a theme that we encounter elsewhere in Franciscan iconographic schemes of roughly the same period. The Maestro di San Francesco, himself responsible for much of the nave glazing at Assisi, included Francis as a thirteenth apostle on the front of the double-sided retable he painted *c.*1272 for the high altar of the Franciscan church in Perugia (fig. 77).[106] In San Francesco in Gubbio, the lunettes of the apse vaults preserve frescoes of Saints Francis and Anthony alongside the apostles Peter and Paul to either side of a central enthroned Christ (fig. 78).[107] On stylistic grounds these images are usually dated to the 1270s or 1280s. Surviving figures of two other apostles (probably Saints Thaddeus and James the Great) on the right pilaster of the *cappella maggiore* suggest that the Gubbio programme originally included all twelve.

These comparisons confirm that the coupling of Saints Francis and Anthony as new apostles was a common, perhaps

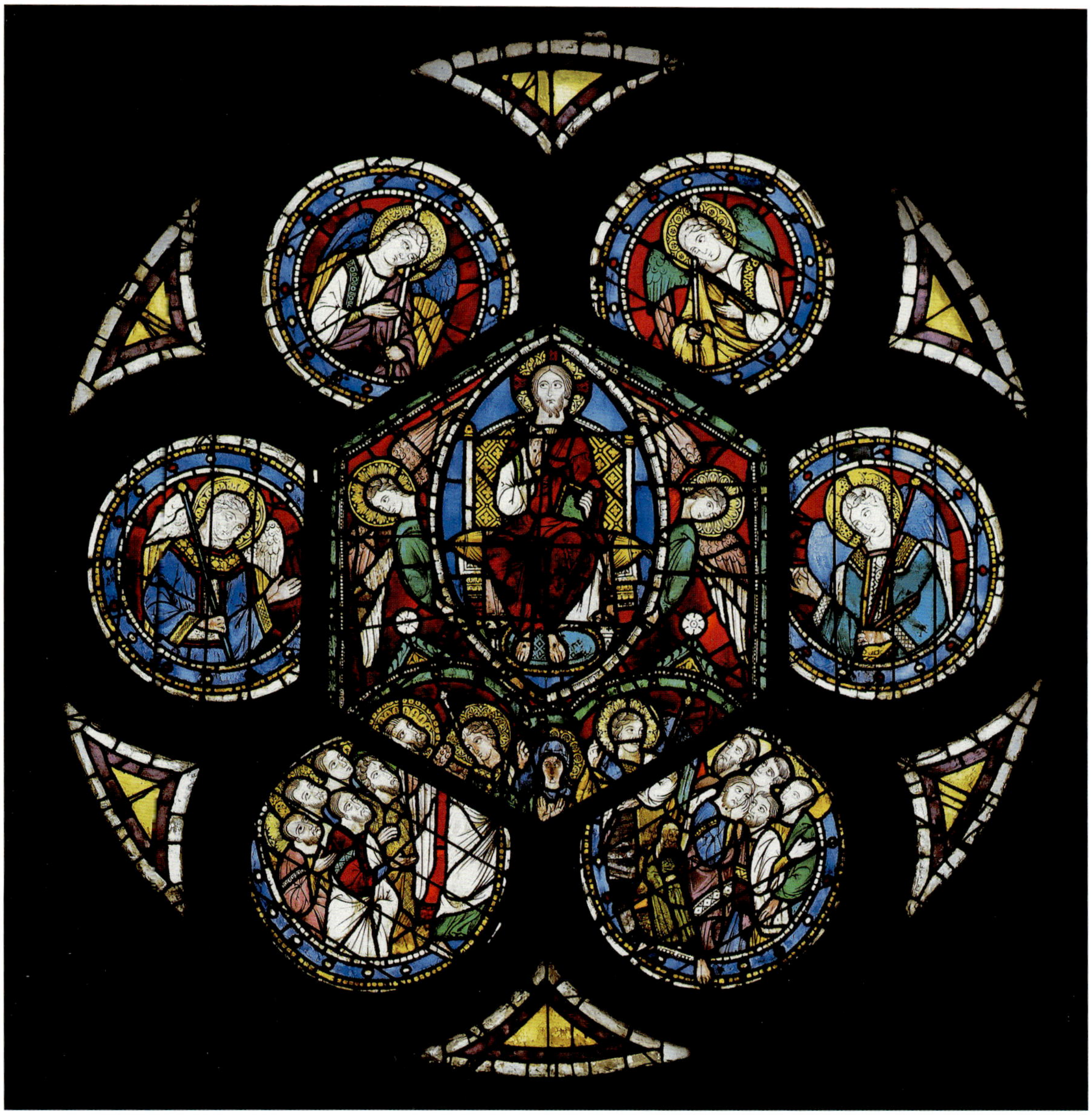

76 Maestro di San Francesco, *Ascension*, *c.*1275–80, stained glass, north transept, Upper Church, Basilica of San Francesco.

even the pre-eminent, mode for representing Saint Francis in Umbria before the 1290s. In the Upper Church the two saints had already been paired to either side of *Christ in Glory* in the south transept glass. But there is a further dynamic at work in the nave window, which clearly privileges Francis above Anthony. In each lancet the narrative cycles read bottom to top. Francis's legend concludes with the *Stigmatization*, which is split between the final quadrant and the upper lunette (fig. 80).[108] Extending the scene over two fields allows for a clear spatial division between Saint Francis below and the Seraph above. Saint Anthony's life culminates in a scene that includes the Paduan saint but more properly belongs to Francis's legend, the *Apparition at Arles*. Like the *Stigmatization* at the top of the neighbouring window, this scene fills the lunette and is split into two levels (fig. 81).[109] In the lower, Saint Anthony preaches to the friars in the open air; in the upper, Francis appears in a vision, frontally posed with his arms outstretched in imitation of the cross. He holds a scroll

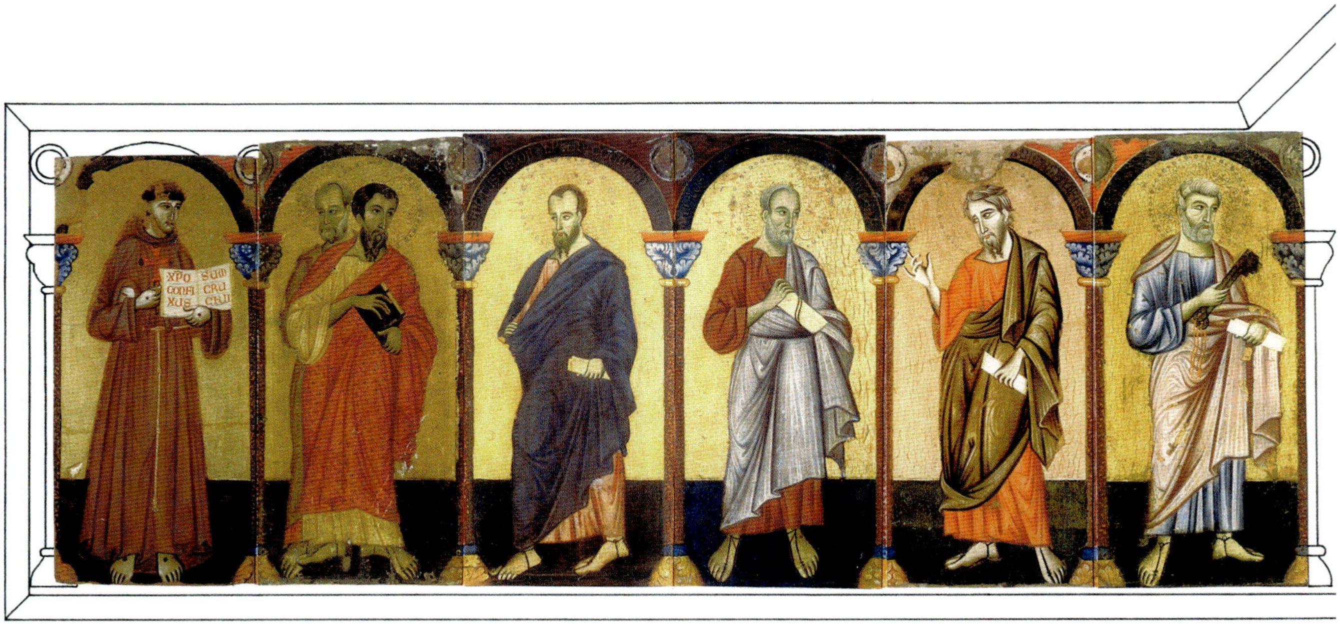

77 Maestro di San Francesco, Saints Francis, Simon with Bartholomew, James, John, Matthew and Peter: reconstruction by Donal Cooper (after Dillian Gordon) of the apostles face (left-hand side) of the double-sided retable, *c.*1272, tempera and gold on wood, for the high altar of San Francesco al Prato, Perugia (Cooper (2000), fig. 10.01, after Gordon (1982), p. 74, fig. 11).

78 Umbrian school, *Christ Enthroned* with Saints Francis, Peter, Paul and Anthony, *c.*1280, fresco, main apse, San Francesco, Gubbio.

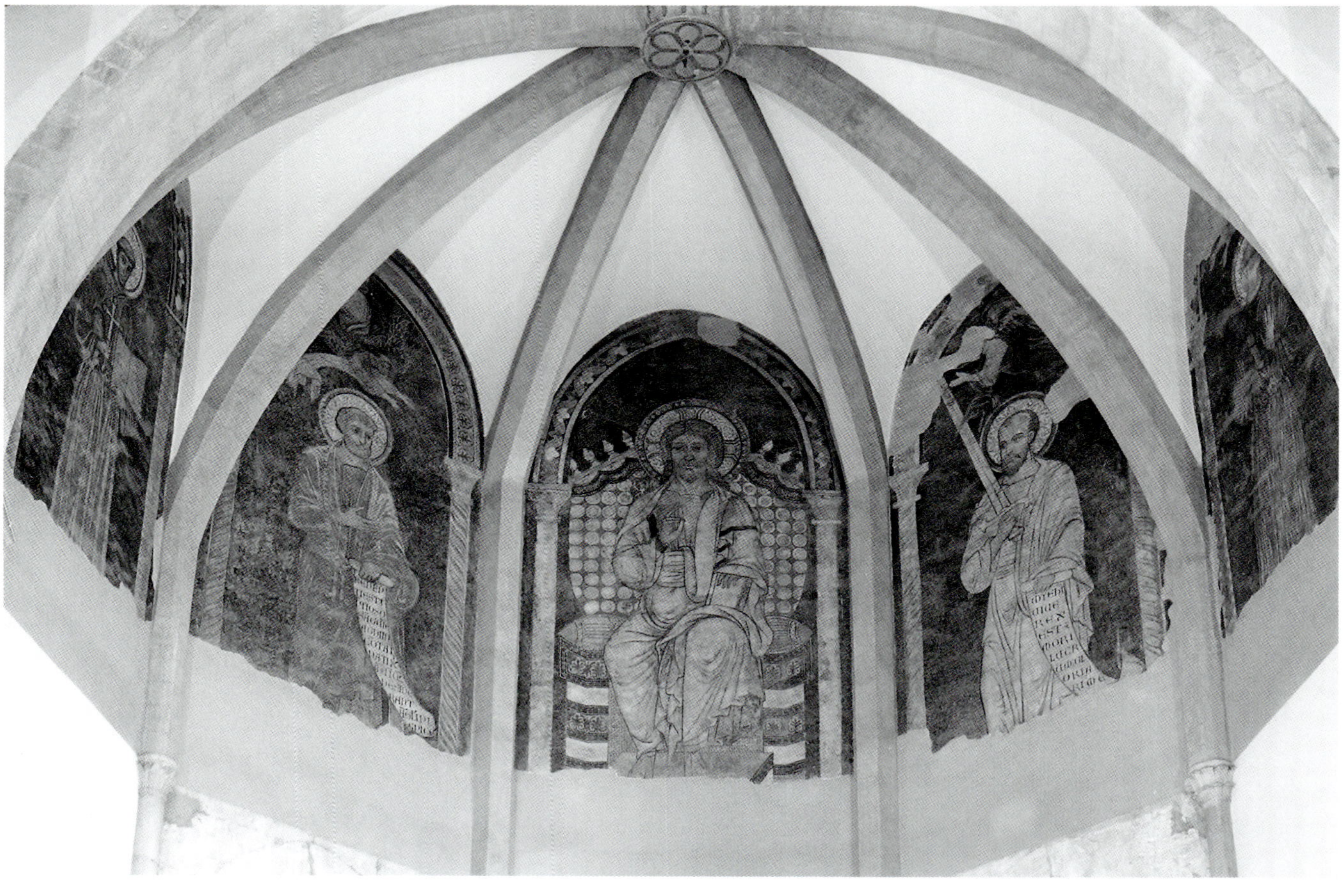

which is now abraded but which almost certainly read 'Benedicat vos Dominus' ('May the Lord bless you'). Francis is depicted without the stigmata, preserving the narrative integrity of his apparition to the provincial chapter at Arles. But his pose and benediction recall his final words to his companions. On the verge of death, the saint had made a cross sign with his arms and blessed all of his brothers, present and absent. Viewed in this light, the stained glass suggests Francis's death and – with Francis's apparition clearly elevated above the friars gathered below – the subsequent ascension of his soul. Franciscans believed that their founder had been transfigured into a seraphic angel at his death, and the Assisi glass makes a similar statement, raising Francis at Arles to the same plane as the Seraph of the *Stigmatization*.

The opposing window on the south side of the fourth bay makes even more extraordinary claims for Francis's status. Its upper sections are filled with six angels, underlining the seraphic resonances of the Francis scenes opposite and giving the window its popular name of the 'Angel Window'.[110] The lowest fields of the twin lancets are reserved for standing figures of Christ and the Virgin, rendered on the same scale as the apostles and two Franciscan saints in the other windows (fig. 79). The depiction of the Virgin in the right lancet is notably archaic: she is frontally posed and holds the Christ Child before her. To the left, Christ holds a diminutive figure of Saint Francis, mirroring the relationship of the Virgin and Child to the right.[111] This relationship is reinforced by various correspondences of gesture and framing. Francis is associated with Christ. He bears the wounds of the stigmata on his hands and feet and the cross that he holds echoes Christ's cruciform halo.

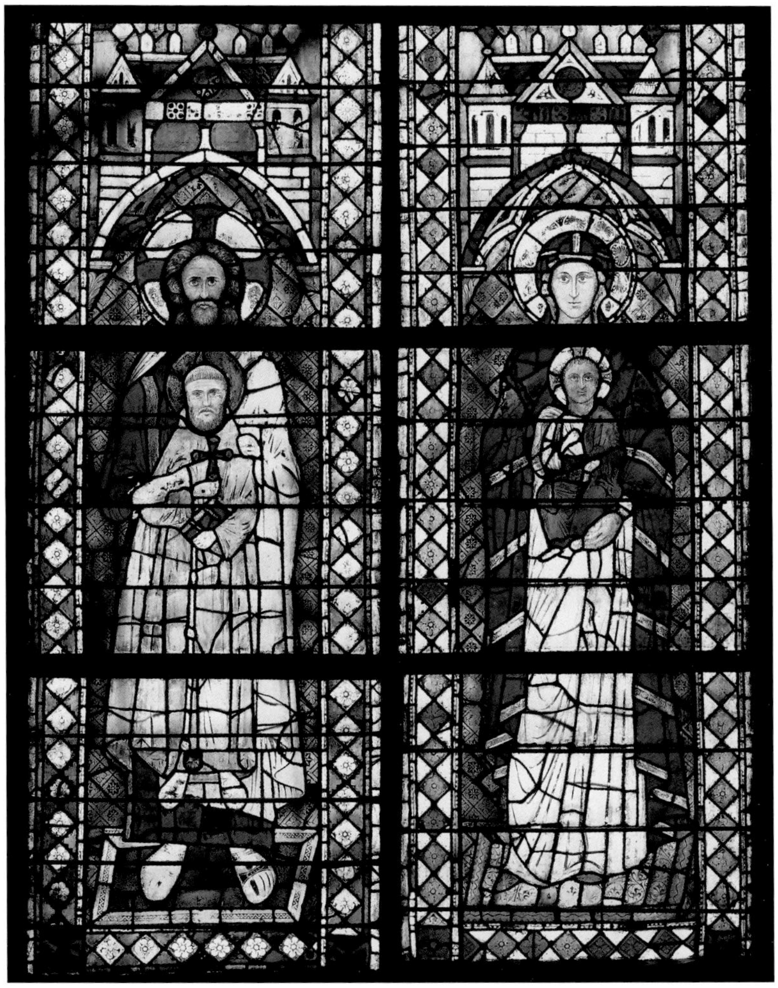

79 Maestro di San Francesco, Christ and Saint Francis, and Virgin and Child, *c.*1275–85, stained glass, fourth bay, south wall of the nave, Upper Church, Basilica of San Francesco.

Nothing comparable to the image of Christ and Francis in the 'Angel Window' at Assisi has survived, and its sources and iconography have puzzled Franciscan scholars. The most convincing explanation has been advanced by Jerôme Poulenc, who linked the window with passages from a roughly contemporary and very popular Franciscan devotional text, James of Milan's *Stimulus amoris*.[112] Certain passages in Chapter 14 of James's work, dedicated to meditations on the Passion, are especially suggestive, for example: 'Not only will I appear crucified with [the Virgin's] Son, I will also return to the crib and lie there with Him as a little child . . . He who was formerly enclosed for sinners in a Virgin's womb, deigns today to carry me, miserable me, in His entrails.'[113] Father Poulenc concluded that the designer of the window must have known the *Stimulus amoris* or at least other devotional texts written in a similar vein. If this relationship is accepted, the 'Angel Window' is not only an assertion of Francis's angelic nature but also presents the saint as a privileged devotional exemplar.

It was in this second sense that the 'Angel Window' was understood by the Franciscan mystic Angela of Foligno. Visiting Assisi in 1291, Angela entered the Upper Church through the façade doors, genuflected and saw – presumably as she looked up from kneeling (and, we might suspect, crossing herself) – 'Saint Francis painted in Christ's breast' ('vidi Sanctum Franciscum pictum in sinu Christi').[114] At this point Angela heard Francis speaking to her, fulfilling an

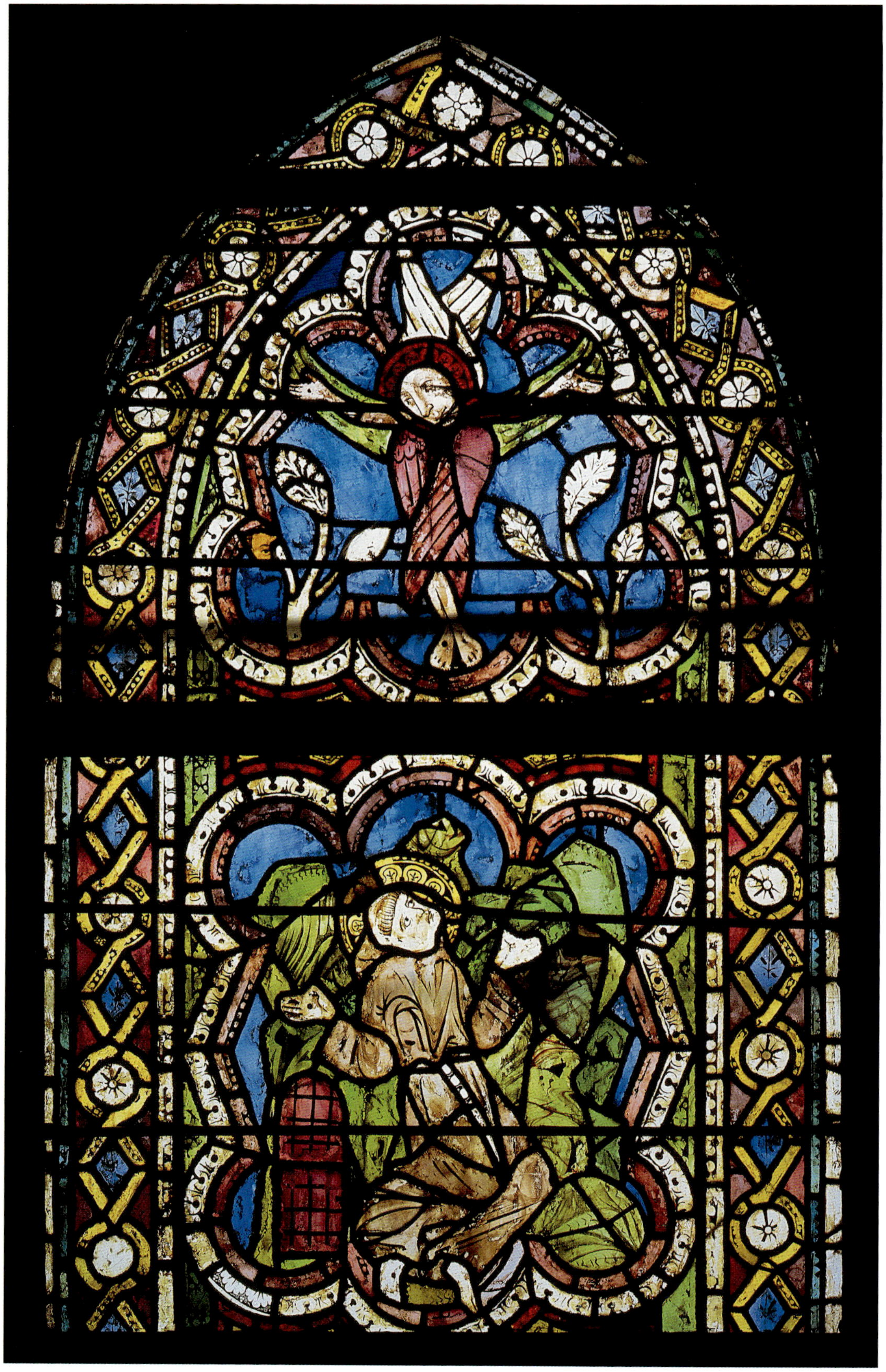

80 Maestro di San Francesco, *Stigmatization*, *c.*1275–85, stained glass, fourth bay, north wall of the nave, Upper Church, Basilica of San Francesco.

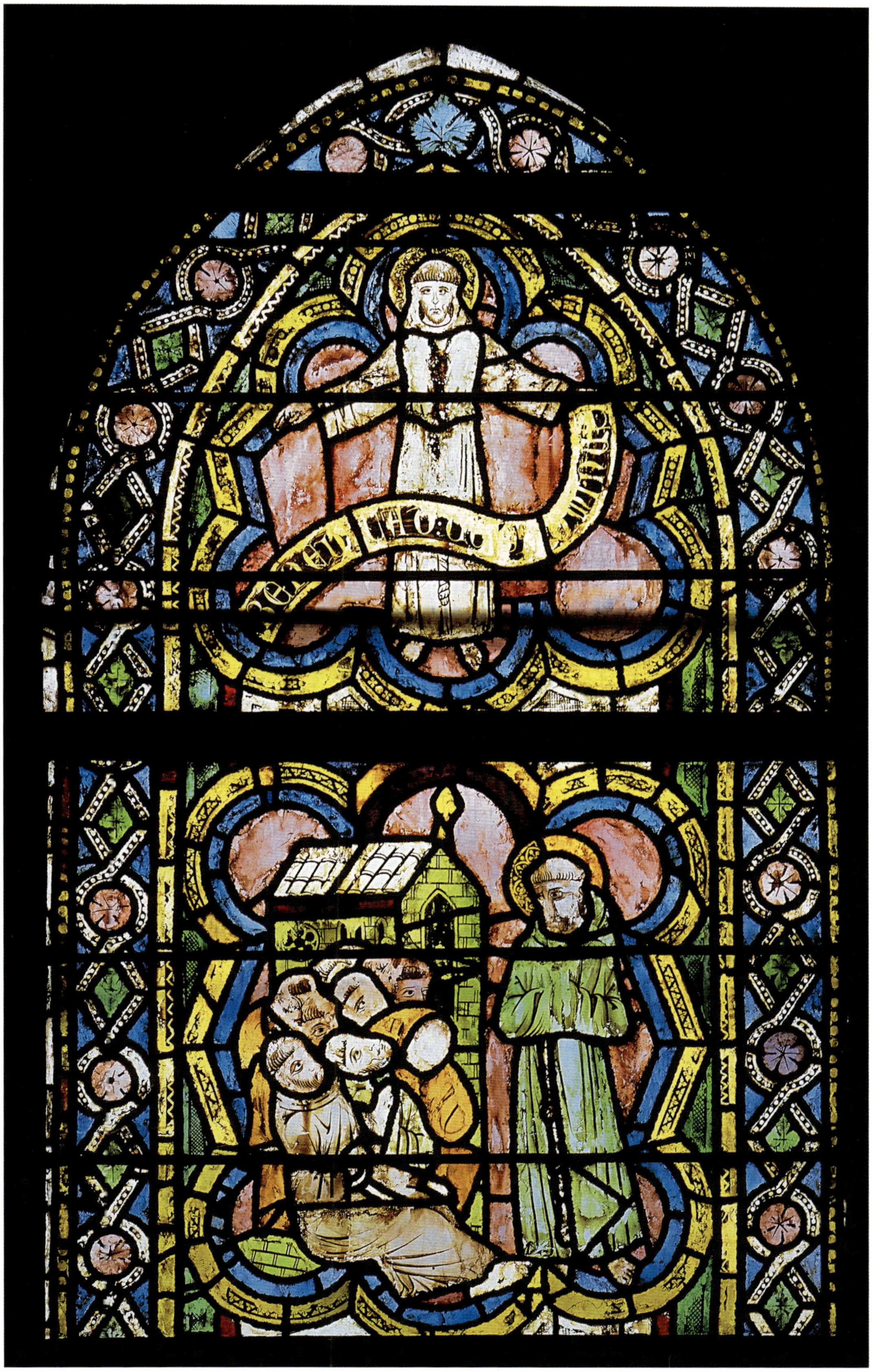

81 Maestro di San Francesco, *Apparition at Arles*, *c.*1275–85, stained glass, fourth bay, north wall of the nave, Upper Church, Basilica of San Francesco.

earlier prophecy she had received. 'I will hold you this closely,' the glazed image of the saint told her, 'even closer than the eyes of the body can see.'[115] This vision provoked a powerful reaction in Angela. Her anonymous confessor witnessed her 'sitting at the entrance of the [Upper] Church, screaming' before an audience of stunned friars and pilgrims. This was hardly proper pilgrim behaviour and her confessor was clearly shamed by the spectacle: 'I told her never to dare to come to Assisi again . . . and I told her companions never to bring her.'[116] Angela's reaction was unusually extreme, but the story reminds us of the prominence and legibility of the stained glass in the Upper Church. For Angela the graphic message of the 'Angel Window' was startlingly clear. Francis had attained a unique mystical union with Christ through the stigmata, offering a devotional path for her and others to follow.

The Frescoes in the Transepts and Crossing

The mural decoration of the Upper Church was probably already under way before the last windows in the nave were glazed. It began in the north transept, where a scaffold was erected up to the full height of the vaults. The first frescoes were executed by a heterogeneous workshop of Italian and non-Italian painters. Much discussion has focused on whether the latter were English, German or French, but there is a general consensus that they came from north of the Alps, like the first glass workers at Assisi.[117] A *Transfiguration* and a *Christ in Majesty* with the symbols of the Evangelists were painted in the lunettes of the transept, echoing the *Ascension* in the adjacent window. The close relationship between the stained glass and the mural programme was continued on the north wall of the transept, where two large standing prophets were painted to either side of the window, their fictive niches with trefoils above echoing the real tracery of the window. Below the lunettes, the two triforium arcades were frescoed with standing figures of the apostles, the six on the western wall executed by the northern workshop, those in the eastern gallery by Italian (probably Roman) painters. Paul Binski has convincingly interpreted the transept programme as an exposition of Christ's dominion over the world, 'the natural end of the evangelical, and Franciscan, mission'.[118] According to this reading, the *Christ in Majesty* stands as the fulfilment of the *Transfiguration*, and the crowned masks at the base of the vaults 'signify those earthly dominions over which Christ is to hold sway'.[119] The apostle friezes in the triforia reinforce this message of Gospel mission, but they also refer to the side altar in this transept, which – as we have seen – was probably dedicated to the Holy Apostles. There is considerable disagreement over the dating of the frescoes in the north transept. The prominent use of fleur-de-lis on the ribs of the vault has been connected to the papacy of Clement IV (1265–8), a Frenchman and staunch ally of both the French King Louis IX and his Angevin relatives in Italy.[120] Several other scholars have preferred a later dating in the 1270s.[121]

The next area to be frescoed was the main apse. Here the northern workshop made a start on the upper wall surfaces, but was soon replaced by the Florentine master Cimabue, who painted scenes from the life of the Virgin, reflecting the Marian dedication of the high altar. After this, a new scaffold was built, filling the crossing bay and the south transept, and Cimabue began work on painting the central vault above the high altar. Whereas the canopies of the north transept and apse had been painted with starred blue heavens, an ambitious figurative programme was conceived for the crossing (see fig. 12). In each web of the vault Cimabue painted one of the four Evangelists, portraying the authors of the Gospels writing at lecterns, their heads touched by descending angels, and their attributes at their feet. Beside them walled cities denoted the regions of the known world – Judaea, Greece, Asia and Italy – that their Gospels were intended to reach. Cimabue applied gold leaf to the backgrounds. Most of this gilding has now flaked off, exposing the white preparatory ground, but the original effect must have been resplendent. The choice of the four Evangelists underlined the centrality of the Gospel to Francis's Rule and the evangelical mission of the Franciscan movement. The crossing vault has therefore been read as a continuation of the theme of Christ's dominion begun in the north transept.

John White and Bruno Zanardi were able to calculate the sequence in which the four Evangelists were painted, concluding that Saint Mark (fig. 82) was painted last.[122] It would not be surprising if this were so, as the city depicted beside the Evangelist is of far greater complexity than the other three and carries a distinct iconographic message: Cimabue might well have wanted to clear the way in order to concentrate on this elaborate scene. Saint Mark was the Evangelist of Italy, and under the banner of 'Ytalia' Cimabue

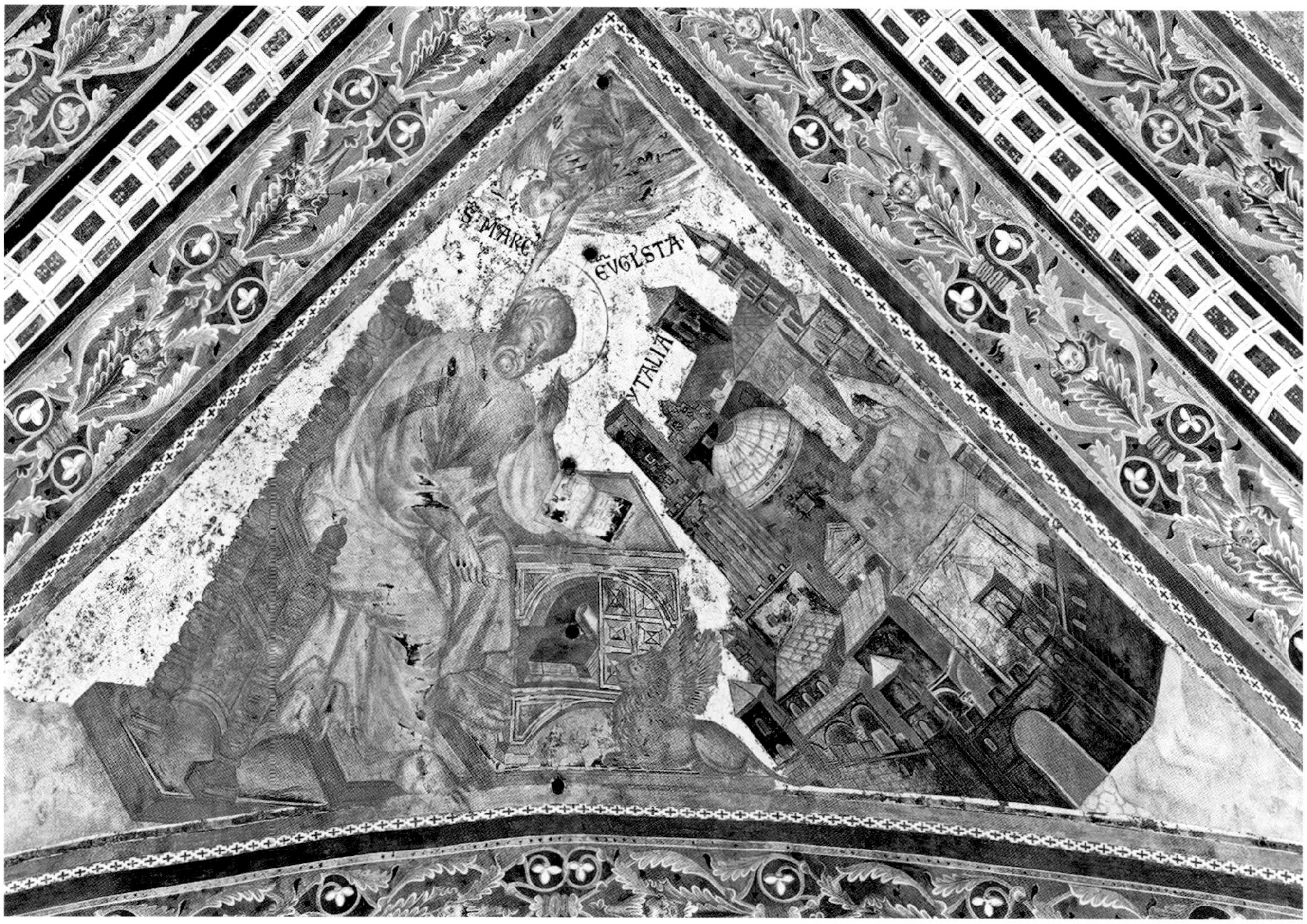

82 Cimabue, Saint Mark, vault of the Evangelists (south web, crossing vault), *c.*1277–80, fresco, Upper Church, Basilica of San Francesco.

painted a remarkably detailed view of the city of Rome, incorporating a number of well-known monuments: the basilica of Saint Peter's, the Pantheon, the Castel Sant'Angelo and the Torre della Milizia are all recognizable (fig. 83).[123] The Palace of the Senate on the Capitol is set directly below the inscription and its façade is decorated with alternating coats of arms of the city of Rome (bearing the initials SPQR) and the Orsini family. This heraldic combination conclusively dates the fresco to the papacy of Nicholas III Orsini (1277–80) and has been convincingly associated with that pope's consolidation of papal authority over the Eternal City. The bull *Fundamenta militantis Ecclesiae*, issued on 18 July 1278, restricted the office of senator to Roman citizens, and Nicholas himself was elected sole senator two months later, though he delegated authority for the first year to his nephew Cardinal Matteo Rosso Orsini as vicar. Matteo Rosso was succeeded by members of other Roman families in September 1279. A series of large Orsini *stemmi*, alternating with civic coats of arms, were discovered on the tympanum of the medieval façade of the Palace of the Senate in 1959. These must have been painted shortly after Nicholas assumed the office of senator, probably during Matteo Rosso's term as vicar from September 1278 to September 1279.

All the evidence points to the Saint Mark vault having been painted between September 1278 and Pope Nicholas's sudden death at his summer villa of Soriano in August 1280. Maria Andaloro's careful analysis of the buildings selected for the 'Ytalia' cityscape demonstrated beyond reasonable doubt that it was conceived as a 'Roma Orsiniana'.[124] Nicholas III lavished attention on Saint Peter's, rebuilding the papal apart-

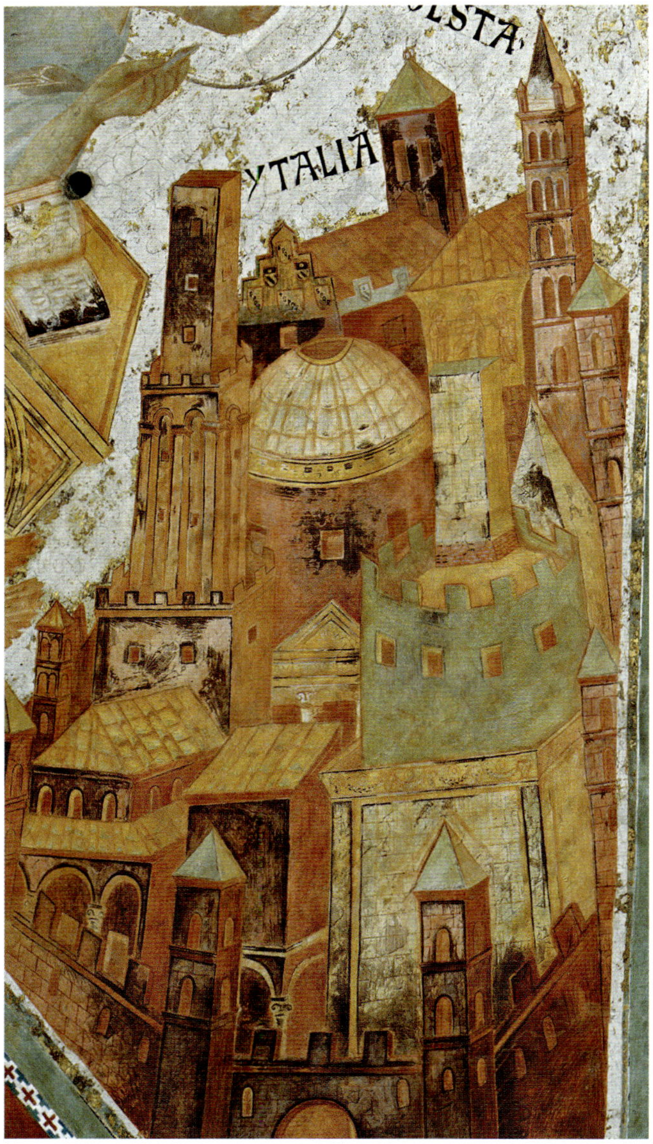

83 Cimabue, 'Ytalia', detail from vault of the Evangelists (south web, crossing vault), *c.*1277–80, fresco, Upper Church, Basilica of San Francesco.

ments there and basing the curia at the Vatican whenever he resided in Rome. In Cimabue's fresco, Saint Peter's, identifiable by its façade mosaic, is emphasized at the expense of the other major Roman basilicas. The Castel Sant'Angelo and the nearby pyramid of the Meta Romuli, both monuments that belonged to the Orsini by the mid-thirteenth century, also figure prominently. Above all, the shields on the fictive Palace of the Senate faithfully rendered the freshly painted heraldry on the actual building. The vault can be read as a coherent pictorial endorsement of Nicholas's glorification of Rome as a new Jerusalem and the fulcrum of papal temporal power.

Does this mean that Nicholas III was personally involved in the creation of the fresco, as several scholars have argued? The Orsini pope was certainly devoted to the Franciscan Order. His father had known Saint Francis and Nicholas had served as the Order's cardinal protector from 1261 until his election in 1277. A fresco above Nicholas's tomb in Saint Peter's portrayed the pope being carried upwards by his heavenly patron saints, Nicholas of Bari and Francis.[125] He personally concerned himself, to a greater degree than any other pontiff, with the interpretation of the Franciscan Rule. The result was the lengthy bull *Exiit qui seminat*, in effect an exposition of the Rule, issued on 14 August 1279.[126] It is surely no coincidence that one of the ideal viewing points for the cityscape in the Saint Mark vault is from the north transept (fig. 84), which is where one would have entered the Upper Church from the papal apartments in the Sacro Convento.[127] The vault is more than eighteen metres from the floor of the Basilica, but the 'Ytalia' fresco is surprisingly legible even in its present abraded state. Before their reds faded and silver leaf grew tarnished, the Orsini shields would have stood out as sharp flecks of primary colour at the summit of the cityscape, immediately below the 'Ytalia' inscription.[128] The level of detail with which Cimabue invested his view of Rome indicates that he had been instructed to produce a recognizable representation of the city. But none of this necessarily means that Nicholas III himself 'commissioned the work and stipulated what he wanted'.[129] He never visited Assisi as pontiff.[130] It is perhaps more likely that the Saint Mark vault was conceived by leading Franciscans at Assisi as an image that Nicholas would understand and appreciate, if and when the Orsini pope visited Assisi – an event the friars of the Sacro Convento surely hoped for and would have had some reason to expect, until Nicholas's unexpected death at Soriano on 22 August 1280 put an end to any such prospect.[131]

Most likely the vault of the Evangelists was completed in time for the Assisi general chapter in May 1279. The upper walls and vault of the south transept were painted using a shared scaffold and so must have been completed in the same campaign as the crossing vault. Here the iconographic scheme reinforced the dedication of the side altar below to Saint Michael Archangel. The triforium passageways were popu-

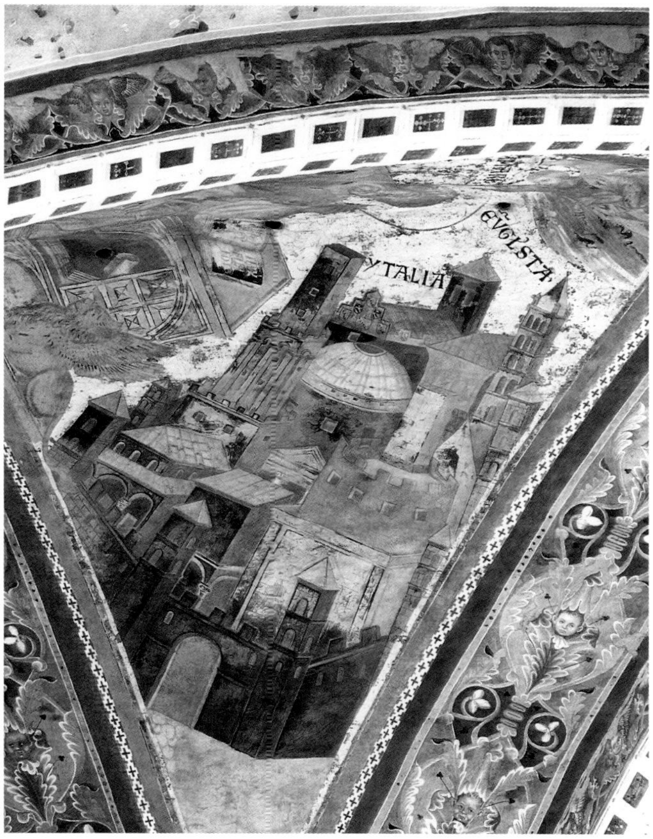

84 Cimabue, 'Ytalia', detail from vault of the Evangelists (south web, crossing vault), *c.*1277–80, fresco, viewed from the entrance into the north transept from the Sacro Convento, Upper Church, Basilica of San Francesco.

lated and surmounted by ranks of angels (fig. 85). One of the lunettes depicted Saint Michael and two other angels overcoming the dragon and other demonic creatures. Colossal standing angels, now almost entirely lost, flanked the window on the end wall of the south transept. There was little attempt in this bay to integrate the frescoes with the existing Genesis cycle or enthroned Virgins in the stained glass.

The fresco decoration of the vaults and upper walls of the transepts, crossing and apse reflected the dedication of the three altars below, albeit to a somewhat uneven degree.[132] The scheme that was chosen for the wall surfaces below the triforium aimed for a much more systematic correspondence. Here Cimabue painted three cycles: five Apocalypse scenes in the south transept to reflect the Saint Michael dedication; four scenes – two to either side of the papal throne – in the central apse covering the Virgin's last days, her Dormition and Coronation, to underline the Marian dedication of the high altar; five scenes in the north transept from the lives of the apostles.[133] As Hans Belting observed, Cimabue's apostle scenes at Assisi faithfully copied a lost Roman model, the mural cycle formerly in the portico of Old Saint Peter's, an iconographic choice that showcased the Upper Church's status as a papal basilica.[134] Cimabue's sanctuary programme was completed by two enormous and symmetrically sited *Crucifixions* on the eastern walls of the transepts behind the side altars (see fig. 5). Distinct from the adjacent cycles, these great Calvaries served as monumental altarpieces, insisting on the liturgical disposition of the transept and the eastward orientation of the side altars. Furthermore, the viewer in the western end of the church would have seen Cimabue's two mural *Crucifixions* linked by the silhouetted verso of Giunta's great panel cross at the head of the nave. Belting also underlined the devotional function of Cimabue's *Crucifixions*.[135] In both versions, a diminutive figure of Saint Francis kneels at the foot of the cross, a devotional exemplar for the friars gathered in the transepts.

The painting of the lower walls did not require such lofty and inflexible scaffolds, and Cimabue was able to work his way around the entire sanctuary end of the church (transepts and apse), executing the frescoes in a clockwise sequence beginning with the *Crucifixion* in the south transept. The two

85 Cimabue, angels, *c.*1277–80, fresco, east wall of the triforium, south transept, Upper Church, Basilica of San Francesco.

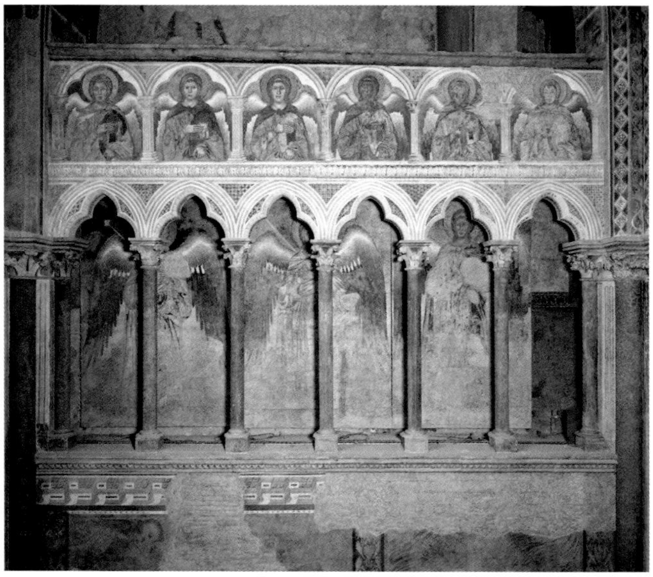

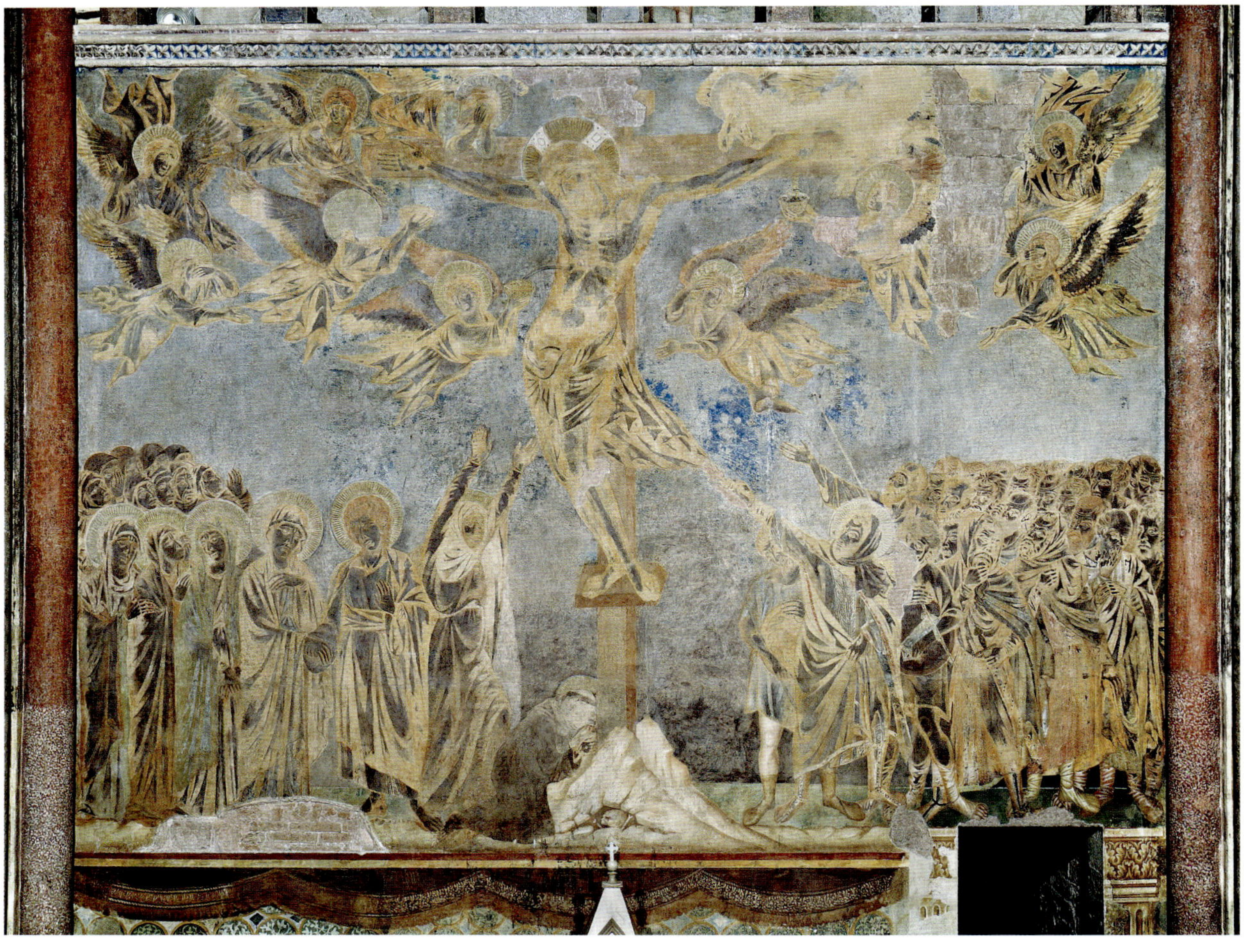

86 Cimabue, *Crucifixion*, *c.*1279–82, fresco, east wall of the south transept, Upper Church, Basilica of San Francesco.

Crucifixion frescoes extended right up to the bases of the triforia passageways and across to the pilasters of the transept bays, covering the maximum mural surface at the expense of any internal frames (fig. 86). But on the other walls, Cimabue used common framing elements to unify the three narrative cycles, devising a heavy fictive cornice to run above the scenes (fig. 87). Below the transept cycles (including the *Crucifixions*) Cimabue painted fictive fabric hangings, using a repeat pattern of roundels that imitated the most luxurious designs of contemporary woven and embroidered silks. The wall surfaces below the Marian scenes in the apse were left bare, a sure sign that some kind of high-backed seating was already envisaged, or *in situ*, to either side of the papal throne. The combination of the architectural frieze above and fictive textiles below was so successful that a refined version was subsequently deployed in the nave when the Saint Francis cycle was painted, thereby providing consistent bands of ornament around the whole Upper Church.[136]

The dating of Cimabue's activity at Assisi continues to stir controversy in scholarly circles, with sharply divergent interpretations of the artist's stylistic development competing against one another.[137] On logistical grounds, it is possible to argue for a break in Cimabue's campaign between the dismantling of the scaffolding in the crossing and south transept and the execution of the cycles on the lower walls, perhaps to allow for the celebration of the general chapter in May 1279.[138] But even then, progress is unlikely to have been delayed for long, and the transept programme was surely complete by the early 1280s at the latest. Innocent IV's quarter-century grant of alms for the Basilica's decoration, prolonged by Clement IV for a further three years, finally expired in 1281.

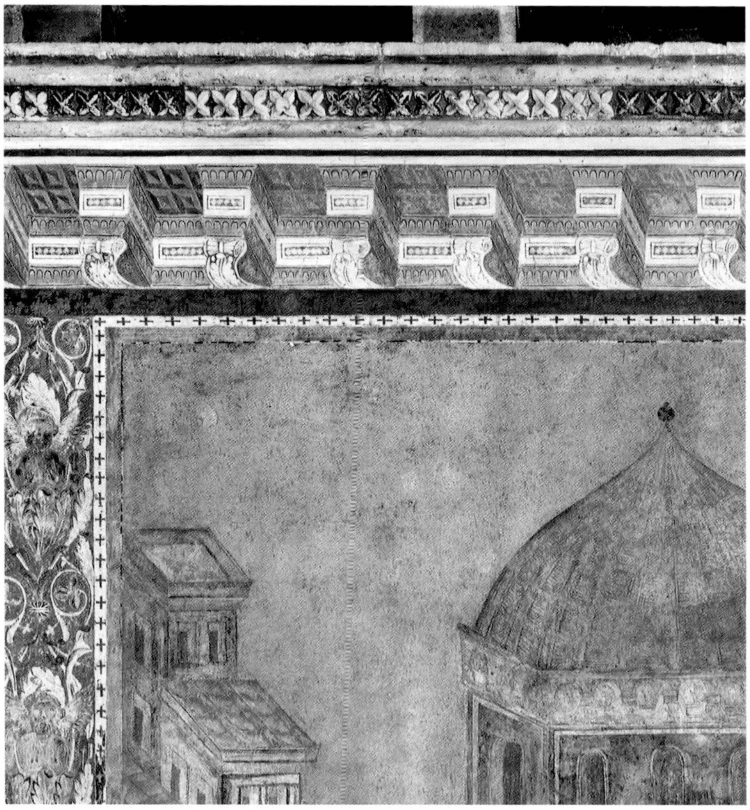

87 Cimabue, framing cornice, detail from *Saint Peter Curing the Lame Man in front of the Temple* (fig. 144), Apostles cycle, *c.*1279–82, fresco, north transept, Upper Church, Basilica of San Francesco.

✳

In May 1288 the Upper Church would have presented a deeply uneven spectacle. Every inch of the apse, crossing and transepts was frescoed, and the newly gilded vault of the Evangelists must have been particularly eye-catching. This splendour was in clear contrast to the bare masonry of the nave, still unadorned three and a half decades after the Basilica's consecration. Here the stained-glass lancet windows gave isolated splashes of colour to an otherwise austere space. More light would have flooded in from the great rose window on the façade, orientated to face the morning sun. The most powerful visual presence in the nave would still have been Giunta Pisano's great panel crucifix, accompanied – we would argue – by lateral panels depicting Saint Michael and Pentecost. These images were mounted on a beam and the mighty crucifix was chained to the vaults above. The memory of Elias's patronage had probably faded, his donor inscription, if not his donor figure, invisible to the naked eye below. In the wake of *Reducentes*, the friars may have removed a masonry screen or barrier at the head of the nave, but the cross and its beam, some six metres clear of the floor, they chose to leave in place.[139] More than that, they considered carefully how to integrate these older artworks into the new programme for the nave's mural decoration.

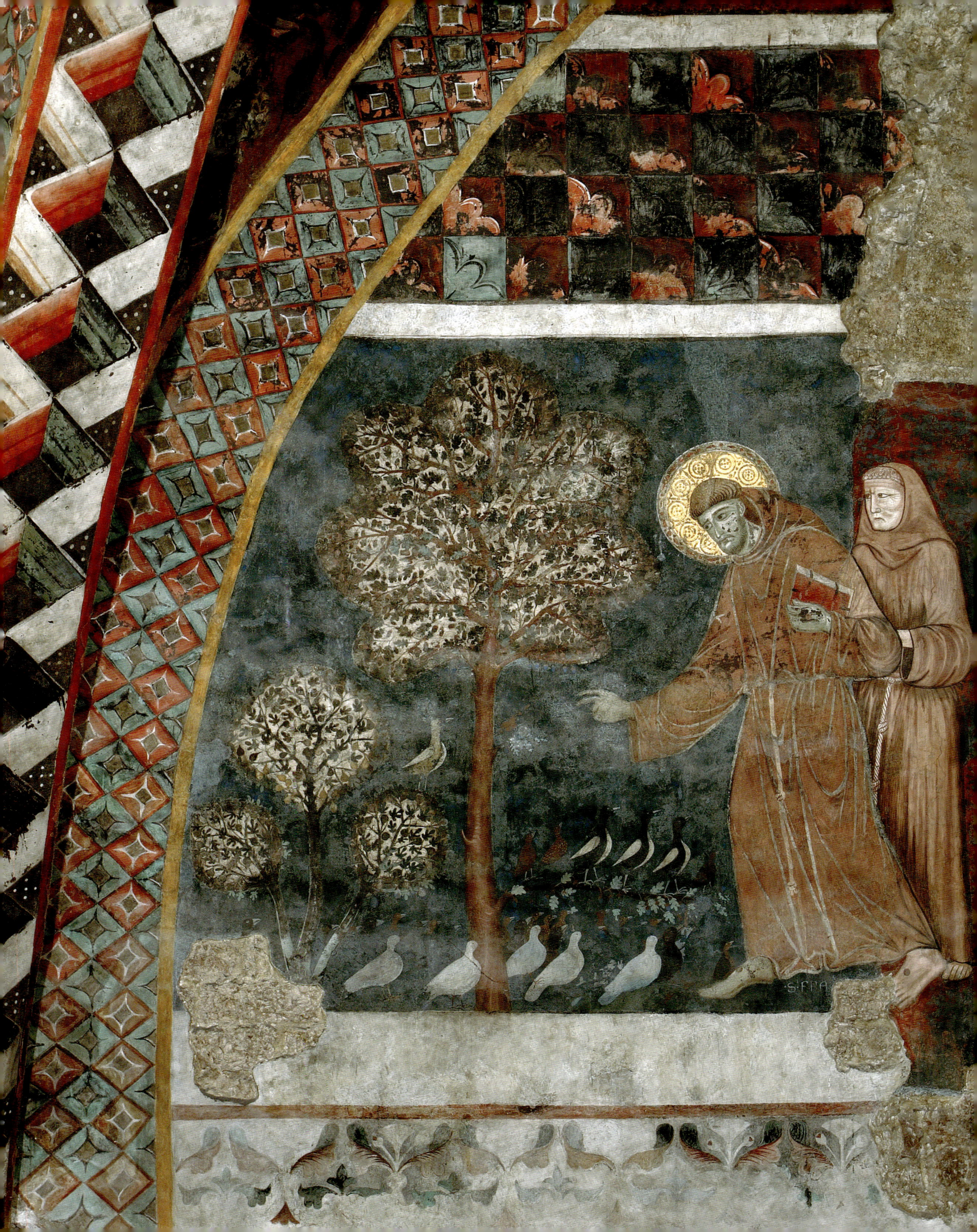

4

Planning the Nave Programme

The Upper Basilica in 1288 was dominated by biblical imagery, with the figure of Saint Francis making only sporadic appearances in its stained glass and wall paintings. That balance would undergo a radical shift with the implementation of the fresco programme devised for the nave (fig. 89). The centrepiece of the new scheme was the Saint Francis cycle, the longest and most famous painted narrative of the saint ever produced in medieval or Renaissance Italy. It was also the most innovative. Its twenty-eight scenes are prominently positioned just above eye level, forming the lowest of the nave's three registers of frescoes. The cycle wraps its way clockwise around the three walls, starting at the altar end of the north wall and continuing across the counter-façade, before completing its circuit by returning along the south wall to the altar.

Biblical stories were still assigned an important role in the pictorial plan, however. Sacred history is played out on each longitudinal wall, with an Old Testament cycle on the north wall facing a New Testament cycle on the south (fig. 90). Each cycle is split into two horizontal registers, one above the other, their narrative sequences running in parallel from the altar end of the nave towards the counter-façade. The sixteen scenes from the Old Testament are all taken from Genesis. The eight in the upper tier begin with the *Creation of the World* and end with *Cain Forsaking Abel*; the lower register continues with eight stories devoted to the Old Testament patriarchs Noah, Abraham, Isaac, Jacob and Joseph. The same pattern is adopted for the sixteen New Testament scenes on the south wall: the upper tier begins with the *Annunciation* and ends with the *Baptism of Christ*; the lower proceeds from the *Wedding at Cana* to the *Three Maries at the Tomb*. On this wall, the altar-to-entrance disposition of the cycle imposed a right-to-left flow on the narrative.

For both the content and the disposition of the biblical cycles, the friars in Assisi looked to Rome: in the naves of all the Constantinian basilicas in the Eternal City, as far as we can tell from the surviving evidence, the early Christian frescoes were arranged in a 'double parallel', Old Testament scenes on one wall facing New Testament scenes on the other.[1] In aping these Roman basilical models, the planners of the Assisi frescoes were following a tradition that had been established in numerous other late medieval Italian churches. But in this chapter we shall demonstrate that the Assisi cycles diverged from their Roman prototypes in some highly creative and unusual ways, to produce a whole iconographic scheme that was tailored to the architectural space of the

facing page 88 Maestro di San Francesco, *Preaching to the Birds* (see fig. 107).

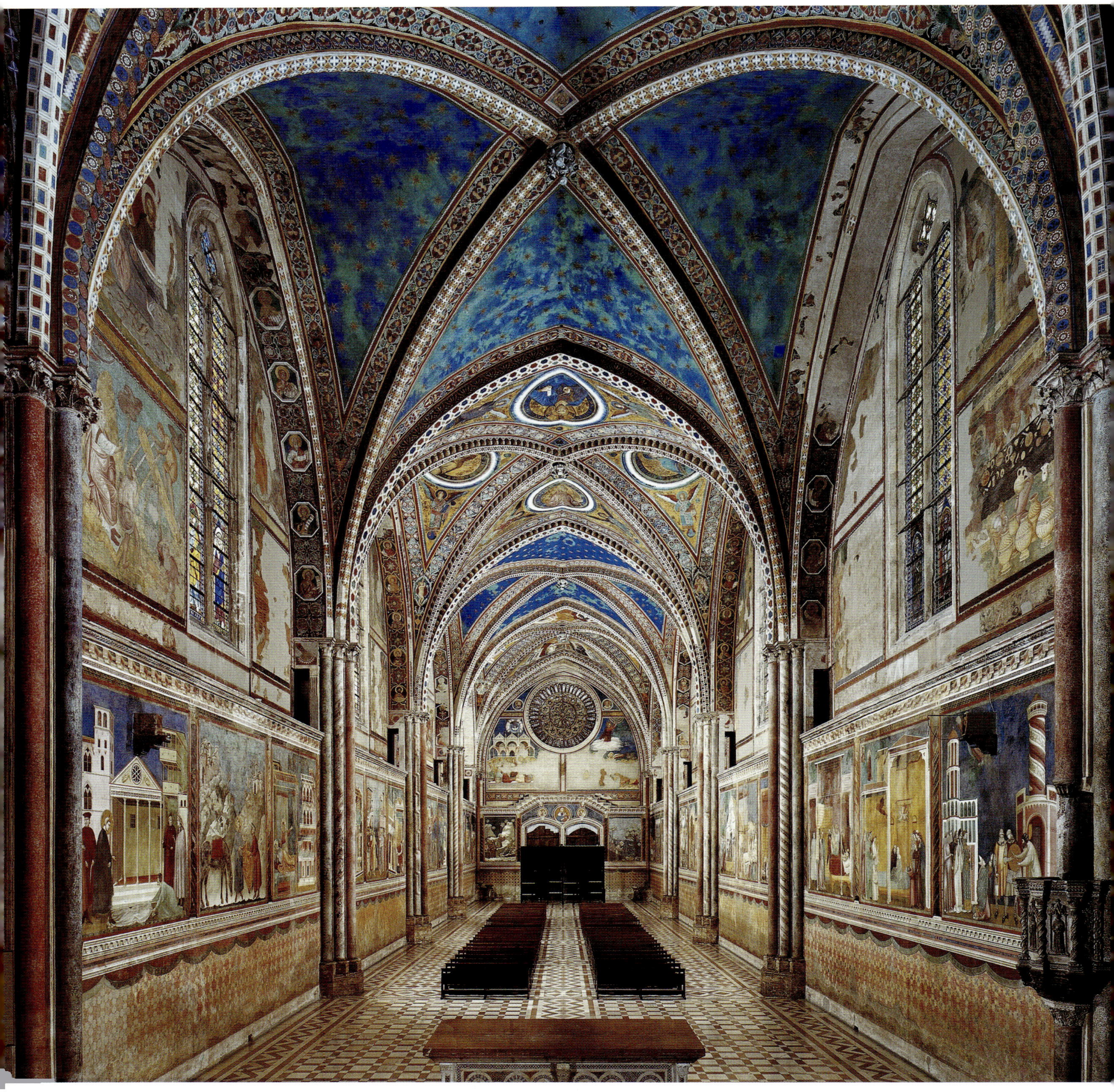

89 Basilica of San Francesco, nave of the Upper Church, looking towards the counter-façade.

facing page 90 Plan of the fresco cycles in the nave of the Upper Church, Basilica of San Francesco.

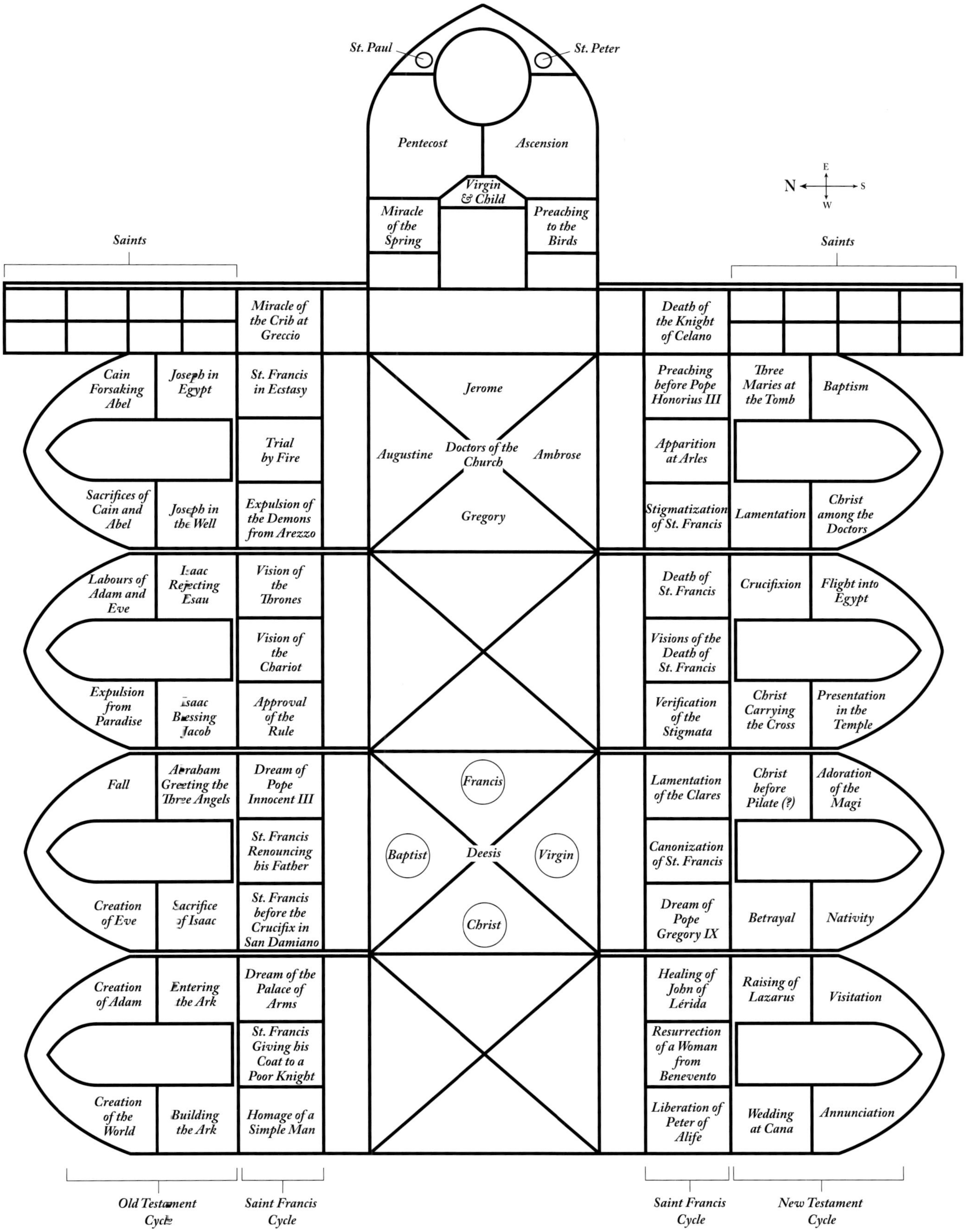
St. Paul
St. Peter
Pentecost
Ascension
Virgin & Child
Miracle of the Spring
Preaching to the Birds
N
E
S
W
Saints
Saints
Miracle of the Crib at Greccio
Death of the Knight of Celano
Cain Forsaking Abel
Joseph in Egypt
St. Francis in Ecstasy
Jerome
Preaching before Pope Honorius III
Three Maries at the Tomb
Baptism
Trial by Fire
Augustine
Doctors of the Church
Ambrose
Apparition at Arles
Sacrifices of Cain and Abel
Joseph in the Well
Expulsion of the Demons from Arezzo
Gregory
Stigmatization of St. Francis
Lamentation
Christ among the Doctors
Labours of Adam and Eve
Isaac Rejecting Esau
Vision of the Thrones
Death of St. Francis
Crucifixion
Flight into Egypt
Vision of the Chariot
Visions of the Death of St. Francis
Expulsion from Paradise
Isaac Blessing Jacob
Approval of the Rule
Verification of the Stigmata
Christ Carrying the Cross
Presentation in the Temple
Fall
Abraham Greeting the Three Angels
Dream of Pope Innocent III
Francis
Lamentation of the Clares
Christ before Pilate (?)
Adoration of the Magi
St. Francis Renouncing his Father
Baptist
Deesis
Virgin
Canonization of St. Francis
Creation of Eve
Sacrifice of Isaac
St. Francis before the Crucifix in San Damiano
Christ
Dream of Pope Gregory IX
Betrayal
Nativity
Creation of Adam
Entering the Ark
Dream of the Palace of Arms
Healing of John of Lérida
Raising of Lazarus
Visitation
St. Francis Giving his Coat to a Poor Knight
Resurrection of a Woman from Benevento
Creation of the World
Building the Ark
Homage of a Simple Man
Liberation of Peter of Alife
Wedding at Cana
Annunciation
Old Testament Cycle
Saint Francis Cycle
Saint Francis Cycle
New Testament Cycle

Upper Basilica and that served a specifically Franciscan agenda. One novel feature, for example, was the treatment of the counter-façade, whose upper sections were used to complete the New Testament sequence with an additional two scenes, the *Ascension* and the *Pentecost*.[2]

Overview of the Saint Francis Cycle

The Gothic architecture of the Upper Church dictated much of the essential structure of the Saint Francis cycle. The nave is divided by heavy clusters of columns into four bays. Each of the first three bays (beginning from the altar end) contains three Saint Francis scenes on either side of the nave; the last bay, adjacent to the counter-façade, contains four, and the counter-façade itself the remaining two (fig. 90). The bays are used to compartmentalize Francis's legend into different sections.

The saint's early life and the process of his conversion are presented in the first two bays of the north wall. The cycle opens in Assisi. Francis is depicted as an elegantly clad young layman who, in the central piazza of his home town, encounters a simple man who lays down his cloak before the future saint, saying that he deserves to be honoured for the greatness of the deeds he will soon perform (Scene 1). The next two scenes are linked: on the plain below Assisi, Francis meets a poor knight, to whom he gives his coat (Scene 2); his charity is rewarded the following night, when he dreams of a magnificent palace full of arms marked with the sign of the cross (Scene 3). When he asks to whom these things belong, he is told that they are for him and his knights. Misunderstanding the divine message, Francis subsequently sets off to join a noble militia. But by the time we see him again, he has already abandoned this plan and returned to Assisi, determined to become a spiritual knight for Christ.

The three scenes in the second bay present the key events in Francis's conversion and the founding of the Order. Praying in front of a crucifix in the dilapidated church of San Damiano, outside the walls of Assisi, Francis hears Christ telling him, 'Repair my house, which as you see is falling into ruin' (Scene 4). Francis's response to this command soon brings him into conflict with his father, the cloth merchant Pietro Bernardone. Having used his father's money to restore San Damiano and other ruined churches around Assisi, Francis is summoned by him before the bishop's court, where Pietro demands the return of his property. In response, Francis strips off all his clothes, and renounces his father, proclaiming that from now on he will acknowledge only 'Our Father, who is in heaven' (Scene 5). The final scene in this bay jumps forward in time. After having begun to live as a poor beggar, and having gathered around him a group of like-minded companions, Francis travels to Rome to seek papal approval for his community. Unimpressed by this dirty and uneducated layman, Pope Innocent III initially refuses to authorize the fledgling order, but the next night the pontiff dreams of a poor little man supporting on his back the church of Saint John Lateran in Rome, which appears on the point of collapse (Scene 6). Innocent is convinced by this that Francis will spiritually restore the Roman Church through his life and teachings, and so grants him and his companions verbal permission to preach. This outcome is suggested through the saint's Franciscan habit, worn for the first time in this scene.

The story of Francis's two decades as a friar unfolds in the long middle section of the cycle, which encompasses the third and fourth bays of the north wall, the counter-façade, and the fourth bay of the south wall. The sequence begins with Francis and his eleven companions kneeling before the pope, who hands the founder-saint a scroll on which the opening words of the Franciscan Rule are legible (Scene 7). In the next scene the communal life of the friars in Assisi commences. Francis has gone to pray in the garden of the cathedral in Assisi while the rest of the friars are sleeping in their first home, an abandoned hovel at Rivotorto, in the fields below the town. Suddenly, they are awakened by the vision of a burning chariot, which bursts into their hut and hurtles around above their heads (Scene 8). Telling the tale in the *Legenda maior*, Bonaventure likens Francis to the Old Testament prophet Elijah, who ascended to heaven in a fiery chariot. A second revelation follows: while praying with Francis, one of his friars experiences a vision of the thrones that were formerly occupied by Lucifer and the rebel angels who fell from heaven (Scene 9). The greatest of these heavenly thrones is now reserved for the humble Francis, making him an *alter angelus* (another angel) as well as an *alter* Elijah. Thus the salvific significance of Francis, having been prophesied by the simple man in the first bay, and revealed to the pope in the second, is unveiled to his brothers in the third bay.

The quartet of scenes in the fourth bay serves to demonstrate both Francis's saintly virtues and his mystical union with Christ. While the preceding bay is primarily concerned with Francis's impact on his fellow friars, the first two scenes in this bay show his ministry in the secular world. First, Francis and another brother cast out demons from the Tuscan city of Arezzo, a metaphor for making peace between violent urban factions (Scene 10). Second, Francis attempts to convert the Sultan of Egypt and his Muslim people to Christianity. Rather than preaching, Francis demonstrates his faith and desire for martyrdom by challenging the sultan's priests to a trial by fire (Scene 11). The third and fourth scenes focus on Francis's inner life of prayer. In Scene 12 Francis is seen by his companions lifted up above the ground in ecstatic contemplation; the fresco expresses in physical terms his spiritual communion with Christ, who leans down from the heavens. The final scene on the north wall is the *Miracle of the Crib at Greccio* (Scene 13), illustrating that Christmas Eve on which Francis set up a nativity scene to demonstrate to the laity the humble circumstances of Jesus' birth. One of the participants sees a vision of the Christ Child in Francis's arms, a miracle that the written legends set within the context of the saint's power of prayer.

That theme is continued on the counter-façade in the *Miracle of the Spring* (Scene 14). Francis prays for water to relieve the thirst of a poor peasant and a spring appears from the rock. This miracle also demonstrates Francis's power over nature, a theme shared by the second scene on the counter-façade, in which Saint Francis preaches to a flock of birds that understand his words (Scene 15). More importantly, though, this scene begins a theme that continues into the fourth bay of the south wall, whose first three scenes are all concerned with Franciscan preaching to diverse audiences. The triad opens with the *Death of the Knight of Celano* (Scene 16). Having been invited to dine at the house of a wealthy nobleman, Francis warns his host of his imminent death and advises him to confess without delay. On the right of the fresco the knight is seen lying dead, surrounded by his lamenting household. In the next scene Francis, inspired by the Holy Spirit, preaches to Pope Honorius III and the curia of cardinals (Scene 17). The triplet is completed by an episode in which an apparition of the absent saint is experienced miraculously by one of the friars attending the provincial chapter of Arles in southern France (Scene 18). But the scene also depicts the preaching of Saint Anthony of Padua, the first Franciscan teacher of theology, to his confrères in the chapter house. Saint Francis's earthly life then reaches its dramatic climax, the moment in which the saint, meditating at the hermitage of La Verna, receives the stigmata, the wounds of the crucified Christ (Scene 19).

The final three bays of the south wall deal in considerable detail with the events surrounding the death, burial and canonization of the saint, followed by a short sequence of post-mortem miracles. The triplet in the third bay focuses on the saint's death, which took place in the convent at the Porziuncola in Santa Maria degli Angeli. The dying Francis lies on the ground, surrounded by his friars, while his soul is seen ascending heavenwards in a shining cloud (Scene 20). The miraculous nature of the event is emphasized by the following fresco (Scene 21), in which two different people (a friar called Agostino, and the bishop of Assisi), in separate places, both experience visions of Francis's passing at the exact time of his death. The bay is completed with the *Verification of the Stigmata* (Scene 22), in which a knight who doubts the truth of Francis's stigmata places his hand into the wound on the saint's torso.

The exequies over Francis's body and the emphasis on the stigmata continue in the trio of scenes in the second bay. First, Saint Clare and her sister nuns at San Damiano lament over Francis's corpse as it is carried towards Assisi for burial (Scene 23). The central, badly damaged, scene of this bay officially confirms the sanctity of Francis, depicting his canonization by Pope Gregory IX (Scene 24), a ceremony that took place while the body was still interred in its temporary burial place in the church of San Giorgio in Assisi. This triplet is completed with the *Dream of Pope Gregory IX* (Scene 25), which, like the final scene in the preceding bay, concerns the authentication of Francis's stigmata. Gregory's doubts about the wound in Francis's torso are dispelled when the saint appears to him in a dream, proffering a vial filled with blood from his side.

The cycle concludes in the first bay with a triplet of post-mortem miracles. It opens with a traditional miracle of healing, but with a new twist. Francis cures a man's stab wounds by placing his own wounded hands upon them; thus, the miracle proclaims the thaumaturgic power of the stigmata (Scene 26). In the second miracle a woman is resurrected through the intercession of Saint Francis, so that she can make her confession and die a second time after having received absolution for all her sins (Scene 27). Finally, Francis frees from prison in Rome the repentant heretic Peter of Alife, to the amazement of the ecclesiastical hierarchy (Scene 28).

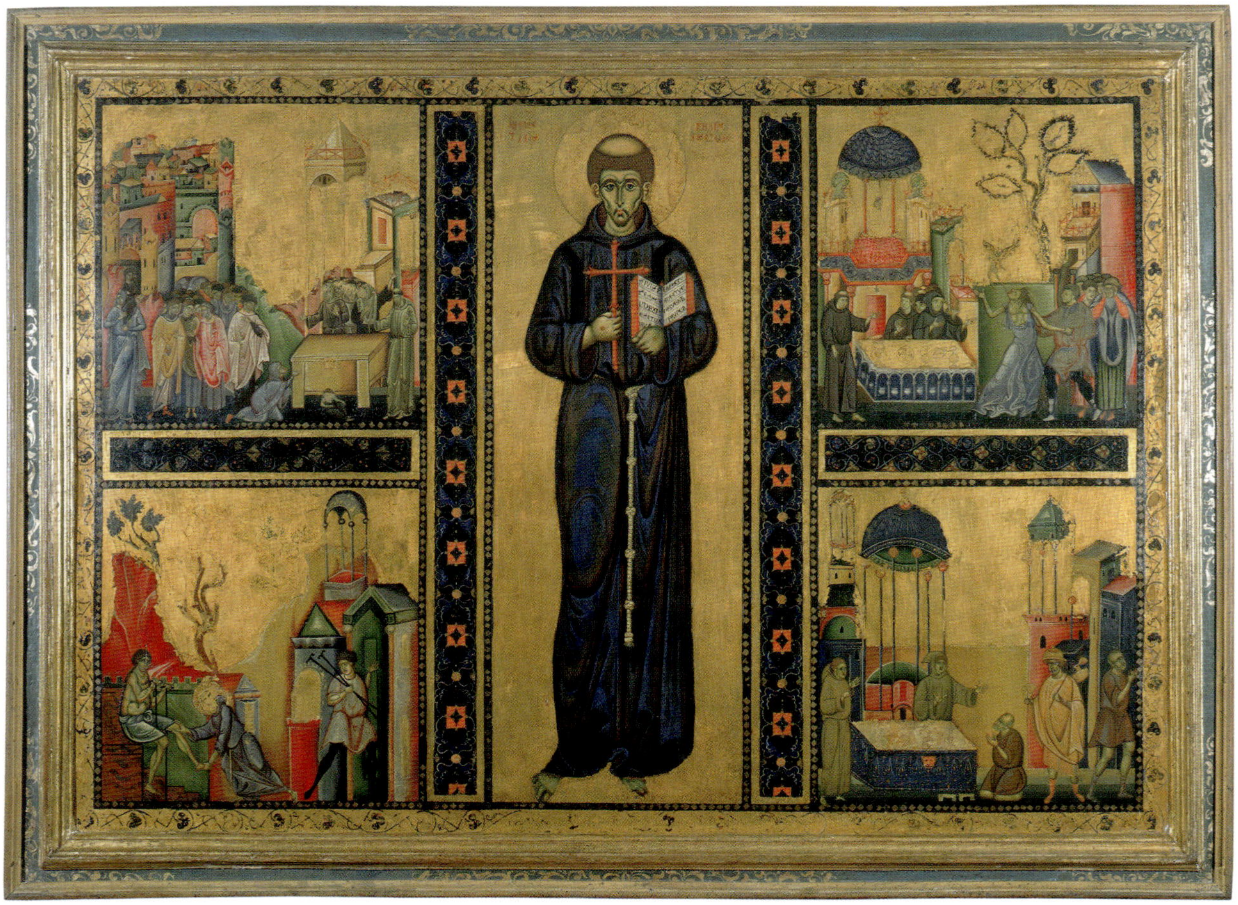

91 Giunta Pisano(?), *Saint Francis and Four Posthumous Miracles*, *c.*1253, tempera and gold on wood (111.5 cm × 154.5 cm), Treasury Museum, Sacro Convento, Assisi.

In these last three scenes, Francis is accredited with the ability not only to rescue his devotees from physical death, but to save their immortal souls as well.

Tradition and Innovation

When the planners of the cycle set about deciding which scenes to include, they had over half a century of material to draw upon in terms of both written and pictorial hagiography of the saint. Within the Basilica itself, there were already four Saint Francis cycles in different media. The oldest of these is on a panel usually dated on stylistic and iconographic grounds to the middle of the thirteenth century, and often attributed to Giunta Pisano.[3] This panel (fig. 91), now in the Treasury Museum of the Sacro Convento, seems always to have been associated with the Lower Church. The earliest record of the painting is a description by Fra Ludovico of Pietralunga of about 1570.[4] By that date the panel was hanging above the doorway to the sacristy in the chapel of Saint John the Baptist at the end of the south transept. But this could not have been its original location, as the Baptist chapel was not constructed until *c.*1300. The Treasury panel features two narrative scenes to either side of a central, standing figure of Saint Francis. All four scenes depict post-mortem miracles. In the lower left is the cure of the cripple Bartholomew of Narni, which probably occurred at one of the natural springs near Narni in southern Umbria. The other scenes all depict miracles occurring at the tomb of Saint Francis. On the upper left, a girl with a twisted neck is cured on the day of Saint Francis's burial in San Giorgio, while the two scenes on the right-hand side of the panel feature exorcisms and healings at the high altar of the Lower Church of San Francesco, following the translation in 1230 of the holy body into its subterranean tomb. But not one of these scenes is repeated in the Upper Church cycle.[5] Indeed, the cycle's entire post-mortem section is highly innovative and singular: seven of the eight scenes following the *Death of Saint Francis* seem to have had no visual precedent, and two of those (the *Lamentation of the Clares* and the *Resurrection of a Woman from Benevento*) never appear again in a fresco cycle.[6]

Much more important models for the Upper Church murals are the two Saint Francis cycles at Assisi attributed to the Maestro di San Francesco. The first is frescoed on the south wall of the nave of the Lower Church, and probably dates to the mid-1260s; the second is in the stained glass of the Upper Church nave. All of the scenes in the Lower Church frescoes reappear in the Upper Church: *Saint Francis Renouncing his Father*, the *Dream of Pope Innocent III*, the *Preaching to the Birds*, the *Stigmatization* and the *Death of Saint Francis*. It was not only the content of this cycle but also its arrangement, facing a Passion cycle on the opposite wall, that was a vital precedent for the pictorial programme of the Upper Church. We shall return to this in more detail below. For now it may be noted that the duplication of the Lower Church Saint Francis scenes probably indicates that at the time the Upper Church cycle was being planned the forthcoming expansion and reconstruction of the Lower Church was at the very least anticipated, if not already under way. When the project was put into action, the Maestro di San Francesco murals had to be sacrificed in the interests of adding a series of side chapels to either side of the nave, which necessitated the piercing of its walls and the semi-demolition of the frescoes.[7] The artist's second Saint Francis cycle, in the stained glass, has survived intact. Only one of its five scenes was rejected by the planners of the Upper Church fresco cycle: generally identified as the cure of Bartholomew of Narni, it is the sole post-mortem episode in the window.[8] Of the four stories that reappear on the walls of the Upper Church, three had already been painted in the Lower Church fresco cycle (the *Dream of Pope Innocent III*, the *Preaching to the Birds* and the *Stigmatization*), but one, *Saint Francis before the Crucifix in San Damiano* (fig. 92), was par-

92 Maestro di San Francesco, *Saint Francis before the Crucifix in San Damiano*, *c.*1275–85, stained glass, fourth bay, north wall of the nave, Upper Church, Basilica of San Francesco.

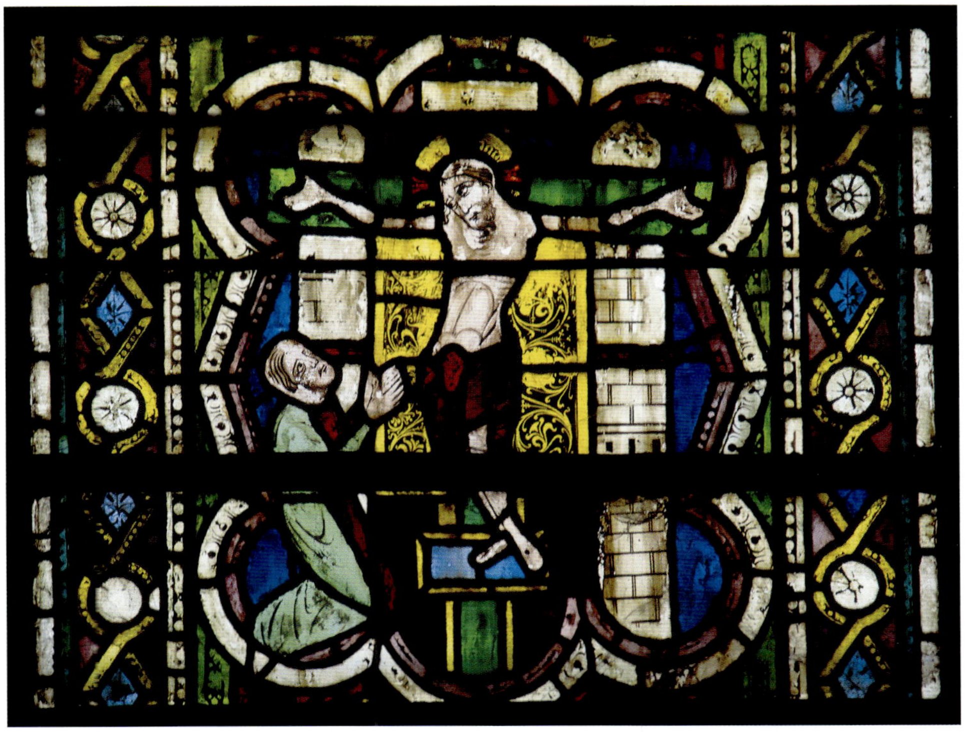

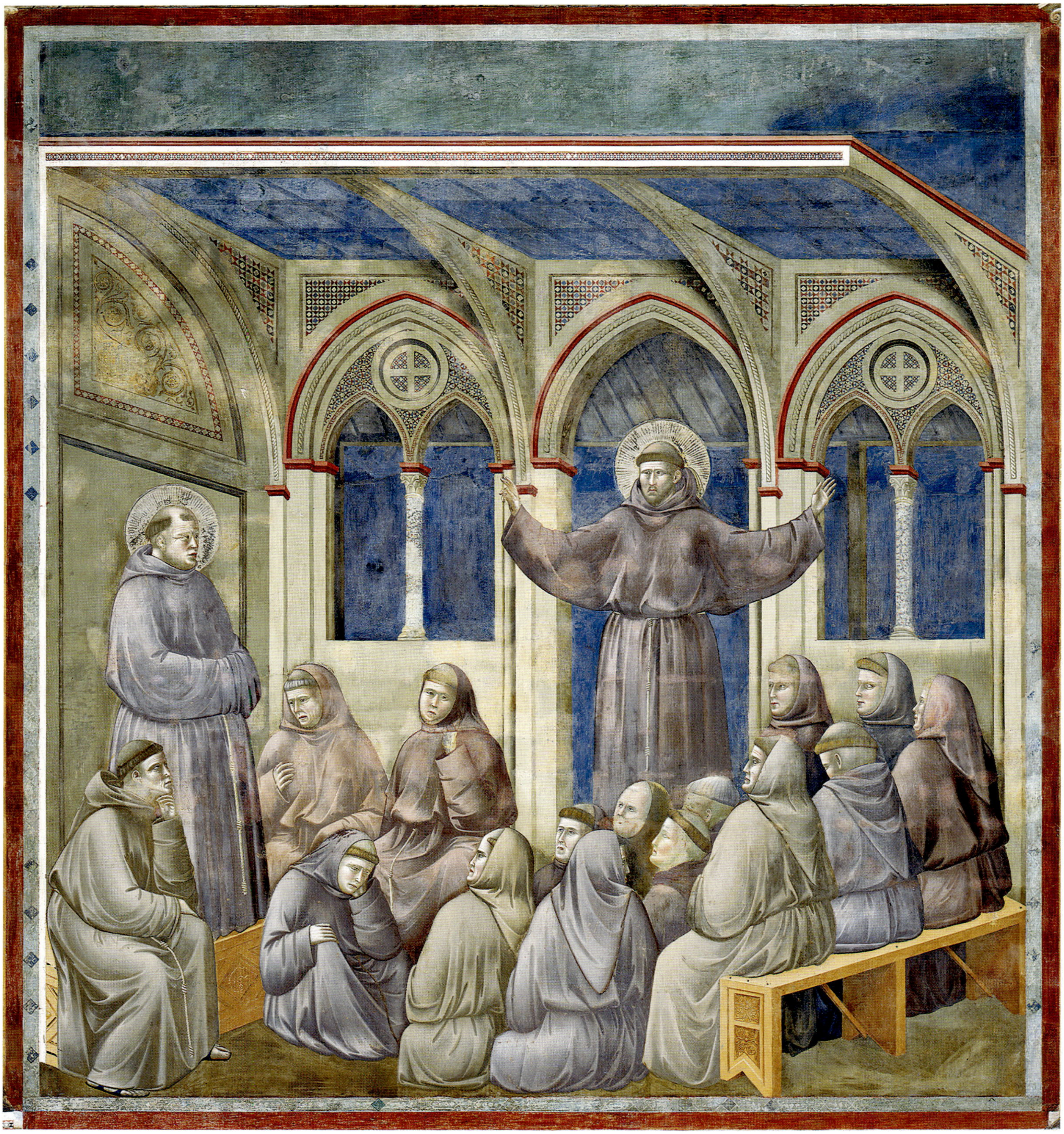

93 *Apparition at Arles*, Scene 18 of the Saint Francis cycle, *c.*1290–96, fresco, south wall of the nave, Upper Church, Basilica of San Francesco.

ticular to the glass. Another scene included in the Upper Church fresco cycle, the *Apparition at Arles*, had a precedent in the same stained-glass window, as part of the Saint Anthony of Padua cycle in the right lancet (see Chapter 3).

One can only speculate about the possible influence of the Saint Francis scenes depicted on the lost orphrey or *paliotto* presented to Assisi by Nicholas IV, which would have been displayed on one of the Basilica's two high altars after its arrival in the late summer of 1289. As discussed in Chapter 2, all we know of its iconography comes from the engravings in Niccolò Catalano's book, along with their accompanying descriptions.[9] The engravings show several figures of friars, copied from two separate parts of the orphrey. The first set of figures clearly comes from a *Death of Saint Francis* (see fig. 32): as Frugoni pointed out, the embroidered scene included the half-length, frontal figure of the saint's soul ascending on a little cloud, but with his hands together rather than displayed, palms out, to the viewer as they are in the Upper Church fresco.[10] Without any evidence about the position of the death scene on the orphrey, we cannot know whether any post-mortem stories followed it.

The comparison between the second engraving and the Assisi cycle is less close, but Frugoni argued that it represents the left side of an *Apparition at Arles*, the trio of figures in the lower section representing some of the friars gathered in the chapter house, and the friar above them the preaching Saint Anthony (see fig. 33). In the Assisi fresco, Anthony stands raised above his brethren, with his joined hands similarly covered by his wide sleeves (fig. 93).[11] If Frugoni was correct, then Nicholas IV's gift could have provided a most important model; the only other surviving version of the Arles story in a Saint Francis cycle is on the Bardi dossal in Florence, where it is depicted in a different fashion altogether. However, as noted above, there was a precedent for the story in the Upper Church in the Saint Anthony window, where the standing saint also has his joined hands covered by his wide sleeves (see fig. 81). Also, the fact that the engraved figure is depicted within a quatrefoil (described as a 'tondo angolato') is a slightly puzzling complication. Could this figure have been an independent portrait, possibly Saint Anthony, inserted between the narrative scenes? If Frugoni's identifications of both scenes are accepted, it would seem that Nicholas's orphrey emphasized Saint Francis as an *alter Christus*, a theme that would be central to the subsequent scheme of frescoes in the Upper Church.

It was therefore in the life scenes rather than the post-mortem miracles that previous pictorial cycles of Francis's legend at Assisi exerted an influence on the new Upper Church murals. Nonetheless, the overall impression of the Saint Francis cycle is one of innovation rather than tradition. Of its twenty-eight scenes, sixteen are without any known precedent, while another four scenes had been represented before, but with very different iconographies.[12] We should be a little cautious about taking this numerical analysis at face value, however. Earlier cycles may have been lost, especially from important Franciscan churches in Rome, while the Assisi cycle is so much longer than all but one of the previous surviving versions that a high degree of originality is inevitable. In addition to the cycles discussed above, six Saint Francis cycles survive on Duecento panels. The only one to contain more than eight scenes is the Bardi dossal in Santa Croce, Florence (fig. 94). Its programme of twenty narrative episodes provides the most meaningful and revealing comparison with the Assisi cycle. The general narrative shape of the two cycles is remarkably similar. Both the Bardi dossal and the Assisi frescoes devote almost exactly one quarter of their cycles to Francis's early life and conversion, up to and including the approval of the Rule; half to his life as a friar, concluding with his death; and a quarter to post-mortem scenes. Yet within this structure the choice of individual scenes differs greatly. Only nine of the twenty episodes from the Bardi dossal appear in the Assisi cycle, and in two of those the iconography is completely new.

The Saint Francis Cycle and Bonaventure

One thing – perhaps the only thing – on which all Assisi scholars agree is that the primary textual source for the Saint Francis cycle is Bonaventure's *Legenda maior*. In 1260 the general chapter of the Franciscan Order, meeting in Narbonne, instructed Minister General Bonaventure of Bagnoregio to compile a new life of Saint Francis. In 1263 Bonaventure presented his completed *Legenda maior* to the subsequent general chapter in Pisa. Three years later, the general chapter of Paris made the *Legenda maior* the official life, directing all earlier texts to be removed from the Order's convents.[13] Before 1266 the most important hagiographical works used by the Order were the three legends written by Thomas of Celano: the *Vita prima* of *c.*1228–9, the *Vita*

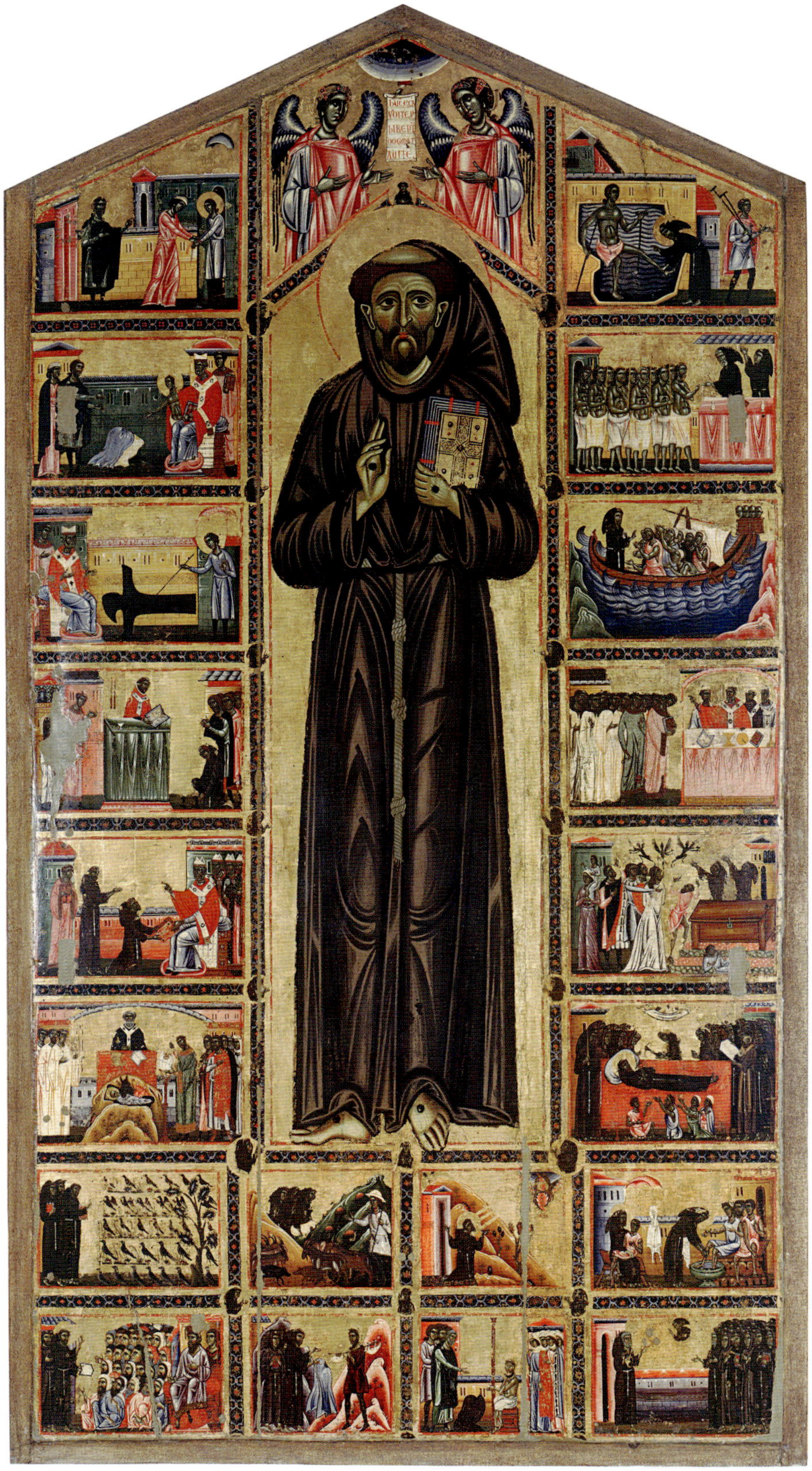

94 Florentine school, Bardi dossal, mid-thirteenth century, tempera and gold on wood (234 cm × 127 cm), Bardi chapel, Santa Croce, Florence.

secunda of *c.*1245–7 and the *Tractatus de miraculis* of *c.*1250–52. A measure of the efficiency with which the Paris general chapter's instruction was carried out is the small number of surviving manuscripts of Celano's works: twenty manuscripts containing the *Vita prima*, or parts of it; nine containing the *Vita secunda* (seven of which are only fragmentary); and only one complete text of the *Tractatus*.[14] In contrast there are around 400 extant manuscripts of the *Legenda maior* from the thirteenth and fourteenth centuries.[15]

Even so, we should not necessarily take it for granted that the *Legenda maior* was the only hagiographical text consulted at Assisi. Curiously, despite the order to destroy earlier *legende*, the versified life of Saint Francis composed by Henri d'Avranches *c.*1230–35 and based on Celano's *Vita prima* was apparently preserved in the Sacro Convento.[16] The library also holds one of the two complete surviving copies of the *Vita secunda*, albeit a late fourteenth-century manuscript whose Assisi provenance is uncertain.[17] While fragments of the *Vita secunda* preserved in Perugia and Poppi offer tantalizingly shadowy clues as to whether any of Celano's texts could have been available to leading friars at Assisi at an earlier date, the Saint Francis cycle provides evidence of its own.[18] All the detail in the *Canonization* scene (fig. 95), for example, could not have come from Bonaventure: the minister general eschewed the colourful reportage of Celano's first life, remarking briskly that the solemn ceremony 'would be too long to describe'.[19] One should, however, be wary of assuming that direct consultation of either Celano's or Henri d'Avranches's texts would have been necessary to design the *Canonization* mural. The more senior friars in the Order in 1288 would have been old enough to have taken their vows before 1266, and therefore would have learned about Francis primarily through Celano's lives. Removal of these books from the convent did not mean the eradication of their contents from the memory, especially a well-trained one. But in any case, the canonization of Saint Francis had taken place in Assisi and the details of such a famous and prestigious local event are likely also to have been passed down orally.

The Franciscans who planned the nave frescoes did not limit themselves to hagiography. As we shall demonstrate in the following chapters, they also drew on their knowledge of a broad range of theological and devotional material, from both before and after 1266. We have already seen one such example in the Upper Church nave: the image of Saint Francis in the 'Angel Window' was most likely devised with a knowledge of James of Milan's *Stimulus amoris* (see p. 79 and fig. 79). Amy Neff convincingly argued that the *Meditatio pauperis in solitudine*, a theological and spiritual treatise written *c.*1282–3 by the Franciscan lector and theologian John of Wales, elucidates the meaning of the images in the third and fourth bays of the north wall.[20] One important set of pre-Bonaventuran texts to survive unscathed was the liturgy for Francis's Office and Mass, which all friars would have sung every year on his feast day and its octave. Papal bulls were another form of text that both preceded and postdated Bonaventure, from *Mira circa nos* (Gregory IX's bull of canonization) to the bulls of Pope Nicholas IV. These were of great authority, and many were preserved at Assisi.[21]

Notwithstanding evidence for the use of other sources, there are many good reasons for characterizing the Saint Francis cycle as Bonaventuran. The first is the simple fact that each of the frescoes has beneath it an explanatory Latin titulus, which is based (often closely) on Bonaventure's text in the *Legenda maior*.[22] In addition, not only are all the episodes depicted to be found there, but they also represent a fairly balanced selection from across its sixteen chapters. Furthermore, the layout of scenes closely follows the order in which the episodes appear in the text (fig. 96). Only three of the scenes in the cycle are placed out of their Bonaventuran sequence – most significantly the two on the counterfaçade, which will be the subject of Chapter 7.

It is important, though, to define more precisely the term 'Bonaventuran'. A comparison between the twenty-eight-scene Assisi cycle and the twenty-scene Bardi dossal is instructive here. Because only nine scenes are common to both works, some scholars have sought to understand the substantial differences between the content of the two cycles by arguing that the Florentine panel (unlike the Assisi cycle) was painted before Bonaventure wrote the *Legenda maior*, and that all its scenes were drawn from Celano's lives.[23] Others have taken a contrary position, insisting that at least some of the Bardi dossal's scenes depend on Bonaventure, and consequently dating the painting after 1263.[24] Such diverse views are possible only because Bonaventure drew heavily on Thomas's earlier texts when he compiled the *Legenda maior,* some thirty-five years after the death of Saint Francis. Consequently, the legends of Bonaventure and Celano share many of the same stories. This is the case for two episodes that appear on the Bardi dossal but not in the Assisi cycle. In the first of these, the young Francis kneels to discard his

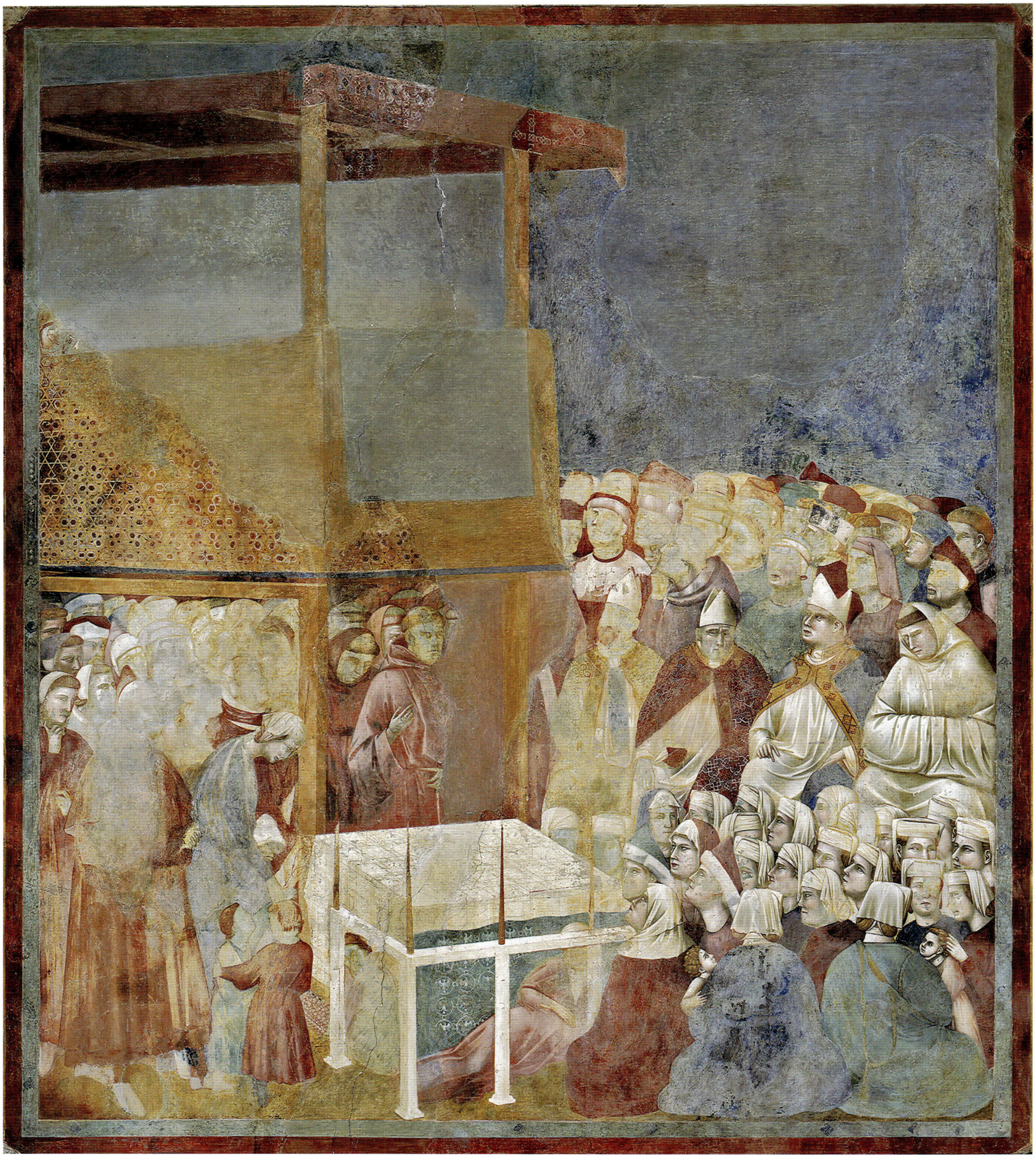

95 *Canonization*, Scene 24 of the Saint Francis cycle, *c.*1290–96, fresco, south wall of the nave, Upper Church, Basilica of San Francesco.

facing page 96 Disposition of fresco cycles in the nave of the Upper Church and correspondence of Saint Francis scenes with Bonaventure's *Legenda maior*.

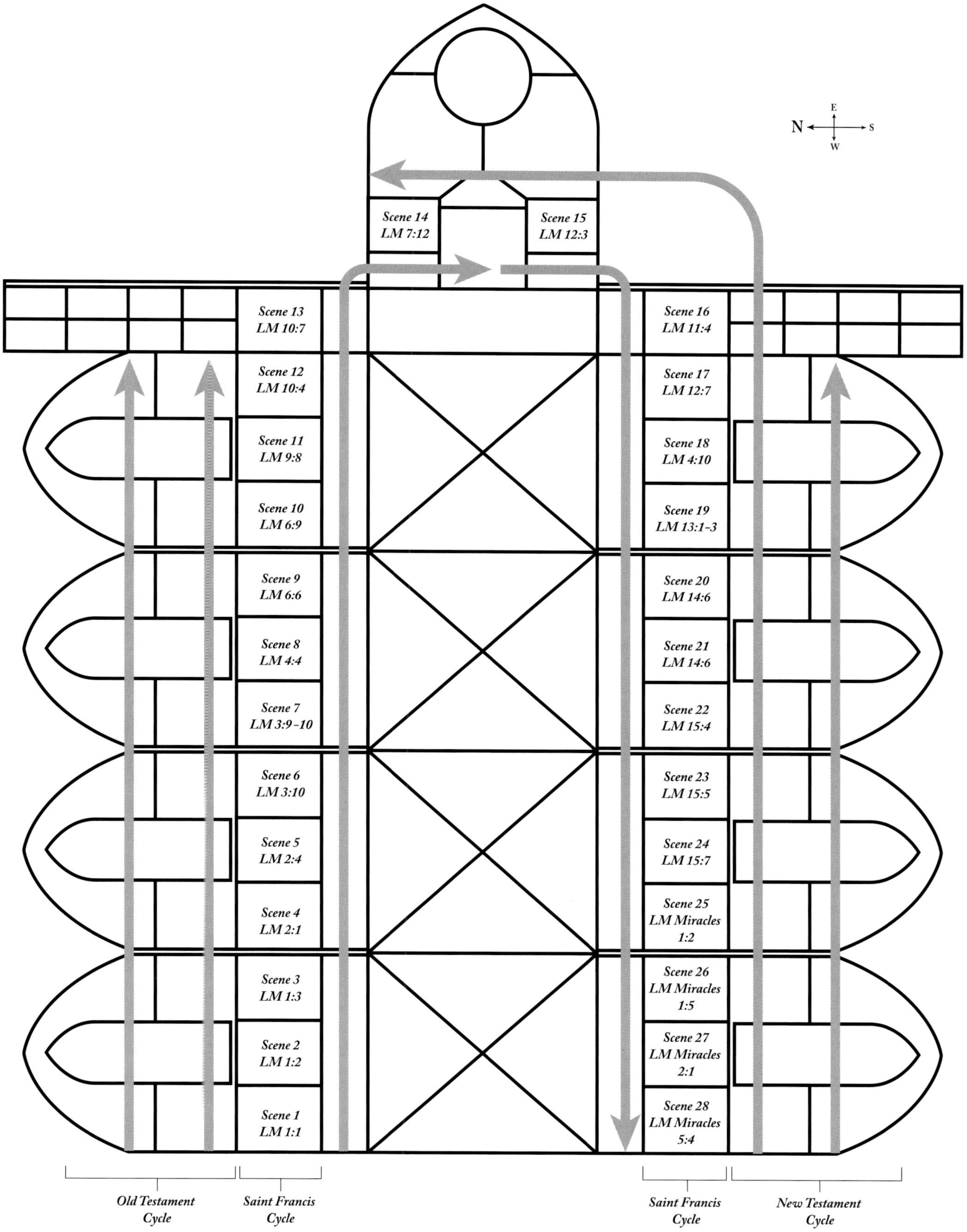
N
E
S
W
Scene 14
LM 7:12
Scene 15
LM 12:3
Scene 13
LM 10:7
Scene 12
LM 10:4
Scene 11
LM 9:8
Scene 10
LM 6:9
Scene 9
LM 6:6
Scene 8
LM 4:4
Scene 7
LM 3:9–10
Scene 6
LM 3:10
Scene 5
LM 2:4
Scene 4
LM 2:1
Scene 3
LM 1:3
Scene 2
LM 1:2
Scene 1
LM 1:1
Scene 16
LM 11:4
Scene 17
LM 12:7
Scene 18
LM 4:10
Scene 19
LM 13:1–3
Scene 20
LM 14:6
Scene 21
LM 14:6
Scene 22
LM 15:4
Scene 23
LM 15:5
Scene 24
LM 15:7
Scene 25
LM Miracles
1:2
Scene 26
LM Miracles
1:5
Scene 27
LM Miracles
2:1
Scene 28
LM Miracles
5:4
Old Testament
Cycle
Saint Francis
Cycle
Saint Francis
Cycle
New Testament
Cycle

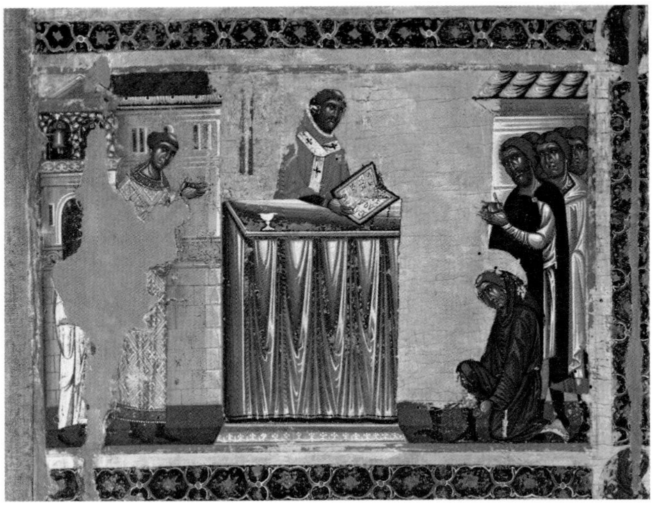

97 Florentine school, *Saint Francis Removing his Shoes*, Bardi dossal, mid-thirteenth century, tempera and gold on wood, Bardi chapel, Santa Croce, Florence.

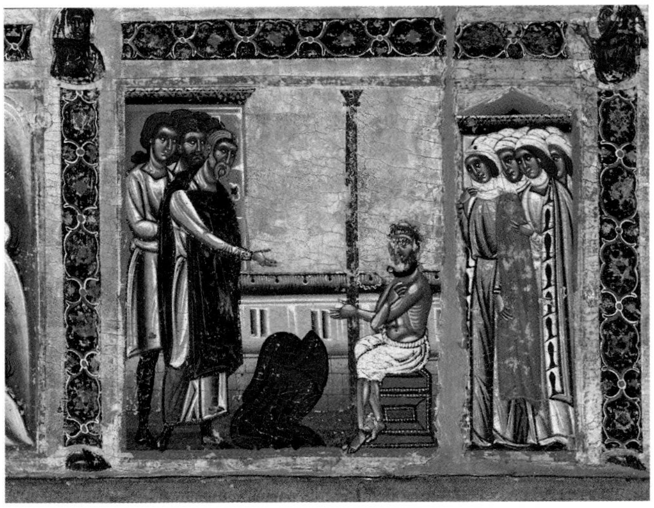

98 Florentine school, *Saint Francis Chained to a Pillory*, Bardi dossal, mid-thirteenth century, tempera and gold on wood, Bardi chapel, Santa Croce, Florence.

shoes as he hears a sermon on Christ's exhortation to his apostles to go out to preach without any money, or an extra tunic, or shoes or a staff (fig. 97).[25] In the second, Francis is shown stripped and chained to a pillory, as a self-imposed penance for some perceived sin of hypocrisy (fig. 98).[26] Since Bonaventure retained both stories, the omission of these scenes at Assisi cannot be ascribed to their not being Bonaventuran, if 'Bonaventuran' is defined simply to mean 'contained in the *Legenda maior*'.

A more convincing explanation emerges through a closer examination of the relationship between Bonaventure and Celano. In order to produce a single text of manageable size, Bonaventure had to cull a good deal of Celano's biographical material. It has been calculated that he discarded around sixty episodes from the *Vita prima* and 120 from the *Vita secunda*.[27] This was not done randomly. By excising material, Bonaventure systematically remodelled Francis's life. He played down several themes, including the saint's severe asceticism; his strictest observance of poverty and hatred for money; his distrust of books and study; and any association with women, including Saint Clare.[28] Similarly, the Franciscan friars who planned the Assisi fresco cycle made their selections from the *Legenda maior* not casually, but thoughtfully, displaying a profound understanding of Bonaventure's intellectual conception of Saint Francis. The same themes that had been played down in the *Legenda maior* were also omitted from the murals. Consequently, there was no place in the Upper Church for the Bardi dossal's scenes of Francis discarding his shoes in literal imitation of Christ's poverty, or his penance chained to the pillory. The Assisi cycle can be described as 'Bonaventuran' in a deeper sense: its iconographic programme displays a profound understanding of Bonaventure's overall vision of what was most important about Francis's life, miracles and sanctity.

The close relationship between the Assisi cycle and Bonaventure becomes even more apparent when we turn to what is original in the *Legenda maior*. In contrast to the substantial amount of biographical detail that the minister general excised, he added very little that was new: only forty episodes in total.[29] Three of the twenty-eight scenes in the Saint Francis cycle – the *Homage of a Simple Man*, *Saint Francis in Ecstasy* and the *Dream of Pope Gregory IX*, all depicted here for the first time – are taken from this small cache of exclusively Bonaventuran material. This is a disproportionately high number. Each of these three scenes, we shall argue, deals with themes that are central not only to Bonaventure's concept of Saint Francis, but also to the preoccupations of the Franciscans at the time the cycle was planned and executed, and to the overall programme of the nave frescoes.

The cycle is Bonaventuran in another sense as well. Bonaventure's intellectual achievement in the *Legenda maior* was to reshape Francis's life within a theological framework, presenting it as a progressive mystical journey towards evangelical perfection, wisdom and union with God. At the heart of this concept is the cross. Bonaventure saw in Francis's early life six manifestations or visions of the cross, all of which prefigure the seventh and final one, the stigmatization.[30] This key Bonaventuran thread is woven through the Saint Francis cycle, which includes four of the seven visions: the palace of arms (Scene 3), the speaking crucifix in San Damiano (Scene 4), the apparition at Arles (Scene 18) and the receipt of the stigmata (Scene 19). Indeed, the supreme importance of the stigmatization of Saint Francis lies at the heart of the iconographic programme of the nave, as we shall argue in Chapter 5.

Story-Telling, Theology and the Iconographic Plan

Any analysis of the content and meaning of the frescoes in the nave of the Upper Church must begin by acknowledging the major contribution of two books, both published in the 1970s, which laid the foundations for much of the current scholarship on the subject, including our own. The first is Alastair Smart's *The Assisi Problem and the Art of Giotto*, published in 1971, which, despite the title, is not a book about Giotto but a study of the Saint Francis cycle. Through a close study of the compositions of the Saint Francis scenes, Smart sought to characterize the aesthetic principles underlying their pictorial language, arguing that it was impossible to consider design and meaning separately.

He believed the cycle was planned to form distinct groups within each bay. The spectator is encouraged to view each bay as a coherent unit by the illusionistic cornices running horizontally above and below the Saint Francis cycle, whose perspective always converges to the centre of the bay. Within each bay (and regardless of changes of artist), the two outer scenes are balanced around the middle one, creating a symmetrical arrangement that Smart likened to 'a triptych, with the central scene as the main panel and the outer scenes as the wings'.[31] In the bays with four scenes, the system had to be adapted, to create an inner and an outer pair. Each unit was further bound together through a broad rising and falling movement, created through the use within the compositions of strong diagonals, which ascend from the left towards the centre and descend again to the right.

Smart believed that the Saint Francis cycle is misunderstood if it is seen as 'mere story-telling': the underlying theme of Bonaventure's *Legenda maior* is 'the theological significance of the saint's life, rather than the drama of that life in itself, and it is this most important aspect of the Assisi cycle that brings it so close in spirit to its principal literary source'.[32] He convincingly argued that the aesthetic principles he had identified were intended to assist in the realization of a theological programme.[33] The structure of the cycle is built on relationships between the scenes within each bay, so that compositional analogies and thematic parallels are constantly interwoven. For example, Scene 4 of the cycle, on the left of the second bay on the north side, depicts Saint Francis inside the dilapidated San Damiano, being called by Christ to repair the church, a calling that is spiritually fulfilled on the right of the bay, where Pope Innocent III sees the saint supporting another falling church, Saint John Lateran in Rome. But Smart also argued that the cycle utilized the physical space of the Upper Basilica and that, in every bay, meaningful comparisons are deliberately set up across the nave, from the north wall to the south. In the second bay, for instance, on the north wall the young Francis is scorned by the people of Assisi when he renounces his father (Scene 5), while directly opposite he is acclaimed by them at his canonization (Scene 24).

Although he doubted whether a medieval viewer would have considered the single row of Saint Francis scenes more worthy of attention than the sublime biblical cycles in the upper two registers, Smart argued that the Franciscan scenes 'could never have been related very closely to the Old and New Testament scenes above them'.[34] For him, the cycle was essentially self-contained. But Padre Gerhard Ruf, in his 1974 study of the Upper Church nave frescoes, took a more holistic view. As a Franciscan friar who lived for fifty years in the Assisi convent, Ruf had little or no interest in the attributional debates about the frescoes in the mother church of his Order. Rather, he was motivated by the desire to explain their religious content to pilgrims and tourists visiting the Basilica. Ruf saw the nave frescoes as a unified whole and he aimed to demonstrate what he saw as an indisputable fact ('il fatto indiscutibile'), the strict theological ties between the Old and New Testament scenes and the frescoes of the life of Saint Francis.[35] He argued that the biblical cycles in the upper tiers of the nave were arranged in strict typological concordance – that is, according to the theological method of understanding the Old Testament primarily in terms of prophecy or prefiguration of the New. The upper register on the north wall, from the creation of the world to Cain's murder of Abel, recounts the Fall of man away from God, as a result of the sin of Adam. In the sequence along the upper row of the south wall, Christ is presented as the antithesis, the 'new Adam', whose Incarnation begins the process of redeeming original sin and leading humanity back to God. While the characters from Genesis in the first tier are sinful figures, the Old Testament patriarchs in the second are virtuous ones; they are no longer antitheses but prefigurations (or 'types') of the adult Christ who is depicted in the Ministry and Passion scenes on the opposite wall. The Saint Francis cycle adds a third dimension to this typology, according to Ruf, with the scenes from the saint's life being intimately connected to the biblical stories in the registers above them, and framed in profoundly theological terms.[36]

Smart's theological structure for the Saint Francis cycle proposes meaningful links between groups of scenes, both within each bay and across from one wall to the other. To this horizontal nexus Ruf adds vertical and diagonal links between the separate narrative cycles. Both hypotheses assume a great deal of planning before any painter laid brush to wall, but Ruf's argument goes further in that it requires the entire pictorial programme of the nave to have been planned as a single unit. Although we agree that the nave scheme was sketched out as a unified whole from the start, we do not believe that this involved devising meaningful links between every scene, in every direction, as Ruf proposed. Rather, the planning must have started with some major decisions about key parts of the programme; less crucial links could have been worked out by the friars and the artists as the work proceeded; and, at a third level, additional links may have emerged fortuitously. The end result was a pictorial programme of light and shade, in which the ties between the different tiers are more emphatic in some places than others, rather than forming a uniform grid of one-to-one connections.

Roman Prototypes: The Old and New Testament Cycles

What evidence is there that the biblical scenes at Assisi were selected and positioned to create meaningful links with the Saint Francis cycle below them? Hans Belting has characterized the biblical cycles in the Upper Church as 'a truly Roman programme in a truly Roman space'.[37] Specifically, they drew on the extensive early Christian cycles of Old and New Testament murals in the papal basilicas of Old Saint Peter's and San Paolo fuori le Mura. At first sight, this may seem a surprising response to *Reducentes*, given Pope Nicholas IV's lack of interest in these particular basilicas (see Chapter 1). But viewed in a broader historical context, such a strategy was only to be expected. The tradition of imitating the pictorial programme of Saint Peter's had been established at San Paolo as early as the fifth century. This practice had become particularly prevalent during the twelfth and thirteenth centuries, when more than a dozen Italian churches commissioned extensive Old and New Testament cycles based on these Roman models, but it also continued after Assisi (for instance, in L'Annunziata at Cori).[38] In comparison, there is a virtual absence of copies of the decorative programmes of Saint John Lateran and Santa Maria Maggiore, the two papal basilicas favoured by Nicholas IV.

For churches wishing to assert their relationship with Rome and the papacy, the ancient fresco cycles in Saint Peter's and San Paolo together represented the great authoritative models. A decade before the nave scheme was devised at Assisi, Cimabue's frescoes devoted to Saints Peter and Paul in the north transept had already emulated the cycle in the portico of Saint Peter's, thereby signalling the special status of the Upper Church as a papal chapel. The same ideological strategy was continued in the nave. Saint Peter's and San Paolo were the most important prototypes not just for the Roman papal basilica, but also for the apostolic burial church (a status that the Lateran and Santa Maria Maggiore could not claim). This was particularly important for Assisi, which was the burial church of Saint Francis. For all these reasons, therefore, it was to Saint Peter's and San Paolo that Assisi addressed itself. At least some of the friars involved in the planning for the nave scheme must have spent periods of time in Rome, and so presumably would have been familiar with the pictures in Saint Peter's and San Paolo. But to produce detailed copies – or careful adaptations – of the compositions of particular scenes, they would surely have relied on the more specialist knowledge and guidance of the artists employed on the nave frescoes.[39] Many had previous experience of painting in Rome and some, among them perhaps Jacopo Torriti, may even have worked on the restoration campaigns in Saint Peter's and San Paolo that had been carried out under the patronage of Pope Nicholas III in the late 1270s.

We do not know exactly how close the iconography of the frescoes in San Francesco was to its Roman antecedents, since neither basilica has survived in either its early Christian or its medieval state. The last part of Old Saint Peter's was demolished at the start of the seventeenth century to make way for the monumental Vatican basilica that still stands today. San Paolo survived much longer, but was ravaged by fire in 1823 and subsequently rebuilt. For both basilicas, our knowledge of the frescoes depends on seventeenth-century copies and descriptions. Although the record they supply is incomplete, they nonetheless provide us with a considerable amount of information, allowing several important conclusions to be drawn.

The frescoes in Saint Peter's are known only from two watercolours by Domenico Tasselli, and descriptions made between 1608 and 1619 by the apostolic notary Giacomo Grimaldi.[40] At that stage, a little less than half of the original nave was still standing: of the forty-six Old Testament paintings originally disposed in two tiers on the right wall, twenty-two remained intact, and Grimaldi was able to describe all but three of them (fig. 99). The surviving section of wall contained the stories of Noah, Abraham, Isaac and Jacob in the upper tier, with eleven scenes from Exodus in the register below, all dealing with Moses in Egypt. We can therefore assume that the destroyed part of the nave, to the left of the surviving section, must have contained in its upper tier the opening narratives of the Genesis cycle (the Creation, Adam and Eve, Cain and Abel), with an extensive sequence of Joseph scenes below. That assumption is largely based on the evidence from San Paolo, whose own Old Testament cycle, painted in the fifth century, was the first copy of the earlier one in Saint Peter's. The frescoes in San Paolo were later restored (or repainted) by a team of painters led by Pietro Cavallini in a campaign that was instigated by Pope Nicholas III (1277–80) and probably completed by 1285, the date inscribed on the new ciborium sculpted by Arnolfo di Cambio.[41] The iconography is well documented through a set of watercolours that were made for Francesco Barberini in 1634 and a sketch by Seroux d'Agincourt; from these copies, the general agreement of the San Paolo Old Testament cycle with that of Saint Peter's is apparent.[42]

In comparison with the extensive Old Testament cycles in Saint Peter's (forty-six scenes) and San Paolo (forty-two), the Assisi cycle is very short, containing only sixteen scenes. Most of the other known medieval cycles based on Saint Peter's are also more extensive than Assisi's: for example, Santa Maria Immacolata, Ceri (sixteen scenes containing twenty-five stories); San Pietro in Valle, Ferentillo (about thirty scenes); the chapel of Saint Thomas Becket in Anagni cathedral (more than twenty); San Giovanni a Porta Latina, Rome (eighteen); and, later than Assisi, L'Annunziata at Cori (twenty-nine).[43] One might reasonably argue that the truncation of the cycle in San Francesco was an inevitable consequence of the architectural form of the Upper Church. The lengthy narratives in the Roman basilicas were able to run unbroken along the expanses of wall above the colonnades of the naves; they did not have to negotiate the large windows and heavily articulated bays of a Gothic church (see fig. 89).[44]

Given that the cycle had to be shortened, how did the Franciscans at Assisi set about selecting their sixteen scenes? Here the comparison with San Paolo (and, through it, Saint Peter's) is instructive. In San Paolo, the first chapter of Genesis was represented in ten scenes, from the Creation to Cain and Abel. The upper register of the Old Testament cycle at Assisi replicates this closely, dropping just two of the episodes. In contrast, the rest of the cycle, which ran to thirty-two scenes in San Paolo, had to be dramatically reduced to fit the eight fields of the lower tier. Some major subjects are omitted: both Saint Peter's and San Paolo contained at least eleven scenes devoted to Moses, who does not appear at all in San Francesco, where the cycle confines itself to Genesis. Nor was it just a matter of excision, since of Assisi's eight episodes two seem not to have appeared in either basilica, probably being newly devised for their particular Franciscan setting. One was *Joseph in Egypt*, which the Franciscans introduced in preference to any of eight other Joseph scenes that were depicted in San Paolo, for instance.[45] The result is a tightly edited and meticulously arranged sequence that is unique to Assisi. Each bay contains two scenes focusing on a single Old Testament figure – Noah, Abraham, Isaac and Joseph – to create what is best described as a cycle of the patriarchs. We believe that Ruf was essentially correct to see these four patriarchs as having been selected in order to provide parallels with the life of Saint Francis in the frescoes below.[46] The Saint Francis cycle can be properly understood only if it is analysed not just as a self-contained narrative, but in relation to the biblical cycles above it, and, more particularly, to the scenes in the register directly above it. (These relationships are the subject of chapters 5–7.)

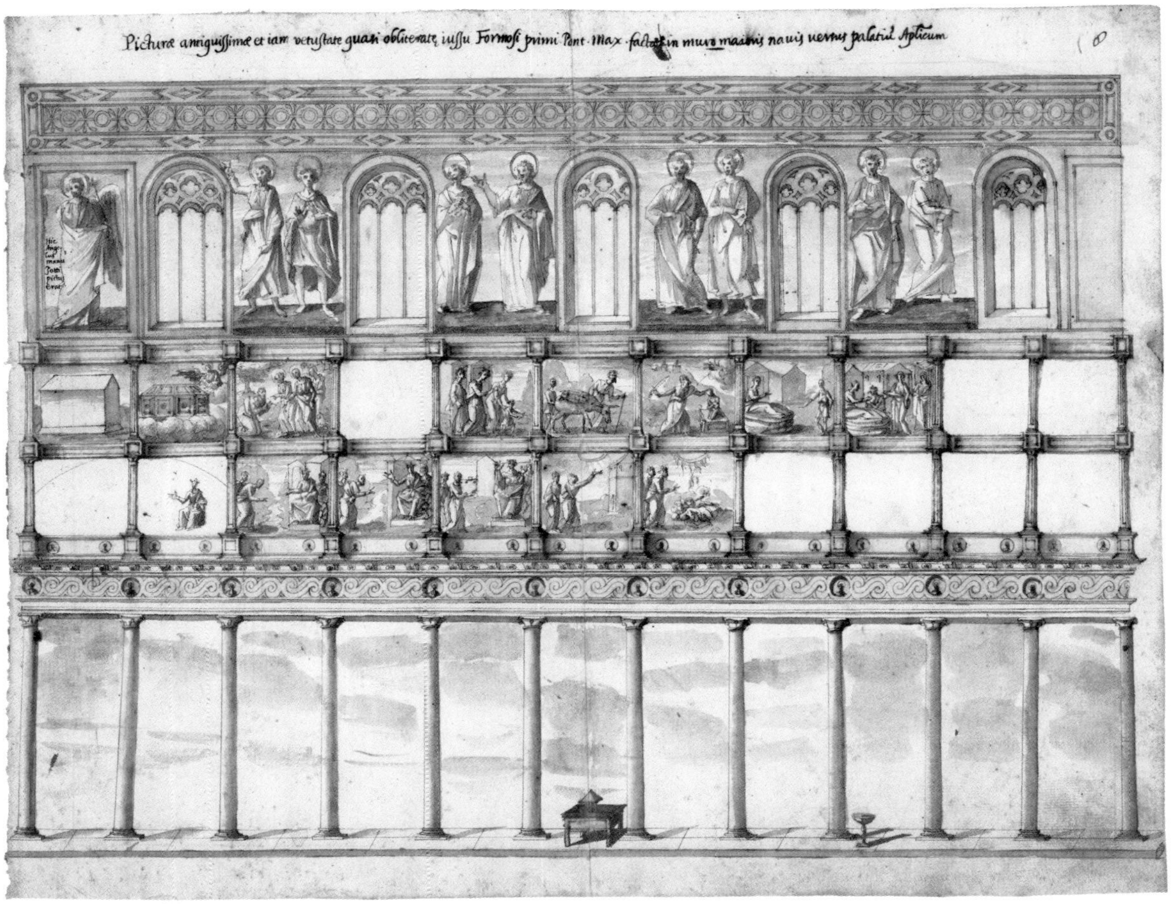

99 Domenico Tasselli, copy of Old Testament scenes in the nave of Old Saint Peter's in Rome, *c.*1619, watercolour, Vatican City, Biblioteca Apostolica Vaticana, Archivio Capitolare di San Pietro, A64 ter., fol. 13r.

The Genesis cycle at Assisi faces a New Testament cycle on the south wall of the nave. The arrangement is the same as in Saint Peter's, but no detailed comparisons can be made of the content, because our knowledge of Saint Peter's is so limited. Of a probable forty-three scenes, Grimaldi could identify only six: the *Baptism of Christ*, the *Raising of Lazarus*, an oversized *Crucifixion*, the *Harrowing of Hell* (or *Anastasis*) and two scenes of Christ appearing to the apostles (fig. 100).[47] Unfortunately, the gaps cannot be filled through comparison with San Paolo, where the New Testament cycle was based on the Acts of the Apostles rather than the Gospels, in order to chronicle the life of the titular saint. The dating evidence for the New Testament cycle in Saint Peter's is also complex. A common view, which followed Grimaldi's, used to be that it dated from the time of Pope Formosus (891–6). The tenth-century chronicle of Benedict, a monk of Sant' Andrea in Flumine, near Ponzano Romano, credited Formosus with having renewed all the pictures in the church of Saint Peter's.[48] Much depends on how one interprets 'renovavit'; a plausible scenario is that the New Testament cycle was originally painted in the fifth century, but that interventions and repaintings were carried out in at least two later periods.[49] The enlargement of the *Crucifixion* may have been done during Formosus's campaign, and the *Anastasis* added at the same time. The latter subject has Byzantine origins and is known in Western art only from the seventh century onwards, so it could not figure in a scheme of the fifth century. The frescoes in Saint Peter's were also, like those in San Paolo, restored under Pope Nicholas III in the late 1270s.[50] Even if the *Crucifixion* had been enlarged before Nicholas's time, it was most likely repainted during his campaign. The iconography of the *Christus Patiens*, fixed to the

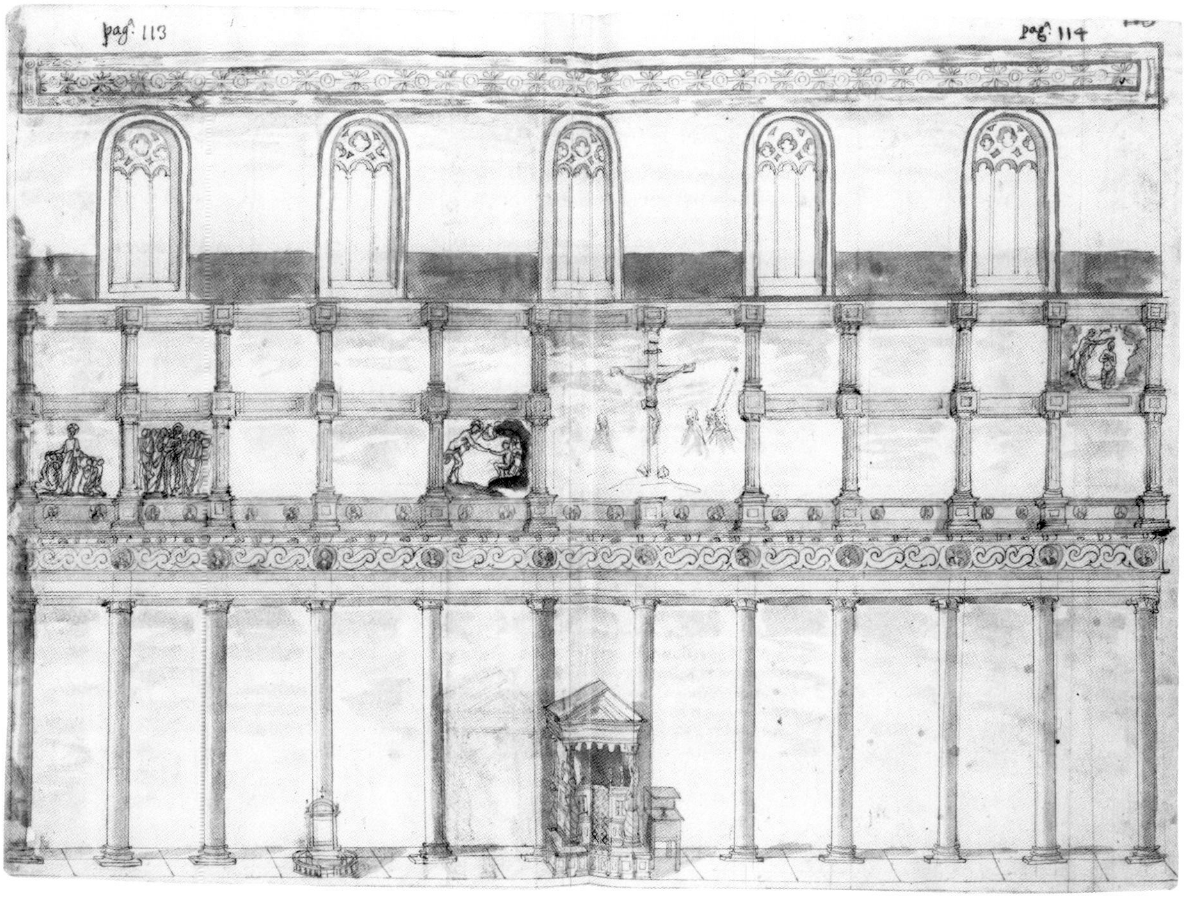

100 Domenico Tasselli, copy of New Testament scenes in the nave of Old Saint Peter's in Rome, *c.*1619, watercolour, Vatican City, Biblioteca Apostolica Vaticana, Ms Barb. lat. 2733, fols 113v–114r.

cross with three nails (assuming Tasselli was accurate in his sketch), was not in use in Italy before the thirteenth century.[51] In this respect, Nicholas III's 'restoration' may have been a response to recent developments in Passion iconography, many of which had been introduced by the Franciscans (see the discussion of the Elias cross in Chapter 3, pp. 63–72).

The position of the *Baptism* on the Tasselli drawing of Saint Peter's is generally agreed to mark the end of the sequence depicting the Infancy of Christ, which would almost certainly have begun with the *Annunciation*: this part of the cycle must therefore have contained thirteen scenes in the upper tier, running from the apse. The problem in the rest of the cycle is how to accommodate the *Crucifixion*, which in its enlarged form straddled both tiers. Tronzo assumed a strict double-parallel sequence, with the Ministry of Christ filling the rest of the top tier (leapfrogging the *Crucifixion*) and then continuing along the lower tier, starting again from the apse and concluding beneath the *Baptism*, a total of twenty-one scenes.[52] However, this would leave only nine scenes to deal with the Passion and Resurrection of Christ. Kessler has instead proposed that the Ministry ran in parallel directly beneath the Infancy (again in thirteen scenes, starting from the apse end), but that the remainder of the cycle, after the *Baptism*, zigzagged up and down over both registers.[53] This would allow for seven Passion and ten post-*Crucifixion* scenes. A factor he cites in support of this slightly clumsy arrangement is that the New Testament cycle in San Paolo may also have been disposed partly as a double parallel and partly as a zigzag.[54]

Despite the uncertainty about the subdivision of the content of the cycle, there is still sufficient evidence to allow one important comparison with Assisi. If the Infancy cycle in Saint Peter's was only thirteen scenes long, then the remaining thirty scenes must all have dealt with the adult Christ. In the Upper Church at Assisi, the Infancy scenes (from the *Annunciation* to the *Baptism*) appear in the upper tier of the south nave wall, while Christ's Ministry, Passion and Resurrection are depicted in the middle tier and on the counter-façade. In other words, the relationship between Assisi and Rome was the same for the New Testament cycles as for the Old: again, it is in the upper register of frescoes that we find the Roman model being most faithfully followed (thirteen scenes being reduced to eight at Assisi), while in the middle tier thirty scenes were compressed down to only ten, which must have entailed making much more carefully considered choices.

The evidence suggests that at Assisi the upper register of the biblical cycles was approached by its planners rather differently from the register below. In the upper tiers, the iconography of the Genesis cycle (certainly) and the Infancy of Christ (probably) closely emulated their Roman papal models, deriving authority from the prototype. The scenes at the top of each wall were intended to call to each other across the space of the nave. It is not necessary to interpret each scene as being specifically typologically paired with its direct counterpart; rather, the story of the Fall in its entirety is reversed in that of the Incarnation. But in the middle tiers of the nave walls, while it is true that the Old Testament patriarchs can and should be understood as prefigurations of Christ, the dialogue was no longer primarily intended to echo across the nave. Instead, the main flow of the discourse is between Saint Francis on the lowest tier of the nave walls and the sacred characters immediately above him – the Old Testament patriarchs on the north wall and Christ on the south. This is not to say that there are never any meaningful parallels across the space of the nave, or between Saint Francis and the biblical figures depicted in the top tiers, but such links are not consistently found. In our opinion, they were a secondary consideration in the overall plan.

Franciscan Biblical Typology and the Precedent of the Lower Church

The two apostolic basilicas in Rome may also have provided Assisi with the ideal prototype for promoting its titular saint through typology. In San Paolo, the narratives depicting the conversion and ministry of the Roman apostle were placed directly opposite the Old Testament cycle. In basing its cycle on Acts rather than the Gospels, the Pauline basilica diverged from the model of Saint Peter's, yet the apparent difference between the two might not have been so great. Kessler argues that the New Testament cycle in the Vatican would have included many scenes featuring Saint Peter, stressing his primacy among the apostles. Furthermore, the long sequence from Exodus on the opposite wall not only depicted Moses (as lawgiver) as a type for Christ but also (as leader of the Chosen People) as a type for Saint Peter, the head of the Church. The same Exodus sequence was repeated in San Paolo, extending the typology to allow the titular saint to be prefigured by Aaron, the brother of Moses. This visual parallel served to promote the idea of an equal partnership between the two papal saints, Peter and Paul; the New Testament cycle at San Paolo ended with their apocryphal meeting.[55] In a sense, by comparing Francis with Old Testament patriarchs in the Assisi frescoes, the friars were comparing him with the two papal apostles as well. The claim that Saint Francis was the direct successor of Saint Peter and Saint Paul was, as we have already seen, boldly proclaimed in Rome in the 1290s through the imagery of the apse mosaics of Santa Maria Maggiore and Saint John Lateran. It would also, more subtly, underlie some of the iconography in the first half of the Saint Francis cycle (see chapters 6 and 7).

At the time when the nave frescoes in the Upper Church at Assisi were being planned in 1288, there was no precedent in Franciscan art for comparing the founder-saint of the Order with Old Testament prophets or patriarchs but, as we shall demonstrate, these typologies already existed in Franciscan writings. The Franciscans at Assisi would certainly have been well disposed to construct such parallels. The friars who probably planned the pictorial scheme in detail all held the kind of administrative posts within the Order for which a high level of theological education was a prerequisite.[56] Given that the Sacro Convento seems to have housed a *studium generale* by 1285, if not before, and also possessed an exceptionally fine library, there would have been plenty of expertise close to hand.[57] But an understanding of typological allusion would not have been restricted to this intellectual elite. A thorough knowledge and understanding of the Bible was a fundamental part of the training of every Franciscan friar, who, even at the lowest level of education in the Order, would have been accustomed to listening to the convent lector reading from a commentary on a biblical book.[58] The dominance of mendicant friars in the production of biblical exegesis during the thirteenth and fourteenth centuries is well known, and Roest points to the importance of 'academic and non-academic biblical teachings as vehicles for innovative religious thought' in the Franciscan Order.[59] But it should not be forgotten that earlier biblical commentaries, in particular that compendium of medieval Christian biblical exegesis, the *Glossa ordinaria*, were still studied and used.[60]

Another insight into the mentality of educated friars is given by sermons. Although their importance for visual cycles has tended to be underestimated (perhaps because the vast majority remains unpublished), sermons on Saint Francis were a means of rapid oral transmission of ideas about the saint, not only from friars to laity, but among the friars themselves.[61] Sermons as a literary genre provide a closer parallel for the Assisi nave programme than Bonaventure's *Legenda maior*. Like pictorial cycles, sermons contain only a small number of biographical episodes and are therefore much more highly selective texts than *vitae*. Secondly – and this is particularly significant for the Upper Church nave – sermons were preached on a biblical text, which then had to be related in a didactic way to the saint. This format would have familiarized both Franciscan preachers and their audiences to the notion of making connections between the Saint Francis cycle and the biblical ones above.

When it came to planning the frescoes on the south wall of the nave and on the counter-façade, where the Saint Francis cycle interlocks with that of Christ, the friars in the Upper Basilica at Assisi would have had no need to look to Rome for inspiration. They already had a precedent for such a scheme beneath their feet: in the nave of the Lower Church, the two Maestro di San Francesco cycles were set out in parallel, with the Saint Francis cycle on the south wall and the Passion cycle on the north. But unlike the biblical narratives in Rome, or the Upper Church, both cycles ran from the entrance towards the high altar, where they terminated at the choir screen (fig. 101).

101 Plan of the fresco cycles in the nave of the Lower Church, Basilica of San Francesco.

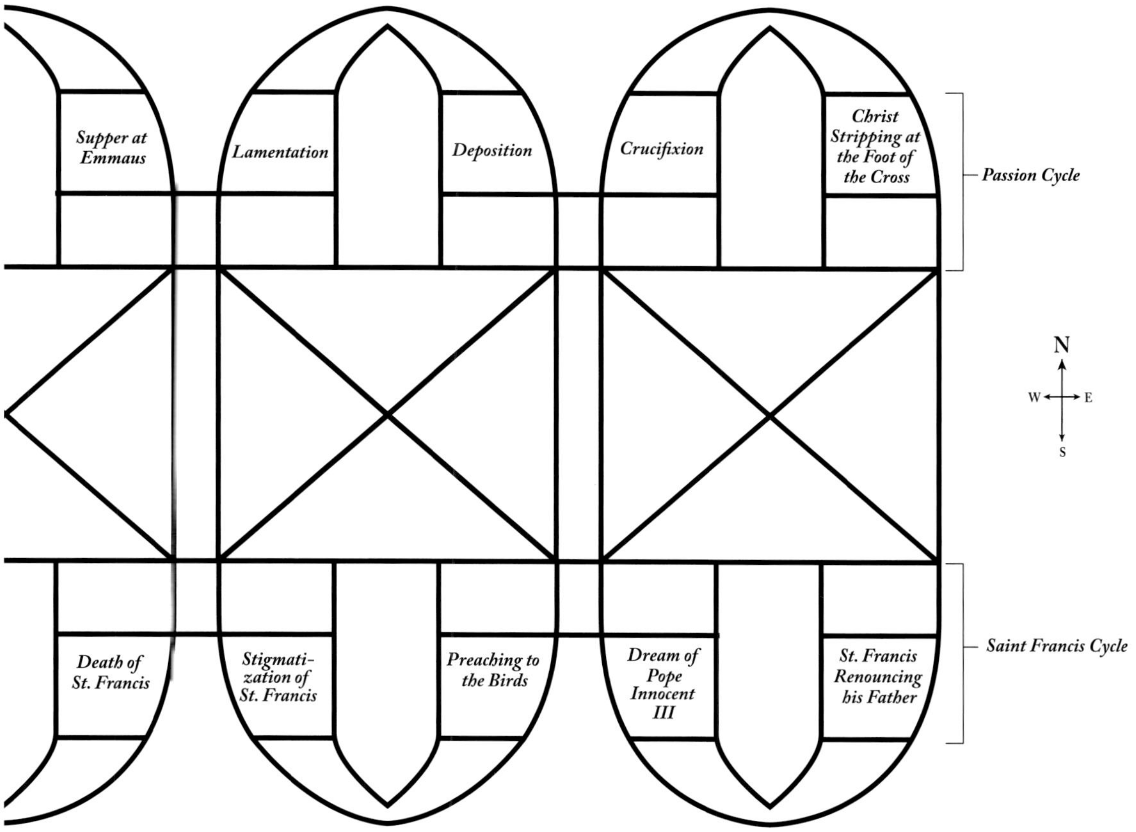

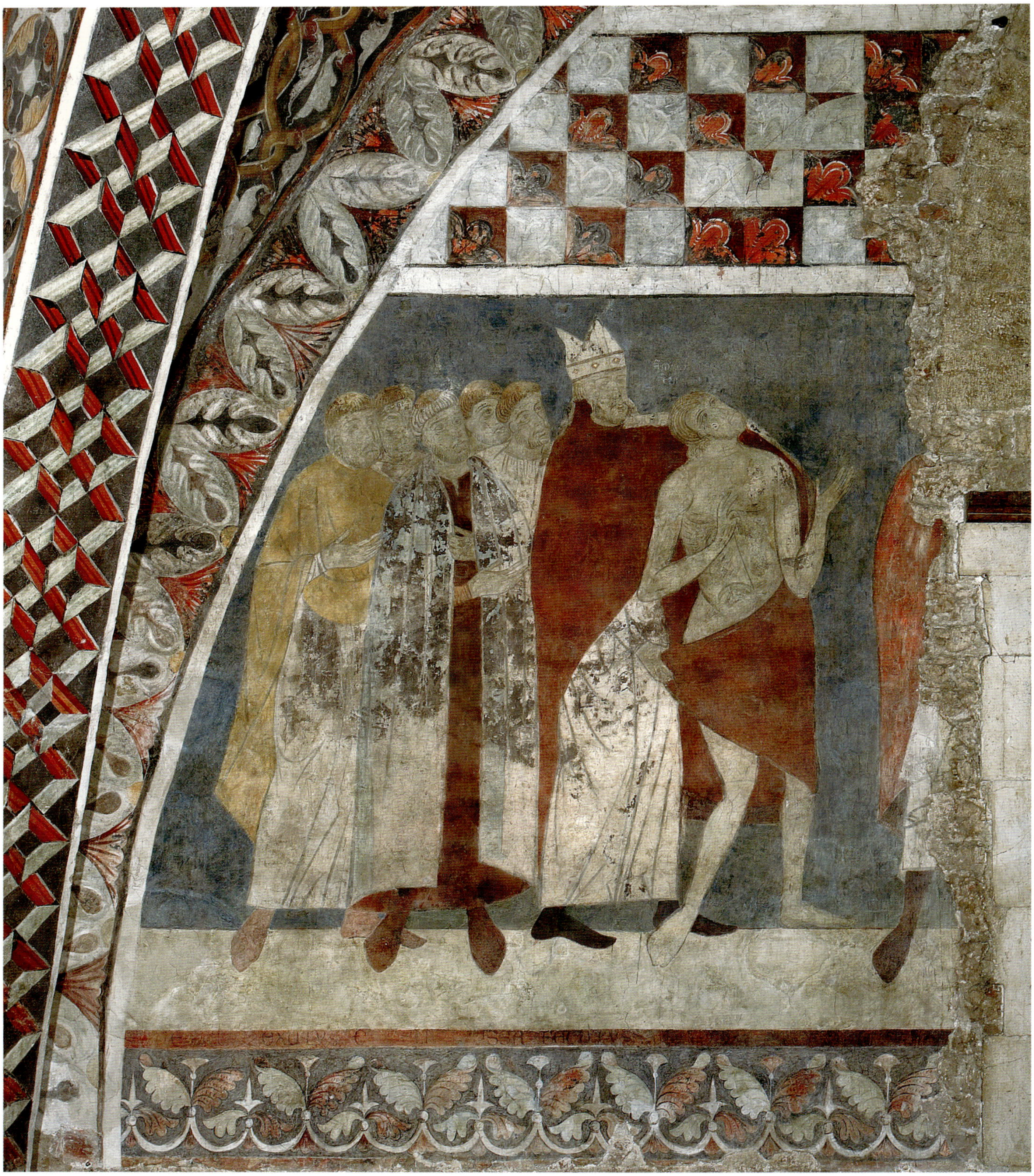

102 Maestro di San Francesco, *Saint Francis Renouncing his Father*, Saint Francis cycle, *c.*1260s, fresco, south wall of the nave, Lower Church, Basilica of San Francesco.

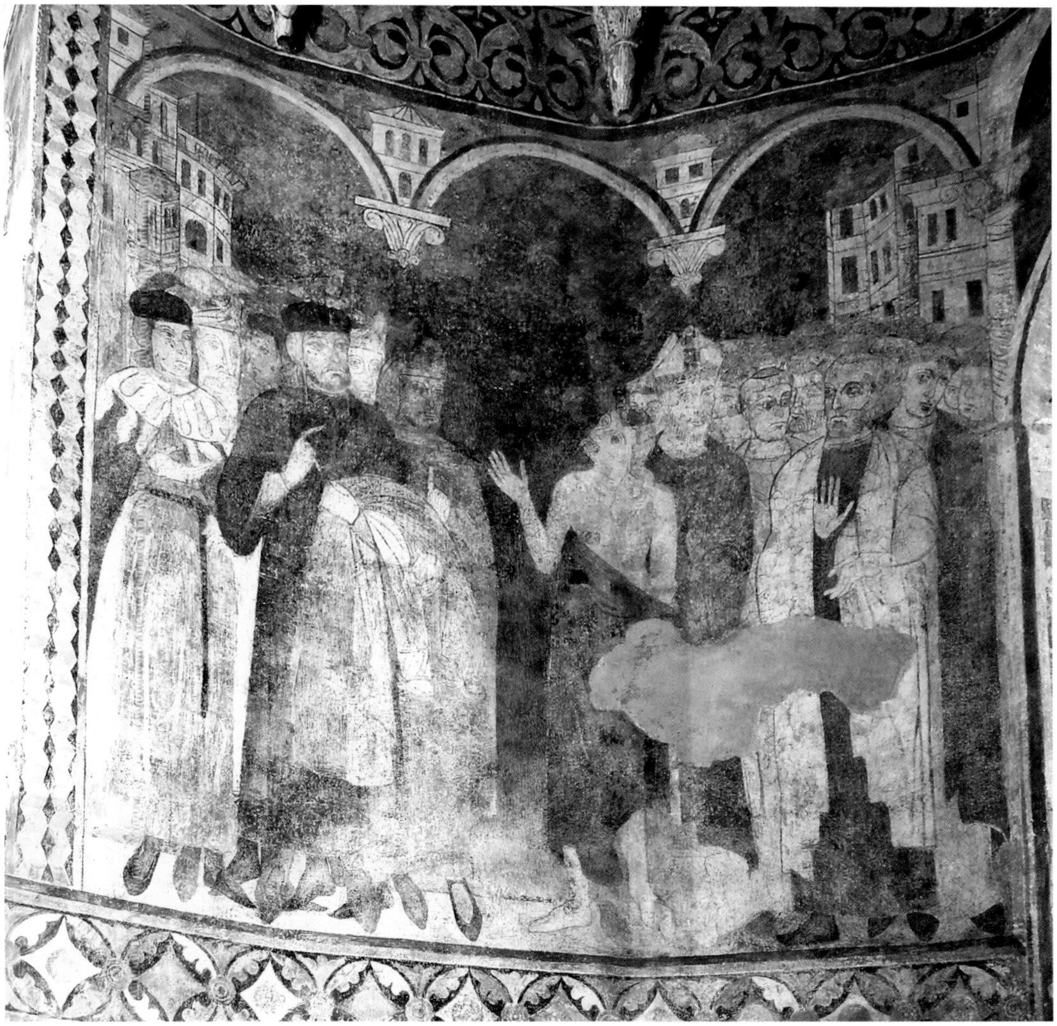

103 Umbrian school, *Saint Francis Renouncing his Father*, *c.*1280, fresco, right apsidal chapel, San Francesco, Gubbio.

The first pair of scenes at the bottom of the nave demonstrates how the two cycles were intended to function together. The initial episode on the south wall is *Saint Francis Renouncing his Father* (fig. 102). Only the left-hand side of the fresco survives, the right-hand side having been destroyed to make way for the entrance arch to the Saint Martin chapel. A related (but reversed) version of the scene in San Francesco in Gubbio helps to fill in the missing information, showing Francis's father, Pietro Bernardone, holding the saint's clothes (fig. 103). The opposite scene in the Lower Church is unprecedented, showing Christ casting off his clothes as he prepares to mount the cross (fig. 104). The episode has no basis in the Gospel texts and no surviving precedents in Italian painting. A related version of the same scene of roughly the same date survives in the Clarissan monastery of San Sebastiano near Alatri, a further indication of a Franciscan genesis for this category of image.[62] But the Christ at Alatri does not hand his clothes over voluntarily to the high priest in the way he does in the Lower Church, in a clear parallel to Francis's act of renunciation on the opposite wall. As Brooke observed, in this instance a Passion story has been deliberately altered 'to bring it into line with an incident in Francis's life'.[63]

The parallels between the next pair of scenes are less extraordinary but still meaningful from a Franciscan point of view. On the south wall, the *Dream of Pope Innocent III* follows (fig. 105); on the north, the *Crucifixion* (fig. 106). The *Stigmatization* or the *Death of Saint Francis* might have been a more obvious parallel to Christ's death on the cross, but the designers of the programme also had to maintain the internal coherence of the separate cycles, so they chose to link the falling façade of the Lateran with the Virgin, as emblems of the Church. Francis will support and renew the Church, just as Saint John (standing for the priesthood) supported the Virgin (standing for the Church) at the Crucifixion. The Virgin leans on John's arms just as the tottering basilica rests on Francis's shoulder. To underscore the point, an inscription in the *Crucifixion* fresco repeats Christ's words from the cross, entrusting the Virgin to Saint John's care.

One struggles to read any such parallels between the next pair of scenes, the *Preaching to the Birds* (fig. 107) and the *Deposition* (fig. 108). In this case the need to maintain the narrative coherence of each cycle seems to have prevailed. A degree of flexibility also allowed the friars to incorporate one of the most popular scenes in the Franciscan canon. But the fourth pair of scenes renewed the parallel reading of the two cycles. Here the *Stigmatization* (fig. 109) faces the *Lamentation* (fig. 110). The depiction of the Seraph in the former is one of the chief pieces of evidence for the dating of the nave frescoes. The vision still follows Celano's formula of an angelic being with six wings rather than the later Bonaventuran version, which had Saint Francis see Christ Crucified in the form of a Seraph. The pictorial iconography of the stigmatization quickly accommodated Bonaventure's innovation, and it is difficult to believe that the friars at Assisi would have lagged behind in this regard. For this reason, the frescoes are generally held to have been painted before the publication of the *Legenda maior* and the suppression of Celano's writings after 1266.[64]

The figure of Saint Francis on the left-hand side of the fresco has all but disappeared, only his knee having survived the demolition of the nave wall, but it is likely that the side wound was prominently depicted on his body. The Maestro di San Francesco had emphasized the side wound in a panel image of Saint Francis now at the Porziuncola, probably painted a few years before the Lower Church frescoes. The increased concern to represent the side wound reflected the stern defence of all five wounds of the stigmata by Alexander IV in the 1250s.[65] On the opposite wall, the Virgin, Saint John and the other witnesses to the Crucifixion weep over Christ's tortured body in the *Lamentation*. This scene, even more than the *Crucifixion* itself, offered the opportunity to emphasize the wounds on Christ's body and, by extension, the wounds of the stigmata on Francis's. As we shall see, the same parallel between the *Lamentation* and the *Stigmatization* would be repeated in the Upper Church.

The stigmata are again prominent in the fifth and final scene on the south wall, the *Death of Saint Francis* (fig. 111). Again, much of the fresco has been lost, but above the obsequies Francis's soul is still visible being borne upwards by angels. Below, the first companions gather around Francis's body, kissing the wounds on his hands and pointing in wonder to the wound in his side. The scene thus functions also as a recognition of the stigmata, and this parallel is brought out by the opposing scene on the north side of the nave. Here the Passion cycle concludes with the *Supper at Emmaus*, where the risen Christ is first acknowledged (fig. 112).

The nave frescoes in the Lower Church represented a clear departure from earlier cycles of Saint Francis's life on painted panels. In format and scale, the saint's legend was treated as an equal to Christ's Passion, and the choice of scenes and iconographic inflections was driven by a desire to draw parallels across the space of the nave. In these respects, the Maestro di San Francesco and his Franciscan patrons encountered some of the same issues that would later have to be dealt with on a larger scale during the frescoing of the Upper Church. They had to maintain a balance between the desire to draw typological parallels between Franciscan legend and biblical stories on the one hand, and the need to maintain the internal narrative coherence of each individual cycle on the other. The ten scenes in the lower nave achieve an effective balance. The two cycles can be read individually, and the Saint Francis cycle includes the most important scenes from the saint's life. But the first and last pairs of scenes offer such meaningful alignments that the alert viewer would have understood that the two cycles mirrored each other across the nave.

The Saint Francis Cycle: Structuring the Analysis

The next three chapters examine the content and meaning of the frescoes of the Upper Church nave in detail. The intention is not to offer a comprehensive description of each Saint Francis scene, in chronological order, but rather to understand the cycle within the broader context of the biblical scenes in the registers above. Each chapter focuses on one

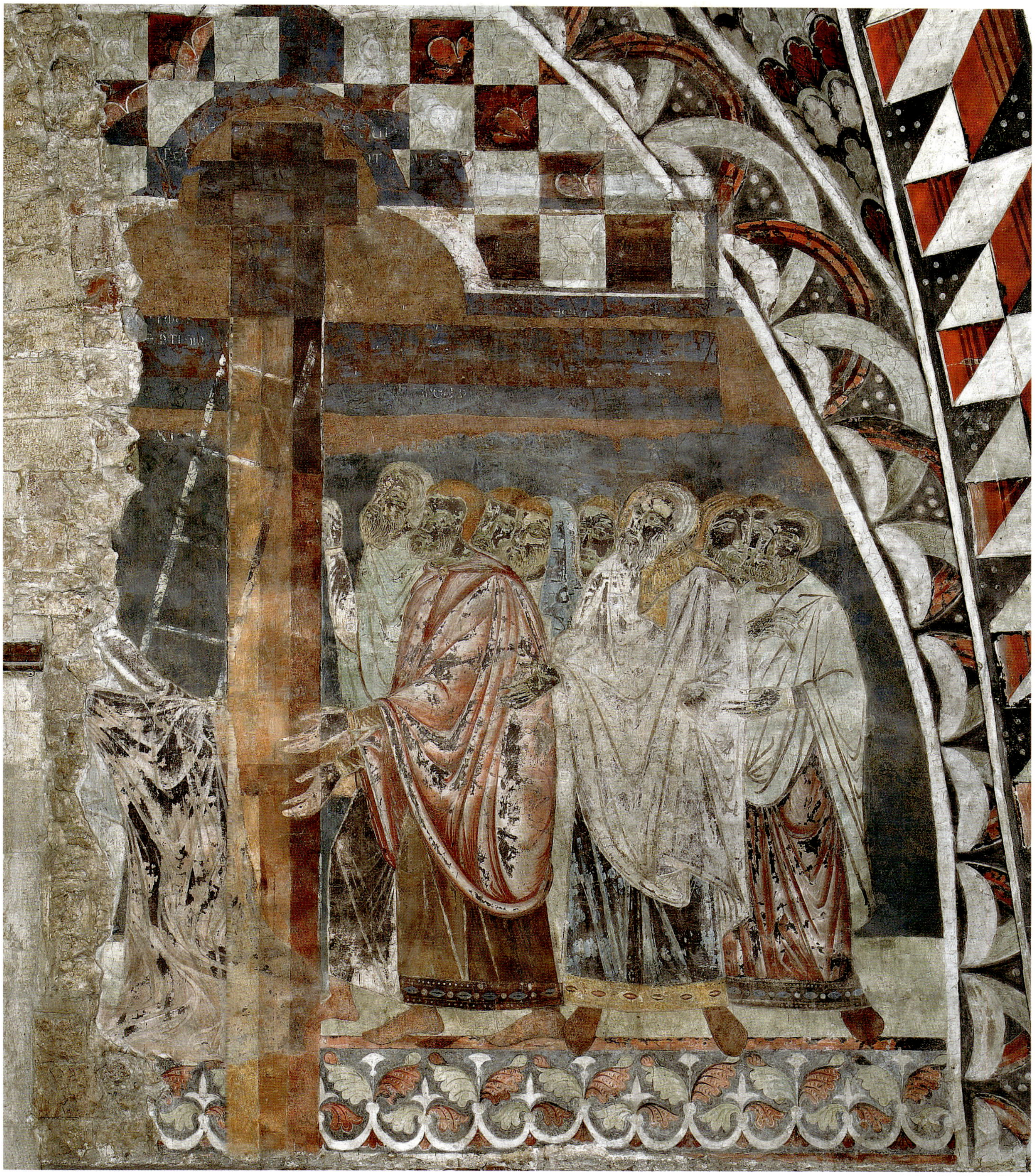

104 Maestro di San Francesco, *Christ Stripping at the Foot of the Cross*, Passion cycle, fresco, *c.*1260s, north wall of the nave, Lower Church, Basilica of San Francesco.

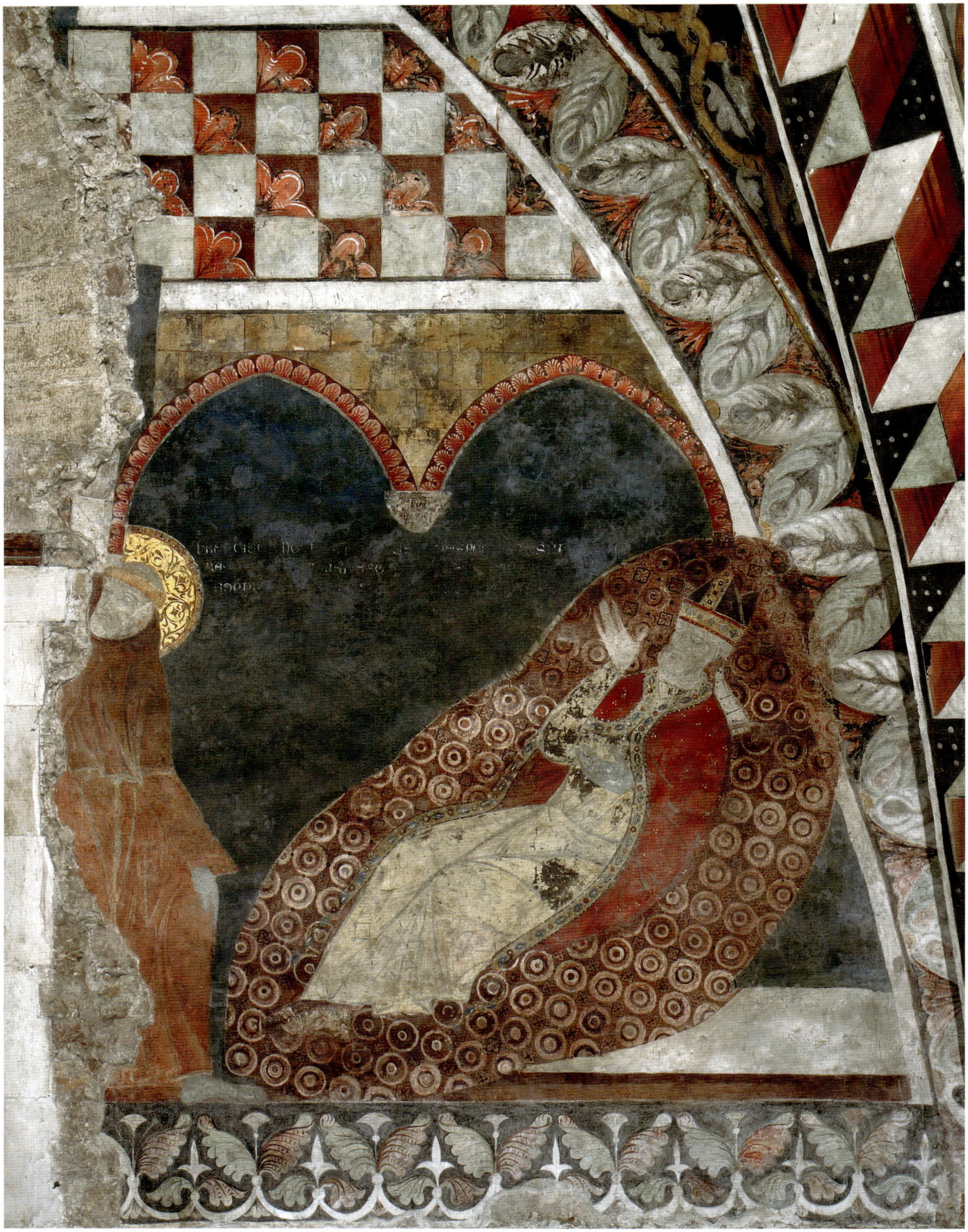

105 Maestro di San Francesco, *Dream of Pope Innocent III*, Saint Francis cycle, *c.*1260s, fresco, south wall of the nave, Lower Church, Basilica of San Francesco.

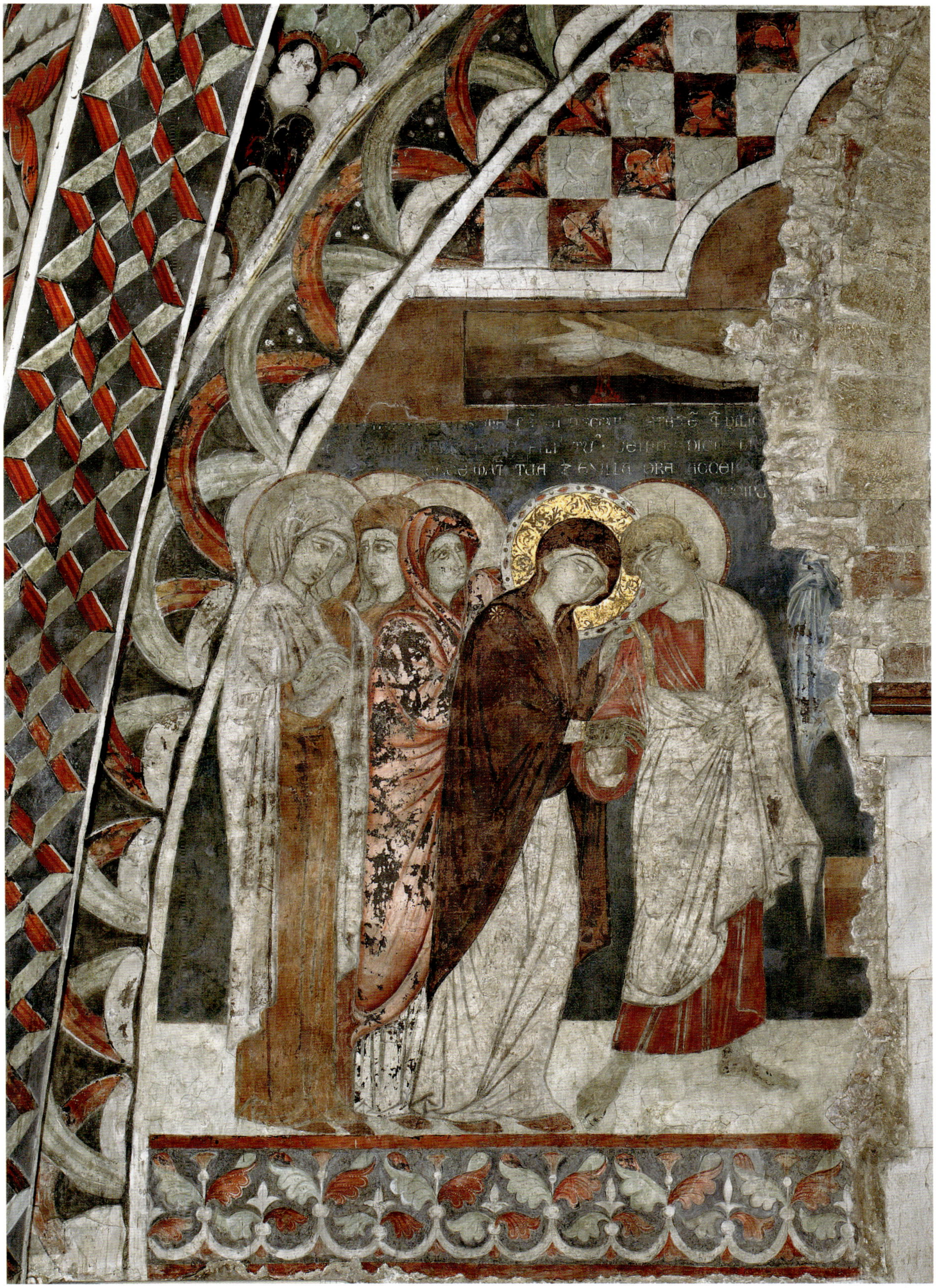

106 Maestro di San Francesco, *Crucifixion*, Passion cycle, *c.*1260s, fresco, north wall of the nave, Lower Church, Basilica of San Francesco.

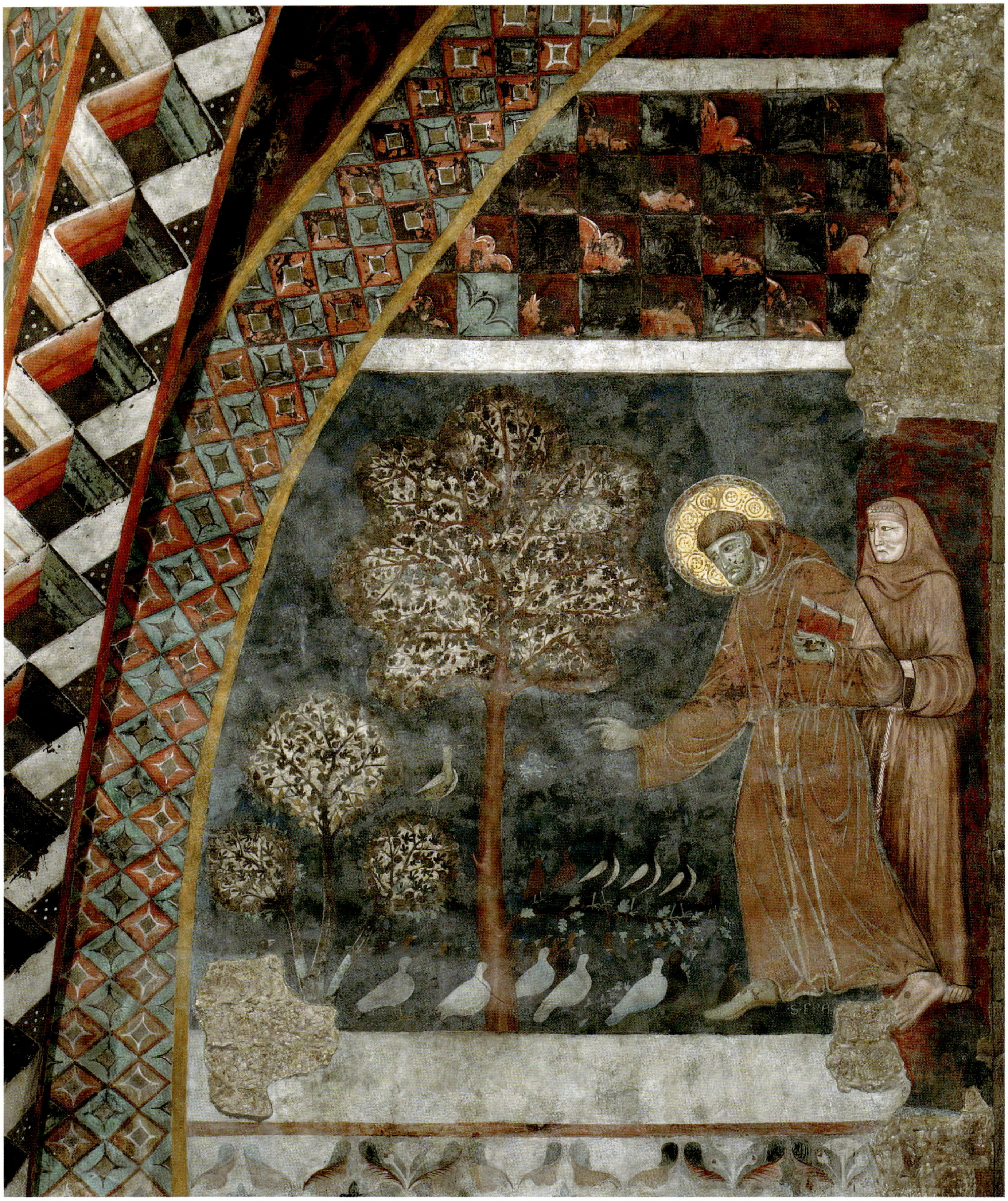

107 Maestro di San Francesco, *Preaching to the Birds*, Saint Francis cycle, *c.*1260s, fresco, south wall of the nave, Lower Church, Basilica of San Francesco.

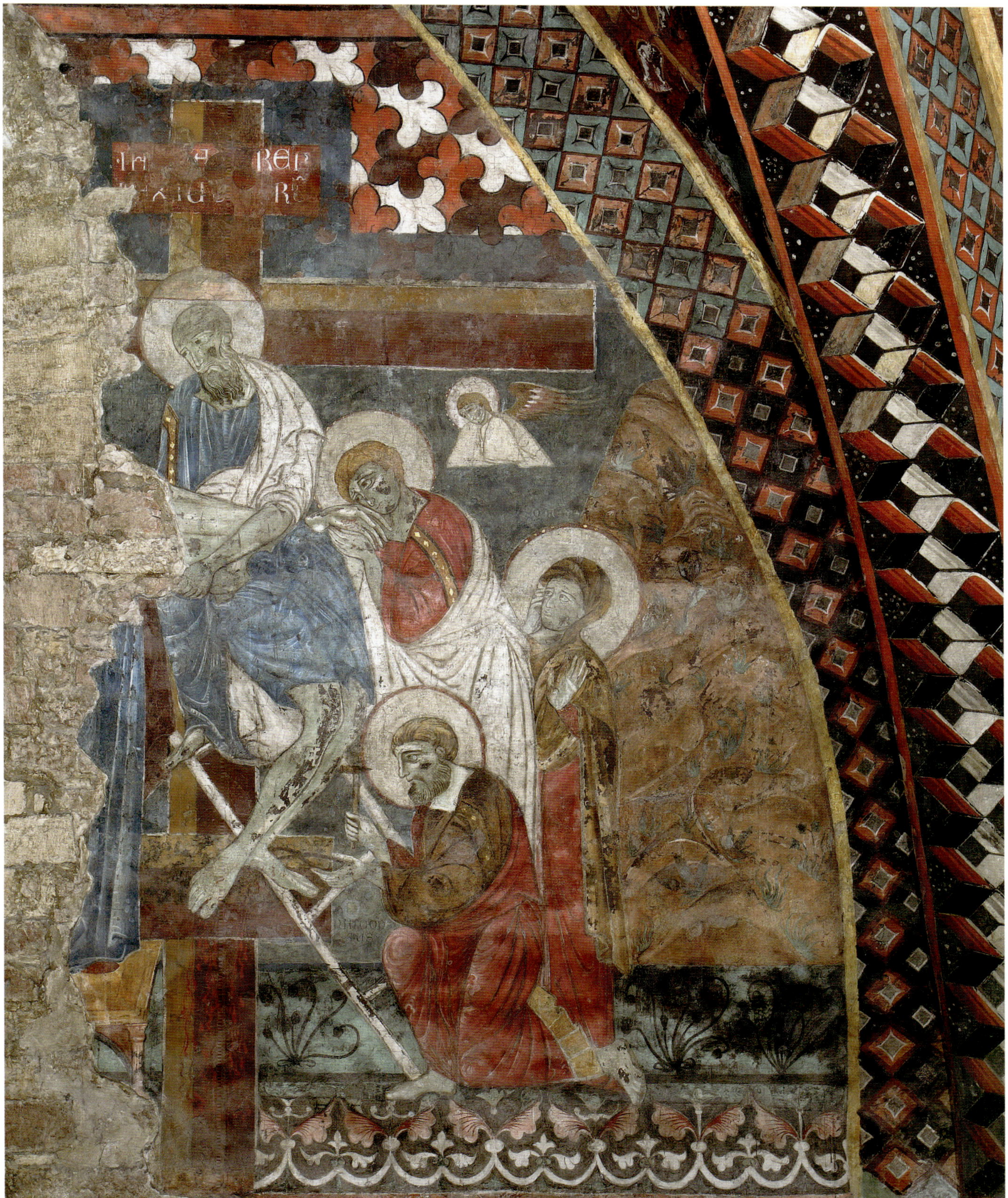

108 Maestro di San Francesco, *Deposition,* Passion cycle, *c.*1260s, fresco, north wall of the nave, Lower Church, Basilica of San Francesco.

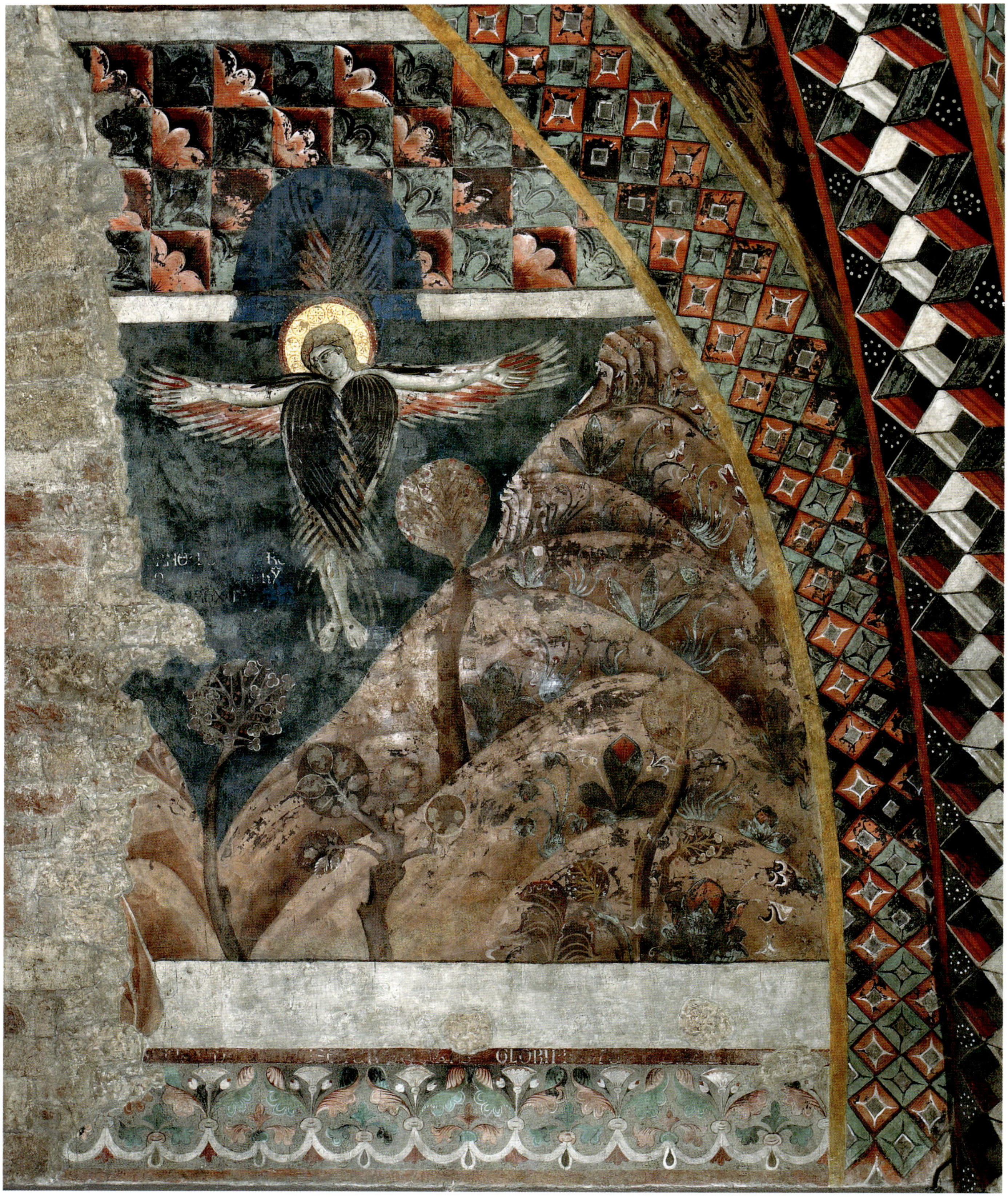

109 Maestro di San Francesco, *Stigmatization of Saint Francis*, Saint Francis cycle, *c.*1260s, fresco, south wall of the nave, Lower Church, Basilica of San Francesco.

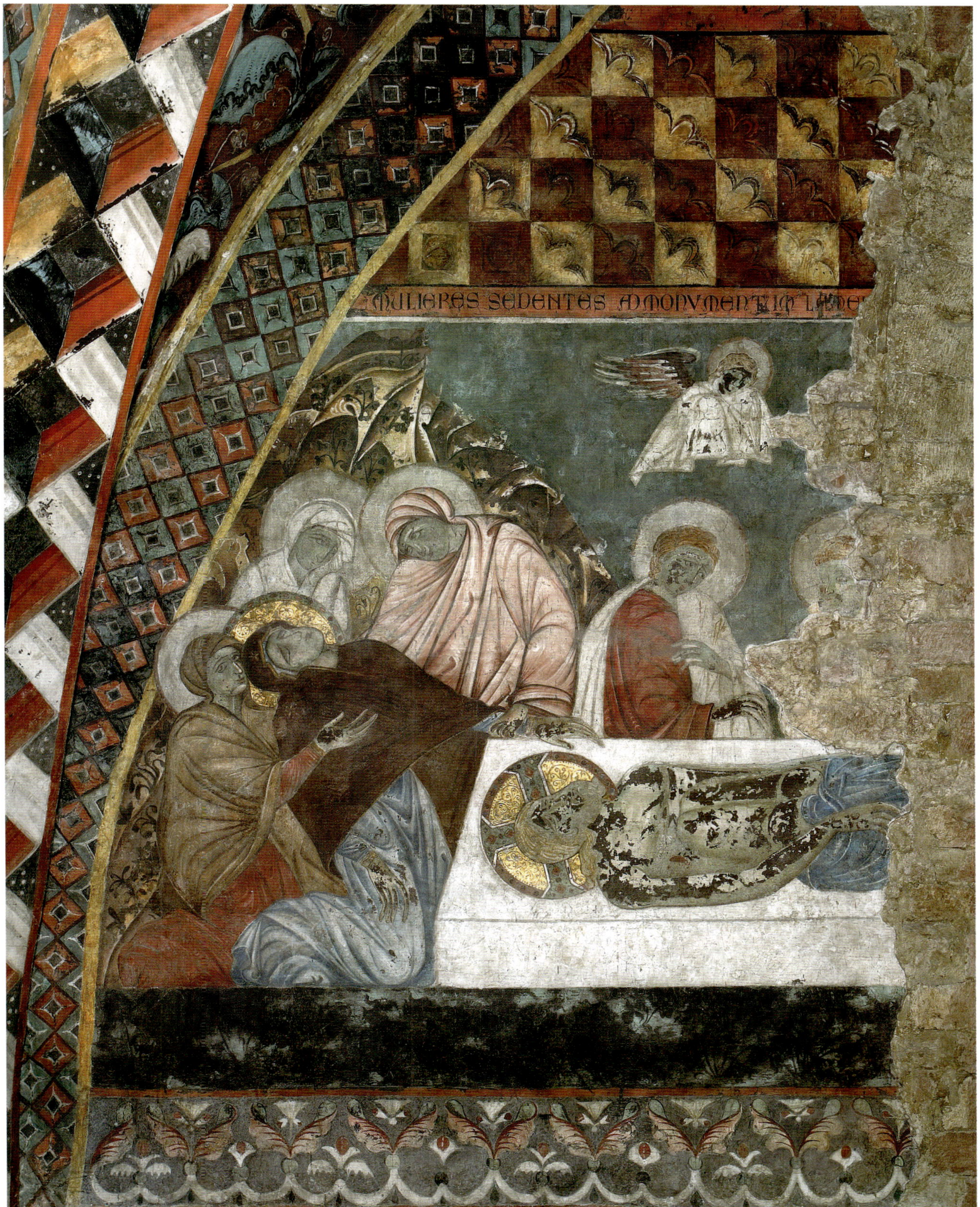

110 Maestro di San Francesco, *Lamentation*, Passion cycle, *c.*1260s, fresco, north wall of the nave, Lower Church, Basilica of San Francesco.

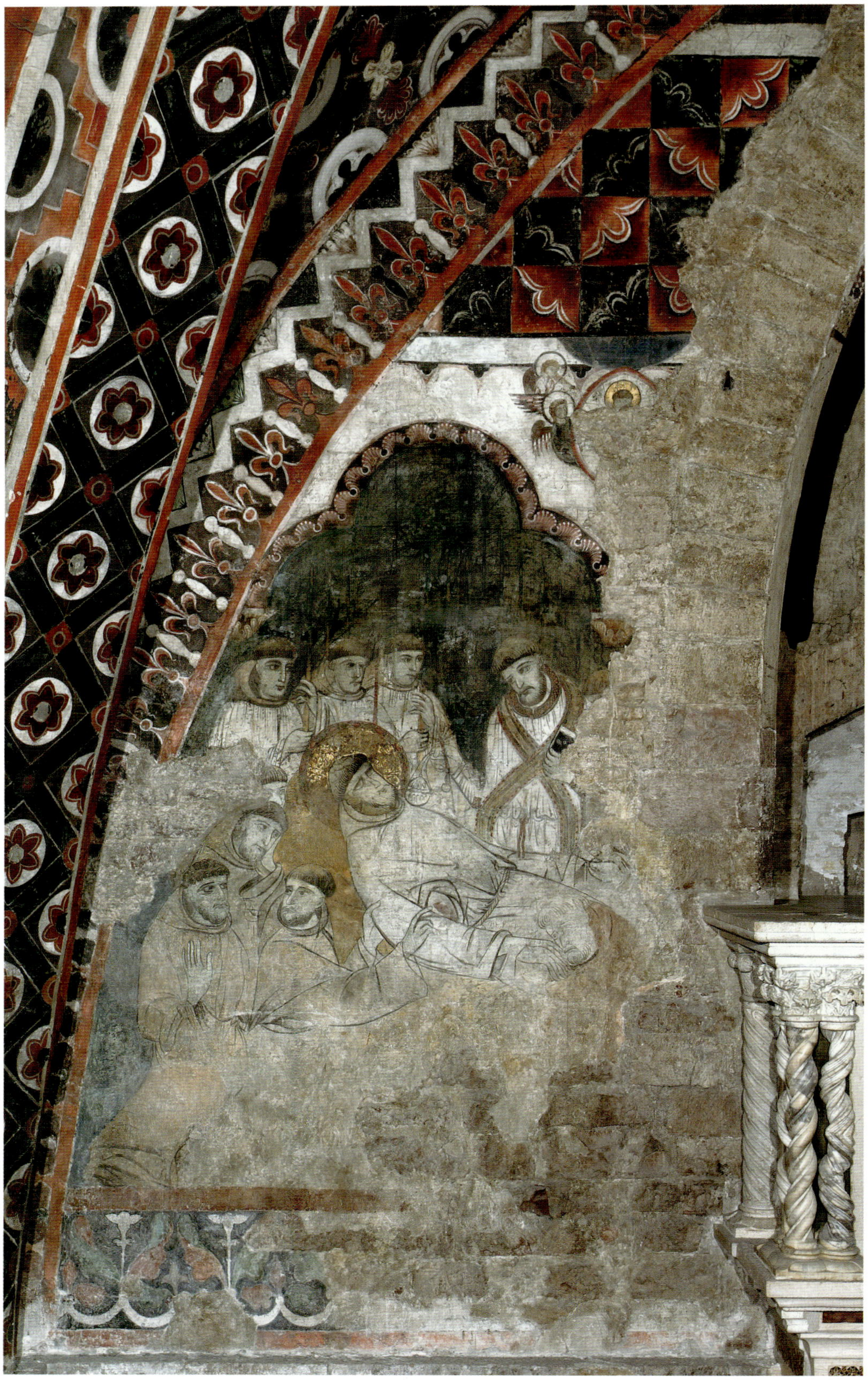

111 Maestro di San Francesco, *Death of Saint Francis*, Saint Francis cycle, *c.*1260s, fresco, south wall of the nave, Lower Church, Basilica of San Francesco.

section of the Saint Francis cycle and highlights a particular set of iconographic themes which convey important and topical ideas about the saint, the friars and the papacy at the end of the Duecento.

Chapter 5 looks at Scenes 19 to 28, on the south wall of the nave. Although this is the last part of the Saint Francis cycle, we have chosen to examine it first because the sequence of scenes depicting the saint's stigmatization, his death and post-mortem miracles is fundamental to understanding the entire cycle. The core theme of Saint Francis as *alter Christus* was promoted by the papacy as much as by Bonaventure. We shall show how the relationships between the Franciscan scenes and those of the Passion of Christ in the tier above are imaginatively and powerfully exploited at key moments. This chapter demonstrates the system of vertical and diagonal links that is consistently used to interlock the separate cycles throughout the nave, and it casts more light on the process of decision-making behind the detailed planning of the scheme.

In Chapter 6, we turn to the north wall and primarily to the scenes of Francis's early life and the foundation of the Order. This part of the scheme is heavily ecclesiological, stressing Francis's role in rebuilding the Church, both literally and figuratively. The use of typological parallels with the Old Testament patriarchs in the middle register of the wall gives prophetic gravitas to Francis's early life. But the north wall is also about prophecy fulfilled, intricately binding together the past and the present, Saint Francis and Pope Nicholas IV. We demonstrate that a particular vehicle for achieving this is the symbolic representation of church buildings in Assisi and Rome, particularly San Damiano and Saint John Lateran.

Chapter 7 examines the long middle section of the cycle, depicting the life of Saint Francis as a Friar Minor. It begins in the third bay of the north wall with the *Approval of the Rule* and concludes in the fourth bay of the south, with the *Stigmatization*. The most visually prominent part of this section is the counter-façade, whose two Saint Francis scenes, the *Miracle of the Spring* and the *Preaching to the Birds*, were taken out of their Bonaventuran sequence to be placed here, below the *Ascension* and the *Pentecost*. The meaningful links between this quartet of scenes are the key to understanding the scenes in the bays either side. The counter-façade communicates fundamental messages not just about Saint Francis himself, but about Franciscan identity and mission at the end of the Duecento.

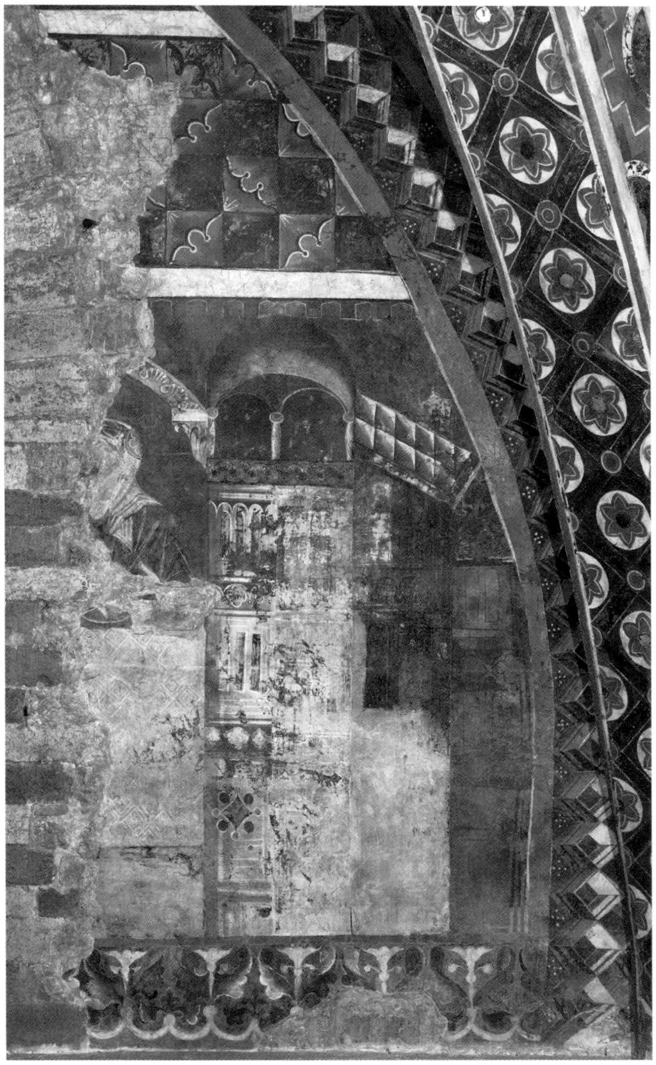

112 Maestro di San Francesco, *Supper at Emmaus*, Passion cycle, *c.*1260s, fresco, north wall of the nave, Lower Church, Basilica of San Francesco.

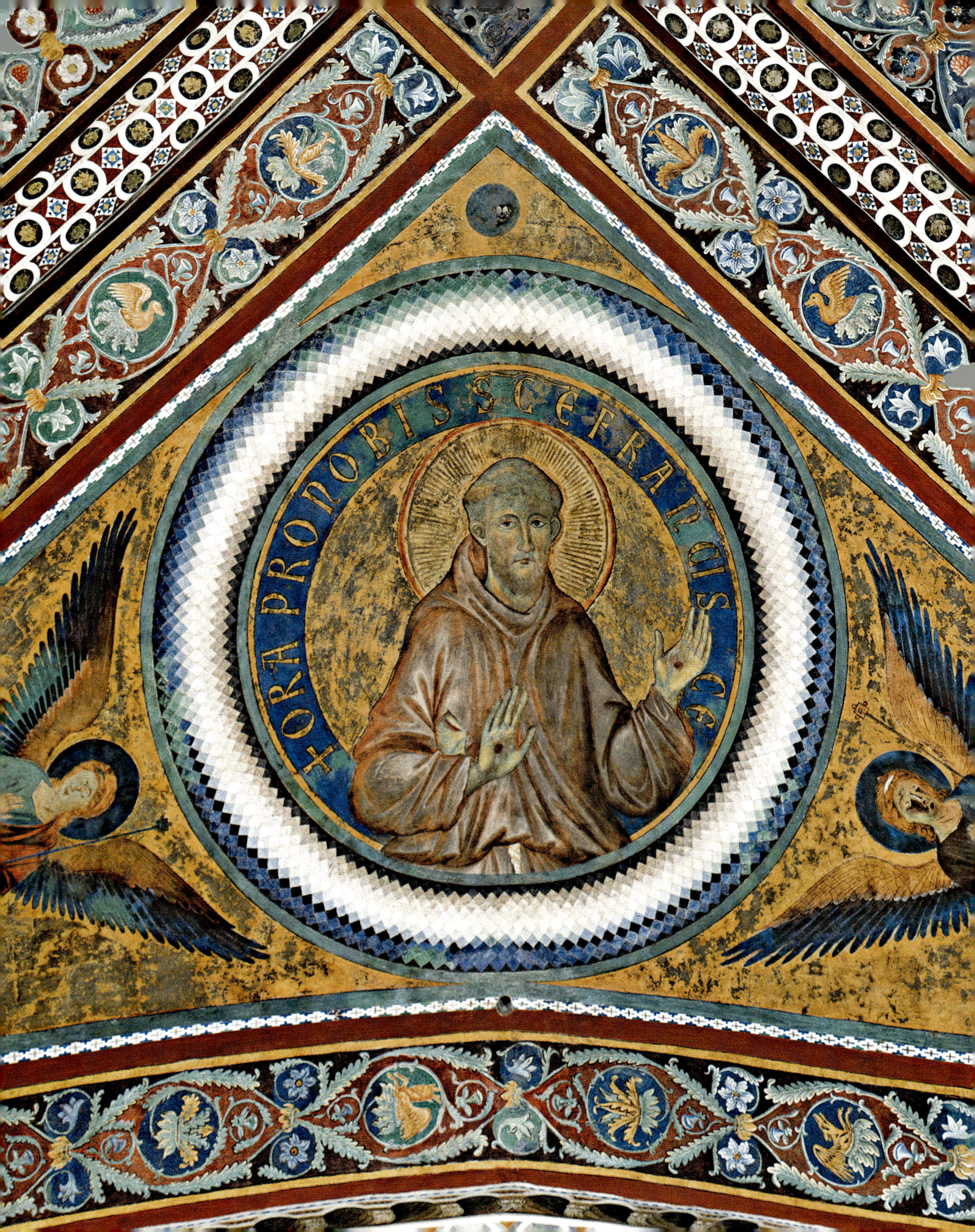
+ORA PRONOBIS SCE FRANCISCE

5

'Franciscus alter Christus'

Promoting Saint Francis as an *alter Christus* (another, or second, Christ) was accorded the highest importance in the programme of the Upper Church nave. Not only did the theme dominate the Saint Francis cycle, it was also a major factor in the detailed iconographic planning of the nave as a whole. The agenda was established from the start, as we can see from the *Deesis* in the vaults, one of the first parts of the nave to be painted. The length of the Upper Church is spanned by five vaults, which alternate figured decorations with starred grounds (see fig. 89). The crossing vault above the high altar had already been decorated before 1288 with the four Evangelists (see fig. 12). The other two figured vaults were painted as part of the Nicholine scheme: the four Doctors of the Church at the east end (see fig. 45) and the *Deesis* spanning the centre of the nave (see fig. 13).

✱

facing page 113 Jacopo Torriti, Saint Francis, *Deesis* vault (east web, second bay of the nave), *c.*1288–90, Upper Church, Basilica of San Francesco.

'Pray for us, Saint Francis'

Each web of the *Deesis* vault features a medallion containing a bust-length figure, framed by angels holding orbs and sceptres, and set against a dazzling gold ground. The basic iconography of the *Deesis* (or intercession) is based on a Byzantine formula, but here it is transformed into something new, a specifically Franciscan image, which both utilizes and orchestrates the spatial possibilities offered by the architecture of the Basilica.[1] For the worshipper who enters the Upper Church through the main façade portal at the east end, the central figure of the *Deesis* is Christ, who holds a scroll and gives a sign of blessing (fig. 114). In the webs to either side are the Virgin Mary (fig. 115) and Saint John the Baptist (fig. 116), who both look out at the viewer while indicating Christ with petitionary gestures. Christ is alpha and omega, first and last, who returns from heaven to judge all souls, living and dead, at the end of time. The Virgin and the Baptist act as the chief advocates for humanity, imploring divine mercy.

Hans Belting suggested that the *Deesis* vault at Assisi functions as an abbreviated *Last Judgment*, an image which does not otherwise feature in the Basilica.[2] Amy Neff, on the

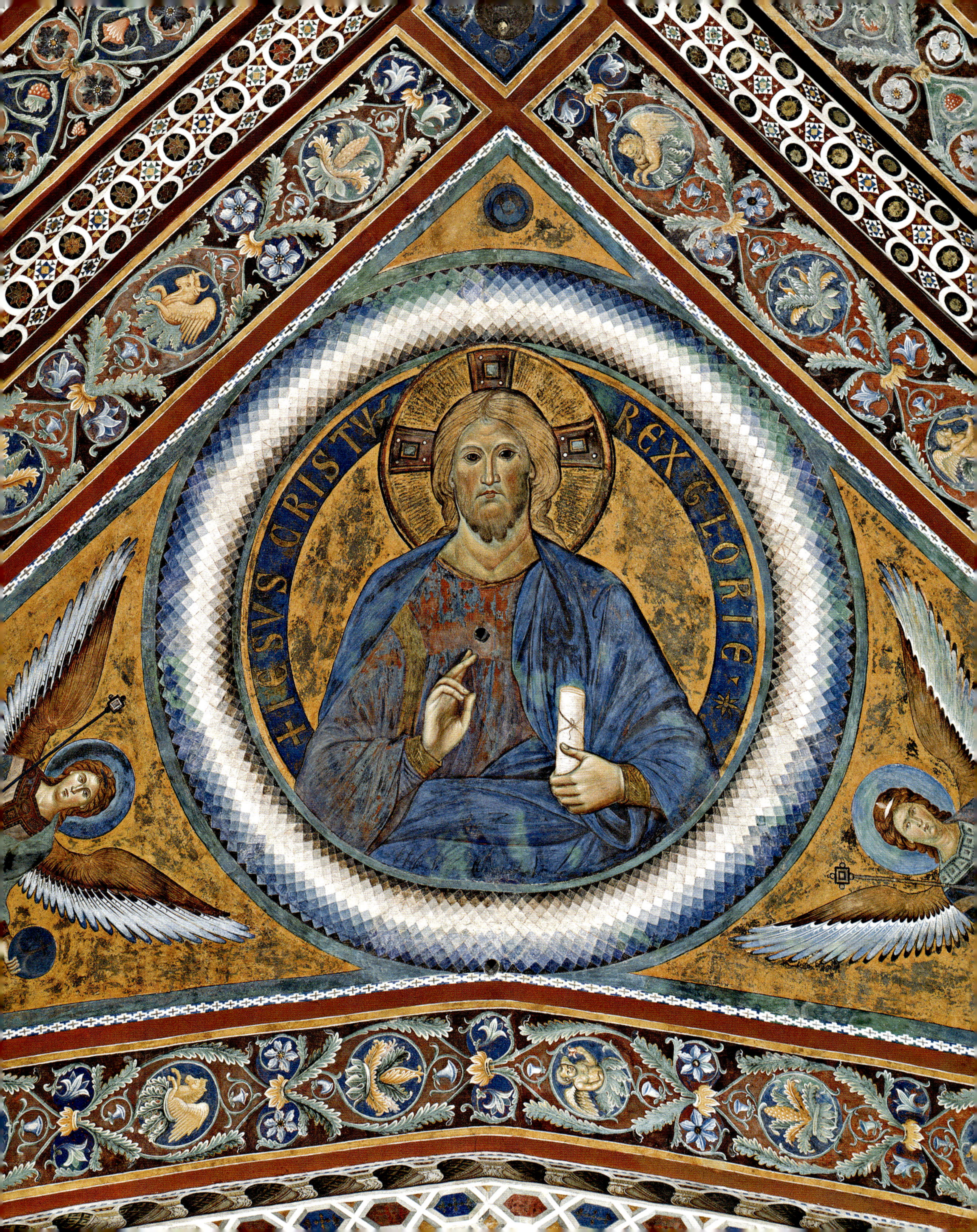
+ IESVS CRISTV REX GLORIE

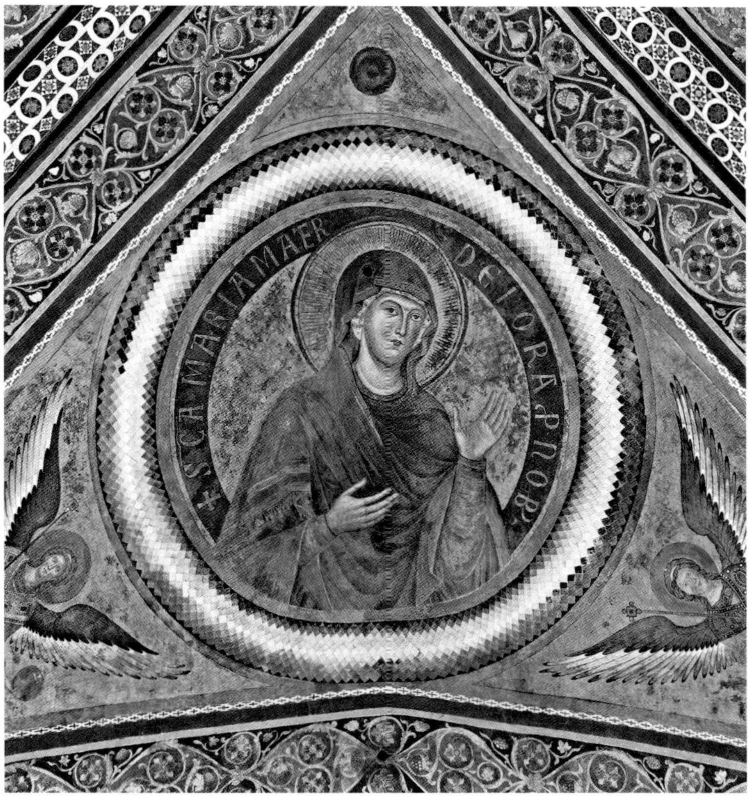

115 Jacopo Torriti, Virgin Mary, *Deesis* vault (south web, second bay of the nave), *c.*1288–90, Upper Church, Basilica of San Francesco.

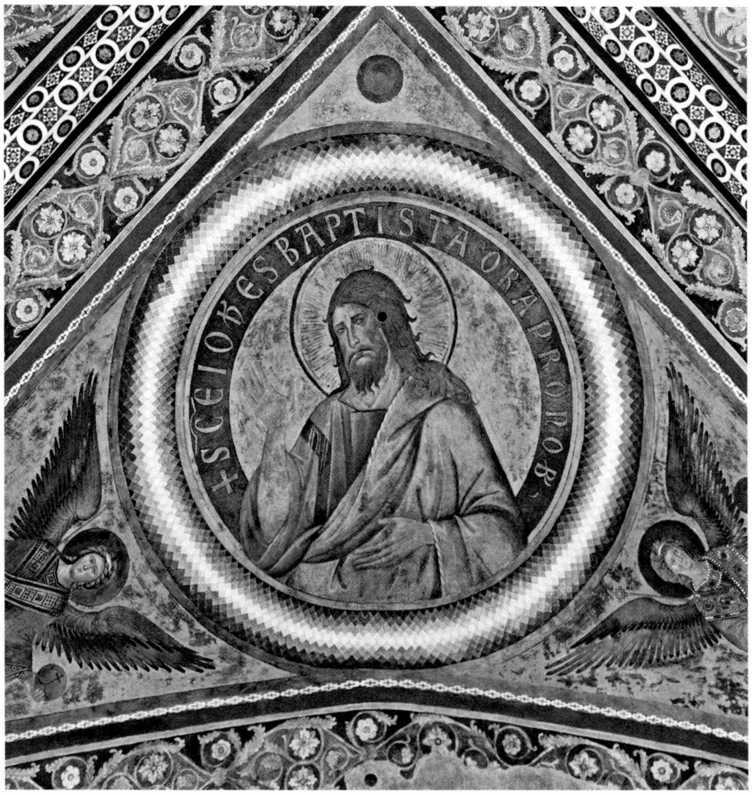

116 Jacopo Torriti, Saint John the Baptist, *Deesis* vault (north web, second bay of the nave), *c.*1288–90, Upper Church, Basilica of San Francesco.

other hand, pointed out that as a Last Judgment it is remarkably optimistic, with no indication of wrath or damnation. Rather than displaying his wounds, the celestial and radiant Christ broadly equates to a Byzantine Pantocrator.[3] The inscription within his medallion hails him as IESUS CRISTUS REX GLORIE ('Jesus Christ, King of Glory'). This nomenclature recalls the *Te Deum laudamus*, a hymn of praise sung at the end of Matins on major feast days, which includes the acclamation 'Tu, Rex Gloriae, Christe.'

The inscriptions in the other two medallions invite the active involvement of the faithful in the nave below, voicing their prayers: SANCTA MARIA MATER DEI ORA PRO NOBIS ('Holy Mary, Mother of God, pray for us'); SANCTE IOHANNES BAPTISTA ORA PRO NOBIS ('Saint John the Baptist, pray for us'). This is the formula of prayer used in the litany of saints, where the name of the saint is invoked by the celebrant, and the congregation responds each time 'ora pro nobis'. But the invocation to the Virgin as 'Mater Dei' more precisely echoes the *Ave Maria*, the best-known of all Marian prayers, which was commonly recited by both lay and religious in the liturgy and in private devotions.[4]

facing page 114 Jacopo Torriti, Christ, *Deesis* vault (west web, second bay of the nave), *c.*1288–90, Upper Church, Basilica of San Francesco.

In the fourth web of the vault, back to back with Christ, is Saint Francis (fig. 113). His role as a heavenly intercessor is clear both from his pose and from the inscription, ORA PRO NOBIS SANCTE FRANCISCE ('Pray for us, Saint Francis'). Adding saints to the traditional triad was not uncommon in *Deesis* groups in Byzantium.[5] At Assisi, from the point of view of the visitor entering the Upper Church from the east, Saint Francis initially seems less important than the Virgin or the Baptist, since his image is inverted. But as Neff argued, Saint Francis's status is elevated above the other two intercessors by the juxtaposition of his image with that of Christ, on the central axis of the nave.[6] And viewed from the west end, the message of the *Deesis* vault is even bolder. For the friars looking up from their choir stalls in the apse, it is Saint Francis who is the central, upright figure while Christ can be seen only obliquely and upside-down.[7]

Saint Francis's hands are also subtly distinguished from those of Mary and John the Baptist. Only he turns both palms outwards to the viewer in a gesture that, while it still signals intercession, is designed to display the stigmata prominently. The wound in his side is also clearly visible through a tear in his tunic. It was surely no accident that in Saint Francis's inscription the two phrases of the formula of prayer used for the Virgin and Saint John are reversed. In the Office of Saint Francis, 'Ora pro nobis, beate Francisce' is the prayer spoken by the celebrant during first and second Vespers, to which the friars respond, 'Ut digni efficiamur promissionibus Christi' ('That we may be made worthy of the promises of Christ').[8] The Office had been composed by Julian of Speyer in *c.*1235 and remained in use throughout the Latin Church right up to the sixteenth century.[9] Consequently, it seems likely that the image of Saint Francis in the *Deesis* vault, with its inscription, would have evoked for the friars the liturgy they sang to celebrate his feast day. That likelihood is increased by the antiphon for the octave, 'Plange, turba paupercula'. Attributed to Pope Gregory IX, who had canonized Saint Francis, the antiphon makes it clear that Francis's stigmata were perceived as giving the saint his unique authority as an intercessor:

> Lament, poor little company;
> To the father of the poor, like orphans cry:
> This sorrowful and plaintive sigh,
> Father Francis, take up and hear,
> And show to Christ those precious brands
> Upon your side, and feet, and hands,
> That to us orphans He may give
> A worthy father in your stead.[10]

Not only do the images in the vault articulate the space below them as a place of prayer, they also cleverly exploit the spatial possibilities of the Upper Basilica, enabling them to serve two distinct audiences with different points of view (both figuratively and literally). By placing Christ and Saint Francis back to back, facing in different directions, the designers of the *Deesis* vault established the iconographic typology and spatial paradigm that would underpin a later generation of double-sided high altarpieces painted for Franciscan houses in Umbria, on which the Christ Child in the arms of the Virgin Mary faced the lay congregation, and *Franciscus alter Christus* the friars in their choir.[11] On the whole, we know remarkably little about how the interior of the Upper Church was used, but the available evidence suggests a versatile and multipurpose space.[12] Angela of Foligno's vision before the 'Angel Window' in 1291 confirms that the nave was open to pilgrims and that laity and friars could mix there.[13] Like thousands of other pilgrims, Angela also came to Assisi for the *Perdono*, the extraordinary plenary indulgence that offered a complete remission of sins committed up to that date. The *Perdono* was available every year to those visiting the Porziuncola in Santa Maria degli Angeli between Vespers on 1 August and Vespers the following day. Although the *Perdono* was not attached to the Basilica itself, much of the spiritual preparation took place there, and Angela described the gathered pilgrims hearing Mass in the Upper Church on the Sunday preceding the two-day indulgence period.[14] There is also evidence that the Upper Basilica was used for the profession of a group of forty-eight male and female Franciscan tertiaries in January 1304.[15] The original document makes it clear that this was a public event, with 'aliis multis testibus' in addition to the seven laymen named as witnesses.[16]

The images in the nave therefore had to cater for a wide, mixed audience of Franciscan friars, pilgrims, other religious orders and lay people, not all of whom would have understood them on the same level. As the *Deesis* vault demonstrates, the design and arrangement of the frescoes take this into account, using the space of the Upper Church as a dynamic force, allowing different depths and shades of meaning to be discerned by the various groups of viewers seeing them from different vantage points within the building. Any Franciscan friar who was familiar with a traditional *Deesis*, composed as a triad, could have been in no doubt about the significance of what he was being offered in the vault. From the friar's viewpoint, Saint Francis took the central place usually occupied by Christ, with the Virgin and the Baptist as subsidiary figures. Suspended over the centre of the nave, the *Deesis* vault acts as a preface for the themes that will be fully elucidated on the walls below: Saint Francis as an *alter Christus*, the unique nature of his relationship with Christ and the power of his stigmata.

A New Version of the Stigmatization

Immediately after Francis's death, his stigmata had been proclaimed to the friars throughout the Order in an encyclical letter from Brother Elias.[17] Specific papal authority for the representation of the stigmata in images of the saint was not far behind. In 1237, Pope Gregory IX, in one of three bulls he issued to defend the authenticity of the stigmata, asked: 'What is the fear, where is the sin, if through the testimony of the picture one makes visible to the eyes of the devoted such a singular privilege, to the great glory of him who conceded it?'[18] The marks of the wounds rapidly became a standard characteristic in portraits of Francis, being shown with increasing prominence and confidence as the thirteenth century progressed. The narrative scene of the *Stigmatization of Saint Francis* was also well established in Duecento Italy, and numerous surviving examples pre-dating the Assisi cycle attest its popularity.[19] Yet, as we shall see, controversy over the authenticity of the stigmata was still not resolved by the time of the Saint Francis cycle in the Upper Church at Assisi.[20]

The first indication of the particular attention given to the *Stigmatization of Saint Francis* in the Assisi cycle (fig. 117) is the introduction of several important iconographic innovations, as Chiara Frugoni convincingly demonstrated.[21] Thomas of Celano, in his *Vita prima* of *c.*1228, described how Francis, while praying at the mountain hermitage of La Verna in Tuscany, experienced in a vision 'a man having six wings like a Seraph . . . affixed to a cross', and how, some time after this mystical encounter, he developed the wounds in his hands, feet and side.[22] It was Bonaventure, in the *Legenda maior*, who stated explicitly that the figure who appeared to Francis was 'Christ . . . under the appearance [*sub specie*] of the Seraph'.[23] The scene in the Upper Church is the first to show this unambiguously: Christ's naked torso with its side wound is clearly visible, he is bearded and has a cruciform nimbus.

The Assisi *Stigmatization* also breaks with tradition in the way it visualizes the interaction between saint and Christ–Seraph. In 1235 the Lucchese artist Bonaventura Berlinghieri, painting the *Stigmatization* on the *vita* panel for San Francesco in Pescia (the earliest securely dated example of the scene), attempted to convey in one image the complex and ambiguous nature of Francis's experience (fig. 118).[24] According to Thomas of Celano while the saint rejoiced in the beauty of the Seraph, he was frightened by the suffering implied by its fixation to the cross; subsequently, he struggled to discern the meaning of this vision, which left him feeling both joy and sorrow. Only *after* all of this did the signs of the nails develop on his hands and feet.

Berlinghieri depicted Francis kneeling in prayer on the mountainside, gazing intently up at the Seraph. Small black dots indicate the stigmata on his hands and feet, but the communion between the two figures is suggested by means of a broad gilded beam, extending down from the sky to bathe Francis's head in light. By such means, the physical phenomenon of the stigmata is separated from the saint's inner, spiritual experience of the vision of the Seraph. Berlinghieri thereby established a prototype which was usually followed in *Stigmatization* images before the Assisi cycle. When artists visually connected the Seraph and the saint (and they did not always do so), they usually depicted three rays of light radiating from the Seraph towards Francis's head.[25]

Bonaventure's account in the *Legenda maior* both compressed the chronology of the events and simplified them. Although he repeated Celano's reference to Francis's mixed feelings of joy and sorrow, the minister general maintained that while Francis was still contemplating the Christ–Seraph he came to understand that 'he was to be totally transformed into the likeness of Christ crucified, not by the martyrdom of his flesh but by the enkindling of his soul. As the vision was disappearing, it left in his heart a marvellous fire and imprinted in his flesh a likeness of signs no less marvellous.' It is at Assisi that Saint Francis is shown for the first time with thin white lines, which were originally gilded, directly linking each of his five wounds with those of the Christ–Seraph. This new iconography retains the impression of light, but fuses the spiritual encounter and its physical outcome into a single moment, a combined event. The titulus beneath the scene, in a careful compression of Bonaventure's text, leaves no doubt that the stigmata came directly from Christ: 'While Blessed Francis was praying on the side of Mount La Verna, he saw Christ under the appearance of a crucified Seraph, who impressed on his hands and feet, and on his right side, the stigmata of the cross of our Lord Jesus Christ.'[26]

In a third innovation, the Assisi scene was also the first to include Francis's companion and confessor, Brother Leo, who sits on the ground in front of the little chapel reading a book. The presence of Leo would have been a reminder of the events leading up to the stigmatization, again according to Bonaventure. Seeking spiritual guidance, Francis had taken

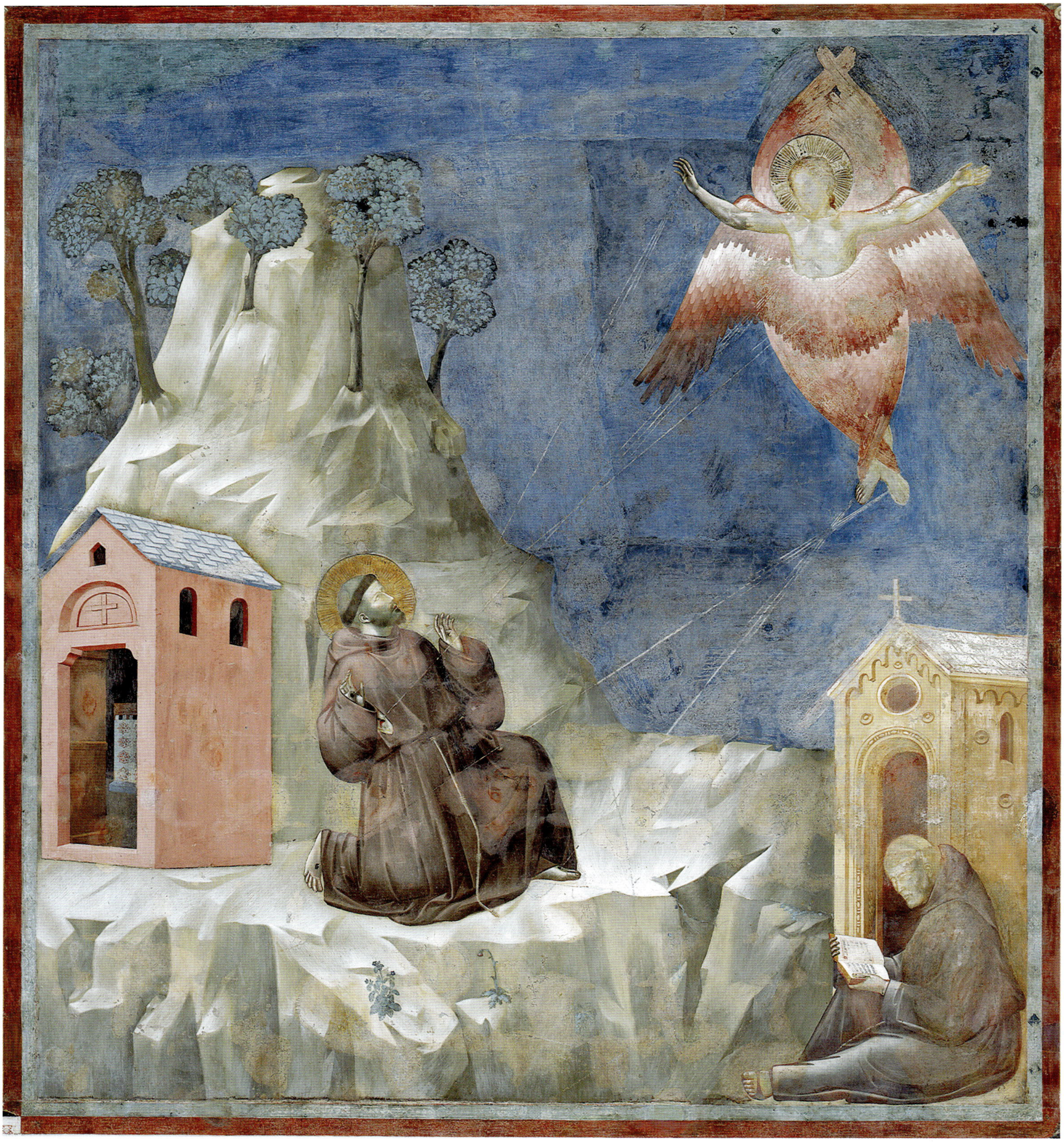

117 *Stigmatization of Saint Francis*, Scene 19 of the Saint Francis cycle, *c.*1290–96, fresco, south wall of the nave, Upper Church, Basilica of San Francesco.

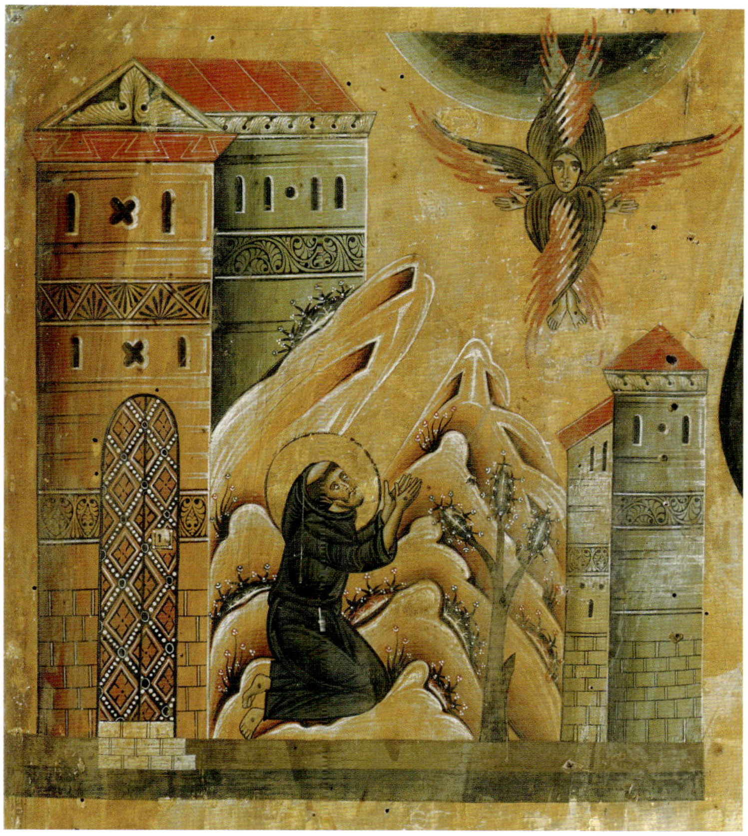

118 Bonaventura Berlinghieri, *Stigmatization of Saint Francis*, Pescia dossal, signed and dated 1235, tempera and gold on wood, San Francesco, Pescia.

the Gospels from the altar and asked Leo to open the book three times: each time it had fallen open at the account of the Passion. Francis then understood that just as he had imitated Christ in life, so must he also be conformed to Christ in his Passion.[27] There may well have been another motive for including Leo: he was a vital witness of the stigmatization, whom Bonaventure may have consulted while preparing to write the *Legenda maior*.[28] Leo was especially significant for the friars in Assisi. After his death, in 1271 or 1272, he was buried in the south transept of the Lower Church.[29] He had, perhaps in the late 1250s, given the Sacro Convento a precious piece of parchment on which Francis had written a blessing for him. Leo had later annotated this parchment, explaining that Francis had written it at La Verna, after receiving in his body the 'impression of Christ's stigmata'.[30] As Brooke observed, for the friars of the Basilica, Leo's annotated blessing was both evidence and relic.[31]

The Body of Francis and the Body of Christ

Not only is the iconography of the *Stigmatization* new, but the scene is given particular emphasis within the Saint Francis cycle. The *Stigmatization* is Scene 19 and it is immediately followed by the *Death of Saint Francis*. As we shall see, this placing was of crucial importance for the nave scheme, and the position of the *Stigmatization* must have been one of the very first major decisions made by the planners of the cycle. The placement is faithful to Bonaventure's concept of the stigmatization as the zenith of the saint's life: in the *Legenda maior* he interpreted six earlier biographical episodes as apparitions of the cross, all pointing towards the seventh and final apparition, the stigmatization itself.

In the Assisi cycle, the scene immediately preceding the *Stigmatization* is the *Apparition at Arles* (see fig. 93). During a provincial chapter meeting at Arles, in southern France, while Saint Anthony of Padua was preaching to the assembled friars on the subject of the inscription on the crucifix, one of the brothers saw in the doorway a vision of Saint Francis, lifted up in the air with both arms extended as if on a cross.[32] This was the sixth of Bonaventure's apparitions of the cross, and the episode prefigures the stigmatization.[33] As Smart pointed out, the figure of the saint hovering in the doorway at Arles is given the same pose and position as the Christ–Seraph at La Verna in the subsequent scene, which emphasizes its typological significance.[34] The use of this visual device may well have been an intentional reworking of the parallel already made in the stained glass devoted to Saints Francis and Anthony in the window facing this bay (see figs 80 and 81).

Considerable advance planning must have been required in order to achieve this juxtaposition of scenes, because the *Apparition at Arles* is one of only three episodes in the Saint Francis cycle to be placed out of its Bonaventuran sequence (see fig. 96).[35] The story was transplanted from Chapter 4 of the *Legenda maior* and inserted between episodes from chapters 12 and 13. Rearranging the episodes of Francis's life in order to bring out their greater meaning was, however, entirely in accord with Bonaventure's principles, as the saint's biographer explained in the Prologue to the *Legenda*: 'To avoid confusion I did not always weave the story together in chronological order. Rather, I strove to maintain a more thematic order, relating to the same theme events that happened at different times, and to different themes events that happened at the same time, as seemed appropriate.'[36]

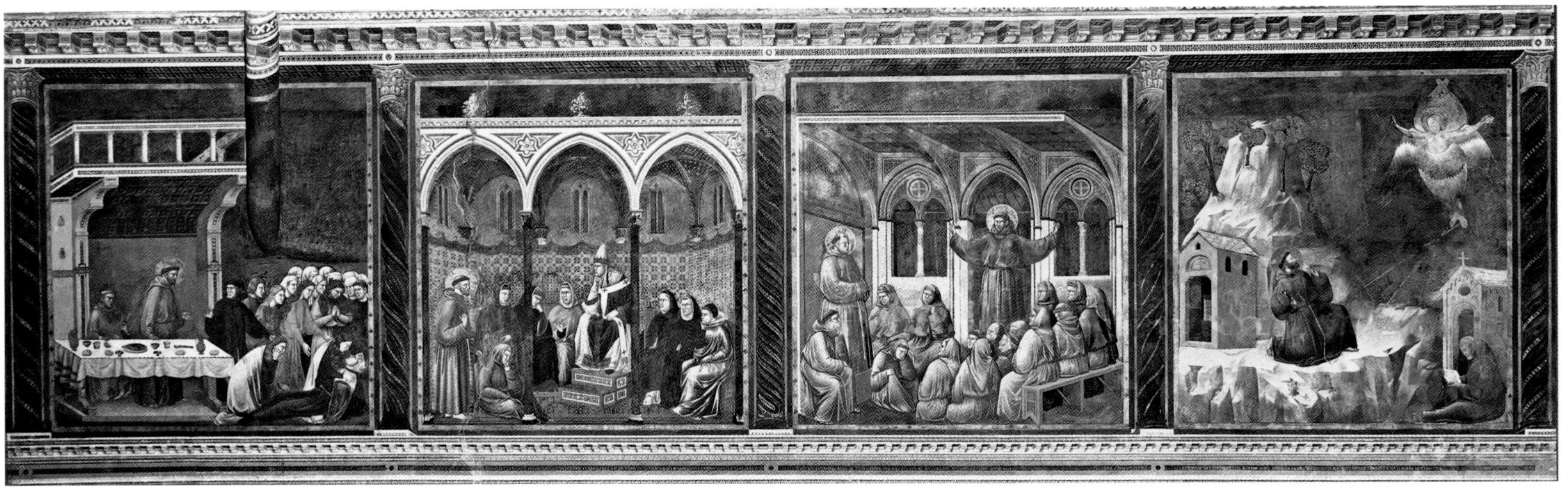

119 Saint Francis cycle, Scenes 16 to 19, *c.*1290–96, fresco, south wall of the nave, Upper Church, Basilica of San Francesco.

But considered within the physical space of the nave, the position chosen for the *Stigmatization* initially seems awkward and even oddly inconsequential. The scene appears on the south wall in the fourth bay, which is closest to the counter-façade (see fig. 90). For structural reasons, the pictorial field for the Saint Francis cycle is wider in this bay than the others. Since the bay contains four scenes rather than three, the *Stigmatization* could not be emphasized by being given the central place. Indeed, as it is placed fourth, the initial impression is that the *Stigmatization* is marginalized, and a comparison with the three preceding scenes only adds to a sense of dislocation rather than harmony within the bay (fig. 119). Those three scenes all have interior settings, and the perspectival treatment of their architecture creates a unified triptych: the building in the *Death of the Knight of Celano* recedes to the left; that of *Preaching before Pope Honorius III* is centrally viewed; while the chapter house of the *Apparition at Arles* recedes to the right. In contrast, not only does the landscape setting of the *Stigmatization* create a disjunction, but Saint Francis turns his back on the preceding scenes.

Only when the *Stigmatization* is viewed within the context of the entire wall does its position start to make sense and its prominence within the cycle become apparent. Bonaventure's identification of the stigmatized Francis with the crucified Christ is powerfully expressed on the south wall of the nave through the dynamic relationship between the Saint Francis cycle and the Passion cycle in the tier directly above. The Saint Francis stories proceed from left to right; those of Christ from right to left. This was not new to the Basilica: in the nave of the Lower Church, in the 1260s, the Maestro di San Francesco had also painted a fresco cycle of Saint Francis running from left to right and a Passion cycle running from right to left. But in the Lower Church the two cycles had been painted on opposite walls of the nave, in a parallel scheme, enabling both narrative sequences to proceed in the same direction, towards the high altar. In the Upper Church, the Saint Francis scenes are not placed opposite the Passion scenes, but below them on the same wall. In the top two registers of the nave, the biblical cycles are again arranged in parallel, each running from the altar end of the wall to the eastern entrance. The novelty results from the decision to arrange the Saint Francis cycle, in the third tier, as a wrap-around scheme. This means that while on the north wall the first half of the Saint Francis cycle proceeds in the same direction as the Genesis cycles above (from the altar towards the counter-façade), on the south wall the second half of the cycle turns to flow back towards the high altar, while, in the tiers above, the Christ cycle runs in the opposite direction.

This unusual arrangement offered new and exciting iconographic possibilities, but to exploit them fully required meticulous planning and creative thinking. One curious feature of the iconography of the *Stigmatization* offers a clue to the means by which the two fresco cycles are visually linked. Both Bonaventure and Celano described the Christ–Seraph being fixed to a cross, but in the Assisi scene, although the figure's arms are outstretched, there is no cross. This

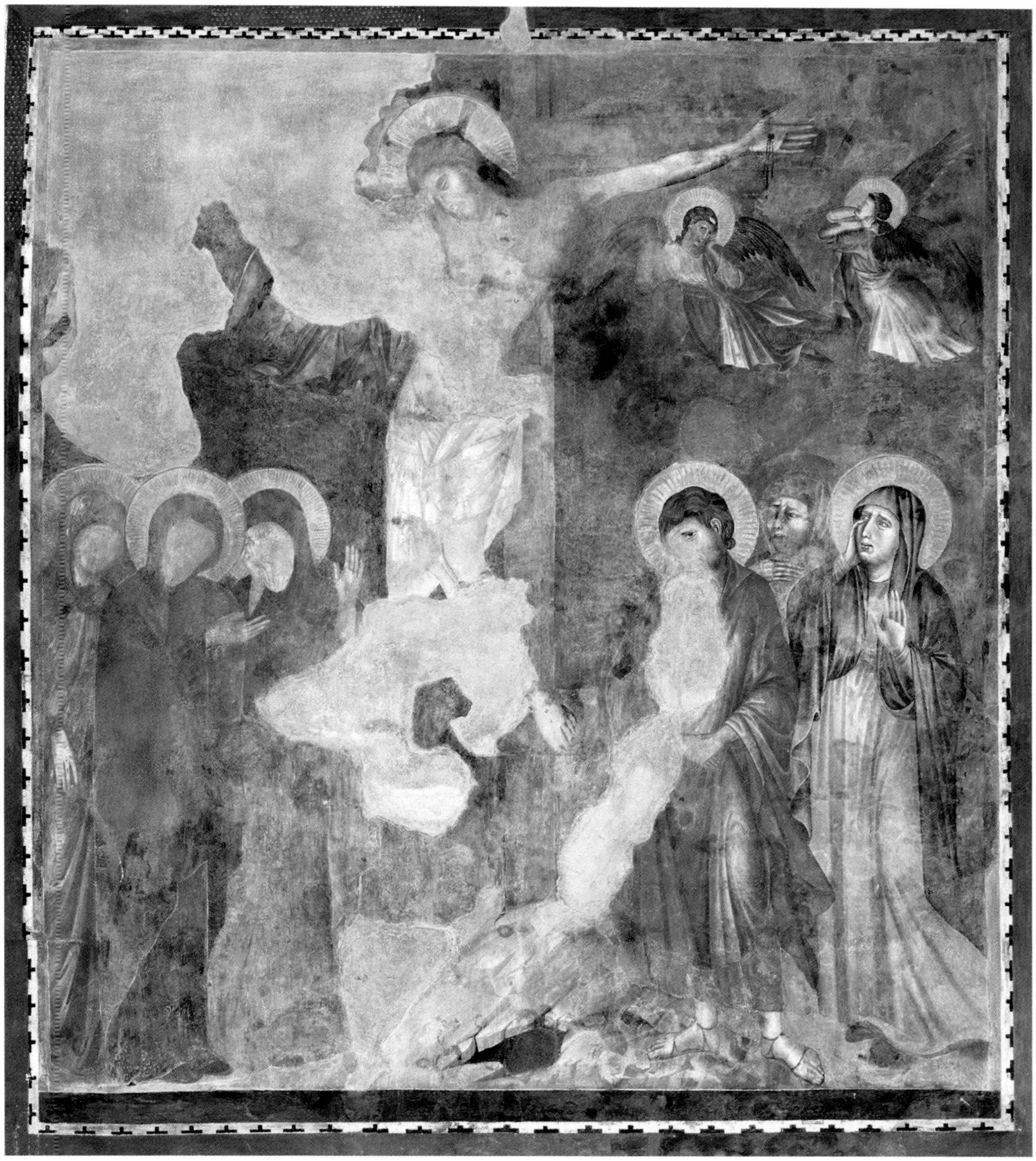

120 *Crucifixion*, New Testament cycle, *c.*1288–91, fresco, third bay, south wall of the nave, Upper Church, Basilica of San Francesco.

omission becomes more explicable when we look at the juxtaposition of the two cycles. Within the scene, Saint Francis kneels and looks up to the right at the Christ–Seraph, but if the diagonal of his gaze is continued beyond the limits of the pictorial frame, it leads up to the first scene on the middle tier of the next bay, the *Crucifixion* (fig. 120). Thus Francis experiences a double vision of Christ Crucified, both literally (within his own narrative) and figuratively (within the Passion cycle) (fig. 121).[37] By means of such visual links between the tiers, the overall nave programme continually becomes more than the sum of its individual parts.

Directly below the *Crucifixion* is the *Death of Saint Francis* (fig. 122). One of the friars who was present when Francis died saw his soul, like a star, carried on a shining cloud up to heaven, and the fresco portrays this vision prominently. Francis's soul is depicted as a half-length frontal figure, carried by angels. His side wound is clearly visible through a tear in his dark-red habit, and he holds his palms aloft to

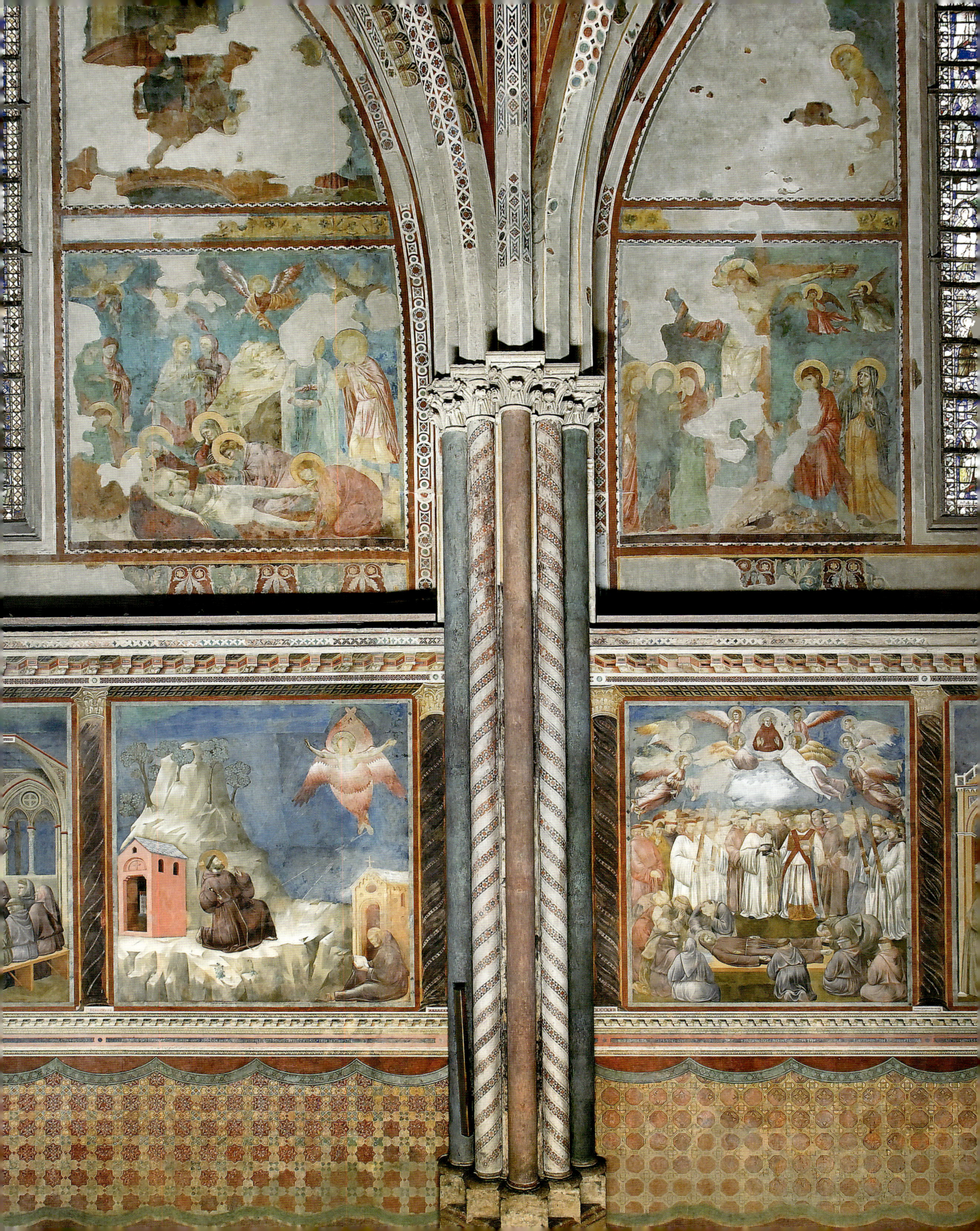

display his wounds to the viewer. Although Francis had borne the stigmata for two years before his death, only his closest companions knew of them. His death was the critical moment, the time of revelation and public recognition of the stigmata. Again, the two cycles are linked, the vertical ascent of Francis's soul leading the eye up to the *Crucifixion* above, asserting the identity of the stigmatized saint with the crucified Christ (fig. 121).

The miraculous nature of Francis's passing is accentuated by the next scene, *Visions of the Death of Saint Francis* (fig. 123). This combines two episodes that happened simultaneously in different places, both coinciding with the moment of the saint's death. In the right-hand section of the picture, we see the sleeping figure of Guido, bishop of Assisi. While Guido was on pilgrimage to Monte Sant'Angelo in Puglia, Francis appeared to him, saying: 'Behold, I am going to heaven.' The bishop later discovered that this had occurred at the exact moment of his friend's death. On the left, a group of friars gathers at the deathbed of Brother Agostino, the provincial minister of the Terra di Lavoro (the province of Naples). Just before he died, Agostino suddenly cried out: 'Wait for me, father, I am coming with you!' When the brothers asked to whom he was speaking, he replied: 'Don't you see our father, Francis, going to heaven?'

The composition of this scene is highly innovative. Given the conventions of left-to-right pictorial cycles, it is unusual to find the main protagonists in the story facing left rather than right. Agostino sits up, stretching out his arms and gazing avidly upwards, apparently at the blank wall above the heads of his confrères. As with the *Stigmatization*, however, the true object of the friar's inner eye lies beyond the confines of the picture frame: what he sees is the ascending soul of Francis in the preceding scene.[38] The pictorial version makes explicit Bonaventure's implication that Agostino is a second eye-witness to the vision of Francis's soul ascending to heaven, and even suggests a third: the friar standing behind Agostino echoes the minister's gaze. That the daring conceit of these two linked scenes (the *Death of Saint Francis* and the *Visions of the Death of Saint Francis*) was carefully planned and coordinated between the artists and the friars of the Sacro Convento is suggested by the titulus describing the *Visions*, which is the only example in the cycle of a single caption extending across more than one scene.[39]

The figures of Agostino and the friar behind him have a further function: rather than leading the eye on to the next scene, they return attention to the preceding one, so underlining the crucial importance of the death of the saint and prompting the viewer to linger on it. Further emphasis is added by another visual link, this time across the space of the nave. The scene opposite the *Death of Saint Francis*, on the north wall, is the *Vision of the Thrones* (fig. 124). One of Francis's companions experiences a vision of heavenly thrones: he is told that the highest throne was formerly occupied by the fallen Lucifer, but it is now reserved for Francis. Placing this scene opposite the *Death of Saint Francis* visually accentuates the ascension of Francis's soul as the fulfilment of this divine prophecy.[40] Neff argued that the red habit of the transcendent Francis, which was once covered in gold striations, emphasizes his bond with Christ.[41] The *Ascension* window in the north transept identified Christ with a prophecy of Isaiah – 'Why then is thy apparel red . . .?' – and he is clad in red consistently throughout the nave frescoes.[42] The red and gold of Francis's tunic also indicate the radiance of his soul as it ascends to the glory of the heavenly seat vacated by Lucifer (whose name means 'light-bearer'). The vacant throne on the north wall mirrors the exact position of Francis's soul on the south; the link must have been intended.

According to the chronicle of the Franciscan friar Salimbene of Parma, when Brother Leo saw the naked body of Francis, he thought he saw before him 'a crucified man who had just been taken down from the cross'.[43] Francis's corpse is surrounded by the hunched figures of his stricken companions who touch his hands and feet, in a composition that echoes the *Lamentation* over the dead Christ. The comparison can easily be made: the *Lamentation* follows the *Crucifixion* in the tier above, which (because of the Passion cycle's right-to-left flow) places it directly above the *Stigmatization*. Consequently, this section of the south wall offers a quartet of scenes that is so tightly bound that it can be read across the heavy cluster of columns that divides the two bays, allowing meaningful links to be made both vertically and diagonally (fig. 121). The body of Christ is directly above the Passion of Francis; the body of Francis directly below the Passion of

facing page 121 *Stigmatization of Saint Francis*, *Death of Saint Francis*, *Crucifixion* and *Lamentation*, New Testament and Saint Francis cycles, *c.*1288–96, fresco, second and third bays, south wall of the nave, Upper Church, Basilica of San Francesco.

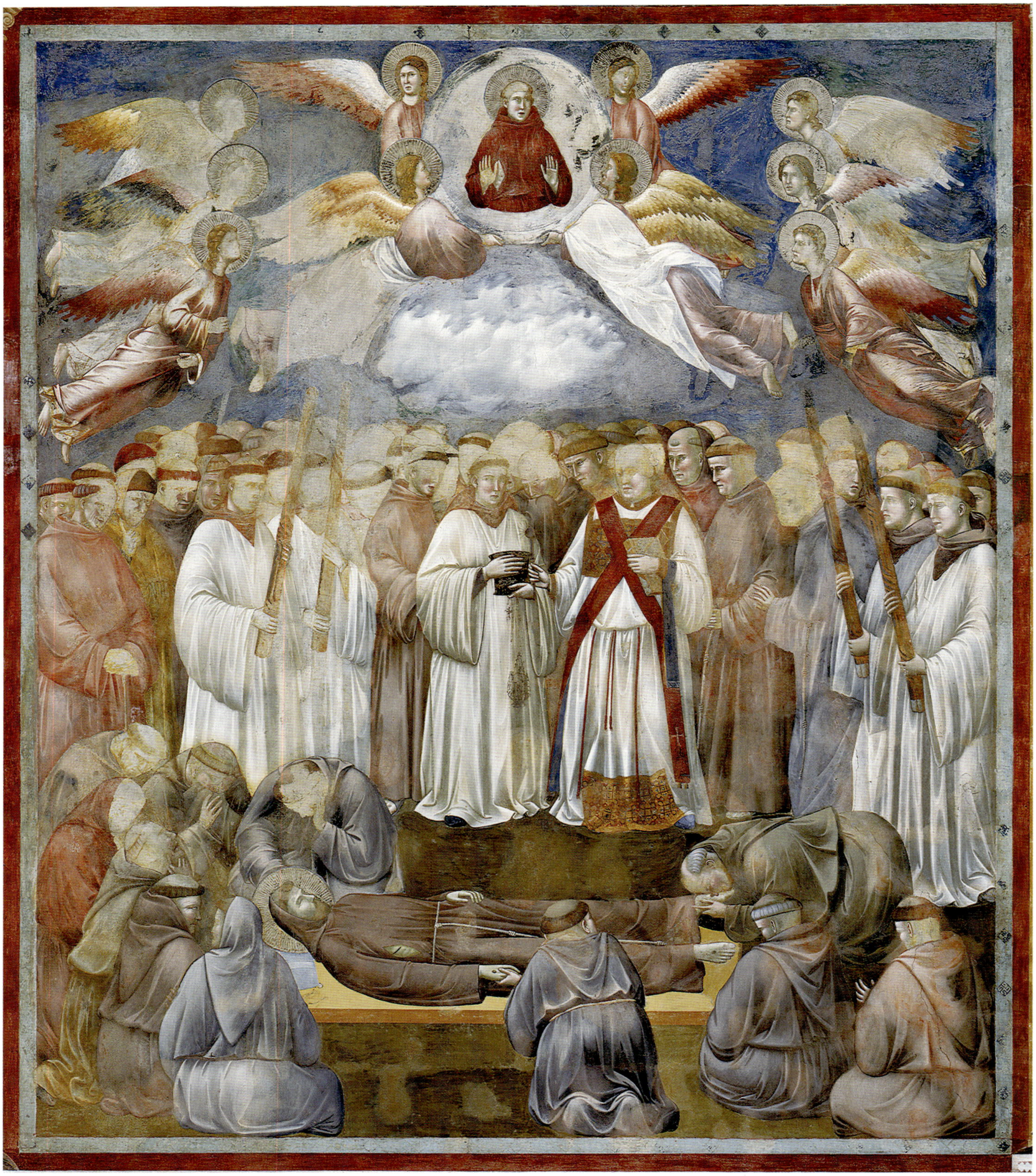

122 *Death of Saint Francis*, Scene 20 of the Saint Francis cycle, *c.*1290–96, fresco, south wall of the nave, Upper Church, Basilica of San Francesco.

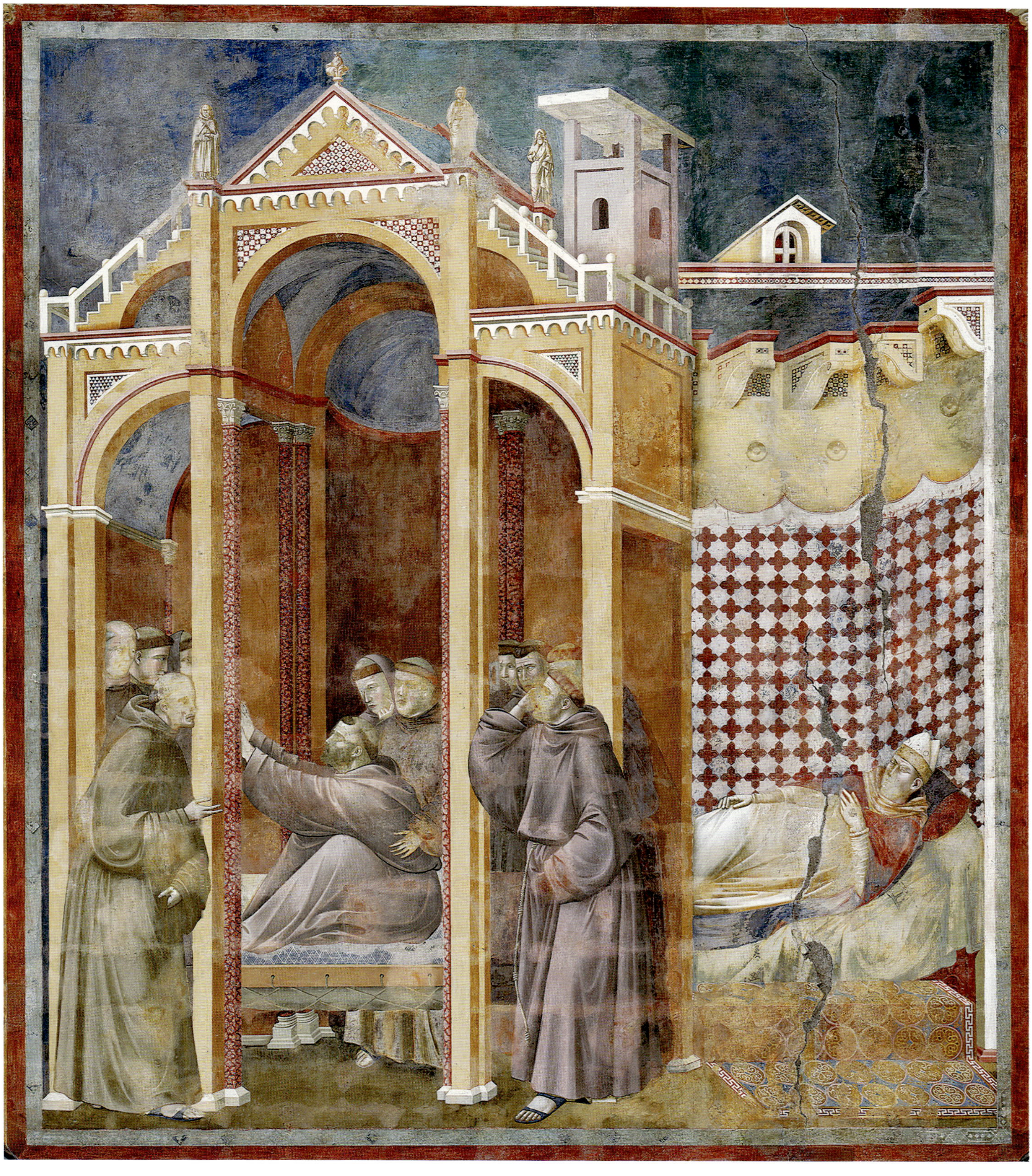

123 *Visions of the Death of Saint Francis*, Scene 21 of the Saint Francis cycle, *c.*1290–96, fresco, south wall of the nave, Upper Church, Basilica of San Francesco.

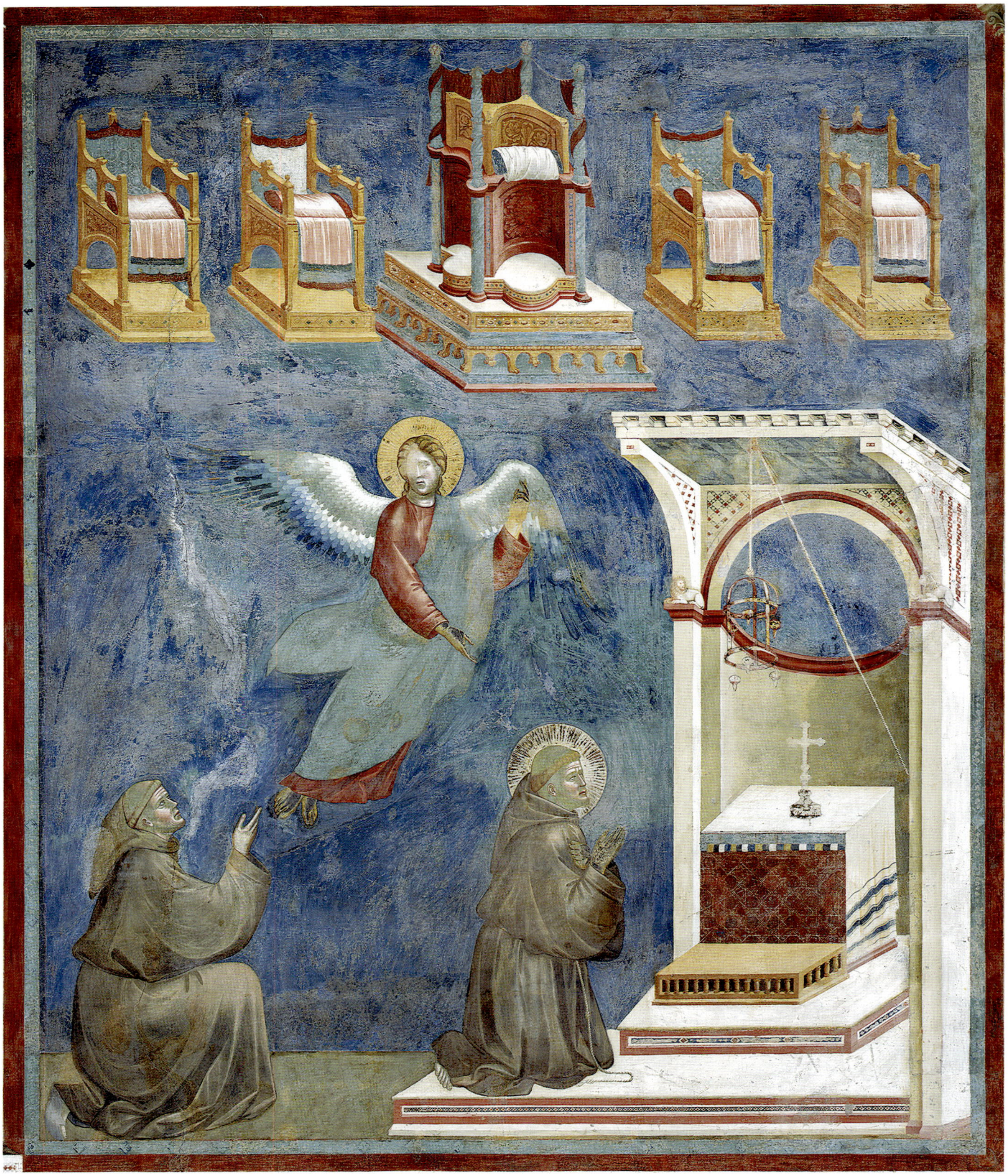

124 *Vision of the Thrones*, Scene 9 of the Saint Francis cycle, *c.*1290–96, fresco, north wall of the nave, Upper Church, Basilica of San Francesco.

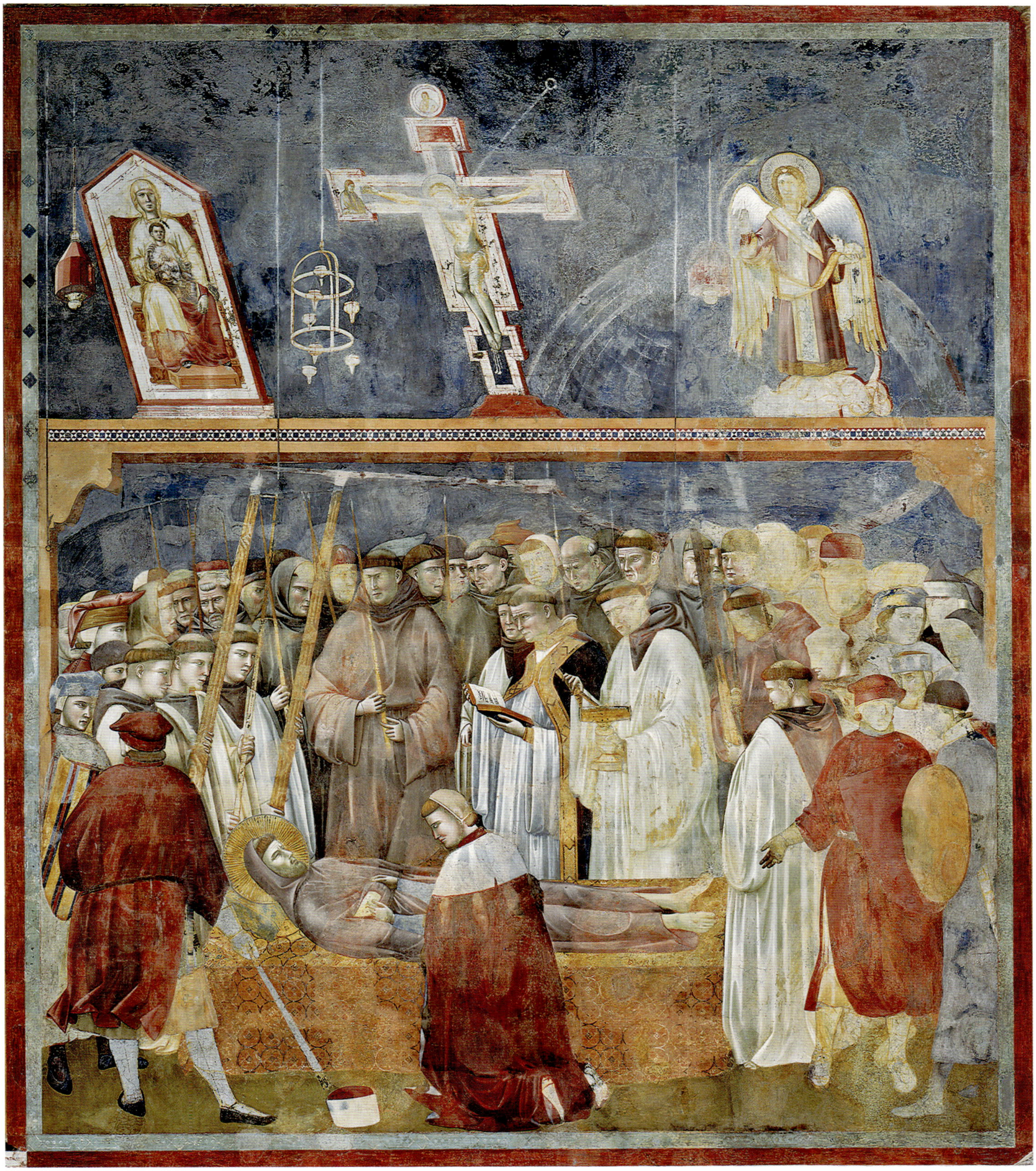

125 *Verification of the Stigmata*, Scene 22 of the Saint Francis cycle, *c.*1290–96, fresco, south wall of the nave, Upper Church, Basilica of San Francesco.

Christ. The first diagonal ties the *Stigmatization* to the *Crucifixion* while the second links the two *Lamentations*: these two intersecting diagonals form another cross. By these means, the suffering and wounded bodies of Christ and Francis are intimately connected.

The triplet of Saint Francis scenes in the third bay is completed with the *Verification of the Stigmata* (fig. 125), which follows the *Death of Saint Francis* and the *Visions of the Death of Saint Francis*. The *Verification* echoes the composition of the *Death of Saint Francis*, while also reiterating its main themes, with the stigmata again being displayed for the veneration of the faithful. This scene includes the figure of Jerome, a learned knight of Assisi, who refused to believe in the miraculous wounds until he had touched them himself. Bonaventure, who introduced this episode for the first time in the *Legenda maior*, likened Jerome to Doubting Thomas, so adding another specific parallel between the stigmatized bodies of Francis and Christ. The link between Francis and the cross of Christ is here asserted twice more: first within the scene, through the inclusion of a painted panel crucifix on the rood beam above the saint's corpse, and then outside it, through a vertical link to the Passion scene directly above, *Christ Carrying the Cross* (fig. 126). The entire bay is composed with meaningful symmetry, so that in both the two outer scenes (the *Death* and the *Verification)* Saint Francis's body, displaying 'the stigmata of the cross of our Lord Jesus Christ', is placed directly beneath images of Christ's cross. The message could hardly be more emphatic.[44]

Celestial Pearls and the Heavenly City

The sequence of scenes from the *Stigmatization of Saint Francis* to the *Verification of the Stigmata*, with their carefully wrought diagonal and vertical links to the Passion narratives above, is one of the most skilful and powerful pieces of image-making in the entire nave. The system of diagonals and verticals that we have demonstrated here is employed as a recurring compositional device throughout the Saint Francis cycle. We do not, however, intend to argue that it is applied consistently for every scene. In our view, it would have been impossible to have done this while still maintaining narrative coherence and balance within each individual cycle. Some links are much stronger than others. Not only that, but the selective application of this compositional device actually makes it a far more effective tool, which functions on one level to highlight and on another to gloss the most important passages within the overall iconographic scheme.

The next bay on the south wall (the second; fig. 127) allows us to make more deductions about the priorities and processes of planning. The Saint Francis cycle continues here with the *Lamentation of the Clares*, the badly damaged *Canonization* and the *Dream of Pope Gregory IX*. The two Passion scenes in the middle tier of the wall are, possibly, *Christ before Pilate* (above the *Lamentation*) and the *Betrayal* (above the *Dream*).[45] Analysis of this bay is somewhat hampered by losses to the frescoes, but nonetheless it is hard to see any strong thematic links between the two tiers. This strengthens the argument that in planning the cycle, the first priority was given to positioning the *Stigmatization* and the *Death of Saint Francis* scenes. The key ideological decision was to make the stories of Francis and Christ, advancing from opposite directions, coincide at the moment of their two deaths. But the contrary flow of the two cycles posed a practical dilemma, in that the greater the amount of space devoted to the life of Francis (as opposed to posthumous scenes), the smaller the space available for the life of Christ in the tier above. The Saint Francis scenes were given precedence and the Passion cycle tailored to fit. This seems the most plausible explanation for Christ's Passion (that quintessentially Franciscan subject) being reduced to only four scenes and his Ministry to just two.[46]

In the second bay, therefore, the Passion scenes had to be chosen primarily to maintain the internal coherence of the Gospel narratives, rather than for their relevance to the Saint Francis cycle. However, that does not imply any lessening in the *alter Christus* theme; rather, different visual strategies were adopted for expressing it within the Saint Francis stories themselves. The *Lamentation of the Clares* (fig. 128), for example, draws on the iconography for a *Pietà*, with Saint Clare taking the role of the Virgin Mary, bending to embrace Francis's body, while her sisters kiss his hands and feet. But it also includes iconographic motifs from a quite different Passion scene, the Entry of Christ into Jerusalem – an episode that had to be omitted from the Passion cycle above. The typical composition of an Entry into Jerusalem has Christ on the left, riding a donkey and followed by his disciples, being acclaimed by a jubilant crowd streaming out of the city on the right. Here, the body of Francis, who had died at the Porziuncola outside Assisi, is being carried back into the city for burial in the church of San Giorgio. The cortège pauses at San Damiano, where Saint Clare was cloistered, to allow the nuns to venerate his body. Bonaventure's account omitted much of the detail that had earlier been provided by Celano, but it retained the description of the crowd taking branches from the trees.[47] It was this that provided the reference to Christ entering Jerusalem, a significance well understood by the planners of the Assisi cycle, who included in the titulus the description of the crowd 'cum ramis arborum'.[48] The fresco itself not only shows three leafy boughs being held by some of the men following the bier, but behind them a boy climbs a tree to reach for another branch.

Youths climbing trees had been a standard motif in the iconography of the Entry into Jerusalem since early Christian times, but the dorsal pose of the Assisi boy seems to have been an innovation. Ever since M. Roy Fisher's 1956 article, which first drew attention to the remarkable similarity between the climbing lad at Assisi and his counterpart in Giotto's *Entry into Jerusalem* in the Arena Chapel, Padua (fig. 129), the 'boy in the tree' has been a *cause célèbre* in the dating and attributional debates over the Saint Francis cycle.[49] Fisher, accepting both cycles as the work of Giotto, believed it more probable that the Assisi boy was copied from Padua than the reverse, and therefore that the whole Saint Francis cycle must post-date the Arena frescoes. He argued that 'the boy in the tree is undeniably a figure associated with the scene of Entry' and that therefore it was unlikely that the innovative figure could have been invented for the Assisi scene 'where it is not an essential requirement'.[50] However, if one accepts that the parallel with the *Entry into Jerusalem* was quite deliberate, then the boy in the tree is far from incidental: on the contrary, he is the vital iconographic motif that makes the reference clear. The Assisi boy is by no means the only figure in the cycle to be depicted from the rear. Indeed, all three scenes in this bay of the south wall contain striking examples of such figures, not least the man bending to set down Francis's bier in the *Lamentation of the Clares*. Might not an artist have felt freer to adapt the pose of the boy in the tree in the context of a new Franciscan scene, untrammelled by iconographic tradition, rather than when depicting Christ's Passion?

Several scholars, noting the allusion to the Entry in the fresco, have suggested that it might explain why the façade of San Damiano in the mural bears no relation to that of the actual church outside Assisi (fig. 130). In marked contrast, the Roman basilica of Saint John Lateran in the *Dream of Pope Innocent III* (see fig. 140) on the north wall is depicted much more accurately. Symbolism rather than naturalism seems the most likely explanation, particularly as this is just one of several important representations of churches in the cycle which (as we shall argue in the next chapter) are also primarily carriers of symbolic and figural meanings. It is telling that the titulus below the scene does not specify where the events are taking place: 'How the crowd from the city of Assisi had assembled, taking up branches from the trees . . . and carried the sacred body . . . so that Blessed Clare and her virgin sisters could see him.'[51] The emphasis on the civic nature of the funerary procession, in conjunction with the Gospel quotation and the iconography of the boy in the tree, all help to draw the parallel with the Entry into Jerusalem. But whereas the living Christ entered the earthly Jerusalem, the dead Francis is about to enter the heavenly Jerusalem, and this is what the façade of San Damiano in the fresco represents.[52] Johannes Tripps has demonstrated that medieval cathedral façades were often intended to symbolize the walls of the celestial Jerusalem, their sculpted figures of saints, prophets and angels representing the guardians and inhabitants of the city.[53] Celebrations for Palm Sunday customarily involved two crowds: the first group, carrying palms, came out from inside the church to meet the second, carrying Christ in the form of the Eucharist. Saintly relics were often carried into the church as well. In Siena, all the people came to the cathedral, where the cantors and clerics stood on top of the steps in front of the central portal to meet them, singing the *Gloria*.[54]

While Francis arrives bodily at the gates of the celestial city, the eagle perched atop the church gable may signal the entry of his soul into heaven. An eagle has numerous symbolic possibilities, but a particularly pertinent one is the ascending Christ, following Saint Jerome's interpretation of Jeremiah 49:22 as a prophecy of the Ascension: 'Behold he shall come up as an eagle, and fly: and he shall spread his wings over Bosra'.[55] The vision of Francis's soul ascending

following spread (left) 126 View of the third bay, south wall of the nave, Upper Church, Basilica of San Francesco.

following spread (right) 127 View of the second bay, south wall of the nave, Upper Church, Basilica of San Francesco.

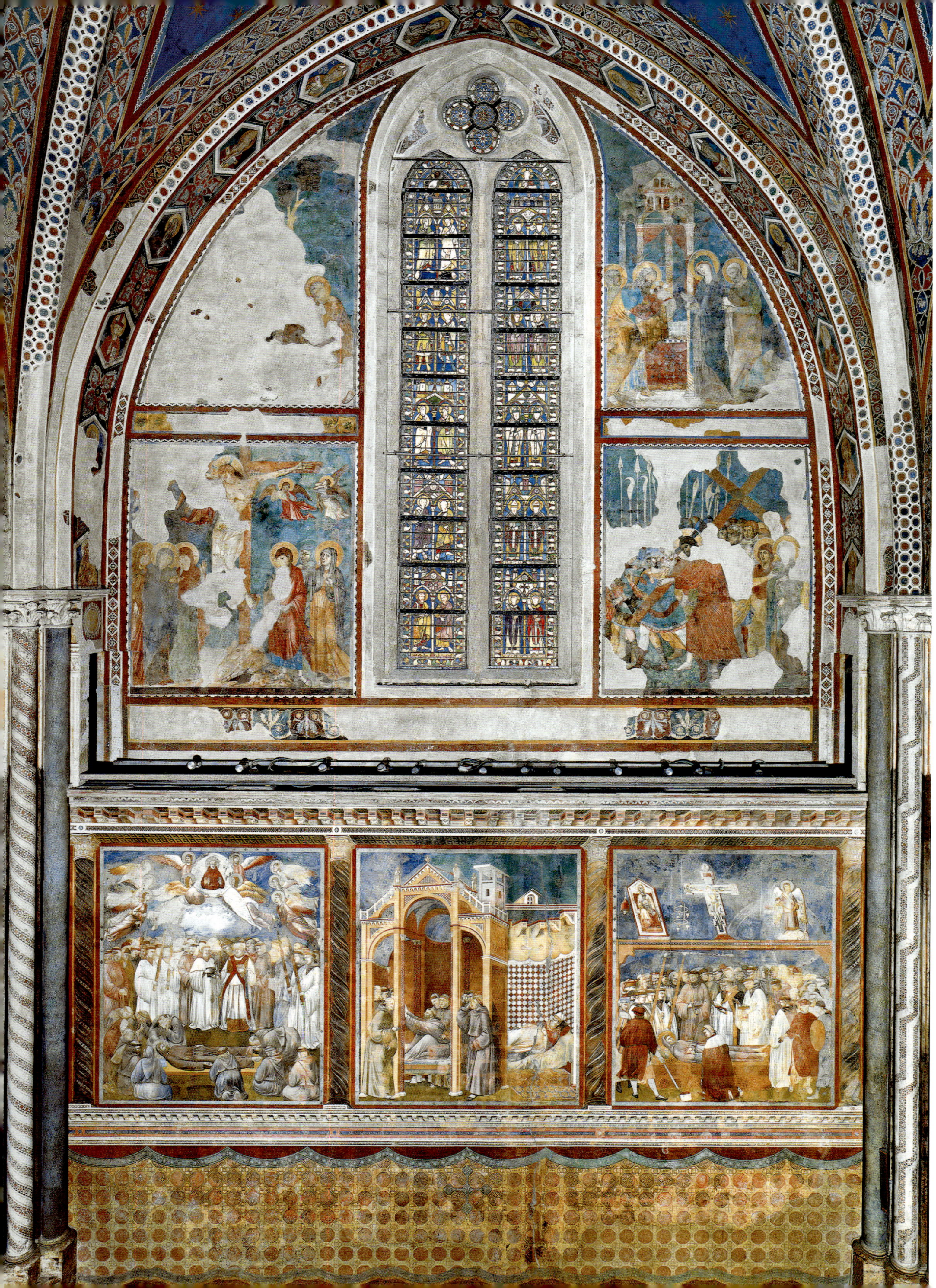

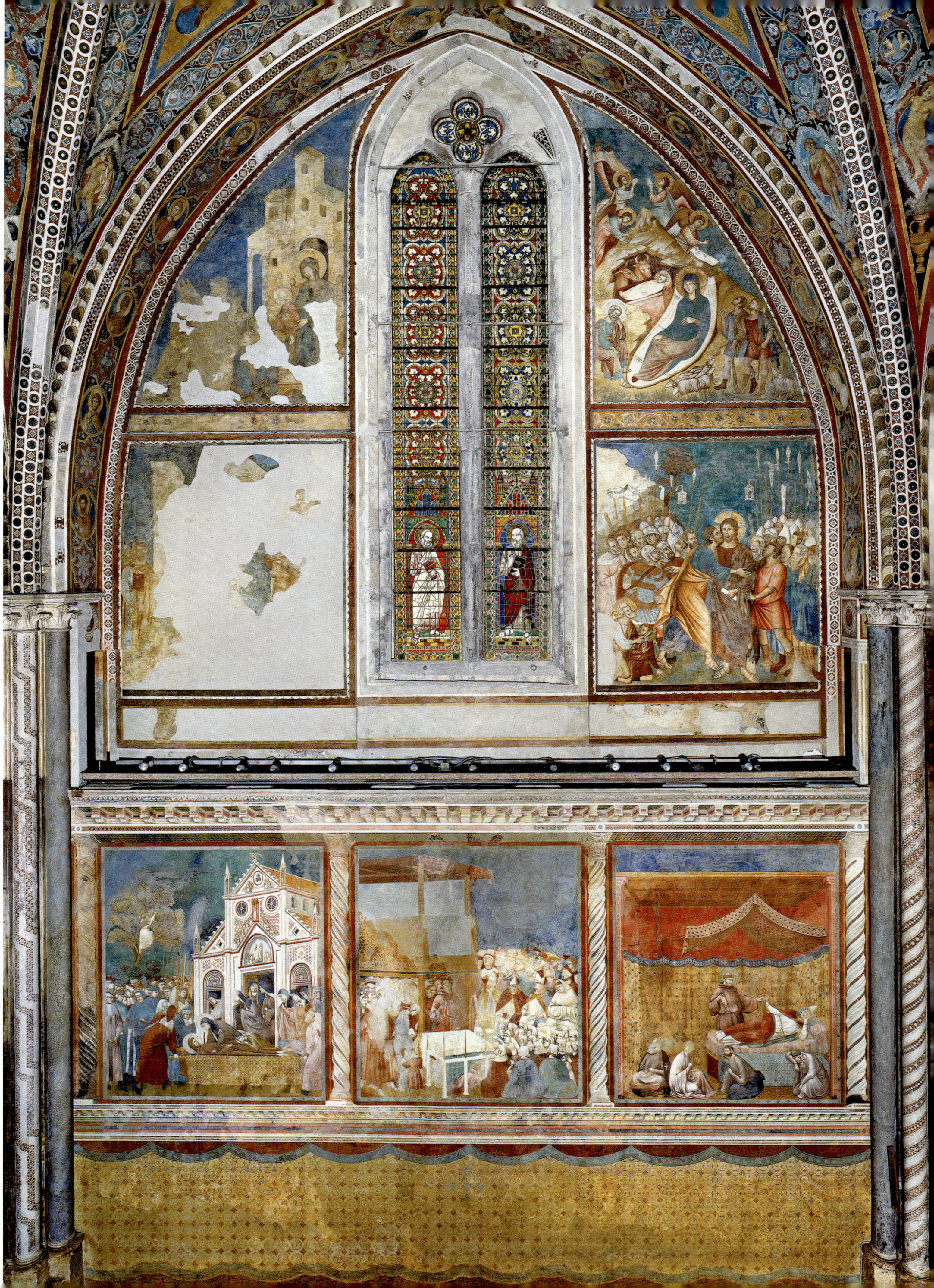

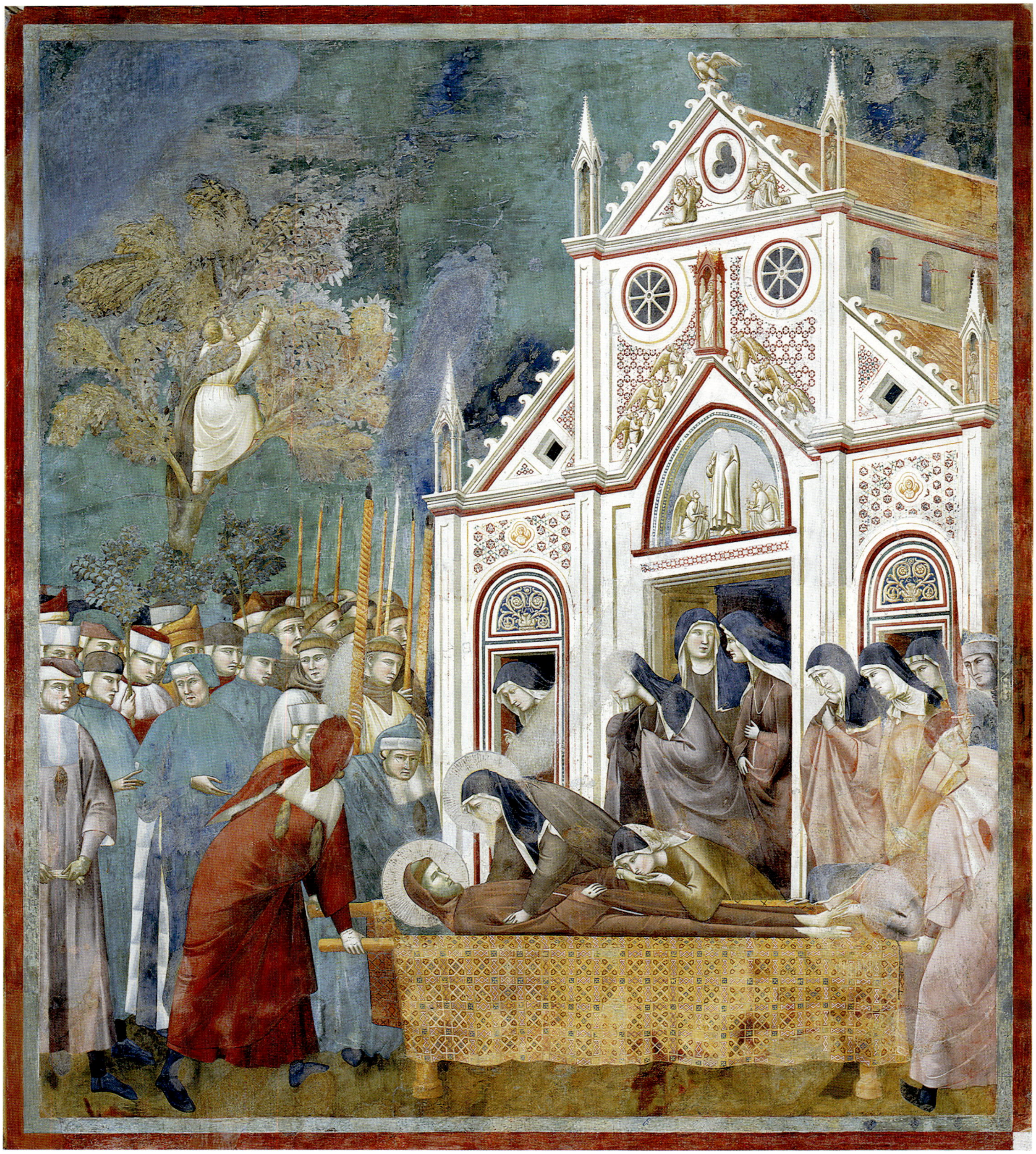

128 *Lamentation of the Clares*, Scene 23 of the Saint Francis cycle, *c.*1290–96, fresco, south wall of the nave, Upper Church, Basilica of San Francesco.

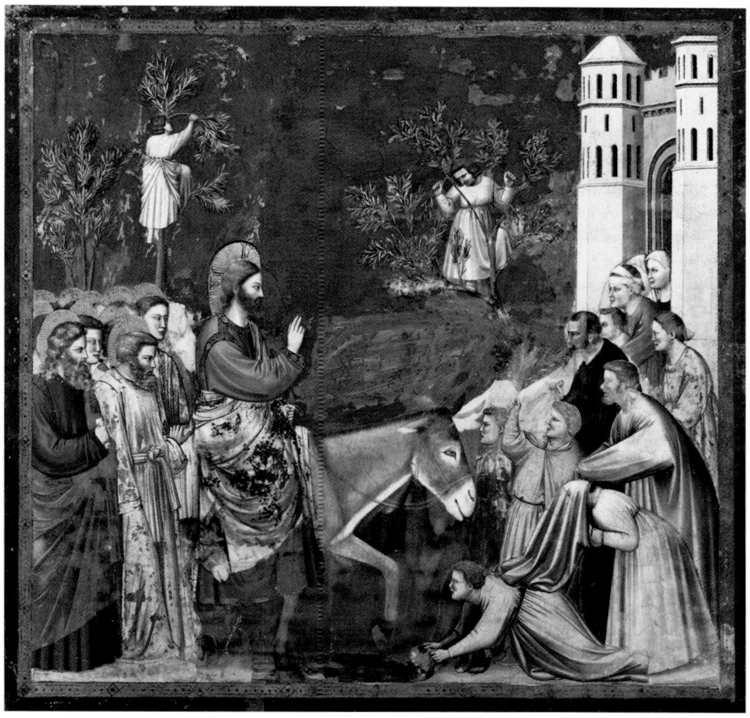

129 Giotto, *Entry into Jerusalem*, *c.*1302–5, fresco, Arena Chapel, Padua.

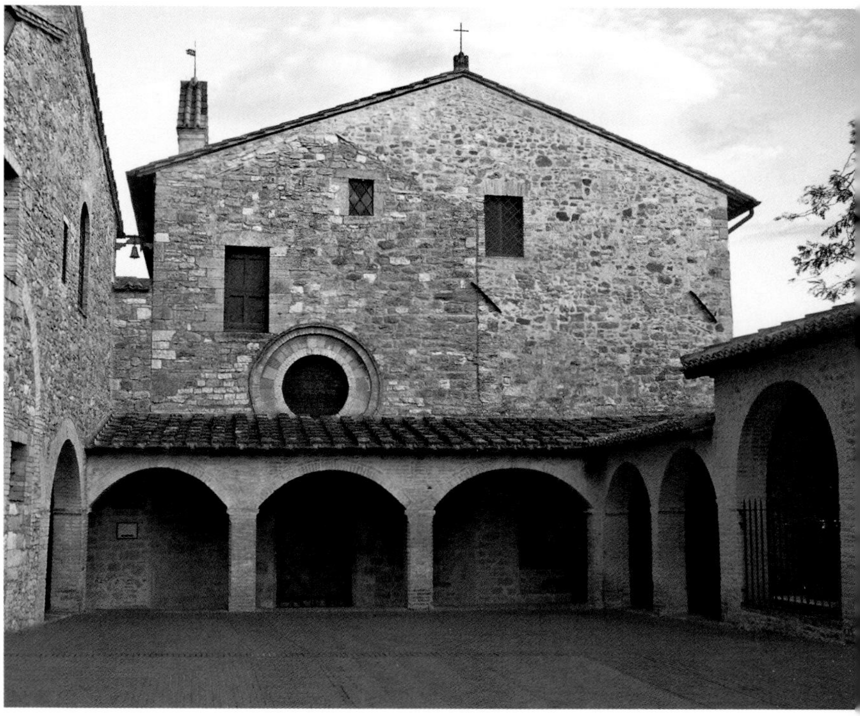

130 San Damiano, Assisi, view of the façade.

on a cloud had already likened him to the ascending Christ,[56] so this interpretation of the eagle would be consistent with that; and, as we shall see, eagles also appear on the counter-façade of the Upper Church in connection with the Ascension (see Chapter 7).

The façade of the fictive San Damiano is covered in multicoloured geometric cosmati-work mosaic. Its appearance may have been intended to evoke the description in the Apocalypse of the walls of the celestial Jerusalem, whose foundations were 'adorned with all manner of precious stones'.[57] Each of the four sides of the city wall had three gates, each gate being made of a single pearl.[58] 'And the gates [of the city] shall not be shut by day . . . And they shall bring the glory and honour of the nations into it'.[59] This is reminiscent of Bonaventure's lyrical description (quoted in the inscription below the fresco) of Francis's sacred body 'adorned with its heavenly pearls'; that is, with the stigmata.[60] After halting at San Damiano the crowd reached the city of Assisi, where 'with all reverence they placed the precious treasure they were carrying in the church of San Giorgio'.[61] An extra overlay of meaning for local viewers of the fresco at the end of the Duecento may have been the knowledge that San Giorgio, Francis's temporary burial place, had by 1257 been transformed into the basilica of Santa Chiara, housing both the tomb of Saint Clare and a Clarissan nunnery.

The Miraculous Power of the Stigmata

The Saint Francis cycle concludes with the *Canonization* (see fig. 95), followed by four post-mortem miracles. The *Canonization* itself may contain a posthumous miracle of healing, since the figure lying in front of the altar/tomb is probably the girl with a twisted neck, who was cured during Francis's funeral at San Giorgio.[62] There is some justification for the transposition of this miracle to the *Canonization* scene, since it was the first in the list of miracles read in the presence of Pope Gregory IX at the ceremony, according to Celano.[63] Although it is not in the *Legenda maior*, the miracle would have been well known at Assisi. It is one of the four post-mortem miracles of Saint Francis depicted on the mid-Duecento Treasury panel (see fig. 91). In the early 1290s, the panel would still have been in the Lower Church. Doubtless the friars would have been used to recounting the story to pilgrims visiting the tomb of Saint Francis.

No earlier pictorial versions exist for the cycle's four post-mortem miracle scenes, which may have been represented here for the first time. Scholars have frequently commented that they make new claims for Francis's posthumous powers. The *Dream of Pope Gregory IX* (fig. 131), which completes the second bay, is one of only three wholly original post-mortem miracles contributed by Bonaventure in the *Legenda maior* (the rest of the collection was imported from Celano's *Treatise of the Miracles*, which had been completed only about fifteen years earlier).[64] Bonaventure discloses that, before the canonization, the pontiff had harboured some doubts about whether Francis had really received a wound in his side. In response Francis, stern of face, appeared to him in a dream and asked him to fetch an empty vial; when Gregory brought it, the vial then seemed to be filled to the brim with blood flowing out of the saint's side. In the fresco, Francis stands beside the sleeping Gregory, holding his torn habit open to display his wound while handing the pope the blood-filled vial. Gregory had no further doubts.

The first scene in the final bay (fig. 132) initially seems to be a traditional miracle of healing but, once again, the story is really about the stigmata. John of Lérida calls on Saint Francis for aid, after having been attacked and viciously stabbed. The saint appears and cures John's lacerations by placing his own wounded hands upon them. Bonaventure is quite categorical: it is the stigmata that give Francis his healing power.[65] This miracle was so important to Bonaventure that he included it in the *Legenda minor*, despite his choir legend having no chapter on posthumous miracles; it is inserted into the chapter on the stigmatization, to demonstrate the thaumaturgical power of Francis's wounded hands.[66] Bonaventure likens Francis to Christ, who healed the whole human race through his wounds. This spiritual power is imaginatively expressed in the fresco, where Francis is accompanied by two angels, one of whom holds an ointment box. This no doubt refers to a detail in Bonaventure's account, that the saint seemed to anoint the man's wounds with ointment, but it might also suggest the Archangel Raphael, whose name was commonly interpreted as 'medicina Dei'.[67] In contrast, the man depicted shrugging helplessly outside the door is probably the doctor who has given up hope of saving the wounded man's life.

The central scene of the bay is the *Resurrection of a Woman from Benevento* (fig. 133). An unnamed woman, who had died without having confessed all her sins, was miraculously resuscitated through the intercession of Saint Francis, allowing her to remedy her omission and receive absolution before expiring a second time.[68] The woman is pictured sitting up in bed, whispering her sins into the ear of a ministering priest, while against the blue sky in the top left a diminutive Saint Francis kneels in prayer before an attentive Christ. Above the woman's head a bright angel swoops down to chase away a bat-winged demon, making it dramatically clear that the purpose of Francis's intercession was not to restore the woman's earthly life but to save her immortal soul. Perhaps this imaginative motif, which is not derived from the text, was suggested by the scene's proximity to the Duecento panel of Saint Michael on the rood beam (see Chapter 3). According to a seventeenth-century description, the archangel was depicted in his role as defender of heaven, doing battle with Lucifer. This juxtaposition of images, for the viewer in the nave, would have had strong apocalyptic overtones. The antiphon for Vespers on Saint Michael's feast day, giving him an intercessory role at the Last Judgment, is loosely based on the Apocalypse: 'While John was beholding the sacred mystery, Michael the Archangel sounded the trumpet: Forgive us, Lord our God, you who open the book and unloosen the seals.'[69] The friars, viewing the woman of Benevento scene from their choir in the Upper Church, would have been able to see only the back of the Saint Michael panel, but they would have had a full view of the Apocalypse fresco cycle in the south transept. The angelic theme in this bay is completed by the first fresco in the Infancy cycle in the top tier, where the Archangel Gabriel announces Christ's Incarnation to the Virgin (fig. 134).

Francis's post-mortem miracles are placed below two miracles performed by Christ during his ministry: on the left the ruined *Raising of Lazarus* and on the right the *Wedding at Cana*. There is a straightforward diagonal link between the *Woman of Benevento* and the *Raising of Lazarus* since both are resurrection scenes. The vertical link between the *Man of Lérida* and the *Raising of Lazarus* is no longer appreciable because of the ruination of the latter. However, in the standard iconography, Christ's disciples free the resurrected Lazarus from his burial bands; similarly, Saint Francis unties John of Lérida's bandages.

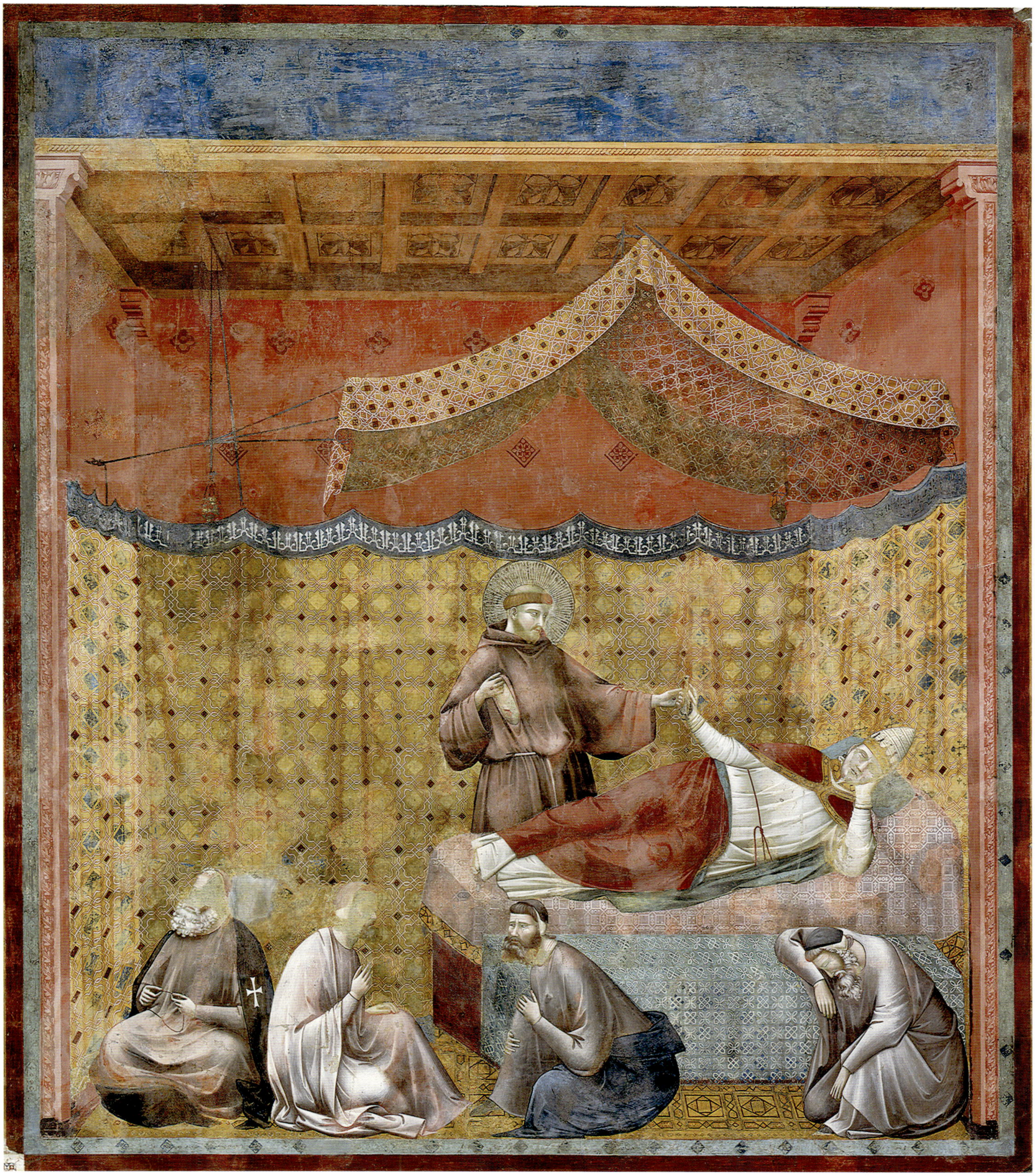

131 *Dream of Pope Gregory IX*, Scene 25 of the Saint Francis cycle, *c.*1290–96, fresco, south wall of the nave, Upper Church, Basilica of San Francesco.

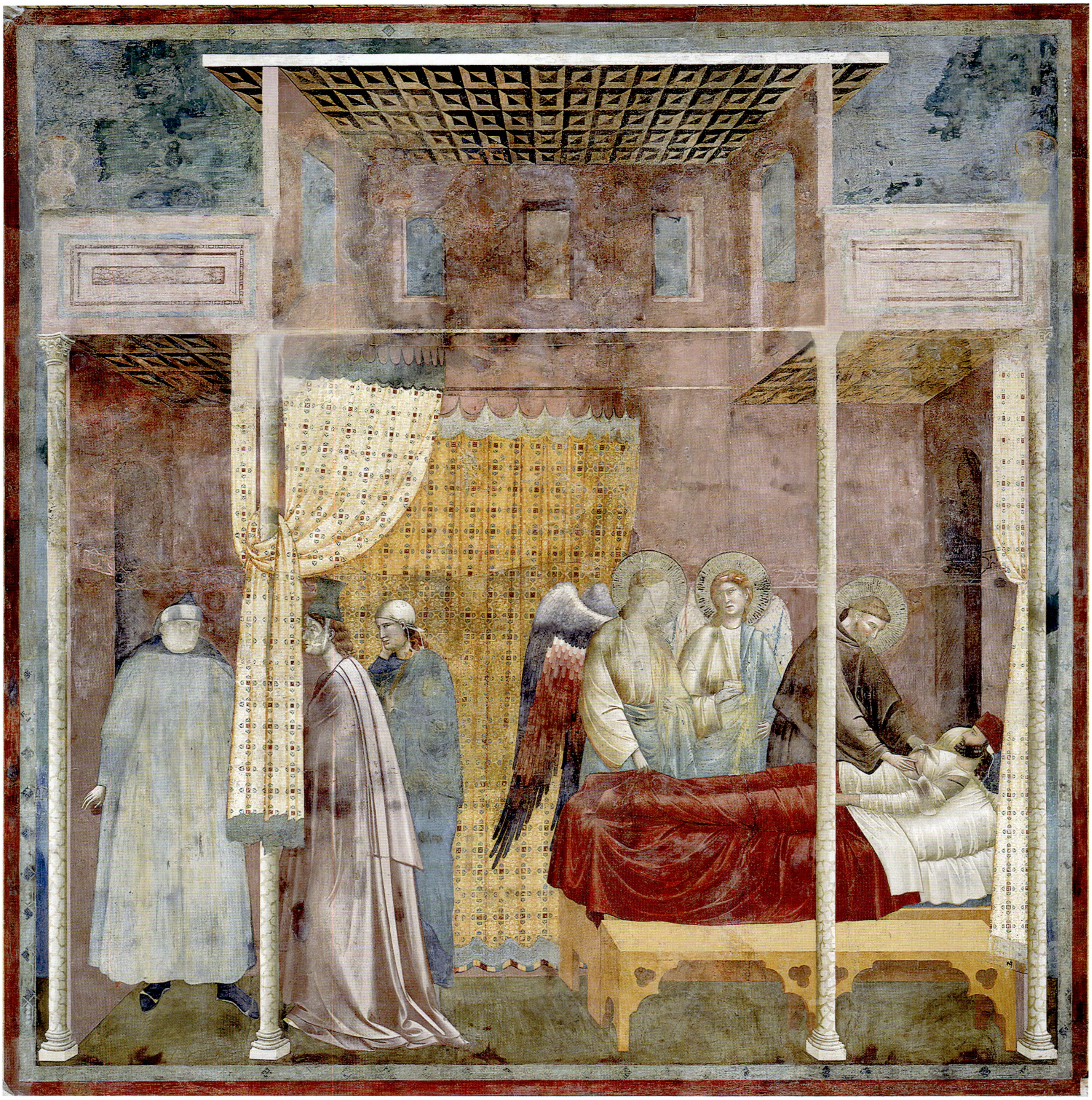

132 *Healing of John of Lérida*, Scene 26 of the Saint Francis cycle, *c.*1290–96, fresco, south wall of the nave, Upper Church, Basilica of San Francesco.

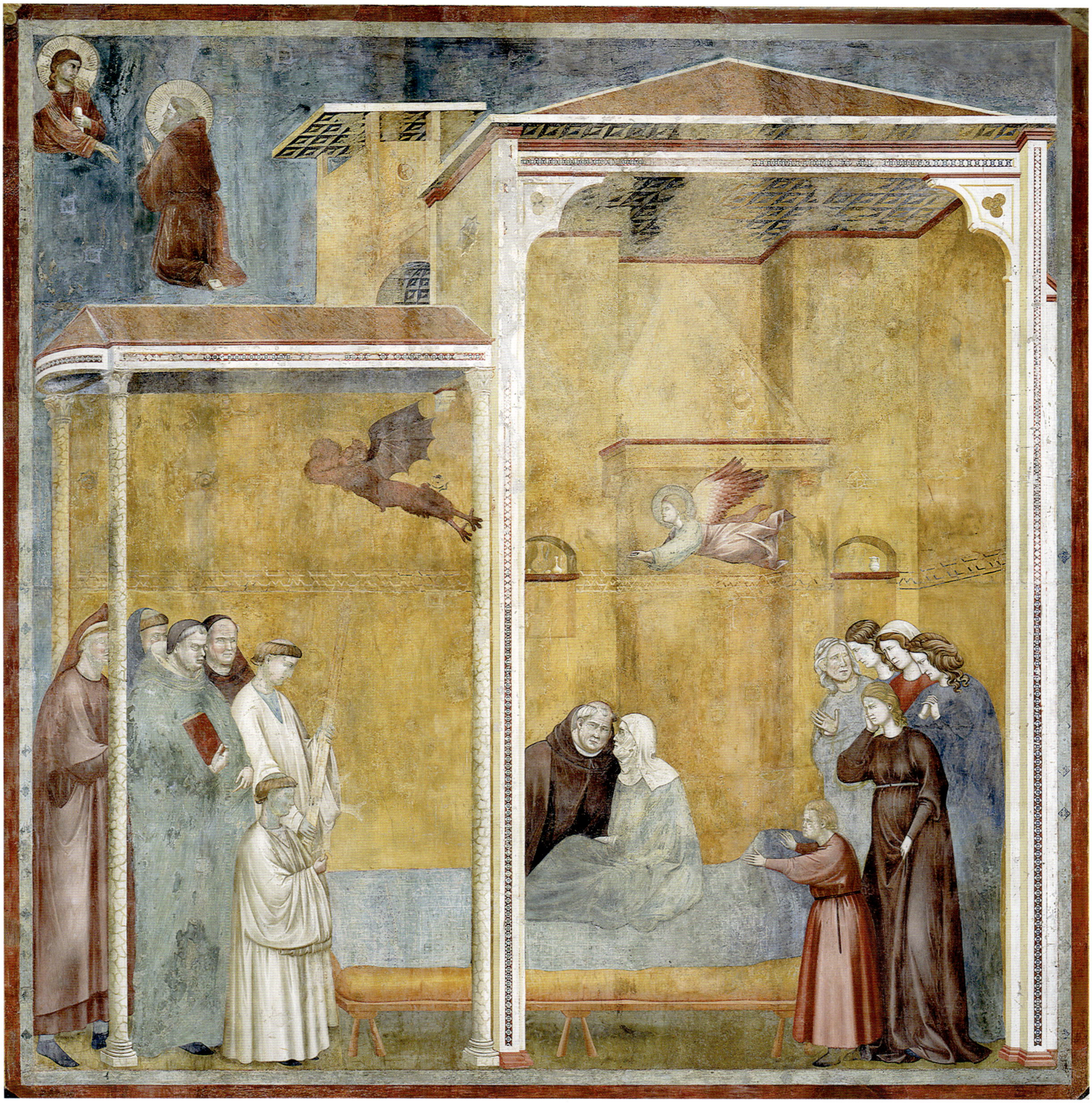

133 *Resurrection of a Woman from Benevento,* Scene 27 of the Saint Francis cycle, *c.*1290–96, fresco, south wall of the nave, Upper Church, Basilica of San Francesco.

But another, more subtle parallel is being made, which would have been understood only by viewers who were well schooled in biblical exegesis. For Franciscan commentators, the unwrapping of Lazarus's bands, in response to Christ's command 'Loose him, and let him go,'[70] represented the absolution of the penitent sinner. The Church claimed its authority to forgive sins from Christ's promise to Saint Peter, the first pope: 'whatsoever thou shalt bind upon earth, it shall be bound also in heaven: and whatsoever thou shalt loose upon earth, it shall be loosed also in heaven.'[71] So Francis removing John of Lérida's bandages, placed below the *Raising of Lazarus*, not only shows his ability to heal physical wounds, but hints at his power to save souls as well. This power of 'binding and loosing' is explicit in the woman of Benevento story, where the Franciscan Order's qualifications for absolving sinners are related to Francis's unique effectiveness as a heavenly intercessor. The hierarchy of intercession is meticulously depicted, with Francis displaying his stigmata to a Christ whose own wounds are clearly visible. Once again, it is Francis's stigmata, his credentials as *alter Christus*, that are crucial to his salvific efficacy in the afterlife.

The final scene of the cycle (see fig. 34) takes place in Rome. Peter of Alife had been accused of heresy and imprisoned by the bishop of Tivoli on the command of Pope Gregory IX. Having repented his heresy, Peter prayed to Saint Francis and the saint entered the prison, breaking Peter's fetters and the cell door through the power of his presence. When the bishop was told what had happened, he went to the prison and, seeing that a miracle had taken place, immediately worshipped God.[72] As discussed in Chapter 2, the bishop in the story was a Colonna, and Frugoni and Binski have argued that the extraordinary spiral column perched atop Peter's prison should be read as a Colonna rebus.[73] The most likely time for the Colonna to have exerted such influence at Assisi would have been after the death of Nicholas IV, during the 1292–4 conclave that eventually resulted in the ill-judged decision to elect Celestine V. If this interpretation is correct, there is at least a possibility that the *Liberation of Peter of Alife*, the last but one scene in the cycle to have been painted, might not have been the original choice to conclude the Saint Francis cycle.[74] Certainly there does not appear to be a strong vertical link with the *Wedding at Cana* in the tier above. The eucharistic significance of the miracle at Cana, where Christ turned water into wine, may well have been the main reason for placing it close to the high altar of the Upper Church.[75] However, the *Liberation of Peter* does share the main themes of the other two Saint Francis miracles in the bay. It is another dramatic story of heavenly intercession, with Saint Francis's power to 'bind and loose' being powerfully visualized in the figure of Peter brandishing his broken leg-irons. As Frugoni noted, Peter of Alife evokes his name-saint Peter, who was twice miraculously freed from prison, first in Jerusalem and then in Rome.[76] Saint Peter's chains were venerated in the Roman church of San Pietro ad Vincula (literally, 'where the chains are'). As the *Golden Legend* explains, the liturgical feast of Saint Peter in Chains on 1 August commemorates not only the apostle's liberation from his physical bonds, but also his ability to free others from the bonds of sin through the intercessory power conferred on him by Christ.[77] For the Franciscans at Assisi, the coincidence of the dates of the *Perdono* (1–2 August), the great plenary indulgence conceded to Saint Francis, and the feast of Saint Peter in Chains was surely considered significant.

The Stigmata, the Side Wound and the Papacy

Throughout the lengthy sequence of scenes displaying Francis's stigmata, there is a constant emphasis on the side wound. In the *Death of Saint Francis* (see fig. 122) the wound is prominent both on the saint's corpse and on his ascending soul. In the *Verification of the Stigmata* (see fig. 125) Jerome slips his fingers into Francis's side, a much more specific emphasis than in Bonaventure's text, which described the doubting knight touching each of the wounds but without stressing any particular one. Likewise, Saint Clare in the *Lamentation* is depicted touching the side wound, a detail not found in the *Legenda maior*.[78] The side wound is dealt with specifically in the *Dream of Pope Gregory IX* (see fig. 131). According to Bonaventure, after experiencing this mystical revelation Gregory felt such devotion for the stigmata that 'he would not allow anyone to obscure these signs with arrogant presumption, without striking him with a severe rebuke'.[79] Bonaventure was evidently alluding to the three

facing page 134 View of the first bay, south wall of the nave, Upper Church, Basilica of San Francesco.

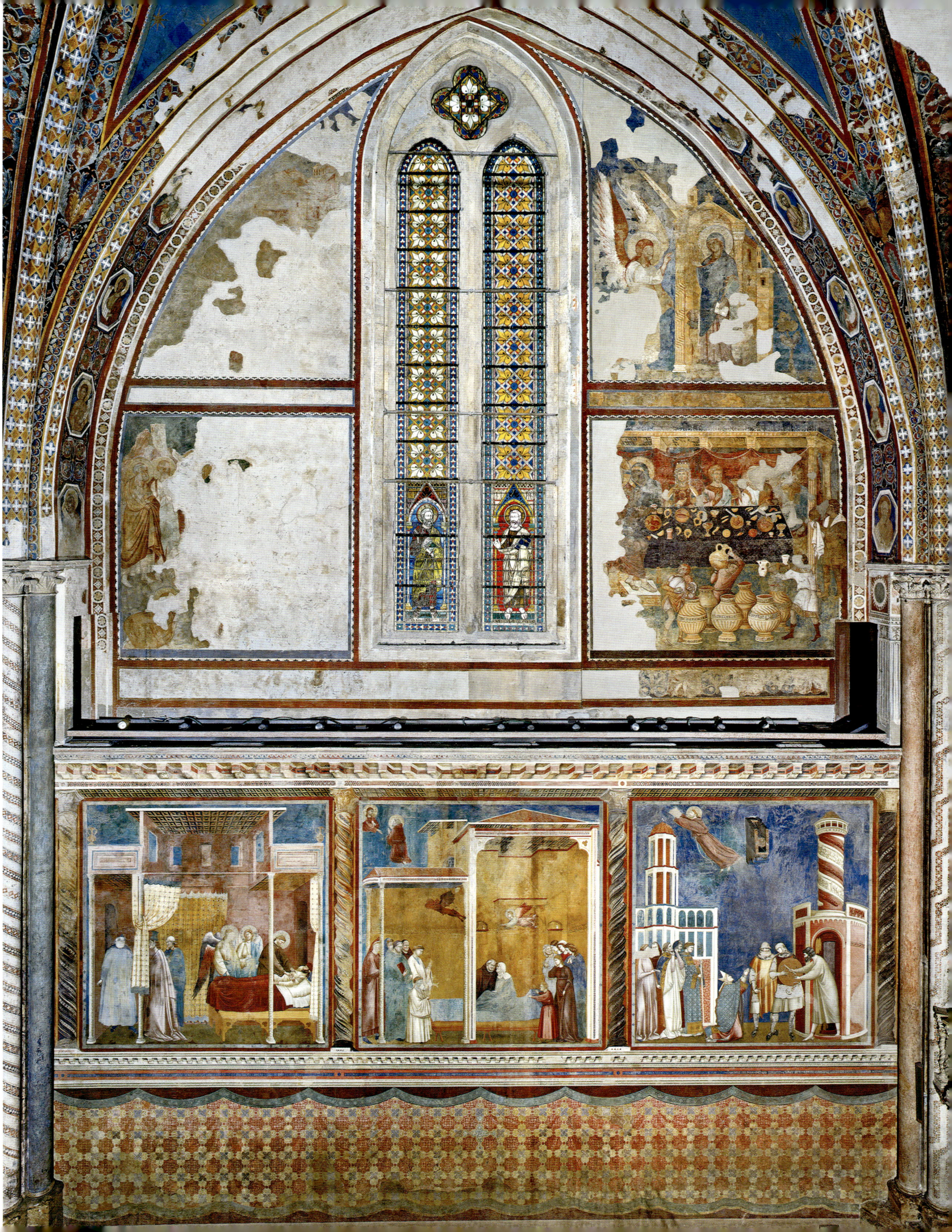

bulls that Gregory issued during the spring of 1237, all of which defended the authenticity of the stigmata against detractors.[80]

The *Legenda maior* was written between 1260 and 1263, during a time of renewed controversy over the authenticity of the stigmata. In the immediately preceding years, Pope Alexander IV had issued a further three bulls on the subject. Before becoming pope, Alexander had served as cardinal protector of the Franciscans, and he continued to hold the post during his pontificate (1254–61). He had known Francis personally and asserted that he himself had seen the stigmata while the saint was still alive.[81] In his bull *Benigna operatio*, addressed to all the bishops of the Church in 1255, Alexander declared: 'we wish . . . to set before your eyes those gratifying insignia of the Lord's Passion, which should be frequently recalled and greatly admired, and which the hand of divine operation impressed on the body of this saint while he was still alive.'[82] In his bulls, Alexander paid particular attention to the side wound. Although this is never spelled out, the reason was surely the unique theological significance of the wound in Christ's side. According to John's Gospel, it was the spear-thrust alone that revealed Jesus as the Messiah, by fulfilling the Old Testament prophecy: 'They shall look on him whom they pierced.'[83] Francis's side wound, therefore, likened him to Christ not only in his humanity, his suffering on the cross, but also in his divinity. The blood and water that flowed from Christ's side were salvific, and were interpreted as symbolizing the sacrament of baptism, with its fundamental power to cleanse original sin.

This was bold stuff. Only after Alexander IV's intervention were the Franciscans in Italy apparently confident enough to depict Francis's side wound; before then, it may well have been regarded as potentially blasphemous.[84] Bonaventure, describing the stigmata on Francis's corpse in the *Legenda maior*, takes care to quote *Benigna operatio* almost verbatim, when asserting that 'the wound in his side . . . was not inflicted on his body nor produced by human means; it was like the wound in the Saviour's side, which brought forth in our Redeemer the mystery of the redemption and regeneration of the human race'.[85] Still the issue did not go away. The need to defend the authenticity of the stigmata was as much a concern for the Franciscans at the time of the Saint Francis cycle as it had been when Bonaventure wrote the *Legenda maior*. During September 1291 Pope Nicholas IV reissued and confirmed two of his predecessors' bulls. The first was a bull of Pope Nicholas III from 1279, which had in its turn repeated and confirmed Gregory IX's *Confessor Domini* of 1237.[86] In *Confessor Domini* Gregory had not only commanded all the faithful to believe firmly in the stigmata, but had specifically stated that this miracle had been a special motive in his decision to canonize the saint (though the stigmata had not, in fact, received any mention in the bull of canonization). In the Assisi cycle, the *Canonization* is firmly embedded in the sequence of scenes devoted to Francis's stigmatized body, and is immediately followed by the *Dream of Pope Gregory IX*.

The second of Nicholas IV's bulls reconfirmed Alexander IV's *Benigna operatio*, which, as discussed above, contained the lengthiest and strongest papal statement on the stigmata; it concluded with a declaration that anyone denying the stigmata would be severely condemned and punished for their blasphemy.[87] In this context, how significant is it that the *Dream of Pope Gregory IX* is placed directly beneath the *Betrayal* of Christ by Judas? One needs to approach this question with caution. First, the *Betrayal* was an essential scene in any Passion cycle and so it had to go somewhere. Second, as we have already seen, the amount of space devoted to the Passion cycle in the Upper Church nave was severely limited, so the options for its placement were few. Nonetheless, the juxtaposition is difficult to ignore, particularly given that the Franciscans frequently used the figure of Judas for didactic purposes. The underlying intent would not, of course, have been to liken Pope Gregory to the traitor Judas, but to present the pair as antitheses. The strategy of using Judas in a meaningful pair of opposites – this time with Saint Peter – would later be consistently pursued in Pietro Lorenzetti's Passion cycle in the south transept of the Lower Church.[88] In the Upper Church, Christ's false disciple, betraying him with a kiss, is also contrasted with all true devotees of Saint Francis, represented by the friars and nuns who reverently kiss the saint's hands and feet in the *Death of Saint Francis* and the *Lamentation of the Clares*.

Another bull of Pope Nicholas IV gives us a telling glimpse of the context in which the Saint Francis cycle was created. On 20 November 1291 Nicholas wrote to the Dominican prior of the province of Tuscany concerning the examination and condemnation of one of his friars, Thomas of Aversa.[89] Preaching in public on the feast of Peter Martyr, the Dominican saint, Thomas had acted 'perniciously and audaciously' in 'disparaging with outrageous criticism the stigmata with which Saint Francis is known to have been marked . . . in such a way as to ascribe the signs of the living God to Saint Peter Martyr, and the signs of the dead God to Saint Francis'. Not surprisingly, the Franciscan pope was furious and promptly banned Thomas from preaching and teaching for seven years, a punishment that, 'as a result of our patience', was more lenient than he deserved. This bull shows that denigrators of the stigmata, often members of rival religious orders, still existed more than sixty years after Francis's canonization.[90] One detail is of especial interest. Thomas of Aversa did not deny that Francis had borne the stigmata on his body, but he claimed that the saint had been marked merely 'in a superficial way, as is perceived in pictures'.[91] It is easy to understand why images of Francis's stigmata were so important, when even an unbeliever cited them as factual evidence. The Dominican friar would presumably have been familiar with *Stigmatization* scenes on thirteenth-century Tuscan *vita* panels, such as the Pescia dossal (see fig. 128), which, as discussed above, typically depicted the kneeling saint with his head illuminated by light emanating from the Christ–Seraph.

The new iconography at Assisi, with its arrow-like rays connecting the bodies of Christ and Francis, wound to wound, certainly makes the stigmatization into a more physical encounter with the divine. But why? One reason may have been the need to assert the fact that Francis's wounds were not superficial, self-induced or faked.[92] Evidence of concern about this can be adduced from the short treatise on the stigmata written on 3 October 1282 by Philip of Perugia, the provincial minister of Tuscany. This text, which has received virtually no attention in the art-historical literature, was written in response to the command of Minister General Bonagrazia, at the general chapter at Strasbourg in May of that year, to investigate the exact day and time when Saint Francis received the stigmata. In his treatise, Philip reports the revelation received by a pious lay brother, Matthew of Castiglione Aretino.[93] Saint Francis appeared to Matthew in a vision while he was praying at La Verna, and confirmed that the encounter with the Christ–Seraph had occurred on the feast of the Exultation of the Cross.

As a lay friar, Matthew probably had little or no Latin.[94] We might speculate on how much of the detail of his vision was crafted by Philip, who was, as well as being a friar of some stature, one of the learned witnesses who signed the donation deed for Matthew of Acquasparta's books, drawn up at the Sacro Convento in Assisi in early 1287.[95] Saint Francis told Matthew exactly how he received the stigmata, in an account that partially echoes the *Legenda maior* but is much more graphic than Bonaventure dared to be: 'The Lord applied his hands to my body, and impressed these stigmata on me, firstly on my hands, secondly on my feet, thirdly on my side; each time with the most intense pain and with a great cry.'[96] The same stress on the physical trauma of the stigmata is evident in Nicholas IV's refutation of Thomas of Aversa in his letter of 1291, which declared that 'the holy Roman Church accepts it as proven through due process by witnesses that the stigmata entered [Francis's] flesh in no superficial way, but into the inner parts through flesh and nerves and bones, in the five parts of the hands, feet and side . . . not through natural forces, but by a miraculous gift of grace'.[97]

The *Stigmatization* in the Assisi cycle shows Francis's hands and feet being penetrated; the scenes focusing on the side wound prove that fingers can be inserted into the gash and that it bleeds. Francis's stigmatized body is displayed for the veneration of the viewers of the frescoes and there is a strong insistence within the painted narratives on authoritative witnesses, from friars and nuns to knights and leading citizens, laymen and -women, ministers and popes. One of those present at the saint's deathbed sees Francis's soul ascending on a cloud; many more both see and touch his body with its sacred wounds.[98] For pilgrims and friars visiting the Basilica, these images would have compensated for the lack of access to Francis's body in the Lower Church, where his remains were interred in a subterranean tomb beneath the high altar, in an area hidden behind the substantial barrier of the *tramezzo* screen.[99] Pilgrims could neither see nor touch the relics, and could witness the unique miracle of the stigmata only through these painted images.

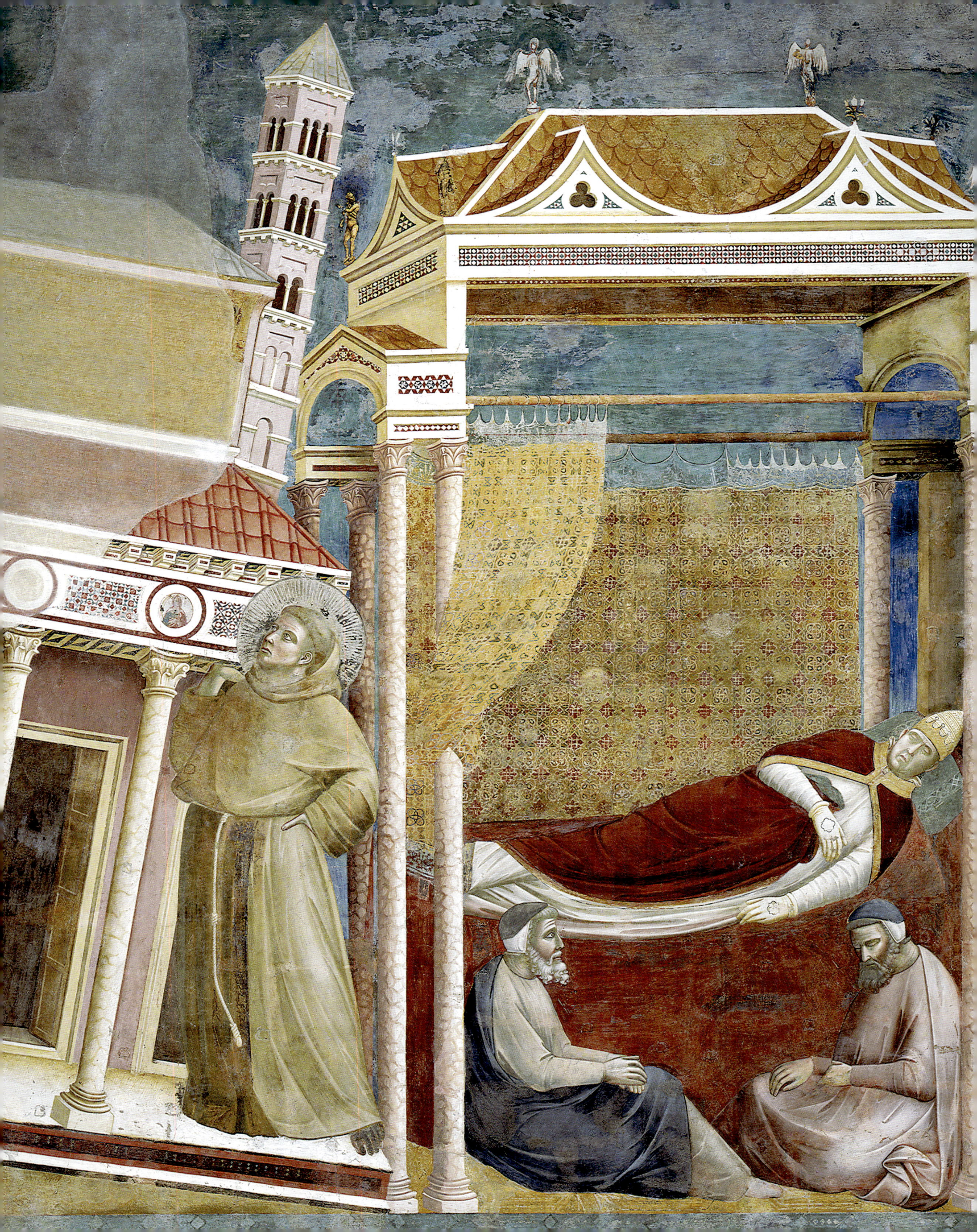

6

Rebuilding the Church

The arrangement of the first half of the Saint Francis cycle was just as carefully planned as the second. At the exact midpoint in the sequence of thirteen scenes arrayed along the north wall of the nave is the *Approval of the Rule* (Scene 7) (see fig. 180), the official birth of the Order. Placing this crucial event at the start of the third bay effectively divides the north wall of the Saint Francis cycle into two halves. The six scenes in the first and second bays depict Francis's secular life and the progress of his conversion. The third and fourth bays begin the long sequence of scenes that portray Francis's life as a friar, which continues across the counter-façade and into the fourth bay of the south wall.

In the preceding chapter we demonstrated how, on the south wall, vertical and diagonal links were used to draw parallels between the Saint Francis cycle and important biblical scenes in the tier above it. This system is consistently employed on the north wall too. While the concept of comparing Saint Francis to Christ in his Passion was worked out and executed with unusual subtlety at Assisi, it was not new. On the north wall, on the other hand, the disposition of the cycles offered novel possibilities, since there was no visual precedent for comparing Saint Francis with the Old Testament patriarchs featured in the register immediately above. Our comparison with the earlier Genesis cycles in Saint Peter's and San Paolo in Rome demonstrated how carefully the planners of the Assisi cycle selected, edited and arranged the eight scenes in the middle tier, depicting the Old Testament patriarchs Noah, Abraham, Isaac, Jacob and Joseph (see Chapter 4).

In recent years, the premise that the Saint Francis and Genesis cycles are meaningfully linked has been accepted and developed by several art historians, but analysis of the specific connections between the tiers has been uneven. Most attention has been given to the two Isaac scenes in the third bay, which have been the subject of contradictory interpretations. While Romano suggested that the blind patriarch Isaac in *Isaac Blessing Jacob* (see fig. 183) was intended to parallel the dying Saint Francis on the opposite wall of the nave, Neff argued that it was not the father but the son, Jacob, who was the type for Francis.[1] Neff's analysis also included the two Joseph scenes in the fourth bay, pointing to a common theme in all four Genesis scenes: the relationship between pairs of elder and younger brothers (Esau and Jacob, Joseph and Benjamin). In each case, it was the younger or 'lesser' brother who provided a type for Saint Francis and the Franciscans, the Friars Minor ('lesser brothers'), in the scenes below them.[2]

facing page 135 *Dream of Pope Innocent III* (detail of fig. 140).

The relationships in the first two bays of the north wall have received far less scholarly attention. Francis's secular life is set below the two Noah scenes in the first bay and the two Abraham scenes in the second. In this chapter we argue that the key relationships in these four Genesis scenes are between fathers and sons, and that this theme is paralleled in the Saint Francis scenes below, in which Francis is transformed from the son of Pietro Bernardone into the father of a new religious order. The focus on fathers and sons in the first and second bays complements that on older and younger brothers in the third and fourth bays. In our view, the Noah and Abraham scenes were arranged with the explicit intention of giving theological weight and prophetic significance to Francis's early life. The first two bays should be viewed as a single, intricately planned and coherent iconographic unit, which sets out to emphasize the place of Saint Francis in the history of salvation, and his rebuilding of the Church.

The Conversion of Saint Francis

The saint's youth is treated in far greater detail here than in any previous pictorial cycle. The scenes in the second bay – *Saint Francis before the Crucifix in San Damiano*, *Saint Francis Renouncing his Father* and the *Dream of Pope Innocent III* – had all appeared before in the Basilica. But the first bay was more innovative, and there are no earlier surviving examples of any of its scenes: the *Homage of a Simple Man*, *Saint Francis Giving his Coat to a Poor Knight* and the *Dream of the Palace of Arms*.

Francis's journey from son of an Assisi cloth merchant to founder of a new religious order was lengthy, meandering and more than a little haphazard. Crafting a coherent image of a conventional founder-saint out of a disparate collection of incidents was one of the great achievements of Francis's thirteenth-century hagiographers.[3] The process was begun by Thomas of Celano, but it was Saint Bonaventure who gave the events of Francis's conversion true gravitas. In the *Legenda maior*, Bonaventure loaded the saint's early life with prophetic import, both for his identification as an *alter Christus* and for his crucial role in the spiritual restoration of the Roman Church.

The artists and planners of the Assisi cycle were just as skilful as the hagiographers at injecting a coherent sense of narrative purpose into the six scenes leading up to the *Approval of the Rule*. As Smart pointed out, clothing is consistently used as a visual motif.[4] In the opening scene we see Francis stepping on the cloak that a simple man of Assisi has spread before his feet, in homage to his future greatness (see fig. 53). In the second scene he gives away his own coat as an act of charity (fig. 137), in the next he is shown a vision of a palace full of armour marked with the sign of the cross (fig. 138), while in the fifth scene he strips off all his clothes to renounce his father (fig. 139). The entire sequence culminates in the *Dream of Innocent III* (fig. 140), where the saint appears clad for the first time in the rough tunic and cord of the Franciscan habit. The gradual discarding of secular clothing becomes a sign of the progress of Francis's conversion. This metaphor would have been quite easy to grasp for both lay and religious viewers, but a religious would have understood it on a more elevated level. In particular, any Franciscan friar who knew his Bonaventure should have been able to spot a literary parallel: the first chapter of the *Legenda maior* is entitled 'De conversatione Sancti Francisci in habitu saeculari' ('Saint Francis's manner of life in the attire of the world').[5]

A second visual device is compositional. The scenes in the second bay form one of the most successfully realized triptychs in the entire cycle. The central scene, the *Renunciation*, divides the secular and religious figures into two separate groups. Such a composition was already customary, and the figures in the Maestro di San Francesco version in the Lower Church (see fig. 102) had probably been similarly arranged. That is hard to appreciate now because of the loss of the right-hand section of the fresco but, as we saw in Chapter 4, a related image in San Francesco, Gubbio, is a good guide to its original composition (albeit reversed) (see fig. 103). The Upper Church fresco takes this convention to new heights of artistic expression, contrasting Francis and Pietro Bernardone through their poses and gestures. But what is really innovative is the empty space marking the centre of the composition. A vertical void divides the two men, a daring conceit that brilliantly conveys the psychological and emotional chasm between father and son.[6]

The symmetry of the central panel of the triptych is complemented by the two outer scenes, which form its shutters: the sloping baseline of the church of San Damiano is mirrored by that of Saint John Lateran (fig. 136). This device encourages the viewer to connect the two scenes. In addition, as Smart pointed out, the detailed attention given to the crumbling edifice of San Damiano was a new develop-

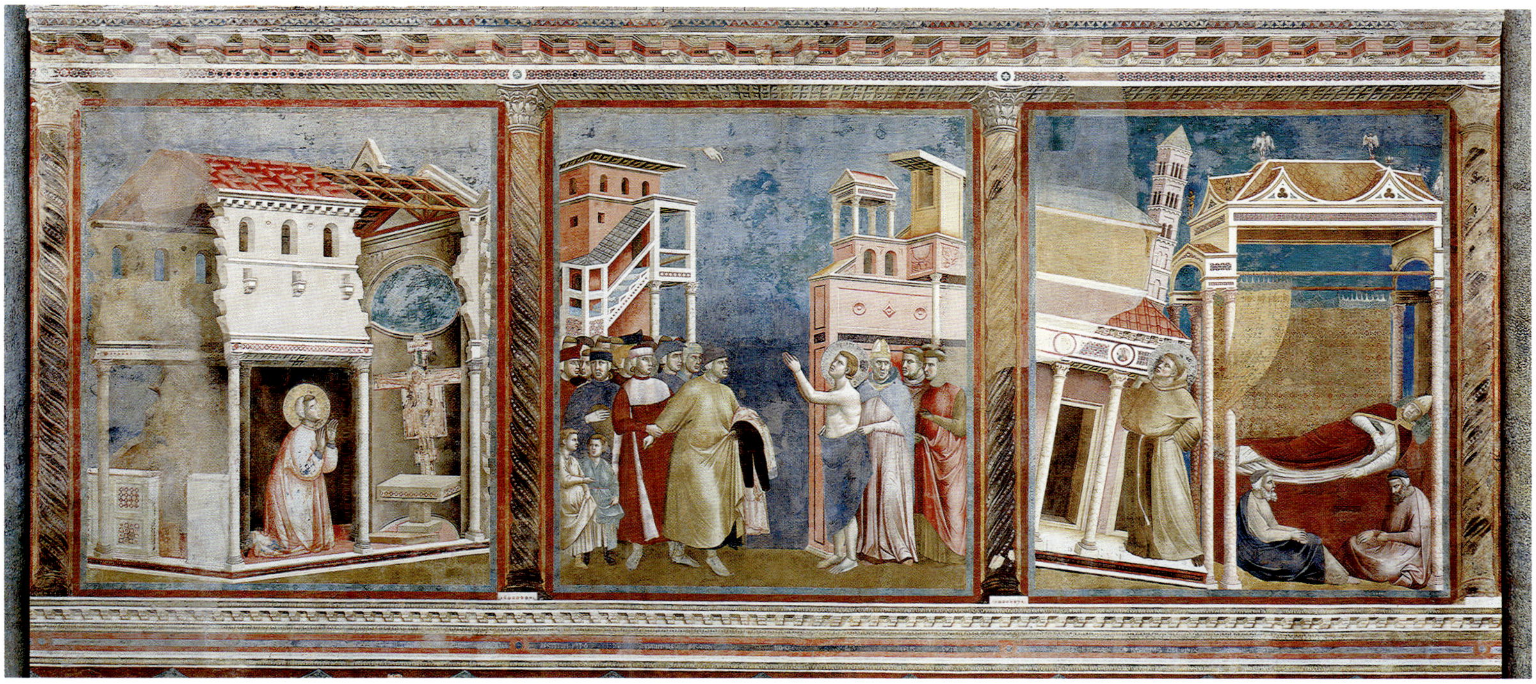

136 Saint Francis cycle, Scenes 4 to 6, *c.*1290–96, fresco, north wall of the nave, Upper Church, Basilica of San Francesco.

ment in the iconography of the scene. The earlier version in the stained glass of the Upper Church shows only the altar with its crucifix (see fig. 92). The dilapidation of San Damiano parallels the toppling Lateran basilica and makes it clear that the two episodes are meaningfully linked.[7] This message is reiterated in the titulus beneath the fresco: 'When Blessed Francis was praying before an image of the Crucified, a voice from that cross said to him three times: "Francis, go and repair my house, which is being completely destroyed"'. This text was derived from the *Legenda maior*, but an original gloss was then added: 'signifying by this the Roman Church'.[8]

In the written legends, the young Francis initially interpreted Christ's call literally, and immediately set about restoring the edifice of San Damiano.[9] In the Assisi cycle, this episode is omitted. By visually linking the San Damiano scene with the *Dream of Innocent III*, and through the explanatory text below the fresco, it is made clear that Christ's call to restore the Church was a spiritual one. This interpretation anticipates the way in which Innocent III understood his dream of a little poor man holding up the falling Lateran: as a prophecy that Saint Francis would spiritually restore the entire *Ecclesia Romana* through his life and teaching. The dream convinced the pope to authorize the Franciscan Order.

The representations of San Damiano and Saint John Lateran in the second bay are just two of the many churches that are depicted throughout the Saint Francis cycle: they include a second version of San Damiano in Scene 23, the chapel at La Verna in the *Stigmatization* (Scene 19), and churches at Bovara (Scene 9), Arezzo (Scene 10) and Greccio (Scene 13).[10] The apparent realism of many of these buildings is often seen in terms of a new artistic interest in naturalism, yet the identification and interpretation of these fictive churches is far from straightforward. For example, Saint Francis died at the Porziuncola, but in the scene of his death (see fig. 122) the fictive rood beam with its three monumental panel paintings evokes the Upper Church at Assisi as much as the tiny interior of Santa Maria degli Angeli.[11] Likewise, as we shall see, it has been argued that the elaborate liturgical space depicted in the *Miracle of the Crib at Greccio* (fig. 141) is more closely related to the Lower Church at Assisi than to Greccio. And the grandiose church façade in the *Lamentation of the Clares* (see fig. 128) bears little or no resemblance to San Damiano, either before or after Francis's rebuilding.[12]

In this chapter, we shall examine more closely the various ways in which representations of buildings in the opening section of the Saint Francis cycle were used to convey sym-

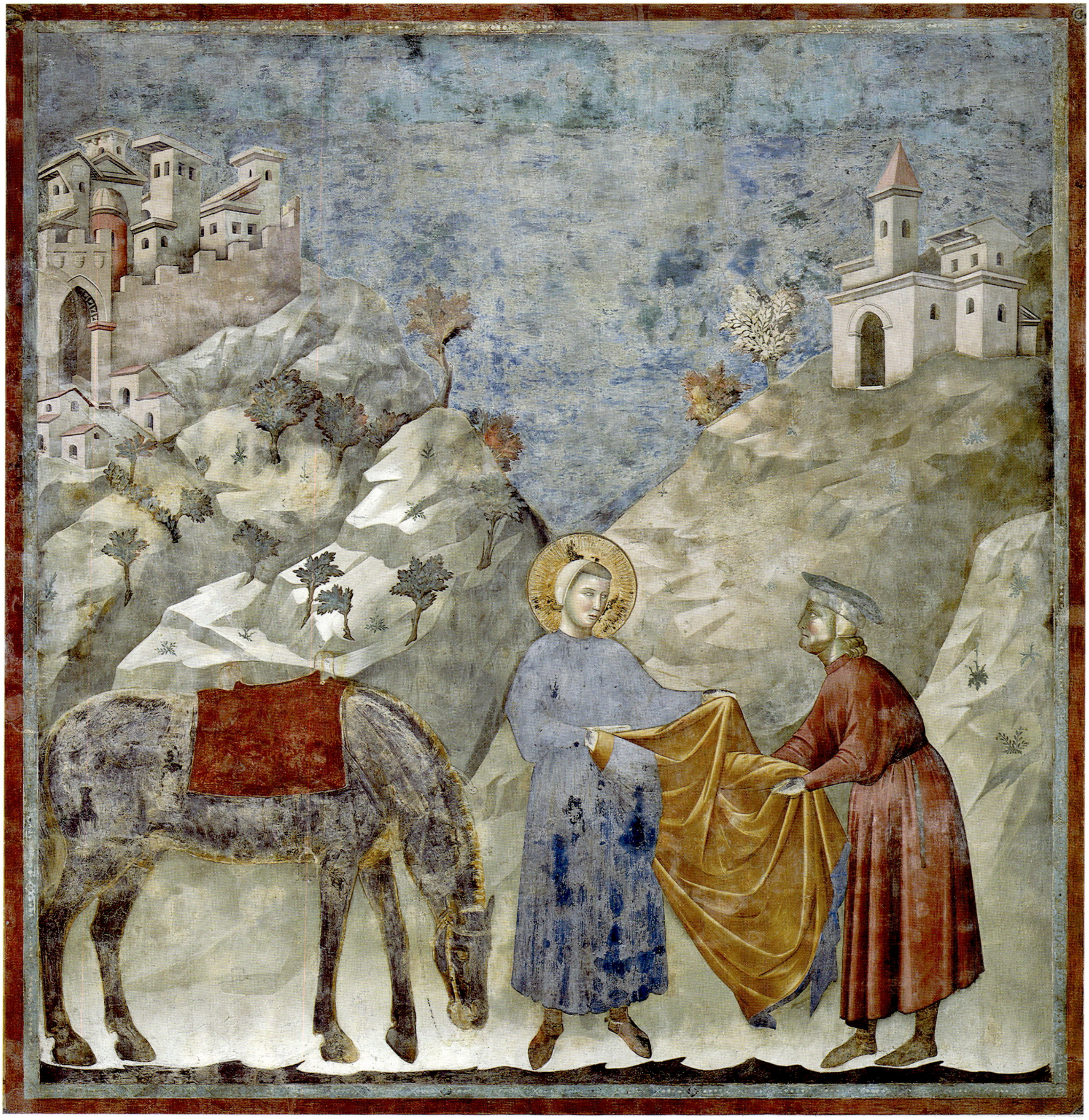

137 *Saint Francis Giving his Coat to a Poor Knight*, Scene 2 of the Saint Francis cycle, *c.*1290–96, fresco, north wall of the nave, Upper Church, Basilica of San Francesco.

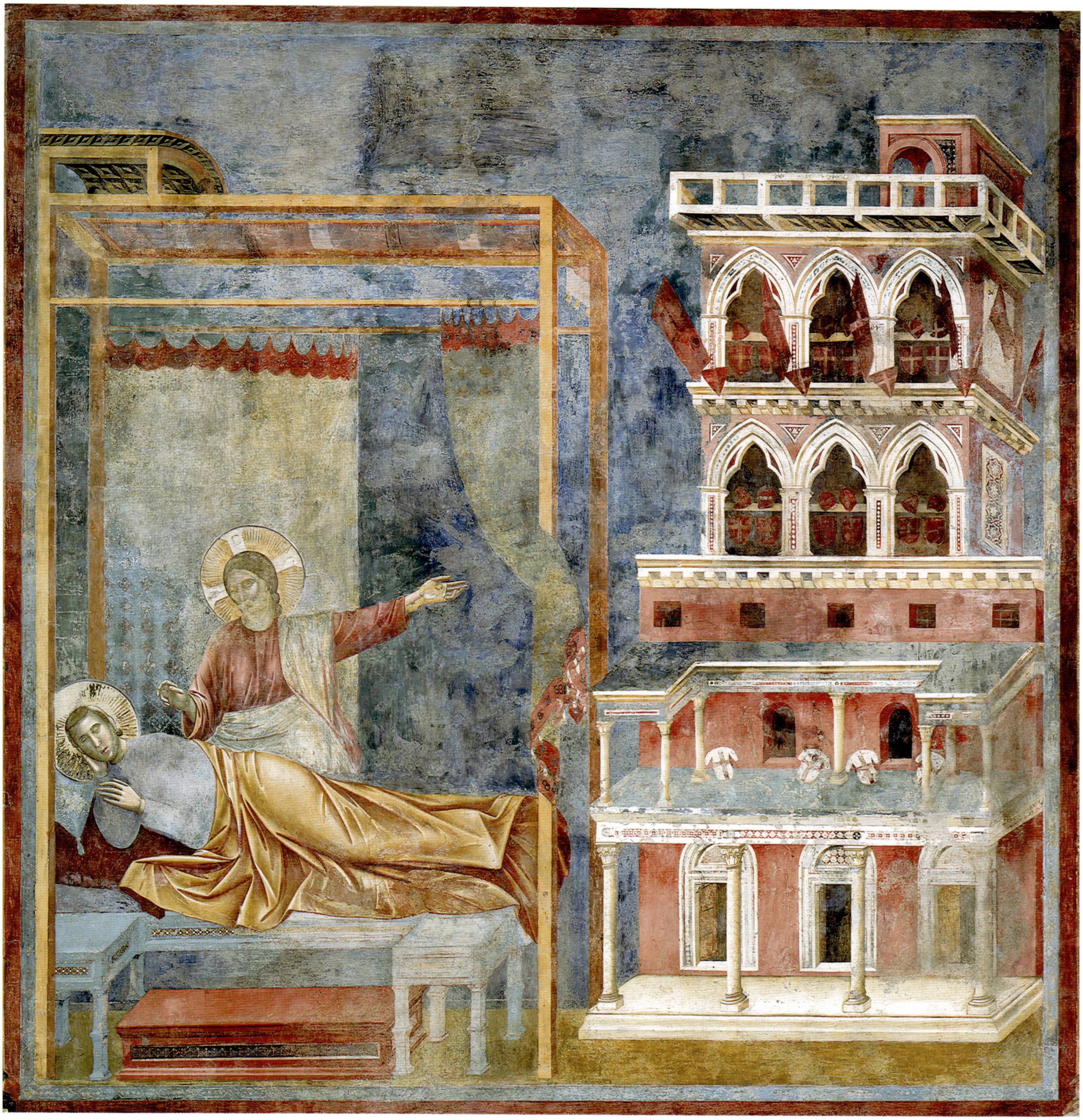

138 *Dream of the Palace of Arms*, Scene 3 of the Saint Francis cycle, *c.*1290–96, fresco, north wall of the nave, Upper Church, Basilica of San Francesco.

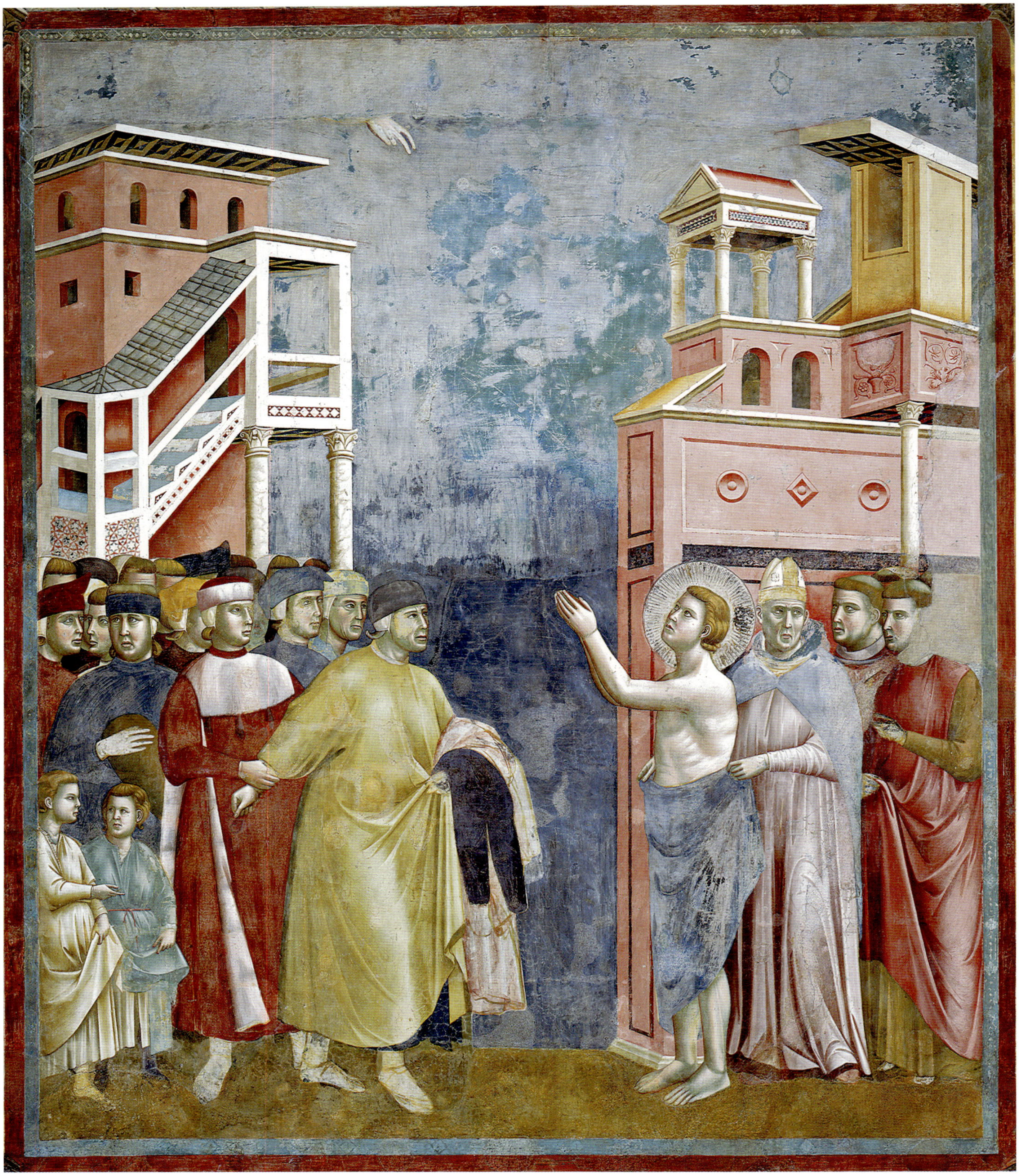

139 *Saint Francis Renouncing his Father*, Scene 5 of the Saint Francis cycle, *c.*1290–96, fresco, north wall of the nave, Upper Church, Basilica of San Francesco.

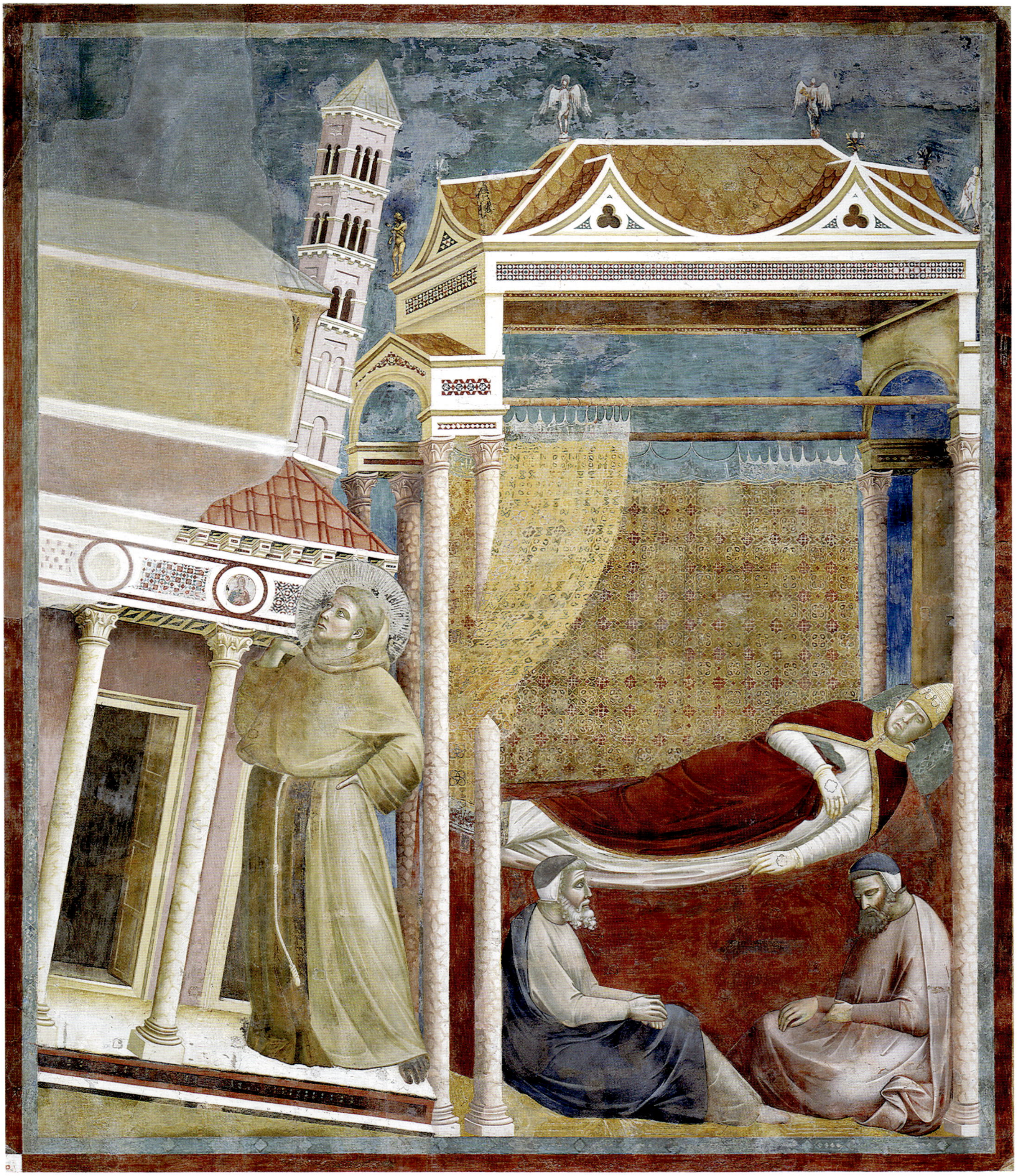

140 *Dream of Pope Inncent III*, Scene 6 of the Saint Francis cycle, *c.*1290–96, fresco, north wall of the nave, Upper Church, Basilica of San Francesco.

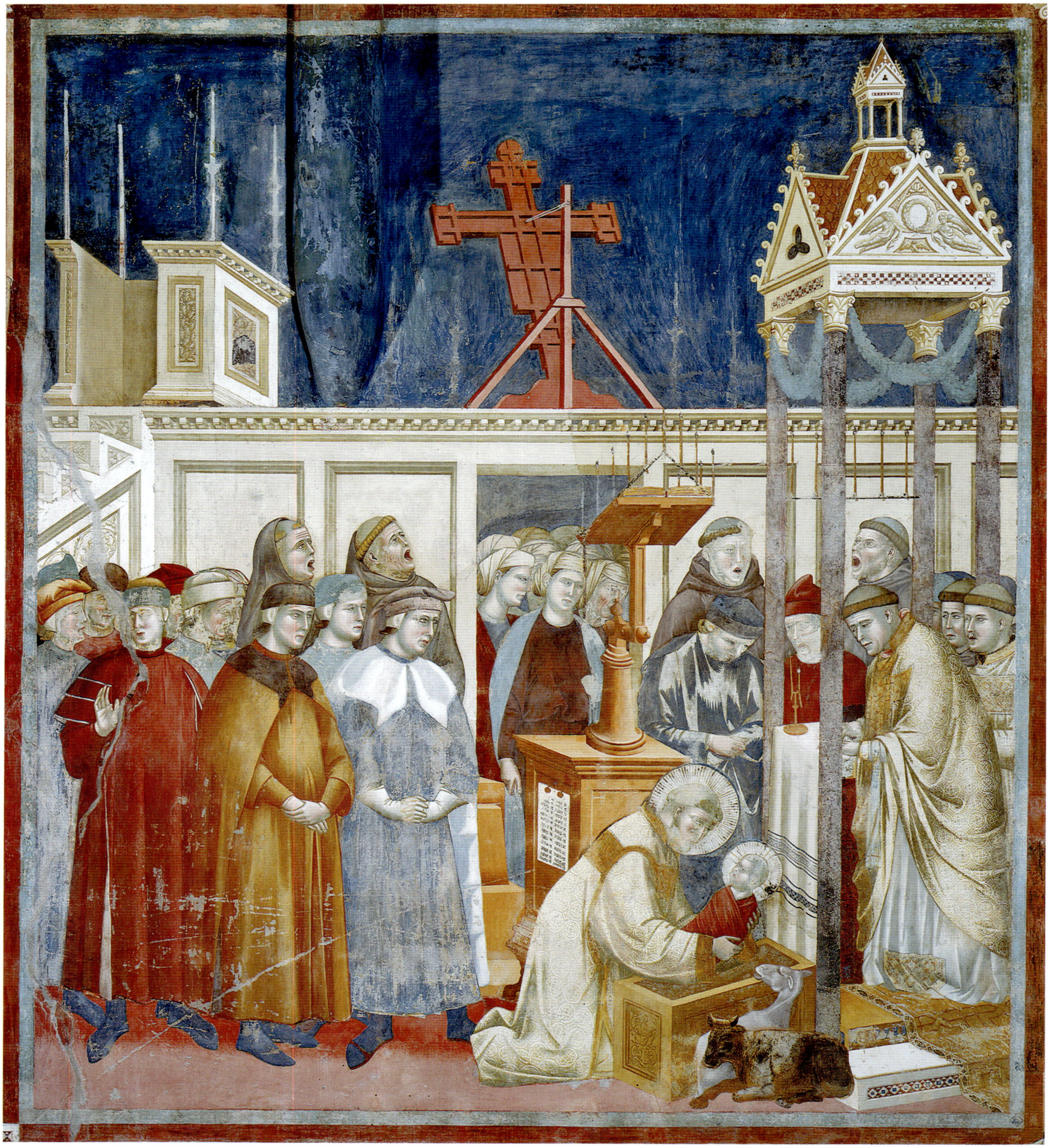

141 *Miracle of the Crib at Greccio*, Scene 13 of the Saint Francis cycle, *c.*1290–96, fresco, north wall of the nave, Upper Church, Basilica of San Francesco.

bolic and figurative meanings. There is a constant interplay between rebuilding churches and restoring the Church.[13] The depiction of churches serves primarily to portray Saint Francis as the spiritual rebuilder of the Church, but it also refers more subtly to the contemporary restoration of basilicas in Rome by Nicholas IV, and how this activity was understood both by the Franciscan pope himself and by the friars at Assisi.

The Temple and the Church

The *Homage of a Simple Man* (see fig. 53), the opening scene of the Saint Francis cycle, is one of the most admired artistically. It depicts one of the few original biographical episodes that Bonaventure contributed in the *Legenda maior*. While Francis was still a carefree youth, as yet unaware of God's plan for him, he met in the streets of Assisi an uneducated man who spread a cloak at his feet. This simple fellow declared that Francis was worthy of such reverence because he was destined soon to do great things and to be magnificently honoured by all the faithful.[14] In the fresco, Saint Francis, wearing a blue costume and fashionably bobbed hair under a white cap, steps forward onto the cloak of the simple man who kneels before him.

The encounter takes place against an impressive urban backdrop. The ancient Roman temple at its heart is readily identifiable as the first-century BCE Temple of Minerva, which still dominates the Piazza del Comune, Assisi's main square (fig. 142). The temple is flanked by medieval buildings, including, on the left, the palace and tower of the Capitano del Popolo. Bonaventure did not specify where the episode took place because, as he explained, the simple man behaved in the same way 'whenever he chanced to meet Francis going through the city'.[15] Smart argued that the local setting of the story offered an imaginative artist 'the opportunity of throwing open a window upon the everyday world and of creating in the process . . . the first modern street-scene in Italian art'.[16]

Yet a little later in the cycle, another episode that took place in a familiar locale inspired no such imaginative re-creation: the confrontation between Francis and his father in front of the bishop of Assisi's palace (fig. 139) is set against entirely generic buildings.[17] One reason for this difference in approach could be that the *Homage of a Simple Man* and the *Renunciation* were not painted by the same artist. Zanardi's technical examination of the sequence of plaster patches has confirmed that the *Homage* was painted after the other two scenes in the same bay.[18] Because of its stylistic similarities to the Saint Francis scenes on the opposite wall, the *Homage of a Simple Man* is generally considered to have been painted by the workshop responsible for completing the cycle.[19] Some scholars have argued that it was painted to replace an earlier, unknown scene, but this seems highly unlikely.[20] More probably, its execution had to be left until last because the planned removal of an earlier screen at the head of the nave had still to be carried out when work on the Saint Francis cycle started (see Chapter 3). In any case, the switch from specific to generic representations of buildings within the cycle cannot be explained simply as a change from one master to the next: in the triplet of scenes in the second bay, which are all attributed to the same workshop, the generalized architectural backdrop of the *Renunciation* is bracketed by the detailed depictions of San Damiano and Saint John Lateran. A more plausible explanation for the disparity of treatment of the fictive architecture within this bay may be that the bishop's palace in the *Renunciation* was not considered essential to the deeper layers of meaning in

142 Temple of Minerva, first century BCE, Piazza del Comune, Assisi.

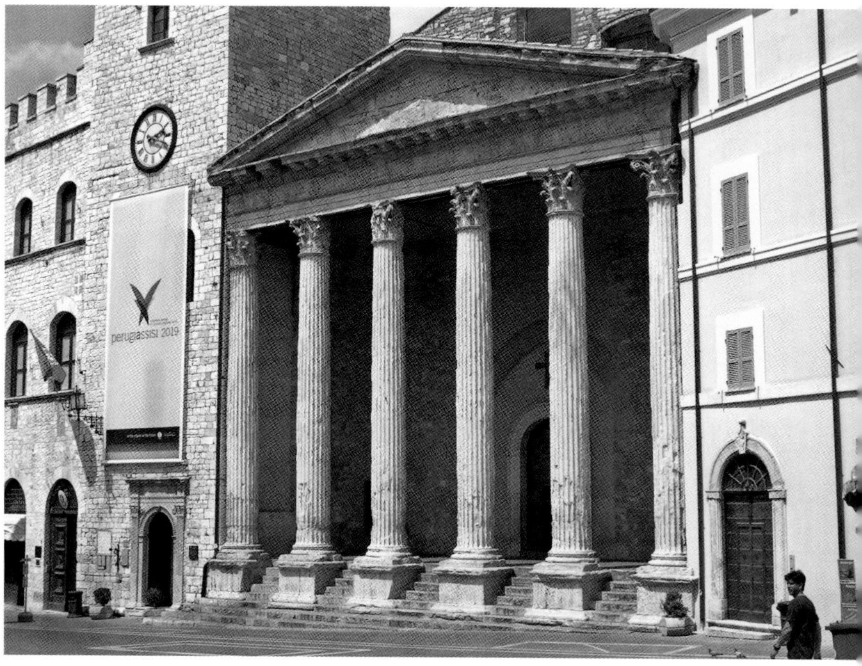

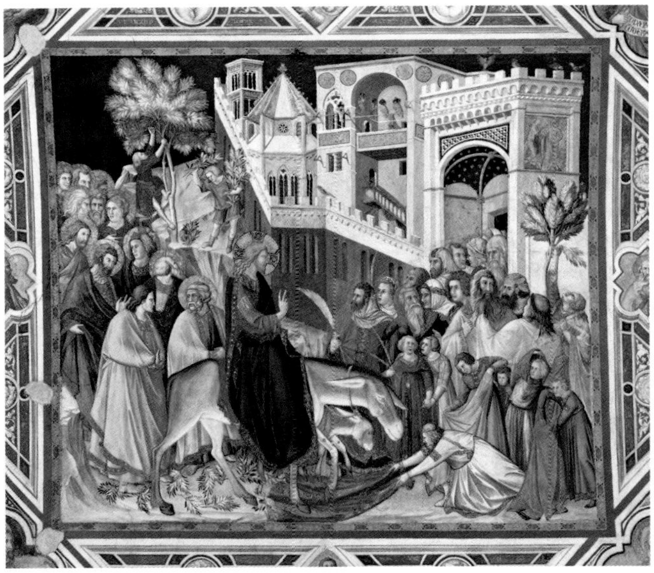

143 Pietro Lorenzetti, *Entry into Jerusalem*, Passion cycle, *c.*1316–19, fresco, south transept, Lower Church, Basilica of San Francesco.

the narrative, as the two churches clearly were. This would suggest that it was the friars, not the artists, who chose the buildings to be depicted throughout the cycle, wherever they were iconographically significant.

The Temple of Minerva is the most prominent building in the *Homage of a Simple Man*. Unobscured by the figures in the foreground, it forms the backdrop for the simple man's act of homage, its central position carefully calculated to accommodate the console supporting the rood beam across the head of the nave. Although it had been converted into a church by the Benedictines in the sixth century, by the late thirteenth century the Temple of Minerva had purely secular functions. In 1212 the temple had been leased to the commune. Its cella had been divided into two floors, the upper containing the living quarters of the *podestà* and the lower the city gaol. This explains the two barred windows included in the fresco. In addition, the portico may already have been in use as a court of justice.[21] A secular setting seems entirely appropriate for a scene depicting Francis as a worldly youth. But more has been read into it. Lunghi, pointing to the civic coats of arms on the Torre del Popolo and the magisterial figures standing in front of the Temple, saw this scene not only as the homage of the city to its saint, but also as a recognition on the part of the Franciscans of the financial support given to the Basilica by the city and its citizens.[22]

Be this as it may, the religious iconography in the scene is strong. The figure of the simple man kneeling to lay his cloak at the feet of the saint is based on the traditional Entry of Christ into Jerusalem (see, for example, the later fresco attributed to Pietro Lorenzetti in the Lower Church, *c.*1316–19; fig. 143). The parallel was already present in the *Legenda maior*, where Bonaventure's reference to how the simple man 'spread his garment' under Francis's feet alludes to Luke's description of the inhabitants of Jerusalem welcoming Christ into their city on Palm Sunday.[23] The visual device makes the point more assertively. It identifies Francis with Christ, and more particularly with the beginning of his Passion, right from the start of the cycle. This reflects Bonaventure's concept of Francis's life as a journey that culminates in union with the crucified Christ through the stigmatization.[24]

The overall composition of the *Homage of a Simple Man* took as its model Cimabue's *Saint Peter Curing the Lame Man in front of the Temple* (fig. 144), in the north transept of the Upper Church. This biblical story also took place in Jerusalem, outside Solomon's Temple.[25] After Pentecost, at the beginning of their missionary activities, Peter and John the Evangelist went every day to pray in the temple. Outside its gate, they encountered a lame man begging for alms. Peter took the cripple by the right hand and healed him. Both frescoes set two groups of figures before a backdrop of three distinct buildings. Saint Francis takes the place of Saint Peter, approaching from the left. In all the scenes in which Francis appears in secular clothing, he wears blue; in the second scene he is pulling off his coat to give to the poor knight, revealing its golden-yellow lining. Although the deteriorated condition of Cimabue's fresco makes it impossible to be sure, Saint Peter was almost certainly clad in golden yellow over blue.[26] *Saint Peter Curing the Lame Man* was a meaningful model: the scene begins the cycle of the apostles in the north transept, just as the *Homage of a Simple Man* begins the Saint Francis cycle on the north wall of the nave. One cycle succeeds the other, and the resemblances between the two opening scenes enable Saint Francis to be presented as a new apostle, the direct successor to Saint Peter and almost a second founder of the Roman Church.

Understood in these terms, the Temple of Minerva becomes considerably more significant. It was not unusual for medieval representations of the Temple of Solomon to envisage it as

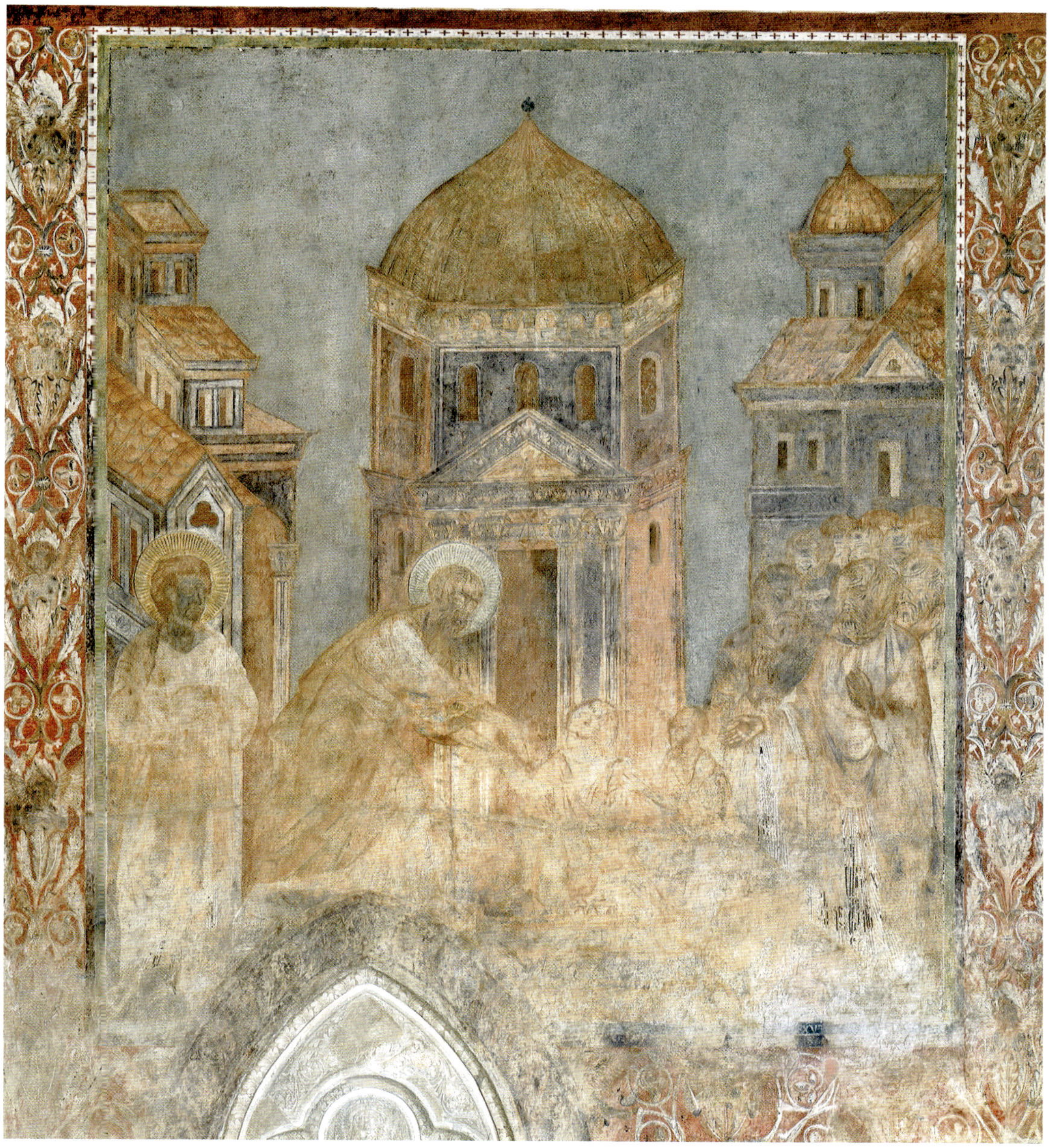

144 Cimabue, *Saint Peter Curing the Lame Man in front of the Temple*, Apostles cycle, *c.*1279–82, fresco, north transept, Upper Church, Basilica of San Francesco.

an antique building. Cimabue's temple is a domed polygonal building with a classical portico, whose pediment is supported, like that of the Temple of Minerva, by fluted columns with Corinthian capitals.[27] Just as the Old Testament patriarchs were understood to be the spiritual ancestors of all Christians, so the temple in Jerusalem was to be revered as a prefiguration of the 'new temple', the Christian Church. This typological interpretation is clear from the opening of Bede's influential commentary *On the Temple*: 'The house of God which King Solomon built in Jerusalem was made as a figure of the holy universal Church'.[28] Christ's promise that the new temple would be founded on his own body is the first link in a long chain of biblical texts describing the Church in terms of architectural metaphors.[29] Individual Christians are exhorted to be 'as living stones' in the temple, which is 'built upon the foundation of the apostles and

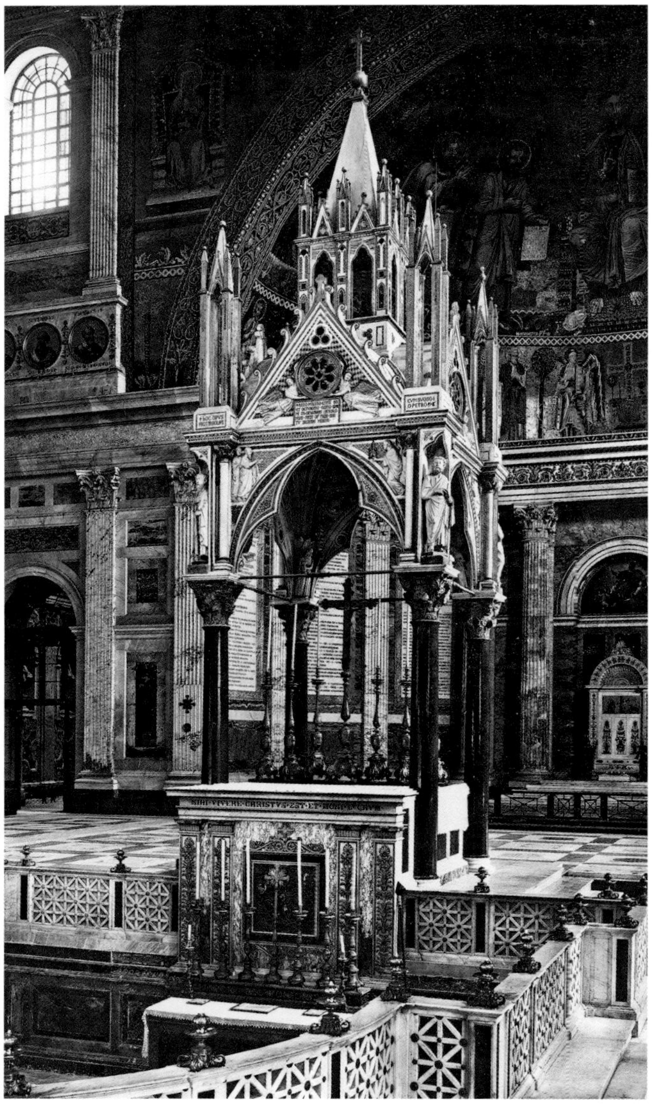

145 Arnolfo di Cambio, high-altar ciborium, signed and dated 1285, marble with cosmati inlay and gilding, on porphyry columns, San Paolo fuori le Mura, Rome.

prophets, Jesus Christ himself being the chief corner stone: In whom all the building, being framed together, groweth up into an holy temple in the Lord.'[30] It is this biblical metaphor that underlies Pope Innocent III's dream, later in the cycle, of Saint Francis physically supporting 'Christ's Church'.

If the Temple of Minerva is understood typologically, this could explain one of the major discrepancies between the painted building and the real one. In the fresco, the tympanum has been adorned with a rose window flanked by sculpted reliefs of angels. The marked similarity between this decorative feature and the micro-architecture of Arnolfo di Cambio's ciborium, installed over the high altar of San Paolo fuori le Mura in Rome in 1285 (fig. 145), was noted by Smart.[31] This embellishment has often been explained in aesthetic terms – the updating of a classical building for contemporary Gothic taste[32] – but it seems unlikely that it was intended purely as an artistic reference. Since the *Homage of a Simple Man* was one of the last scenes in the cycle to be painted, the decorative detail on the temple could have been an opportunistic response to the *Miracle of the Crib at Greccio* (see fig. 141), already completed at the other end of the same wall. The Greccio story takes place in a church whose high altar is covered by a Gothic ciborium that has also been compared with Arnolfo's for San Paolo.[33] The allusion to a ciborium within the architecture of the Temple of Minerva may have been intended to strengthen the building's typological significance as a prefiguration of the Church.

Francis and Adam: Creation and Reformation

The *Homage of a Simple Man* is a scene of prophecy, signalling the advent of change that Francis will bring for the Church. When the Saint Francis scenes are placed in the context of the entire wall, they can be read within a theme of new beginnings that runs throughout the first two bays. The top tier opens with the *Creation of the World* and the *Creation of Adam* (fig. 147) in the first bay, followed by the *Creation of Eve* and the *Fall* (figs 148 and 146) in the second. In the middle tier of the first bay God is ready to devastate the world in a mighty deluge, but he decides to spare Noah. He instructs him to build an ark and to take on board his family and every kind of animal, so that they can survive the flood and make a fresh start, repopulating the world. In the first scene, Noah is shown twice, on the left being summoned by the hand of God and on the right overseeing his sons building the ark (fig. 149). In the second scene, now badly damaged, the animals enter the ark (fig. 147).

As we saw in Chapter 4, the Genesis scenes in the top tier of the north wall closely emulated Roman papal models. Parallels between Saint Francis and the biblical figures in these eight scenes cannot be consistently found, and were probably only a secondary consideration in planning the cycles. However, in this part of the nave, arguably, the friars would have seen a meaningful link between Francis and

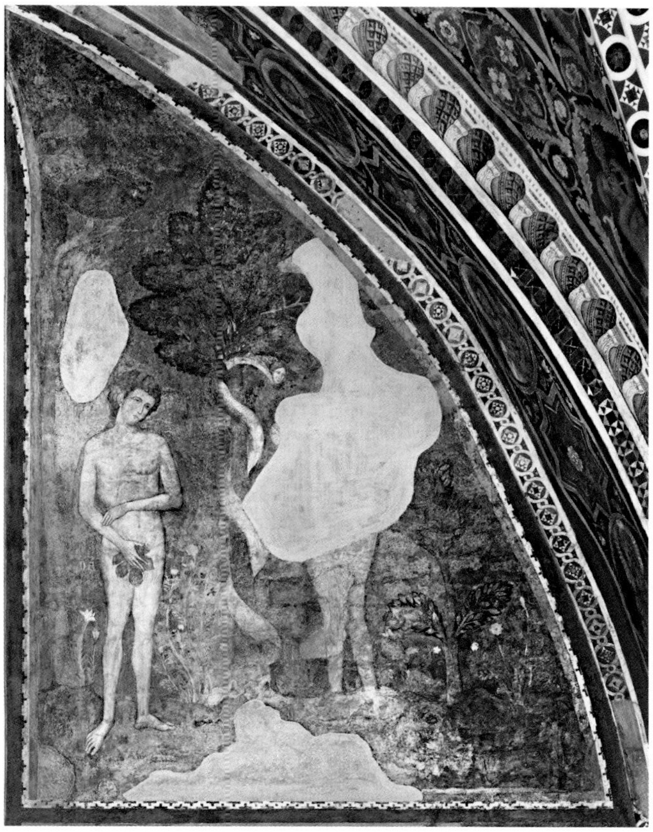

146 Jacopo Torriti, *Fall*, Old Testament cycle, *c.*1288–90, fresco, second bay, north wall of the nave, Upper Church, Basilica of San Francesco.

Adam, given the evidence that can be found in Franciscan sermons. Bougerol found sixteen Saint Francis sermons in thirteenth- and fourteenth-century manuscripts with the incipit 'Creavit Deus hominem ad imaginem' (Genesis 1:27), the verse that describes the creation of Adam. Most have been attributed to leading Franciscan thinkers, notably Jean de la Rochelle and Matthew of Acquasparta, but there are some by non-Franciscan preachers as well.[34] Matthew's sermon may have been especially influential for the friars at Assisi because the only complete collections of the former minister general's sermons (including his autograph copies) are in the Sacro Convento library:

> "So God created humankind in his image" . . . blessed Francis was conformed to and like Jesus Christ because he was sealed with the stigmata of the Crucified. As humans were made in God's image at the beginning of the world, so at the end of time God formed a singular man in the likeness of the Crucified so that the image of God almost lost, darkened and deformed in the first man, was, as it were, repaired and reformed in Francis.[35]

Matthew reasons that Francis's likeness to the crucified Christ (the perfect image of God in human form) was the proof of his power to reform a sinful world. Since Christ was seen as a new Adam because his sacrifice on the cross reversed Adam's sin, Francis as an *alter Christus* could be cast in the same salvific role.[36]

In the second bay, the motif of clothing that is used to symbolize the progress of Francis's conversion also serves to contrast his renunciation with Adam's fall. Bonaventure's version of the renunciation in the *Legenda maior* makes no mention of Adam, but the iconographers at Assisi had many other texts at their disposal in the library of the Sacro Convento. One of these may well have been the life of Saint Francis composed in verse by Henri d'Avranches for Pope Gregory IX and his court between 1230 and 1235.[37] Describing Francis's renunciation, the poet writes:

> Without a stitch, stark naked he stands, for all the world like Adam.
> But he differs from Adam in this: he suffers freely what Adam
> Was forced to endure; he suffers by merit what Adam endured for sin;
> And yet he is penalized as Adam was – though in a different way:
> Exposed was the shamefulness of Adam, while no shame
> Is discovered in him. Where is the shame in a naked body
> When the vesture of its soul is honour? Wherein did this
> Manliness lie? In scorning the world, in making himself disdained
> By the world; in caring not a whit for his property or person,
> In putting up with derisive taunts, in leaving an earthly father
> For his Father in heaven . . .[38]

following spread (left) 147 View of the first bay, north wall of the nave, Upper Church, Basilica of San Francesco.

following spread (right) 148 View of the second bay, north wall of the nave, Upper Church, Basilica of San Francesco.

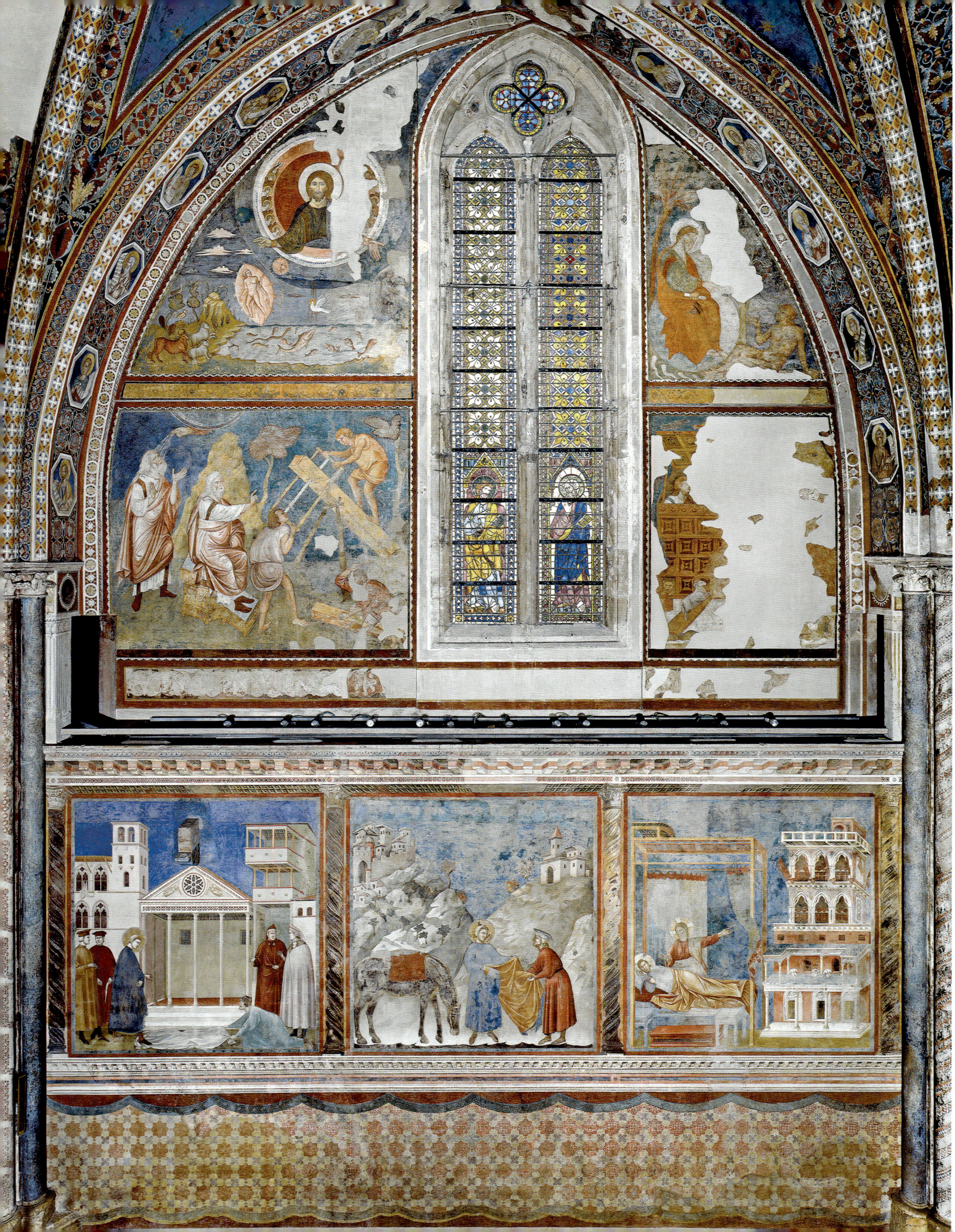

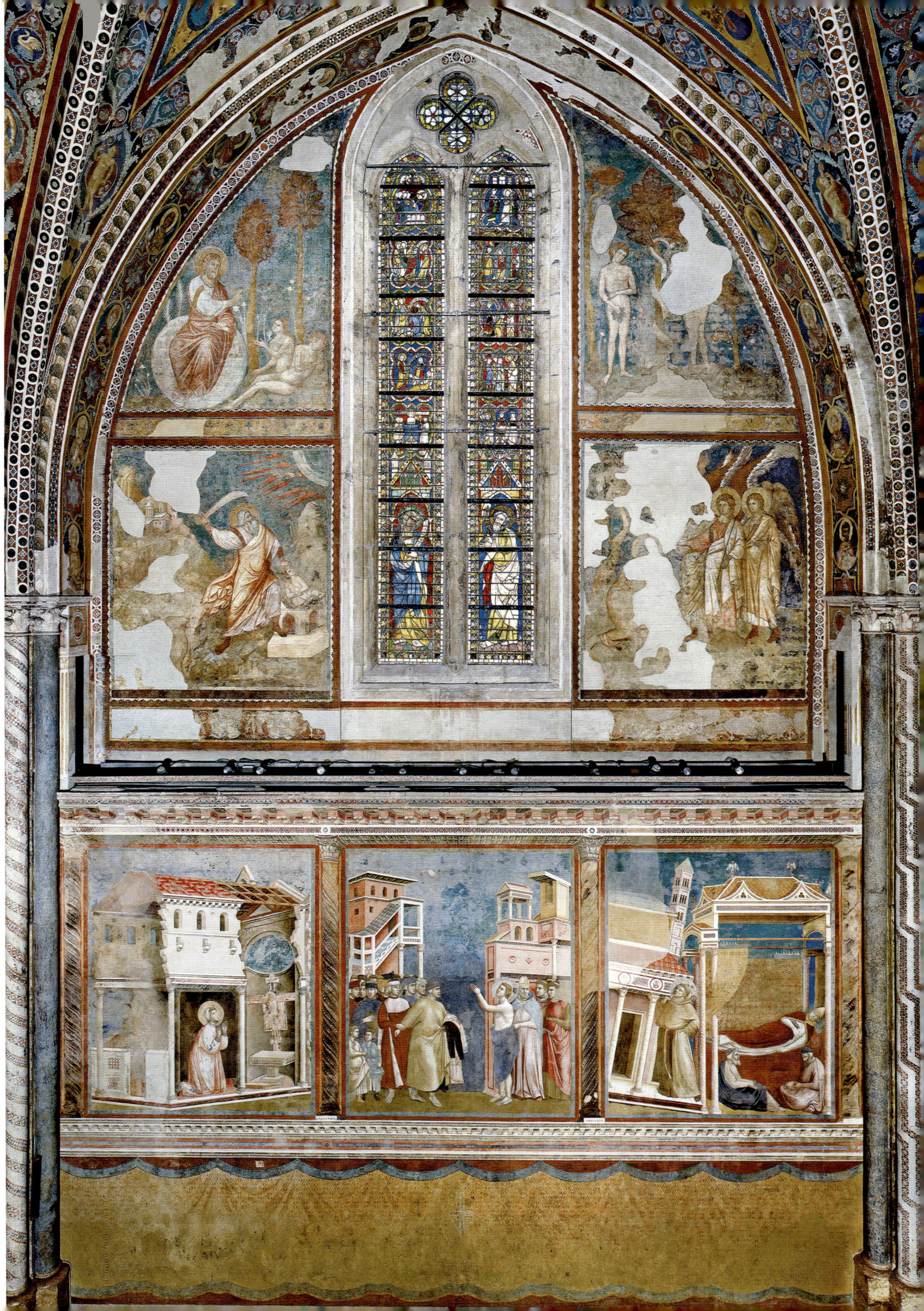

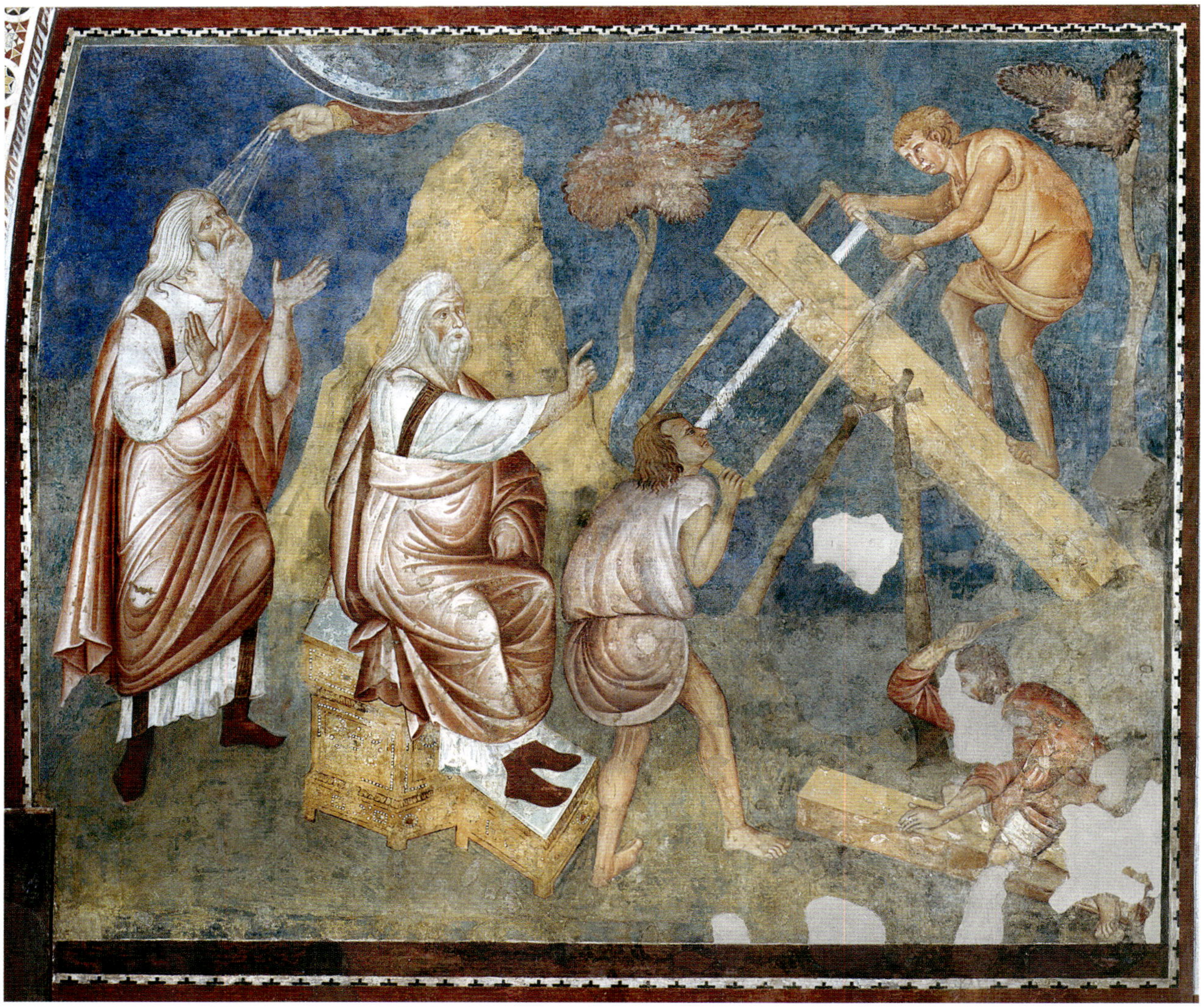

149 Jacopo Torriti, *Building the Ark*, Old Testament cycle, *c.*1288–90, fresco, first bay, north wall of the nave, Upper Church, Basilica of San Francesco.

The *Fall* (fig. 146), placed diagonally above *Saint Francis Renouncing his Father* (see figs 139 and 148), emphasizes Adam's shame: he tries to cover his nakedness with the figleaf, while Francis, in contrast, is quite unabashed, and it is left to the quick-thinking bishop of Assisi to protect the young man's modesty with his own mantle. Although Francis's stripping is often interpreted in terms of Franciscan poverty, both Henri d'Avranches's verse and the composition of the scene emphasize rather Francis's rejection of his earthly father for his heavenly one. In Bonaventure's text Francis speaks to Pietro Bernardone, but in the fresco he looks up and communes directly with God the Father, the remnants of whose hand can be glimpsed emerging from the heavens. Francis's obedience to God is contrasted with Adam's disobedience, and is seen in terms of the restoration of man's proper relationship with God.

Francis and Noah: Ark, Cross and Church

Unlike Adam, Noah seems to have held little or no interest for Franciscan hagiographers or preachers. Scholars have therefore been at something of a loss to find any meaningful links between Noah and Saint Francis in the opening bay of the nave. Quality compensates for lack of quantity, however, as the one relevant reference can be found in *Mira circa nos*, Pope Gregory IX's bull canonizing Francis in 1228.[39] The authority of this papal document was of fundamental importance for the Order.

In an extended metaphor, Gregory talks about the state of the world before Saint Francis, likening it to a vineyard that has been laid waste by godless men. These wicked people were destined to be destroyed, but God raised up his servant Francis, just as, when he sent the Flood, he saved 'the just man by a contemptible piece of wood'.[40] This last was a quotation from the book of Wisdom, and we are fortunate in having a mid-Duecento commentary written by Bonaventure on this biblical book.[41] Through typology, Bonaventure identifies 'the just man' as Noah and 'the contemptible piece of wood' as the ark.[42] The wood of the ark prefigured that of the cross, because while the cross was contemptible to unbelievers it was venerable to believers.[43]

The identification of the ark with the cross goes back to Saint Augustine. This was not the only typology he found for the ark: he also identified it with the body of Christ. The crucified Christ had his side pierced by a spear, and the blood and water that flowed out symbolized the sacrament of baptism. Likewise, the door of Noah's ark was in its side and so, Augustine argued, just as the animals could enter the ark only through this one door, Christians could enter the Church only through the wound in Christ's side – that is, through baptism. These references, obscure to those without exegetical education, may have had particular resonance for the Franciscans, given the strong emphasis on Francis's side wound on the opposite wall of the nave.[44] Both the ark and the cross were the means by which humanity was saved from sin. Therefore the ark – like Solomon's Temple – also prefigured the Church, because it offered salvation to Noah's family, just as the Church offered salvation to the whole Christian family. The second Noah scene at Assisi is badly damaged, but the animals are shown entering the ark, while Noah and his family are already safe inside; the head of one of Noah's sons is still just visible (fig. 150). All these ideas were succinctly presented in the medieval *Glossa ordinaria*, which explained: 'Noah is set free through water and wood, as is his family. Similarly the family of Christ [is set free], through baptism and the cross.'[45]

In the first bay, the typological connection between the ark and the cross is expressed visually by linking the two

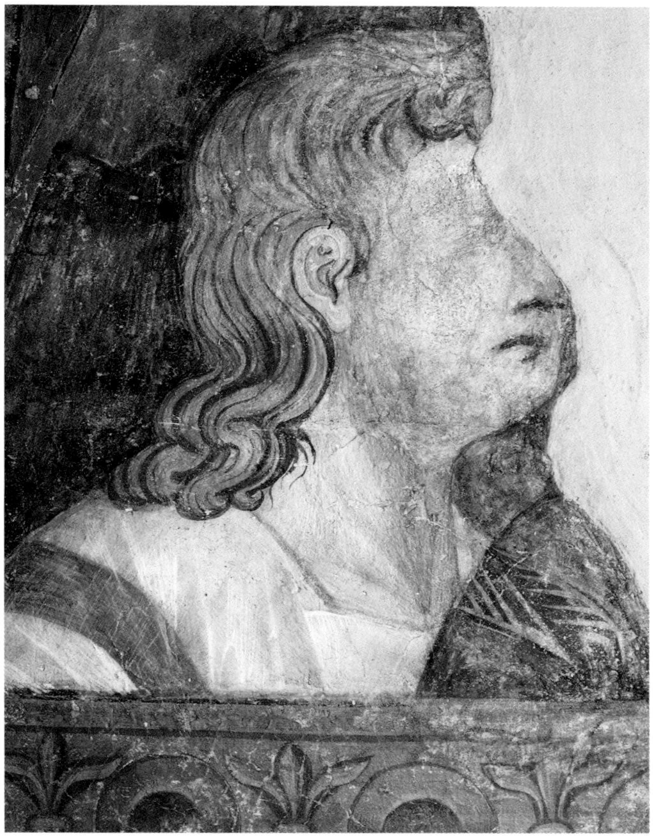

150 Head of Noah's son, detail from Jacopo Torriti, *Entering the Ark*, Old Testament cycle, *c.*1288–90, fresco, first bay, north wall of the nave, Upper Church, Basilica of San Francesco.

Noah scenes with the third scene in the Saint Francis cycle, the *Dream of the Palace of Arms* (see fig. 138). The ark itself is placed directly above the palace, while in the preceding scene the huge wooden beam being sawn by two of Noah's sons points diagonally towards it (see fig. 147). The armour, shields and banners in the palace are all marked with the sign of the cross of Christ (fig. 151). This detail is specifically mentioned in the inscription below the scene, which would have helped to draw viewers' attention to the typological link between the two tiers: the ark above and the cross below.[46] Evidence that the diagonal was contrived deliberately is suggested by the seventeenth-century copy of *Building the Ark* in San Paolo fuori le Mura in Rome (fig. 152), whose Old Testament cycle was one of the models for Assisi.[47] Jacopo Torriti adapted the Roman composition, reversing the group of sons on the right in order to change the angle of the plank.[48] The creation of this typological link is thoroughly

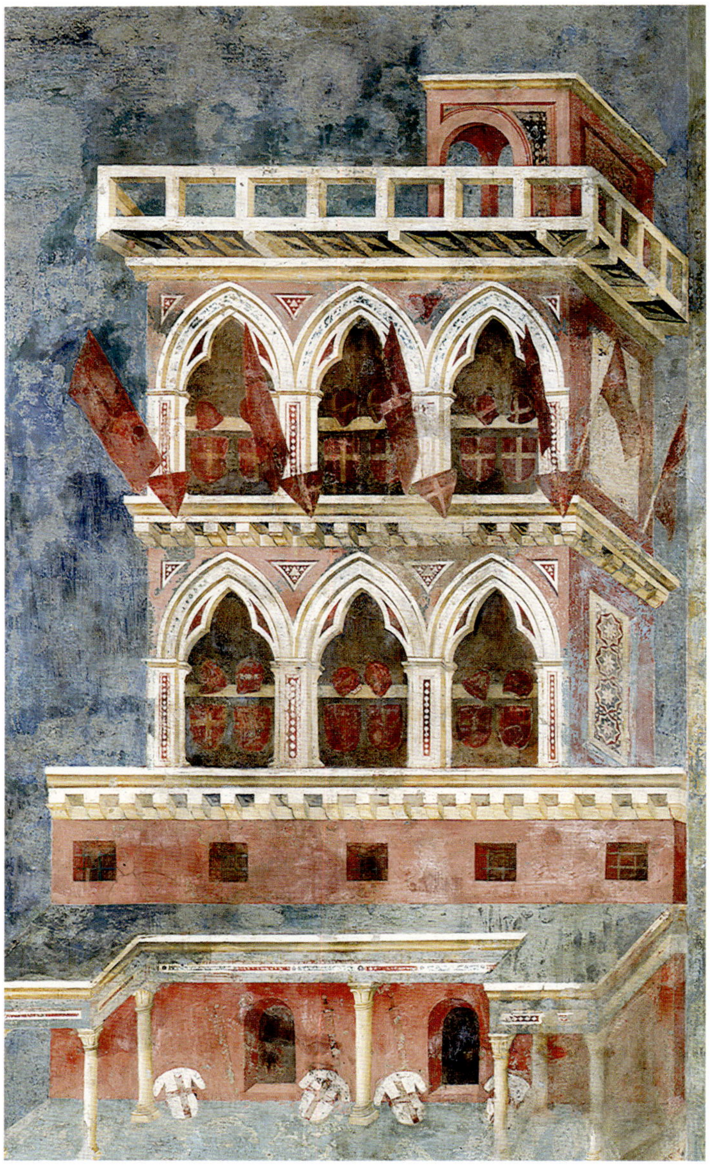

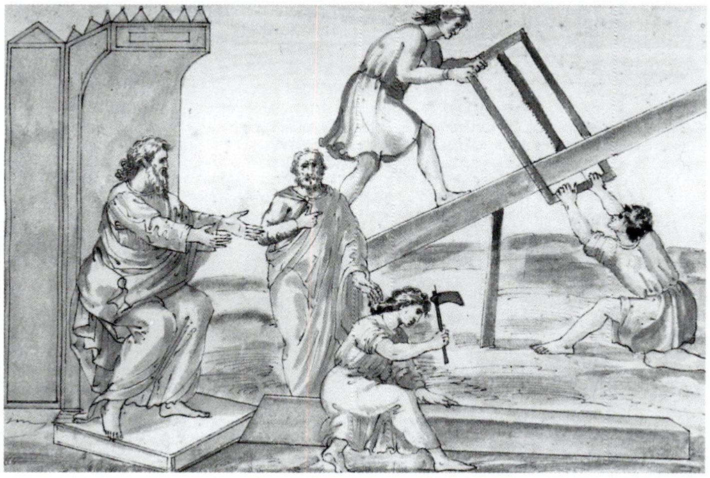

in keeping with Bonaventure's interpretation of Francis's dream of the palace as the first of the six visions of the cross that prefigured his stigmatization.[49]

The ark/cross typology could have been suggested to the friars in the Upper Church through another visual parallel as well. The two long, squared beams that are being sawn into planks by Noah's sons are not only highly suggestive of the cross, which they prefigure, but also of the battens on the reverse of a monumental panel crucifix. Those ideally situated to make such a comparison would have been the friars seated in their choir stalls behind the high altar. From that position, both the wood of the ark and Giunta Pisano's gigantic cross, its rood beam fixed into the wall directly below the Noah scene, would have been clearly visible. The friars would, of course, have been looking at the carpentered back of the panel crucifix, with its grid of wooden battens, a viewpoint perfectly captured in the *Miracle of the Crib at Greccio* (see fig. 141). This is typical of the kind of site-specific design opportunity that could only have been conceived through the collaboration of artists and friars, working within the space.

Francis, Abraham and Isaac: Fathers and Sons

After being prefigured in the first bay, the Church and the cross materialize in the second bay, with its representations of San Damiano and Saint John Lateran. The close association between the Church and the body of Christ is stressed inside San Damiano, where a panel crucifix stands on the altar (fig. 153). Directly above this scene is the *Sacrifice of Isaac* (fig. 154). Abraham was ordered by God to take his son Isaac to Mount Moriah and to sacrifice him as a burnt offering. Abraham obeyed, but at the last moment God intervened and saved Isaac, providing a ram caught in a thicket by its

top 151 Armour marked with signs of the cross, detail from *Dream of the Palace of Arms*, Scene 3 of the Saint Francis cycle, *c.*1290–96, fresco, north wall of the nave, Upper Church, Basilica of San Francesco.

bottom 152 Copy of *Building the Ark*, early Christian fresco in San Paolo fuori le Mura, Rome, seventeenth century, watercolour, Vatican City, Biblioteca Apostolica Vaticana, Ms Barb. lat. 4406, fol. 36.

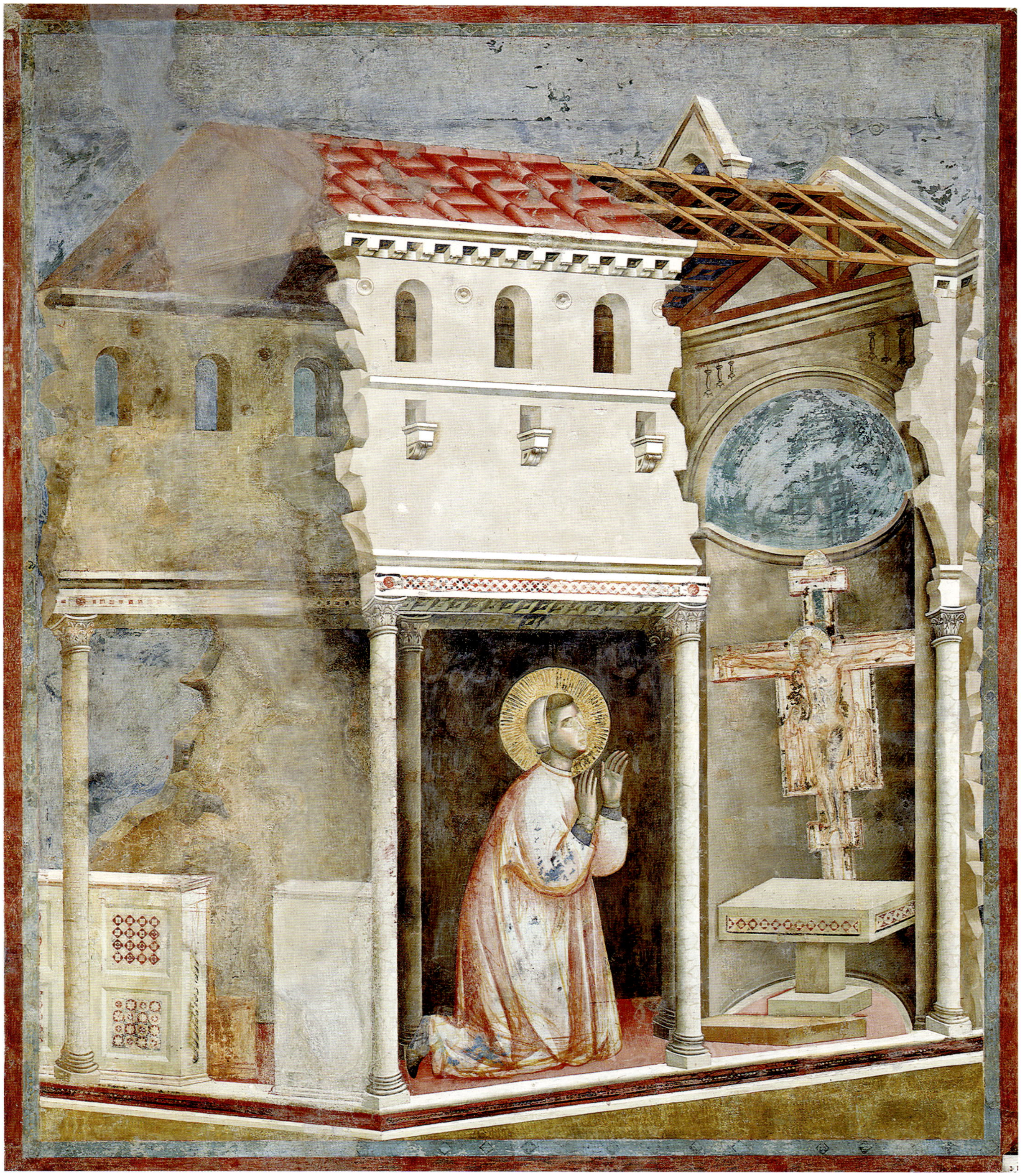

153 *Saint Francis before the Crucifix in San Damiano*, Scene 4 of the Saint Francis cycle, *c.*1290–96, fresco, north wall of the nave, Upper Church, Basilica of San Francesco.

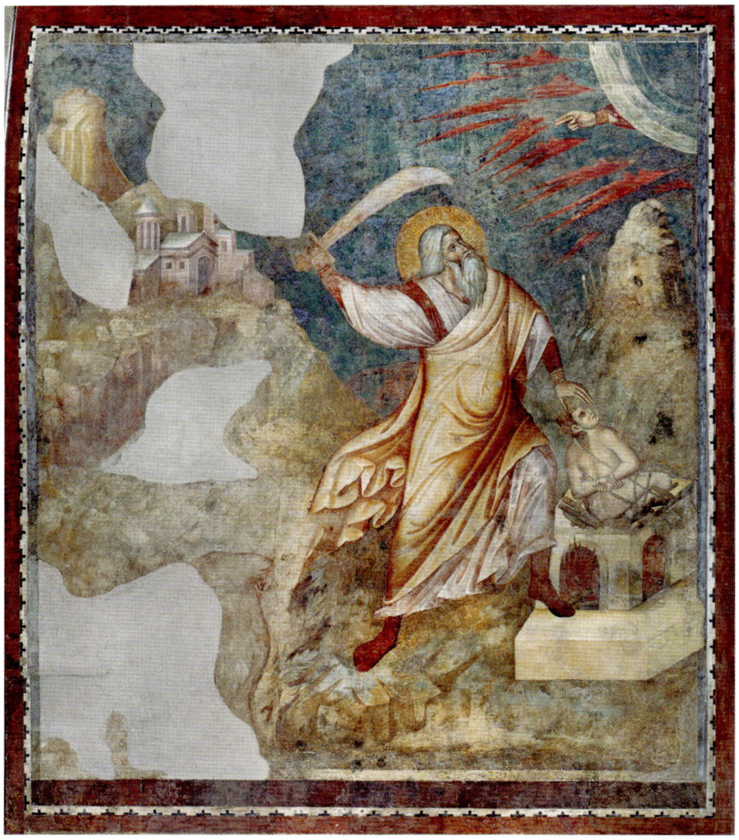

154 Jacopo Torriti, *Sacrifice of Isaac*, Old Testament cycle, *c.*1288–90, fresco, second bay, north wall of the nave, Upper Church, Basilica of San Francesco.

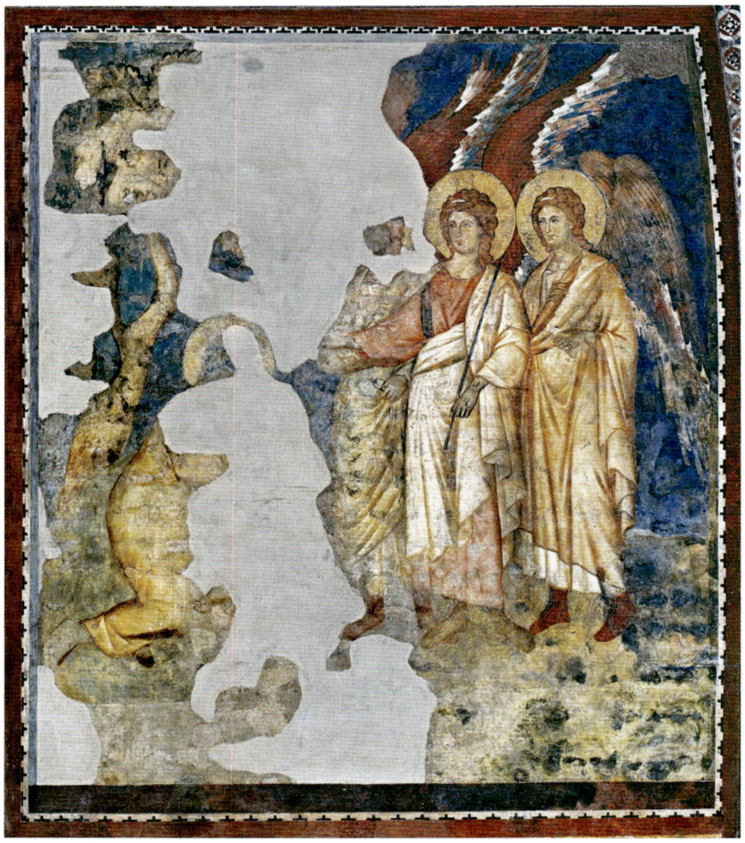

155 Jacopo Torriti, *Abraham Greeting the Three Angels*, Old Testament cycle, *c.*1288–90, fresco, second bay, north wall of the nave, Upper Church, Basilica of San Francesco.

horns to be sacrificed instead.[50] There was a long theological tradition of interpreting this difficult story as a prefiguration of the Crucifixion. Abraham was likened to God the Father who sacrificed his beloved son Jesus, prefigured by Isaac. Mount Moriah itself was triply significant: it was believed that King Solomon had built his temple over the site of Abraham's altar; and that Christ was later crucified on the same spot.

It is highly likely that the typology of the *Sacrifice of Isaac* influenced the decision to place the crucifix on the altar of San Damiano directly beneath the figure of Isaac on Abraham's altar (see fig. 148). A friar would have understood that the *Sacrifice of Isaac* prefigured not only the historical Crucifixion but also the ritual re-sacrifice of Christ's body in the Mass. Further evidence in support of this argument is that the two Abraham scenes have been chronologically reversed: according to Genesis, the events depicted in *Abraham*

156 *Abraham Greeting the Three Angels*, late twelfth century, fresco, San Pietro in Valle, Ferentillo.

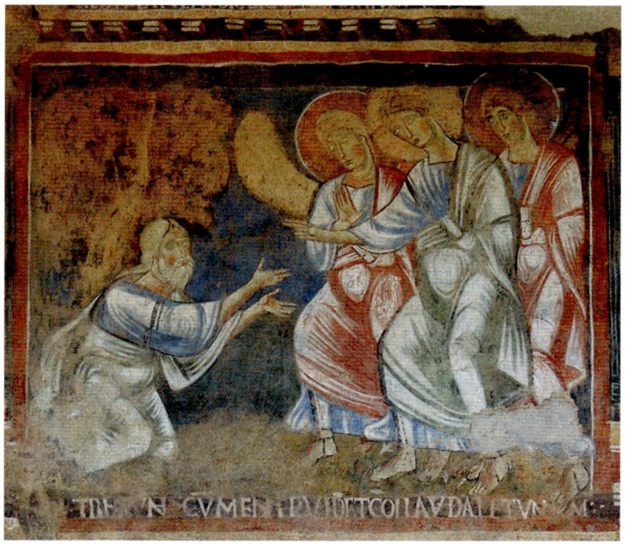

Greeting the Three Angels (fig. 155), on the right, happened before Isaac was born.[51] These are the only biblical scenes in the nave to have been placed in the wrong sequence; nor was this inversion the norm, because the Old Testament cycles from which the Assisi scheme was derived ordered the scenes correctly.[52] It is hard to avoid the conclusion that the Abraham scenes were deliberately rearranged at Assisi to make the parallels between Saint Francis and Abraham clearer, by forging strong vertical and diagonal ties between the two tiers of narratives.

The diagonal link is created by means of Francis's gaze towards Christ on the painted cross, as he prays in San Damiano. Continued beyond the picture frame, its direction leads up to the scene of *Abraham Greeting the Three Angels*. The basic iconography of this Genesis scene, as it had been established in the early Christian murals in Old Saint Peter's, can be seen in the surviving medieval cycles derived from that Roman prototype; a good example is the late twelfth-century fresco from the Benedictine abbey church of San Pietro in Valle, Ferentillo (fig. 156). While Abraham was sitting outside his tent, 'the Lord' appeared to him. Lifting up his eyes, he saw three men ('tres viri') standing before him, but Abraham, falling to the ground in adoration, called them 'Lord', as if only one person were present.[53] Later, two of the mysterious visitors travel to Sodom, where they are referred to as 'angels'.[54] Meanwhile, Abraham is described as remaining with 'the Lord'.[55] The true nature of the 'tres viri' puzzled early theologians. Were they all angels, or was one of them the Lord? And if 'the Lord' was Jesus Christ, how would Abraham have been able to see him, in the time before the Incarnation? Saint Augustine explained the figures typologically, as a prefiguration of the Holy Trinity, and his interpretation became standard in the Latin Church. A number of depictions before Assisi, including the prototype of Old Saint Peter's in Rome, annotated the scene not with the text from Genesis but with Augustine's oft quoted phrase, 'Tres vidit et unum adoravit' ('He saw three but adored one'), alluding to the figural meaning of the episode.[56]

While the Trinitarian meaning had been conveyed in Saint Peter's only through the titulus, at Ferentillo the typology is transmitted visually too: the central figure has a different-coloured costume and halo from his two winged companions, and his scroll and gesture are attributes normally associated with Christ.[57] The Assisi *Abraham Greeting the Three Angels* is badly damaged, but a comparison with Ferentillo helps to fill in the gaps. Again, the central angel is subtly distinguished from the others through his different-coloured robe, his gesture and the rod that he holds. He alone has a cruciform halo, which in this period was reserved for images of Christ (fig. 157). These details would have signalled to medieval viewers the underlying identity of the three figures as the Trinity.[58] Positioning Christ literally as the central person of the Trinity would have made complete sense to a Franciscan friar. Bonaventure, for example, calls Christ the 'persona media trinitatis' and it is Christ the 'mediator' who leads every Christian soul back to God.

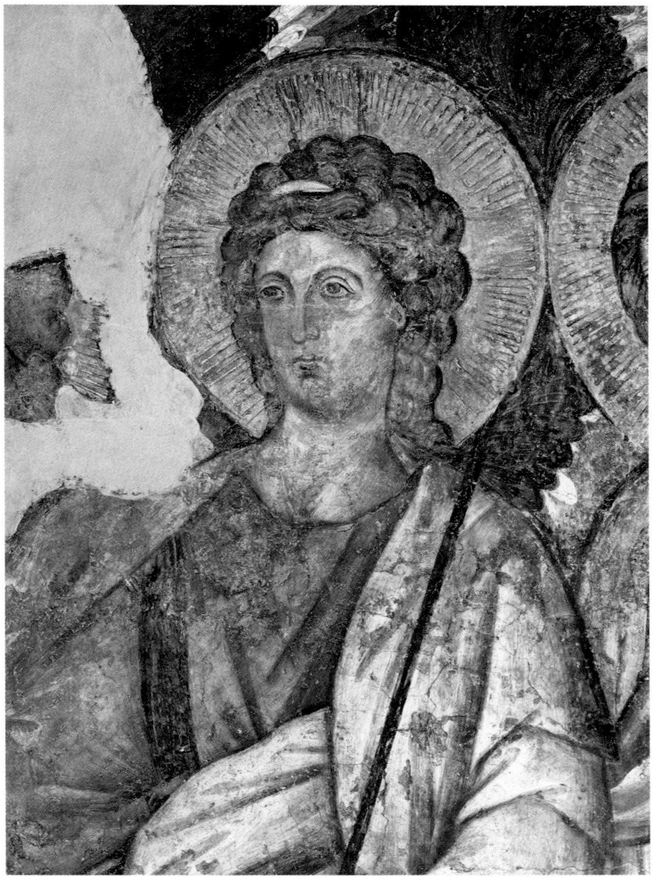

157 Central angel with cruciform halo, detail from Jacopo Torriti, *Abraham Greeting the Three Angels*, Old Testament cycle, *c.*1288–90, fresco, second bay, north wall of the nave, Upper Church, Basilica of San Francesco.

There are some obvious visual similarities between *Abraham Greeting the Three Angels* and *Saint Francis before the Crucifix*, which would have been much more striking before the loss of Abraham's arms. Abraham and Francis both kneel in prayer on the left of their scenes, arms extended and palms raised, looking up at divine manifestations on the right. A uniquely valuable insight into the parallels that contemporary Franciscans might have seen between the patriarch and the saint is offered by one of Matthew of Acquasparta's Saint Francis sermons, preserved in the Sacro Convento library. This sermon was extremely unusual: in Bougerol's study of 540 Saint Francis sermons from the thirteenth and fourteenth centuries, this is the only one preached on the text 'Abraham is our father' (John 8:39).[59] After a standard Trinitarian explanation of Abraham's meeting with the angels, Matthew turned his attention to Francis, asking rhetorically, 'Who is more faithful, sincere, simple than Francis, who believed most strongly in all that faith teaches: namely, God one and three, our Lord Jesus Christ true God and true man?' In this passage, by using the nature of God as a linking theme, Matthew was able to leap directly from the Trinity to Christ, on whom he then focuses exclusively. Linking Abraham and Francis through the metaphor of the seal, which he interprets as a sign of divine approval, Matthew argues that Abraham was sealed by circumcision because he had lived before the birth of Christ, but that Francis was 'sealed with Christ crucified in the limbs of his Passion': that is, by the stigmata.[60]

It has frequently been noted that both the pose of Francis before the crucifix – his hands raised in the *orans* gesture of prayer – and the overall composition of the scene allude to the stigmatization. By means of this visual language, the episode's additional function as one of Bonaventure's six manifestations of the cross, prefiguring the stigmatization, is conveyed to the viewer. What has not been remarked is that *Abraham Greeting the Three Angels* also contains elements of stigmatization iconography. Abraham sees a Christ-like figure in the guise of an angel, just as Francis sees a vision of Christ 'under the appearance of a Seraph'. The three angels between them even present six wings. The praying Saint Francis regards Christ on the painted cross, but beyond the picture frame he sees the prefiguration of Christ who appears to Abraham. The spatial relationship between these two scenes foreshadows the arrangement on the south wall, where the praying Saint Francis in the *Stigmatization* looks diagonally up to see not only the vision of the Christ–Seraph, but also the crucified Christ beyond (see fig. 121). An understanding of the San Damiano scene as a prefiguration of the stigmatization is reinforced by this repetition.

The *Sacrifice of Isaac* and *Saint Francis Renouncing his Father* can also be linked diagonally. Given the emphasis throughout the cycle on *Franciscus alter Christus*, we might have expected Francis to be compared with Isaac, but instead he is likened to Abraham, who puts his relationship with God before all human family ties. Both Abraham and Francis are depicted looking up towards the hand of God. Modern viewers see the young Francis as the son of Pietro Bernardone, but Franciscan friars had a different understanding. As Matthew of Acquasparta's sermon explains: 'It is customary to call the founders of religious orders and monasteries fathers . . . Among all peoples the Lesser Brothers can glory in their father, since their father is Francis, a person of wonderful perfection . . . who was prefigured by Abraham, the main patriarch.'[61] The vertical and diagonal links between Francis and Abraham are continued with the final scene in the second bay, the *Dream of Pope Innocent III* (see fig. 140). As a result of his dream, Innocent believed that Francis would be 'the one who will hold up Christ's Church by what he does and what he teaches'. Saint John Lateran was also known as the *Basilica Salvatoris*, so the building that Francis supports is 'Christ's Church' both literally and metaphorically. Careful attention has been given to its depiction. There is a large area of loss on the façade, which has been restored as a blank area. However, the same scene on the predella of the *Stigmatization* panel signed by Giotto, made for San Francesco in Pisa, with Assisi as its model, includes an accurate rendition of the Lateran's façade mosaic: Christ flanked by the archangels Gabriel and Michael (fig. 158).[62] It is all but certain that this detail was originally included in the Upper Church scene, where it would have provided a vertical link with the three angels – the central one prefiguring Christ – in the scene above, *Abraham Greeting the Three Angels*.[63]

Francis's stance and the direction of his gaze create the diagonal link with the *Sacrifice of Isaac*. This scene had unique typological significance in the mythology of the Lateran Basilica, whose high altar (distinct among the papal basilicas of Rome) was fashioned from wood instead of marble. In the early thirteenth century Pope Honorius III, attempting to explain this peculiarity, claimed that when the basilica was founded, its altar had been established 'in the form and likeness of the altar of Abraham, whose wood prefigured the cross of the Passion of Christ'.[64] In addition, the Lateran styled itself as the new temple, the direct successor to the destroyed

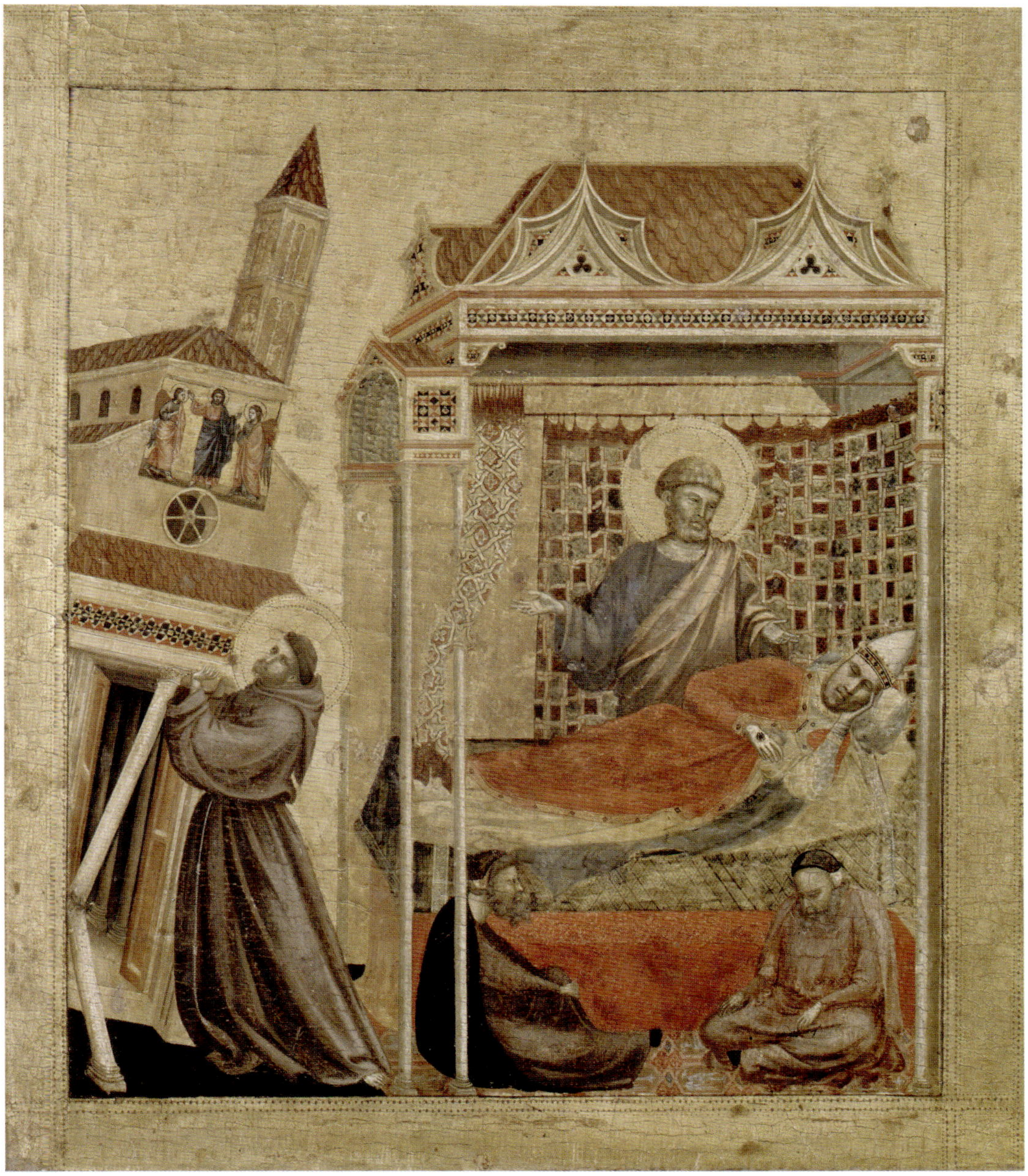

158 Giotto, *Dream of Pope Innocent III*, predella of the *Stigmatization*, *c.*1297–1300, signed, tempera and gold on wood, Musée du Louvre, Paris (originally San Francesco, Pisa).

Temple of Solomon in Jerusalem, which had been built on the site of Abraham's altar. Medieval visitors were shown the bronze columns of the pergola in front of the high altar, and were told they were spoils from Solomon's Temple.[65] Hence the Lateran was doubly prefigured in the *Sacrifice of Isaac*.

The sextet of scenes dealing with Francis's conversion from rich layman to poor friar both opens and closes with depictions of buildings that allude to the transformation of the Temple of Solomon into the *Ecclesia Romana*: the Temple of Minerva and the Lateran basilica. The architectural metaphor is reinforced by the various Old Testament prefigurations of the Church in the biblical cycles above. In the *Dream of Pope Innocent III*, Saint Francis takes his place in salvation history as the figure who will continue the process of renewing and rebuilding the Roman Church. Recalling the biblical metaphor of Christians as living stones in the temple, Francis does not prop up the falling Lateran from beyond its confines but stands on its plinth, so becoming part of the edifice – a literal pillar of the church.

The portico may be significant not only as an accurate rendition of the basilica in the time of Pope Nicholas IV, but also because some of its features tally with biblical descriptions of the temple in Jerusalem. The entrance to Solomon's Temple was framed by two mighty pillars which, as discussed above, the Lateran basilica claimed to possess. Biblical commentators interpreted all the parts of the temple symbolically. Bede, for example, referring to Saint Paul's description of the apostles James, Cephas and John as pillars (Galatians 2:9), understood the pillars of the temple to signify not only the apostles but all spiritual teachers. The two pillars stand either side of the temple door, which symbolizes Christ, who said: 'I am the door. By me, if any man enter in, he shall be saved'.[66] Innocent III had been convinced by his dream that Francis would support Christ's Church 'by what he does and what he teaches'. Francis as the pillar of the temple is a spiritual teacher who shows the way to Christ. The door to the Lateran stands open, inviting the spectator to enter. In contrast, the Temple of Minerva in the opening scene has no door at all, and the closed nature of the edifice is further emphasized by its two barred windows.

Rebuilding the Church: From Saint Francis to Nicholas IV

The full import of the *Dream of Innocent III* becomes apparent only when the Saint Francis scenes on the north wall are considered together with those opposite them. The distinctive status of this bay as a spatial unit is signalled by the *Deesis* in the vault: marking the central point in the length of the Upper Church, it functions as a pictorial bridge, connecting the two nave walls (see fig. 89).[67] The central scenes in the triplets on either side of the bay, Francis's *Renunciation* (see fig. 139) and his *Canonization* (see fig. 95), juxtapose the beginning of the saint's spiritual life with its culmination.[68] The depiction of Francis's relationship with churchmen in these two scenes is emblematic. His entry into religious life is symbolized by the protective gesture of the bishop of Assisi, accompanied by his clerics, while its triumphant finale is the public acclamation of Francis's sanctity by the pope and the whole ecclesiastical hierarchy.[69]

The outer scenes on each wall are linked across the void by two crossing diagonals, tracking the same lines as the ribs of the vault above. The first pairs the two dreaming popes, Innocent III and Gregory IX; the second the two representations of San Damiano.[70] The correspondences between the directly facing scenes, though less remarked, are also striking. At the west end of the bay, the stigmatization is prefigured by *Saint Francis before the Crucifix in San Damiano* (see fig. 153); opposite, the *Dream of Pope Gregory IX* (see fig. 131) asserts the inviolable truth of the sacred wounds. Above, in the *Deesis*, the saint's efficacy as a heavenly intercessor is assured through the display of his stigmata. These images, at the heart of the Upper Basilica, inextricably link Francis's potency in the Church Triumphant to his unique status as an *alter Christus*.

At the east end of the bay, Saint Francis supporting the falling Lateran in the *Dream of Innocent III* faces the magnificently restored San Damiano in the *Lamentation of the Clares*. In this comparison between Francis as a restorer of church buildings and as the restorer of the spiritual Church, San Damiano would at first sight appear to represent the material church. This was where Christ had called Francis to 'repair my house' and it was the building he had literally rebuilt in response. However, it was also at San Damiano that Francis had established the Second Order, the Poor Clares, which Thomas of Celano had judged to be 'a spiritual building much nobler than that earthly one'.[71] San Damiano may have been intended not only to represent the material church but also the more noble building of the Franciscan Order.[72]

In 1209 or 1210 Pope Innocent had interpreted his dream of the Lateran in spiritual terms, as a prophecy of Francis's restoration of the *Ecclesia Romana*. Almost eighty years later, its significance was transformed by the election of Jerome of Ascoli as the first Franciscan pope. The most recent events in Rome could not have been far from the minds of any Franciscans viewing the *Dream of Innocent III* at Assisi. As we saw in Chapter 1, Nicholas IV's campaign to renovate and redecorate Saint John Lateran seems to have been pushed forward with sufficient speed for his dedicatory inscription to have been placed in the church by the early months of 1291. After opening with Innocent III's dream, and his belief that Francis would 'bear the collapsing Church and faith', the inscription recounted how 'A child of Francis, Jerome, arising under the name of Nicholas the fourth, as Roman leader, the first among those whose lot is of that of the Minors', seeing that parts of the Lateran were falling into ruin, set about restoring the building.[73] In Nicholas's inscription, as in the Saint Francis cycle at Assisi, the material and spiritual restoration of the Roman Church are closely linked. The *Dream of Innocent III* assumed deep personal significance for Nicholas's sense of historical mission; he seems to have sincerely understood both his restoration of the Lateran basilica and his pontificate as the fulfilment of Innocent's prophecy. It is highly likely that the detailed depiction of the Lateran in the Assisi fresco would have been seen by leading friars at Assisi in the 1290s as a symbol of the restoration of the Roman Church, not only by Saint Francis but also by Nicholas IV. It was an institutional statement of the mission of the Franciscan Order.

The north wall of the nave concludes with the image of another church, which also contains allusions to Rome.[74] The *Miracle of the Crib at Greccio* (see fig. 141) shows, according to its titulus, 'How Blessed Francis, in memory of the birth of Christ, had a crib prepared, that hay and that an ox and an ass be brought in, and afterwards he preached to the people about the birth of the poor king. Then a knight [John of Greccio] saw the Child Jesus in the place of that child placed there by the saint.'[75] The scene is set inside a church, whose furnishings – a choir screen supporting an ambo and a monumental panel crucifix – are typically Franciscan. Scarpellini argued that the close correspondences between this fictive church and the Lower Basilica at Assisi suggest that what was being depicted was not an anachronistic version of the events at Greccio (which, it is clear from the written sources, took place outdoors) but the annual Christmas liturgy at Assisi.[76] We know that such a ceremony took place at least as early as 1253, because the canonization process for Saint Clare of Assisi recounted her vision of the Christmas celebration in San Francesco, in which she saw 'el presepio del Signore nostro Iesu Christo'.[77] Moreover, while in Bonaventure's account the knight sees the Christ Child appear in an empty crib, the titulus to the fresco has a real child appear in place of the one put there by Francis. This modification to the legend suggests that by the late thirteenth century the Christmas vigil at Assisi included a model Christ Child in the crib.[78]

Like the *Verification of the Stigmata* scene, whose fictive setting references both the Porziuncola and the Upper Basilica, yet without literally depicting either one, the *Crib at Greccio* does not offer a straightforward replication of the Lower Church, but a loose amalgam of architectural allusions. While the rood screen with its panel crucifix may suggest Assisi, the liturgical furnishings of the Lower Church could never have included a ciborium: it would have been impossible to build such a structure over the exceptionally wide altar *mensa*.[79] The similarity of the frescoed canopy to Arnolfo di Cambio's high altar ciborium for San Paolo fuori le Mura, completed in 1285 (see fig. 145), points instead towards Rome. Since, by the late Duecento, Roman ciboria had unmistakably papal connotations, perhaps the ciborium in the *Crib at Greccio* – depicted in the most modern style and in a setting that evoked the Lower Church – was intended to suggest the status of San Francesco, Assisi, as a papal basilica.[80]

The painted ciborium may have been intended as a more particular reference. Among the papal basilicas, the unique combination of a ciborium and a crib scene was applicable only to Santa Maria Maggiore. In the seventh century relics of the Nativity were brought from Bethlehem to this Roman church, earning it the denomination Santa Maria ad Praesepe. By the eleventh century a complex Christmas stational liturgy had developed. The nocturnal papal Mass was celebrated in the Cappella del Presepio, which opened off the north side of the nave, after which the singers and other participants returned to the choir for the *laudes matutinales*, followed in turn by a solemn Mass at the high altar (fig. 159).[81]

Until its replacement in the fifteenth century, the ciborium over the high altar of Santa Maria Maggiore was one that had been translated from Saint Peter's by Pope Leo III in 809. Although it would not have had the Gothic features of the frescoed version at Assisi, it seems to have had unusually elaborate decoration for an ancient ciborium. Before it was moved from Saint Peter's, Leo III had its columns embellished with the figures of gilded silver cherubim above the capitals.[82] De Blaauw believes that the porphyry shafts of its four supporting columns probably dated back to the earliest baldachin in Saint Peter's, erected by Gregory the Great (590–604), which established the prototype for such columns on subsequent papal ciboria.[83]

The shafts of the Assisi ciborium, which are painted in purple to resemble porphyry, could therefore have suggested the high altar ciborium of Santa Maria Maggiore. But by the

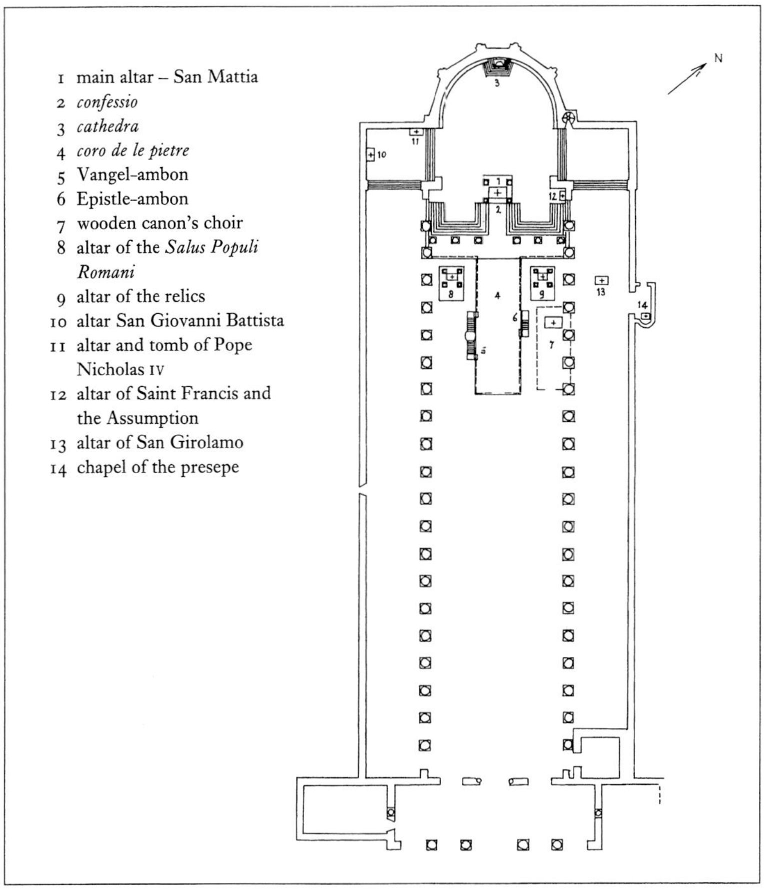

159 Plan of Santa Maria Maggiore, Rome, *c.*1400 (Israëls (2003), p. 116, fig. 54, after de Blaauw (1994), fig. 18).

1290s, the Marian basilica possessed at least one other ciborium supported on porphyry columns, the Capocci tabernacle.[84] Dated by inscription to 1256, it was built to house relics, including the *cunubulum* (manger) in which the baby Jesus was believed to have lain. During Nicholas IV's pontificate, the lead casket housing the *cunubulum* was replaced with a new one of engraved silver. The Capocci tabernacle stood on the north side of the choir enclosure, close to the Cappella del Presepio (see 9 and 14 on fig. 159). The tiny chapel was enhanced *c.*1289–91 with a sculpted Nativity group (or *presepio*) commissioned from Arnolfo di Cambio. This survives only in fragmentary form, but includes figures of Joseph, the three Magi, an ox and an ass (figs 160 and 161).[85] The precise patronage for Arnolfo's *presepio* is uncertain. Both Vasari and Onofrio Panvinio named a certain 'Pandolfo', perhaps Pandolfo da Pontecarvo, who is documented in 1288 as a *scriptor papae* of Nicholas IV and in 1291 as a canon of Santa Maria Maggiore.[86] But Romano considered it 'almost certain or extremely probable' that the initiative was that of Nicholas or his close circle.[87]

When he suggested that the *Crib at Greccio* depicted the Christmas liturgy in the Lower Church at Assisi, Scarpellini pointed to the diminutive ox and ass, which seemed to him to be closer to painted terracotta statues than to the live beasts of the Greccio story.[88] Once the miracle had been transformed into sacred drama, it would have been natural for the friars at Assisi to allude to the Roman basilica that was at the heart of the papal liturgy of the Nativity, and that at the time was being transformed by Nicholas IV and his Colonna allies. But the relationship between Assisi and Rome may have been more complex. The Greccio episode made Saint Francis the instigator of the use of *presepe* in Christmas celebrations: consequently, Nicholas IV's decision to upgrade and embellish the accoutrements of the Nativity cult in Santa Maria Maggiore may well have been another expression of his Franciscanism.

What we do not know is whether subtle references in the Upper Church frescoes to Nicholas's artistic patronage in Rome were planned and executed while he was still alive. If so, we could see them almost as reportage, intended to flatter Nicholas, should he or his representatives visit Assisi. But if the details of the scene were not worked out until after the pope's death, arguably the references could have been even more meaningful. Unlike the rest of the Saint Francis scenes on the north wall, the *Crib at Greccio* does not appear beneath Genesis scenes. It is adjacent to the counter-façade and directly below the pairs of saints painted in the archivolt (fig. 162). As discussed in Chapter 2, the presence here of Agapitus, the obscure patron saint of Palestrina, makes sense only as a reference to Nicholas IV, cardinal priest of Palestrina until his elevation to the papacy, and to the Colonna.[89] It was the Colonna, controllers of Santa Maria Maggiore, who completed Nicholas's Roman projects after his demise.

Not only that, but the *Crib at Greccio* is beneath the vault of the Doctors of the Church (see fig. 45). Of the four doctors, Saint Jerome (fig. 163) was given the most prestigious position, adjacent to the counter-façade and visible along the entire longitudinal axis of the Upper Church.[90] In fact, Jerome occupies the equivalent web of the vault to Saint Francis in the *Deesis*, so that a viewer from the apse

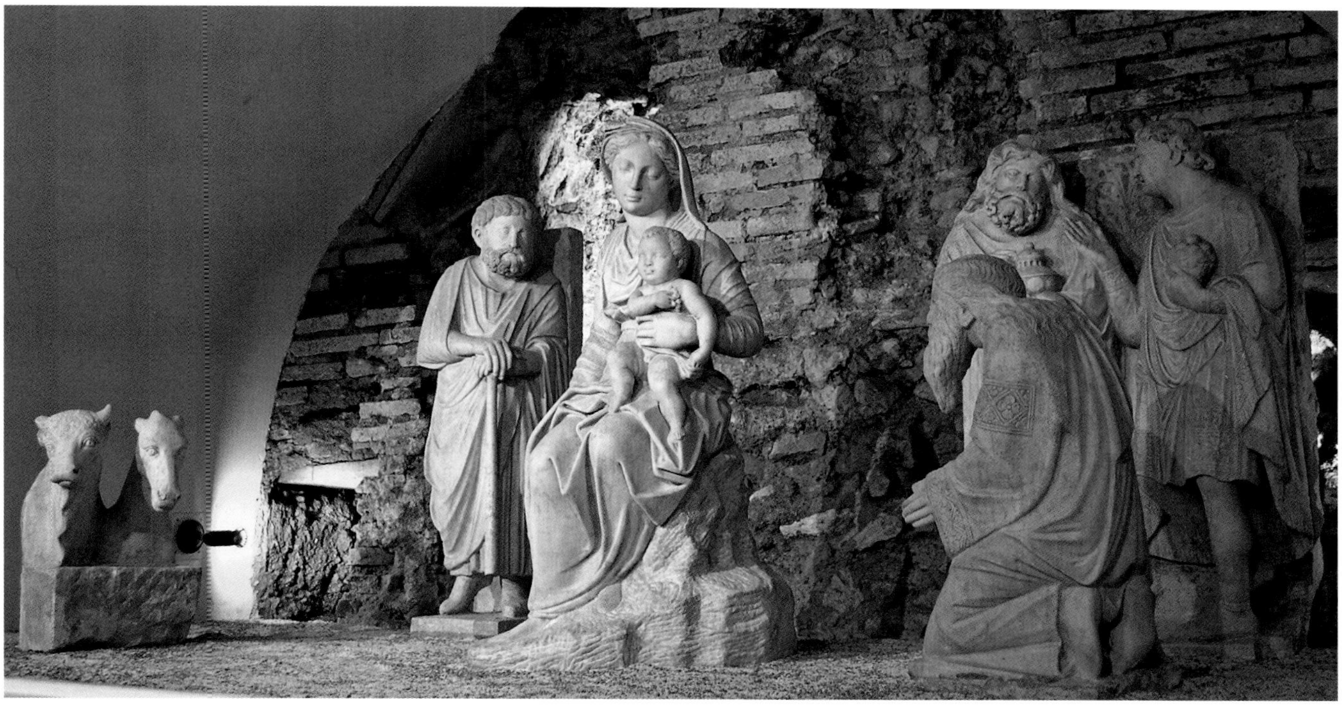

would look from Francis to Jerome. It is plausible that one reason Jerome was given this place was to honour Nicholas, whose name-saint he was; it is also suggestive that Jerome is placed back-to-back with Gregory, the only doctor to have been a pope.

Saint Jerome was strongly connected with the Nativity and had been buried in Bethlehem. His cult in Rome flourished after the translation of his relics to Santa Maria Maggiore, probably in the thirteenth century. There is no archival record of the presence of Jerome's remains in the Roman basilica before 1398, when they were referred to as lying under an iron grate in front of the Cappella del Presepio.[91] But elsewhere within the Esquiline basilica, in the

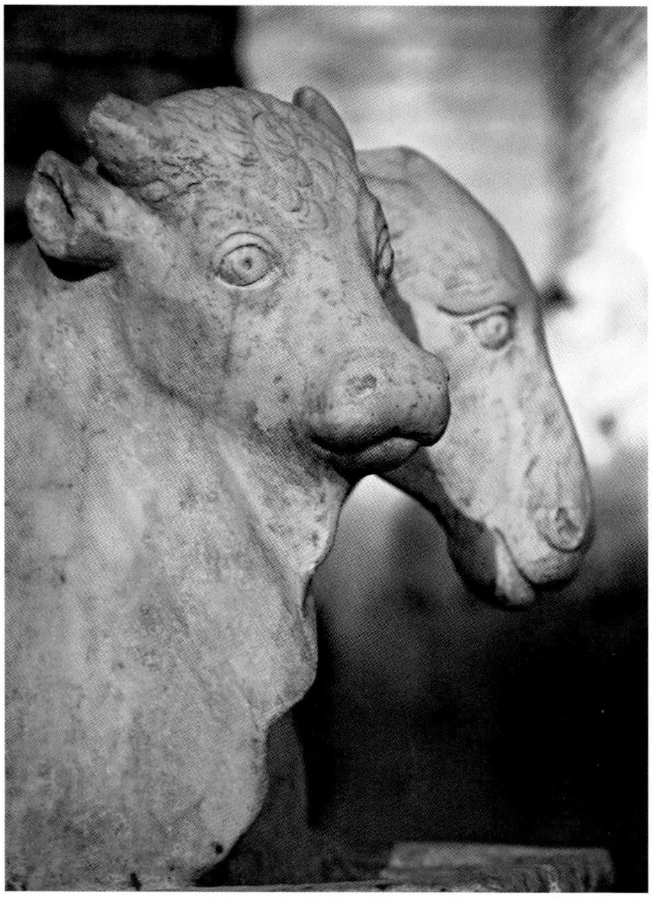

top 160 Arnolfo di Cambio, figures from a Nativity, *c.*1289–91, marble: Saint Joseph (85 cm × 23 cm × 26 cm), kneeling Magus (53 cm × 28 cm × 22 cm), and two standing Magi (80 cm × 60 cm × 15 cm), with Virgin and Child by an unknown sixteenth-century sculptor, Museum of Santa Maria Maggiore, Rome (originally Cappella del Presepio, Santa Maria Maggiore).

bottom 161 Arnolfo di Cambio, ox and ass from a Nativity, *c.*1289–91, marble (37 cm × 28 cm × 27 cm), Museum of Santa Maria Maggiore, Rome (originally Cappella del Presepio, Santa Maria Maggiore).

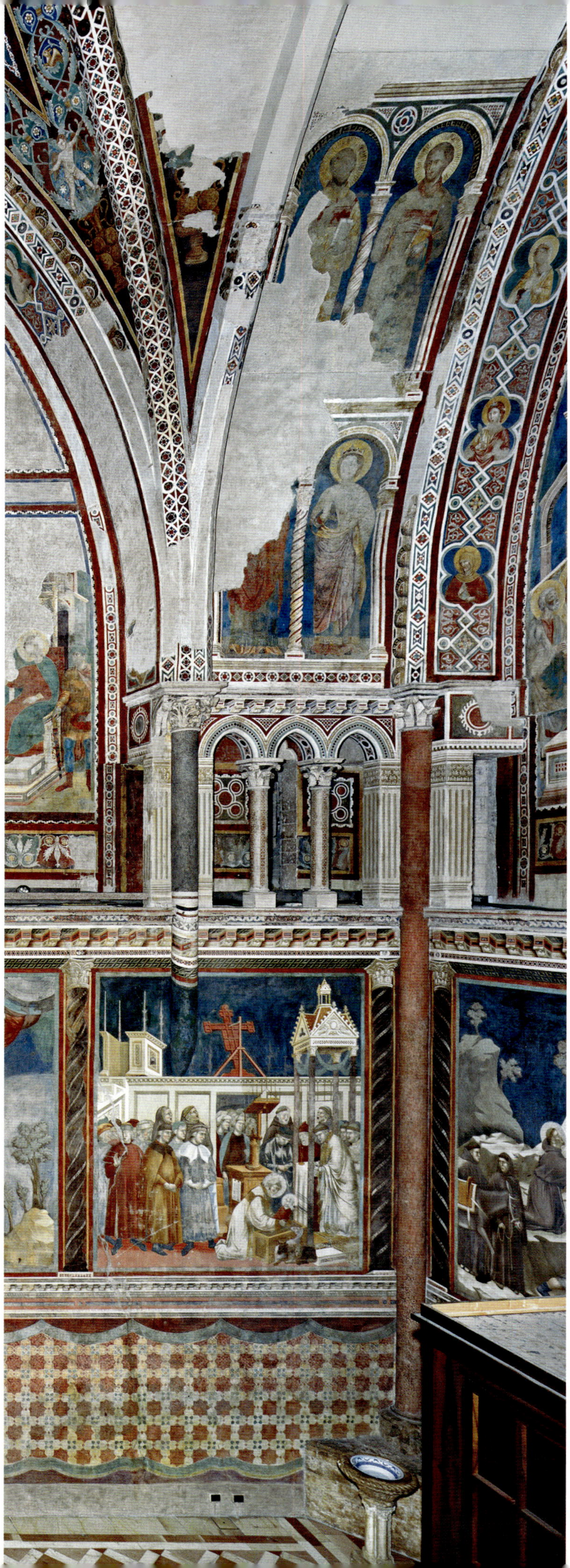

mosaic lunette of the tomb of Cardinal Rodriguez Consalvo, who died in 1299, Saint Jerome displays a scroll referring to the location of his own body: 'I recline near the grotto of the crib.'[92] So it is apt that the figure of Jerome appears in the vault at Assisi above the *Miracle of the Crib at Greccio*. Images of Saint Jerome were also part of Nicholas IV's planned new mosaic decorations for the Roman basilica, on the triumphal arch and on the façade, both completed by the Colonna before 1297 (see fig. 27).[93] Nicholas was buried at Santa Maria Maggiore beneath a simple floor slab. This may have been in the right aisle, close to the Capocci tabernacle, the Cappella del Presepio and the altar-tomb of his name-saint Jerome (see fig. 159).[94] Although not all of this could have been foreseen when the nave programme at Assisi was being planned, by the time the frescoes were completed, the proximate images of the *Crib at Greccio*, Saint Agapitus and Saint Jerome may have acquired an extra layer of commemorative meaning.

The nexus of Saint Francis scenes in the second bay, on the other hand, must have been intended as a focal part of the nave programme from the start. Nicholas IV united in one person two poles of power, the papacy and the Franciscan Order. The sextet of Saint Francis scenes does likewise: each takes place either in Rome or in Assisi, bringing together popes and prelates, friars, nuns and laity into the combined body of the Church Militant, exalting Saint Francis as an *alter Christus*. We have seen that Nicholas combined institutional power with personal humility, and that he continued to maintain his identity as a Friar Minor throughout his papacy. As pope, Nicholas was father of the entire Church; yet as friar he remained the son of his spiritual father, Francis, as his donor inscriptions in the Lateran proclaimed.[95] But in the eyes of others, perhaps, Nicholas had been elevated from son to father, in the same way that Saint Francis, after repudiating Pietro Bernardone, had been transformed into the founder and patriarch of his Order, another Abraham. The *Dream of Innocent III* was one of the most important scenes in the entire cycle, celebrating the power and success of the Franciscan Order. The titulus below it begins simply 'Quomodo papa videbat' without identifying the pope in question. This lack of specificity

162 View of the north-east corner of the nave, Upper Church, Basilica of San Francesco.

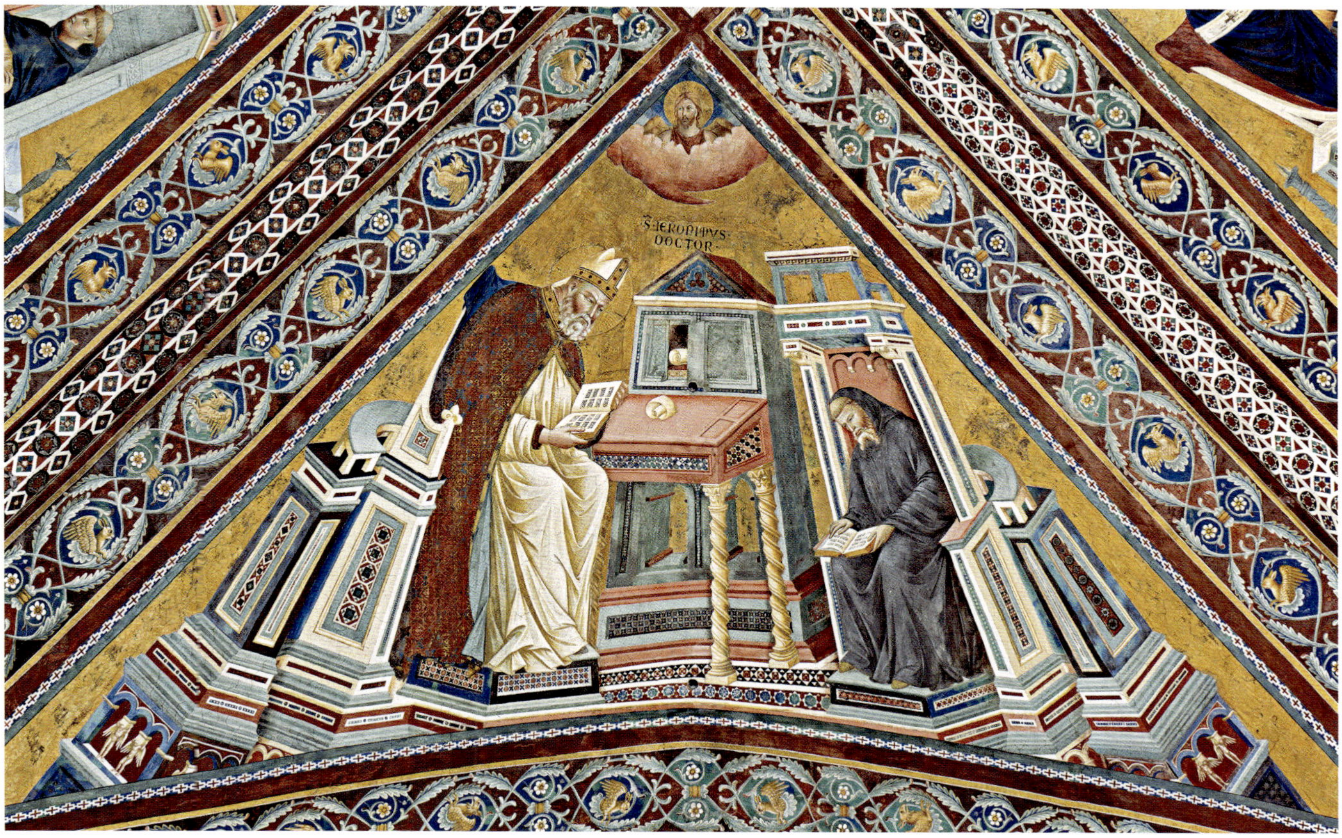

163 Saint Jerome, vault of the Doctors of the Church (east web, fourth bay of the nave), *c.*1288–91, fresco, Upper Church, Basilica of San Francesco.

opens up the scene for multivalent readings, allowing for the possibility of superimposing one pope upon another. Nicholas IV's own understanding of the dream of the Lateran transformed it from a prophecy to a prophecy fulfilled. For the friars at Assisi, the *Dream of Innocent III* honoured both their founder-saint and their papal patron, the father of their own Order and the father of the Roman Church. It was due to both of them that the Church was no longer ruined, either materially or spiritually, but magnificently restored.

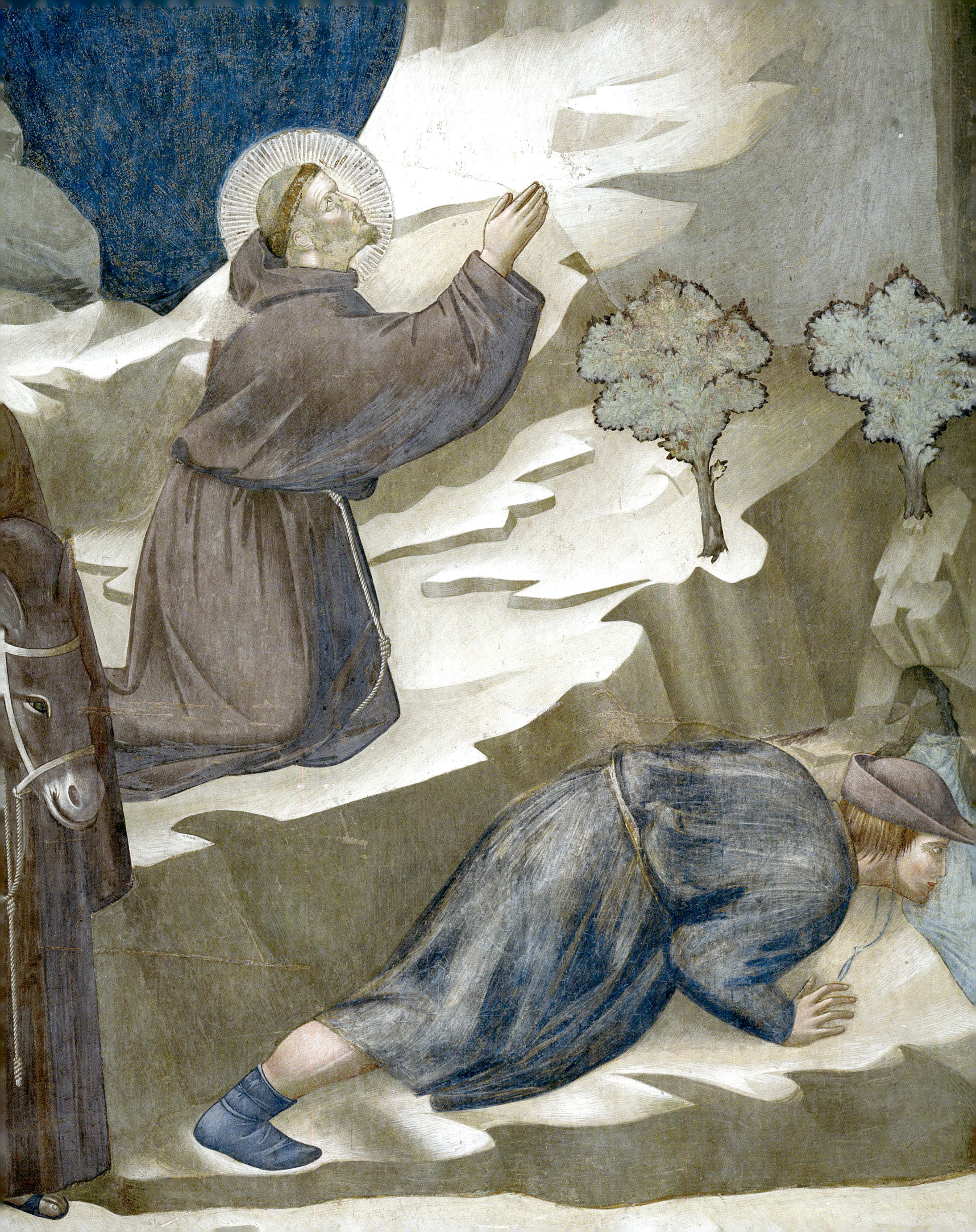

7

Ascending to God, Descending to Neighbour

When Giorgio Vasari first asserted Giotto's authorship of the Saint Francis cycle, in the 1568 edition of his *Lives of the Artists*, he singled out just one detail from the entire scheme for particular praise: 'One of the most beautiful scenes is of a man showing signs of great thirst kneeling down to drink eagerly at a fountain; the incident is conveyed so exactly and movingly that one might be looking at a real person.'[1] Who was this thirsty man, who so caught the imagination of Vasari? He appears on the counter-façade, in the story of the *Miracle of the Spring* (fig. 164). One hot summer's day, Saint Francis and his companions were journeying to a mountain hermitage. Because he was weak from illness, Francis was riding on a donkey belonging to a peasant who was accompanying the friars. This poor fellow, exhausted by the heat and the steep climb, finally exclaimed that he would die unless he got something to drink. In response to the man's distress, Francis immediately dismounted and knelt on the ground, praying unceasingly until a stream of water sprang from the hard rock.[2]

facing page 164 *Miracle of the Spring* (detail), Scene 14 of the Saint Francis cycle, *c.*1290–96, fresco, counter-façade, Upper Church, Basilica of San Francesco.

On first reading, the *Miracle of the Spring* does not seem to be one of the more important episodes in Saint Francis's life, but the prominent position of the scene in the Upper Church suggests otherwise, and helps to explain why it caught Vasari's eye. The counter-façade represents one of the most important ensembles of frescoes in the entire Basilica (fig. 165). It is here that the Saint Francis cycle reaches its mid-point, and where the stories of Francis and Christ first interlock. The New Testament cycle, having advanced from the transept along the south wall of the nave, culminates on the upper part of the counter-façade with the *Ascension* (fig. 167) and the *Pentecost* (fig. 166). Beneath, and proceeding chronologically in the opposite direction, are two Saint Francis scenes, the *Miracle of the Spring* (fig. 168) and the *Preaching to the Birds* (fig. 169). Since the counter-façade is visible down the entire length of the nave, its four scenes are much more prominent than those on the north and south walls. The counter-façade would also have been legible to friars gathered in the choir behind the high altar, and to the pope seated (ideally, if not actually) on his throne in the apse.

In Chapter 5 we argued that one of the first major decisions taken by the planners of the nave murals must have been to fix the positions of the *Stigmatization* and the *Death of Saint*

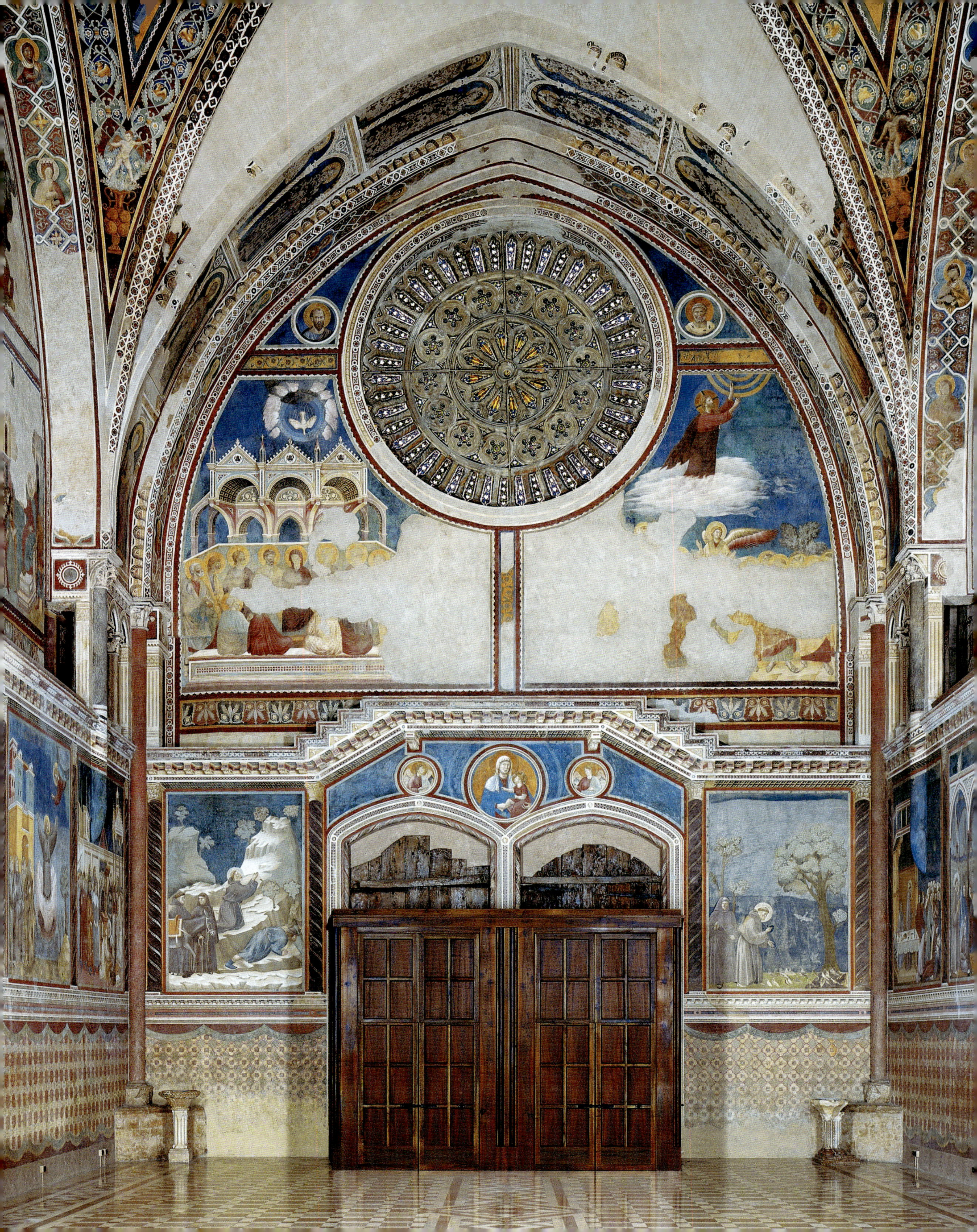

Francis on the south wall. Placing them below the *Crucifixion* and the *Lamentation* over the body of Christ created a powerful quartet of images, bound together through strong vertical and diagonal links. Perhaps the next key decision was the choice and arrangement of scenes on the east wall. As we shall see, the counter-façade comprises another quartet of narratives whose extended meanings are articulated by means of verticals and diagonals. The idea that the counter-façade was given special treatment in the nave plan is strongly suggested by the choice of the *Miracle of the Spring* and the *Preaching to the Birds* for its two Saint Francis scenes. Both had to be plucked out of their sequence in the *Legenda maior* in order to be placed here (see plan, fig. 96).[3] Scholars have frequently remarked on this fact, yet the rationale behind it has rarely been explored further. Smart noted 'the pairing of these two country scenes' but made no additional comment.[4] Cook saw them functioning 'like windows at the back of the church', their contrasting landscapes anticipating the topography visible on exiting the Basilica: to the left Mount Subasio rises up beyond Assisi, while to the right the plain of the Spoleto valley spreads out below the city walls.[5] While this observation is borne out by experience, given the intellectual depth of the decorative scheme it does not seem credible that these two Franciscan scenes were placed on the counter-façade purely for aesthetic reasons. To explain their selection, deeper layers of meaning in the fresco programme need to be uncovered.

Although this chapter argues that the quartet of images on the counter-façade was designed to make sense as a self-contained unit, its two Franciscan stories are embedded within a much longer set of narratives depicting the saint's life as a friar. This long middle section of the cycle encompasses the third and fourth bays of the north wall, the counter-façade and the fourth bay of the south wall. It starts with the *Approval of the Rule* (Scene 7) (see fig. 180) and concludes with the *Death of Saint Francis* (Scene 20) (see fig. 122): fourteen scenes in all, exactly half the cycle. It is perhaps only to be expected, in the mother church of the Order, that this part of the cycle should deal not just with the singular sanctity of Saint Francis, but with broader questions like the religious vocation and pastoral mission of the Friars Minor as an institution. Within this thematic sequence, as we shall see, the counter-façade plays a very special role. It is, in effect, a microcosm of the entire middle section of the cycle, and the scenes on the lateral walls to either side of it were carefully arranged to complement and complete its central message.

facing page 165 View of the counter-façade (post 1997), Upper Church, Basilica of San Francesco.

The Miracle of the Spring and the Preaching to the Birds

The significance of the *Miracle of the Spring* and the *Preaching to the Birds* as a pair is key to understanding the iconography of the counter-façade as a whole. Of the two scenes, it is not difficult to explain the choice of the *Preaching to the Birds* for this privileged position (fig. 169). The episode had been important in Franciscan iconography from the start, and there are notable examples on three Duecento Saint Francis panels in Tuscany.[6] Within the Basilica, the scene had already been depicted in the Maestro di San Francesco fresco cycle in the Lower Church, and in the stained glass of the Upper Church. In its allegorical sense, the story of Francis preaching to a mixed flock of birds, which seemed to understand his words, signified a divine mandate for the Franciscan mission to preach to all peoples. Had the *Preaching to the Birds* been positioned in the Upper Church according to the *Legenda maior*, it would have appeared on the south wall, below the Passion cycle. By deciding to lift the scene out of sequence, the planners of the Saint Francis cycle may have sought to improve on the example of the Maestro di San Francesco's Lower Church murals from the 1260s, which had failed to find a convincing parallel between the *Preaching to the Birds* and its opposing Passion scene.[7] In the Upper Church, transplanting the *Preaching to the Birds* to the counter-façade avoided that problem, while increasing the visibility of an important scene.

The prominence of the *Miracle of the Spring* (fig. 168) is more difficult to understand. The story does not seem to have been depicted before, nor did it gain much currency afterwards: only three later medieval examples are known.[8] The miracle recalls Moses, who drew water from a rock by striking it with his staff, a comparison made by Bonaventure in the *Legenda maior*.[9] In one sense, then, this scene completed the sequence of typological parallels that had been made between Francis and the patriarchs on the north wall.[10] The fact that Moses does not appear in the Old Testament cycle does not necessarily preclude the parallel, for in the *Vision of the Chariot* (see fig. 182) Francis was likened to

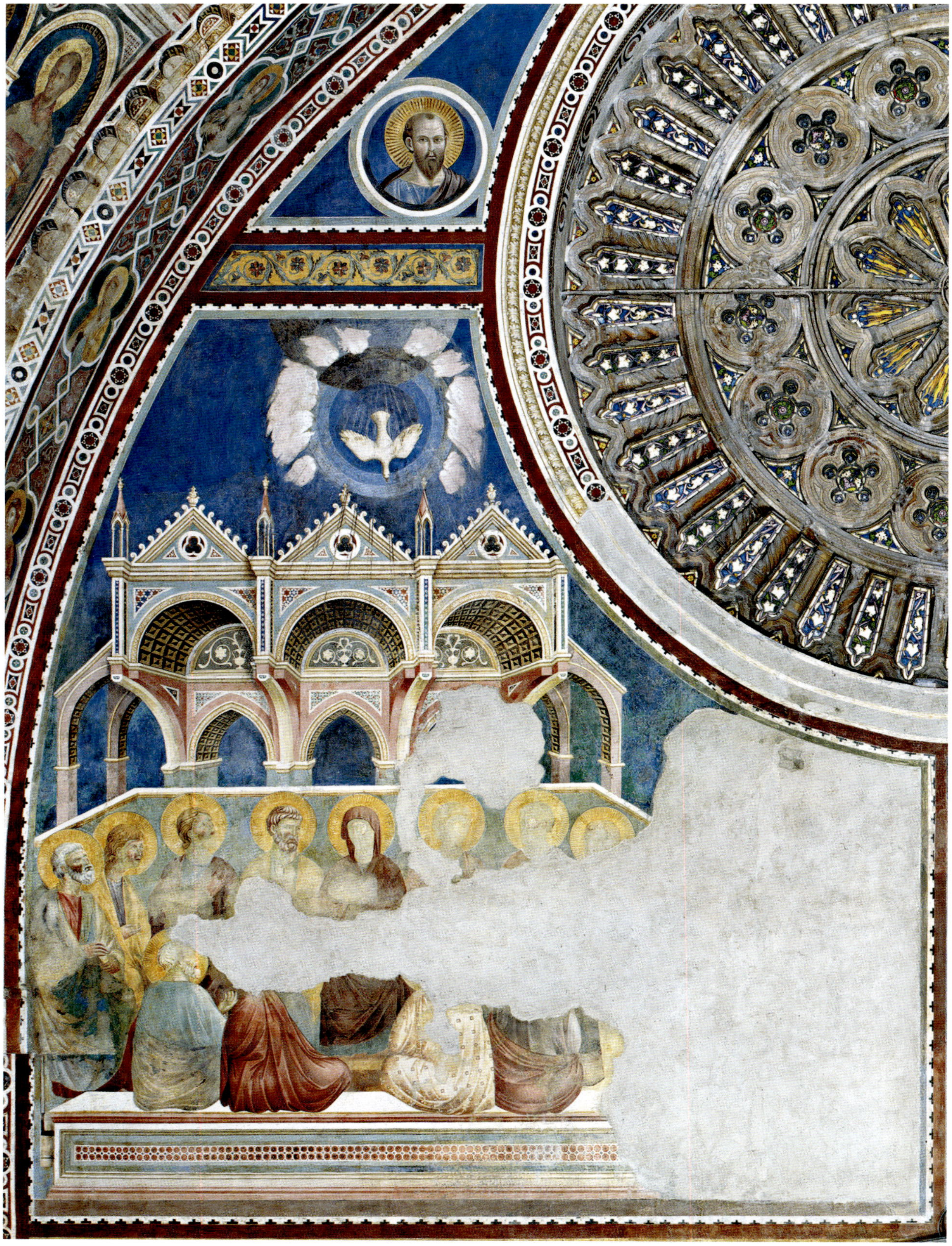

166 *Pentecost*, New Testament cycle, fresco, *c.*1288–91, counter-façade, Upper Church, Basilica of San Francesco.

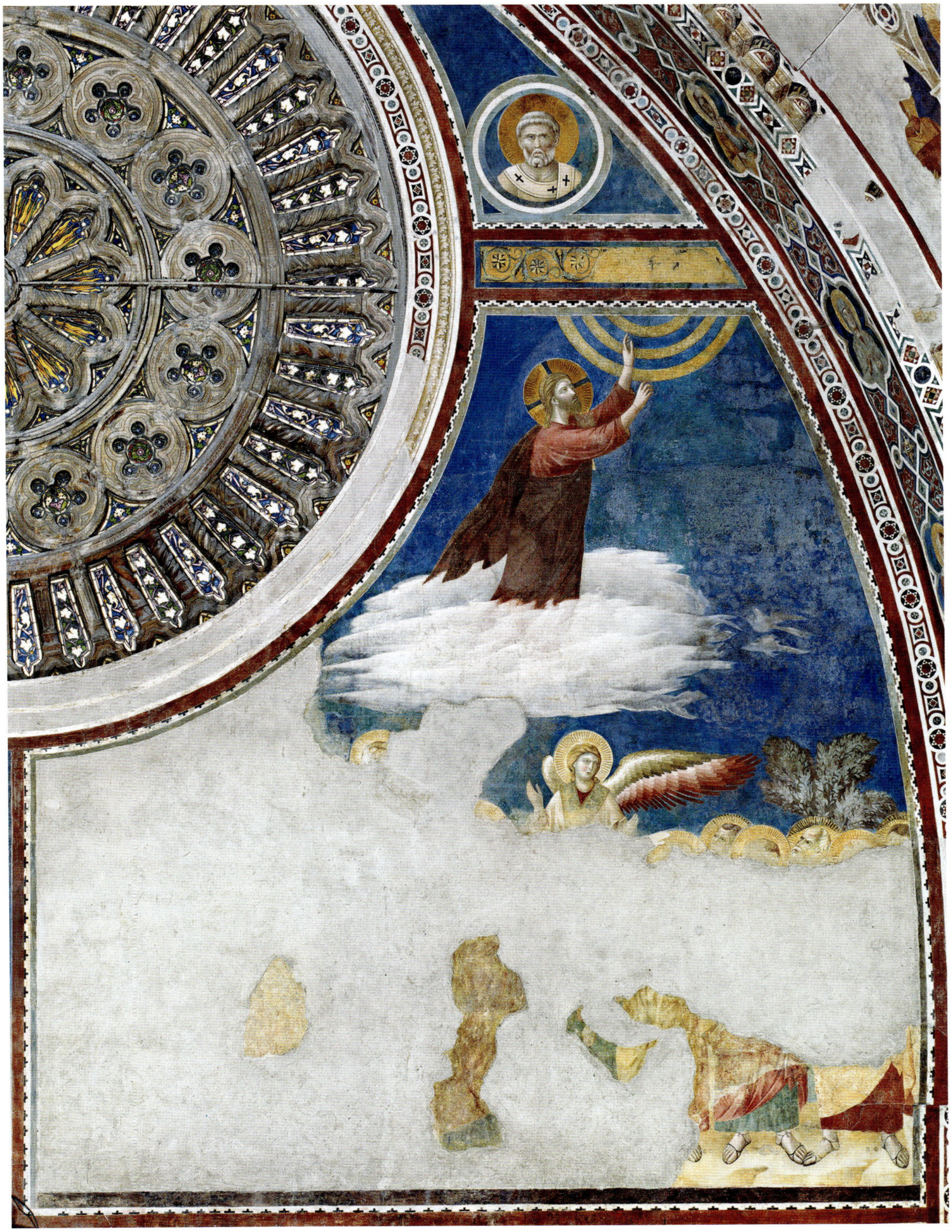

167 *Ascension*, New Testament cycle, fresco, *c.*1288–91, counter-façade, Upper Church, Basilica of San Francesco.

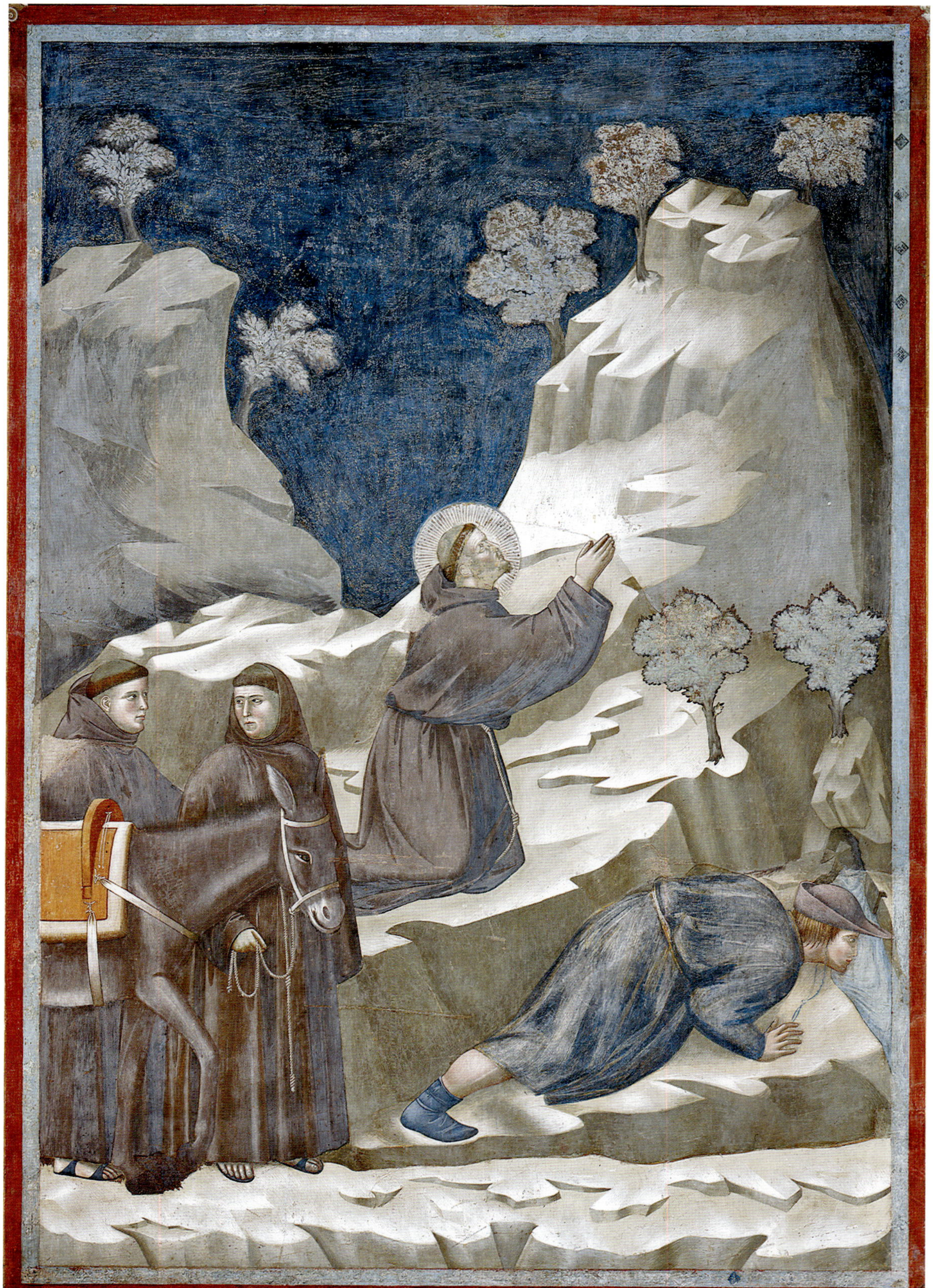

168 *Miracle of the Spring*, Scene 14 of the Saint Francis cycle, *c.*1290–96, fresco, counter-façade, Upper Church, Basilica of San Francesco.

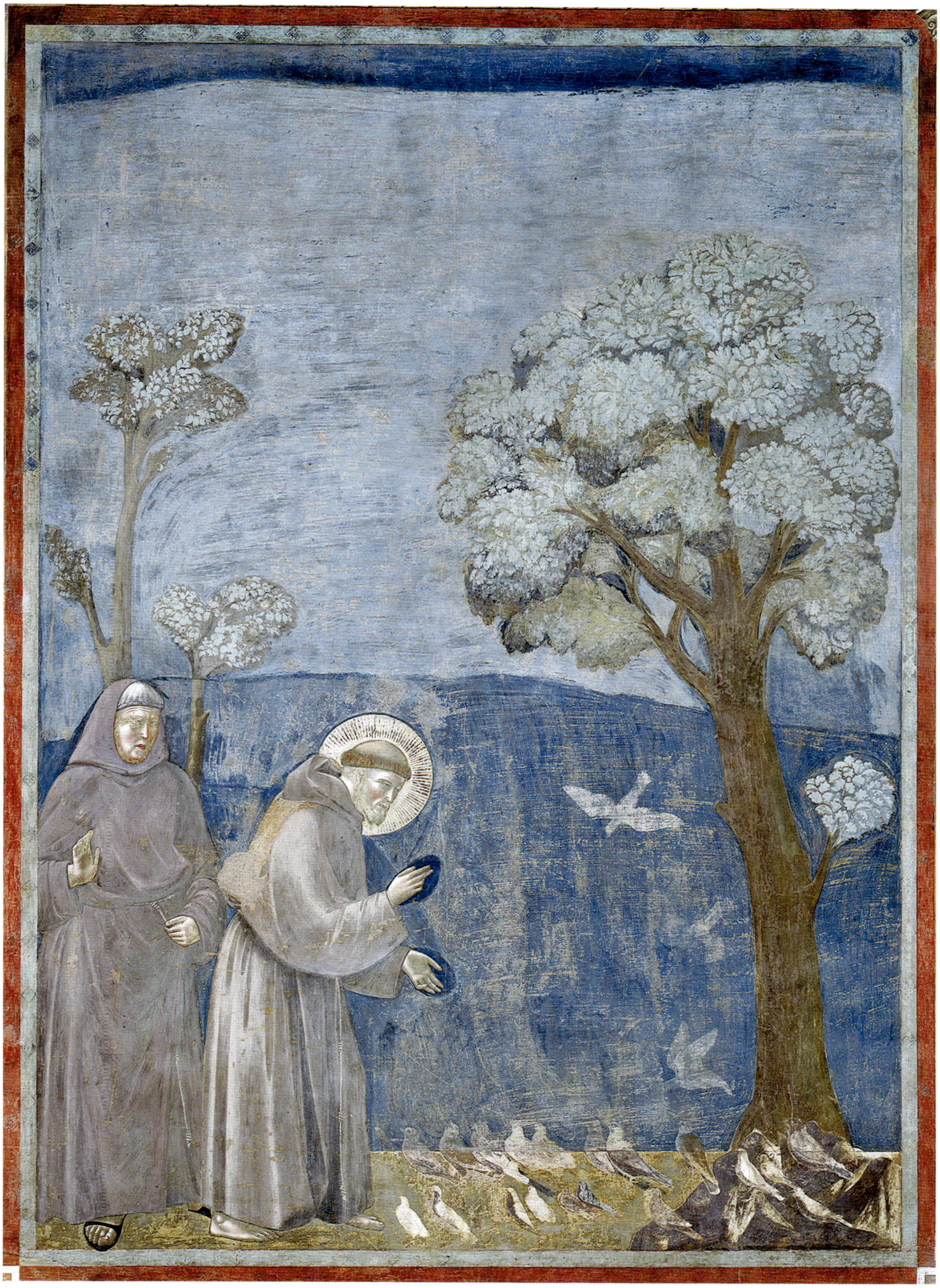

169 *Preaching to the Birds*, Scene 15 of the Saint Francis cycle, *c.*1290–96, fresco, counter-façade, Upper Church, Basilica of San Francesco.

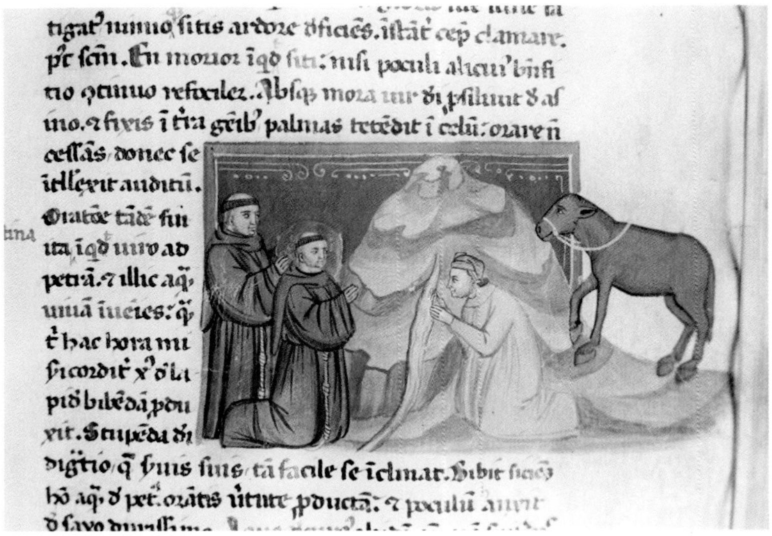

170 *Miracle of the Spring* from Bonaventure, *Legenda maior*, *c.*1330–50, manuscript illumination, Madrid, Biblioteca Cardenal Cisneros (Archivo Ibero-Americano), Cod. 768, fol. 39.

Elijah, who does not appear either. However, it is significant that the *Miracle of the Spring* was not set below an episode from the Old Testament; instead, it is the first Saint Francis scene to be placed beneath stories from the New Testament. Directly above is the *Pentecost* and, diagonally to the upper right, the *Ascension*. Neither scene invites the viewer to make the connection between Francis and Moses, nor is the parallel with the prophet mentioned in the titulus below the *Miracle of the Spring*.[11]

The broader significance of the *Miracle of the Spring* for the counter-façade can be deduced from its unusual composition, which must have been designed specifically for the context of the Upper Church. Comparison with a later image of the same scene confirms the idiosyncratic nature of the Assisi version. The episode was illustrated in an illuminated manuscript of the *Legenda maior* of *c.*1330–50: here the peasant drinking from the spring is placed at the centre of the composition while Francis and his companion kneel to one side (fig. 170).[12] The focus, as one might expect, is on the miraculous font of water. But at Assisi, the spring beside which the poor man crouches to slake his thirst is jammed up against the right-hand picture frame. The marginalization of the miracle allows the dominant central figure of Francis to command the viewer's attention, as it does in the *Preaching to the Birds*.[13] It is this focus on the comparative actions of the saint that allows the two scenes to function as a meaningful pair: on the one hand, Francis is praying; on the other, he is preaching. These activities represent broader religious concepts. In the *Legenda maior*, Bonaventure began his chapter on the stigmata with a crucial passage in which he described the saint's vocation: 'It was a custom of the angelic man Francis never to rest from the good, rather, like the angelic spirits on Jacob's ladder, he either ascended into God or descended to his neighbour. For he had so prudently learned to divide the time given to him for merit, that he spent some of it working for his neighbour's benefit and dedicated the rest to the tranquil excesses of contemplation.'[14] The two counter-façade scenes encapsulate this notion visually. The praying Francis looks and reaches heavenwards, while the preaching Francis inclines his head and hands towards the earthbound birds.

For an audience of friars, Saint Francis would have functioned on the counter-façade as an exemplar for the dual aspects of the Franciscan vocation.[15] The *vita contemplativa* and the *vita activa* were the two traditional forms of religious life. In the early Middle Ages, monks had devoted themselves to a secluded, contemplative life of prayer, study and meditation, while the secular priesthood pursued an active pastoral ministry, serving the laity. One of the novel characteristics of the friars, however, was that they practised a mixed life (*vita mista*, or *vita apostolica*), which combined the *vita contemplativa* and the *vita activa*. This was true of all the mendicant orders, but there were differences in the mix, with contemplative seclusion playing a more important part in Franciscan than in Dominican life. That emphasis is physically manifest in the numerous small and often remote Franciscan hermitages scattered across the hills and mountains of central Italy.[16] Saint Francis even wrote a brief Rule for Hermitages, which insisted on meticulous observance of the devotional hours, silence and strict enclosure.[17]

In medieval exegesis several biblical figures were interpreted as models for the contemplative and active lives, but the most important were Mary Magdalen and her sister Martha, two of Christ's followers. According to Luke's Gospel, when Jesus visited Martha's home, she busied herself serving the meal, but Mary sat at Christ's feet to listen to his words. Martha appealed to Jesus to tell her sister to help with the serving, but he demurred, explaining: 'Mary hath chosen the best part, which shall not be taken away from her.'[18] Hence, *contemplativa* was traditionally interpreted by the Church as a more perfect form of religious life than *activa*. Abbo of Fleury, for example, at the very end of the tenth century, ranked the laity, the clergy and the monks in ascending order of excellence.[19]

The Franciscan Order was, at the start, a predominantly lay movement, but it rapidly became clericalized. To begin with there were qualms about how high office could be compatible with Franciscan principles, but obedience to the pope took priority and Friars Minor were soon rising rapidly through the ecclesiastical hierarchy.[20] The virtue of humility, demonstrated by an initial reluctance to accept high office, long remained a Franciscan characteristic. Bonaventure, for example, having refused the archbishopric of York, became cardinal bishop of Albano only in 1273 (the year before his death) and apparently much against his will.[21] Even Nicholas IV cogitated for a week before accepting the papal tiara in 1288. Once the majority of the friars were clerics, and many also priests, the active side of their ministry became more important.[22] Numerous thirteenth-century Franciscans, of all persuasions, wrote to vindicate the mixed life of their Order. Bonaventure, for example, in the prothemes of his Sunday sermons (designed by him to be a model sermon collection for the use of his friar–preachers), united the call to preaching with the invitation to pray.[23] Gilbert of Tournai, in a sermon on the translation of Saint Francis, presented the active life of preaching and charity as a necessary counterweight to the inner life of contemplation.[24] Even Peter John Olivi, who was one of the leading thinkers of the spiritual wing of the Order, conceded that while contemplation surpasses other actions, the mixed life is best.[25] But perhaps the most authoritative voice of approval for the mendicant *vita apostolica* was Pope Gregory X. Defending the Franciscans and Dominicans against the criticisms of the seculars at the Council of Lyon in 1274, the pope is said to have retorted: 'If you lived as they live and studied as they study, you would have the same success. Like Mary they sit at the feet of the Lord, and like Martha they do everything to serve him.'[26]

The Ascension and the Pentecost

Considered together, the *Miracle of the Spring* and the *Preaching to the Birds* act as pendants, but they are also linked to the other images on the end wall. Indeed, the entire counter-façade was designed to function as a self-contained unit. Consequently, if the full meaning of the Saint Francis scenes is to be unlocked, the significance of the *Ascension* and the *Pentecost* scenes above them needs to be understood.[27]

The dominance of these two biblical scenes is now somewhat reduced by the loss of substantial areas of the painted surface, but they are nearly four times larger than the other Old and New Testament stories on the upper registers of the nave. Even though the Upper Church diverged from the Roman models of Saint Peter's and San Paolo in the iconographic programme of its counter-façade, these monumental biblical scenes were not entirely unprecedented. In the New Testament cycles frescoed in the Benedictine abbey church of Sant'Angelo in Formis, *c.*1100, and in the Roman church of San Giovanni a Porta Latina, *c.*1170, three scenes were given enlarged fields: the *Entry into Jerusalem*, the *Crucifixion* and the *Ascension*. Both these cycles are seen as medieval imitations of Saint Peter's. Since the Vatican basilica certainly featured a monumental *Crucifixion*, Saint Peter's is sometimes seen as the prototype for the other oversized scenes as well. However, since no other enlarged fields are shown on the Tasselli drawing (see fig. 100), it remains unclear whether the prominent *Ascension* at Assisi could have had a Roman papal model.[28] The papal identity of the Upper Church is certainly emphasized on the counter-façade through the roundels of Saint Paul and Saint Peter, placed at the top of the wall to either side of the rose window. Their physiognomy is traditional and comparable with their customary representations on papal seals, as we can see from Nicholas IV's lead seals, which are still attached to his bulls preserved in the Sacro Convento (see figs 3 and 4).[29] The images of Saints Peter and Paul on the counter-façade face the papal throne in the apse, with its portraits of two sainted popes frescoed in roundels to either side.[30]

This is not the only way in which the design of the counter-façade reflects pre-existing imagery at the other end of the church. It is often claimed that the powerful T-shape formed by the horizontal border above the two New Testament scenes, and the vertical border between them (which, conceptually, meet in the centre of the rose window) consciously refers to a Tau cross. The connection with Giunta's crucifix, which confronted this 'T' down the length of the nave, is rarely made however. Nor was it only the axial power of Giunta's crucifix that resonated with the counter-façade; so did the iconographic programme presented by the lateral images on the beam (see Chapter 3).

To the south, the panel of Saint Michael overcoming the dragon would have faced Christ's *Ascension*. Saint Michael was commonly identified as the archangel who led souls into paradise, and so was often linked to the Ascension. In the fourteenth-century *Meditations on the Life of Christ*, one of the most popular devotional Franciscan texts, Michael is said to have hurried to heaven ahead of Christ to announce his Ascension to the heavenly host.[31] The importance of Michael for the migration of souls was stressed in Franciscan hagiography, as it was in the Order's liturgy.[32] Bonaventure, following Thomas of Celano before him, stated that Francis was 'devoted with a special love to blessed Michael the Archangel in view of his duty of presenting souls to God'.[33] The Ascension was also a prophecy of Christ's Second Coming and, as such, prefigured Saint Michael's prominent role in the Last Judgment. In the biblical account of the Ascension, two angels console the apostles with the knowledge that one day Christ will return from heaven in the same way that he has entered it.[34] Much of the left side of the counter-façade scene is now lost, but a nineteenth-century drawing by Johann Anton Ramboux (fig. 171) clearly captures the second angel, who was visible before the paint surface deteriorated further in the following century.[35]

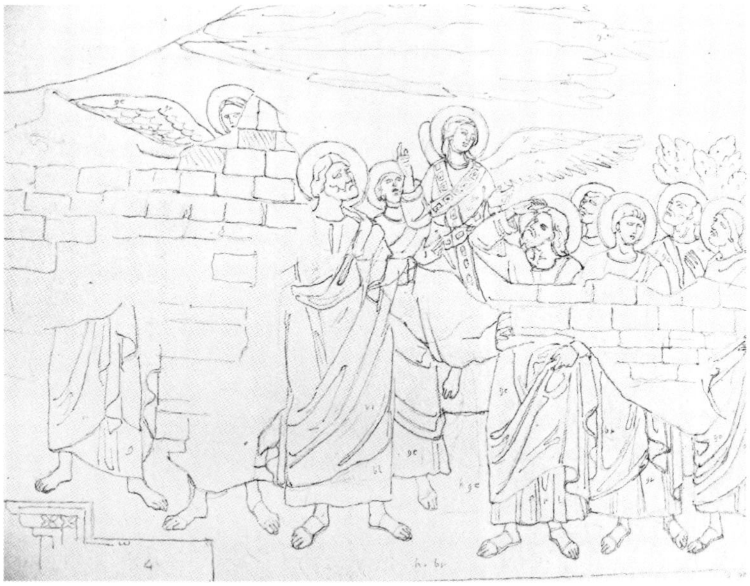

171 Johann Anton Ramboux, copy of the *Ascension* on the counter-façade of the Upper Church, *c.*1818–43, drawing, Frankfurt, Städel Museum, *Sammlung von Umrissen und Durchzeichnungen dienend zur Geschichte der bildenden Künste des Mittelalters in Italien*, vol. III, p. 224 (nr 220).

On the north side of the nave, the *Pentecost* fresco on the counter-façade would have faced the panel of the same subject mounted on the beam to the right of Giunta's crucifix. Although Pentecost symbolized the institution of the Church, there is no evidence that the scene was given any particular emphasis in the early Roman papal basilicas, so its prominence on the counter-façade at Assisi must be due to its Franciscan connotations. From an early date, the Franciscans had prepared for Pentecost by keeping a 'fast of the apostles' which began at Ascension. Its observance is recommended in Bonaventure's *Instructions for Novices*, written *c.*1260.[36] According to Dominic Monti, this 'mini-Lent' was a novena to petition for the gift of the Holy Spirit.[37] In so doing, the friars were emulating the apostles, who in the ten days after Ascension prepared themselves for the coming of the Holy Spirit by 'fasting, praying and groaning'.[38]

The importance of Pentecost at Assisi is shown by its inclusion among the list of feasts and their octaves on which visitors to the Basilica could gain the maximum indulgence granted in 1291 by Nicholas IV (three years and forty days).[39] The indulgence would have benefited the friars as much as the laity. An indication of the particular celebrations accompanying the liturgy for Pentecost can be found in a surviving record from 16 May 1388, which detailed payments made for ropes 'for the representation of the Holy Spirit in the Upper Church'.[40] This suggests a spectacle in which a model dove was let down onto the altar, possibly through the hole in the keystone of the vault of the Evangelists.[41]

Pentecost was of central importance to the Assisi Basilica in its function as the Franciscan mother house: general chapter meetings of the Order had always been held at that time of year. This probably influenced the choice of subject for the lateral panel on the rood beam, as well as the dedication of the side altar in the north transept of the Upper Church. Hueck argued that, given the large number of friars usually attending general chapters, only the Upper Church would have been large enough to accommodate the crowd gathered for the solemn Mass for Pentecost at the general chapter of Assisi in 1279.[42] The Constitutions of Narbonne in 1260 established a detailed procedure for the opening of general chapters. After hearing the Mass, the participating friars were instructed to enter the chapter singing the hymn 'Veni, creator Spiritus'.[43] The iconography of the counter-façade could well have been chosen (at least in part) to serve this occasion, in the reasonable expectation that the Basilica, as the head and mother of the Order, would often host future general chapters – as indeed it did in 1295 and regularly thereafter.[44]

Saint Francis and the Struggle for Vocation

Both Ascension and Pentecost were essential to the advent of the Holy Spirit, as John's Gospel makes clear. Before ascending to heaven, Christ told his disciples that he had to return to the Father: 'if I go not, the Paraclete [the Holy Spirit] will not come to you; but if I go, I will send him to you'.[45] This causal relationship is powerfully visualized on the counter-façade. On one side of the rose window, Christ ascends above the clouds to pierce the celestial spheres; on the other, the dove of the Holy Spirit plummets from the heavens, scattering the clouds as it comes.

Beneath the biblical narratives, the Saint Francis scenes also combine an ascent with a descent. In the *Legenda maior*, the episodes are non-sequential and apparently unconnected. However, once the two scenes are understood as signifying the contemplative life and the active life, the relationship between them is transformed. Bonaventure related Francis's miraculous encounter with the birds at Bevagna as the first example of his preaching mission.[46] But he prefaced the story with a lengthy passage recounting Francis's 'great struggle' over how he should best please God: should he spend his time in prayer, or travel around preaching?[47] Francis argued for the superiority of prayer, which drew one closer to God and to the angels. Although he could muster only one counter-argument, it carried supreme weight: Christ himself had preached, and Christ was Francis's model. To resolve his dilemma, Francis asked Saint Clare and Brother Sylvester to pray for God's guidance. When both separately received a divine revelation that he should preach, Francis immediately took to the road for Bevagna. This carefully crafted passage is one of the few pieces of original biographical material in the *Legenda maior*. By adding this episode, Bonaventure placed a justification of the mixed life practised by the Order of his own day into the mouth of the founder-saint. As we saw above, such vindications were common in thirteenth-century Franciscan texts. Although Christ declared that Mary had chosen 'the best part', Martha also had a valuable role to play.

Another pair of biblical sisters who were seen as types for *contemplativa* and *activa* were Rachel and Leah, the two wives of Jacob in Genesis. In *Mira circa nos*, his bull of canonization of 1228, Pope Gregory IX had described how Francis, 'not wishing to benefit only himself by remaining on the mountain, clinging to Rachel's embraces alone, that is to a contemplation that is beautiful but sterile . . . came down to Leah's forbidden bedchamber, to lead his flock'.[48] Because Rachel was more beautiful than Leah, Jacob loved her more, but Leah was more fertile than her sister and bore him many children. Likewise, contemplation was beautiful but sterile because it dealt exclusively with the individual's inner relationship with God; active ministry was fruitful because it brought others to salvation. In the accounts of Pope Gregory IX and Bonaventure, Francis abandoned prayer for preaching. Likewise, in the Saint Francis cycle, the *Preaching to the Birds* follows the *Miracle of the Spring*. But the spiritual journey from the *vita contemplativa* to the *vita activa* is given a more complex treatment on the counter-façade by interlocking the Franciscan and biblical scenes.

Compositionally, the counter-façade forms two strong, crossed diagonals (see fig. 165). The praying Francis in the *Miracle of the Spring* (see fig. 168) looks up to the right, where he is linked by his pose to the Christ of the *Ascension* (see fig. 167). The motif of Christ ascending in profile was somewhat archaic by this time and was probably used here deliberately to forge the visual link between Francis and Christ.[49] The corresponding diagonal descends from the *Pentecost* to the *Preaching to the Birds*, the plunging dove of the Holy Spirit (see fig. 176) being echoed by at least two other doves (now largely effaced) (see fig. 177), which flutter down from the tree towards Francis with outstretched wings.

Ascending to God: The Mountain and the Ladder

The ascending diagonal starts with the praying figure of Saint Francis. The classic definition of prayer, coined in the eighth century by Saint John of Damascus, is 'the ascent of the mind into God'.[50] One of Bonaventure's most popular and influential devotional works, the *Itinerarium mentis in Deum* ('The Journey of the Mind to God'), characterized the contemplative life as a progressive ascent towards God, its goal being complete union with the divine. This could be fully achieved only after death, when the blessed would see God face to face in heaven, but Saint Francis exemplified the most perfect contemplation that could be achieved on earth.

In the final chapter of the *Itinerarium*, Bonaventure described Francis's experience of the Christ–Seraph on La Verna, which culminated in his receipt of the stigmata, as a mystical transport of the soul that allowed him to transcend the sensible world and pass over into God.[51] The *Stigmatization* (see fig. 117) would surely have been the obvious choice to represent *contemplativa* on the counter-façade, especially as there were already numerous examples of the scene being paired with the *Preaching to the Birds*. The germ of the idea goes back to the Pescia panel of 1235, on which these were the only two life scenes represented.[52] In the Basilica at Assisi, the *Preaching to the Birds* immediately precedes the *Stigmatization* in both of the Saint Francis cycles attributed to the Maestro di San Francesco (the frescoes in the Lower Church and the stained glass of the Upper Church; see Chapter 4). A particularly pertinent precedent is an illumination pairing the *Stigmatization* and the *Preaching to the Birds* in a Duecento manuscript now in the Vatican Library in Rome (fig. 172), which shares several features with the counter-façade.[53] The two scenes are framed together at the head of a table of antiphons, forming a self-contained diptych; the chronology of the episodes is reversed to enable *contemplativa* to appear before *activa*; and Saint Francis's ascending and descending gestures are strongly contrasted.[54]

Why, then, does the *Stigmatization* not appear on the counter-façade of the Upper Church? The answer may be straightforward: the scene was needed elsewhere. As we argued in Chapter 5, an overriding imperative for the friars in planning the nave frescoes was to link the *Stigmatization* with the *Crucifixion*, stressing Francis's unique status as *alter Christus*. Having committed the *Stigmatization* to the south wall, the friars were then obliged to select something else for the counter-façade. It seems reasonable to assume that they would have chosen a scene that could meaningfully substitute for the *Stigmatization* but, at first sight, the *Miracle of the Spring* does not seem the obvious candidate. In comparison to the vision of the seraphic Christ and the unprecedented gift of the stigmata, the *Miracle of the Spring* is focused on a commonplace prayer of petition (albeit a highly effective one).

But one important characteristic that the *Miracle of the Spring* and the *Stigmatization* share is their location. In the Bible, mountains are places of revelation, where men can separate themselves from earthly matters and get closer to God. The apostles Peter, James and John witnessed Christ's Transfiguration when they ascended Mount Tabor. In the Old Testament, Moses received the tablets of the law on Mount Sinai, and Elijah ascended to heaven in his fiery chariot from Mount Carmel, prefiguring Christ's Ascension from the Mount of Olives. For the mountain as a place of prayer and contemplation, Christ himself provided the model. Before choosing the twelve apostles, he ascended a mountain to pray; indeed, ascending the mountain is analogous with prayer as John of Damascus defined it.[55] Franciscan devotional literature often used the mountain as a metaphor for contemplation. James of Milan, for example, concluded his *Stimulus amoris* with a chapter in which he employed the motif extensively, beginning: 'Whoever wants to come to the summit of the mountain of God through contemplation . . . shall ascend through elevation of the soul.'[56] It was therefore no coincidence that in *Mira circa nos* Pope Gregory IX described the contemplative Francis 'remaining on the mountain, clinging to Rachel's embraces'.[57]

It was, of course, on the mountain of La Verna that Francis received the stigmata. The miracle of the spring also took place during the ascent to a mountain hermitage. It was not named in the *Legenda maior* and the titulus below the Assisi fresco has the friars climbing simply 'quemdam montem'. It is hard, however, to imagine any Franciscan mountain other than La Verna being referred to in such a familiar manner. The *Miracle of the Spring* and the *Stigmatization* (see fig. 117) are the only scenes in the Assisi cycle with mountain settings, and the similarity of their vertiginous craggy landscapes is surely meant to suggest that both represent La Verna. In Franciscan texts written after the Assisi cycle, in the fourteenth century, La Verna is specified as the location of the miracle of the spring.[58]

The mountain as a symbol of prayer and contemplation linked Saint Francis at La Verna with Christ on the Mount of Olives. This was not the first time that the contemplative Francis had been visually connected with the Ascension of Christ in a Franciscan context. The opening miniature in a gradual made for San Francesco in Cortona, some thirty miles north-west of Assisi, *c.*1280–85, depicts Francis kneeling in prayer in the midst of the apostles, who shield their eyes from the light as they witness Christ ascending seated on a rainbow (fig. 174).[59] A second Cortona gradual, *c.*1285–90, depicts the *Stigmatization* in the border medallions of an

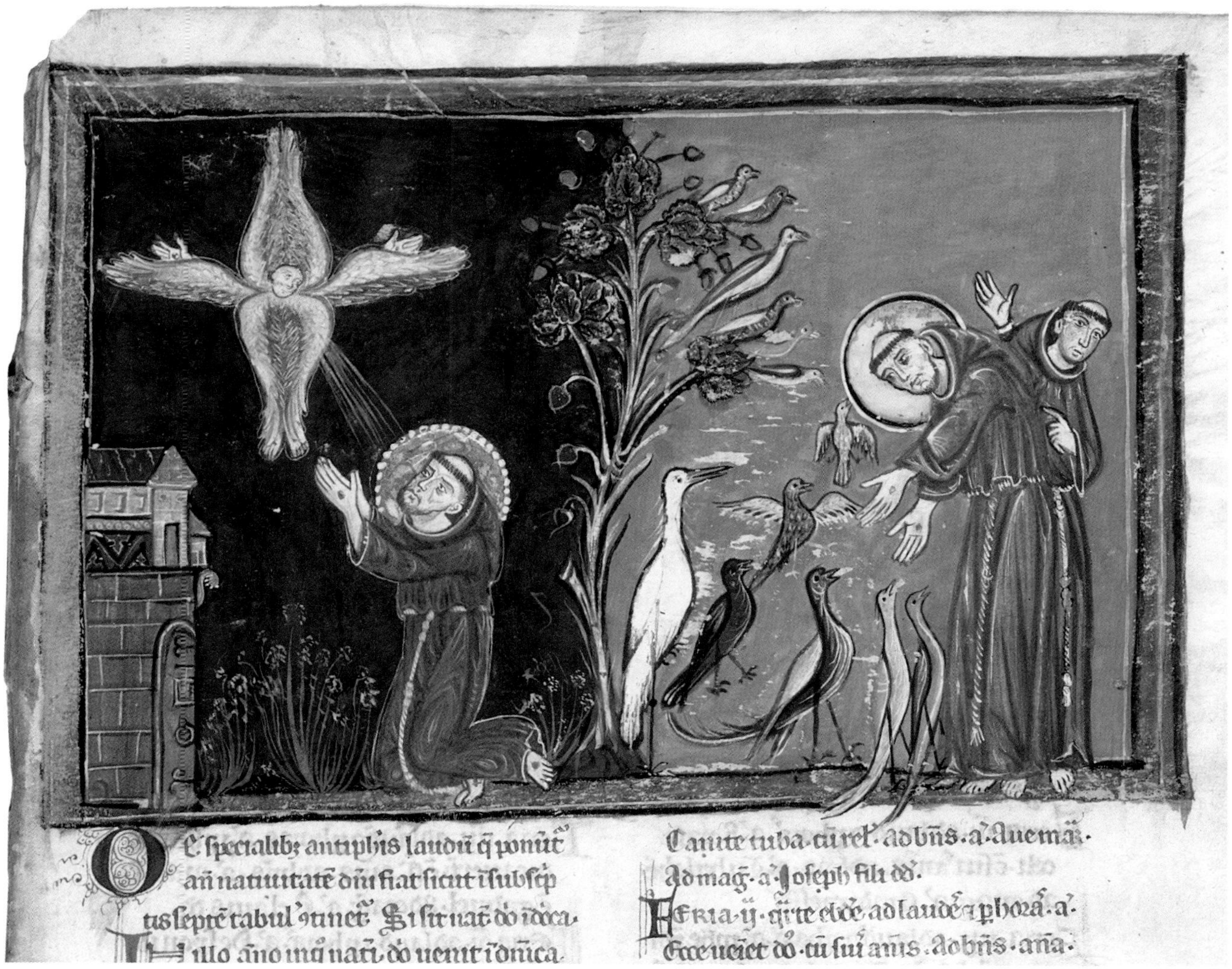

172 *Stigmatization* and *Preaching to the Birds*, *c.*1290, manuscript illumination, Vatican City, Biblioteca Apostolica Vaticana, Archivio Capitolare di San Pietro, Ms B87, fol. 78r.

illumination that depicts the twelve apostles and the Virgin gazing up at Christ in a mandorla, flanked by two angels (fig. 173).[60] Both these miniatures (which combine iconographic elements of the Ascension with Christ in Majesty) illuminate the initial 'A' in the text from Psalm 24: 'Ad te [Domine] levavi animam meam' ('To thee[, O Lord,] have I lifted up my soul').[61]

The nature of the relationship between the contemplative Saint Francis and the ascending Christ becomes much clearer through an examination of Bonaventure's Ascension sermons. These give us the greatest insight into how this Christian mystery was interpreted by the friars in the Duecento. In salvation history, Christ's Ascension signified the moment when heaven was reopened for the first time since the Fall. When he ascended, Christ led the way back to the Father for all Christians to follow. In spiritual terms, Christ's Ascension was a model for how the pious soul should seek to ascend to God through contemplation.

In one of his Ascension sermons, Bonaventure took as his text the same verse from the Psalms that he had used as the opening for the *Itinerarium*: 'Blessed is the man whose help is from thee: in his heart he hath disposed to ascend by steps.'[62] Bonaventure argued that since Christ had reached heaven by ascending higher than all the angels, he must have ascended to the perfection of sanctity via all the steps in the celestial hierarchy. Popularized in the late medieval period through

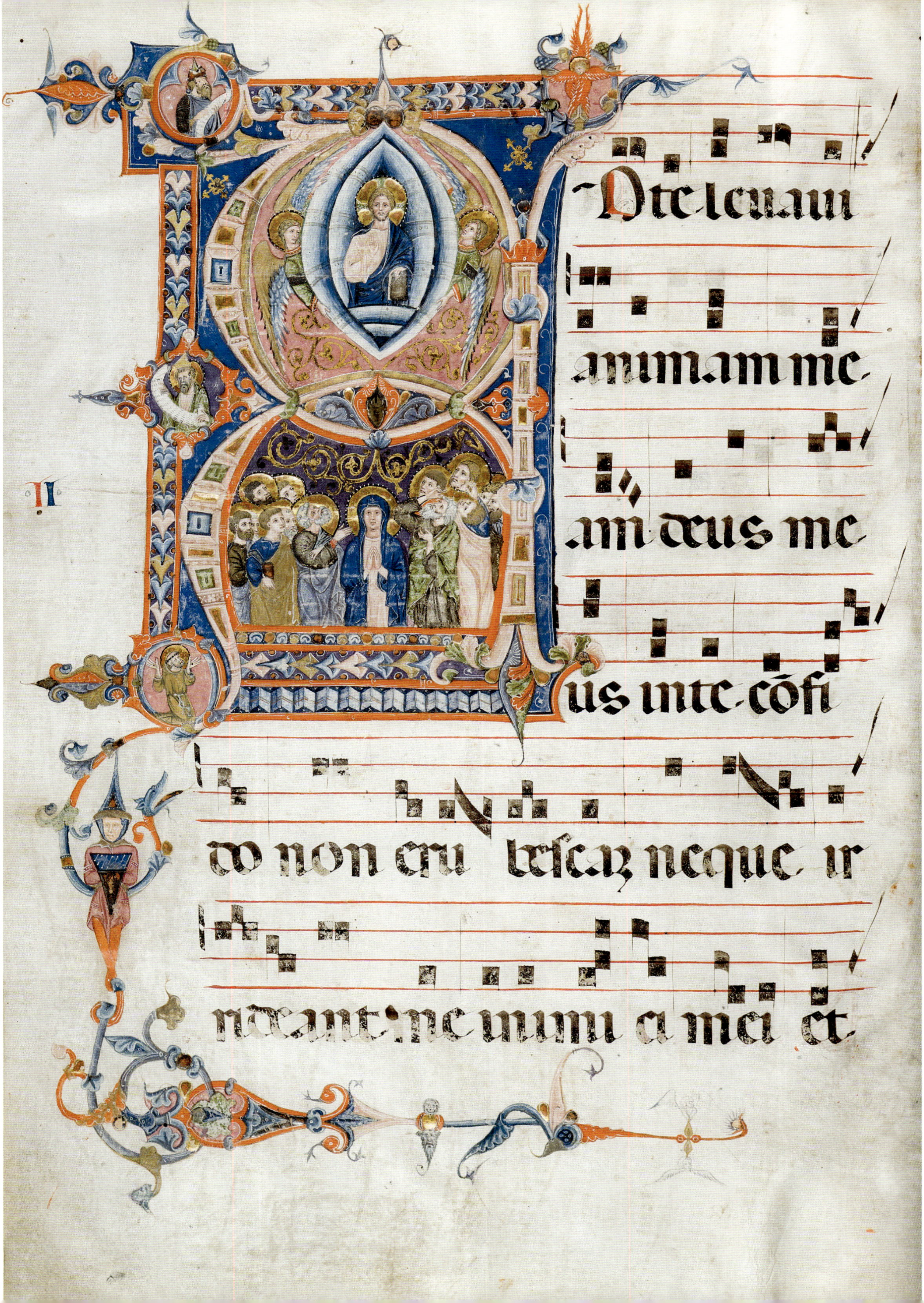
D te leuaui
animam me
am deus me
us in te cōfi
do non eru bescā neque ir
rideant me inimi ci mei et

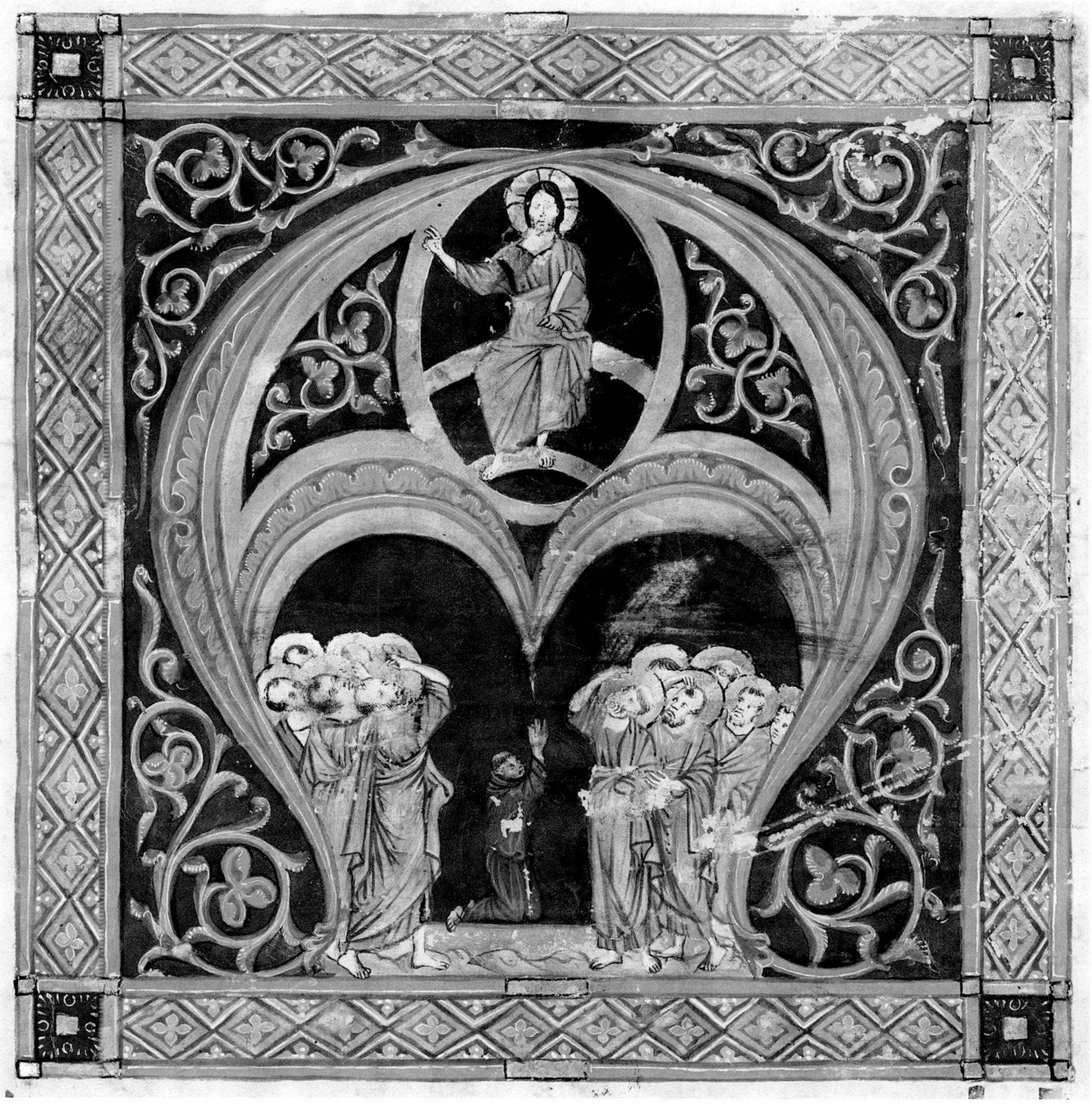

174 *Ascension/Christ in Majesty*, *c.*1280–85, manuscript illumination, Graduale temporale, Cortona, Biblioteca del Comune e dell'Accademia Etrusca, Cod. 2A, fol. 1r (originally San Francesco, Cortona).

the writings of Pseudo-Dionysius, the celestial hierarchy ranked angelic beings into nine orders. Angels were at the bottom (closest to mankind) and seraphim at the top (closest to God). Bonaventure describes Christ ascending through each of these orders, like steps on a ladder: in the final seraphic step, the soul is swept away in an 'excess of exultation' and becomes oblivious, carried out of itself and almost completely absorbed in God.[63] Bonaventure later employed virtually the same terminology to describe Saint Francis, in collations he gave to the friars in Paris in 1273. In one collation Bonaventure divided the ecclesiastical hierarchy into nine orders, each equivalent to one of the celestial orders. He characterized the Franciscans and the Dominicans as contemplatives, equated to the penultimate order of angels, the cherubim. For Bonaventure, only Saint Francis had attained the

facing page 173 *Ascension/Christ in Majesty*, *c.*1285–90, manuscript illumination, Graduale temporale, Cortona, Biblioteca del Comune e dell'Accademia Etrusca, Cod. 1, fol. 2v (originally San Francesco, Cortona).

ultimate seraphic level, exemplifying those who reached God 'by means of elevation, that is, through ecstasy and rapture'.[64]

Another of Bonaventure's Ascension sermons, probably preached in 1267, is particularly pertinent because it was given on the feast of the Translation of Saint Francis (25 May), which in that year fell on the vigil of the feast of the Ascension. In this sermon, he gave the ascending Christ a more specific function in aiding contemplatives. Preaching on the text 'Friend, go up higher' (Luke 14:10), Bonaventure explained that the Lord addressed Saint Francis in the same words: 'as if to say to him on the feast of the Ascension, "Go up" with my help by calling on me in prayer . . . The Lord says to him: "Go up" with my help, for I am the ladder on which you can ascend. This is signified by the ladder which Jacob saw: "set up on the earth and the top of it reached to heaven".'[65] Bonaventure was referring to the Old Testament story of Jacob, who dreamed of a ladder reaching from earth to heaven, on which angels were ascending and descending.[66] There was a long tradition of interpreting Jacob's ladder spiritually, especially in monastic devotional literature. The ladder usually symbolized the monk's life and its steps the virtues he must practise to ascend towards heaven.[67] But, in keeping with the Christocentric nature of Franciscan theology, Bonaventure interpreted Jacob's ladder rather differently in his Saint Francis sermon, asking: 'What is this ladder other than our Lord Jesus himself, the Son of God who through his humanity is set up on earth and by his divinity transcends the heavens?'[68]

On the counter-façade, a connection between the Christ of the Ascension and the Christ Child held by the Virgin in the roundel above the central portal is suggested by the use of wine-red garments for them both – a motif already used in the Ascension window in the north transept (see Chapter 3; fig. 76). The Child is a reminder that Christ descended before he ascended, because it was through the Incarnation that Christ became human. This was spelled out in detail in another of Bonaventure's Ascension sermons: '[Christ] indeed is a ladder that . . . penetrates the heavens thanks to the sublime dimension of divinity and that descends to contact with the earth through the slime of our flesh . . . and on that ladder angels ascend and descend upon the Son of Man, and this is signified by Genesis 28, where Jacob was elevated to his vision.'[69]

Another visual allusion to Jacob's ladder on the counter-façade of the Upper Church may be found in the stepped gable that frames the Virgin and Child above the portal (see fig. 165). Each of the small triangular spaces beneath these steps contains an eagle. Although they could be purely decorative motifs, the eagles have been carefully painted, stalking down the gable in two alternating poses (fig. 175): in the first, the eagle walks with stooped head and folded wings; in the second, it twists around to look back and up, with wings spread. As we saw in Chapter 5, an eagle often symbolizes the ascending Christ (based on Jerome's interpretation of Jeremiah 49:22: 'Behold he shall come up as an eagle, and fly: and he shall spread his wings over Bosra'). The ascending eagle could also symbolize contemplation, because it was believed to be able to fly higher than any other bird without being blinded by the sun. Matthew of Acquasparta, for example, explained that Saint Francis, 'Like an eagle . . . meditated on God without turning aside the eyes of his mind, and so was perfectly transformed into God, not only in his mind but also in his flesh.'[70] But the eagle had a dual aspect, as Saint Gregory explained: 'For it is the eagle's custom to look at the rays of the sun with an unaverted, piercing gaze, but when set by the need for food, the same keen gaze that had been fixed on the sun turns down to look for a carcass, and however high he may fly, he makes for the earth to lay hold of flesh.'[71] For Gregory, the descent and ascent of the eagle symbolized Christ's Incarnation and Ascension, a model that would neatly fit the imagery of the counter-façade.[72]

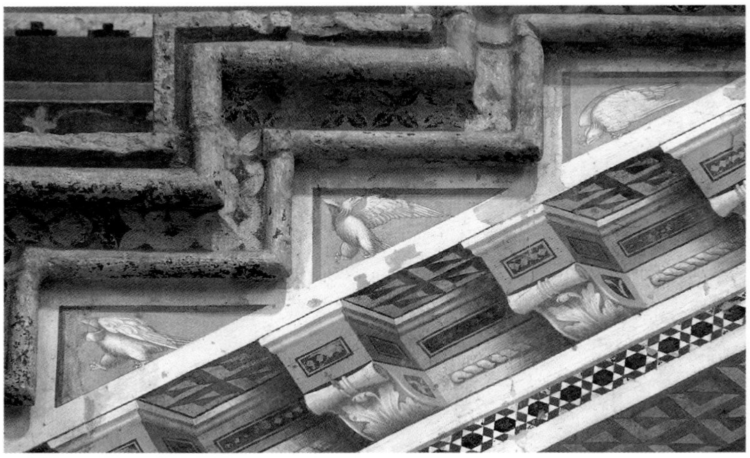

175 Eagles in the stepped gable above the portal (detail), *c.*1290–96, fresco, counter-façade, Upper Church, Basilica of San Francesco.

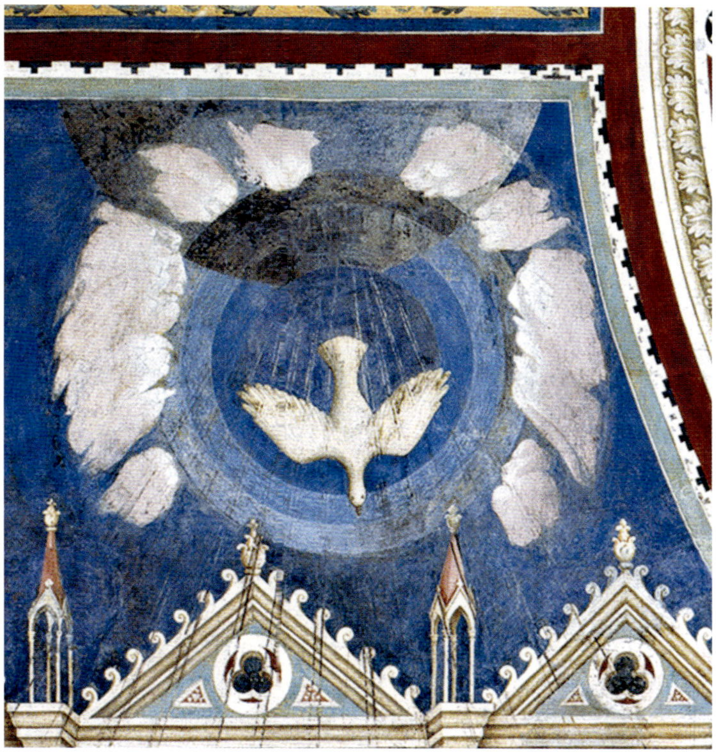

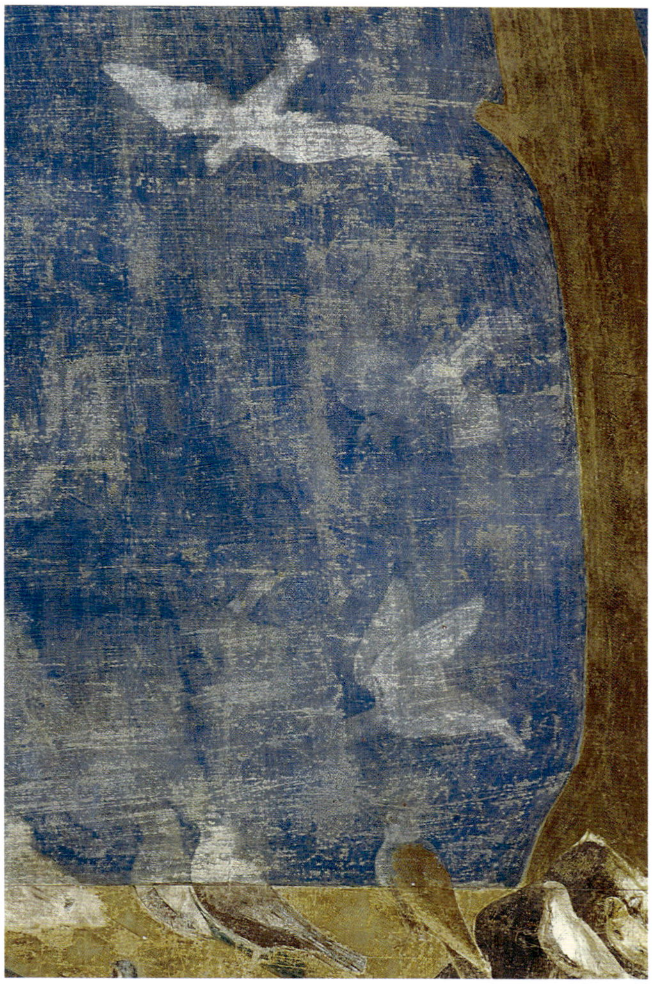

left 176 Descending dove of the Holy Spirit, detail from *Pentecost*, New Testament cycle, *c.*1290–96, fresco, counter-façade, Upper Church, Basilica of San Francesco.

right 177 Doves flying down from a tree, detail from *Preaching to the Birds*, Scene 15 of the Saint Francis cycle, *c.*1290–96, fresco, counter-façade, Upper Church, Basilica of San Francesco.

Descending to Neighbour: Water and the Holy Spirit

While the contemplative Saint Francis ascends to Christ through prayer, the active Saint Francis descends to his neighbour by preaching, in a direct line of succession from the apostles at Pentecost. When all the apostles were gathered together, the Holy Spirit descended upon them, its presence made visible through 'parted tongues, as it were of fire'.[73] Once they were filled with the Spirit, the apostles were transformed. This was immediately apparent: when they went out to preach, they were able to speak in diverse languages, to the amazement of the various peoples gathered in Jerusalem.[74] At the top of the counter-façade, a white dove dives down from the heavens towards the apostles (fig. 176): the idea that the Holy Spirit's descent encompassed Saint Francis in the *Preaching to the Birds,* as well as the apostles at Pentecost, was originally suggested by at least two – if not three – other doves, all fluttering down from the tree in similar poses, to join their companions on the ground (fig. 177). These swooping white doves are now almost entirely effaced, but when they were freshly painted they would have stood out clearly against the blue sky. The gathered birds, which were of many kinds, were miraculously able to understand Francis's words. The implication is that the preaching of Francis, like that of the apostles at Pentecost, has been inspired by the Holy Spirit.

As well as the diagonal connection from the *Pentecost* to the *Preaching to the Birds*, there are strong vertical links between the *Pentecost* and the *Miracle of the Spring*. While the advent of the Spirit is signalled in the Pentecost by the descending dove, there is another symbol of its presence in the *Miracle of the Spring*. Pope Nicholas IV's unpublished sermon 'De missione Spiritus Sancti' begins with a simple assertion: 'The Holy Spirit is signified by water.'[75] This was a standard Franciscan topos. Of Bonaventure's seven sermons for Pentecost published in the *Opera omnia*, four have water as the major theme. One of these sermons includes an exhaustive list of all the metaphorical prefigurations of the Holy Spirit as water that Bonaventure could find in scripture: the river watering paradise; the gushing spring; the river that flows from the throne of God and the Lamb; the well of 'the living one who sees me'; the well of living water; the streaming river; and the waters of Gideon.[76]

One of the most fully argued of Bonaventure's Pentecost sermons takes as its text John 7:38: 'He that believeth in me, as the scripture saith, Out of his belly shall flow rivers of living water.'[77] Bonaventure explains that 'rivers of living water' refers to the flowing in of the gift of the Holy Spirit. Christ is the origin of this river: as the incarnate Christ he is the font of grace; as the crucified Christ the font of pardon; and as the exalted Christ the font of glory.[78] Bonaventure reminds his readers that Christ will never refuse those who come to him spiritually thirsting; rather, he will refresh them with the waters of eternal life. And he quotes Christ's words to the Samaritan woman at the well: 'Whosoever drinketh of this water, shall thirst again; but he that shall drink of the water that I will give him, shall not thirst for ever.'[79] This water is the grace of the Holy Spirit.[80]

Bonaventure's exegesis seems to be beautifully encapsulated in the Assisi fresco by the poor man drinking eagerly from the miraculous spring, 'living water' that has sprung out of the rock as a result of Francis's ardent prayer (see fig. 164).[81] When Vasari's eye was drawn to the counter-façade, almost three centuries after the murals were painted, the Aretine artist clearly sensed the importance of the thirsty peasant kneeling at the spring, although he understood the power of the figure in naturalistic terms – 'the incident is conveyed so exactly and movingly that one might be looking at a real person' – rather than its iconographic significance.[82] The theological symbolism of water – an element not shared by any other story of Saint Francis in prayer or ecstatic contemplation – was surely a major motive behind the choice of the *Miracle of the Spring* as the scene to set below the *Pentecost*. It also explains why the spring is pushed over to the edge of the pictorial frame: this allowed the water to be placed directly below the descending dove in the *Pentecost*, making the meaningful vertical link between the two scenes perfectly clear to anyone aware of the water symbolism associated with the Holy Spirit.

A further vertical parallel is that between Saint Francis and the apostles, who are all depicted in prayer. As Johnson has demonstrated, Bonaventure constantly exhorted his friars to emulate the apostles by praying for the advent of the Spirit.[83] Continuing his water metaphor, Bonventure described prayer as the vessel by which the grace of the Holy Spirit could be drawn down. Although the Spirit is a gift, sent from both the Father and the Son, the friars should direct their prayers to Christ, who is the font of living water. Seeking the Spirit through prayer was at the heart of the liturgy of Pentecost, expressed in hymns such as 'Veni, creator Spiritus', and was an important aspect of Franciscan spirituality. Matthew of Acquasparta, for example, inscribed his books with the sequence for the Pentecostal Mass, 'Sancti Spiritus adsit nobis gratia' ('The grace of the Holy Spirit be present with us').[84] On the counter-façade, as Saint Francis kneels and prays towards the ascending Christ, he draws down the gift of the Spirit in the form of the miraculous spring.

Although the quartet of scenes on the counter-façade is an entirely novel ensemble, similar theological ideas can be found in earlier Christian iconography. Of especial interest is the apse mosaic of Saint John Lateran in Rome (see fig. 19). As discussed in Chapter 1, Nicholas IV commissioned Jacopo Torriti to restore and embellish the apse mosaic as part of his renewal of the Lateran basilica. In the central section (see fig. 20), the dove of the Holy Spirit descends from the celestial Christ towards a jewelled cross standing on a small hill. Golden rays emanate from the dove, streaming over the cross to collect in a pool of water at its foot. Four rivers, labelled Phison, Gehon, Tigris and Euphrates, flow out from the pool to quench the thirst of four deer and two sheep. The deer symbolize the Christian soul, according to a traditional interpretation of Psalm 41:2: 'As the hart panteth after the fountains of water; so my soul panteth after thee, O God.' The four rivers derive from the description of the Garden of Eden in Genesis 2:10: 'And a river went out . . . to water paradise'.[85] The watered garden of paradise was interpreted as the Church, through which the Holy Spirit continually flows in the form of the sacraments, which cleanse and satiate Christian souls.

In the *Miracle of the Spring*, the water streams down to the thirsty peasant crouching on the rocks, but then its course turns to run out of the right-hand frame of the picture. By implication, it flows on towards the *Preaching to the Birds*, to join the dove as a symbol of the Holy Spirit inspiring Franciscan preaching. The friars would have been very familiar with such imagery, since both Thomas of Celano and Pope Gregory IX had already used biblical water metaphors to describe Francis's preaching. Thomas declared that Francis, 'like one of the rivers of paradise, has poured out the streams of the Gospel in a holy flood over the whole world',[86] while in *Mira circa nos*, Gregory had proclaimed:

> Filled with the zeal of the Holy Spirit, he took up the jawbone of an ass, preaching in simple words, not with the plausible words of human wisdom, but with the mighty strength of God . . . There flowed forth . . . from that same jawbone abundant waters, which refreshed the fallen, cleansed the filthy and irrigated the dry. This spring, gushing up to eternal life, could be purchased without money and without price; its stream spread far and wide, watering the vineyard, sending out its branches to the sea and its shoots to the river.[87]

Divine Illumination on the Counter-façade

The symbolic possibilities of the mountain and the spring were prime motives for placing the *Miracle of the Spring* on the counter-façade. While both these elements were derived from Bonaventure's text in the *Legenda maior*, a third prominent feature in the fresco was not. Intense light, apparently emanating from the rose window, illuminates Saint Francis's upturned face and the mountainside around him. Why was this radiant lighting included, and what does it signify?

There are several possibilities. One is completely site-specific. In the Prologue to the *Legenda maior*, Bonaventure likened Saint Francis to one of the angels that Saint John saw in the Apocalypse, his prophetic vision of the end of the world.[88] After the sixth seal was opened, John says: 'And I saw another angel ascending from the rising of the sun, having the sign of the living God.'[89] This *alter angelus* would play a crucial role in salvation history, because its function was to mark with the sign of the Tau the foreheads of those who were to be saved at the end of time.[90] The key to the identification of Saint Francis with this apocalyptic angel was the stigmata, which Bonaventure called 'the seal of the likeness of the living God'.[91] The architecture of the Upper Church offered an extraordinary opportunity for visualizing Saint Francis as the *alter angelus* of Apocalypse 7:2. Because the Basilica is occidented, the rose window on the counter-façade faces east, towards the dawn. The short periods during which rays of morning sunlight pierce the rose are maintained in perpetuity by the fictive light illuminating Saint Francis in the *Miracle of the Spring*. For an audience of friars, this may have suggested the angel 'ascending from the rising of the sun'.

Apocalyptic interpretations of Saint Francis have sometimes been seen as the exclusive property of the spiritual wing of the Franciscan Order. However, it was Bonaventure's *Legenda maior* that made the claim widely known, and it was subsequently repeated by many other mainstream Franciscan exegetes in the last third of the thirteenth century, including Matthew of Acquasparta and John Pecham.[92] As David Burr has pointed out, these leading Franciscans were very careful to interpret Apocalypse 7:2 morally rather than literally.[93] Many of them identified the *alter angelus* with Christ first, and only then with Saint Francis; in this sense, *Franciscus alter angelus* was simply another aspect of his identity as *Franciscus alter Christus*.

A particularly relevant example for Assisi is the interpretation of Matthew of Acquasparta, whose sermons on Saint Francis and unpublished Apocalypse commentary, all autograph, are preserved in the Sacro Convento. In his biblical gloss, Matthew decides that, although the 'vidi alterum angelum' of Apocalypse 7:2 refers principally to Christ, it can also be understood to refer to Francis. He recommends this as the best theme on which to preach about the saint and, following his own advice, took it as the text for the first of his four sermons for Saint Francis's feast day.[94] In this homily Matthew begins with a categorical statement that Francis was the Angel of the Sixth Seal who 'was sent at the end of the world'.[95] He then goes on to analyse the biblical verse in detail. Francis was an *alter angelus* because he was sent by God ('angel' means messenger). The 'sign of the living God' is, of course, the stigmata, through which Francis was conformed to Christ. But most interesting of all is his interpretation of 'ascending from the rising of the sun'. By 'ascending', Matthew understands that Francis was raised up through the elevation of his mind, and by 'from the rising of the sun' that he achieved this elevation through fervent love, 'which is the principle of elevation and upward striving [*sursumactio*]'.[96] In other words, Matthew's discussion of Francis as *alter angelus* is couched in very similar terms to Bonaventure's interpretation of his stigmatization. Not only are both phenomena seen as unique manifestations of Francis as *alter Christus*, they also exemplify the contemplative ecstasy of the saint and his mystic ascent into God. If the image of Francis in the *Miracle of the Spring*, bathed in the light of the rising sun, evoked for some his identification as the Angel of the Sixth Seal, that was perhaps more compatible than we might think with the representation of Francis, praying to the ascending Christ, as the perfect exemplar of the *vita contemplativa*.

It is significant that light descending upon Saint Francis was another feature that the *Miracle of the Spring* shared with the *Stigmatization*, further reinforcing the parallel between the two episodes. In the earliest known version of the *Stigmatization*, on the Pescia dossal of 1235 (see Chapter 5; fig. 118), the saint's mystical experience was signalled by a broad gilded beam, streaming down from the Seraph. Light descending from the Christ–Seraph to the head of the saint was a common feature of *Stigmatization* scenes throughout the Duecento. The Vatican illumination discussed above is a striking example (see fig. 172), as is a sculpted relief from La Verna, *c.*1260s (fig. 178).[97] It is hard to imagine how anyone familiar with images such as these could not have associated the figure of Saint Francis in the *Miracle of the Spring* – kneeling in prayer on both knees, in profile, uplifted face suffused by light – with the *Stigmatization*.

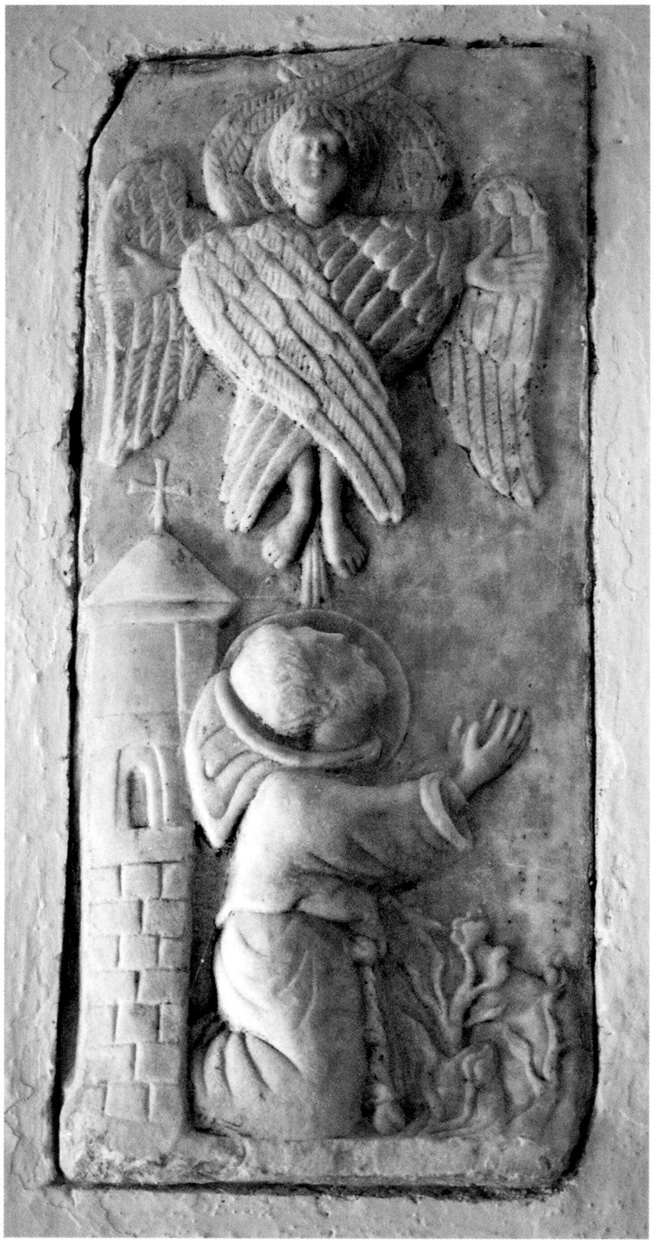

178 *Stigmatization of Saint Francis*, *c.*1260s, stone relief sculpture, entrance to the Chapel of the Stigmatization, La Verna.

The origins of the supernatural light in the *Stigmatization* seem to have lain in Duecento narrative images, not in written sources. There is no reference to luminary phenomena in the *legende* of Celano or Bonaventure, and beams of light seem to have been introduced as an artistic device to make visible Saint Francis's mystic union with God. Art historians, commenting on the increased emphasis on light emanating from the Christ–Seraph in Trecento versions of the *Stigmatization*, have connected this development with the emergence of the theme in Franciscan writings. Paul Hills highlighted the importance of the *Considerations of the Sacred Stigmata*, which described how 'the whole mountain of La Verna then appeared burning with resplendent flame, which shone forth and illuminated all the mountains and valleys around'.[98] The *Considerations* formed the second part of a later edition of the *Fioretti*, a popular collection of stories about Saint Francis and his companions. Although the earliest manuscript of the *Fioretti* is dated 1396, the text had probably been in circulation for much longer, as most of it is an Italian translation of the *Actus beati Francisci* (*Deeds of Blessed Francis and his Companions*), written by friars in the Marche, *c.*1328–37.[99] The account of the stigmatization in the *Deeds* describes the vision of the Christ–Seraph appearing 'at night with such splendour that it illuminated the mountains and valleys all around more than if the brilliance of the sun had appeared there'.[100] The writers of both the *Deeds* and the *Considerations* clearly had knowledge of Philip of Perugia's treatise on the stigmatization of 1282 (see Chapter 5). The Fifth Consideration includes an account of the visionary appearance of Saint Francis to Brother Matthew of Castiglione Aretino, first reported by Philip. And it is in his text on the stigmata, composed just a few years before the planning of the Assisi Saint Francis cycle, that we find the oldest specific textual reference to light radiating from the crucified Seraph: 'At the presence of the Crucified, the whole mountain shone with golden light.'[101]

Light is a fundamental metaphor for God in Christian theology. Consequently, the language of mystical contemplation is permeated with light metaphors, because the higher the contemplative ascends towards God, the nearer he gets to the source of divine light, which illuminates him with ever increasing intensity and clarity. Divine illumination was the theory employed by thirteenth-century Franciscan scholastics to try to explain human cognition.[102] These theologians maintained that although the human mind had some innate ability to know, it could not truly understand without the assistance of divine light, because God was the only source of immutable truth and goodness. Most argued that this illumination was not communicated directly to the human mind by God (*lux*, the uncreated light) but by lesser forms of light (termed *lumen*, *radium* or *splendor*) that proceeded from *lux*, just as the physical sun radiates beams.

For medieval exegetes, the poetic descriptions in the biblical book of Wisdom confirmed the concept of wisdom as light descending from God: 'For she [wisdom] is the brightness of eternal light, and the unspotted mirror of God's majesty, and the image of his goodness . . . For she is more beautiful than the sun, and above all the order of the stars'.[103] Within the Trinity, it was Christ (the Word) who was considered the source of all wisdom and true knowledge.[104] Bonaventure's sermon, 'Christ, the one teacher of all', begins by stating that Christ is the one fontal principle of cognitive illumination, and he quotes Sirach (Ecclesiasticus) 1:5: 'The word of God on high is the fountain of wisdom'.[105]

The fullest Franciscan exposition on divine light in the thirteenth century was the *Tractatus de luce*, written by Bartholomew of Bologna some time before 1290.[106] Although Bartholomew's works are little known today, he was a Franciscan theologian and teacher of some substance.[107] He trained and taught in Paris (possibly succeeding Matthew of Acquasparta as regent master), attended the Assisi general chapter in 1279, and was, alongside Philip of Perugia and others, involved in drafting Nicholas III's bull *Exiit qui seminat*. By 1282 he was teaching theology in Bologna, where he also served as provincial minister from 1285 to 1289. Although the *Tractatus de luce* does not set out to be a tract on cognition, it is solidly rooted in the theory and terminology of divine illumination and it focuses exclusively on Christ. The basis of Bartholomew's argument is Christ's declaration in John 8:12 that he is the light of the world ('Ego sum lux mundi'). Bartholomew explains that Christ calls himself *lux*, rather than *lumen*, *radium* or *splendor*, because he is the source of all other sources of light; all intellectual knowledge and every spiritual illumination emanate from him.[108] In Franciscan writings, the close relationship between Christ as light and as wisdom is frequently underpinned by analogies between physical and spiritual illumination, between sight and understanding. In his *Commentary on Luke*, for example, Bonaventure interprets Christ's curing of the blind beggar in terms not only of physical sight, but also of the light of wisdom.[109]

Although Franciscan theologians considered divine illumination an essential part of the normal mental process of cognition, they differentiated this from the supernatural way in which God revealed wisdom to mystics. For Bonaventure, there was a higher knowledge of the divine essence that could be received only while the mind was joined to God in ecstatic contemplation.[110] It is in terms of this special privilege, granted only to a select few, that we should understand the light that illuminates Saint Francis in the *Miracle of the Spring*, as he contemplates the ascending Christ. It was Christ, through his Ascension, who taught mankind to spurn the wisdom of the world and to seek after divine wisdom, which comes from above.[111]

In the final chapter of the *Itinerarium*, Bonaventure spoke of Saint Francis's encounter with the Christ–Seraph on La Verna as a passing over into God, which offered a model of contemplation to others:

> If this passing over is to be perfect, all intellectual operations must be given up, and the sharp point of our desire must be entirely directed toward God and transformed in him. Such a motion as this is something mystical and very secret, and no one knows it except him who receives it, and no one receives it except him who desires it, and no

one desires it unless the fire of the Holy Spirit, whom Christ sent to earth, inflames him to the very marrow. That is why the apostle [Saint Paul] attributes to the Holy Spirit the revelation of such mystical wisdom.[112]

This mystical wisdom is primarily experiential rather than intellectual.[113] Saint Francis at La Verna, 'on fire with an ever intense flame of heavenly desires', was able to experience 'an overflow of the sweetness of heavenly contemplation'.[114] Wisdom, the highest gift of the Spirit, is linked to charity, the highest virtue, because only through ardent love of God can the soul enjoy this affective knowledge of the divine. This is why the Holy Spirit, who is the bond of love in the Trinity, uniting humanity to God, plays a dynamic role in the spiritual ascent.[115] Saint Francis is frequently portrayed as having been able to enter into hidden mysteries, 'enlightened by the splendour of eternal light', not through intellectual endeavour but because of the strength of his ardour.[116] As we saw above, Matthew of Acquasparta, in his sermon on Francis as the *alter angelus*, interpreted 'ascending from the rising of the sun' as a reference to the elevation of mind that Francis achieved through fervent love.

In the third part of the *Tractatus de luce*, Bartholomew of Bologna argued that imitation of Christ, and therefore possession of all the virtues, is the condition that renders the human mind capable of receiving divine illumination. Among the virtues, charity's power is transformative. Using the analogy of a seal, he likened Christ to a matrix, which carries the engraved image of all that is knowable. The human mind is the wax, ready to receive the imprint of the seal. Charity (or love) warms and liquefies the wax, so that when the matrix is stamped into it, the impressed image adheres more strongly.[117] This analogy is remarkably similar to Bonaventure's description in the *Legenda minor* of the twofold impact of Saint Francis's encounter with the Christ–Seraph. Inwardly, the saint was inflamed with seraphic ardour; outwardly, his flesh was impressed with a likeness conforming him to the Crucified. 'It was', Bonaventure explained, 'as if the liquefying power of fire preceded the impression of the seal'.[118]

The verbs used for love's actions – kindling, inflaming, burning – are related to the account of Pentecost in Acts. As the apostles sat together in prayer, 'there appeared to them parted tongues, as it were of fire: and it sat upon every one of them'.[119] But in the *Pentecost* at Assisi, the Holy Spirit is not shown as a flame on the head of each apostle (a more popular iconography in the later Middle Ages); instead, the dove, symbolizing the Spirit, descends in the midst of a burst of thin gold rays. The rays are paired, perhaps to suggest the 'parted tongues', but they resemble light more than fire. This is quite compatible with Franciscan thought: Bartholomew of Bologna, writing about the actions of divine light, remarks that, just as in nature light produces heat, divine light likewise has two effects, illumination and heat. The golden rays of light in the *Pentecost* make clear the connection between the transforming effect of the Holy Spirit on the apostles, and the illumination of Saint Francis below.

Prayer and Preaching in the Saint Francis Cycle

As we have seen, the composition of the counter-façade is dominated by two powerful diagonals, one ascending from the *Miracle of the Spring* to the *Ascension*, the other descending again, from the *Pentecost* to the *Preaching to the Birds*. The entire wall is locked into a continuous flow of narrative around the light of its central rose. This great circular motion at the heart of the Saint Francis cycle intertwines the life of the saint with the lives of Christ and the apostles; it demonstrates the transforming power of the Holy Spirit in Francis and the symbiotic relationship between his inner life of prayer and his pastoral mission.

The way that *contemplativa* and *activa* are presented on the counter-façade is entirely consistent with how the relationship between these dual aspects of the Franciscan vocation was understood by the friars. The author of the *Meditations on the Life of Christ*, in a discussion of the ministry of Mary and Martha, divided the active life into two parts. The first part concentrates mainly on trying to eradicate the vices and acquire the virtues in one's own life, through prayer and reading, but also by helping others through acts of justice and charity. This is a model for the laity, and it is the type of life that the young Francis is shown leading in the first few scenes of the Saint Francis cycle, before he renounces his father and enters religious life. The second part of the *vita activa* is concerned principally with 'teaching and helping in the salvation of souls, as do prelates, preachers, learned doctors, and others of this kind'.[120] Between these two parts of the active life comes the contemplative life, which is devoted to God alone. Only when the first part of the active life *and* the contemplative life have 'imbued him with virtues and true wisdom, illumined him and made him fervent' will the Franciscan friar be ready to devote himself to the salvation of others.[121]

True wisdom, illumination and fervency: these are the fruits of contemplation that a friar must acquire if he is to become an effective preacher. This ideal progression from *contemplativa* to *activa* is encapsulated on the counter-façade, but is not confined to it. The reordering of the *Legenda maior* that enabled the *Miracle of the Spring* and the *Preaching to the Birds* to be paired on the entrance wall was not so extreme as to disrupt the overall narrative arc of the Saint Francis cycle. These two episodes are embedded within a sequence of thirteen scenes devoted to Francis's life as a friar, from the *Approval of the Rule* (Scene 7) to the *Stigmatization* (Scene 19).

The sequence begins in the third bay of the north wall, where Saint Francis is depicted receiving from the pope's hand a scroll on which the opening words of the Franciscan Rule can be read (fig. 180). This image seems deliberately to superimpose the events of 1223, when Honorius III had confirmed the Rule with a papal bull, onto those of 1209/10, when Innocent III had approved the fledgling Order only verbally. The titulus beneath the scene (as reconstructed by Marinangeli) is equally ambiguous, emphasizing papal authority for the friars' preaching mission, but without naming the pontiff: 'How the pope approved the Rule and gave a mandate to preach penitence, and to the brothers who had come with the saint he gave tonsures, so that they could preach the word of God.' Despite this, neither Francis nor any of his friars is seen preaching in any of the next seven scenes. The first depiction of this quintessential mendicant activity is the *Preaching to the Birds*. Only after the counter-façade, in a triplet of scenes in the fourth bay of the south wall, is there a focus on the active ministry of the friars. The first two show Saint Francis exhorting a knight to penitence and preaching a sermon to Pope Honorius III, while in the third scene it is another Franciscan saint, Anthony of Padua, who lectures to the friars in the chapter house at Arles.

Conversely, of the eight scenes before the *Preaching to the Birds*, no fewer than five show Saint Francis in attitudes of prayer or contemplation. The implication is that the entire sequence of scenes depicting Saint Francis as a friar was intended to expand the contemplative–active diptych of the counter-façade. In order to achieve that, preaching was purposely suppressed in the first half of the cycle. This thesis is supported by a comparison with the Bardi dossal. On the

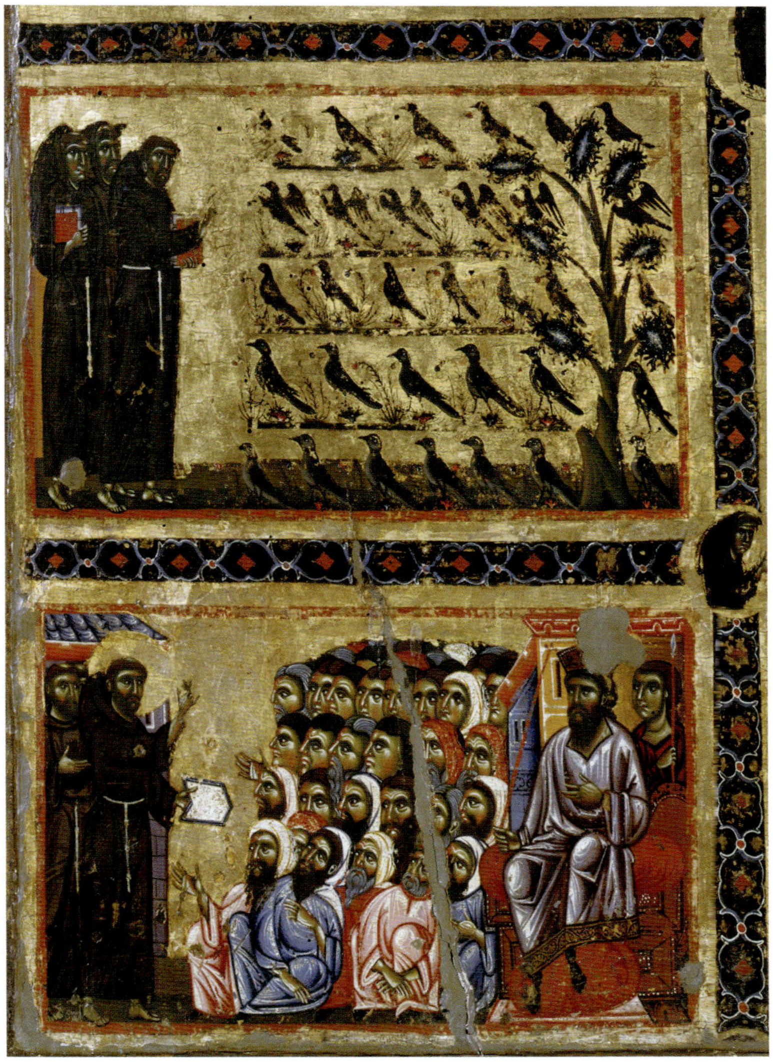

179 Florentine school, *Preaching to the Birds* and *Preaching before the Sultan*, Bardi dossal, mid-thirteenth century, tempera and gold on wood, Bardi chapel, Santa Croce, Florence.

Florentine panel, which comprises the longest Saint Francis cycle we know of before that at Assisi, the *Approval of the Rule* is followed immediately by three scenes depicting the saint's active ministry. In the *Miracle of the Crib at Greccio*, Francis is seen in church, reading the Gospel in his liturgical function as a deacon. Then comes the *Preaching to the Birds*, and below it the saint's encounter with the Sultan of Egypt in Damietta. The similarity of the latter two compositions, with their serried ranks of attentive listeners, clearly invites comparison (fig. 179). At Damietta, as Saint Francis addresses the assembled Muslims he brandishes an open book and uses

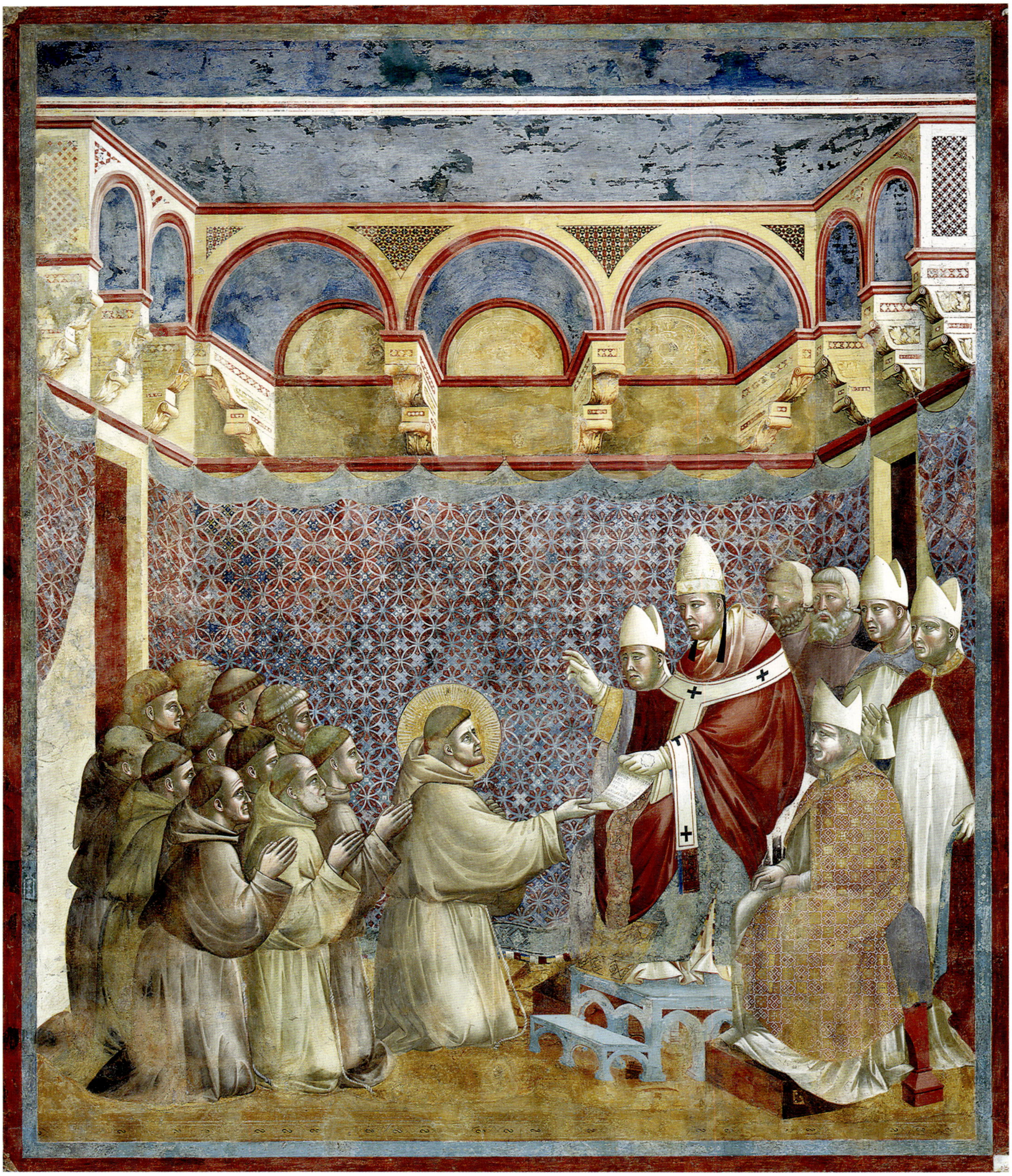

180 *Approval of the Rule*, Scene 7 of the Saint Francis cycle, *c.*1290–96, fresco, north wall of the nave, Upper Church, Basilica of San Francesco.

his fingers as an *aide-memoire* for the structure of his sermon. But in the Assisi cycle, not only is the *Preaching to the Birds* deferred until much later, the iconography of the other two episodes is significantly altered. In Egypt, Francis does not preach, but challenges the Sultan's priests to a test of faith by fire (fig. 181). The emphasis is the saint's ardent love of God and desire for martyrdom. And at Greccio, Francis no longer reads the Gospel, while the pulpit on top of the screen is conspicuously empty (see fig. 141).[122]

The treatment of the saint's religious vocation in the third and fourth bays of the north wall is consistent with Franciscan understanding of the *vita contemplativa*. The first scene after the *Approval of the Rule* immediately establishes the themes of prayer and ascent. In the *Vision of the Chariot* (fig. 182), Saint Francis appears flying above the heads of his confrères in a burning chariot, his hands folded together in a gesture of prayer. The episode depicts Saint Francis as a second Elijah, whose ascent into heaven in a chariot of fire was understood typologically to prefigure Christ's own Ascension. Already, the messages of the counter-façade are being anticipated.

The 'Vita contemplativa': Jacob, Benjamin and Paul

The Saint Francis scenes in the third bay of the north wall are set beneath the two Genesis scenes dealing with Isaac and his sons. On the left, the patriarch Isaac, now old and blind, gives his blessing to his younger son Jacob (fig. 183). By passing himself off as Esau, Jacob obtains his elder brother's birthright through deception. In the second Isaac scene, Esau arrives too late at his father's bedside, while behind him Jacob and his mother Rebecca are seen fleeing the house (fig. 184). Neff convincingly argued that it is Jacob, not Isaac, who is the prototype for Saint Francis here.[123] Her interpretation largely depends on the *Meditatio pauperis in solitudine* ('The meditation of a poor man in the desert'), a mystical and moral treatise written in the early 1280s by the respected Franciscan lector and master of theology John of Wales.[124] Reflecting on the mission of Saint Francis and his Order, John focuses on fraternity, pointing out that among religious orders only the Franciscans are called 'brothers'. Throughout the *Meditatio pauperis* not only does he consistently interpret 'Friars Minor' (*fratres minores*) to mean 'younger brothers', but he goes so far as to assert that Jacob 'truly is Francis, who, although he is the younger brother [*frater minor*], fully attained the inheritance of the older through his father's blessing'. What is more, the legacy Jacob inherits from Isaac is the founding of Israel, which is seen typologically as the founding of the Franciscan Order. Turning to the Assisi frescoes, *Isaac Blessing Jacob* is placed directly above the *Approval of the Rule* (fig. 185). Isaac blesses his younger son Jacob, just as the pope, father of the Church, gives his blessing to Francis, the *frater minor*.

It is important to note that the typology of Jacob for Francis was well established long before John of Wales's *Meditatio pauperis*, and was fundamentally related to contemplation. In his bull of canonization of 1228, Pope Gregory IX had already cast Francis as a new Jacob, wedded both to Rachel, symbolizing the *vita contemplativa*, and Leah, the *vita activa*.[125] But according to Bonaventure it was not only Rachel who was a model contemplative. In Genesis, after struggling all night with an angel, Jacob was given a blessing and the name Israel, which medieval exegetes interpreted as 'one who sees God'.[126] Likewise, Bonaventure described how Saint Francis, during his vision of the Christ–Seraph at La Verna, was 'carried out of himself [and] passed over to God, becoming a model of perfect contemplation – another Jacob now become Israel'.[127]

Biblical exegesis routinely justified Jacob's theft of his brother's birthright by denouncing Esau for a plethora of vices. In the *Meditatio pauperis*, John of Wales followed this tradition, identifying Esau with the proud Lucifer, who was rightly cast down into hell. He argued that Francis, like Jacob, deserved his father's blessing because of his exemplary poverty, charity and humility. John then recounted Brother Pacifico's vision of the celestial thrones vacated by the fallen angels, in which he was told that Lucifer's throne was reserved for the humble Francis (see fig. 124).[128] Neff argued that it is surely not by chance that the *Vision of the Thrones* is depicted at the end of the third bay, directly below *Isaac Rejecting Esau* (fig. 185).[129] This concordance between the nave frescoes and the *Meditatio pauperis* appears to confirm either that the friars at Assisi had direct access to John's text, or that his ideas permeated mainstream Franciscan thought in the final decades of the thirteenth century.

In the *Vision of the Thrones*, Francis's self-abasement is apparent as he prays before the altar, his fist clenched to his chest (fig. 186). The detail does not derive from this episode in the *Legenda maior*, but elsewhere Bonaventure describes

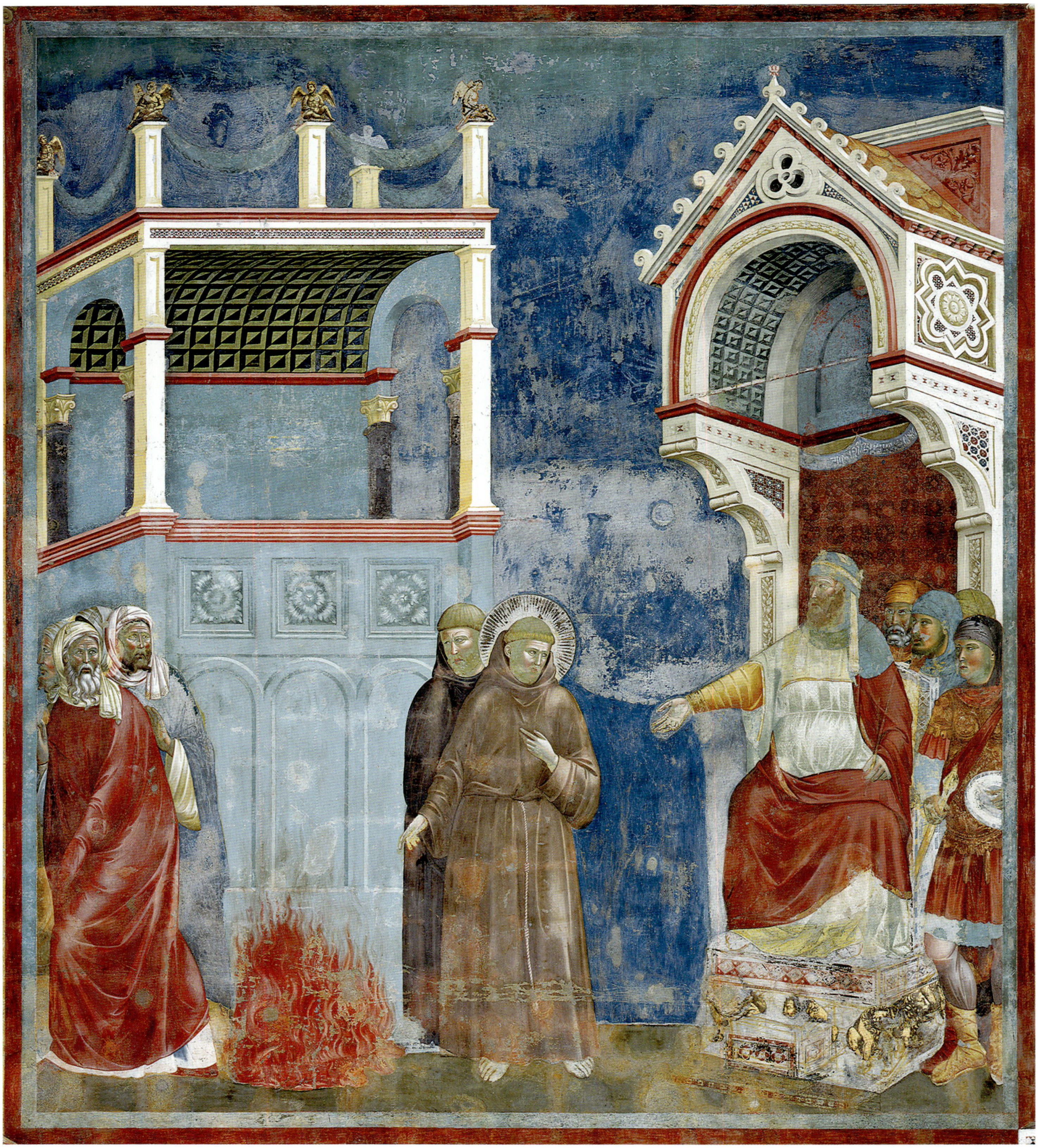

181 *Trial by Fire*, Scene 11 of the Saint Francis cycle, *c.*1290–96, fresco, north wall of the nave, Upper Church, Basilica of San Francesco.

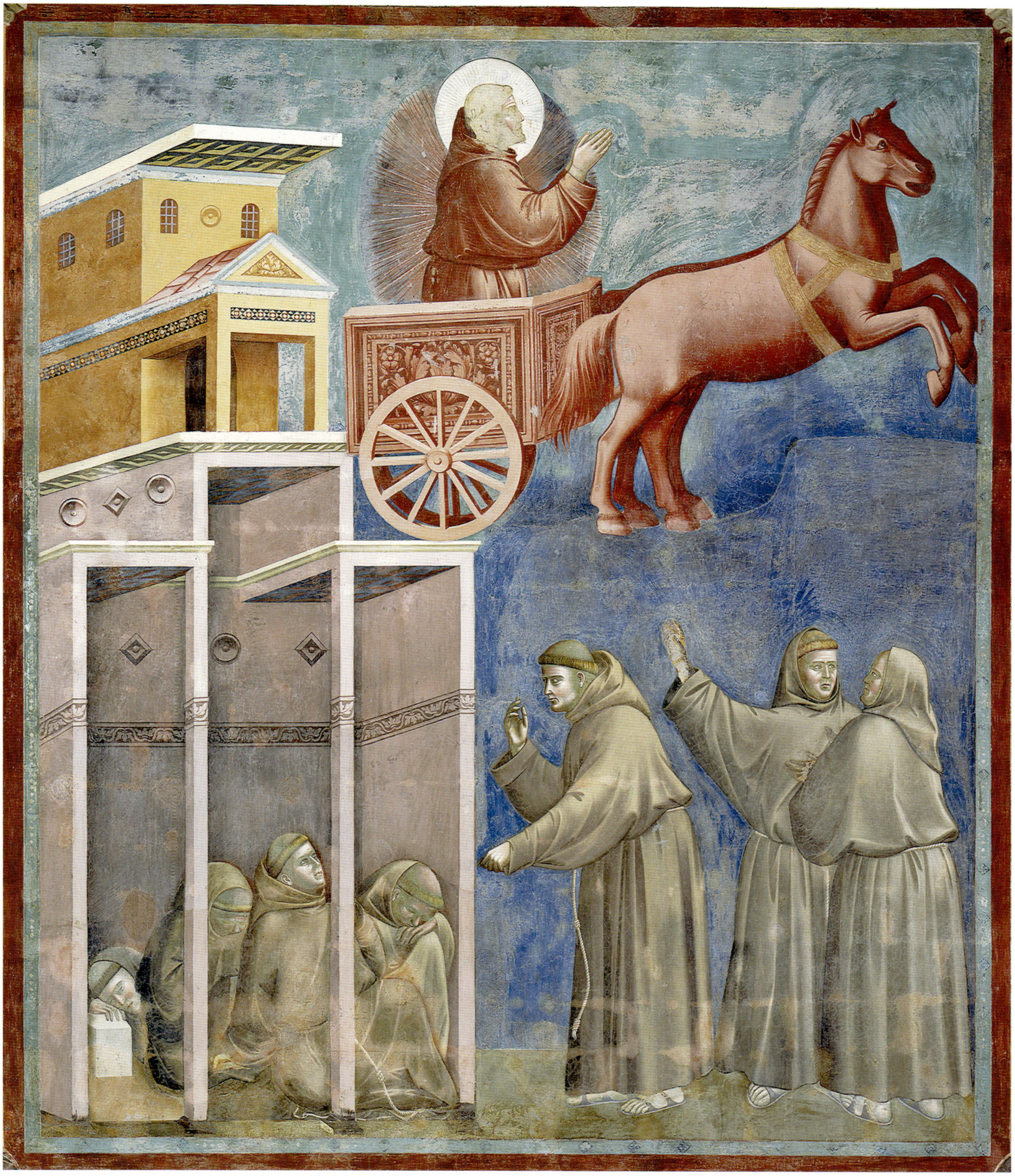

182 *Vision of the Chariot*, Scene 8 of the Saint Francis cycle, *c.*1290–96, fresco, north wall of the nave, Upper Church, Basilica of San Francesco.

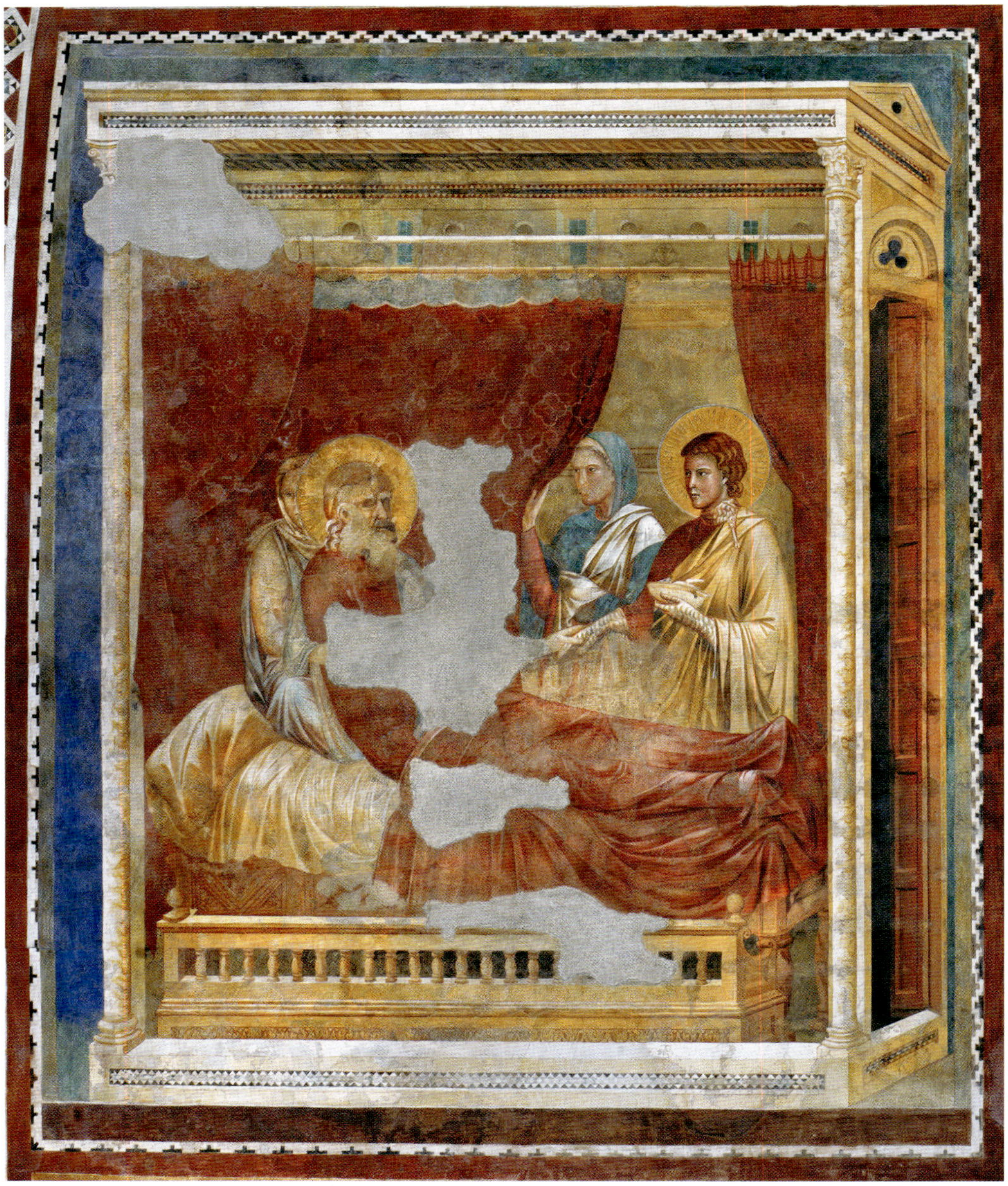

183 *Isaac Blessing Jacob*, Old Testament cycle, *c*.1288–91, fresco, third bay, north wall of the nave, Upper Church, Basilica of San Francesco.

how the saint in solitary prayer would 'strike his breast with his hand'.[130] This imaginative addition reflects a common penitential gesture which was ultimately derived from Christ's parable of the Pharisee and the publican in Luke's Gospel. The humble publican, who beat his breast to show his sorrow for his sins, was understood as an exemplar for prayer.[131] Glossing this passage, and clearly addressing his fellow friars, Bonaventure commented: 'Wherefore, it is also part of our custom in confession, and in saying that we are guilty in a chapter of faults, to beat our breasts in accusation of and repentance within our hearts and in testimony of our consciences.'[132]

The depiction of Francis's prayer life continues in the fourth bay (fig. 188), which opens with the casting out of demons from the city of Arezzo (fig. 189). Francis is shown kneeling in supplication, having sent his companion Brother

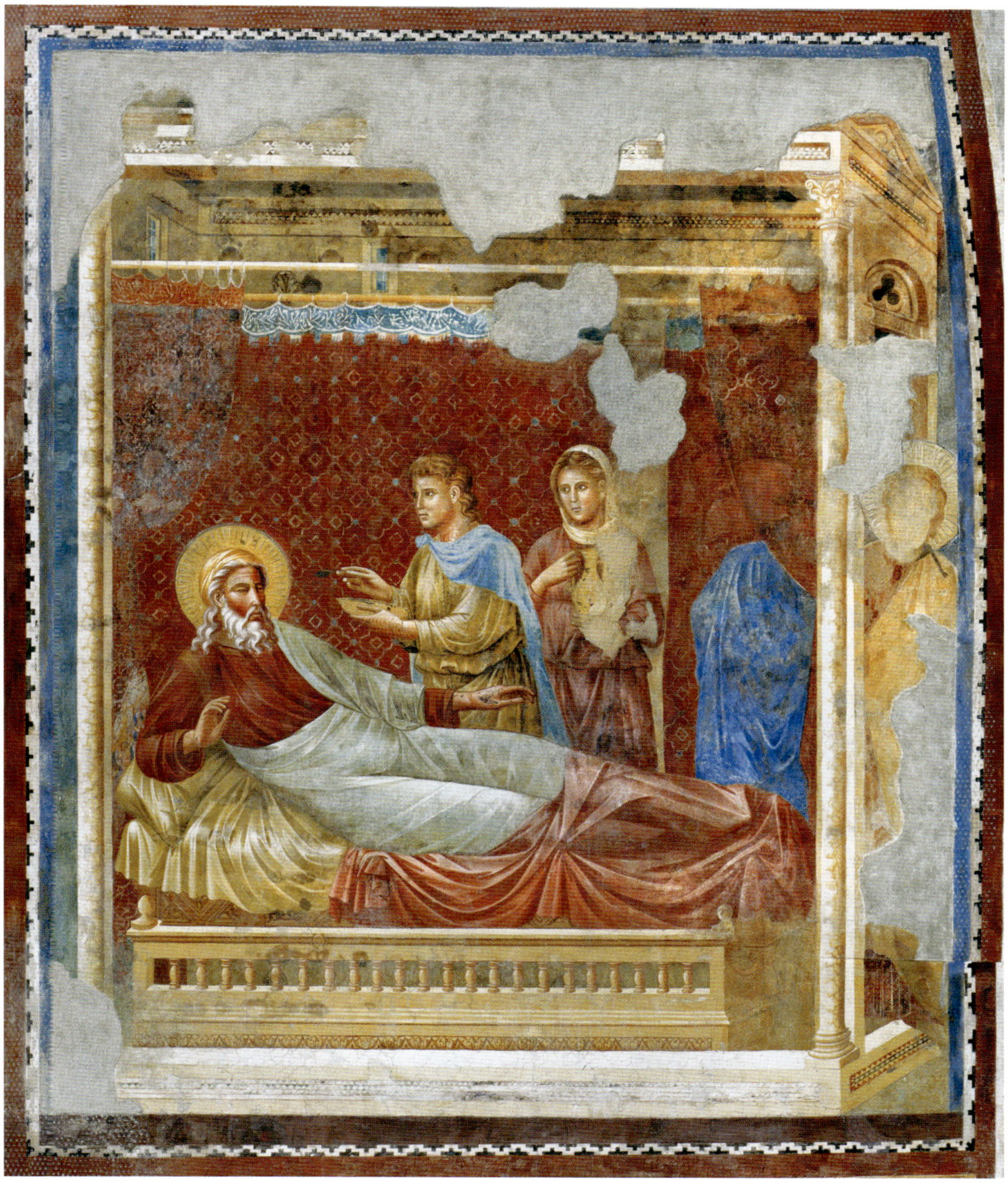

184 *Isaac Rejecting Esau*, Old Testament cycle, *c.*1288–91, fresco, third bay, north wall of the nave, Upper Church, Basilica of San Francesco.

Sylvester to command the demons to depart (as a priest, Sylvester was qualified to perform exorcism). In Chapter 6, we argued that the first scene in the Saint Francis cycle, the *Homage of a Simple Man*, took as its point of departure Cimabue's *Saint Peter Curing the Lame Man in front of the Temple* in the north transept. The intention was to portray Saint Francis as a new apostle. A similar strategy was adopted for the *Expulsion of the Demons from Arezzo*, but this time using Cimabue's *Fall of Simon Magus* (fig. 187) as the model. There are parallels between the Franciscan story and the apocryphal tale of Saints Peter and Paul, as recounted in the *Golden Legend*. In Rome, the two apostles are challenged by the magician Simon Magus, who holds sway over Emperor Nero. Simon claims he is God and can ascend to heaven. When he jumps off the top of a high tower, 'Paul said to Peter: "I'm the one to pray now; you're the one to command!" . . .

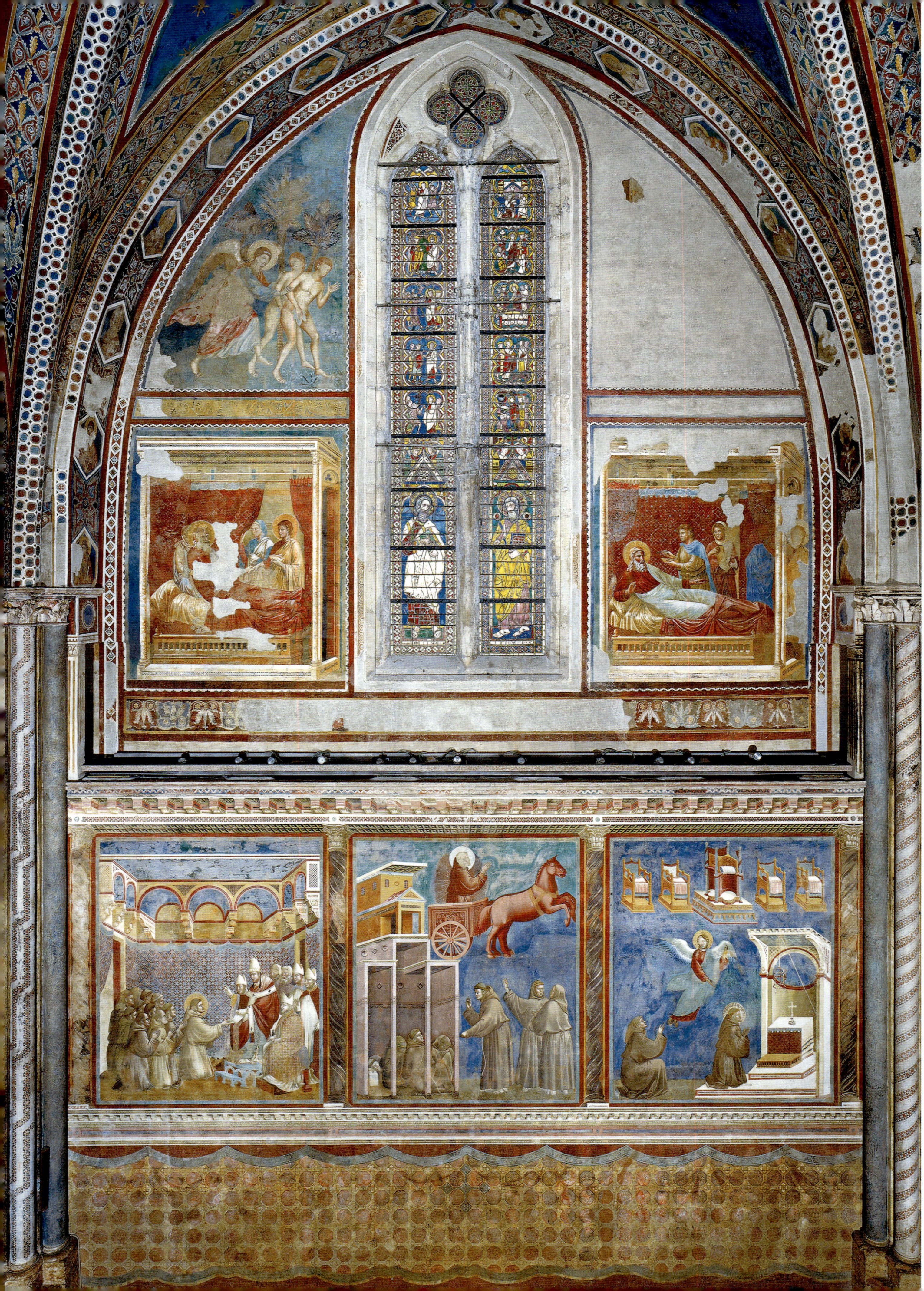

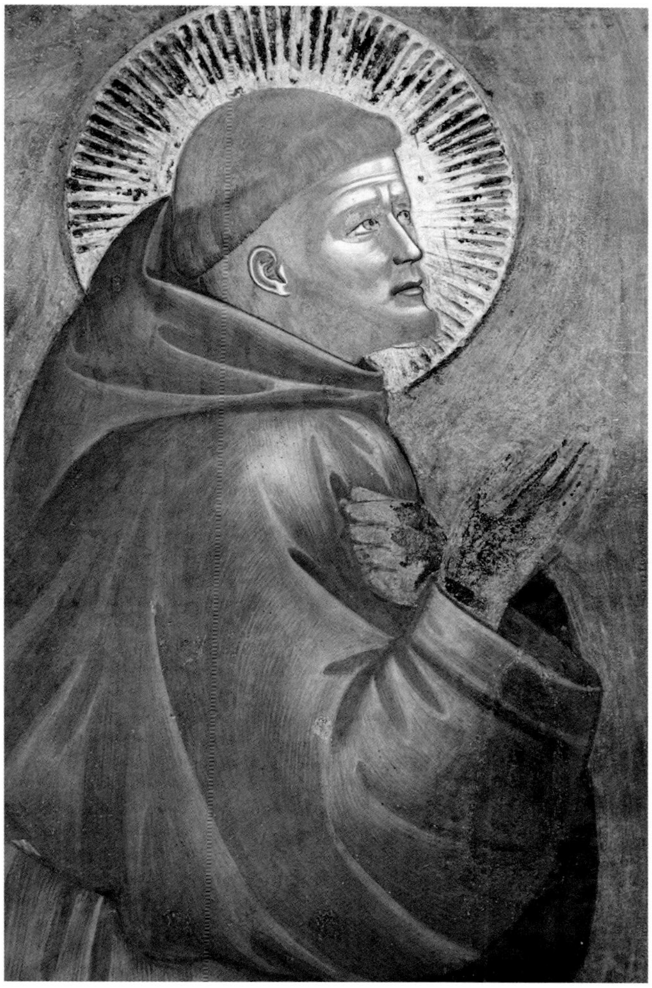

186 Saint Francis in prayer, detail from *Vision of the Thrones*, Scene 9 of the Saint Francis cycle, *c.*1290–96, fresco, north wall of the nave, Upper Church, Basilica of San Francesco.

Peter said: "I adjure you, angels of Satan, you who are holding Simon up in the air, I adjure you in the name of Jesus Christ our Lord! Stop holding him up and let him fall!" They released him at once and he crashed to the ground, his skull was fractured, and he expired.'[133] In the Arezzo scene, the two friars are given the same positions and poses as the two apostles. But it is the priest Sylvester who is likened to Saint Peter, while Francis is cast in the role of Saint Paul.[134] In effect, this is another pairing of *activa* and *contemplativa*. As we shall see, the parallel between Saint Francis and Saint Paul is particularly significant. Paul was commonly seen as a model contemplative, and his epistles contain crucial descriptions of ecstatic experiences of God, which were applied to Saint Francis by Minorite writers.[135]

facing page 185 View of the third bay, north wall of the nave, Upper Church, Basilica of San Francesco.

Saint Francis's contemplative journey along the north wall culminates with his *Ecstasy* (fig. 190), the third scene of the fourth bay. In one of the few new stories he contributed in the *Legenda maior*, Bonaventure described the saint seeking solitude in the forest at night, where his brothers saw him praying, his hands outstretched in the shape of a cross and his whole body lifted up above the ground. While Francis was raised up, he was 'surrounded by a sort of shining cloud, so that the extraordinary illumination around his body was a witness to the wonderful light that shone within his soul'.[136] Bonaventure explained that while Saint Francis was in this ecstatic state 'unknown and hidden secrets [*occulte*] of

187 Cimabue, *Fall of Simon Magus*, Apostles cycle, *c.*1279–82, fresco, north transept, Upper Church, Basilica of San Francesco.

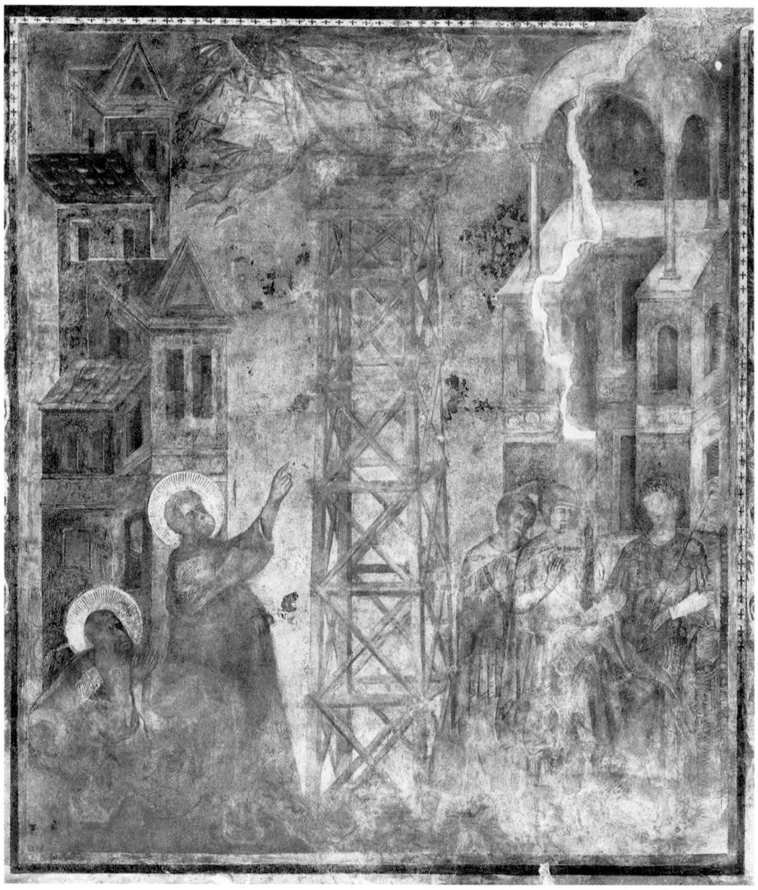

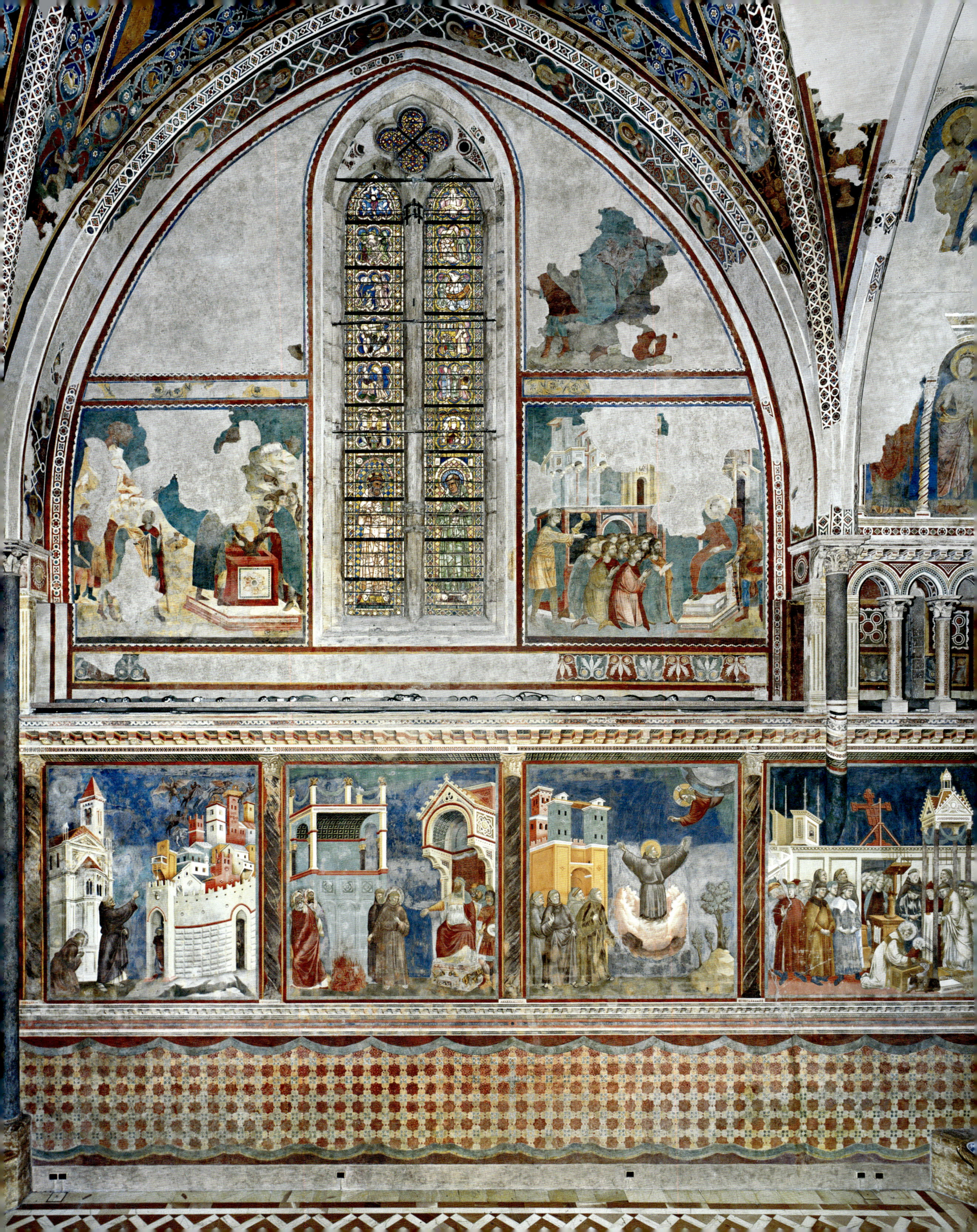

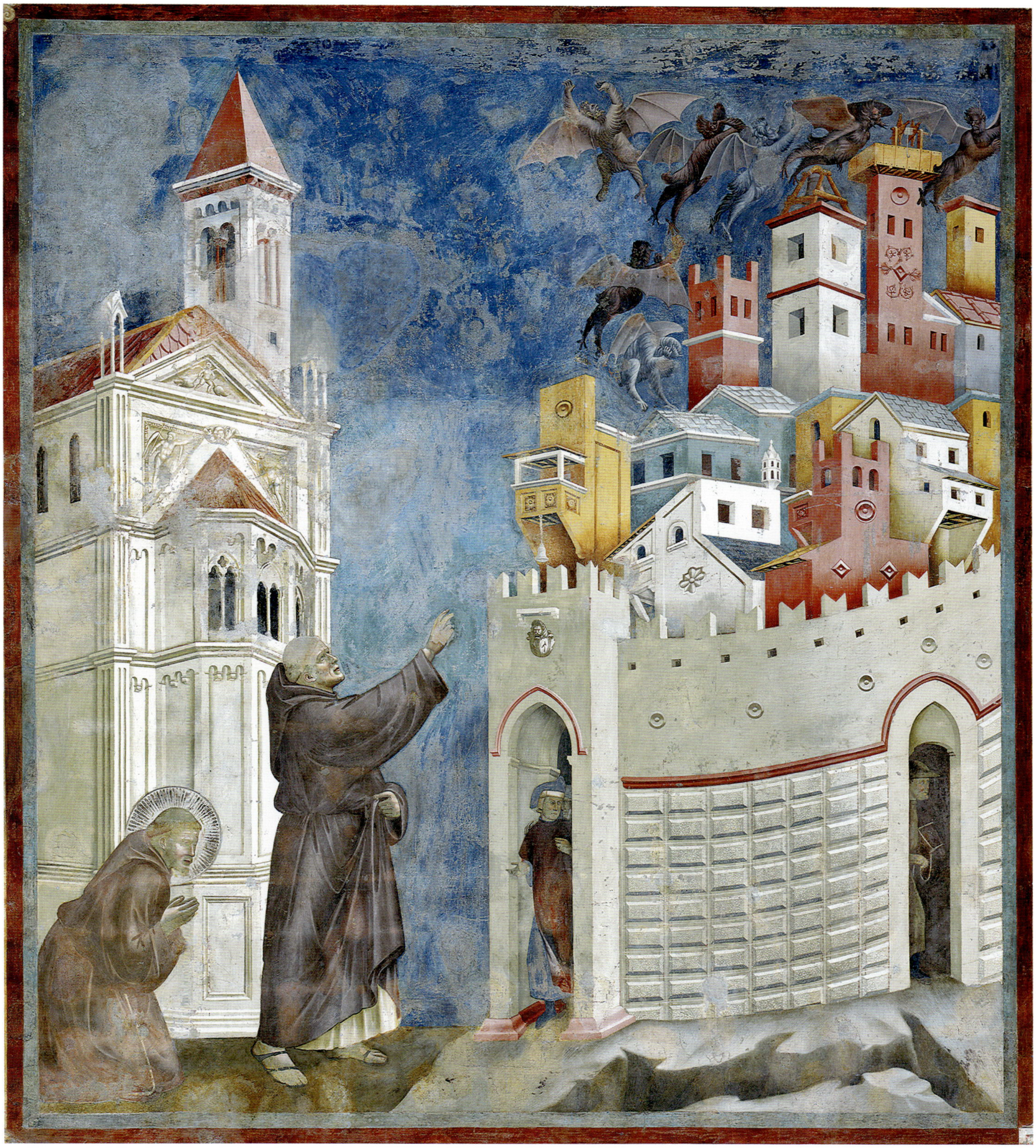

189 *Expulsion of the Demons from Arezzo*, Scene 10 of the Saint Francis cycle, *c.*1290–96, fresco, north wall of the nave, Upper Church, Basilica of San Francesco.

facing page 188 View of the fourth bay, north wall of the nave, Upper Church, Basilica of San Francesco.

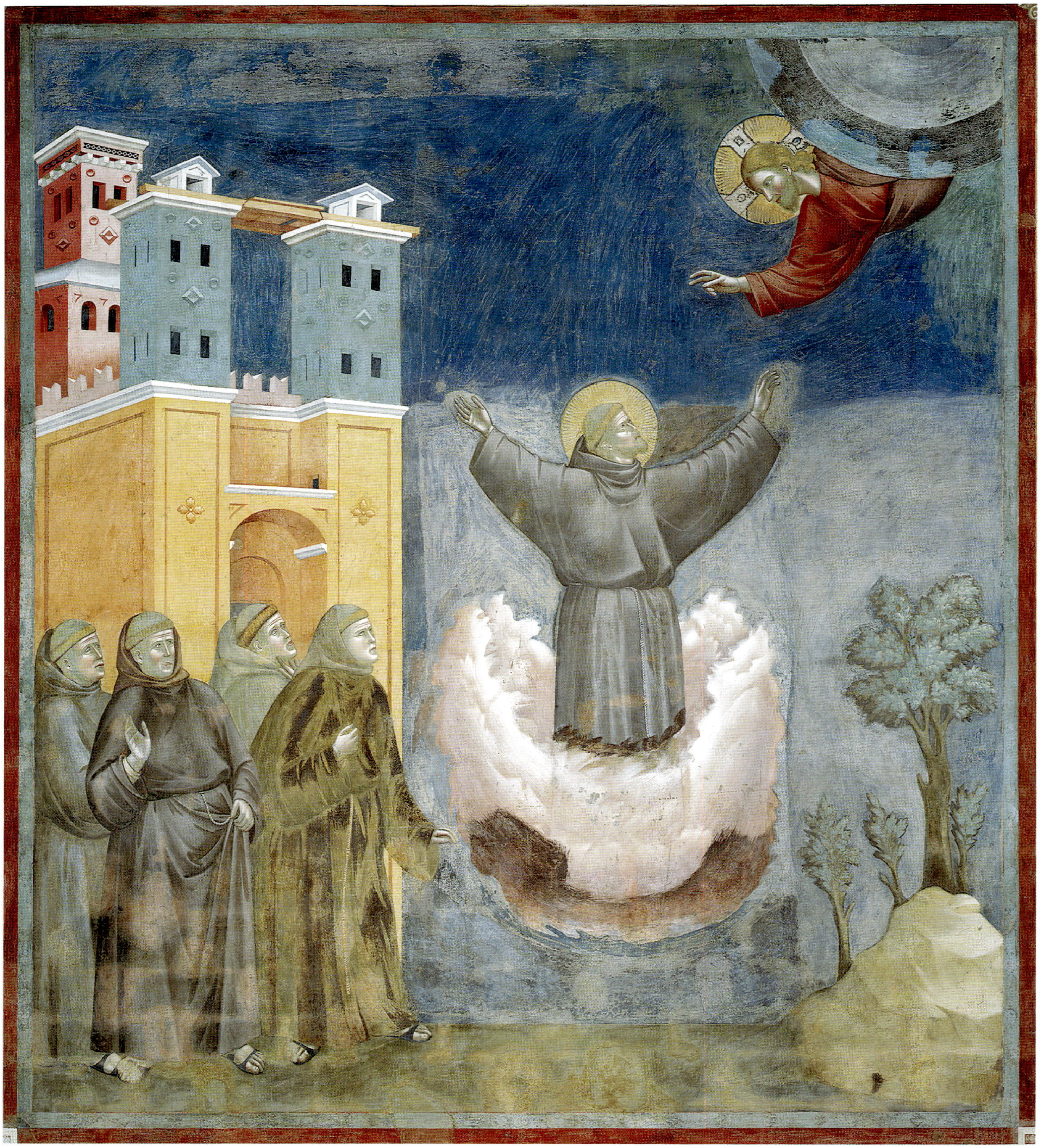

190 *Saint Francis in Ecstasy*, Scene 12 of the Saint Francis cycle, *c.*1290–96, fresco, north wall of the nave, Upper Church, Basilica of San Francesco.

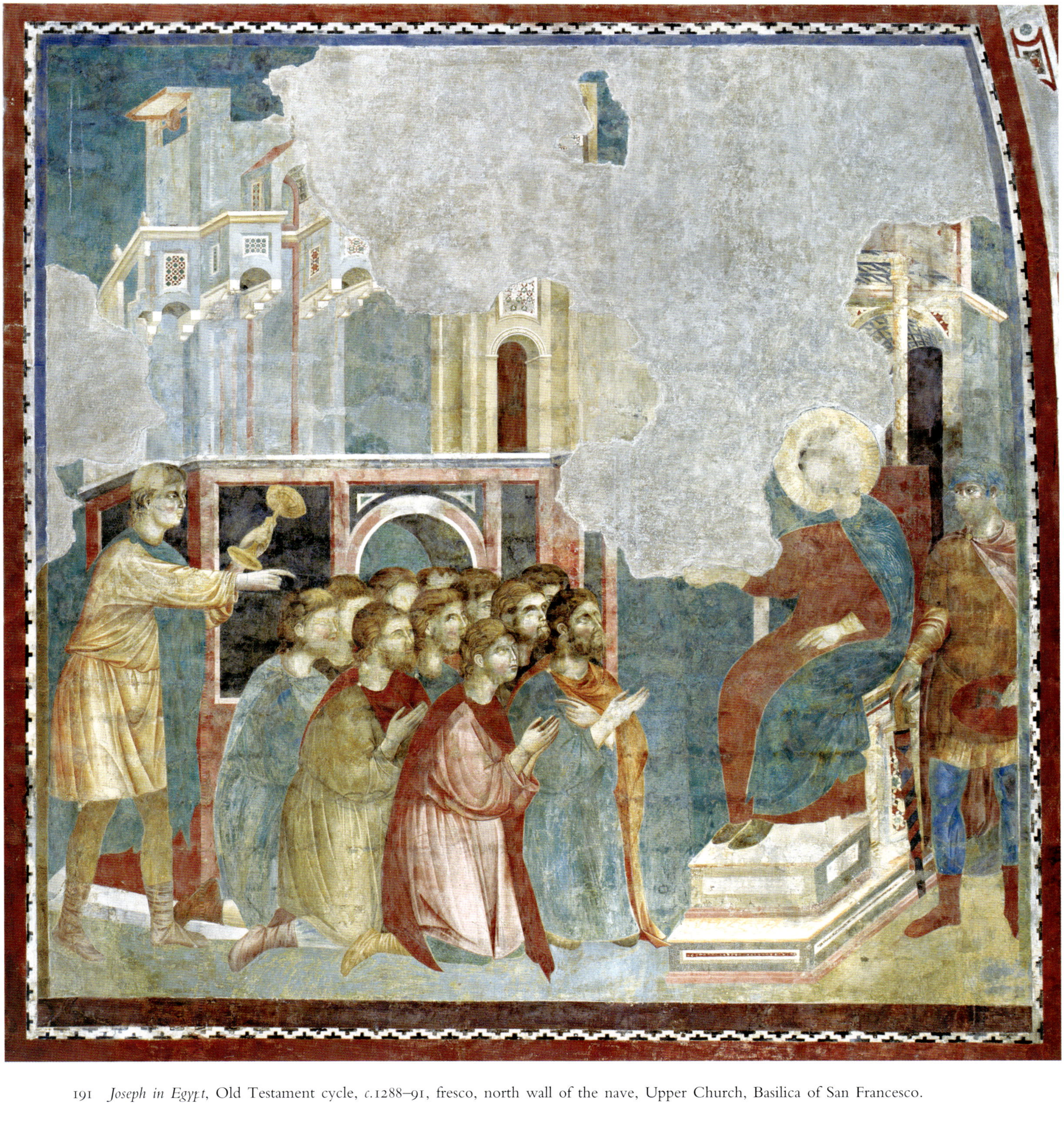

191 *Joseph in Egypt*, Old Testament cycle, *c.*1288–91, fresco, north wall of the nave, Upper Church, Basilica of San Francesco.

divine wisdom were opened up to him'. As we have seen, medieval scholastics differentiated between the normal process of cognition, in which God through his eternal light communicated openly (*aperte*), and the extraordinary process by which God revealed knowledge of supernatural things through revelation, more secretly (*occulte*).[137]

In the fresco, the figure of Christ stoops down from heaven to bless the levitating saint. This detail is not found in the *Legenda maior*, but its addition reveals a profound understanding of the subtext behind Bonaventure's account. The inclusion of Christ could express Francis's burning desire for union with God, which led him through prayer to seek – in Bonaventure's words – 'the Beloved [Christ] from whom only the wall of the flesh separated him'.[138] But this iconographic touch also suggests more precisely the state of intimate colloquy in which 'unknown and hidden secrets of divine wisdom' were revealed to Francis by Christ.

In his account of the stigmatization, Bonaventure linked Saint Francis's mystical experience with that of Saint Paul. The apostle described being 'caught up to the third heaven', in which ecstatic state he 'heard secret words, which it is not granted to man to utter'.[139] Bonaventure cited Paul's experience when he claimed that the words the Seraph uttered to Francis were so secret that he never disclosed them to anyone.[140] Matthew of Acquasparta understood Francis's ecstasy in the same way. In his first sermon on Saint Francis, he declared: 'There is no doubt that, while [Francis] shone with these heavenly splendours and was in these excesses of mind, "he heard things that are not to be told, that no mortal is permitted to repeat" [2 Corinthians 12:4] . . . It is not improper to think that in such rapture he was, like Paul, raised to a vision of the divine essence.'[141] In the Assisi fresco, Francis's communion with Christ, his outstretched arms and the trees standing on a little outcrop of rock (almost a La Verna in miniature) all seem to prefigure the stigmatization.

It is the getting of divine wisdom that provides a thematic link between *Saint Francis in Ecstasy* and the scene above, *Joseph in Egypt* (fig. 191), which concludes the Genesis cycle. As discussed in Chapter 4, there was no model for this story among the extensive Joseph scenes in the Roman basilica of San Paolo, and it seems to have been devised for the Assisi cycle.[142] Joseph, one of the twelve sons of Jacob, was sold by his jealous brothers and sent into Egypt as a slave. But, after he correctly interpreted the Pharaoh's dreams as a prophecy of famine, he was made governor of Egypt and became a wise ruler who provided for his people. Years later, when his brothers came to buy grain in Egypt, Joseph accused them of stealing a silver cup which, unbeknownst to them, he had had planted in the sack of his youngest brother, Benjamin. The Assisi scene depicts the moment of discovery: as Joseph's brothers kneel before him, his steward brandishes the cup and points an accusing finger at Benjamin (in the foreground, wearing pink).

According to Neff, the key to the significance of *Joseph in Egypt* in the Assisi cycle is the symbolic interpretation of the twelve sons of Jacob, found in the last part of the *Meditatio pauperis*.[143] This was based on Richard of Saint Victor's popular mid-twelfth-century tract, the *Beniamin minor*. Of Jacob's progeny, only Joseph and Benjamin were the sons of Rachel, and so identified with *contemplativa*. John of Wales followed Richard in associating Joseph with 'the clear vision of wise discretion' and Benjamin with 'the ecstatic excess of sweet consolation', but he added his own peculiarly Franciscan gloss, seeing the younger brother Benjamin as 'truly the consummation of perfection of the Friar Minor'.

The parallels between the Saint Francis scenes and the biblical scenes in this bay are certainly not the most visually accomplished in the Upper Church. The compositions lack the strong verticals and diagonals that we have seen being used to link scenes elsewhere. Nevertheless, Benjamin is positioned above Saint Francis in the *Ecstasy*, and Joseph roughly above Christ (see fig. 188), the latter pair being likened through their dark-red clothes and elevated positions. The Joseph/Christ parallel was unlikely to have been missed by observers since Joseph was one of the strongest figures for Christ in medieval typology. Not only was he sold by his brothers, prefiguring Christ's sale by Judas, but in Egypt he was given the name *Salvator Mundi* ('Saviour of the World').[144]

The parallel between Benjamin and Saint Francis is more obscure, and was probably confined to Franciscan circles, but Neff convincingly observed that the prominence of the cup being flourished by Joseph's steward in the fresco suggests that the analogy was intended. Because Joseph's cup was used for divination, it was usually interpreted as a symbol of divine wisdom. But the cup was not found until the steward searched the sack of the youngest brother, Benjamin, which allowed John of Wales, in a complicated metaphor, to point out that 'although others pride themselves on having sacks full of grain, with which they are able to feed others with

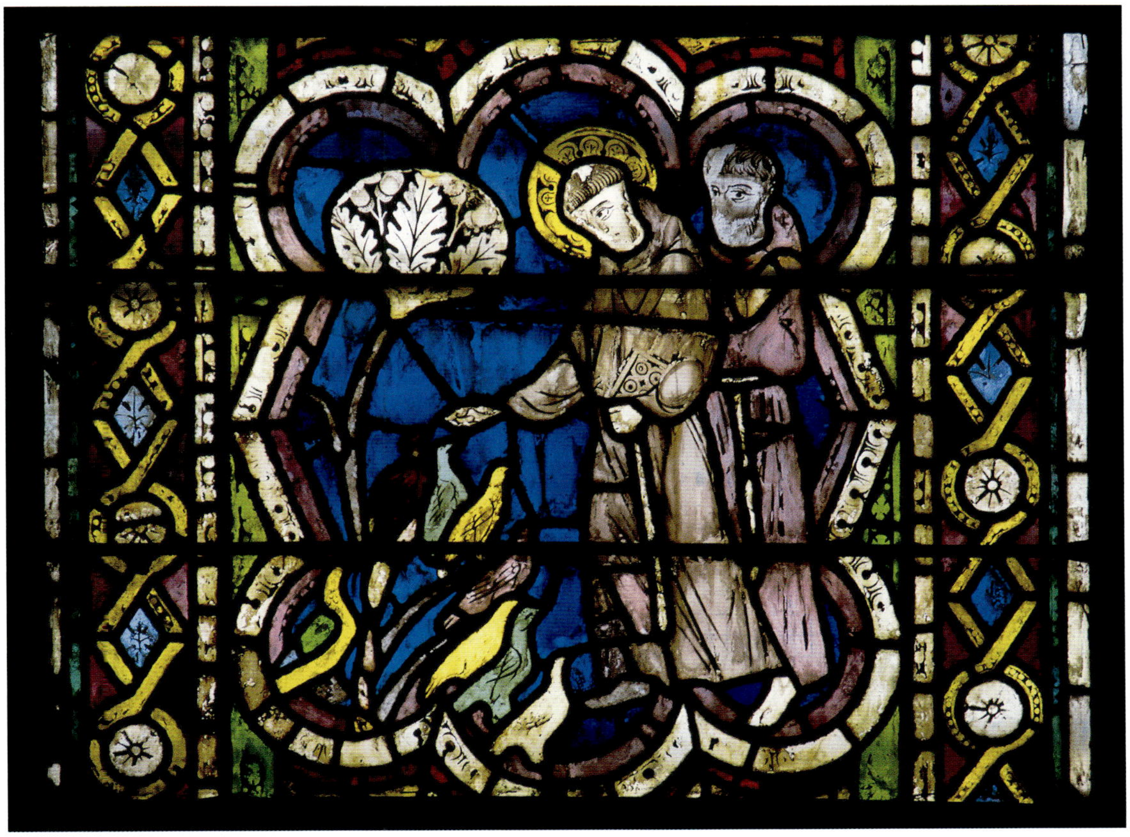

192 Maestro di San Francesco, *Preaching to the Birds*, *c.*1275–85, stained glass, fourth bay, north wall of the nave, Upper Church, Basilica of San Francesco.

the word of preaching, only the Lesser Brother has a cup on top of the grain. He alone is able to "feed" others "with the bread of life and understanding and the water of wholesome wisdom to drink [Sirach (Ecclesiasticus) 15:3]".'[145] John turned the story of Benjamin's cup into a polemic on the superiority of Franciscan ministry. The juxtaposition of *Saint Francis in Ecstasy* and *Joseph in Egypt* enabled those viewers who knew the significance of the cup to recognize it as a gloss on the scene below, signifying the gift of divine wisdom, which Francis had received.

The 'Vita activa': Solving the Problem of Saint Francis

The shimmering cloud surrounding the ecstatic Saint Francis on the north wall and the light illuminating the praying Saint Francis on the counter-façade communicate the same message. The saint was instructed not by human teachers but through divine revelation. The point is underlined throughout the sequence of four consecutive scenes dealing with Francis's *vita activa*: the *Preaching to the Birds*, the *Death of the Knight of Celano*, *Preaching before Pope Honorius III* and the *Apparition at Arles*. In the *Preaching to the Birds*, Francis has no preaching aid other than the Holy Spirit, in the fluttering form of the descending dove. This was evidently a deliberate choice: as has often been noted, the plaster patches on which Francis's hands are painted were hacked out and replaced during the execution of the cycle, which suggests that the friars considered his preaching gestures important.[146] The earlier versions of the scene in the Basilica, in the Upper Church glass (fig. 192) and in the fresco in the nave of the Lower Church (see fig. 107), both depict the preaching saint clutching a book.[147]

The parallel that is made on the counter-façade between Saint Francis and the apostles at Pentecost can also be found elsewhere. Discussing divine illumination in the *Tractatus de luce*, Bartholomew of Bologna remarked that often it is the most devoted men, approaching God by means of excellent contemplation and fervent love, who receive the clearest understanding, even though they know little of the secular sciences.[148] A marginal note on the manuscript, in another hand, comments: 'This is shown by the apostles. When they were inflamed by love at Pentecost, they understood everything . . . and they had divine knowledge; just as the unlearned Francis ['Franciscus idiota'] understood great things, so that all men were amazed.'[149] While the description of Francis as 'idiota' might sound derogatory to modern readers, the phrase was a reference to the apostles. The preaching of Saint Peter and Saint John in Jerusalem after Pentecost caused an immediate stir and they were arrested by the temple authorities, who knew them to be illiterate and ignorant men ('sine litteras et idiotae').[150] The comparison was made by Bonaventure in the *Legenda maior*: 'For the exalted Teacher is accustomed to opening his mysteries to the simple and the little ones, as first appeared in David, the best of the prophets; and then in Peter, the prince of the apostles; and finally in Francis, the little poor man of Christ. For when these simple men were unskilled in letters, they were made illustrious by the teaching of the Holy Spirit.'[151] This became a standard trope. Several of Matthew of Acquasparta's sermons also place Saint Francis 'illiteratus et simplex', taught only by the Holy Spirit, within the tradition of the apostles, most of whom were also 'illiterati, simplices'.[152]

The constant reiteration of this notion by Bonaventure and Matthew suggests some underlying anxiety about Saint Francis's credentials for pastoral ministry, which becomes understandable if we consider the rapid development of the Franciscan Order over the course of the thirteenth century. In 1209 or 1210, Saint Francis had received for his fledgling order a verbal mandate from Pope Innocent III to preach penitence. The first brothers were virtually all laymen and preaching was normally the sole preserve of priests. Francis himself never entered the priesthood and never received formal theological instruction, but over the subsequent decades the Order rapidly became clericalized. In the period when the Saint Francis cycle was being created, the typical Franciscan preacher would no longer have been a lay brother, but a priest trained in the new academic method of the *sermo modernus*. This was a thematic sermon liberally peppered with biblical authorities and expounded through a disciplined system of divisions and distinctions.[153] He would have had to acquire proficiency in preaching techniques, four years of theological instruction in a *studium*, and sufficient maturity before being examined and licensed by his provincial chapter.[154] Representing Saint Francis in the Assisi cycle as a model Franciscan preacher of the late Duecento would therefore not have been easy.

At the same time, the whole issue of Franciscan pastoral ministry was politically sensitive. Their level of training made the friars the most effective preachers of the age, but their success caused friction with the secular clergy, who saw them as rivals. A conflict flared up in the 1280s and 1290s after Pope Martin IV issued the bull *Ad fructus uberes* in 1281, which granted the Franciscan and Dominican orders the privilege of preaching and hearing confessions without restriction (previously, friar–preachers and confessors had required permission from their local bishop).[155] This provoked vehement protests from the seculars, especially in France and England. Representatives of the French bishops were in Italy in 1289–90 to petition Pope Nicholas IV, but their protests were contemptuously rejected in November 1290 at the Council of Paris, under the presidency of Cardinal Benedetto Caetani.[156]

It is possible, therefore, to see the three scenes that follow the *Preaching to the Birds* in the Saint Francis cycle as something of a manifesto for the Franciscan pastoral mission. Each deals with a different aspect of preaching. In the *Death of the Knight of Celano* (fig. 193), Saint Francis, a guest at dinner in a noble household, exhorts his host to confess his sins because his death is imminent.[157] The saint stands up from the table to pronounce his prophecy; on the right, the body of the knight lies where he has fallen, supported by his stricken womenfolk. The knight's confession is not pictured, and this crucial part of the narrative is explained only in the titulus below the scene. Perhaps the planners of the cycle thought it more important to exploit the opportunity for a visual link with the lamentation over the dead Christ in the Passion cycle in the tier above (fig. 195). They may also have wanted to avoid replicating the deathbed confession of the woman from Benevento, at the far end of the same wall (see fig. 133).[158] Be that as it may, the omission meant that another problem could be avoided. For all that he exhorted the knight to repent, Saint Francis could not have administered the sacrament, because he was not ordained.[159] The confessor must have been the friar who is seated at the dinner table (fig. 194).[160] His presence there would have been

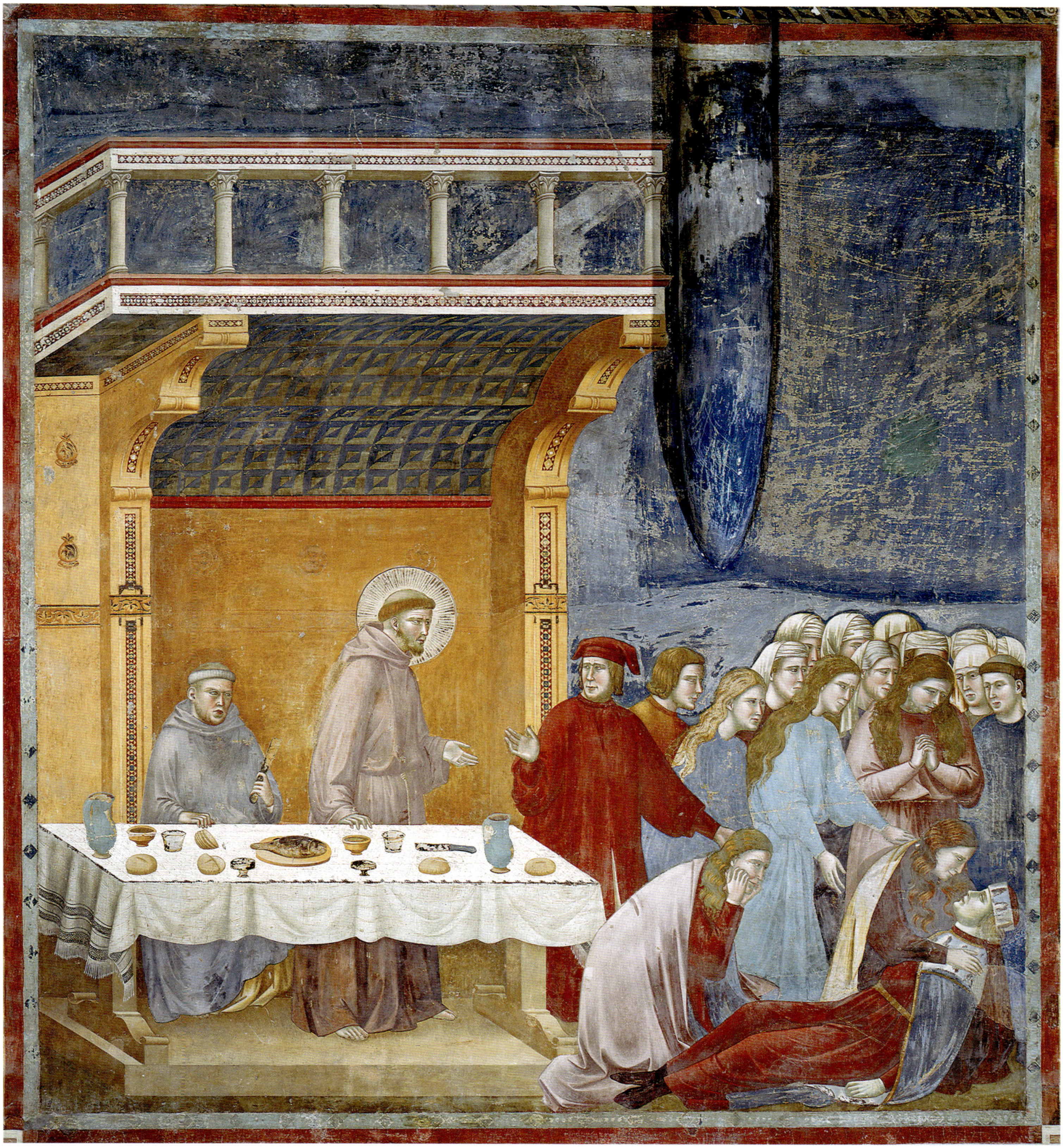

193 *Death of the Knight of Celano*, Scene 16 of the Saint Francis cycle, *c.*1290–96, fresco, south wall of the nave, Upper Church, Basilica of San Francesco

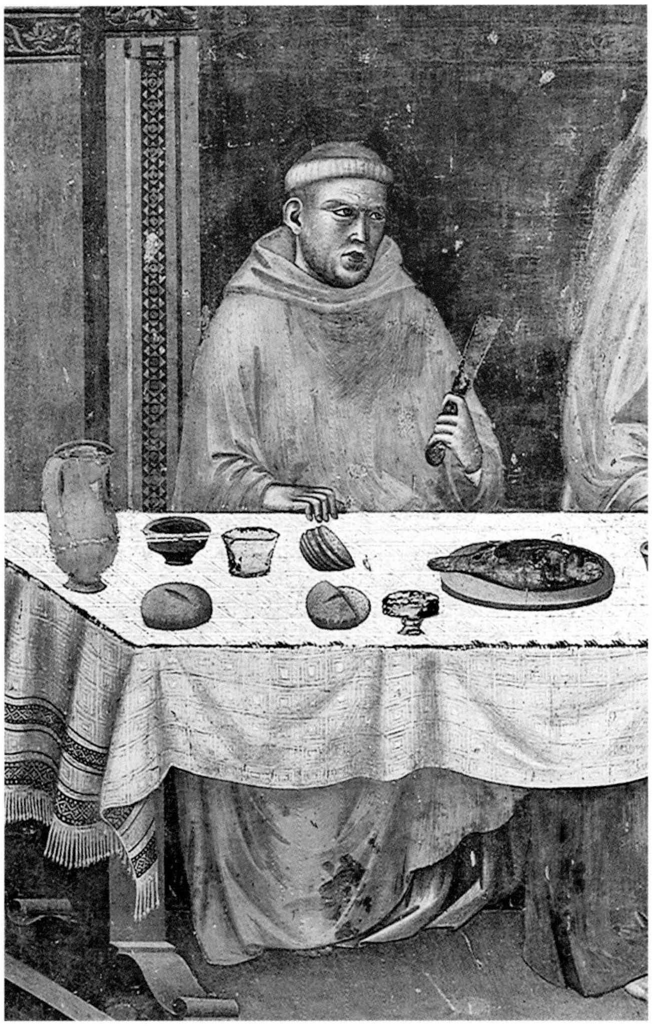

194 Friar–confessor, detail from *Death of the Knight of Celano*, Scene 16 of the Saint Francis cycle, *c.*1290–96, fresco, south wall of the nave, Upper Church, Basilica of San Francesco.

perfectly plausible: Franciscan confessors were granted the privilege of taking their meals outside the convent refectory in the line of duty, because they needed to be able to hear confessions in the domestic setting, especially in the case of deathbed repentance.[161] With his lined face and grey hair, Francis's companion is an accurate portrait of a Franciscan confessor. According to provincial regulations, an aspiring confessor had to be well trained, of good character and at least thirty years old before he could apply to his provincial minister to be licensed.[162]

The central place in the preaching triplet is given to the *Preaching before Pope Honorius III* (fig. 196). According to Bonaventure, Francis had composed and memorized a sermon, but when he stood up to begin the homily his mind went blank. However, after invoking the grace of the Holy Spirit he began to preach with eloquence and power.[163] The episode was elaborated from a much shorter version in Celano's *Vita prima*, and it seems likely that the minister general was responding to two considerably less flattering accounts by the Dominican Stephen of Bourbon, one a more concise version of the other, both written before 1261.[164] In Stephen's lengthier account, some prominent prelates in Rome wanted to hear Francis preach because they knew him to be a simple man of little learning, 'who had usurped that office for himself'. A high-ranking cleric who was a friend of Francis, fearing his disgrace, supplied him with 'a soundly composed and well ordered sermon'; when Francis forgot his memorized homily, rather than being inspired by the Spirit, he opened his psalter and extemporized upon the first passage that met his eyes.

At Assisi, both image and text insist on the direct inspiration of the Holy Spirit. Once again, the preaching Francis has no book. This is one of the places in the nave where there are meaningful parallels between the Saint Francis cycle and the biblical stories on the uppermost tier of the wall. The *Baptism of Christ* (fig. 197) appears vertically above the *Preaching before the Pope*. Although the fresco is badly damaged, the dove of the Holy Spirit can still be made out as it descends towards Christ and, by association, to Saint Francis directly below. Diagonally above the preaching saint, in *Christ among the Doctors* (fig. 198), the boy Jesus amazes the scholarly Jewish priests of the temple with his wisdom, as Francis does the cardinals of the papal curia. The text below the fresco of Saint Francis preaching stresses that he spoke 'not in the words of learned human wisdom, but from the divine spirit', a reference to Saint Paul's first letter to the Corinthians.[165] The composer of the titulus knew exactly what he was doing: by using these words, he was equating Saint Francis with the apostle.[166] Finally, the significance of the episode is further emphasized through its placement directly opposite *Saint Francis in Ecstasy* (see fig. 190) on the north wall. As we saw above, Bonaventure had described the enraptured Francis as being carried into God and having 'unknown and

facing page 195 View of the fourth bay, south wall of the nave, Upper Church, Basilica of San Francesco.

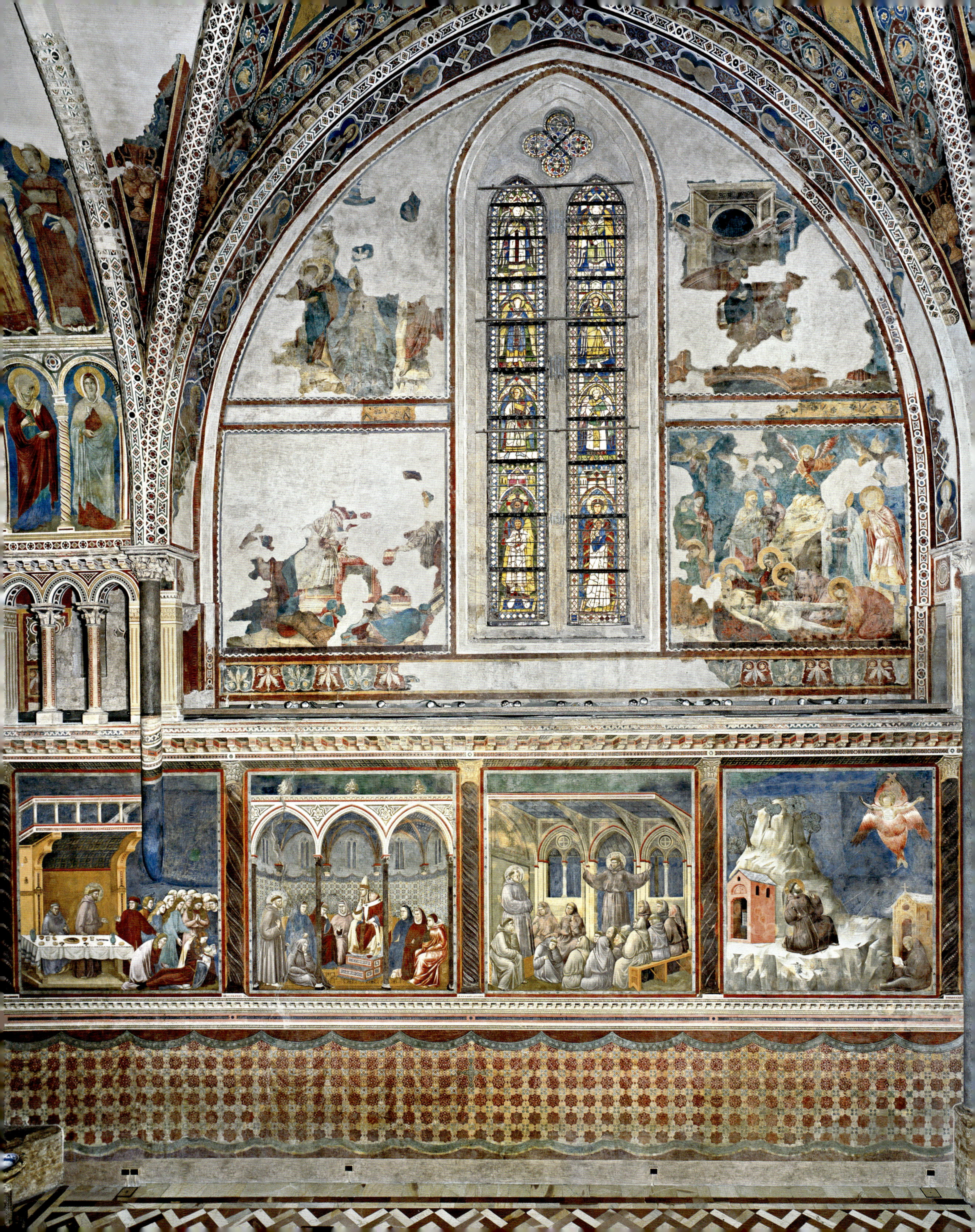

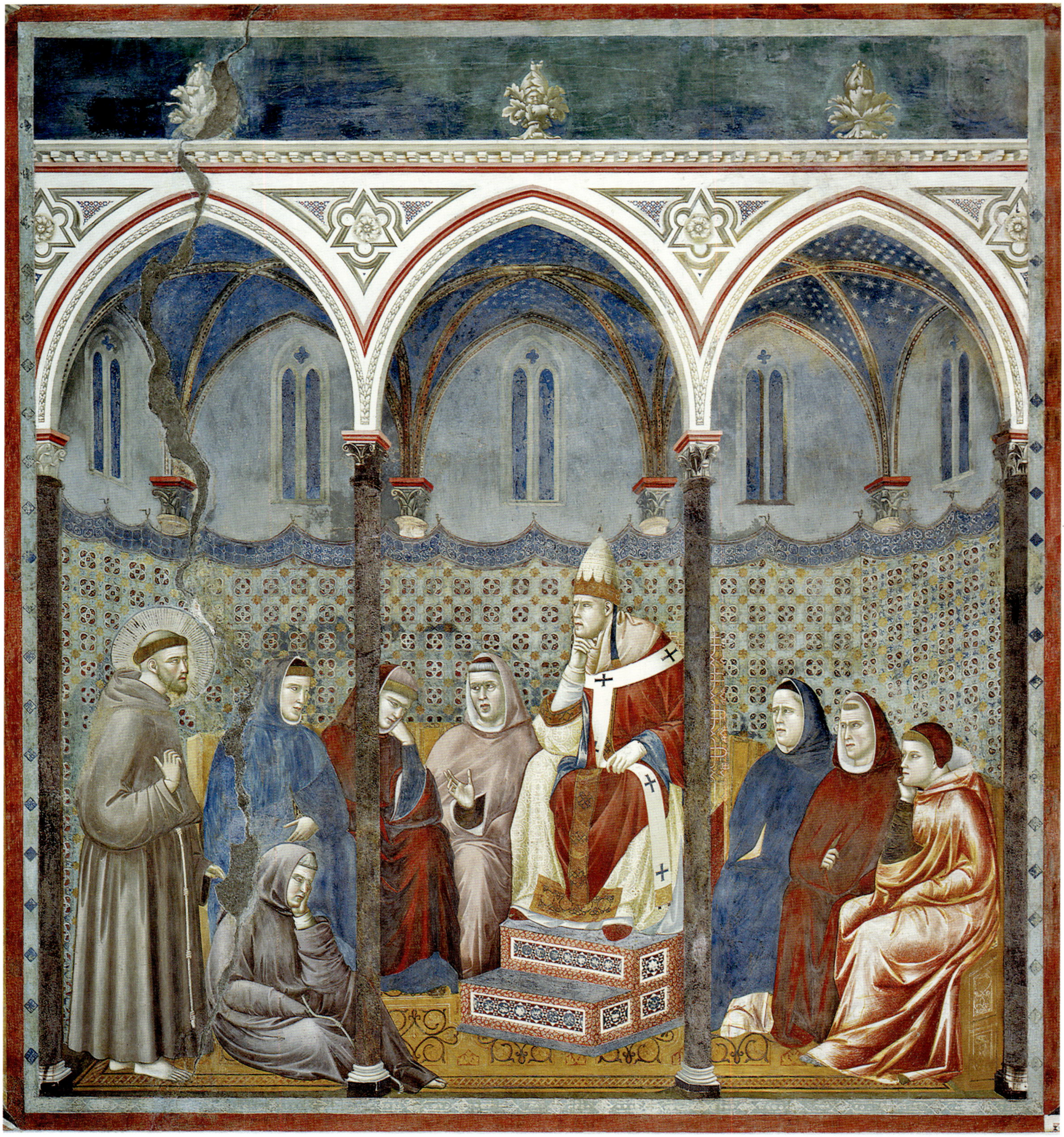

196 *Preaching before Pope Honorius III*, Scene 17 of the Saint Francis cycle, *c.*1290–96, fresco, south wall of the nave, Upper Church, Basilica of San Francesco.

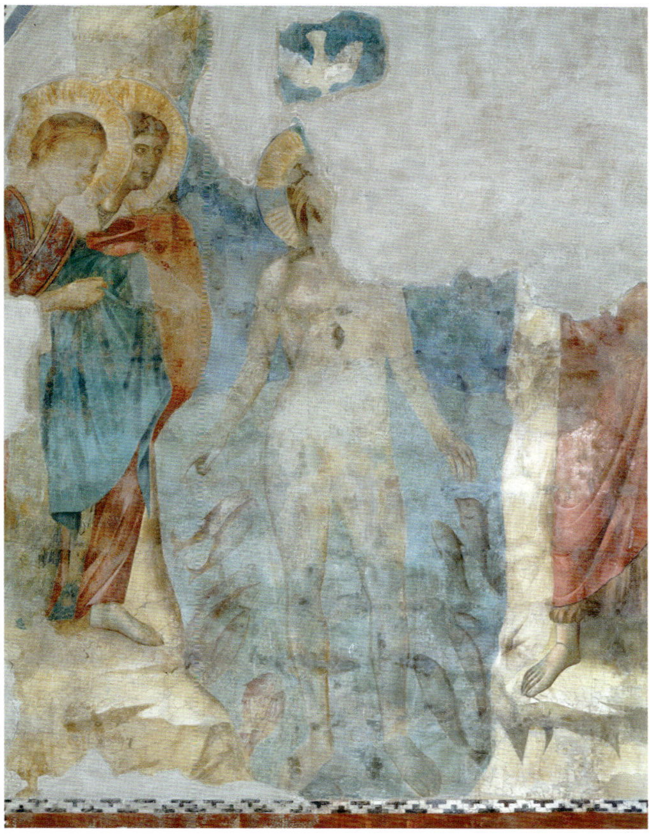

197 *Baptism of Christ* (detail), New Testament cycle, *c.*1288–91, fresco, fourth bay, south wall of the nave, Upper Church, Basilica of San Francesco.

hidden secrets of divine wisdom' revealed to him by Christ – an experience that Matthew of Acquasparta had likened to that of Saint Paul.

The third preaching scene is the *Apparition at Arles* (see fig. 93). While Saint Anthony of Padua was preaching in the chapter house at Arles, Francis, though absent in the flesh, appeared in the doorway, blessing his brothers and filling them with a great consolation of the Spirit. The situation would certainly have spoken to the experience of late Duecento friars. Sermons were a primary tool in their education, from the convent schools to the universities. The fifty-four seasonal sermons in Bonaventure's edited collection were all delivered to his confrères in chapter.[167]

How should we interpret the three scenes of preaching that are depicted in this bay? Brooke argued that by placing the *Preaching before the Pope* and the *Apparition at Arles* side by side, the cycle shows two different facets of Minorite preaching, the charismatic homily of Saint Francis and the doctrinal preaching of Saint Anthony, giving equal weight to both.[168] Frugoni, on the other hand, believes that the *Apparition at Arles* stresses the importance of theological training for friar–preachers. Unlike Francis, they could not rely on the intervention of the Holy Spirit to rescue them. In order to preach effectively, the friars must study and be ordained; Francis's blessing signals his approval of the new direction the Order has taken. It is Anthony rather than Francis who is being offered to the Franciscans as a model here.[169]

A useful way to differentiate these scenes is by the type of people being addressed. The successful preacher had to be capable of adapting his material to the appropriate intellectual level of his audience. John of Wales addressed this issue

198 *Christ among the Doctors* (detail), New Testament cycle, *c.*1288–91, fresco, fourth bay, south wall of the nave, Upper Church, Basilica of San Francesco.

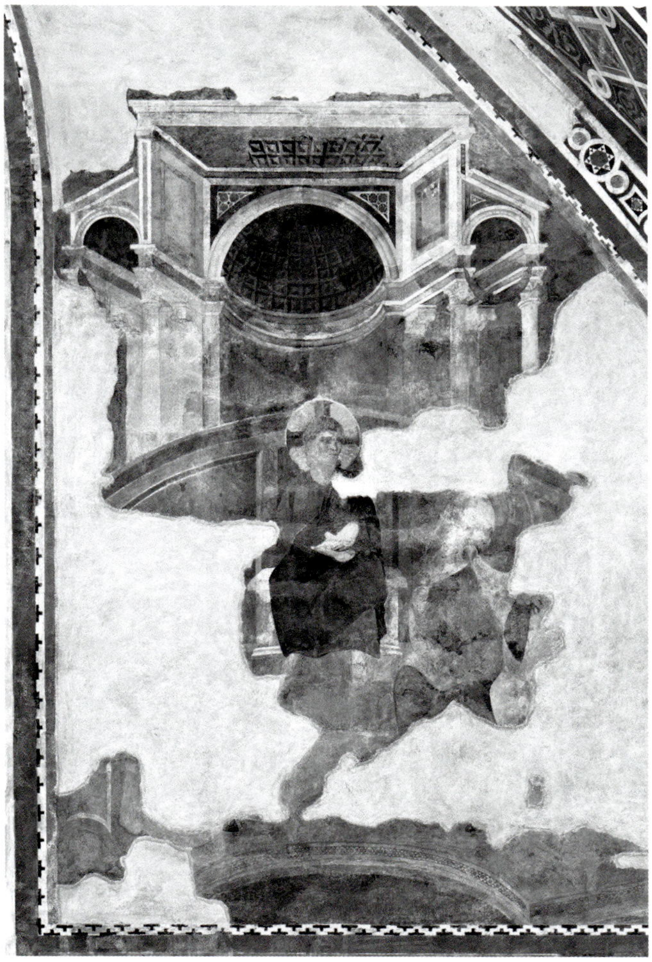

in the Prologue to the *Communiloquium*, his popular manual for preachers, completed *c.*1270.[170] A preacher should know how to speak usefully to those of every station in life, to instruct them doctrinally and admonish them effectively – not only by means of the declamatory sermon, but also through everyday encounters, because 'often familiar and mutual conversation is more effective for instructing than public preaching or lecturing'.[171] Christ did not only preach publicly in the city and the temple, but also at the dinner table, using parables. As an example, John described Christ, while having supper in the house of Simon the Pharisee, teaching his host about repentance and forgiveness.[172] Even a university lector of theology like John of Wales, therefore, would have regarded the example of Saint Francis in the home of the knight of Celano with approval.

But the next scene presents a completely different situation. Addressing the pope and his cardinals would have called for a full-blown academic sermon of the kind the historical Francis certainly never gave. Many of the manuals on preaching technique (the *artes praedicandi*) that were produced for the education of the friars categorized sermons into different types. These *artes praedicandi* did not ignore the inspired style of homiletic preaching practised by Saint Francis, but by associating it with the heroic beginnings of the Church they tended to present it nostalgically. They explained that the holy Doctors of the Church did not need to structure their sermons into themes and divisions, because they were inspired directly by the Holy Spirit. But, as the Franciscan master of theology Géraud du Pescher warned his early fourteenth-century readers: 'modern men, who are not saints, nor illuminated by divine grace, before they preach need first to order their preaching material'. If their preaching is to be fruitful they must study and prepare, rather than improvising or presuming on divine help.[173] An opinion written between 1286 and 1292 by another Franciscan master, probably Raymond Rigaud, sets forth the same view more bluntly. Any friar accepting the office of preacher or confessor was obligated to do whatever he could to acquire sufficient learning to equip himself for the role; not to do so would be a most grievous sin. As Şenocak puts it: 'Preaching by an uneducated friar, even with a disposition for holiness, is simply out of the question.'[174]

Thirty years earlier, Bonaventure had already expressed similar sentiments, in his earliest recorded sermon on Saint Francis, preached in 1255 to the friars at Paris, on the text 'Learn from me.' Saint Francis could teach others without error, because he had been taught by divine revelation. The proof was in his own life: when he had to prepare something himself, or was taught by another man, Francis had nothing to say (this was presumably a reference to his preaching before Honorius III). In this, however, the saint was more to be praised and wondered at than imitated. 'Hence it is not without reason that his sons attend the schools. To arrive at knowledge without a human teacher is not for everyone, but the privilege of a few. Though the Lord himself chose to teach Saint Paul and Saint Francis, it is his will that their disciples be taught by human teachers.'[175] It seems clear, therefore, that the constant emphasis on divine relevation and the inspiration of the Holy Spirit throughout the sequence of scenes depicting Francis's *vita activa* was intended both to deal with the problem of his lack of learning and, by equating him with the apostles (especially Saint Paul) and early Fathers of the Church, to bolster his authority as a preacher.

But there is another strategy at work here too. In the cycle, Saint Francis's life does not end with his active ministry, but with the *Stigmatization* (see fig. 117), which follows the preaching scenes as the fourth scene in the same bay. In his Saint Francis sermon, Bonaventure candidly admitted that the saint's teaching could not have had lasting character in the eyes of others on the strength of Francis's own authority, 'for he was an uneducated merchant and no learned doctor'. Therefore, God himself confirmed it through the stigmata, that 'awe-inspiring seal from on high'. Ultimately the stigmata constitute the divine endorsement guaranteeing the authenticity and orthodoxy of Francis's teaching, his doctrine and his Rule.[176]

Regarding the Counter-façade

What messages would a Franciscan audience have drawn from the counter-façade and its adjacent scenes? This chapter has suggested that the *Miracle of the Spring* and the *Preaching to the Birds* could be viewed as exemplars of the *vita contemplativa* and the *vita activa*, reminding the friars of the dual aspect of their vocation. Whether or not Saint Francis is being offered as a model for imitation – either in the *Legenda maior* or in the Assisi cycle – is a question that has been much debated. Art historians have, for example, puzzled over why Saint Francis is shown barefoot throughout the cycle, while all his confrères wear sandals. Is this a recognition that Francis's practice of poverty was more perfect than that of his brothers, or an indication that times had changed?

The stigmatization is, as so often, at the heart of the matter. Dalarun argued that Bonaventure stressed Francis's unique identification with Christ in order to discourage the brothers from imitating him literally, and that is why the stigmata were given central place in his vision of Francis.[177] Similarly, Frugoni argued that the new iconography of the stigmatization in the Assisi cycle was a visual refinement of Bonaventure's image of a Francis whose sanctity was inaccessible, and who should be venerated rather than imitated.[178] But other scholars have taken a different view. Johnson, for example, believes that the stigmatization 'serves as a paradigm for those wishing to ascend by means of contemplation into God'.[179]

It is possible that the friars distinguished between different aspects of the saint. In the *Apologia pauperum*, written to defend Franciscan *imitatio Christi*, Bonaventure asked: If Christ is the exemplar of perfection, does that mean we should imitate him in all his actions? And the answer is no. Bonaventure argued that Christ did some things to demonstrate his power (like walking on water) or to demonstrate the light of his wisdom (like penetrating the secrets of people's hearts, or prophesying). No one can imitate these things, unless they are given a special privilege through grace. But other things that Christ did simply demonstrate the perfect way of life, and these should be copied, including his poverty, chastity, obedience and prayer.[180] The first three are, of course, the subjects of the traditional monastic vows, which also introduce the Franciscan Rule.[181] Could Saint Francis in the Assisi cycle have been seen in the same way? As a friar, Saint Francis is very often depicted demonstrating his special gifts of grace, but on the counter-façade he also demonstrates actions that are capable of being imitated: that is, prayer and preaching. On the other hand, the *Miracle of the Spring* and the *Preaching to the Birds* are so loaded with symbols – mountain, water, light, dove – that they seem closer to allegory than narrative. The interlocking of the Franciscan stories with those of Christ, the Holy Spirit and the apostles further elevates Saint Francis's actions to a higher level of meaning. Saint Francis goes beyond a personal model to become an institutional and metaphorical one.

The Order was founded on the Rule, written by Francis and confirmed by Pope Honorius III's bull. We have already noted the resemblance of the roundels of Saint Peter and Saint Paul on the counter-façade to the imagery of a papal seal. The two apostles function here as stamps of papal approval for the powerful Franciscan manifesto that surrounds them.[182] But the Rule was also confirmed by a higher authority, the seal impressed on the saint's body by 'Christ, the Supreme Pontiff'.[183] On the counter-façade, the praying Saint Francis is illuminated directly by Christ, while the Holy Spirit authenticates his apostolic preaching mission.

The group of learned Franciscans who devised the nave programme, and probably plenty of their brothers as well, would have remembered the words of Pope Nicholas III in *Exiit qui seminat* as they contemplated the counter-façade. This bull of 1279 was the most famous papal clarification of the Franciscan Rule. In the late thirteenth century *Exiit* was both the definitive interpretation of the Rule and a fundamental expression of the Order's identity within the Church. One of the Assisi lectors, Philip of Perugia, had helped to draft it.[184] The future Nicholas IV, as Cardinal Jerome of Ascoli, had ensured that copies were widely disseminated throughout the Order.[185] *Exiit qui seminat* upheld all those who professed

> that holy Rule, a rule founded on the teaching of the Gospel, confirmed by the example of Christ, and approved by the words and actions of his apostles, the founders of the Church Militant. This then is religion pure and undefiled before God the Father. Coming down from the Father of lights, it was passed on by his Son to the apostles in word and example, and finally, through the work of the Holy Spirit, it inspired blessed Francis and his followers. It bears then, so to speak, the witness of the whole blessed Trinity. To cite Saint Paul, it is something about which 'no one ought henceforth to make trouble' [Galatians 6:17], since Christ has sealed it with the brand marks of his passion, desiring to distinguish its author in a visible way with the signs of his own suffering.[186]

It is not only sunlight from the central rose window that beams down the nave from the counter-façade, but a luminous image of the identity and mission of the Franciscan Order at the apex of its power.

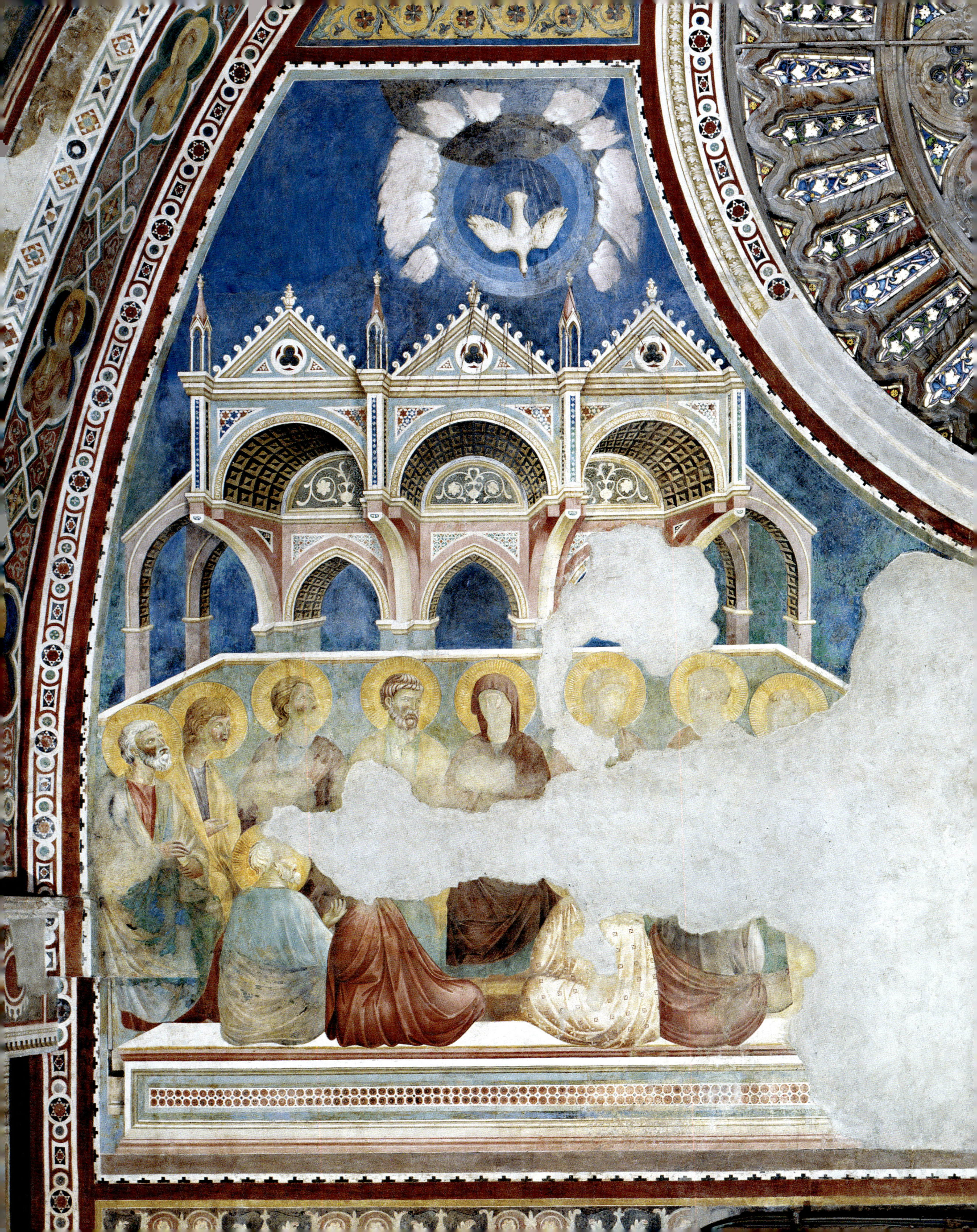

Conclusion

In the spring of 1295 Franciscans from every province of the Order converged on Assisi at Pentecost to attend the general chapter meeting hosted by the Sacro Convento. Whether all the frescoes of the Upper Church were finished by then we do not know, but such a large and prestigious gathering of the Order would have provided a strong incentive to complete the mural decoration and clear the nave of painters' scaffolds and materials. The earlier general chapter held at Assisi, in 1279, had probably been the spur for the realization of Cimabue's vault of the Evangelists above the high altar. Sixteen years on, the eyes of the assembled friars would have been dazzled by a spectacle of colour, light and artistic virtuosity far beyond anything seen before in a Franciscan church.

We may picture the scene, with hundreds of friars filling the Upper Church for the Pentecostal Mass on Sunday 22 May 1295.[1] Directly above their heads, the life-sized figures of the Saint Francis cycle would have appeared as a mythical extension of the congregation. For some friars, the frescoes must have been a triumphant assertion of the unique nature of Francis's sanctity and the destiny of their Order; for others, a betrayal of everything the *poverello* had most cherished. The impact of such splendour resonated down to 1312, when the leaders of the Franciscan community had to acknowledge the 'sumptuousness' of the paintings in their mother church and to defend them on the basis that they had been commissioned by Nicholas IV rather than the Order.

In the absence of eye-witness accounts, any discussion of responses to the newly painted Saint Francis cycle is necessarily speculative. But the general chapter of 1295, as the greatest assembly of senior and learned Franciscans in Assisi at the end of the Duecento, was in many ways the ideal audience for the frescoes. A core proposition of this book is that the Saint Francis cycle can be properly understood only within the intellectual and spiritual world of the Franciscans, in the very particular moment of Nicholas's papacy and its immediate aftermath. When the Franciscan pope instructed the Assisi friars in 1288 to renew their church, issuing privileges and indulgences to finance the work, he was following in the footsteps of previous papal supporters of the Basilica, notably Innocent IV. Under Nicholas, however, the ties that bound Rome and Assisi were tighter than they had ever been

facing page 199 *Pentecost*, New Testament cycle, Upper Church, Basilica of San Francesco (detail of fig. 166).

before, or would ever be again. During his four-year pontificate, the major building and decorative programmes that Nicholas instigated – in Rome at the Lateran and Santa Maria Maggiore, as well as in Assisi – consistently used the image of Saint Francis to assert the prominence of the Friars Minor at the heart of the Latin Church.

This book has cast Nicholas IV as the catalyst and facilitator for the design and execution of the fresco cycles in the nave of the Upper Church, rather than their hands-on patron. What we know of Nicholas's Roman projects indicates a man who understood and exploited the potential of art to communicate important and complex ideas. The visual amalgam of Church history and Franciscan ideology fashioned by Nicholas in Rome would be perfected at Assisi by the 'wise brothers' of the Umbrian province. The terms of the *Reducentes* bulls were very clear: in 1288 Nicholas delegated the implementation of the wide-ranging programme he had in mind for the Basilica to the Franciscan community of the Sacro Convento. Assisi-based friars, rather than the pope or his cardinals, were most probably the true intellectual authors of the nave frescoes.

The leaders of the Umbrian province in the crucial years around 1290 had impeccable credentials for the task. They were able administrators and men of learning: university trained, academically minded and well travelled. They were able to draw on a wide range of cultural experiences, and all the latest trends in Franciscan thought and literature. Brother Philip of Perugia, for example, had helped to compose the definitive papal commentary on the Franciscan Rule, *Exiit qui seminat*, before investigating the circumstances of the stigmatization and composing a short but influential treatise from his findings. We have no positive evidence connecting Philip with the mural decoration of the Upper Church but he was – unlike most of the other candidates who have been associated with the programme's design – in the right place at the right time to make a contribution, documented as a lector at the Sacro Convento in 1287. Philip is only one of several eminent friars to emerge from the Assisi archives and there were doubtless others whose identities are now lost to us.

The nave scheme was forged from a mixture of tradition and innovation. The concept of the three registers of narratives, the two biblical cycles in double parallel with the Saint Francis stories below them, again had its roots in Rome, in the extensive early Christian cycles in the apostolic tomb basilicas of Saint Peter's and San Paolo fuori le Mura. But the friars at Assisi boldly diverged from these prestigious models, especially in the middle register of each longitudinal wall. The reduction in number and the reordering of the Roman scenes, as well as the addition of new ones, provide strong evidence for believing that the entire nave programme was conceived from the start as a single holistic scheme. The prime organizing principles were to draw correspondences between Saint Francis and the Old Testament patriarchs on the north wall, and between Saint Francis and Christ on the south wall and the counter-façade. Within this overarching framework, the arrangement of the particular scenes revolved around certain fixed points: the interlocking of the *Stigmatization* and *Death of Saint Francis* with the *Crucifixion* and *Lamentation* on the south wall; the typological paralleling of the saint with the patriarchs of Genesis on the north; the creation on the counter-façade of a *contemplativa–activa* diptych that presented a dynamic relationship between Francis, the ascending Christ, the apostles and the Holy Spirit. These choices must have been some of the first decisions taken during the planning of the fresco programme.

The key relationships in the Upper Church scheme were established by the confident alignment of scenes from the different cycles, so the gush of water in the *Miracle of the Spring* (Scene 14; see figs 164 and 168) was forced into the extreme lower right corner of the picture, plumb below the descent of the Paraclete in the Pentecost above (see fig. 166). Rather than cascading out of the fresco's lower border, the stream veers sideways, exiting to the right and implicitly flowing into the second half of the Saint Francis cycle. Elsewhere the designers drew symmetries across the space of the nave: one especially clear case is that of Saint Francis's ascending soul in Scene 20 (see fig. 122), set directly opposite the empty throne vacated by Lucifer in Scene 9 (see fig. 124). As far as we can tell from surviving or recorded precedents, nothing like this level of geometric sophistication had ever been achieved before in medieval mural painting. In this respect the Upper Church programme moved far beyond any of the known Roman prototypes. The primary impulse for this feature of artistic innovation at Assisi was ideological: the desire to map Saint Francis's life against the Old and New Testament scenes above, to claim an epochal status for Francis alongside Christ and the patriarchs in the Christian scheme of history.

The Assisi cycle has often been characterized as an institutional statement, and we would concur with that. The portrait of Saint Francis projected from the nave walls is recognizably that of Bonaventure in the *Legenda maior*, the official life of the saint. One would hardly have expected anything else in the 'caput et mater' of the Order. But if Bonaventure's biography provided, metaphorically, the programme's underdrawing, the colour and shading came from elsewhere – from biblical exegesis, sermons, theological treatises and devotional tracts. The resulting ensemble of images served an ambitiously wide remit: honouring Nicholas IV as well as Saint Francis, while also advancing confident and grandiose statements about the Franciscan mission in the Church and the world. In the process, the example of Francis's life was elevated to new symbolic and allegorical planes of meaning.

The role of the papacy and the Franciscans in the creation and realization of the nave frescoes has been the focus of this volume, not the artists' contribution. Nonetheless, it remains true that for all their intellectual fascination, the nave frescoes would not be as celebrated nor so fiercely debated were it not for the enduring brilliance of their artistic achievement. Without concrete evidence from documents or preparatory drawings, exactly how the collaboration between friars and painters may have functioned as work progressed in the nave can only be hypothesized. Detailed conjecture on this question lies beyond the scope of this study, although we hope our book may stimulate further debate on the subject.

We shall limit ourselves here to some brief observations. The paralleling of the Franciscan and biblical cycles throughout the nave had its intellectual origins in long-established medieval practices of typology and in the hagiography of Saint Francis. But the *visual* success of the concept is due to the use of strong vertical and, especially, diagonal axes to link compositions in the different registers. As Smart recognized, it is the use of rising and falling diagonals that is so distinctive in the compositions of the Saint Francis cycle, and that gives them such rhythm and dynamism. This device may very well have been a serendipitous response to the practical problem presented by the Gothic architecture of the Upper Church. Only by means of diagonals could the central Saint Francis scene in each bay, always positioned below a window, ever be linked to a biblical scene on the tier above. And only by means of diagonals could scenes be pulled together across the colossal clusters of columns that separated the bays.

Was this visual expedient conceived by one of the friars, or by one of the painters? It may be more than coincidence that the first master to set his brush to the nave walls was both an artist and a friar and therefore uniquely qualified to make such a contribution. Was the suggestion Jacopo Torriti's? It is a tantalizing question, though ultimately unanswerable. The favoured artist of Nicholas IV, Torriti would have been able to contribute first-hand knowledge of painting in Rome, and he probably adapted his composition of the *Building of the Ark* from San Paolo (see figs 149 and 152) in order to launch a diagonal towards the *Dream of the Palace of Arms* in the Saint Francis cycle below. Whatever Torriti had in mind for the Franciscan scene, the link was left for other painters to complete. The friar–artist had already been recalled to Rome before work on the Saint Francis cycle began.

The degree of success with which the vertical and diagonal links between the tiers are achieved varies considerably in different bays. This suggests that the concept had been established at the outset and that each succeeding workshop on the scaffolds was instructed to employ it. Evidently some proved more able (or willing) than others to apply the schema effectively and creatively. One peculiarity of the changes in workshops was that the painters of the Saint Francis cycle had the difficult task of connecting their scenes to biblical cycles that had already been completed by other artists. That sometimes created problems. On the upper walls of the third bay, Torriti was replaced by the Isaac Master, whose revolutionary compositions have often led to his identification as the youthful Giotto. But the powerful horizontal connection between the two Isaac scenes, established by the meticulously duplicated bedchambers with matching oblique settings, arguably limited the options for dynamic compositional links with the Saint Francis scenes below.

*

Even before the painters had completed their work in the nave of the Upper Church, the second phase of the response to *Reducentes* was getting under way downstairs. Over the next quarter-century, the friars embarked on a radical rebuilding and expansion of the Lower Church: pulling down the *tramezzo* screen, building a series of side chapels and repainting the entire sanctuary. Compared to the painting of the Upper Church, the interventions in the Lower were more varied and more extensive, meeting the full breadth of Nicholas's call to 'maintain, repair, build, modify, enlarge, furnish, and decorate' the Basilica. By the time the chapter general gathered at Assisi in 1295, construction had already begun on the Saint Nicholas and Saint John the Baptist chapels off the transept.

The remaking of the Lower Church would take place under very different historical circumstances from the frescoing of the Upper Church. In May 1295 one era was drawing to a close and another was about to open. The death of Nicholas IV in April 1292 had been followed by a tumultuous period in the Roman Church. Factionalism between the Colonna and their rivals resulted in two years of deadlock in the college of cardinals, followed by the disastrous five-month papacy of Celestine V. Having persuaded the hapless Celestine to abdicate, Cardinal Benedetto Caetani was himself raised to the papal throne on Christmas Eve 1294, taking the name Boniface VIII. Despite these convulsions, the Nicholine project at Assisi remained relatively intact. The Colonna cardinals continued to support the Franciscans and protected Nicholas IV's legacy, including his artistic projects. They also wielded considerable political power in Umbria during the lengthy interregnum in 1292–4. In the Basilica, the friars honoured the Colonna in the closing scene of the Saint Francis cycle (see fig. 34), through the spiral Roman column that referenced the family's name and coat of arms.

The Colonna's revolt against Boniface VIII in May 1297 changed everything. The family's influence across central Italy was swiftly and systematically eradicated by the vengeful pope. This dramatic turnabout in fortunes would once more be visualized in Franciscan iconography. Around 1300 the Pisan Franciscans commissioned Giotto to paint a gabled panel of the *Stigmatization*, modelled on the scene in the Assisi cycle, for their church of San Francesco. The first of three smaller narratives below the main field depicts the *Dream of Pope Innocent III* (see fig. 158). This image also depends on the version in the Upper Church, but with two telling additions: Saint Peter stands beside the sleeping pope and a column of the Lateran's portico – the only column visible – violently breaks, cracking against the scene's border. Chiara Frugoni argued persuasively that this shattered column, the collapse of which threatens to destroy the church, is a reference to the fall of the Colonna.[2] Saint Francis, as ever, averts disaster by supporting the collapsing basilica. In fact, under Boniface, the Lateran – so symbolic for Nicholas IV and the Franciscans – would be sidelined. The plenary indulgence proclaimed by the Caetani pope for the Jubilee year of 1300 could be earned only by visits to Saint Peter's and San Paolo. The Petrine emphasis of Boniface's reign was underlined in Giotto's image by the presence of Saint Peter at the pope's bedside.

In the decades after Nicholas's death, the ties between Assisi and Rome slackened, especially once the papal court decamped to Avignon in 1305. Although San Francesco remained a papal church, Boniface VIII seems to have been the last pope to grant any substantial indulgences to the Basilica.[3] As the remaking of the Lower Church gathered pace in the early Trecento, different players would come to the fore. With the papacy now far away in France, the most significant figures would once again be those closer to hand; in particular the papal legate to Umbria, Cardinal Napoleone Orsini, and the Franciscan bishop of Assisi, Teobaldo Pontano. On the cusp of the fourteenth century, the Franciscan project at Assisi was about to shift its focus again, away from the visions of popes and towards the needs of pilgrims.

List of Abbreviations

AF — *Analecta Franciscana* (1885–), ed. Collegio San Bonaventura (Quaracchi)

ASC — Assisi, Archivio del Sacro Convento

BF — G. Sbaralea *et al.*, eds (1759–68). *Bullarium franciscanum romanorum pontificum: Constitutiones, epistolas, ac diplomata continens tribus Ordinibus Minorum, Clarissarum, et Poenitentium a seraphico patriarcha Sancto Francisco institutis concessa ab illorum exordio ad nostra usque tempora*, 4 vols (Rome)

Celano I — Thomas of Celano, *Vita prima Sancti Francisci*, in *FF*, pp. 275–424; Eng. trans. as 'The Life of Saint Francis' in *FAED*, vol. I, pp. 180–308

Celano II — Thomas of Celano, *Vita secunda Sancti Francisci*, in *FF*, pp. 443–639; Eng. trans. as 'The Remembrance of the Desire of a Soul' in *FAED*, vol. II, pp. 239–393

DBI — *Dizionario biografico degli Italiani* (1960–) (Rome)

FAED — Regis J. Armstrong, William J. Short and J. A. Wayne Hellman, eds (1999–2001). *Francis of Assisi: Early Documents*, 3 vols (New York)

FF — Ernesto Menestò, Stefano Brufani and Giuseppe Cremascoli, eds (1995). *Fontes franciscani* (Assisi)

LM — Bonaventure of Bagnoregio, *Legenda maior Sancti Francisci*, in *FF*, pp. 777–961; Eng. trans. as 'The Major Legend of Saint Francis' in *FAED*, vol. II, pp. 525–683

LMin — Bonaventure of Bagnoregio, *Legenda minor Sancti Francisci*, in *FF*, pp. 965–1013; Eng. trans. as 'The Minor Legend of Saint Francis' in *FAED*, vol. II, pp. 684–717

Notes

Introduction

1 The standard edition of the bulls is *BF* IV, pp. 22–3 (nrs 28 and 29). There is some confusion regarding their precise sequence. The *Bullarium* dates both to 15 May, but the copy of nr 29 conserved at Assisi is clearly dated to the preceding day ('Datum Reate II Id. Maii pontificatus nostri anno primo'). In fact, nr 28 seems to refer back to nr 29 ('per alias nostras litteras'), suggesting that the latter was composed first. The editors of the *Bullarium* seem to acknowledge this in their footnote: 'Nimirum sequentes per errorem postpositas.'

2 ASC, Bollario, VII/220 and 220bis, VIII/225 and 225bis.

3 *BF* IV, p. 23 (nr 29): 'Dilectis filiis Ministro Provinciae et Custodi Beati Francisci salutem et apostolicam benedictionem. Reducentes ad sedulae considerationis examen, quod continua Ecclesiae Beati Francisci de Assisio conservatio non modicum noscitur sumptuosa, et quod ad eam, in qua ipsius Sancti Corpus gloriosissimum requiescit, ac etiam ad Ecclesiam Sanctae Mariae de Portiuncula ob ipsius Sancti reverentiam innumera Fratrum vestri ordinis confluit multitudo; quodque Assisii Civitas brevi concluditur spatio et propterea minus sufficiens redditur ad subventionem Fratrum ipsorum necessitatibus impendendam; paternae solicitudinis studio ducimur, ut super his provisionis opportunae remedium apponamus. Cum itaque nostrae intentionis existat, ut omnia, quae in quibuscumque pecuniis, seu monetis in Ecclesiis, sive locis eisdem a Christifidelibus offeruntur, in hujusmodi conservationem ejusdem Ecclesiae Sancti Francisci, ac subventionem Fratrum ad Ecclesias confluentium supradictas, et eorum etiam, qui commorantur inibi, convertantur: Discretioni vestrae per Apostolica scripta mandamus, quatenus aliquam, vel aliquas personas idoneas, et fideles, de qua, vel quibus expedire videretis, et quae de vestro ordine non existant, nomine Romanae Ecclesiae, ac pro ipsa, quoties, et prout expedire putabitis, deputare, ac in ipsorum loco aliam, vel alias personas de Ordine non existentes eodem, sicut et quoties vobis videbitur, subrogare curetis, quae praedicta omnia, quae in quibuscumque pecuniiis, seu monetis in Ecclesiis, sive locis praefatis a Christifidelibus, prout praemittitur, offeruntur, solicite colligant, diligenter custodiant, et conservent. Datum Reate II idus Maii, Pontificatus nostri Anno Primo.' English translation by Daniel Hadas.

4 *BF* IV, p. 22 (nr 28): 'Dilectis filiis Generali Ordinis Fratrum Minorum et Provinciae Sancti Francisci Ministris salutem et apostolicam benedictionem.'

5 *BF* IV, p. 22 (nr 28): 'Tibi, Minister Provinciae, ac etiam dilecto filio Custodi Beati Francisci per alias nostras litteras iniungimus, ut aliquam, vel aliquas personas idoneas, et fideles etc.'

6 *BF* IV, p. 23 (nr 28): 'Gerentes itaque de circumspectione vestra fiduciam in Domino specialem, vobis, filii Ministri, et

utrique vestrum communiter, et divisim ex nunc praesentium auctoritate committimus, ut de oblationibus, seu eleemosynis supradictis possitis de discretorum Fratrum ejusdem Ecclesiae Sancti Francisci consilio facere conservari, reparari, aedificari, emendari, ampliari, aptari, et ornari praefatas Ecclesias, et loca earum, cum, et prout vestra discretio viderit expedire. Ac si aliquod de oblationibus, et eleemosynis praelibatis residuum fuerit, in necessitates Fratrum ad Ecclesias, et loca confluentium praelibata et eorum etiam, qui commorantur inibi, cum integritate converti, donec per Nos, vel Successores nostros Romanos Pontifices per eorum patentes litteras, et apostolica Bulla munitas aliud in hac parte contigerit ordinari. Datum Reate idibus Maii, Pontificatus nostri Anno Primo.' English translation by Daniel Hadas.

7 For the burial of Saint Francis below the high altar of the Lower Church, see Cooper (2005).

8 For the references to the Upper Church in Fra Vincent of Kielce's *Vita sancti Stanislai Cracoviensis episcopi*, see Nessi (1995) and Chapter 3 below for further discussion.

9 We shall address the remaking of the Lower Church and its early Trecento context in a future volume. For some preliminary observations, see Cooper (2005); Robson (2005); Cooper and Robson (2011).

10 We follow the majority of scholars in dating Cimabue's activity in the Upper Church to the pontificate of Pope Nicholas III Orsini (1277–80), rejecting the minority view advanced most forcefully by Luciano Bellosi, who argued that the Florentine painter's work was the first response to *Reducentes* and therefore dated to 1288 or 1289. For the latter position, see Bellosi (1998), pp. 160–67; for a full consideration of the arguments for the earlier dating, see Chapter 3.

11 '. . . nec vidimus in ecclesiis fratrum sumptuositatem magnam pictorarum nisi in ecclesia Assisii, quas picturas dominus Nicolaus IV fieri precepit propter reverentiam Sancti, cuius reliquie iacent ibidem.' We were the first scholars to bring the significance of this text for the dating and patronage of the Assisi frescoes to the attention of art historians, in Cooper and Robson (2003); we have since discussed this text more extensively in Cooper and Robson (2009). The passage was first published by Delorme (1945), p. 78. The manuscript source is Rome, Sant'Isidoro, Cod. 1/146, fol. 263r.

12 The integrity of the mural decoration has been scarred within living memory by the earthquake of 26 September 1997. After minor damage caused by an initial quake at 2.33 a.m., a more powerful tremor at 11.42 a.m. destroyed the Saint Matthew web of the vault of the Evangelists and the Saint Jerome web of the vault of the Doctors, as well as the upper registers of standing saints on the archivolt of the counter-façade. Two technicians and two friars were killed by the falling masonry. For a full photographic record of the damage to the vaults, see Bonsanti (1998), including a moving account of the quakes by the photographer Ghigo Roli (pp. 15–18). Following a painstaking sift through 300,000 tiny fragments of fresco identified from the rubble, reconstructed mosaics of the originals have now been replaced on the vaults, but at the time of writing, much work remains to be done; see the interview with the chief restorer of the Basilica, Sergio Fusetti, in *La Repubblica*, 23 June 2011.

13 See in particular Binski (2009) and Chapter 2 below for further discussion.

14 For recent statements of the case for the post-Arena dating of the Assisi frescoes, see de Wesselow (2005), and Schwarz with Zöschg (2008), pp. 238–54, 331–44, arguing for a dating between 1294 and 1298 for the painting of the vaults and upper walls of the nave, and *c.*1308 for the Saint Francis cycle.

15 For summaries of the technical data on the Saint Francis cycle, see Zanardi (2002), pp. 85–113; Zanardi (2004).

16 Zanardi (2004), p. 57, drew an analogy with the 'viridario' (or 'pleasure garden') of the papal palace in Avignon, which we know from documents was frescoed in 1365–6 by as many as twenty-one painters, led by Matteo Giovannetti.

17 The rather later analogy of Sassetta's high altarpiece for the Franciscan church in Sansepolcro (in north-eastern Tuscany), painted in 1437–44, may be instructive here. Sassetta's polyptych does not compare in scale to the Upper Church frescoes, but the extensive documentation associated with the commission reveals the close supervision exercised by the local Franciscan community over the design and iconography of its altarpiece. See Banker (1991); and now the definitive collaborative study of the altarpiece, Israëls, ed. (2009), especially the anthology of documents edited by James Banker in vol. II, pp. 566–83.

18 See note 11 above.

19 For this approach, see especially Ruf (2004).

20 Smart (1971).

21 Ruf (1974); rather confusingly, Ruf's volume was subsequently marketed in a new dust jacket with the different title *Giotto in Assisi: Nuova presentazione degli affreschi di Giotto nella Basilica Superiore* (the new emphasis on Giotto – doubtless intended to broaden the book's appeal – is ironic given that the painter is scarcely mentioned in the text).

22 In numerous publications, but pre-eminently Frugoni (1993).

23 Brooke (2006).

24 Neff (2006).

25 From the Annals of Worcester for the year 1290, referring to both Nicholas's pontificate and the contemporary archbishop of Canterbury, the Franciscan John Pecham (†1292): 'Fratres de Papa Nicholao et de archiepiscopo Johanne Cantuariensi

sic dicebant: "Solem et lunam sub nostro habitu nos habemus."' Luard, ed. (1864–9), vol. IV, p. 509.

26 Burr (2001) provided a magisterial account of how this basic fault-line in the Franciscan movement widened into division and heresy.

1 *Nicholas IV: A Franciscan Pope*

1 For Nicholas's patronage of art see Ciardi Dupré dal Poggetto (1991); Gardner (1997). Also fundamental is Gardner (1973c).

2 For Nicholas IV's biography, see Franchi (1990); Barone (2000); and, most recently, Brooke (2006), pp. 439–53. The suggestion that Jerome chose his papal name in homage to his mentor, Nicholas III, seems plausible; see Franchi, p. 95, quoting Chacón (1677), vol. II, p. 255: 'Hieronymus, qui in memoriam Nicolai III, a quo cardinalis creatus fuerat, Nicolai IV nomen assumpsit.'

3 For Jerome's reception of Mongol ambassadors at this time, see Franchi (1990), p. 92; Montgomery, trans. and ed. (1927), pp. 56–9.

4 According to the near contemporary *Historia ecclesiastica* by Ptolemy of Lucca: 'Hic [Jerome] dum essent cardinales inclusi in sancta Sabina ad electionem faciendam post mortem Honorii, dum alii cardinales fugissent locum propter infirmitatem, ipse solus ibidem remansit in loco infirmiori, et tamen evasit. Et causa fuit, quia in profunda aestate semper habuit prunas copiosas in aula sua et in camera et in aliis officinis.' See Ptolemy of Lucca (2009), p. 627; quoted by Franchi (1990), pp. 91–2 n. 5.

5 Franchi (1990), p. 92.

6 The surname Massi or Masci, although often cited in the modern literature, was not linked with the pope until 1586. As papal legate in Constantinople in the 1270s, he was simply named as 'Jerome of Ascoli' in both the Latin and Greek sources; for references and further discussion, see Franchi (1990), pp. 15–16. On the problem of Nicholas's armorial, see Le Pogam (2005), pp. 372–4. Discussing the unidentified shields accompanying an inscription of 1288 on the front of the loggia added to the papal palace in Rieti, Le Pogam cautions that the earliest evidence for Nicholas's coat of arms dates from the fifteenth century, 'et il n'en a probablement jamais porté, ce qui coïnciderait bien avec ses origines modestes et avec le fait qu'il ait été franciscain'.

7 In his first encyclical, *Judicia Dei*, of 23 February 1288, Nicholas recalled joining the Franciscan Order in his youth; *BF* IV, p. 2 (nr 1): 'Propter quod a nostrae juventutis auspiciis Ordinem Fratrum Minorum intravimus'.

8 The quotation is from Brentano (1974), p. 179.

9 Gregory X's letter *Qui miseratione*, of 24 October 1272, naming brother 'Hieronymum de Asculo' as the first of four ambassadors (all Franciscans) to the Byzantine emperor Michael VIII Palaeologus, is the earliest known reference to Jerome; see Cenci (1993), p. 486. Gregory's letter was transcribed in full by Wadding (1931), vol. IV, pp. 386–93 (Jerome reference at p. 391).

10 Jerome was apparently elected to this office at the first general chapter of Lyon chaired by Bonaventure, in 1272; see Franchi (1990), p. 207, citing Arnaldo of Sarrant's *Chronica XXIV generalium Ordinis Minorum*, compiled *c.*1374, *AF* III, p. 407: 'factus fuit Minister in provincia Sclavoniae'. For the possible significance of Dalmatian monuments for Jerome's later artistic patronage, see Gardner (1997), p. 1. However, given his short tenure of office, it is unlikely that Jerome had much opportunity to tour his province. On his election to the papacy, in the biographical introduction to *Judicia Dei*, he recalled having held several offices in the Order before becoming minister general; *BF* IV, p. 2: 'Occupati namque fuimus ex obedientiae debito in variis ministeriis dicti Ordinis, et demum in Ministri Generalis officio.'

11 Franchi (1990), pp. 44–5; Gardner (1997), p. 2; the description of the shipwreck is from Pachymeres (1865), cols 850–52; the ambassadors sailed from Constantinople on 11 March 1274, only finally disembarking at Cape Leuca on 5 April.

12 Franchi (1990), p. 51.

13 Jerome spent nearly thirty months in Paris from 1276 to 1279; see Franchi (1990), p. 57. He recalled these travels in the encyclical *Judicia Dei*: 'et inscii aliquid de hoc agi reformandae concordiae inter clarae memoriae Philippum Francorum, et Alphonsum Hispaniae Reges de mandato Sedis ipsius in ultramontanis partibus vacaremus'; *BF* IV, p. 2 (nr 1).

14 For the Pentecost seal, see Bihl (1911), discussing the impression reproduced here (attached to Gent, Rijksarchief, fonds Sint-Pietersabdij, charter nr 644), which is datable to 1254 and the ministership of John of Parma. Another impression, now in the Archives Nationales in Paris (J. 462, nr 28/11; Douët 9747), is still attached to a document from Jerome's ministership, reproduced by Franchi (1990), p. 53. This charter was composed in Paris on 17 February 1278, so Jerome must have taken the great seal with him to France; see Callebaut (1914), pp. 257–8. In 1279 the general chapter at Assisi required the minister general to use a new seal, as the old one was now too worn and could not be repaired; Bihl, p. 433.

15 Franchi (1990), p. 81.

16 Franchi (1990), pp. 59, 81–2. In his letter *Convenientibus vobis* of 16 May 1279, Nicholas III assured the friars gathering in Assisi that 'dilecti filii nostri Hieronymi Sanctae Romanae Ecclesiae Cardinalis' would arrive in time for the chapter ('ad

dictum Capitulum posset decenti tempore pervenire'); see *BF* III, pp. 393–4 (nr 116).

17 The source is the *Catalogus generalium ministrorum Ordinis Fratrum Minorum* of *c.*1304, attributed to Bonaventure's secretary, Bernard of Besse, which claimed that Jerome and his fellow Franciscan cardinal Bentivenga of Todi, 'presentibus et coagentibus', worked with Nicholas III, minister general Bonagrazia of Giovanni in Persiceto and other leading friars on the revision of the Rule at the papal residence of Soriano during the summer of 1279; see Bernard of Besse (1905–13), p. 667. The same passage was later integrated into the *Chronica XXIV generalium Ordinis Minorum*; see *AF* III, p. 369. Both are quoted by Franchi (1990), p. 83.

18 The source concerned is Nicholas Glassberger's *Chronica* (composed in the early sixteenth century from earlier sources), in *AF* II, p. 93, quoted by Franchi (1990), p. 83: 'fratrem Hieronymum cardinalem, qui nolens thesaurizare in terra, sed in coelis, pro declaratione super Regulam nostram et aliis privilegiis, quae sunt impetrata ad praesens pro universis et singulis Provinciis Ordinis, pretium quod ascendit, ut creditur, fere ad ducentas quinquaginta libras Turonenses facit solvi, ut omnes fratres recommendatum habeant specialiter in Missis et aliis orationibus apud Deum.'

19 Salimbene of Parma (1905–13), pp. 169, 498, quoted by Franchi (1990), p. 82: 'Matheus Rubeus est Ordinis fratrum Minorum . . . gubernator, protector et corrector; et papa Nicholaus [III] assignavit eum et Ordini dedit, cum prius domnum Ieronimum petivissent, qui fuerat Generalis minister eorum.'

20 Bernard of Besse (1905–13), p. 666, quoted by Franchi (1990), p. 255: 'lector non parve litterature'.

21 For Jerome's supposed corpus of works, see Franchi (1990), pp. 29–30; 254–5; the seventeenth-century Ascoli historian Sebastiano Andreantonelli (†1643) reported that fragments of a commentary on the *Sentences* by Jerome were extant in Ferrara, presumably in the Franciscan convent there.

22 Rome, Biblioteca Casanatense, Cod. 1184; the manuscript was copied in the early fourteenth century, probably in Venice or nearby, but was in the Marches by the early sixteenth; see Cenci (1995), esp. pp. 487–8, for the volume's likely provenance, and p. 491 for the hypothesis that Jerome as lector of the Aracoeli may have come to Bonaventure's attention when the latter was in Rome for the coronation of Gregory X in March 1272. For further discussion of Jerome's possible connection with the Aracoeli, see Bolgia (forthcoming).

23 Franchi (1990), pp. 56–7, quoting the *Chronica XXIV generalium* in *AF* III, p. 361.

24 Frugoni (2001), p. 387 n. 121, citing López (1908). See also Franchi (1990), pp. 55–7; Brooke (2006), pp. 442–4.

25 Franchi (1990), p. 85; Eubel (1913), pp. 9–10.

26 The causation was suggested by Gardner (1997), p. 3.

27 The cosmati altar frontal at Palestrina was first published by Gardner (1981), pp. 30, 35 n. 16, plate 3.3, who noted how the design incorporated the column device of the Colonna and suggested a date in the second half of the thirteenth century. Gardner was surely correct to associate the frontal with the high altar of the medieval cathedral, although it is now located in the chapel of San Lorenzo off the north side aisle; see Borzi (1984), p. 130. The Barberini coat of arms at the centre dates from after 1630, when the Colonna sold the city to Carlo Barberini, brother of Urban VIII. It may well have replaced an earlier Colonna emblazon. Virtually nothing else of the medieval interior survives, as the cathedral has been redecorated several times, the last and most comprehensive campaign being completed between 1882 and 1917. The integration of the column device on the Palestrina frontal finds a close parallel in an early medieval marble panel at Santa Prassede, Rome, where the three crosses of the original design were subsequently carved back to form columns, probably at the Colonna's behest in the late thirteenth century; for this suggestion, see Osborne (2012).

28 Franchi (1990), pp. 85–6.

29 Franchi (1990), pp. 86–8; Jerome is specifically named in two of Honorius IV's letters concerning the establishment of Margherita Colonna's community at San Silvestro: *Ascendit fumus* of 24 September and *In mandatorum suorum* of 9 October 1285; see *BF* III, pp. 544–6 (nr 11), pp. 548–9 (nr 15). The letters were addressed to 'Herminiae abbatissae monasterii Sancti Silvestri in Capite de Urbe', who may have been another member of the Colonna family. For the new foundation, see Barone (1983).

30 Bolgia (2003b), pp. 191–2; Gardner (2011).

31 The following discussion depends on Gardner (2011), pp. 461–5 (we are very grateful to the author for the opportunity to consult his text before publication). Gardner, p. 467 n. 29, transcribed the 1285 inscription accordingly: . . . ECCLESIA VESTRA QUE IN HONORE SANCTI SALVATORIS CONSTRUCTA ESSE DIGNOSCITUR ET QUE PER VENERABILEM FRATRUM NOSTRUM IERONIMUM EPISCOPUM PENESTRINUM . . . A PENESTRINO RENOVATA CAPELLA SACRATUR CUI TITULUS DATUS EST SALVATORIS . . . HOC CAMPANILE MURI PICTURA SEDILE TESTUDO ROSA PECTOQUERALIA CONGRUA FACTA TEMPORE SUBMODICO SUNT PLENE CUNCTA FACTA. . . . The marble panel is illustrated in Manacorda (1982), p. 106, fig. 33; the inscription was transcribed and translated in Manacorda (2001), p. 132, and also discussed by Bolgia (2003b), pp. 191–2.

32 Gardner (2011), p. 463, noted that rose windows were incorporated into the transept façades of the Franciscan basilica of

Santa Maria in Aracoeli, not far from San Salvatore in Pensilis, around this time, and would soon appear on the new façade of Santa Maria Maggiore, one of Jerome's major projects after his accession to the papacy.

33 Gardner (2011), p. 465.

34 In 1288 Pentecost fell on 16 May. The Franciscan Matthew of Acquasparta also figured among Nicholas's new creations, balanced by the Dominican Hugues Aycelin de Billom; see Eubel (1913), p. 11. For Pietro Colonna, see Waley (1982c), who rejected as anti-Colonna propaganda Giovanni Villani's claim that Pietro had married as a young man and consigned his wife to a nunnery on being raised to the cardinalate.

35 For a description of the celebrations and itineraries of Nicholas's first Easter as pope, see Montgomery, trans. and ed. (1927), pp. 68–71.

36 Le Pogam (2005), p. 76: 'Rappelons que Nicholas IV, tout comme Honorius IV, n'a résidé au Vatican que ponctuellement. Mais c'est justement en 1288, qu'il y a séjourné le plus longuement, notamment au printemps, pendants plus d'un mois, ce qui renforce la présomption d'authenticité du résumé.'

37 By the twelfth century, the feast of the Enthronement (22 February) was celebrated using the so-called *Cathedra Sancti Petri*, a ninth-century wooden throne, believed to be the original episcopal throne of Saint Peter; see Maccarrone (1971), pp. 15–16. In 1287, shortly before Nicholas's coronation, the Mongol ambassador, Bar Sauma, saw in Old Saint Peter's 'that throne of Mar Peter, on which they seat the Reverend Pope when they consecrate him'; see Montgomery, trans. and ed. (1927), p. 59. Its use for Nicholas's coronation is confirmed by an English source, the chronicle of Thomas Wykes: 'in festo Cathedrae Sancti Petri solemniter consecratus, jam Petri successor effectus, eodem die in eadem cathedra, qua princeps Apostolorum Petrus sedere promeruit, summo cum honore collocatus, mutato nomine pristino de Jeronimo vocatus est Nicholaus quartus'; see Luard, ed. (1864–9), vol. IV, p. 313, cited by Maccarrone, p. 26 n. 121. We are grateful to Chiara Frugoni for drawing the significance of the *Cathedra* for Nicholas's coronation to our attention.

38 For the movements of the curia during Nicholas's pontificate, see Le Pogam (2005), p. 20.

39 Ptolemy of Lucca (2009), pp. 627–8, noted that Nicholas IV 'in sancta Maria maiori suam curiam tenet'. Onofrio Panvinio's much later claim (1570) that Nicholas rebuilt the palace at Santa Maria Maggiore is probably unfounded; see Le Pogam (2005), pp. 270, 758.

40 Le Pogam (2005), pp. 570–71, citing Bortolan (1887); see, for example, p. 427: 'ipse papa [Nicholas IV] stetit apud Sanctam Mariam Maiorem et fecit audienciam literarum aput Sanctam Potencianam'. The calendar was compiled by Guidotto Spiapasto, procurator of the commune of Vicenza at the papal curia.

41 Pipino (1726), col. 728: 'Iste Romanus Pontifex [Nicholas] etiam in eodem Libello, qui intitulatur, *Incipit initium malorum*, describitur in hunc modum. Est enim inclusus Columnae, ita ut nonnisi caput appareat mithratum, et ante se alias duas habet columnas, in quarum una est caput avis, rostro sustinens nidum, in quo est caput senis Clerici. Est etiam ibi subscriptio talis: *Nicolaus Papa IV, confusio, error concitabitur.*' Cited by Gardner (1973c), p. 42 n. 10; Brooke (2006), p. 442.

42 De Angelis (1621), p. 55, quoting Giacomo Colonna's testament of 1321. Of the six priests endowed at Santa Maria Maggiore by Giacomo's will, two were to celebrate Mass daily 'in Cappella sanctae memoriae quondam Sanctissimi Patris Domini Nicolai Papae Quarti, quam dictus Dominus Cardinalis aedificari fecit ob reverentiam, et memoriam praedicti Sanctissimi Patris Domini Papae'. For Nicholas's tomb and its subsequent renewals, see Mann (1928), pp. 47–9.

43 For Giacomo's vision of his sister, experienced when he was studying law in Bologna, see Brentano (1974), pp. 177–8. Giovanni's life of Margherita was edited by Oliger (1935); see pp. 111–88 for Giovanni's text; Giacomo's Bologna vision is described at pp. 113–16. A miracle recorded in the other early life of Margherita Colonna, written by a nun of San Silvestro *c.*1288–92, gives a strong hint at Colonna attempts to promote her canonization. The story concerns the anger and subsequent repentance of a sick man from San Vito Romano, whose doctor had gone to Margherita's tomb in Castel San Pietro with Giovanni Colonna rather than treating him as promised. On hearing this, the sick man protested: 'Look here! It is embarrassing and degrading the way the lords of Colonna impetuously try to add their sister to the choirs of saints.' ('Videte ludibrium et funestum quod domini de Columpna violenter Sanctorum choris germanam ipsorum satagunt aggregare.'). The implication is that the doctor's visit was to verify miracles at Margherita's tomb for a possible canonization process. See Oliger (1935), pp. 83, 213–14; English translation adapted from Brentano, pp. 178–9.

44 Salimbene of Parma (1905–13), p. 169; quoted by Gardner (1973c), p. 1: 'domnus Jacobus de Columna, qui totaliter est amicus ordinis Fratrum Minorum'.

45 The surviving section of this mosaic, now in the Palazzo Colonna, was first discussed by Oliger (1911). It has traditionally been associated with the final side chapel in the left aisle at Santa Maria in Aracoeli, but its original location within the church is unclear. For full discussion and bibliography, see Bolgia (2007), pp. 78–94. Giovanni died at some point

between April 1292 and March 1294; for his biography, see Waley (1982b).

46 '"Vere", inquit, "hic ille est, qui opere et doctrina Christi sustentabit Ecclesiam."' The same wording is used by both Celano II, 17, and *LM* 3:10 (*FAED* II, pp. 256, 548; *FF*, pp. 459, 802).

47 On the competing mendicant claims for this legend in the thirteenth century, see Cannon (1982). The Dominican version first appeared in Constantine of Orvieto's legend of Saint Dominic composed in 1246–7; see Scheeben, ed. (1935), pp. 301–2.

48 For the Aracoeli mosaic and its likely connection with Nicholas IV, see Andaloro (1984b); Piazza (2010), pp. 130–31.

49 Andaloro (1984b), p. 33, fig. 7.

50 The subject matter of the Aracoeli mosaic was first recognized by Casimiro of Rome (1736), pp. 28, 493, who also recalled the presence of mosaics on the 'cornicione' of the façade, 'consumato a poco a poco dal tempo' and removed in sections by the workmen (or 'festaroli') who decorated the façade for major festivities; a large section was sold during the canonization of the Franciscan saints James of the Marches and Francis Solanus in December 1726 (the decoration of the Aracoeli for the occasion evidently rendered the upper sections of the façade accessible). Casimiro's remarks indicating the existence of a more extensive mosaic programme are confirmed by Pompeo Ugonio's description from the 1590s, quoted by Bolgia (2003b), p. 141. Ugonio mentioned traces of mosaic on the façade as well as on the upper right face (presumably the *Dream* mosaic). Bolgia (2003b), pp. 133–49, perceptively noted that the marble string-course moulding that extends across the façade and around its left corner is absent on the right face. This frees a much more expansive area of brickwork for the *Dream of Innocent III*, a further indication that the image was distinct from (and larger than) any other mosaics originally on the façade. For further discussion of the Aracoeli façade mosaics, see Bolgia (forthcoming) (we are very grateful to the author for discussing her research on the Aracoeli with us before publication).

51 On the scope of Nicholas IV's rebuilding programme at the Lateran, see de Blaauw (1994), vol. I, pp. 217–20; Brooke (2006), pp. 446–8; Claussen (2008), pp. 92–113.

52 Tomei (1990), p. 13; the unusual wording of Torriti's signature may result from the nineteenth-century reconstruction of the mosaic.

53 PARTEM POSTERIOREM ET ANTERIOREM RUINOSAS HUIUS SANCTI TEMPLI A FUNDAMENTIS REEDIFICARE FECIT ET ORNARI OPERE MOSYACO NICOLAUS PAPA IIII FILIUS BEATI FRANCISCI ET SACRUM VULTUM SALVATORIS INTEGRUM REPONI FECIT IN LOCO UBI PRIMO MIRACULOSE POPULO ROMANO APPARUIT QUANDO FUIT ISTA BASILICA CONSECRATA. ANNO DOMINI M CC NONAGESIMO I. Claussen (2008), pp. 96, 106–7, 341, adapting the transcription published by Forcella (1869–84), vol. VIII, p. 14 (nr 14). The current inscription, entirely renewed in the 1880s, ends NONAGESIMO II (1292), but most scholars prefer 1291 on the basis of Forcella and other earlier transcriptions. For Torriti's mosaic and its dating, see Tomei (1990), pp. 77–98.

54 The origins of this legend are obscure. A connection with the original dedication of the basilica seems unlikely, given the absence of this story from the legends of Saint Sylvester, pope between 314 and 335 and the Lateran's traditional founder. The *Liber pontificalis* likewise makes no reference to any such miraculous apparition at the Lateran. Philippe Lauer cautiously suggested that it may have been associated with the restoration of the Lateran basilica after Rome was sacked in the fifth century: Lauer (1911), pp. 215–16.

55 Torriti's apse mosaic was demolished between March 1883 and October 1884. Some sections of the 1:1 squeezes, taken before the mosaic's destruction, came to light a century later; see Tomei (1987). The lower register is also recorded through a late seventeenth-century drawing now in Edinburgh; see Gardner (1973b). For a full discussion of the nineteenth-century demolition, with marginally different dates, see Claussen (2008), pp. 92–104.

56 Tomei (1990), p. 91; Claussen (2008), p. 105.

57 For the likely appearance of the earlier apse mosaic, see Christe (1970).

58 On the water imagery in the Lateran apse mosaic, see Lloyd (2002), esp. pp. 41–4. The iconography of Torriti's mosaic is fully described by Claussen (2008), p. 108.

59 'Sicut areola praeparata ad inrigationes aquarum sic anima mea praeparata est ad te Deus.' Quoted (in English translation) by Lloyd (2002), p. 39.

60 See Chapter 7 below.

61 On the relationship of the *Deesis* with the earlier mosaic, see Matthiae (1967), pp. 347–54; Tomei (1987), p. 193; Tomei (1990), pp. 91–2.

62 FR[ATER] IACOB[US] DE CAMERINO SOC[IUS] MAG[IST]RI OP[ER]IS RECOMM[EN]DAT SE MIS[ERICORDIAE] XPI ET MERITIS BEATI IOH[ANN]IS. Tomei (1990), p. 78; Claussen (2008), p. 109. Jacopo is usually said to be breaking a piece of stone (or glass) into mosaic tesserae.

63 Claussen (2008), p. 108, believed the rectangle to stand either for a stone 'Reißboden' for inscribing 1:1 designs or a large sheet of parchment. For the recent discovery of a marble slab incised with an architectural design at the Aracoeli, see Bolgia (2003a).

64 On the identification of this friar as Jacopo Torriti, see Pace (1996), who convincingly allays the doubts expressed by

Tomei regarding the lack of an accompanying inscription beside the portrait, and the absence of 'frater' or similar expression of Franciscan identity from Torriti's signature in the main apse field. The set-square and compass are the traditional attributes of the architect. For the most recent analysis of the two friars, see Bolgia (2012), pp. 158–66 (with documents identifying Jacopo of Camerino at work on Orvieto cathedral from the late 1290s until the 1320s, at p. 162 n. 90).

65 Pace (1996), p. 214; endorsed by Claussen (2008), p. 108.

66 See below, pp. 36, 231.

67 Brooke (2006), p. 448 (however, the author rejected the identification of the unnamed friar as Torriti).

68 De Kerval, ed. (1904), pp. 125–6; the miracle appears among the additions made to the *Legenda prima* of Saint Anthony (also known as the *Assidua*) in a manuscript now in the Capuchin convent in Lucerne. The manuscript was copied in Switzerland in 1337, so the story must have been in circulation well before this date. It has often been cited in relation to Torriti's apse: Gandolfo (1983), p. 68; Tomei (1990), pp. 80, 94 n. 19. On the Lucerne manuscript, see Huber (1948), pp. 100–01; for a description see de Kerval, ed., pp. 16–17.

69 De Kerval, ed. (1904), pp. 125–6: 'Cui depingendae deputati sunt duos [*sic*] fratres minores in illa arte periti plurimum et experti . . . ex instinctu proprio depinxerunt imagines sanctorum Francisci et Antonii.'

70 De Kerval, ed. (1904), p. 126: 'Dimittatis illum sanctum, quia, ut videmus expresse, possemus plus perdere quam lucrari.'

71 The following reprises the arguments put by Gandolfo (1983), pp. 68–71.

72 After his coronation in Saint Peter's on 23 January 1295, Boniface immediately moved to the Lateran, where the curia is documented from 24 January until 7 May; see Le Pogam (2005), p. 20.

73 On the Lateran ambulatory, the so-called 'Portico Leoniano', see de Blaauw (1986–7), esp. pp. 106–7. De Blaauw presents evidence for an earlier ambulatory, dating from the fifth century, but concludes that any prior structure was completely demolished during the construction of Nicholas's new apse. Furthermore, he observes that descriptions of the apse exterior from the early 1860s (before its destruction) indicate that its four windows were originally longer, their lower edges being raised to make space for the ambulatory, suggesting that the passageway was not initially part of the Nicoline project.

74 This possibility, proposed by Gandolfo (1983), pp. 86–7, was rejected by Tomei (1990), pp. 86–8. The arguments on both sides were weighed by Claussen (2008), pp. 109–13. Much depends on the interpretation of a seventeenth-century drawing of the lower apse, now in Edinburgh.

75 Salvi (1990). For the panel's original location, see Claussen (2008), p. 137.

76 Salvi (1990), pp. 191–3; Claussen (2008), pp. 137–40, 342–3: + TERTIUS ECCL[ES]IE PATER INNOCENTIUS HORA QUA SESE DEDERAT SOMPNO NUTARE RUINA HANC VIDET ECCL[ES]IA[M] MOX VIR PANNOSU[S] [ET] ASP[ER] DESPECT[US] Q[UE] HUMERU[M] SUPPONE[N]S SUSTINET ILLA[M] AT PATER EVIGILANS FRANCISCU[M] P[ER]SPICIT ATQ[UE] VERE E[ST] HIC IN QUID QUE[M] VIDIMU[S] ISTE RUENTE[M] ECCL[ES]IAM Q[UE] FIDEM Q[UE] FERET SIC ILLE PETITIS CUNCTIS CONCESSIS LIBER LETUSQ[UE] RECESSIT FRANCISCI PROLES PRIMUS DE SORTE MINOR[UM] HIERONYMUS QUARTI NICOLAI NOMINE SURGE[NS] ROMANUS PRESUL PARTES CIRCUMSPICIT HUIUS ECCLESIE CERTA IAM DEPENDERE RUINA ANTE RETRO Q[UE] LEVAT DESTRUCTA REFO[R]MAT [ET] O[R]NAT ET FUNDAMENTIS PARTEM COMPONIT AB YMIS POSTREMA QUA PRIMA DEI VENERA[N]DA REFULSIT VISIBUS HUMANIS FACIES HEC INTEGRA SISTENS Q[U]O FUERAT STETERAT Q[UE] SITU RELOCATUR EODE[M] PRESULIS ECCE TUI DEUS HEC AMPLECTERE VOTA QUE TIBI P[ER] SOLVIT DOMUS HUIUS AMANDO DECORE[M] SERVA VIVIFICA CELO TERRA Q[UE] BEATUM EFFICE NEC MANIB[US] TRADAS HUNC HOSTIS INIQ[UI] INGREDIE[N]S POP[U]LUS DEVOTUS MUNERA SUMAT QUE BON[US] HI[C] PAST[OR] DEDIT I[N]DULGE[N]DO BENIGNE ET LARGA PIETATE PATER PECCATA REMITTENS ANNO AB INCARNATIONE DOMINI N[OST]RI IE[S]U CHR[IST]I M. CC. XC. I. PONTIFICATUS EIUSDEM QUE NICOLAI P[A]P[E] IIII ANNO III. English translation by Daniel Hadas. It has not hitherto been noted that the reference to the third year of Nicholas's papacy should fix the inscription's date to January or February 1291 (the pope having been crowned on 22 February 1288).

77 Claussen (2008), p. 97.

78 Claussen (2008), pp. 38–56, believed that the upper part of the Lateran's façade was rebuilt by Nicholas. The mosaic roundel of the Saviour, attributable to Jacopo Torriti and later integrated into the eighteenth-century façade, is an isolated survival of Nicholas's façade scheme. The origins of the Lateran's transept are the subject of continuing debate. De Blaauw (1994), vol. I, pp. 221–7, 230–3, dated its construction to the 1130s; Claussen (2008), pp. 154–5, argued that the transept was begun under Nicholas IV or shortly after his death, before being completed by Boniface VIII, a proposition now accepted by de Blaauw (2011), pp. 161–2.

79 The lower apse inscription read: HEC EST PAPALIS SEDES ET PONTIFICALIS PRESIDET ET XPI DE IURE VICARIUS ISTI ET QUIA IURE DATUR SEDES ROMANA VOCATUR NEC DEBET VERE NISI SOLUS PAPA SEDERE ET QUIA SUBLIMIS ALII SUBUNDTUR IN IMIS. ('This is the papal and pontifical seat, and the vicar of Christ sits on it by law. And because it is granted by law it is called the Roman seat, nor indeed should anyone except only the pope sit [there]. And because it is on high, the others are

subjected beneath.') Claussen (2008), p. 345. The opening words also appeared in a mosaic inscription on the steps of Nicholas's new papal throne at the bottom of the apse; see Claussen, pp. 131–2. As Gandolfo (1983), pp. 88–9, observed, the throne inscription echoed a similar inscription below Innocent III's apse mosaic in Old Saint Peter's: SUMMA PETRI SEDES EST HAEC SACRA PRINCIPIS AEDES. ('This is the most high seat of Peter, the holy temple of the prince.') English translations by Daniel Hadas.

80 Claussen (2008), pp. 137–40, 343–5.

81 The seminal analysis of Nicholas's renewal of Santa Maria Maggiore is Gardner (1973c). For a more recent treatment, with particular reference to the role of the Colonna, see Romano (2006).

82 For the insertion of the transept, see Gardner (1973c), pp. 2–3; de Blaauw (1994), vol. I, pp. 359–62.

83 Tomei (1990), pp. 99–125.

84 A *Last Judgment* seems to have been frescoed on the counter-façade, from which a fragmentary Lamb of God survives; the exterior façade was mosaiced by Filippo Rusuti. See Gardner (1973c), p. 20, fig. 17 (for the *Agnus Dei* fresco), pp. 22–9 (for Rusuti's mosaics).

85 Gardner (1973c), p. 4. The Pope conceded a year and forty days 'quandocumque manum porrexerint ad conservationem et reparationem basilicae Sanctae Mariae Majoris'; another bull of the same date gave forty additional days to those visiting the basilica 'vere poenitentibus et confessis'. Earlier that year, on 11 August 1288, Nicholas had already granted substantial indulgences of a year and forty days on each of the basilica's three consecration feasts, and three years and 120 days at Christmas and Easter and on the feasts of the Purification, the Annunciation and Saint Matthias. Summaries of these bulls are given by Langlois, ed. (1905), p. 128 (nrs 632–5), the full texts by Tomei (1990), pp. 153–6.

86 For the prioritization of the Lateran, see Romano (2006), p. 303.

87 The date is now incomplete, but was read as 1296 by a sixteenth-century source; for further discussion, see Tomei (1990), p. 13.

88 See Nicholas IV's letters of August to September 1288, published in full by Tomei (1990), pp. 153–6 (with analysis at pp. 103–6), addressed to 'Dilectis filiis Iacobo . . . archipresbytero ac priori et capitulo basilice Sancte Mariae Maioris de Urbe'.

89 Gardner (1973c), p. 2; this information is taken from De Angelis (1621), pp. 55–6. For the extent of Colonna patronage on the Esquiline, see Romano (2006), pp. 298–301, who argued that the family turned the basilica into 'una sorta di grande cappella palatina'.

90 De Angelis (1621), p. 55, and see above, note 42.

91 From a document of 6 September 1290, first noted by Gardner (1973c), p. 50 n. 181: 'quod ipsa ecclesia [Orvieto cathedral] . . . nobilis et solempnis ad instar S. Mariae maioris de Urbe . . . construatur'.

92 For the shrine of the crib and associated cult of Saint Jerome at Santa Maria Maggiore, see Romano (2006), pp. 300–01, who noted that Nicholas's floor-tomb may have been close to the altar dedicated to Saint Jerome in the right side aisle. Two images of Jerome were incorporated into the new mosaic programme. The scene of Saint Jerome with Paula and Eustochius on the left side of the triumphal arch refers to the *Epistola ad Paulam et Eustochium de Assumptione Beatae Virginis Mariae*, then attributed to Saint Jerome, which furnished the readings for the feast of the Assumption (15 August) in the Franciscan breviary; see Tomei (1990), p. 114. This image therefore pertained to the Assumption iconography of the main apse as well as the relics of Saint Jerome in the basilica. Indeed, the cult of Saint Jerome at Santa Maria Maggiore was generally associated with the veneration of the Virgin. The Doctor of the Church was also depicted on the upper register of the façade mosaics. This figure of Jerome was destroyed when Fuga's loggia was attached in the 1740s, but is visible in earlier drawings of the façade; see Gardner (1973b), pp. 584, 586 (fig. 28), 589 (fig. 30).

93 For a formal analysis of Torriti's mosaic and its possible sources, see Gardner (1973c), pp. 6–12; Brooke (2006), pp. 448–51.

94 At the foot of the *Dormition* kneel a pair of friars and a layman. Brooke (2006), p. 451, suggested that the layman may be Jacopo Torriti, rejecting his identification as a friar. But it is also possible that the layman depicts Filippo Rusuti, who had probably started work on the façade mosaics before Torriti completed the apse, while the two friars are Torriti and Jacopo of Camerino.

95 MARIA VIRGO ASSUMPTA EST AD ETHEREUM THALAMUM IN QUO REX REGUM STELLATO SEDET SOLIO + EXALTATA EST SANCTA DEI GENETRIX SUPER CHOROS ANGELORUM AD CELESTIA REGNA. ('The Virgin Mary has been assumed into the celestial bridal chamber at whose starry threshold sits the King of kings; the holy mother of God has been lifted above the angelic choirs to Heaven's realm.') The mosaic inscription was originally intended to encircle the Coronation clipeus, and traces of lettering are still visible to the upper left of the Virgin; see Tomei (1990), p. 104, plate XIXb.

96 See Nicholas's letter of 11 August 1288: 'Hec est mulier amicta sole et luna sub pedibus eius [Apocalypse (Revelation) 12:1], que cum virginitate fecunda nobis genuit Salvatorem. Hec est illa que mater et virgo Deum habuit filium, super choros angelorum ad regna celestia exaltata.' Quoted by Tomei (1990), p. 104, with full transcription at p. 154.

97 Torriti's source for the riverscape was almost certainly the fourth-century cupola mosaic of Santa Costanza, Rome, extant until 1620; see Andaloro, ed. (2006a), pp. 72–8; and for the connection with Santa Maria Maggiore, see Brenk (2010), pp. 22–3. It is also tempting to draw a link with the extensive Nile mosaic from the Temple of Fortune at Palestrina, the Colonna stronghold and Nicholas's old cardinal bishopric. This mosaic was created in the first century BCE and was traditionally thought to have been rediscovered in the 1620s, but recent research has demonstrated that it was already visible around 1500; see La Malfa (2003).

98 QUARTUS PAPA FUIT NICOLAUS VIRGINIS AEDEM HANC LAPSAM REFICIT FITQ. VETUSTA NOVA PATER APOSTOLICUM SERVET FRANCISCUS ALUMNUM PROTEGAT OMNIPOTENS MATRE ROGANTE BEET. Forcella (1869–84), vol. XI, p. 11 (nr 7); Gardner (1973c), p. 42 n. 25. The inscription no longer survives.

99 Langlois, ed. (1905), pp. 925–6 (nr 6926): the money was to be spent 'in reparatione parietum ecclesie Sancte Marie Majoris de Urbe' and had to be paid within eight days; see Gardner (1973c), p. 4.

100 Romano (2006), pp. 304–5, went significantly further, suggesting that the representation of Nicholas IV in Torriti's apse, executed several years after his death, can be read as a Colonna polemic against the legitimacy of the popes that succeeded him, Celestine V and Boniface VIII.

101 Forcella (1869–84), vol. XI, p. 11 (nr 6): HIC TUMULUS TUMULAT HUMILEM QUI FASCIBUS AUCTUS SIC MORIENS STATUIT OSSA MANERE SUA HUNC FRANCISCUS ALIT CARDO UT SIT ALMAQ. PETRI SEDES MAGNIFICAT GRATIA DEI BEAT. QUARTUS PAPA FUIT NICOLAUS VIRGINIS AEDEM HANC LAPSAM REFICIT FITQ. VETUSTA NOVA PETRUS APOSTOLICUS SOCIUM FRANCISCUS ALUMNUM PROTEGAT OMNIPOTENS MATRE ROGANTE BEET. English translation by Daniel Hadas.

102 We accept Julian Gardner's arguments for dating the façade mosaics to before 1297; see Gardner (1973c), pp. 28–9.

103 Gardner (1973c), pp. 22–3, fig. 20; Gardner (1973b), pp. 584–7, fig. 28.

104 Romano (2006), pp. 293–4: 'La presenza del cardinale Jacopo Colonna . . . è dunque da considerare eclatante.' Giacomo's portrait at Santa Maria Maggiore contrasts with Honorius III's apse mosaic of *c.*1220 at San Paolo fuori le Mura, where the abbot and the sacristan of the basilica were depicted on a lower register relative to the donor figure of the pope himself, see Pace (1991).

105 For a classic account of the Colonna rebellion against Boniface, see Boase (1933), pp. 159–85.

2 *Power and Patronage at Assisi*

1 For the interpretation of the 'great sumptuousness' of *Contra quasdam* as an allusion to the Upper Church, see Cooper and Robson (2009), p. 660.

2 The classic studies of the formation of the Papal States remain Waley (1961), esp. pp. 212–25, for Nicholas IV and the Colonna; and Partner (1972).

3 Giovanni was appointed rector of the March of Ancona on 27 June 1288, a title he held until the summer of 1291, although in practice he had been replaced by his son Agapito as vicar from April 1290, when Nicholas appointed him senator of Rome; see Waley (1982a) for Agapito; Waley (1982b) for Giovanni.

4 Stefano was first appointed rector of Ascoli on 17 May 1288, before moving to the rectorship of the Romagna in August 1289; see Waley (1982d); Paschini (1955), p. 13.

5 For that date Nicholas's registers contain a letter addressed to 'Landulpho de Columpna de Urbe, ducatus Spoletani rectori', and one to the inhabitants of Cesi and the surrounding area in southern Umbria, ordering them to submit to Landolfo's authority. Another letter of 1 March ordered all the nobles, *podestà* and communities of the Duchy to obey Landolfo; see Langlois, ed. (1905), p. 939 (nrs 6955–8). Paschini (1955), p. 12, perhaps on the basis of sources in the Colonna archive, stated that this was the day of Landolfo's appointment. Waley (1961), p. 214, followed this reasonable assumption: '[Nicholas] at once proclaimed his intention to rely on the Colonna for the government of the Papal State, appointing Landulf rector of the Duchy [of Spoleto] a week after his consecration.'

6 On the Perugia–Foligno conflict, see Waley (1961), pp. 215–16.

7 Landolfo Colonna 'de Urbe' is addressed as 'Rector' of the Duchy of Spoleto in a papal letter of 13 April 1288, composed at Saint Peter's and dispatched to Bevagna, where it is still preserved in the local archive; see Guarino (2007), p. 13 (nr 11). The letter concerns a long-running dispute between the commune of Bevagna and the rebel Raynaldo di Napoleone, which Nicholas urged Landolfo to resolve.

8 For the centres frequented by the rector's court in the period 1250–1324, see Waley (1983), p. 194. The court is documented in Assisi *c.*1254; see Fausti (1917–19), p. 321, for a document dated 29 May, probably in that year, 'apud hospitale sancti Georgii de Asisio'.

9 Langlois, ed. (1905), p. 947 (nr 7019): 'Dilecto filio nobili viro . . . potestati Asisinati. Ei mandat, sub poena mille marcharum argenti et privationis postestariae Asisii, ut Landulpho de Columpna de Urbe, ducatus Spoletani rectori, assistat contra Perusinos, si ab eo de hoc requisitus fuerit.'

10 See Presutti (1910), p. 318, citing Rome, Archivio Colonna II, A, 3, fol. 372B.

11 Rainerius is first named as 'ducatus Spoletani Sabiniеque rectori' in a papal letter of 5 March 1291; see Langlois, ed. (1905), p. 999 (nr 7316).

12 Rome, Archivio Colonna, perg. LIV, 5, published by Presutti (1910), pp. 329–31: Landolfo named 'fratrem Nicolaum de Penestre ordinis minorum' as one of his five executors. The same brother Nicholas is named alongside two other Franciscan friars among the eight witnesses. Landolfo also named one of his two sons Francesco. For Landolfo's allegiance to Boniface VIII from 1297, see Brentano (1974), p. 182.

13 For the burning of the communal records in 1442, see Monacchia (2002), p. 394.

14 Armaleo of Antignano entrusted his sons to the care of Giovanni Colonna in 1291; see Sensi (2009), pp. 299–302.

15 Sensi (2009), p. 286, quoting Jacobilli (1646), p. 65: 'Ermanno di m. Guidone Ermanni da Foligno per due mesi, maestro Giovanni Cenci romano sopradetto [he had previously deputized as *podestà* for Pope Martin IV in 1284], per il cardinale Pietro Colonna, per altri dieci mesi, nel 1290'. (Sensi appears to make an uncharacteristic slip when claiming that Giacomo Colonna, rather than his nephew Pietro, had been elected *podestà*.)

16 An argument made most forcefully by Bellosi (2007), who dates almost the entire mural decoration of the Upper Church to the four-year window of Nicholas's pontificate. See also Brooke (2006), p. 453. We first discussed the *Contra quasdam* passage in Cooper and Robson (2003).

17 Tomei (1990), pp. 45–7. Many scholars also identify the hand of the young Torriti alongside that of the so-called 'Northern Master' in the frescoes of the north transept of the Upper Church; see Boskovits (2000a), pp. 75–6, and Chapter 3 below for further discussion.

18 Boskovits (2000a), p. 76, attributed at least twelve Old and New Testament scenes directly to Torriti, and argued that he produced the sinopia preparatory drawings for even more.

19 Tomei (1990), p. 55, suggested that Torriti worked briefly at Assisi in 1288–9, perhaps for one season, before being recalled to Rome by Nicholas in 1289–90. See also Brooke (2006), p. 443.

20 *BF* IV, p. 2 (nr 2): the bull records the donation of 'nonnulla diversi coloris paramenta, pontificalia serica, vasa argentea, certam summam pecuniae, ac quaedam alia in cedula praesentibus interclusa'. The gifts were accompanied by a priest from Nicholas's retinue, 'Magistrum Petrum de Sora Clericum, et familiarem nostrum'.

21 Kleinschmidt (1915–28), vol. III, pp. 31–5.

22 For this reliquary, see Morello and Kanter, eds (1999), pp. 164–5. The object was described thus in the Basilica's 1338 inventory: 'In primis una capsa de argento deaurata, plena multis reliquiis, ornata lapidibus pretiosis, cum cristallis in modum portarum; super quam est una crux de argento deaurata, in qua est lignum vere Crucis coopertum cristallo; quam misit dominus Nicholaus papa quartus, de Ordine Minorum.' See Kleinschmidt (1915–28), vol. III, p. 31. Hueck (1982), p. 177, noted that the presence of Pudenziana among the saints depicted on the reliquary's exterior referred to Nicholas's titular church between 1278 and 1281; this date range would also accord with the object's archaic style. Makers' marks confirm that the reliquary was made in Rome.

23 Morello and Kanter, eds (1999), pp. 182–3; the base of the stem bears the inscription: GUCCIUS MANAIE DE SENIS FECIT. NICHO[L]AUS PAPE QUARTUS. The chalice is described thus in the 1370 inventory: 'unus magnus calix de argento, inauratus, cum smaltis et figuris; quem misit dominus Nicholaus papa quartus, de Ordine Minorum; et in signum huius, dictus Papa est ibi figuratus et nomen suum descriptum; et est ponderis XLV unciarum.' See Alessandri and Pennacchi (1914), p. 298. Nicholas's cup is almost certainly the 'calix magnus de argento inauratus, cum smaltis', also weighing 45 ounces, recorded at the very beginning of the 1338 inventory: Kleinschmidt (1915–28), vol. III, p. 30.

24 *BF* IV, pp. 92–3 (nr 146): 'quod vobis quoddam Aurifrisium nuper de mandato nostro contextum, tam materia, quam opere pretiosum, prout ex ejus apertius inspectione colligitur, quod eidem Ecclesiae ad ornatum Altaris ipsius de Apostolicae Sedis plena liberalitate donamus'. The orphrey had been entrusted to Peter of Sora, the same priest who had escorted Nicholas's previous gifts to Assisi in February 1288. For the orphrey itself, see Nessi (1980), p. 15; and the important article by Frugoni (2011a) (we are very grateful to the author for the opportunity to read her article before publication).

25 *BF* IV, p. 93 (nr 146): 'auctoritate Apostolica districtius inhibentes, ne Aurifrisium ipsum vendere alienare, seu distrahere quomodolibet attentetis: Nos enim ex nunc irritum et inane decernimus, si secus per quemcumque quavis auctoritate contigerit attentari'. On the gift's potential violation of Franciscan legislation, see Cooper and Robson (2009), p. 661 n. 50.

26 Although no document refers specifically to Guccio's chalice we can assume, given the enamel plaque on the cup's base depicting the Franciscan pope, that it too was commissioned only after Nicholas's election.

27 *BF* IV, pp. 92–3 (nr 146): 'nuper de mandato nostro contextum'.

28 The altar *mensa* of the Lower Church measures 372 cm across, that of the Upper Church 322 cm; see Ludovico of Pietralunga (1982), pp. 257, 364. Frugoni (2011a), p. 216, believes that the high altar of the Lower Church was the more likely

destination, as the bull *Excitamur ab intimis* mentioned the tomb of Saint Francis, the orphrey being gifted to 'ipsius Ecclesiam, in qua gloriosum requiescere noscitur Corpus eius'; but this was a relatively standard clause in Nicholas's bulls (appearing in *Reducentes*, for example). Nicholas's orphrey was destined 'ad ornatum Altaris ipsius [Ecclesiae]', which could refer to the high altar of either the Upper or Lower Church.

29 Kleinschmidt (1915–28), vol. III, p. 32: 'unum aurifrigium cum ystoria beati Francisci, de auro et argento tracto, ornatum pernis, valde nobile et pretiosum; quod misit dominus Nicholaus papa IV, de Ordine Fratrum Minorum' (from the 1338 inventory). On the disappearance of the orphrey, see Frugoni (2011a), p. 217.

30 The engravings, taken from drawings by the local Assisi artist Giampaolo Zampa, were published by Catalano (1652): 'in un pallio fatto per l'Altare di S. Francesco dal medesimo Papa veggonsi molte pitture de' Santi e de' frati' (p. 124); engravings, pp. 319–20; Zampa's testimonial p. 324. Catalano's volume focused on identifying the original form of the Franciscan habit, then the subject of an acrimonious controversy between the Conventual and Capuchin Franciscans, and copied early images for evidence.

31 Frugoni (2011a), p. 221.

32 The height of the textile is more difficult to deduce; an orphrey should properly be a narrow decorative frieze attached to the front edge of the altar table. However, Nicholas's orphrey was often referred to as a 'palio' or 'paliotto' in later documents – for example, when the 'palio' was recorded in Rome in 1608 where it had been sent for repairs, see Zaccaria (1964), p. 174 – and by Catalano (1652), p. 124 ('pallio'), pp. 319–20 ('palleotto/palliotto'). These are terms for an altar frontal, i.e. a textile hanging that covered the full height of the altar block. This suggests that the lost embroidery was comparable in size to the only historiated altar frontal of this period to survive from a Franciscan context, the lavish embroidery intended for the high altar of the Cordeliers church in Toulouse, now conserved in the Musée Paul-Dupuy in the same city. Generally dated to *c.*1315–20, the Toulouse frontal is 88 cm high and 267 cm wide, but has been cut down on its right-hand side; its original width may have been as great as 346 cm. It combines scenes from Saint Francis's life with narratives from the Passion, the life of the Virgin and the lives of other saints. For the Toulouse embroidery, see Durliat (1995) and now Frugoni (2012a).

33 A later Franciscan pope, Sixtus IV, commissioned another embroidered altar frontal for the Basilica in the 1470s, which very likely imitated the example of Nicholas's orphrey. Sixtus's frontal, still conserved in the Basilica's treasury, measures 377 cm across, and its orphrey frieze is divided into fifteen pictorial fields; see Bonito Fanelli (1980), pp. 81–5.

34 Chiara Frugoni highlighted the similarities between the Catalano engravings and the relevant scenes in the Saint Francis cycle, observing that the paintings could hardly have inspired the embroidery; instead, the orphrey could have provided a rich source for the planners of the frescoes. Indeed, the iconographer of the orphrey may have had a hand in designing the Upper Church programme; see Frugoni (2011a), p. 223.

35 For example, see *Dum solicitae considerationis* of 30 April 1288 (forbidding the foundation of non-Franciscan monastic houses in Assisi) and *Praeclara gloriosissimi* of 14 May 1288 (exempting the Basilica from papal interdicts), *BF* IV, pp. 16–17 (nr 17), pp. 21–2 (nr 26).

36 Brooke (2006), pp. 418–19, 444, argued that Jerome of Ascoli and Matthew of Acquasparta had together drawn up the decorative plan of the Upper Church in the 1270s.

37 Although the Basilica can hardly be considered a typical Franciscan building, elsewhere in central Italy the Friars Minor were content for patrons' coats of arms to be visible throughout their churches; see Cooper (2011).

38 Binski (2011) (we are very grateful to the author for the chance to consult a draft of his article before publication).

39 It is generally accepted that the *Liberation of Peter of Alife* was the penultimate scene to be painted, followed by the *Homage of a Simple Man* (the first scene of the cycle, directly opposite); see Zanardi (2002), p. 85, and plates L, LXIX, for the relevant *giornata* plans.

40 Two other representations of the story survive. It is unclear if a column featured in the now fragmentary fresco painted *c.*1295 in the *cappella maggiore* of San Francesco in Rieti, but the extant sections of the scene clearly depend on the Assisi mural, see Cook (1995a), esp. pp. 139–41. A Bolognese manuscript leaf of *c.*1320–42 now in the Metropolitan Museum, New York (accession number 1994.516) offers a simplified version of the story, with no column above Peter of Alife's prison.

41 The miracle appeared in Thomas of Celano's *Treatise of Miracles* (*c.*1250–52) before being included in Bonaventure's *Legenda maior*; see *LM, Miracles* 5:4 (*FAED* II, pp. 437–9, 667; *FF*, pp. 703–4, 937–8). The events narrated in the story are usually dated to 1231 or 1232. An excellent summary of the miracle and its later political connotations is provided by Frugoni (2010b), pp. 174–8.

42 Frugoni (2004a), esp. pp. 108, 122.

43 Frugoni (2004a), p. 124 n. 49.

44 Brooke (2006), p. 443, and Romano (2006), p. 297 n. 33.

45 Binski (2009); for a development of the column rebus theme

with regard to Giotto's *Stigmatization of Saint Francis* panel in the Louvre, see Frugoni (2010a).

46 Bolgia (2007), pp. 75, 78 (fig. 14); the same chapel also preserves another Colonna blazon, with a fluted column on a blue mosaic ground.

47 The building to the left of the column in the fresco has so far defied convincing explanation. Most recently Curzi (2011), pp. 9–16, argued for a reference to the polygonal exterior of the newly built apse of Santa Maria Maggiore in Rome, reinforcing the homage paid to the Colonna family. For alternative identifications, see Wolff (1996).

48 It may be significant that the column seems not to have been included in the later version of the same scene at Rieti, which otherwise copies closely the prototype at Assisi; see Cook (1995a), p. 140.

49 For a comprehensive photographic record, see Bonsanti (1998), pp. 30–41.

50 Several additional letters, since disappeared, are visible under magnification, beside these figures, in an early photograph marked 'Hautes études, Millet C815 / Assise-St. François' conserved in the Fototeca Berenson at the Harvard University Center for Italian Renaissance Studies, Villa I Tatti (Box F14). We are indebted to Giovanni Pagliarulo, Agnes Mongan Curator of the Fototeca Berenson, for scanning this photo at very high resolution.

51 This figure is sometimes mistaken for a male saint; see Bonsanti (1998), p. 32.

52 Saint Agapitus does not appear as a dedication in the tithe lists of Umbrian parish churches from the period: see Sella (1952). One of Franco Sacchetti's *novelle* refers to a church of 'Santo Agapito' in Perugia, but this seems to be entirely fictitious, as no church of that dedication is documented in the city; see Sacchetti (1860–61), vol. I, p. 317 (Novella 134).

53 For Saint Agapitus's legend and cult, see Borzi (1997) and Petrini (1793). There is a long-standing confusion between the Agapitus venerated at Palestrina, a 15-year-old boy thought to have been martyred under the Emperor Aurelian on 18 August 274, and another Agapitus, named alongside Saint Lawrence among the seven deacons of Rome martyred under the Emperor Valerian in August 258. The youthful deacon saint at Assisi, paired with Saint Lawrence and the two other deacons on the opposite side of the arch, seems to reflect this conflation.

54 For the reliquary, see above, note 22. However, it has not been recognized until now that a much fuller list of the 'multis reliquiis' originally contained within the casket was included in a separate inventory of the Basilica's relics compiled shortly after 1348. Among them were 'De reliquis . . . Sancti Agapiti martiris'; see Faloci Pulignani (1886), p. 148.

55 For this Agapito (†1302), see Waley (1982a).

56 Digard *et al.*, eds (1884–1939), vol. II, col. 588 (nr 3416; 13 June 1299): 'In ecclesia vero Beati Agapiti martyris posita juxta eam [Palestrina], que quidem ante destructionem civitatis extitit ecclesia cathedralis . . . construi altare in honorem Beati Bonifatii.' Pope Boniface had already destroyed the old city of Palestrina and ordered a new town to be built lower down the hillside, named 'Civitas Papalis'. The June 1299 edict implies that the cathedral of Sant'Agapito, the only building spared the general destruction of the old city, would be rededicated to Saint Boniface. For the Caetani pope's use of the cult of his seventh-century namesake, Pope Boniface IV, for political ends, see Maccarrone (1983), esp. pp. 754–7 for his burial chapel dedicated to Saint Boniface in Old Saint Peter's.

57 For the links between the Colonna cardinals, their retinues and Umbria, see Rehberg (1999), pp. 349–64, 523–4, 526.

58 The document was seen by Ferdinand Gregorovius in the Colonna archives; see Gregorovius (1859–72), vol. V, p. 504 n. 1 (citing the collocation Armadio I, fasciculo I, n. 5).

59 The link is made by Sensi (2009), p. 302. For the text and date of Giacomo's approval, see Alberzoni (1999).

60 Sensi (2009), pp. 300–01.

61 According to some scholars, the college of cardinals, including the two Colonna, was instrumental in establishing and decorating the Saint Nicholas chapel in the Lower Church at Assisi during this period, as a votive offering for Cardinal Napoleone Orsini's young brother Gian Gaetano, who had died suddenly during the conclave. Gian Gaetano was laid to rest in the Basilica while a marble wall-tomb was prepared for him in the Saint Nicholas chapel. Much depends on the interpretation of the eight kneeling cardinals depicted on the inner face of the chapel's entrance arch, who were effaced soon after they were painted, the two innermost cardinals being replaced with portraits of Napoleone Orsini and Gian Gaetano. For Hueck (1983), the eight cardinals represented those who participated in the Perugia conclave, and the subsequent repainting was necessitated by the disgrace of the Colonna in May 1297. However, Hueck's hypothesis has recently been challenged by Romano (2010), who argued that the Saint Nicholas chapel was a purely Orsini foundation from the outset, the eight cardinals representing the extended Orsini family. The lost cardinals were rediscovered only in 1913, and the restored fresco now presents a mixture of the two schemes; see Supino (1926–7); Maginnis (1975), p. 515. We shall discuss the patronage of the Saint Nicholas chapel in our forthcoming book on the Lower Church.

62 Kleinschmidt (1915–28), vol. III, pp. 30, 31: 'Item una crux de argento deaurata, cum ligno vere Crucis, et ymagine Salva-

toris relevata, et cum pede de argento deaurato simplici, et lapidibus pretiosis; quam misit dominus Iacobus de Columpna.' 'Item aliud thuribulum cum castris, de argento, deauratum; quod misit dominus Iacobus de Columpna.'

63 Kleinschmidt (1915–28), vol. III, p. 35: 'Item planeta, dalmatica et tonicella de panno tartarico deaurato, cum campo nigro, et in frigio planete sunt arme Ursinorum.' This ensemble of black vestments was probably related to the chantry masses for Gian Gaetano Orsini that would have been celebrated in the Saint Nicholas chapel.

64 See Kleinschmidt (1915–28), vol. III, p. 33, for two altar orphreys: 'Item unum aurifrigium valde pulcrum, cum campo aureo et vite aurea; quod fuit domini Bonifatii pape octavi.' 'Item unum aurifrigium, cum armis domini Bonifatii pape octavi.' See pp. 33–4, 41, for a red cope decorated with the lives of saints: 'Item unum pluviale rubeum, valde pulcrum, cum ystoriis beati Stephani, sancti Laurentii et plurimorum Sanctorum, cum frigio ad medias figuras, et quinque boctonis de pernis, et tribus deauratis; quod misit dominus Bonifatius papa octavus.' The 1338 list of altar frontals includes 'unus pannus, cum armis domini Bonifatii pape' (Kleinschmidt, p. 33). This hanging is probably identical with the green altar dossal with Boniface's arms described in 1473: 'Ibidem aliud dossale cum campo viridi, et armis ad undas; quod misit dominus papa Bonifatius VIII' (Kleinschmidt, p. 42).

65 Digard *et al.*, eds (1884–1939), vol. IV, p. 49 (nr 5522; 7 March 1298): 'Nos igitur, hujusmodi devotionem vestram benignius attendentes, et considerantes maxime grata et accepta servitia, que contra Columpnenses, scismaticos et rebelles nobis et ipsi ecclesie, impendistis et prosecutione continua exhibetis ac ad beneplacitum nostrum exhibere proponitis in futurum.'

66 Brooke (2006), p. 419, emphasized Matteo Rosso Orsini's likely role as a patron at Assisi in his capacity as cardinal protector of the Order: 'After the death of his uncle [Pope Nicholas III] in 1280 the chief responsibility for ensuring that work was carried out will have fallen on the shoulders of Matteo Rosso. The employment of Roman artists and their workshops after the departure of Cimabue is likely to have been due to his interpretation of his role as Nicholas III's executor.' Despite Matteo Rosso Orsini's longevity as cardinal protector (from 1277 to 1305), there is no evidence to link him with the Basilica's fresco decoration. On the contrary, the complete absence of any donations associated with Matteo Rosso in the 1338 inventory suggests a lack of engagement on the part of the cardinal protector; Kleinschmidt (1915–28), vol. III, pp. 30–37. The 1370 inventory records a single white dalmatic 'que fuit domini Mathei cardinalis de domo Ursinorum'; Alessandri and Pennacchi (1914), p. 301. Indeed, Lunghi (1997), pp. 265–6, has astutely observed that *Reducentes* undercut Matteo Rosso's authority at Assisi by transferring responsibility for the Basilica's decoration from the cardinal protector to the minister general of the Order.

67 The most complete biographical account remains Longpré (1928).

68 For the pre-eminence of the University of Paris in the thirteenth century, and the Franciscan *studium generale* there as the Order's most important educational centre, see Roest (2000), pp. 11–21; Şenocak (2012b), pp. 232–4. According to the Constitutions of Narbonne in 1260, each province of the Order was allowed to send two friars each year to Paris, but was obliged to provide their books (Roest, p. 15).

69 An autograph note in Matthew's Commentary on the Sentences, now at Assisi, suggests that he also taught at Bologna; he succeeded John Pecham as the lector at the papal curia after his former master was nominated archbishop of Canterbury on 28 January 1279; see Longpré (1928), col. 375; see also Şenocak (2012a), p. 228. Matthew was still in Paris on 18 May 1279; see Doucet (1935).

70 Menestò (1993), with a full transcription of the donation deed at pp. 281–4. Matthew divided his books between the two convents, giving forty to Todi and thirty-six to Assisi. The charter's date is given only as 1287, but Honorius IV is named as the regnant pontiff, fixing its composition before that pope's death on 3 April. Unfortunately the original parchment can no longer be found in Todi's Archivio Capitolare.

71 Şenocak (2012b), pp. 119–20, noted that Matthew may also have been following Francis's advice that a minister general should not be a book collector.

72 For the entries in the 1338 inventory, see Kleinschmidt (1915–28), vol. III, p. 30 (nr 19: the coral and silver cross), p. 33 (nr 128: a set of three altar frontals with images of the Virgin and the Tree of Jesse, scenes of the Passion and Resurrection, and the lives of the Virgin and Saint Cecilia), p. 34 (nrs 169, 186, 198, 201: various liturgical vestments).

73 This pattern is suggested by an early inventory of Matthew's bequests of liturgical textiles to San Fortunato, Todi, which is divided into two sections: 'Iste sunt res quas venerabilis frater Matheus Cardinalis dedit conventui ante quam esset Cardinalis'; and another list 'postquam effectus esset cardinalis'; Tenneroni (1888), pp. 265–6. Further gifts, which after Matthew's death had passed in succession to the Franciscan cardinals Giovanni di Mino and Vital du Four, finally came to Todi and Assisi in the early 1320s; for the related documentation, see Porzio, ed. (1982), p. 26.

74 See Menestò (1993), p. 272, for the inclusion of the invocation 'Sancti Spiritus adsit nobis gratia' ('The grace of the Holy Spirit be present with us') at the beginning and end of several of Matthew's manuscripts. Matthew's devotion to

the cult of the Holy Spirit is further suggested by his request for a mass in honour of the Holy Spirit in May 1291, see below, note 92

75 For Matthew's seal, see Gardner (1975), pp. 89–91; Cioni Liserani (1979), pp. 49–51 (advancing Guccio's authorship more confidently). The matrix does not survive, but the design is preserved in two impressions from July 1294. The seal bore the legend: + S[IGILLUS] F[RAT]RIS MATH[E]I ORD[INIS] MINOR[UM] DEI GRA[TIA] EP[ISCOP]I PORTUEN[SIS] ET S[AN]C[T]E RUFINE. Matthew was elevated to the cardinal bishopric of Porto and Santa Rufina in 1291, and the matrix would have been commissioned soon afterwards. The seal represented Matthew kneeling below an image of the Crucifixion and two standing saints framed by niches. The male saint on the right is recognizable as Saint Francis; the female saint on the left is likely to be either Saint Clare or Saint Rufina.

76 For the Aracoeli monument, see Pace (1993), pp. 316–30; and Gardner (1992), pp. 83–4, who noted the unusual choice of fresco over mosaic in the context of Roman tomb design, suggesting that it may have been a mendicant preference.

77 In *Paradiso*, Canto XII, 124–6, Dante has Bonaventure say: 'but it will not be from Casale or from Acquasparta, whence come such to the writing that one shuns it and the other contracts it' ('ma non fia da Casal né d'Acquasparta / là onde vegnon tali a la scrittura / ch'uno la fugge e altro la coarta'); Dante Alighieri (1971–5), vol. III/1, pp. 136–7. The passage is generally interpreted to mean that, in Dante's mind, Matthew was betraying the Franciscan Rule ('la scrittura'), while Ubertino da Casale was interpreting it too rigidly. Certainly, Matthew did not let Franciscan poverty hold back his career as a cardinal. Peter Herde suggested that Nicholas IV's promotion of Matthew from cardinal priest of San Lorenzo in Damaso to cardinal bishop of Porto and Santa Rufina in 1291 was driven by Acquasparta's desire to increase his income; see Herde (1993), pp. 90–91. This isolated promotion within the college, for which we do not know the precise date, was unusual. Along with his fellow cardinals, Matthew accepted an annual pension (of 100 gold ounces, in his case) from Charles II of Naples in November 1291; Del Giudice (1896), p. 222.

78 For the date of Matthew's appointment, see Herde (1993), p. 90, citing Langlois, ed. (1905), p. 220 (nr 1013; 21 July 1289), which names 'Matthaeum, Sancti Laurentii in Damaso presbyterum cardinalem, poenitentiarum suum.'

79 For Matthew's duties as penitentiary, see Pásztor (1993), pp. 39–41.

80 Herde (1993), p. 96, quoting (in Italian translation) Stefaneschi's *Opus metricum*, in *Monumenta Coelestiniana* (1921), p. 31: 'Qualiter conabantur aliqui impedire fratrem Mattheum de Aquasparta Portuensem episcopum in officio penitentiarie.' The 'aliqui' concerned, although unnamed by Stefaneschi, were almost certainly the Colonna cardinals, attempting to deprive Matthew of the office of papal penitentiary during the Perugian conclave. In the preceding summer of 1293, Matthew had led the papal forces against Narni after the southern Umbrian city – incited by the Colonna – had threatened the papal fortress of Stroncone; see Calpini (1975), p. 5.

81 Benedetto Caetani is documented as a prior and canon in Todi in 1257 and 1260, where his uncle Pietro Caetani was bishop from 1252; see Herde (1993), pp. 85–6.

82 Ehrle (1892), p. 123 n. 2: 'Ordinat insuper generalis minister de consensu et beneplacito capituli generalis, quod conventus loci sacri de Assisio totaliter remaneat et sit in manibus et dispositione ipsius generalis ministri, qui teneatur et debeat de ydoneo custode eidem conventui providere.' The legislation can be traced back to the constitutions approved at the general chapter in Paris in 1292. It was reversed at the general chapter in Barcelona in 1313, when authority over the Sacro Convento was returned to the Umbrian province: 'Item, determinatum est per Generalem Ministrum et Generale Capitulum, quod locus sacer de Assisio reducatur ad curam Ministri et Provincie Sancti Francisci, ita tamen, quod Generalis Minister illum conventum, prout et quando sibi videbitur, per specialem Visitatorem faciat visitari.' Abate (1933), p. 33.

83 Our principal sources for these officials at the end of the thirteenth century are the charters of the Sacro Convento, now published in Bartoli Langeli with Bossa and Fiumi, eds (1997). For the provincial ministers of the Umbrian province, see also Bartolomasi (1824), republished – with some alterations – as Bartolomasi (1932). A chronological sequence for the custodians of the Sacro Convento, based on archival sources, has been compiled by Nessi (1994), pp. 476–80.

84 Menestò (1993), p. 282: 'fratris Iacobi de Assisio custodis sancti Francisci'.

85 For the charter of 19 August 1288 naming 'religioso viro domino fratre Galgano de Eugubio custode loci Beati Francisci de Asisio', see Bartoli Langeli with Bossa and Fiumi, eds (1997), pp. 289–91.

86 Bartoli Langeli with Bossa and Fiumi, eds (1997), p. 250: 'fratris Galgani guardiani fratruum conventus de Perusio' (3 or 29 October 1282); Menestò (1993), p. 282: 'fratris Galgani inquisitoris' (1287, before 3 April). For 'Fr. Galgano da Eugubio' as inquisitor in 1285, see Bartolomasi (1824), pp. 14–15; Bartolomasi (1932), p. 207.

87 For a document of 2 July 1293 naming Bonaventura of Montedoglio as custodian, see Bartoli Langeli with Bossa and Fiumi, eds (1997), p. 308: 'Frater Bonaventura de Montedol [Montedoglio] ordinis Minorum, custos ecclesie Beati Fran-

cissci de Asisio et conventus ipsius ecclesie'. For Bonaventura as provincial minister, see below, note 97.

88 For Monaldo as custodian in 1294, see Nessi (1994), p. 476. For documents placing Monaldo at Assisi, see Bartoli Langeli with Bossa and Fiumi, eds (1997), p. 203 (27 September 1278), p. 219 (4 October 1280: 'fratre Monaldo de Urbeveteri'), p. 228 (17 April 1281), p. 248 (27 October 1282: 'fratri Munaldo sacriste loci Sancti Francisci'), p. 263 (11 May 1284: 'fratre Monaldo sacristano'), p. 278 (28 August 1286).

89 See Bartoli Langeli with Bossa and Fiumi, eds (1997), p. 267, for the bequest of 3 lire to 'fratri Bartulo nunc ministro provinciali' in a testament of 13 September 1284. For the 1280 date, see Bartolomasi (1932), p. 207: 'An: 1280. Fr. Bartholus Perusinus.'

90 See below, note 99.

91 Bartolomasi (1824), p. 14; Bartolomasi (1932), p. 207.

92 The following instruction is written on the verso of a bull of Nicholas IV granting an indulgence to the Franciscan church at Farneto: 'Dicatur I [una] missa pro domino Matheo cardinali de Aquasparta de Spiritu Sancto qui solvit. Rogetur pro domino vicecancellario frate Matheo Theatino, fratre Francisco Parveri . . . domini Gentili notarii qui laboraverunt pro dictis licteris.' The Farneto indulgence is preserved among the charters of the Perugian house San Francesco al Prato, now held in the Archivio di Stato in Perugia; see Monacchia (1984), p. 67 (nr 42), with transcription of the verso note; the indulgence itself was edited in *BF* IV, p. 248 (nr 462).

93 For the 1289 notice, see Bartolomasi (1824), pp. 14–15; Bartolomasi (1932), p. 207. Angelo of Todi was still provincial minister on 27 November 1290, when a bull was addressed to 'Fratri Angelo ministro . . . Provinciae Beati Francisci'; *BF* IV, p. 192 (nr 363).

94 See Pennacchi (1919), p. 471, for the papal letter of Nicholas IV addressed to 'frater Mattheus fratrum provintie Sancti Francisci minister' (undated but sent after 1290). Bartolomasi (1824), p. 15, recorded that 'Fr. Matthaeus nobilissimae familiae romanae de S. Eustachio' was the Umbrian provincial minister in 1292.

95 For Matthias's tomb slab, see Garms, Juffinger and Ward-Perkins (1981), pp. 128–9 (nr XXVIII, 21). Matthias's engraved effigy is surrounded by the following inscription: + HIC IACET REVE[RE]NDUS PATER FRATER MATIAS DE [S]A[N]CTO EUSTACIO Q[UI] FUIT MI[NI]STER P[RO]VI[N]C[I]ARUM S[ANCTI] FRA[NCISCI ET RO]MANE OBIIT AN[N]O D[OMINI] MCCC. Although no letters have been lost, the inscription is probably incomplete. It was very likely carved during Matthias's lifetime, in the expectation that the year and date of his death would be added to the end; Garms *et al.* date the slab to *c.*1310–12. Zazzera (1628) described Matthias's tomb 'nel tempio d'Aracelli fra la Cappella dell'apparizione ad Augusto, e la porta della Sacristia' (unpaginated); the location was a fitting one, as the Sant'Eustachio family claimed descent from Caesar Augustus. The slab is now immured in the nave wall between the third and fourth chapels of the left side aisle. According to Zazzera, Matthias had originally been baptized Ottaviano, changing his name on joining the Order. The 'Mathias de S. Heustachio' cited as owning property in the Roman rione of Sant' Eustachio in 1279 may be another member of the family, and was evidently a layman, at least at that date; see Federici (1899–1900), p. 412.

96 For the tomb slab of Fra Bernardo Colonna (†1318 or 1328), which remains *in situ* at the foot of the Acquasparta monument, see Garms, Juffinger and Ward-Perkins (1981), pp. 140–41 (nr XXVIII, 37). Fra Bernardo had succeeded Matthias as minister of the Roman province, suggesting that the Aracoeli transept was reserved for the highest-ranking friars. According to Casimiro (1736), pp. 178–9, Matthias was buried close to a tomb of the Colonna ('sepultus in eodem loco prope sepulcrum Columnensis').

97 Bartolomasi (1824), p. 15; Bartolomasi (1932), p. 207; Bonaventura was from the noble family of the counts of Montedoglio, in the Upper Tiber valley to the north of Sansepolcro.

98 Menestò (1993), pp. 281–2.

99 Menestò (1993), p. 282: 'fratris Angeli de Perusi[o, fratris] Guillelmi de Fulgineo, fratris Mathei de Theate, fratris Philippi de Perusio, fratris Iacobi de Tuderto, fratris Rainaldi de Tuderto lectorum'.

100 Bartoli Langeli with Bossa and Fiumi, eds (1997), p. 198 (19 September 1278: 'venerabilis vir frater Angelus de Perusio minister aministrationis Sancti Francisci'), p. 208 (10 April 1279: 'Frater Angelus minister administrationis Sancti Francisci'), p. 267 (13 September 1284: 'fratri Angelo de Perusio lectori'). Bartolomasi (1824), p. 14, listed 'Fr. Michael Angelus de Perusia' as provincial minister under the year 1278, and noted his involvement with the enquiry into the Porziuncola indulgence. This date was changed to 1273 in Bartolomasi (1932), pp. 206–7. Sensi (2002), p. 25, gave Angelo's term of office as 1274–80.

101 For Philip of Perugia, recorded as chaplain to Nicholas III, author of the *Libellus de stigmatibus beati Francisci*, and provincial minister of Tuscany, see Pásztor (1993), pp. 22–3; Paravicini Bagliani (1972), vol. I, p. 326. His treatise on the stigmata was edited in *AF* III, pp. 641–5. A brief biography of 'Maestro F. Filippo da Perugia Teologo dottissimo' is found in Papini (1797), pp. 8–9. In October 1278 Philip was one of a group of four 'Lectores Ordinis Minorum' dispatched to Constantinople by Nicholas III to negotiate with the Byzantine

emperor Michael Palaeologus the union of the Byzantine and Latin Churches; see *BF* III, pp. 349, 354, 355, 359. Philip may be identifiable with the 'fratre Filippo lectore' named among the witnesses in a document dated 4 October 1280 in the Sacro Convento, although if so one might have expected him to be named as Tuscan provincial at this time; see Bartoli Langeli with Bossa and Fiumi, eds (1997), p. 219.

102 The account is found in the *Epistola de cardinalibus protectoribus Ordinis Fratrum Minorum*, composed by 'frater Philippus de Perusio senectutis eius' for Gonsalvo of Valboa during his ministership of the Order (1304–13); text edited as an appendix to Salimbene of Parma (1905–13), pp. 678–84; see also Delorme (1915). For the *Exiit qui seminat* discussions, see Brooke (2006), pp. 96–101.

103 As recorded in the 1338 inventory, see Kleinschmidt (1915–28), vol. III, p. 32: 'Item unus corallus magnus, que fuit Fratris Henrici de Syola.'

104 For the length and structure of the lectorate programme, see Roest (2000), pp. 87–97.

105 When the general chapter of Milan in 1285 legislated on the status of the *studium generale* of Toulouse within the Order, it set Assisi on a par with Oxford and Bologna as destinations for students wishing to study beyond the confines of the Aquitaine province; see Ehrle (1892), p. 56: 'Provintia Aquitanie potest mittere unum studentem Oxonie, Assisii unum, Bononie unum'; cited by D'Alatri (1978), p. 66, as a *terminus ante quem* for the existence of a *studium generale* at the Sacro Convento. For the earlier date, see Roest (2000), p. 28. For further discussion of the various Franciscan *studia* in Umbria, see Nicolini (1982), pp. 119–22. On the status of Assisi as one of seventeen Franciscan *studia generalia* in the early fourteenth century, see Şenocak (2012a), pp. 231–2; Şenocak (2012b), p. 222.

106 Only the Franciscan *studia generalia* at Paris, Oxford and Cambridge could confer degrees by virtue of their university associations; see Roest (2000), p. 11.

107 For instance, Toulouse; see above, note 105.

108 Şenocak (2012a), p. 229.

109 It is just possible that our friar may be the 'sagacissimus quondam Mathias' referred to as an expert on his family's history in the long-running dispute between the Sant'Eustachio and Venturini clans over their respective nobility; see Schuster (1912), p. 580; quoted by Garms, Juffinger and Ward-Perkins (1981), p. 128.

110 A similar network is suggested for the Tuscan province by Giorgio Vasari's report of Cimabue gaining commissions from the Pisan Franciscans on the basis of the recommendation of the guardian of the Florentine convent of Santa Croce: 'parendo al guardiano [of Santa Croce] esser stato servito bene, ch'e' lo conducesse in S. Francesco di Pisa loro convento'; see Vasari (1966–87), vol. II: *Testo*, p. 38. Although some of Vasari's attributions to Cimabue in this passage are mistaken, his reference to the guardian's role may depend on specific information preserved among the friars of Santa Croce.

111 Boskovits (2000b), p. 406, raised the appealing possibility that John of Murrovalle, an eminent Franciscan theologian, appointed lector of the papal curia in 1291, could have been responsible for devising and commissioning the nave scheme. The proposal would reconcile Vasari's report that John had called Giotto to Assisi with an early date for the Saint Francis cycle during or shortly after Nicholas's pontificate. However, Vasari claimed that John commissioned Giotto to paint in the Upper Church when he was minister general of the Order ('allora Generale de' Frati di San Francesco'), an office he did not attain until 1296. Vasari (1966–87), vol. II: *Testo*, p. 100.

112 Some caution, however, is advisable here, as we have notices of lost Franciscan cycles painted at the end of the thirteenth century in the Order's Roman churches of Santa Maria in Aracoeli and San Francesco a Ripa. Some border fragments survive from the Aracoeli scheme, painted on the walls of the south transept, which served as a chapel for the Savelli (Pope Honorius IV's family); see Cellini (1955). According to the seventeenth-century Franciscan historian Ludovico of Modena, Pietro Cavallini had painted the nave and transepts of San Francesco a Ripa with 'many miracles of our Holy Father'; see Smart (1978), p. 30; Brooke (2006), pp. 445–6.

3 *The Upper Church in 1288*

1 For the relevant text from Vincent of Kielce's *Vita sancti Stanislai Cracoviensis episcopi* (written *c.*1260) and analysis, see Nessi (1995). The canonization was held in the 'locum superiorem, basilicam videlicet beati Francisci' and the ceremony was illuminated by lamps hanging from the middle of the vaults, spaced evenly around the church ('luxerunt luminaria in media testudine per girum ordinata proporcionaliter'). Nessi is surely correct to say that the fact that the Upper Church was chosen for the canonization is evidence in itself that the architecture was complete. See also Nessi (1994), pp. 53–5. The newly built vaults would have been unadorned save for mosaic tesserae applied to their keystones (precisely the points from which the lamps would have been suspended); see Andaloro (2001), pp. 73–7.

2 *BF* I, p. 666 (nr 489); for the full text of the bull, see below note 87.

3 Clement IV extended the privileges on 28 March 1266; see Nessi (1994), p. 57.

4 The high altar now stands at the junction of the nave and crossing, and was also in this position by the middle of the eighteenth century, before being moved to the centre of the crossing by Giovanni Battista Cavalcaselle in 1873; it was moved back in 1898. The earlier location of the altar block is unclear: it may have been shifted from the centre of the crossing bay to the mouth of the nave when the floor was relaid in 1720; alternatively it may always have been there. For these movements and restorations, see Iacovilli (1972); Hueck (2001), pp. 50, 53–4, who noted that the foundations below the floor of the crossing allow for both the central and offset positions for the altar platform.

5 For the decoration of the high altar, see Andrea Franci's entry in Bonsanti, ed. (2002), vol. IV: *Schede*, p. 619 (dating the altar block to *c.*1250, i.e. immediately before the 1253 consecration).

6 Ludovico of Pietralunga, describing the Basilica in the mid-sixteenth century, noted that the altar platform had four steps ('se ascende da ciascheduna banda a quattro scaloni'). The ceramic tiles were removed from the altar steps in 1940 and are now conserved in the sacristy of the Upper Church; see Hueck (2001), pp. 51, 54.

7 The Saint Michael altar block bears the inscription: HOC ALTAR ERECTUM EST IN HONORE BEATI MICHAELIS ARCHANGELI. See Andrea Franci's entry in Bonsanti, ed. (2002), vol. IV: *Schede*, p. 561.

8 Van Dijk (1963), vol. II, p. 421: 'Fiat duplex officium in festo angelorum de septembri secundum morem Romane ecclesie.'

9 The dedication to the apostles is given by Andrea Franci in Bonsanti, ed. (2002), vol. IV: *Schede*, p. 608.

10 In San Francesco, Gualdo Tadino, the altar of the apostles is recorded by an inscription on the pulpit (on the left side as one enters the church): NOBILES VIRI IACOBUTIUS ET DOMINUS SIMON DE FINAGUERRE FECERUNT FIERI ISTUD ALTARE AD HONOREM XII APOSTOLORUM QUI ORNAVERUNT IPSUM OPTIMIS PARAMENTIS, CALICE ET MISSALI QUICUNQUE HIC CELEBRAVERIT ORET PRO EIS. The inscription is undated but Simone di Finaguerra is named in a local notarial document of 1307; see Guerrieri (1933), p. 381. The altar seems to have been located below the pulpit, or the choir screen of which it originally formed a part. The dedication was probably a common one for early Franciscan foundations. Another example is documented for San Francesco in Pisa, where one of the transept chapels was dedicated to the apostles, probably before the end of the thirteenth century; see Pisa, Archivio di Stato, Comune D, Opera di San Francesco 1386, fol. 29v, for an inventory notice of 1368 recording liturgical textiles designated 'pro altari Apostolorum'.

11 For an overview of the literature on the papal throne see Andrea Franci's entry in Bonsanti, ed. (2002), vol. IV: *Schede*, pp. 574–5.

12 Nessi (1994), p. 157.

13 Hueck (2001), pp. 43–6, suggested a date for the throne in the late 1270s, assuming that it was completed in time for the general chapter celebrated at Assisi in 1279. Presumably some sort of throne must have been in place during Innocent IV's protracted residencies at Assisi during the summers of 1253 and 1254.

14 Franci, in Bonsanti, ed. (2002), vol. IV: *Schede*, p. 575, argued that the lions and lower elements of the throne could have been sculpted before 1253, while the seat back and the baldachin above may be rather later (based on analogies with Arnolfo di Cambio's ciborium of 1285 in San Paolo fuori le Mura). However, Wiener (1991), pp. 162–91, has argued for the homogeneity of the throne's structure and a date *c.*1278–80.

15 The inscription reads: SUPER ASPIDEM ET BASILIS[CUM AMBULABIS ET CON]CULCABIS LEONEM ET DRACONEM. See Nessi (1994), p. 157.

16 For the relationship between the two thrones, see Gandolfo (1983), pp. 88–95.

17 Noted first by Hertlein (1964), pp. 109–12; see also Gandolfo (1983), p. 97.

18 Hueck (2001), pp. 49–50, following initial observations by Schöne (1957), pp. 63–76. The distinctive design of the bases of the column clusters at the head of the nave may indicate that they were intended to connect to a screen structure.

19 Hueck (2001), p. 52.

20 See the entry by Enrica Neri Lusanna in Bonsanti, ed. (2002), vol. IV: *Schede*, p. 548. For the payment in 1347 to Fra Martino 'pro pergulo, ubi predicatur in superiori ecclesia', see Alessandri and Pennacchi (1914), p. 80. For a later dating, *c.*1400, see Hueck (2001), p. 51 n. 38.

21 Hueck (2001), pp. 51–2, cited examination of the surrounding plaster by Sergio Fusetti.

22 Nessi (1995), pp. 88–9: the legend of Saint Stanislas specified that Pope Innocent preached from the pulpit ('Romanus pontifex ascendit ad pulpitum').

23 Hueck (2001), pp. 47–8. The lower borders of Cimabue's apsidal cycle were examined when the Renaissance stalls were removed in 1999 during the conservation campaigns following the 1997 earthquake. The condition of the plaster suggested an arrangement with wooden stalls rather than integral stone seating.

24 For a summary of the San Rufino contract, see Cenci (1974–6), vol. I, p. 105 (the original document is Assisi, Archivio di San Rufino, pergamena iv, 40); in this document the Opera

of San Rufino commissioned three local craftsmen 'facere et construere et ordinare in dicta ecclesia superiori [of San Rufino], videlicet in tribuna . . . unum chorum de bono lignamine, omnibus eorum sumptibus et expensis, cum sediis illius amplitudinis et longitudinis ac etiam laborerio prout sunt facte sede chori existentis in ecclesia superiori beati Francissci de Assisio, cum colundellis a parte inferiori ac etiam bactetoriis et cum duobus legeis parvulis'.

25 For Domenico da Sanseverino's choir, see Roberto Paolo Novello's entries in Bonsanti, ed. (2002), vol. IV: *Schede*, pp. 608–19.

26 Cenci (1974–6), vol. II, p. 857. Antonio was to build 'in ecclesia superiori predicta, unum corum secundum longitudinem cori veteris', but was also instructed 'facere et fabricare, iuxta dictum corum, iuxta murum usque ad hostium sacristie dicte ecclesie et altare posito ab alio latere, similiter sediles prout in coro predicto'. These must be the banks of stalls that currently surround the walls of the two transepts, and the wording of the contract implies that the earlier choir did not extend into these areas.

27 Theis (2004) and (2006).

28 These cosmati fragments, now integrated into the singing gallery and Magdalen chapel in the Lower Church, are usually connected with the thirteenth-century choir screen of the Lower Basilica; see Hueck (1984).

29 Theis's proposition (2006, p. 61) that the hypothetical *schola cantorum* could have been removed in the early fourteenth century, following the papacy's transfer to France with the election of Clement V in 1305, depends on dating the Saint Francis cycle to after that date, as later proposed by Schwarz with Zöschg (2008), pp. 238–54, 331–44. See pp. 12, 41–3 above for the problems associated with this proposed chronology.

30 Recently the specific subject of two articles: Gieben (2001) and Nessi (2005).

31 The occasion was the investiture of Francesco Boncompagni, nephew of Gregory XV, as bishop of Fano; our principal source for this event is a letter written on 3 August 1624 by bishop of Assisi Marcello Crescenzi to Cardinal Federico Borromeo. Crescenzi described 'che l'anno passato, mentre dovevo consecrare l'Illustrissimo Cardinale Buoncompagni all'hora Legato di Perugia, nella Chiesa superiore di San Francesco di qui, havendo per tal funtione fatto calare à basso il Crocefisso che stava sopra un trave in mezo della medesima Chiesa'; Rotondi (1927), pp. 190–91. Nessi (2005), pp. 698–9, clarified that Francesco's investiture was held during autumn 1622, not 1623 as is often supposed from the wording of Crescenzi's letter.

32 It was seen in this position shortly after 1652 by the anonymous Capuchin author of the *Guida del pellegrino*: 'fu levato el trave che stava sopra l'altare [for the investiture ceremony] . . . in mezzo del quale stava quella gran croce ch'ora si vede sopra la porta maggiore'; L'Aquila, Biblioteca Provinciale, Ms J 44, fol. 25r, first quoted by Supino (1924), p. 41; see also Nessi (2005), p. 702.

33 Angeli (1704), p. 32: '[Giunta] fecit Crucifixi imaginem, super Altare majus superioris Templi olim locatem, dein super primarium Januam, nunc temporis dente quasi corrosam depositam cernimus.'

34 At the end of the eighteenth century, Sebastiano Ranghiasci noted that after the cross had been 'trasportato sopra la porta interiore della stessa chiesa, in occasione d'una solenne festa . . . quindi pochi anni dopo per l'umido, e la pioggia, che spingevasi dal mal custodito finestrone superiore della facciata a levante, si disfece in pezzi cadendo'; Fea (1820), p. 14.

35 In July that year Ranieri Tempesti looked in vain for Giunta's cross; see Nessi (2005), pp. 703–5.

36 Described in the biography of Margaritone d'Arezzo as 'dipinto alla greca, sopra un legno che attraversa la chiesa'; Vasari (1966–87), vol. II: *Testo*, p. 92; Vasari is known to have visited Assisi in May 1563 and April 1566; see Nessi (2005), p. 697.

37 The discovery of the inscription must have been made soon after the cross was taken down, for an accurate transcription was already appended to Bishop Crescenzi's letter of August 1624. Other readings, however, were less reliable; for a full consideration of the various versions, see Nessi (2005), pp. 700, 708–10.

38 Giunta's image was quickly taken up by both sides in the contemporary debate on the original form of the Franciscan habit, which pitted Capuchin friars against Conventuals. Fig. 61 is the copperplate engraving made by Adriaen Lommelin and Lucas Vorsterman for Carolus van Arenberg (1593–1669), the Capuchin historian from Antwerp; it was intended for a polemical tract on the Franciscan habit and was finally published in *Icones antiquae quibus ostenditur Fratres Minores Capucinos eamdem gerere habitus formam* (Brussels, 1666). The print reverses the direction of the figure; the original copperplate (preserved in the Museo Francescano at the Collegio di San Lorenzo da Brindisi in Rome) has the correct orientation; see Gieben (2001), pp. 108–9, figs 3–4. We are indebted to Padre Servus Gieben of the Istituto Storico dei Cappuccini for sharing with us his expert knowledge of van Arenberg's work.

39 Lunghi (1995b), p. 231, attributed this painting to the Bolognese artist Francesco Providoni, who executed the engravings for Angeli's 1704 volume. It was first published by Krüger (1992), p. 158, fig. 294.

40 Nessi (1994), p. 204, fig. 85 and (2005), plate 4.

41 Boverio (1640), p. 57 (first published as an appendix to Boverio (1632–9), vol. I, p. 900): 'At celebris est Fratris Eliae effigies, qui in superiori aede S. Francisci, ad pedes cuiusdam *ingentis molis Crucifixi*, qui ante maius altare altius in trabe prominebat [our italics].' Catalano (1652), p. 298: 'à piede d'una gran mole d'un Crocifisso'. The *Guida del pellegrino* referred to 'quella gran croce'; see above note 32.

42 Nessi (1994), pp. 206–7, associated Angela's vision with Giunta's cross, although Lunghi (2000), pp. 18–19, has instead linked Angela's description of Christ 'quasi tunc noviter de cruce depositi' with the fresco of the *Lamentation* in the Passion cycle on the south wall of the nave. For Angela's account, see Thier and Calufetti, eds (1985), pp. 486–9. The fact that Angela had the vision during Mass at the high altar when the Host was elevated may indicate that Giunta's cross, which was axially set above the altar, was the more likely visual stimulus.

43 Cannon (2002), p. 577.

44 For the late thirteenth-century cross in San Francesco, Arezzo, one of the largest examples, at 576.5 × 372 cm, see Droandi (2010), pp. 189–92. For the crucifix attributed to the Maestro di San Francesco, dated 1272 and measuring 489 × 352 cm, from the Perugian church of San Francesco al Prato (and often regarded as especially close to the lost Elias cross), see the catalogue entry by Serena Romano in Bon Valsassina and Garibaldi, eds (1994), pp. 63–5.

45 For Cavalcaselle's interventions, see Hueck (1981a), esp. pp. 147–8, fig. 5; and Mozzo (2003), p. 133, for documents fixing the installation of the facsimile to 1874; see also Mozzo (2003), figs 10 and 95, for early photographs showing the new cross and beam *in situ*. The reconstruction of the cross and beam seems to have been removed when Cavalcaselle's other interventions in the Upper Church were reversed in 1892.

46 Vasari used the same phrase – 'alla greca' – to describe the surviving crucifix in San Francesco, Arezzo, which he also attributed to Margaritone; Vasari (1966–87), vol. II: *Testo*, p. 90.

47 For the Santa Maria degli Angeli crucifix, see Lunghi (1995a), pp. 47–63. The fragmentary inscription reads: [GIU]NTA PISANUS [CAP]ITINI ME F[ECI]T. The cross measures 174 × 131 cm and is undated. The dimensions of the cross suggest that it may originally have been painted for the Porziuncola; see Sperandio (2001), pp. 65, 104, fig. 28.

48 Belting (1981), pp. 220–21, translated as Belting (1990), pp. 144–5, fixed the development of the *Christus Patiens* to Giunta's Assisi period in the 1230s.

49 Catalano (1652), p. 287: 'che il pittore di queste immagini [in Santa Chiara], come somigliantissime di mano, e nel colorito à quel Crocifisso, che fe far frat'Elia (che noi esamineremo appresso) fosse discepolo all'Autore di quest'altro Crocifisso più antico, e per conseguenza dal suo maestro apprendesse la forma di dipingere dette immagini'.

50 For the Santa Chiara cross and Abbess Benedicta's donor figure, see Lunghi (1995a), pp. 60–62. The inscription consciously echoes Elias's: D[OMI]NA BENEDICTA POST S[ANCTAM] CLA[RAM] P[R]IMA ABBATISSA ME FEC[IT] FIERI. The general similarities between the Elias cross and the Santa Chiara crucifix probably account for the frequent attribution of the latter to Giunta in the early sources. See Angeli (1704), p. 104: 'Servatur tres imagines in tabula [in Santa Chiara], a Giunta Pisano Graecorum alumno delineatae, quae Crucifixum Dominum, B. Matrem Virginem, et S. Claram exprimunt: postque majorem Aram locatae conspiciuntur.' The Santa Chiara cross is conventionally dated between 1255 (the canonization of Saint Clare, also depicted on the *suppedaneum*) and 1260 (the death of Abbess Benedicta), but Andrea De Marchi has now suggested a date in the late 1270s, arguing that the cross celebrated Benedicta's patronage after her death; see De Marchi (2009), pp. 608–11.

51 This idea can be traced back to Oertel (1937), p. 230, and continues to be repeated in the literature: see Hueck (1984), pp. 196, 201 n. 34; Ciatti (2001), p. 32 ('the lost [crucifix] of Fra Elia, of 1236, for the lower Basilica in Assisi'). The presence of a cross in the Lower Church at the end of the thirteenth century is confirmed by a passage in the *Libro* of Beata Angela of Foligno, who stood beside it while Mass was sung ('Et dum cantabatur Missa, posuit se iuxta crucem inter crates ferri'); Thier and Calufetti, eds (1985), pp. 260–61. There is, however, no reason to connect this reference to the Elias cross. Nessi (1994), pp. 208–9, suggested that the Lower Church cross may have been the smaller painted crucifix by Giunta now at Santa Maria degli Angeli.

52 The theory of a Giotto crucifix has been aired most recently by Bellosi (2001). See Nessi (2005), pp. 694–5, for a comprehensive critique.

53 These measurements are taken from the cross-section of the Basilica in Rocchi (1982), plate XV. On the placement of the Elias cross in the Lower Church, we can only concur with the dismissive judgement of Nessi (2005), p. 695, that this is an idea without any documentary or logical support ('un'idea . . . senza alcun sostegno documentario e logico').

54 Hueck (1984), p. 201 n. 34, refers to payments of 1513 relating to the cross's support as evidence that the crucifix was moved from the Lower to the Upper Church at that date. For the documents, see Cenci (1974–6), vol. II, p. 1024: the first 'in agutis, causa atandi pontem in ecclesia superiori, den. 6' (3 May 1513); the second 'pro fune causa ponendi crucem ecclesie superiori, sol. 5' (4 May 1513). However, Nessi (2005), p. 697, is surely correct to relate these modest expenses to the

erection of a temporary platform for the general chapter of the Order celebrated at Assisi that spring.

55 See Zanardi, Frugoni and Zeri (1996), pp. 66–77. In the closing scene, the *Liberation of Peter of Alife*, the background *giornate*, nrs 492–3, again reflect the position of the beam; see pp. 352–62 (*giornata* map at p. 355). As we have already seen in Chapter 2, this and the *Homage of a Simple Man* were the final scenes of the cycle to be painted. We may also exclude the possibility that the beam was inserted shortly before the Saint Francis cycle was painted as a replacement for a screen structure at the head of the nave, as suggested by Hueck (2001), p. 52. While monumental crosses are known to have been mounted directly onto screens, it is scarcely credible that the friars at Assisi repositioned their cross in the knowledge that its new beam would interrupt the planned frescoes in such striking fashion. It is much more likely that the beam would have been juxtaposed with a screen below; similar arrangements are documented for other Italian churches in this period, see De Marchi (2009); and below, note 57.

56 The recent conservation of the Santa Maria Novella cross established that the panel, weighing around three hundred kilograms, was primarily supported at its base and pitched forward, with the hooks on the rear providing subsidiary stabilization; see Ciatti (2001), p. 58.

57 For a consideration of the evidence for the original location of Giotto's crucifix, see Ciatti (2001), pp. 55–9. Since the publication of Ciatti and Seidel, eds (2001), Schwartz (2005) has advanced an appealing amendment to the *tramezzo* setting, proposing that the cross was supported on a beam, above and separate from the screen, more than nine metres clear of the floor.

58 For the building history of the Dominican church, see Lunardi (2001). Traces of late thirteenth-century frescoes have been discovered on the arch above the *tramezzo* screen, an indication that work had progressed this far by the time Giotto painted his crucifix; see Ciatti (2001), p. 58.

59 For an up-to-date survey of Elias's life, see Vecchio (1993).

60 'Frater Helias dominus et custos ecclesie Sancti Francisci asisinatis' is named in a document composed in the Basilica on 27 May 1239; see Bartoli Langeli with Bossa and Fiumi, eds (1997), pp. 23–5. For the two bells cast by Bartholomaeus Pisanus and his son Loteringio for Brother Elias in 1239, see Brooke (2006), pp. 60–61. As Brooke notes, the bell commissions imply that the Basilica's campanile was well advanced if not complete in 1239, which would in turn mean that substantial sections of the Upper Church were also standing by then.

61 The surprise rediscovery of the donor portrait in 1622 appears to confirm its prior invisibility; see Boverio (1640), p. 57: 'Mirabile dictu, cum trabs, cui lignea Crucifixi imago innitebatur, tam alte a terra emineret, ut fratris Eliae effigies penitus videri non posset.'

62 For the Cortona reliquary, probably given to Elias on his mission to Constantinople and Nicaea on behalf of Emperor Frederick II in 1243, see Goldschmidt and Weitzmann (1979), vol. II, pp. 48–9 (nr 77); Venuti (2004).

63 Maines (1986).

64 For a schematic reconstruction of Suger's great cross, see Gerson (1986), p. 192, fig. 10.

65 Suger's inscription read: REX BONE, SUGGERI DIGNARE PIUS MISERERI; DE CRUCE PROTEGE ME, PRO CRUCE DIRIGE ME. ('Good King, deign mercifully to pity Suger; From the Cross protect me; for [the sake of] the Cross direct me.') English translation from Maines (1986), p. 85. Elias's 1236 inscription mirrored Suger's in both sentiment and wording: 'pie' / 'pius'; 'miserere' / 'misereri'. Both echoed the penitential supplication 'miserere nobis' of the Agnus Dei.

66 Maines (1986), p. 79: 'they do not commemorate him as a worthy donor; rather the Suger they commemorate is presented as a sinful suppliant, insistently asking for mercy'.

67 We should, however, note the early links between the Franciscans and the abbey of Saint-Denis. The first friars reached Paris *c.*1218–19 but were refused leave to reside within the city itself and instead settled at Saint-Denis with the blessing of the abbot (this seems to have been the earliest Franciscan house in the Île-de-France). Haymo of Faversham, later minister general, joined the Order at Saint-Denis in 1226. The abbey's early hospitality towards the friars is witnessed in a letter written by Gregory of Naples (provincial minister from 1219) to Abbot Eudes Clément in 1231: 'Cum dudum apud Sanctum Dyonisium peregrini venissemus, non habentes ubi possemus capita reclinare, vos in domo vestra propria collocastis.' See Callebaut (1917), pp. 291–3, 303–4.

68 Lunghi (1995a), pp. 55–6; Ariberto is depicted beneath the feet of the dead Christ, holding a model of the basilica, in memory of his rebuilding of San Dionigi. The Milan cross's original setting is unknown but its monumental dimensions (257 × 190 cm) suggest that it occupied a central position similar to the Elias cross.

69 Desiderius's inscription on the apsidal arch of the Montecassino basilica was recorded by Leo of Ostia; see Hoffmann, ed. (1980), p. 397. For a recent overview of the abbot's artistic patronage, see Toubert (1994).

70 Mariano, writing before 1518, noted Elias's death in 1253 'cum laboraret in constructione ecclesie et conventus Cortone'; for Mariano's text, see 'Compendium chronicarum Fratrum Minorum' (1909), p. 311. Lunghi (1995b), p. 233, citing the example of the Ariberto cross, argued that Elias was portrayed

on the 1236 crucifix in the double aspect of donor of the cross and architect of the Basilica.

71 Two notarial acts from 1245 and 1246 record the transfer of the site for the new Franciscan church in Cortona to Elias himself; Inga (1978) (documents transcribed on pp. 50–52). For the Cortona church see also Cadei (1978). For the tradition recording Elias as an architect, see Nessi (1994), pp. 66–70.

72 For Elias's diplomatic activities on behalf of both Pope Gregory IX and Emperor Frederick II, see Vecchio (1993), pp. 452–3.

73 Rather than looking back to medieval precedents, Silvestro Nessi saw Elias as 'un precursore del Rinascimento'; see Nessi (1994), pp. 84–5.

74 For this process, see Krüger (1992), pp. 156–61.

75 Angeli (1704), p. 32: 'duae aegregiae icones, hinc Spiritum Sanctum super B. Virginem, & Apostolos discendentem, illic S. Michaelem Arcangelum in Luciferum Praeliantem demonstrant. At Juncta alio vocatus opus deservit'; this passage was noted by Scarpellini (1978), pp. 110–11, in relation to Giunta's cross and the *Verification* fresco.

76 Assisi, Biblioteca del Sacro Convento, Fondo Moderno 244bis, fol. 50v: 'In eclesia superiori sunt due tabule una representat Spiritus Sanctus super apostolos descendens, altera immago S. Micaelis Ar: et demonstrat prelianter cum Dracone at Iuncta aliò vocatus opus deservit anno d: 1236.' For a description of the manuscript, see Casagrande, d'Alessandro and Gigante, eds (1988), pp. 120–21, who dated the notebook to the seventeenth century but claimed that the two images by Giunta were frescoes when they were clearly panels ('tabule').

77 The suggestion was made by Scarpellini (1978), pp. 110–11, but has not found great favour in subsequent Assisi scholarship.

78 For the reconstruction of the Santa Chiara beam ensemble, comprising the Benedicta cross, the *vita* retable of Saint Clare and a panel of the Virgin and Child, see Hueck (1997), p. 290, who proposed that the latter two panels, being nearly identical in size and both preserving traces of attachment on their lower edges, were originally placed on a beam to either side of the Benedicta cross, in an arrangement similar to that depicted in the *Verification of the Stigmata* scene. ('Man könnte überlegen, ob nicht die fast gleich großen Tafeln der thronenden Madonna und der heiligen Klara, die beide den Ansatz eines Standartenfußes zeigen, eine Aufstellung zu Seiten des großen Kreuzes haben sollten, vergleichbar den Bildern auf dem Tramezzobalken in der "Prüfung der Stigmata" aus der Franzlegende in der Oberkirche von S. Francesco.') The suggestion that these three images could have been mounted on a beam was first made by Bracaloni (1939), p. 209 n. 1.

79 De Marchi (2009).

80 For the setting of Giotto's *Stigmatization* in Pisa and the related ensemble of images in Santa Croce, see Cooper (forthcoming).

81 The significance of the painted panels does not seem to have travelled well: they are, curiously, omitted from the only close copy of the *Verification* scene, in San Fortunato, Todi, painted around the middle of the fourteenth century, where a beam bereft of images runs along the top of the composition; see Lunghi (1988), pp. 140–43; Blume (1983), pp. 54–7, 173.

82 The archangel in the *Verification* fresco also bears comparison with the stained-glass windows, and – as Hayden Maginnis reminded us – the use of silhouetted panels was known in this period. The fragility of their wooden supports probably explains the meagre rate of survival. See Maginnis (1980). The frontal pose of the Virgin might appear somewhat archaic for the late thirteenth century, but it may have echoed not only the image in the 'Angel Window' but also the lost Pentecost panel from the Upper Church beam, which, according to Angeli's description, depicted the Virgin seated amid the apostles. Both the Pentecost fresco on the counter-façade and the minister general's seal of the same subject incorporated a frontally posed Virgin; on the modernity of the seal's iconography in the thirteenth century, see Gardner (2011), p. 465.

83 Conservation work suggests the presence of a beam at the Porziuncola; see Sperandio (2001), pp. 64–5; and, for further analysis, Frugoni (2001), pp. 368–71.

84 Innocent would return to Assisi in spring the following year, arriving on 21 April 1254 and staying for the whole of May until Pentecost; according to his biographer, the Franciscan bishop of Assisi Nicholas of Calvi, he would have stayed longer but for the political need to return to Rome. See Pagnotti (1898), pp. 113–14. It is likely that Innocent regarded Assisi as his preferred summer base in Italy, and would probably have returned again had he not died in Naples in December 1254. Clement IV's brief residence between the end of August and 6 September 1265 is the only other securely documented visit of the curia to Assisi in the thirteenth century.

85 The pope arrived at Assisi from Perugia on 27 April 1253 and stayed until Monday 6 October, having celebrated the feast of Saint Francis in the Basilica the preceding Saturday, as recorded by Nicholas of Calvi: 'Celebrato postmodum ibi sollempniter festo beati Francisci die sabbati, die lune sequenti egrediens de Asisio cum tota curia'; Pagnotti (1898), p. 111; quoted by Nessi (1994), p. 54 n. 56.

86 The movements of the curia can be tracked to within a few days via the papal registers: Berger, ed. (1884–1920), vol. IV, p. 567 (first bull given at Assisi: 30 April 1253), p. 568 (last

bull given at Assisi: 4 October 1253), p. 570 (first bull given at Assisi: 5 May 1254), p. 571 (last bull given at Assisi: 31 May 1254).

87 *BF* I, p. 666 (nr 489): 'Dilecto filio Fratri Philippo de Campello Ordinis Minorum Magistro et Praeposito operis Ecclesiae Sancti Francisci Assisiat. salutem et apostolicam benedictionem. Decet, et expedit honorificas illis aedificare Basilicas, qui suis gloriosis meritis praecelsum aulae caelestis habitaculum sunt adepti; ut qui digni habiti sunt honore in regione superna perpetuo sublimari, omnimode in terris devotione a Christifidelibus merito venerentur; fiantque sibi ab illis Ecclesiae celebres, in quibus convenienter adoretur Omnipotens, et eorum memoria solemniter percolatur; ut dum sic decor domus Dei diligitur, et tabernaculum studiose componitur suae laudis, ejus propitiatio Sanctorum ipsorum intercessionibus facilius, et uberius impetretur. Hinc est, quod cum Venerabilis Ecclesia Sancti Francisci Assisiat. nondum sit decenti, prout convenit, opere consummata; Nos cupientes ob reverentiam Sancti ejusdem seduli apud Deum pro populo christiano patroni dictam Ecclesiam et nobili compleri structura, et insignis praeminentia operis decorari; ut oblationes in pecunia tu, et alii, qui Praepositi operis ejusdem Ecclesiae pro tempore fuerint, ad Altaria ipsius Ecclesiae, ac alias etiam pro eodem opere recipere valeatis in idem opus totaliter, et fideliter expendendas; prout Venerabilis Frater noster Ostiensis, et Velletrensis Episcopus, vel alius Romanae Ecclesiae Cardinalis, qui Ordinis Fratrum Minorum Protector extiterit, ordinandum, vel disponendum duxerit; contrariis ejusdem Ordinis Statutis et inhibitionibus Generalis, seu Provincialis Ministrorum, aut Custodis, vel Guardiani loci, seu aliorum Fratrum ipsius ordinis nequaquam obstantibus; auctoritate Apostolica indulgemus. Nulli ergo omnino hominum liceat hanc paginam nostrae concessionis infringere, vel ei ausu etc. Praesentibus post vigesimum quintum annum minime valituris. Datum Assisii VI. Idus Julii Pontificatus Nostri Anno Undecimo.' English translation adapted from Brooke (2006), pp. 66–7.

88 Theis (2004), p. 154: '[Innocent IV] dürfte dabei jedoch nicht nur die dekorative Gestaltung von Ober- und Unterkirche gemeint, sondern sicherlich auch ihre liturgische Einrichtung im Blick gehabt haben.'

89 The standard work on the Basilica's glass is Martin and Ruf (1997). For the apse glass, see also Martin (1993).

90 For Lyon cathedral's two rose windows from the 1240s and the apsidal lancets from the early thirteenth century, see Inventaire Général des Monuments . . . de la France (1986), pp. 296–300. The impressive rose in the north transept was commissioned by Arnoud de Colonges, a cathedral canon from 1241 to 1250, and includes his donor figure holding the window, accompanied by the inscription: LI DOIENS ERNOUS ME FECIS FACERE. The Lyon glass was not taken into account by Brooke (2006), p. 309, when she dismissed Innocent's French exile as a meaningful source of inspiration for *Decet et expedit*: 'During the almost seven years he spent [in Lyon] in exile, Innocent IV had naturally no opportunity to visit any of the Gothic cathedrals in northern Europe . . . there is no evidence that he was personally acquainted with any of the glorious stained glass that was being installed in cathedrals and churches throughout northern Europe in this period.'

91 According to Bonaventure, Alexander had seen the stigmata with his own eyes; for this tradition, see below, Chapter 5, note 81.

92 Nessi (1994), pp. 55–6.

93 For the apse glass, see Martin and Ruf (1997), pp. 19–40, 235–52 (with a dating of *c.*1255); for the 'Gothic workshop' in the transepts, see pp. 41–52, 253–67 (with a dating of *c.*1275).

94 For the Maestro di San Francesco workshop, see Martin and Ruf (1997), pp. 53–78, 267–90 (with a dating of *c.*1275–80 or the final quarter of the thirteenth century). For a useful English language introduction to these windows, see Martin (1996).

95 Martin and Ruf (1997), pp. 76, 88, observed that the scenes of Saint Anthony of Padua's life depend in part on the *Vita benignitas*, commissioned from John Pecham by Jerome of Ascoli during his term as minister general (1274–8), probably at the general chapter in Padua in 1276. For Jerome's role, see Franchi (1990), pp. 56–7, and above, p. 19.

96 Some of the idiosyncrasies of the apse and transept glass may result from elements being re-used from the windows of the Lower Church, a possibility considered by Rocchi Coopmans de Yoldi (2002), pp. 72–3.

97 Martin and Ruf (1997), pp. 39–40. However, Amy Neff identified a number of unusual and distinctively Franciscan inflections in the choice of scenes in the apse windows, material presented in her lecture 'Landscapes of Prayer in Franciscan Stained Glass and Painted Panel: Cave, Revelation and Word', given at the Courtauld Institute of Art, 1 June 2011. Gerard of Borgo San Donnino's *Introductorium in Evangelium Æternum*, which had identified the Franciscans as the Order destined to rule the Roman Church in the approaching age of the Holy Spirit, had been condemned in 1255. John of Parma's passion for the same apocalyptic speculation that underpinned Gerard's work forced his resignation in 1257; see Burr (2001), pp. 29–32; Brooke (2006), pp. 252–4.

98 Martin and Ruf (1997), p. 261 (cat. nr 80).

99 Martin and Ruf (1997), p. 261 (cat. nr 81).

100 Martin and Ruf (1997), p. 274 (cat. nr 116).
101 Brooke (2006), p. 317.
102 Martin (1996), pp. 183–5; Brooke (2006), p. 318.
103 See below, Chapter 7, pp. 133, 198.
104 A further window, on the south side of the second nave bay, depicts images of prophets and bishop saints. The images do not appear to fit the apostolic scheme evident in the other nave windows, and it has been suggested that these lights may have been formed of glass re-used from the Lower Church; see Pietro Scarpellini's commentary in Ludovico of Pietralunga (1982), p. 360.
105 For the scenes in this window, see Martin and Ruf (1997), pp. 274–8 (cat. nrs 117–28). For the proposal that the Saint Francis and Saint Anthony narratives were originally intended for one of the transept windows, see Cadei (1983), p. 156, fig. 26.
106 The format of the Perugian altarpiece was established by Gordon (1982).
107 For the Gubbio frescoes, see Rosati (1983), pp. 27–43.
108 Martin and Ruf (1997), pp. 276–7 (cat. nr 122).
109 Martin and Ruf (1997), p. 278 (cat. nr 128).
110 For the 'Angel Window', see Martin and Ruf (1997), pp. 287–90 (cat. nrs 157–64). Before the Second World War the 'Angel Window' was set in the south light of the third bay and was only moved to its current position in the fourth bay during the post-war reinstallation of the Upper Church glass. For a photomontage of the window in the third bay, see Frugoni (2001), p. 372, fig. 9, with further analysis of the iconographic links between the glass and the surrounding frescoes on pp. 374–7. The pre-war arrangement of the nave windows is described by Giusto (1911), pp. 187–248 (the 'Angel Window' at pp. 234–7).
111 Martin and Ruf (1997), p. 288 (cat. nr 157).
112 Poulenc (1983); Martin and Ruf (1997), pp. 84–6.
113 English translation from Brooke (2006), p. 330.
114 For Angela's vision before the window, see Thier and Calufetti, eds (1985), pp. 184–5.
115 Thier and Calufetti, eds (1985), pp. 184–5: '[Francis] dixit mihi: Ita te astrictam tenebo et multo plus quam possit considerari cum oculis corporis.'
116 Thier and Calufetti, eds (1985), pp. 170–71: 'Et dixi sibi quod nunquam de cetero iterum auderet venire Assisium . . . et dixi sociis eius quod nunquam ducerent eam.'
117 The most thorough treatment of this problem is Binski (2001), proposing that the visual sources used by the northern workshop suggest links with the Rhineland as much as with France or England.
118 Binski (2001), p. 95.
119 Binski (2001), p. 92.
120 The heraldic implications of the lilies were first noted by Poeschke (1983), p. 162; the same point was amplified by Lunghi (1995b), pp. 240–41.
121 Based on comparisons between the painted canopies above the triforia arcades and the architectural detail of Strasbourg cathedral, Binski (2001), p. 136, indicated that a date earlier than *c.*1275 for the north transept frescoes is unlikely, noting: 'Even at a date of *c.*1280 the Assisi work is tellingly up to date.' This is echoed by Brooke (2006), p. 342.
122 White and Zanardi (1983), esp. p. 105.
123 The following discussion is indebted to the definitive analysis of the city view by Andaloro (1984a).
124 Bellosi (1998), pp. 161–2, accepted the accuracy of Andaloro's topographical analysis but not her ideological reading. For a tough critique of Bellosi's position, see Brooke (2006), p. 350.
125 For this iconography and its possible sources, see Gardner (1973a), p. 437 n. 118, quoting an English Franciscan source, the *Chronicon de Lanercost* (see Stevenson, ed. (1839), p. 99), which described the now lost fresco: 'Hic [Nicholas III] beato Francisco in tantum extitit devotus ut supra altare capellae suae [the chapel of Saint Nicholas on the right hand side of the nave in Old Saint Peter's] depingi faceret sanctum Nicholaum se ad superiora ducentem et sanctum Franciscum a tergo impellentem.'
126 *BF* III, pp. 404–16 (nr 127).
127 For the original location of the papal palace in the north wing of the Sacro Convento, see Pietramellara *et al.* (1988), pp. 19–21. The palace was in use as early as 1239: Elias of Cortona was accused of residing there before his deposition that year; see Salimbene of Parma (1966), vol. I, p. 235.
128 We simply do not concur with the judgement of Bellosi (1998), p. 162, on the visibility of the Orsini armorials: 'tre piccoli stemmi . . . che è impossibile vedere distintamente a quell'altezza, se non armandosi di un potente binoccolo'. Brooke (2006), p. 343, gives the height of the crossing vaults as 18.5 metres.
129 Brooke (2006), p. 350.
130 Brooke (2006), p. 97 n. 104, is mistaken in claiming Nicholas III's presence at the 1279 general chapter at Assisi on the basis of a passage in *Exiit qui seminat*. The chapter was held at Pentecost, which fell on 21 May in 1279; see Abate (1935), p. 60. Nicholas is documented at Saint Peter's in Rome throughout May, issuing bulls there on 20 and 22 May. He remained in Rome during June before travelling to his villa at Soriano, near Viterbo, between 1 and 11 July, where he stayed until mid-September. For the pope's movements, see Gay and Vitte, eds (1938), p. 423. The relevant passage from *Exiit* has been translated as: 'The brothers of the Order

themselves, assembled in a general chapter, have given occasion to this desire [to clarify the Rule]. Our beloved sons, the general minister and several of the provincial ministers who had gathered at the chapter, appeared in our presence on that occasion.' See *FAED* III, p. 741. This must refer to the visit to Soriano of the new minister general, Bonagrazia, and provincial ministers, following the general chapter, to request the appointment of a new cardinal protector. (Nicholas appointed his nephew Matteo Rosso Orsini after studying a secret ballot taken among the friars.) The original Latin of *Exiit* reads: 'ut Fratres ejusdem Ordinis nuper in Generali Capitulo congregati providerant; dilectis Filiis Generali, et nonnullis aliis Provincialibus ejusdem Ordinis Ministris, qui in Capitulo ipso convenerant, in Nostra praesentia constitutis'. As the editors of the *Bullarium Franciscanum* observed in their notes, the meeting must have been at Soriano; see *BF* III, p. 405 note (g). For Philip of Perugia's first-hand account of this embassy, see Salimbene of Parma (1905–13), pp. 682–4.

131 The pope died suddenly, probably of a stroke; see Allegrezza (2000), p. 445.

132 Hueck (1981b) showed that the choices of scenes reflected the liturgical readings from the Franciscan breviary and missal for the relevant feasts corresponding to the three altar dedications.

133 For an iconographic survey of these cycles, see Brooke (2006), pp. 353–65.

134 Belting (1983), p. 93: 'Gli affreschi del transetto, con scene della vita degli Apostoli, citano quasi letteralmente i prototipi nel portico dell'antico S. Pietro a Roma.'

135 Belting (1977), p. 53, categorized Cimabue's twin *Crucifixions* as large-scale devotional pictures ('großformatige Andachtsbilder'), directed towards the Franciscan community.

136 Nessi (1994), pp. 229–30.

137 The arguments advanced by Bellosi (1985), pp. 149–54, and repeated in subsequent publications – for example, Bellosi (1998), pp. 160–67; Bellosi (2007) – for Cimabue's cycles being painted as late as 1288, as the first response to *Reducentes*, are not convincing.

138 Hueck (2001), pp. 45–7, following a suggestion of Elvio Lunghi's, observed that the friars would have known three years in advance that their general chapter would convene at Assisi in 1279, providing ample time and motivation to commission and complete the transept programme.

139 The measurement is calculated from Rocchi (1982), plate XV. For a reconstruction of another combined beam and screen arrangement, see Schwartz (2005).

4 *Planning the Nave Programme*

1 Lavin coined the term 'double parallel' for the arrangement of the two narrative cycles on opposite walls, both running in the same direction. The early Christian mosaics in the nave of the papal basilica of Santa Maria Maggiore in Rome are also arranged in a double parallel, but in this case there is only one horizontal register, with Old Testament scenes on both walls. For an overview of double-parallel schemes in early Christian churches, mainly in Rome, see Lavin (1990), pp. 15–27.

2 Belting (1977), p. 71, observed that this represented a departure ('ein Novum') with respect to the Roman prototypes.

3 Morello and Kanter, eds (1999), pp. 54–9; Cook (1999), pp. 62–3 (cat. nr 27).

4 Ludovico of Pietralunga (1982), pp. 79–80.

5 With the possible exception of the girl with the crooked neck, who perhaps appears in a new context, the *Canonization* (see Chapter 5, p. 143).

6 The eighth, the *Canonization*, had already been pictured on the Bardi dossal in Florence (for which see pp. 99–102).

7 For the rebuilding and redecoration of the Lower Church, see Cooper (2005) and Robson (2005).

8 The iconography is ambiguous: the saint holds the leg of the cripple, who has crutches, but no water is represented. Cook (1999), pp. 44–7 (cat. nr 21), argues that the usual composition for the Bartholomew of Narni miracle may have been adapted to turn it into a scene of Saint Francis caring for a leper.

9 Catalano (1652), pp. 124, 324 (descriptions), 319–20 (engravings).

10 Frugoni (2011a), pp. 219–20; she also noted that the iconography of the saint's ascending soul was not understood by the painter who copied it, who described it only as 'un'altro frate più elevato sopra nubi, con le mani giunte'.

11 Frugoni (2011a), p. 221.

12 Those without precedent are scenes 1, 2, 3, 9, 10, 12, 14, 16, 17, 21, 22, 23, 25, 26, 27 and 28; those with new iconographies are scenes 11, 13, 18 (if one discounts the *paliotto*) and 24.

13 See Little, ed. (1914), p. 678.

14 Many of the manuscripts were preserved in non-Franciscan libraries; see Michael Bihl's preface to *Legenda S. Francisci Assisiensis: Saeculis XIII et XIV conscriptae ad codicum fidem recensitae*, *AF* X, pp. ix–xix, xxx–xxxvi. For a recent critical study of the surviving *Vita secunda* manuscripts, see Thomas of Celano (2011).

15 *AF* X, p. lxxix n. 2.

16 The earliest surviving text of the poem is found in Assisi, Biblioteca Comunale, Ms 338, which has been preserved in

the Sacro Convento since at least 1381, the date it appeared in the library's earliest inventory. Bihl (1929), p. 5, argued that the 'codex maximam partem fuit ante an. 1279'; however, Cenci (1981), pp. 236–7, has given it to a fourteenth-century Assisian hand. For recent discussion, see Giuseppe Cremasoli's introduction to the edition of the poem in *FF*, pp. 1125–30.

17 The manuscript (Assisi, Biblioteca Comunale, Ms 686) was discovered in a cupboard by Giovanni Giacinto Sbaraglia between 1752 and 1758. It was not included in the 1381 inventory of the library compiled by Fra Giovanni di Iolo; whether it was produced before or after that date (and where) is impossible to ascertain. See Thomas of Celano (2011), pp. xxvi–xxviii. The second surviving manuscript of the *Vita secunda* is preserved in Rome, Archivio Generale dei Cappuccini, Ms AB.23, fols. 1r–39v; the only known complete text of the *Tractatus de miraculis* follows, on fols. 40r–73r. See Thomas of Celano (2011), pp. xxviii–xxix.

18 Perugia, Biblioteca Comunale Augusta, Ms 1046 (M.69) is an early fourteenth-century manuscript whose provenance from the Sacro Convento library at Assisi is secure, as it is marked 'quaternatura assisiensis' in the hand of Giovanni di Iolo. However, poignant evidence of the destruction of Celano's text are the cut-down pages used to bind a copy of Papias, *Elementarium doctrinae rudimentum* (Poppi, Biblioteca Comunale Rilliana, Ms 13). Cenci (1981), vol. II, p. 489 (nr 935), identified the Papias with an entry in the 1381 Assisi inventory: according to a marginal note on fol. 4, the book was at some time in the possession of the Franciscan cardinal Gentile Partino of Montefiore. Cardinal Gentile was at Assisi in March 1312, and was the patron of the Saint Martin chapel in the Lower Church. See Thomas of Celano (2011), pp. xxxviii–xli (Poppi), lxi–xcii (Perugia).

19 *LM* 15:7 (*FAED* II, p. 648; *FF*, p. 910). For Celano's description, see Celano I, 124–6 (*FAED* I, pp. 293–7; *FF*, pp. 403–6).

20 Neff (2006); see also Chapter 7 below.

21 The text of *Mira circa nos* (19 July 1228) was published in *BF* I, pp. 42–4 (nr 25); see Brooke (2006), pp. 36–9. For Nicholas IV's bulls concerning Assisi, see Introduction and Chapter 1.

22 The tituli were transcribed by Marinangeli (1911). He reconstructed the effaced sections with reference to the *Legenda maior*, and to transcriptions made by Fra Ludovico Pietralunga in the late sixteenth century, when considerably more was legible. Marinangeli's reconstructed texts have been generally accepted and are used throughout this book; they were reprinted by Smart (1971), pp. 162–95, along with the relevant Bonaventuran passages. Frugoni (2010b) reproduces the Marinangeli reconstructions together with the more recent reading by D'Acunto (2009). For English translations, see Dozzini (2006).

23 Frugoni (1988), for example, dated the Bardi dossal as early as 1243, arguing for the *Vita prima* as its only textual source; for a similar dating, see Cook (1996). Stein (1976) placed the dossal *c.*1254–7, after Celano's *Tractatus de miraculis* but before Bonaventure.

24 Duffy (1997) and Brooke (2006), pp. 176–92, argued that the Bardi dossal drew on both Celano and Bonaventure – i.e. that it was painted in the three-year window before 1266 when both texts were available, although Duffy, p. 232, believes 'it is at least possible that it could have been painted in the early 1270s or even later'.

25 See Celano I, 22 (*FAED* I, pp. 201–2; *FF*, pp. 296–7), and *LM* 3:1 (*FAED* II, p. 542; *FF*, pp. 794–5).

26 See Celano I, 52 (*FAED* I, pp. 227–8; *FF*, pp. 326–7), and *LM* 6:2 (*FAED* II, p. 570; *FF*, pp. 823–4).

27 Dalarun (2002), p. 249.

28 See Dalarun (2002), pp. 249–55.

29 Dalarun (2002), p. 238.

30 *LM* 13:10 (*FAED* II, pp. 637–9; *FF*, pp. 897–8).

31 Smart (1971), pp. 15–16.

32 Smart (1971), p. 17.

33 For the rest of this paragraph, see Smart (1971), pp. 17–29.

34 Smart (1971), pp. 8, 14.

35 Ruf (1974), p. 232.

36 Ruf (1974), p. 23. In his last book, Ruf (2004) examined the entire Upper Church, but did not alter his interpretation of the Saint Francis cycle.

37 Belting (1977), p. 68: 'ein genuin römisches Programm an genuin römischem Bildort'.

38 Kessler (1989), p. 126 n. 36, listed these churches: Santa Maria Immacolata, Ceri (originally dedicated to San Felice); the chapel of Saint Thomas Becket, Anagni cathedral; Santa Maria Montis Domini, Marcellina; San Pietro in Valle, Ferentillo; San Paolo in Vineis, Spoleto; San Nicola, Castro dei Volsci; San Giovanni a Porta Latina, Rome; San Benedetto in Piscinula, Rome; San Sebastiano in Laterano, Rome; Santa Maria in Vescovio, Torri in Sabina; Santa Cecilia, Rome; L'Annunziata, Cori. For discussion of the medieval copies of Saint Peter's, see Kessler (1989) and (2002c).

39 Kessler (1989), p. 134, argued that the frescoists at Anagni, Ceri, Cori, Marcellina, and perhaps even at San Paolo fuori le Mura, must have used modelbooks to effect the transfer of images from Saint Peter's.

40 The Domenico Tasselli watercolours are Vatican City, Biblioteca Apostolica Vaticana, Archivio Capitolare di San Pietro A64 ter., fol. 13r (Old Testament wall), and Biblioteca Apostolica Vaticana, Barb. lat. 2733, fols. 113v–114r (New Testament wall). For Giacomo Grimaldi's descriptions, see Grimaldi (1972).

41 For Cavallini's work in San Paolo, see White (1956); Gardner (1971); Tomei (2000), pp. 134–42.

42 Waetzoldt (1964), pp. 56–8; figs 328–65 for Vatican City, Biblioteca Apostolica Vaticana, Barb. lat. 4406; fig. 408 for Biblioteca Apostolica Vaticana, Vat. lat. 9843.

43 See Kessler (1989) and (2002c).

44 The contrast with Assisi is abundantly clear from the beautiful graphic reconstructions of the fresco cycles in the naves of Saint Peter's and San Paolo in Andaloro, ed. (2006b), pp. 32–3, plate V, and p. 34, plate VI (for Saint Peter's); pp. 106–11, plate V, and pp. 114–19, plate VII (for San Paolo). Belting (1983), p. 95, pointed out that the lengthy biblical cycles of the Constantinian basilicas were not well suited to Assisi's Gothic architecture.

45 Neff (2006), p. 676, argued that both *Joseph in Egypt* and *Isaac Rejecting Esau* were probably new scenes; for further discussion of these scenes, see Chapter 7.

46 Ruf (1974), pp. 39, 129; Ruf (2004), p. 197.

47 There is a discrepancy between Tasselli's sketch, which does not include the *Raising of Lazarus*, and Grimaldi's description, which placed it somewhere between the *Baptism* and the *Crucifixion*.

48 Zucchetti, ed. (1920), p. 156: 'Renovavit Formosus Papa ecclesia principis apostolorum Petri picture tota.'

49 Kessler (2002c), pp. 75–80. For an alternative dating of the New Testament cycle to the late seventh century, see Tronzo (1985). For a recent review of the arguments, see Viscontini (2006).

50 According to Ptolemy of Lucca (2009), Liber XXIII, 28, p. 607; cited by Kessler (2002d), p. 8 n.18.

51 Kessler (2002d), p. 10.

52 Tronzo (1985), pp. 96–7.

53 Kessler (2002c), p. 78.

54 However, Viscontini (2006), p. 415, considers the evidence of San Paolo to be too compromised by later restorations to be convincing.

55 Kessler (2002c), pp. 80–82.

56 In particular, Şenocak noted that from the second half of the thirteenth century onwards provincial and general ministers were almost exclusively lectors. By 1310–12, Ubertino da Casale was complaining that friars were seeking to become lectors precisely in order to gain political power in the Order; Şenocak (2012b), pp. 187, 194–6.

57 For the *studium generale* at Assisi, see Chapter 2, note 105.

58 Şenocak (2012b), p. 219; Roest (2000), pp. 129–30. The Constitutions of Assisi (1279) and Paris (1292) required all clerical friars to attend the lectures of the convent lector; see Roest (2000), p. 81.

59 Roest (2000), p. 130. For Franciscans and biblical exegesis, see Courtenay (2009); for the popularity of biblical commentaries among library books loaned to Franciscan lectors and magisters, see Şenocak (2004), pp. 151–2. A snapshot of the importance of biblical exegesis for the intellectuals of the Franciscan Order is provided by the large number of biblical commentaries, glosses, postillae and concordances in the list of books donated by Matthew of Acquasparta to the convents of Todi and Assisi in 1287; see Menestò (1993).

60 Roest (2000), p. 130, cites Pope Benedict XII's Ordinations of 1336: 'Magistri quoque et lectores alii legentes textum Bibliae debeant insistere circa dubia quae fiunt iuxta ipsum et circa dicti sanctorum catholicorum Patrum ac Glossarum ordinariarum Bibliae memoratae.'

61 See Brooke (2006), pp. 331–2.

62 A later Clarissan example of the scene was painted in the early fourteenth century in Santa Maria Donnaregina, Naples. For illustrations of these two examples, see Derbes (1996), figs 83 and 85; for more on the Franciscan significance of Christ's stripping and his ascent of the cross, see pp. 149–57.

63 Brooke (2006), p. 291.

64 Cannon (1982); Cook (1999), pp. 33–6 (cat. nr 11).

65 This will be discussed below in Chapter 5. For the Porziuncola panel, see Cook (1999), pp. 67–8 (cat. nr 32).

5 *'Franciscus alter Christus'*

1 Jacopo Torriti's composition at Assisi is unusual but Belting (1977), pp. 74, 223–4, argued that it was probably derived from a Byzantine model similar to the one in the early eleventh-century mosaic in the narthex of Hosios Loukas in Greece.

2 Belting (1977), pp. 73–4, 78.

3 Neff (2007), pp. 371–2, 379.

4 The *Ave Maria* contains the line 'Sancta Maria Mater Dei, ora pro nobis peccatoribus', while in the litany of saints the Virgin is invoked as 'Sancta Dei genetrix'.

5 See Cutler (1987).

6 Neff (2007), p. 370.

7 As Neff (2007), p. 373, pointed out, the rood beam with its panels would probably partially have obscured the view of the *Deesis* vault from the choir stalls. Nonetheless, a position behind the altar represents the conceptual vantage point for the friars.

8 The Divine Office of Saint Francis, *FAED* I, p. 329.

9 See the introduction to the liturgical texts in *FAED* I, pp. 311–18.

10 *FAED* I, p. 344; *FF*, p. 1121. Neff (2007), p. 371, made the same point, quoting Thomas of Celano's prayer in the *Vita prima*, 'O father [Francis], place before Jesus Christ, son of the Most High Father, His sacred stigmata; and show Him the signs of the cross on your hands, feet, and side, that He may

mercifully bare His own wounds to the Father, and because of this the Father will ever show us in our anguish His tenderness.' Celano I, 118 (*FAED* I, p. 287). Celano's prayer slightly predates Julian of Speyer's Office, and makes clearer the hierarchy of intercession. However, we believe that Gregory's hymn is more relevant to the Assisi *Deesis*, because firstly Christ does not display his own wounds here; secondly, Celano's text had been suppressed after 1266; and thirdly, 'Plange, turba paupercula' would have been known by all the friars, and sung in close proximity to the *Deesis* vault.

11 On the development of double-sided altarpieces commissioned for the Order's Umbrian churches, see Cooper (2001), esp. pp. 32–9 for the likely role of the Upper Church as a paradigm for the spatial organization of the other churches in the Umbrian province.

12 We shall consider the distinctive functions of the various spaces within the Basilica complex in our forthcoming book on the Lower Church.

13 See Chapter 3 for the account of Angela's vision by her biographer.

14 See Cooper and Robson (2011), p. 483, for Angela's visit to Assisi for the *Perdono*. For an overview of the *Perdono*, see Sensi (2002).

15 Hueck (2001), p. 54, citing Zaccaria (1963), p. 291 n. 144.

16 ASC, Istromenti III, 2.

17 A copy of Elias's letter was first published in 1620 in the *Speculum vitae Beati Francisci et sociorum ejus* of William Spoelberch, and then by Luke Wadding. No original manuscript has been found and some scholars doubt its authenticity (see *FAED* II, pp. 485–8, where the text is dated after 1253). However, contemporary evidence that Elias wrote such a letter, and that it referred to the stigmata, is provided by Jordan of Giano († after 1262). See Salter, trans. (1926), pp. 173–4.

18 *Usque ad terminos* (variously dated 31 March and 12 April 1237), *BF* I, pp. 211–12 (nr 220), at p. 212: 'Quae temeritas? quod peccatum? si tam singulare privilegium ad indulgentis gloriam picturae testificatione pateat oculis devotorum?' The original copy of this bull seems to be lost: the 31 March copy is the one held at Assisi. For the dating issues, see *BF* I, p. 212 note (a); and Brooke (2006), p. 167 n. 14.

19 Cook (1999) catalogued seventeen extant examples, which he dated to before 1288. For further examples of *Stigmatization* scenes in illuminated manuscripts, see Frugoni (1993).

20 See Vauchez (1968).

21 For a useful summary in English of her work on Francis's stigmatization, see Frugoni (1998), Chapter 6. See also Frugoni (1993), esp. pp. 210–12.

22 Celano I, 94 (*FAED* I, pp. 263–64; *FF*, pp. 369–70). Celano's description drew on Ezekiel 1:1, 8:1.

23 *LM* 13:3 (*FAED* II, pp. 632–3; *FF*, pp. 891–2).

24 Cook (1999), pp. 165–8 (cat. nr 141).

25 The earliest example of a *Stigmatization* with three rays is probably the Bardi dossal, Santa Croce, Florence; Cook (1999), pp. 98–102 (cat. nr 68). For others, see Cook (1999), pp. 108–9, 120, 205–6, 209–11 (cat. nrs 76, 90, 176, 180), which are all either Florentine or Sienese. A further example, with a single beam, is on a panel whose current whereabouts are unknown; Cook (1999), p. 245 (cat. nr 214).

26 'Cum Beatus Franciscus oraret in latere montis Alvernae, vidit Christum in specie seraphim crucifixi, qui impressit in manibus et pedibus et etiam in latere dextro stigmata crucis eiusdem domini nostri Iesu Christi.'

27 *LM* 13:2 (*FAED* II, p. 631; *FF*, pp. 890–91).

28 In the *Itinerarium mentis in Deum* 7:3, Bonaventure referred to Francis having received the vision at La Verna 'as I and several others were told, at that very place, by the companion who had been with him at the time'; English translation from Bonaventure (1960), p. 56. See also Brooke (2006), p. 401.

29 Bernard of Besse, in his *Liber de laudibus Beati Francisci*, *c.*1277–83, recorded that Leo, along with Brothers Bernard Quintavalle, Rufino and Angelo, was buried in San Francesco (see *FAED* III, p. 35). According to Fra Ludovico of Pietralunga, writing before the destruction of the shrine in 1604–5, the remains of Leo, Masseo, Rufino and Angelo were interred in the wall beneath Pietro Lorenzetti's *Crucifixion* fresco in the south transept. The shrine was accompanied by effigies of the four friars, presumably also in fresco; see Ludovico of Pietralunga (1982), p. 76. Another five friars, including Bernard, were interred in the equivalent position in the north transept; ibid., pp. 71–2.

30 The blessing of Brother Leo is currently displayed in the former chapter house, adjacent to the north transept of the Lower Church. Brooke (2006), p. 356, believes that Leo bequeathed it to the Basilica when he died, in 1271 or 1272, but Frugoni (1998), pp. 125–7, suggested that Leo may have added the note and given the parchment to the Basilica at the same time as he presented a breviary used by Francis to the convent of Santa Chiara, Assisi. Leo's letter of donation was addressed to Abbess Benedicta and the nuns of Santa Chiara, so it must have been written between 1257, when the Clares transferred from San Damiano, and 1260, when Benedicta died.

31 Brooke (2006), p. 403.

32 *LM* 4:10 (*FAED* II, p. 557; *FF*, pp. 810–12).

33 *LM* 13:10 (*FAED* II, p. 638; *FF*, pp. 897–8).

34 Smart (1971), p. 27.

35 The other two, the *Miracle of the Spring* and the *Preaching to the Birds*, both appear on the counter-façade and are the subject of Chapter 7.

36 *LM*, *Prologue* 4 (*FAED* II, pp. 528–9; *FF*, p. 780). As it happens, the placement of the *Apparition at Arles* in the Assisi cycle is more chronologically correct than in the *Legenda maior*. The historical chapter meeting at Arles most probably took place either in 1224 (the same year as the stigmatization) or 1226 (the year Francis died); see Péano (1983).

37 Ruf (1974), p. 201.

38 Duccio later employed a similar device to link two adjacent scenes on the back predella of his *Maestà* altarpiece for Siena cathedral, *c.*1308–11. As White (1979), p. 122, pointed out, the blind man cured by Christ looks up to the right, beyond the picture frame, to 'see' the *Transfiguration* in the next panel.

39 It starts beneath the *Death of Saint Francis*: 'Quomodo in hora transitus Beati Francisci unus frater vidi animam eius sub specie stellae prefulgidae in coelum ascendere. Minister terrae laboris cum laboraret in extremis et diu iam perdidisset loquelam'; continues beneath the *Visions of the Death*: 'clamavit et dixit: Expecta me, pater, ecce venio tecum. Et statim defunctus secutus est Sanctum Patrem. Episcopus insuper Assisii cum esset in Monte Sancti Michaelis Archangeli vidit Beatum Franciscum dicentem sibi: Ecce, vado ad coelum' and concludes beneath the *Verification of the Stigmata*: 'Et tali hora ita inventum est.' ('How at the hour of the death of Blessed Francis, one of the friars saw his soul ascend into heaven under the appearance of a radiant star. A minister in Terra di Lavoro, at his last hour and long without the faculty of speech, / began to cry out, saying "Wait for me, Father. I am coming with you". He died then and there and followed his holy father. At the same time, the Bishop of Assisi, who was at the mountain of St. Michael the Archangel, had a vision of Blessed Francis who said to him, "Behold, I am going to heaven". / And in fact this occurred at the very same hour.' English translation from Dozzini (2006), pp. 46, 48.)

40 See Frugoni, in Zanardi, Frugoni and Zeri (1996), p. 272; Neff (2006), p. 688. The demon's head in the clouds through which Francis's soul ascends, discovered by Frugoni (2011b), can also be understood in relation to the *Vision of the Thrones*. Frugoni (2012) draws attention to the medieval belief that, after Lucifer's fall, demons were confined to the misty, turbulent atmosphere around the earth, whence they try to impede mankind's way to heaven.

41 Neff (2006), p. 684. Zanardi notes the original presence of gold striations; see Zanardi, Frugoni and Zeri (1996), p. 274.

42 Isaiah 63:2; for the *Ascension* window, see Chapter 3, p. 76.

43 Salimbene of Parma (1966), vol. I, p. 282: 'sicut unus crucifixus de cruce depositus'.

44 Thus we would strongly refute the view of Brooke (2006), p. 374, who, although she acknowledged the linkages between the *Stigmatization*, the *Death of Saint Francis* and the *Crucifixion*, contended that 'the lives of Jesus and Francis pass as ships in the night'.

45 The first is hard to identify as most of the fresco is lost. Ruf (1974) and (2004), with the benefit of modern photography, argued that it is *Christ before Pilate*. Some earlier scholars, such as Venturi (1908), p. 101, identified it as the *Flagellation*. Scarpellini, in his commentary on Ludovico of Pietralunga, pointed out that *L'anonimo secentesco* (Assisi, Biblioteca Comunale, Cod. 148, fols 49r–53v), the earliest known source for the iconography of the scene, described it as 'quando fu flagellato alla colona'. See Ludovico of Pietralunga (1982), pp. 120, 400.

46 See Derbes (1996), pp. 16–24, for a discussion of Franciscan sponsorship of Passion narratives in Duecento Italy.

47 *LM* 15:5 (*FAED* II, p. 647; *FF*, pp. 907–8).

48 [cum ramis arb]oru(m); see D'Acunto (2009), p. 191. For comparison with the Entry into Jerusalem, see Matthew 21:8 and John 12:13.

49 Fisher (1956).

50 Fisher (1956), p. 52.

51 English translation from Dozzini (2006), p. 52.

52 The idea was first put forward by Ruf (1974), p. 212. It was argued more fully by Finnegan (2008).

53 Tripps (2005) argued that sculpted figures such as those on the façade of Siena cathedral were intended to evoke Isaiah 62:6: 'Upon thy walls, O Jerusalem, I have appointed watchmen'.

54 Tripps (2005), p. 9, quoting Odericus Canonicus (1766), pp. 116–17.

55 'Ecce quasi aquila ascendit et evolabit et expandet alas suas.' This was taken as the text for an Ascension sermon by the Franciscan friar Bartholomew of Bologna (Paris, Bibliothèque Nationale, Cod. 10.698, fols 50rb–52rb); see Squadrani (1932), p. 206. See Finnegan (2008), pp. 34–7, for other interpretations of the eagle.

56 Note, for example, Bonaventure's sermon on the feast of the Translation in 1267: 'We can say of him what Scripture says of Christ: *A cloud took him out of their sight*.' *FAED* II, p. 746.

57 Apocalypse (Revelation) 21:19.

58 Apocalypse (Revelation) 21:21.

59 Apocalypse (Revelation) 21:25–6.

60 '. . . sacrum corpus margaritis caelestibus insignitum'; see *LM* 15:5 (*FAED* II, p. 647; *FF*, p. 908).

61 *LM* 15:5 (*FAED* II, p. 647; *FF*, p. 908).

62 Celano I, 127 (*FAED* I, p. 298; *FF*, pp. 406–7); Smart (1971), p. 221.

63 Celano I, 127.

64 Gregory's dream is *LM*, *Miracles* 1:2 (*FAED* II, p. 651; *FF*, pp. 913–14). Of the other miracles Bonaventure added, one con-

cerned the resurrection of a woman struck by a stone falling from the pulpit in the Lower Basilica at Assisi, which happened after Celano III had been compiled; see *LM, Miracles* 3:4 (*FAED* II, pp. 660–61; *FF*, p. 927). Another dealt with the punishment of a man in Poitiers, for working on Francis's feast day, and his subsequent repentance, which included a vow to visit Francis's tomb; see *LM, Miracles* 9:1 (*FAED* II, pp. 676–77; *FF*, pp. 952–3). In addition to these three new miracles, Bonaventure appended to Celano's account of the healing of a girl in Ancona a brief mention of the cure of another girl, from Catalonia. For further analysis of the miracle stories of Bonaventure and Celano, see the very helpful discussion in Brooke (2006), pp. 269–79.

65 In the *Legenda*, this point is made three times: *LM, Miracles* 1:5 (*FAED* II, pp. 653–4; *FF*, pp. 915–17).

66 *LMin*, Chapter 6, Lesson 7 (*FAED* II, p. 712; *FF*, pp. 1004–5). The *Legenda minor* was composed in nine lessons, for liturgical use, replacing the earlier choir legend written by Thomas of Celano (*FAED* I, pp. 319–26; *FF*, pp. 427–39).

67 For example, Bonaventure, *De sanctis angelis*, sermon 5; Bonaventure (1993), vol. II, p. 725.

68 *LM, Miracles* 2:1 (*FAED* II, pp. 655–6; *FF*, p. 919).

69 'Dum sacrum mysterium cerneret Joannes, Archangelus Michael tuba cecinit: Ignosce Domine Deus noster, qui aperis librum et solvis signacula ejus.' As Meyer (2003), pp. 87–8, noted, the antiphon has little precise biblical authority. In Apocalypse (Revelation) 11:15, it is the seventh angel who blows the trumpet; Michael is named only in Apocalypse (Revelation) 12:7 ('And there was a great battle in heaven, Michael and his angels fought with the dragon'). Nor is the appeal for forgiveness in the biblical text. But the antiphon reflects common beliefs about Michael's multiple apocalyptic functions: he is the defender and protector of the elect, whose souls he leads into paradise; he will kill the Antichrist; the dead will arise at the sound of his voice; and it is he who will present the symbols of Christ's Passion at the day of Judgment. See Jacobus de Voragine (1993), vol. II, p. 201.

70 John 11:44.

71 Matthew 16:19.

72 *LM, Miracles* 5:4 (*FAED* II, p. 667; *FF*, pp. 937–8).

73 Frugoni (2004a); Binski (2009).

74 Frugoni (2004a), p. 129, hypothesized that both this scene and the *Homage of a Simple Man* were the result of a rethink of the original programme.

75 For a different interpretation, see Neff (2007), pp. 374–8, and Neff (2011).

76 Frugoni (2004a), p. 110; Frugoni (2010b), p. 175.

77 Jacobus de Voragine (1993), vol. II, p. 38.

78 Cook (1999), p. 60.

79 *LM, Miracles* 1:2 (*FAED* II, p. 651; *FF*, p. 914).

80 *Usque ad terminos* (see note 18 above); *Non minus dolentes* (31 March 1237), *BF* I, p. 213 (nr 221); and *Confessor Domini* (31 March 1237); but the copy published in *BF* I, p. 214 (nr 223) is dated 5 April 1237: see Brooke (2006), p. 167 n. 14.

81 Bonaventure asserted in the *Legenda maior* that Alexander IV, 'in a sermon preached to the people at which many of the brothers and I myself were present, affirmed that he had seen the sacred stigmata with his own eyes while the saint was still alive'; *LM* 13:8 (*FAED* II, p. 636; *FF*, p. 896). In his bull *Benigna operatio* (19 October 1255), Alexander alluded to his service as a young cleric in the household of Cardinal Ugolino (later Pope Gregory IX), during which time he had 'an intimate knowledge of this confessor [i.e. Francis]' ('cum ea Nobis dudum nota fecerit plenior fides rerum, quando videlicet in minoribus constituti Confessoris ejusdem familiarem ex munere Divino meruimus habere notitiam'); *FAED* II, p. 781; *BF* II, p. 86 (nr 120).

82 *Benigna operatio* (29 October 1255), *BF* II, p. 86 (nr 120): 'signanter vobis ante oculos proponere volumus recolenda frequentius et vehementius admiranda illa saltem jocunda dominicae passionis insignia, quae in ejusdam sancti corpore manus caelestis operationis impressit'; English translation from *FAED* II, p. 780. According to Frugoni (1993), p. 282, this was the first use of the verb *imprimere* in relation to the stigmata; the same expression was then used by Thomas of Celano in his *Legenda ad usum chori*. But for an earlier dating of Celano's choir legend to *c.*1230–32, see *FAED* I, p. 311.

83 John 19:37; cf. Zachariah 12:10; see Frugoni (1993), pp. 56–7 and (1998), p. 121.

84 Frugoni (1993), p. 57. Cook (1999), pp. 67–8 (cat. nr 32), argues that the Saint Francis panel painted for the Porziuncola (Santa Maria degli Angeli), which he dated to Alexander IV's pontificate (1254–61), was probably the first Italian painting to show Francis with the side wound (earlier depictions exist in northern Europe); this is supported by Brooke (2006), pp. 299–300.

85 *LM* 15:2 (*FAED* II, p. 646; *FF*, p. 906).

86 Nicholas IV's bulls were *Quasdam litteras* (13 September 1291) and *Tenorem quarumdam* (17 September 1291), both *BF* IV, p. 293 (nrs 549, 550). Nicholas III's bull was *Litteras felicis* (25 August 1279), *BF* III, p. 417 (nr 129).

87 *BF* II, p. 86 (nr 120): 'volumus et mandamus, ut cum sanae menti restituat judicialis severitas disciplinae; ita quod districta proprii praelati castigatione correctus Dei opera blasphemare dediscat, et fidei catholicae fructus de pia mirabilium Domini credulitate pullulans non arescat'. Cook (1999), p. 60, connected the insistence on the side wound in the cycle to disputes over the stigmata during Nicholas IV's pontificate.

88 See Robson (2004). For a prominent example of the use of Judas in a pairing of opposites, this time in a non-Franciscan context, see Derbes and Sandona (2008), Chapter 2: 'Judas and Mary: The Chancel Arch Antithesis'.

89 *Cum ad aures* (20 November 1291), *BF* IV, pp. 307–8 (nr 574). The bull is mentioned by Vauchez (1968), pp. 603–4, and by Frugoni (1993), p. 92 n. 63, but neither discussed it in relation to images of Saint Francis. We would like to express our gratitude to David d'Avray for translating this bull.

90 See Vauchez (1968), esp. pp. 608–12, for the opposition from within certain quarters of the Dominican Order.

91 *BF* IV, p. 307 (nr 574): '. . . Beato Francisco mortui Dei signa, et haec superficialiter, sicut cernitur in picturis, ascriberet'.

92 Brooke (2006), p. 404, perceptively suggested that one reason for the new addition of the rays may have been a concern to make it clear visually that Francis's wounds were not self-inflicted.

93 The brother is not named in Philip's report, but is identified in the late fourteenth-century *Considerations of the Stigmata*, which draws on the same material: McKay, ed. (1963), pp. 127–8. Philip's treatise, *Instrumentum de stigmatibus beati Francisci*, was published by the Quaracchi fathers in *AF* III, pp. 641–5; for further discussion of Philip's presence at Assisi, see Chapter 2 above.

94 A curious detail in the account of the apparition of Francis to Matthew is that the saint initially addressed the lay brother in Latin, then switched to the *volgare*; see *AF* III, p. 642.

95 See Chapter 2, pp. 49–50.

96 *AF* III, p. 644: 'Dominus manus suas corpori meo applicuit et primo manibus, secundo pedibus, tertio lateri mihi stigmata ista impressit cum vehementissimo doloris sensu et cum magno qualibet vice clamore'.

97 *BF* IV, p. 307 (nr 574): 'Sancta Romana Ecclesia de Beato Francisco, et stigmatum eius infixione sollicita, illa in carne ipsius non superficialiter, sed in interiora per carnem, et nervos, et ossa in quinque partibus manuum, pedum, et lateris . . . ingressa itaut non virtute naturae, sed miraculoso gratiae dono . . . per Testes legitime comprobatum accepit'.

98 Frugoni (2004a), p. 115, pointed out that throughout the scenes on this wall many of the people who exalt Francis are named in the inscriptions below the frescoes.

99 Cooper (2005).

6 *Rebuilding the Church*

1 Romano (1998); Neff (2006), p. 680.

2 See Chapter 7 for a more detailed analysis of this part of the nave programme.

3 For some of the problems they faced, see Peters (1986), esp. pp. 232, 235–6.

4 Smart (1971), p. 152.

5 *FAED* II, p. 530; *FF*, p. 781.

6 Smart (1971), p. 164; Frugoni (2010b), p. 113.

7 Smart (1971), p. 163.

8 'Cum Beatus Franciscus oraret ante imaginem crucifixi, vox dilapsa est de cruce ter dicens: Francisce, vade repara domum meam, quae tota destruitur; per hoc Romanam significans ecclesiam.'

9 See Celano II, 11, 13–14 (*FAED* II, pp. 250, 252–3; *FF*, pp. 453, 455–6); *LM* 2:1, 2:3, 2:7 (*FAED* II, pp. 536–8, 540; *FF*, pp. 786–9, 792).

10 The *Legenda maior* does not specify where the *Vision of the Thrones* (Scene 9) took place, but another Franciscan text, translated and published by Brooke in 1970 as the *Scripta Leonis*, dated to *c.*1244–6, identified the church as San Pietro at Bovara, near Trevi; see Brooke (1970), pp. 126–31. Subsequently, some scholars have argued that the *Scripta Leonis* is an early fourteenth-century text; however, Brooke (2006), pp. 104–5, maintained her early dating.

11 See Frugoni (2001), especially pp. 368–71. For the existence of a rood beam in the Porziuncola, see Sperandio (2001).

12 See Chapter 5.

13 For the use of the word *Ecclesia* in the medieval period to symbolize the entire Church, and the restoration of churches by ecclesiastics, especially in Rome, see Peters (1986), pp. 219–27.

14 *LM* 1:1 (*FAED* II, p. 531; *FF*, p. 782).

15 *FAED* II, p. 531; *FF*, p. 782: 'cum aliquando per civitatem eunti obviaret Francisco'.

16 Smart (1971), p. 152.

17 Gardner (2005), p. 280, argued that the buildings suggest Assisi's *platea comunis*, but Lunghi (1997), p. 255, believed the scene to be set in a 'luogo generico', with no attempt to depict the episcopal palace, which stood next to the church of Santa Maria Maggiore, to the south of the Piazza del Comune.

18 Zanardi, Frugoni and Zeri (1996), p. 68; see also Zanardi (2002), p. 85, and plates L and LXIX, for the relevant *giornata* plans.

19 As long ago as 1864, Crowe and Cavalcaselle proposed that Scenes 1 and 24–8 were the work of a single, anonymous artist, who had not painted the rest of the Saint Francis cycle; see Crowe and Cavalcaselle (1864), p. 227. Some, but not all, scholars have identified this artist with the painter of the Saint Cecilia altarpiece now in the Uffizi in Florence. Offner (1927), p. 97, gave to this 'Saint Cecilia Master' only Scenes 1 and 26–8. Smart (1971), pp. 39–40, concurred. It is interest-

ing to note that Crowe and Cavalcaselle's position, reached on stylistic grounds, is very close to that of Zanardi, who, on the basis of studying painting techniques, believes Scenes 1 and 23–8 to be the work of a single workshop; see Zanardi (2004) for a convenient summary in English of his analysis.

20 See Coletti (1949), p. 45.

21 The court is amply documented after 1313, but Lunghi (1997), p. 259, argued that a document of 1279 implies its presence there by that date.

22 Lunghi (1997), p. 261.

23 Luke 19:36.

24 Milizia (1994), pp. 39–41, seems to have been the first to suggest an *alter Christus* motif in this scene.

25 Acts 3:1–10.

26 Although the colours used for Peter's robes were never completely uniform in Duecento Italian painting, Lisner (1990), pp. 352–66, pointed out that blue seems to have been the 'official' colour for Peter's tunic in both Rome and Florence. Two important Roman and papal models for Cimabue's north transept frescoes both depict Saint Peter in blue and yellow: fragments from the lost Apostles' cycle from the portico of Old Saint Peter's; and the dedication scene in the Sancta Sanctorum, in which Pope Nicholas III as donor is accompanied by apostles Peter and Paul.

27 The historical first temple in Jerusalem was built by King Solomon; it was destroyed by the Babylonians in 586 BCE. Its successor, the second temple, was razed in 70 CE, during the Roman sack of Jerusalem, and was never rebuilt. Medieval Christian knowledge of Solomon's Temple was therefore based on legend and on the Bible, where it was described in considerable detail (see 3 Kings (1 Kings) 6:2–10, 15–36; 7:13–51; 2 Paralipomenon (2 Chronicles) 3:1–17; 4:1–22).

28 Bede (1995), p. 5.

29 Ephesians 2:19–22; 1 Peter 2:4–10.

30 1 Peter 2:5; Ephesians 2:20–21.

31 Smart (1971), pp. 152–3.

32 Smart (1971), p. 152; Scarpellini (1978), pp. 98–9; Frugoni (2010b), p. 101.

33 See below, pp. 177–80.

34 Bougerol (1982). With seven extant versions, of which two copies are in the Sacro Convento at Assisi, the sermon of Jean de la Rochelle (†1245) seems to have been particularly influential. Among the others on Bougerol's list are sermons attributed to the Dominican Nicolas de Gorran (†*c.*1295) and the fourteenth-century Franciscan cardinal Bertrand de la Tour (*c.*1262–1332). The authorship of Bonaventure's third sermon on Saint Francis, published in Bonaventure (1882–1902), vol. IX, pp. 582–585, has been widely disputed. Brady (1976) argued that it was preached to the friars in Paris on the evening of 4 October 1262 by Cardinal Eudes of Châteauroux, chancellor of the University of Paris and legate of Pope Urban IV. Brady's thesis was accepted by Doyle (1983) and by the editors of *FAED*, who reprinted Doyle's English translation in *FAED* II, pp. 811–18. Bougerol was unconvinced; see Bonaventure (1993), vol. I, pp. 37–8; vol. II, p. 431.

35 English translation by Father Campion Murray, published online at http://www.franciscans.org.au/spirituality/campion/Aquasparta-3/St%20Francis.htm. For the Latin texts, see Matthew of Acquasparta (1962), p. 22. Autograph copies of Matthew's Saint Francis sermons are preserved in the Sacro Convento library (Assisi, Biblioteca Comunale, Mss 420–421). These books do not appear in Matthew's 1287 donation, or in the 1381 inventory of the Sacro Convento library. Instead they seem to have been donated in the early fifteenth century by Nicholas of Bettona, a Franciscan lector of theology who was elected provincial minister of the Umbrian province in 1385 and later became Bishop of Foligno. However, Nicholas had spent the 1370s and early 1380s in the Sacro Convento, serving several terms as custodian, and is known to have taken books from the library there (which the Assisi friars made several attempts to recover). The presence of Mss 420–421 in Assisi before 1381 appears to be confirmed by the fourteenth-century transcriptions of Matthew's sermons copied in Biblioteca Comunale, Ms 682 (a volume which is listed in the 1381 inventory). These two versions represent the only complete collections of Matthew's sermons, a strong indication that the manuscript tradition was associated with Assisi from the beginning. See Cenci (1981), pp. 39–40, 351–2, 391–2; Matthew of Acquasparta (1962), pp. 7*–8*.

36 For the theology of Christ as the new Adam, see Ruf (1974), pp. 71–4.

37 Assisi, Biblioteca Comunale, Ms 338. See Chapter 4 above.

38 Henri d'Avranches (1999), pp. 449–50.

39 *Mira circa nos* (19 July 1228), *BF* I, pp. 42–4 (nr 25); *FAED* I, pp. 565–9.

40 *BF* I, p. 42: 'Ecce in hora undecima Dominus, qui cum diluvii aqua terram deleret, justum per lignum contemptibilem gubernavit; super sortem justorum virgam peccantium non relinquens, excitavit servum suum Beatum Franciscum virum utique secundum cor suum'. English translation, *FAED* I, p. 566.

41 Wisdom 10:4: 'Propter quem cum aqua deleret terram iterum sanavit sapientia per contemptibile lignum iustum gubernans'.

42 *Commentarius in Librum Sapientiae*, Bonaventure (1882–1902), vol. VI, p. 172.

43 Bonaventure (1882–1902), vol. VI, p. 172b: 'Lignum autem illud significabat crucem, quia contemptibilis est infidelibus, licet fidelibus sit venerabilis.'

44 See Chapter 5.
45 *Biblia latina cum glossa ordinaria* (1992), vol. I, p. 35, marginal gloss on Genesis 6:9: 'Noe per aquam et lignum liberatur et familia eius. Sic familia Christi per baptismum et crucem.'
46 'Cum Beatus Franciscus nocte sequenti se sopori dedisset, palatium speciosum et magnum *cum militaribus armis crucis Christi signaculo insignitis* vidit, et cum quaereret cuius essent, illa omnia sua fore militumque suorum superna fuit assertione responsum' [our emphasis]. This titulus is no longer extant.
47 See Chapter 4.
48 We are grateful to Laura Jacobus for this observation.
49 See *LM* 13:10 (*FAED* II, pp. 637–8; *FF*, p. 897).
50 Genesis 22:1–18.
51 Genesis 18:1–5.
52 According to Garber (1918), pp. 24, 26, 32, 34, 36, 39, the two Abraham scenes appear correctly ordered in the early Christian or medieval Old Testament cycles in the following churches: Saint Peter's, Rome; San Paolo fuori le Mura, Rome; San Pietro in Valle, Ferentillo; Sant'Angelo in Formis; Cappella Palatina, Palermo; Monreale cathedral.
53 Genesis 18:1–2.
54 Genesis 19:1.
55 Genesis 18:22.
56 *Contra Maximinum* 24:7, Augustine of Hippo (1886), col. 809. Grimaldi's description of the scene from Saint Peter's as 'Abraham tres vidit et unum adoravit' is assumed to have been copied from its titulus; Grimaldi (1972), p. 140. The same phrase is used as the titulus beneath the frescoed scenes in the Cappella Palatina, Palermo, and Sant'Annunziata a Cori, Rome.
57 After the 1990s restoration of the frescoes, the remains of the inscription were transcribed as TRE . . . N . . . CUM EI . . . T VIDET CO . . . LAUDAT ET UNUM. See Tamanti (2003), p. 13.
58 The cruciform halo was first noted by Ruf (1974), pp. 48–50, who argued that it symbolized the pre-existence of Christ and the promise of salvation, which is how the Abraham story was understood by the fathers of the Greek Church before iconoclasm. However, given the closeness of the iconography of the Assisi scene to earlier Italian examples, there seems little reason to doubt the traditional Western exegesis.
59 There is also one sermon on the text 'Abraham pater multarum gentium' (Sirach (Ecclesiasticus) 44:20). See Bougerol (1982), pp. 708–9, for the incipits. For the text of Matthew's sermon, see Matthew of Acquasparta (1962), pp. 46–73.
60 As we have seen, the seal was commonly used as a metaphor for Francis's stigmata. For Abraham's circumcision, Matthew cited Romans 4:11, which calls it 'a seal of the justice of the faith, which he had'.
61 Translation by Murray: http://www.franciscans.org.au/spirituality/campion/Aquasparta–3/St%20Francis.htm.
62 For the iconography of the *Dream of Innocent III* on the Pisa predella, see Gardner (1982), p. 228, Gandolfo (1983), pp. 70–71 and Frugoni (2010a). The panel is now in the Louvre. A manuscript dated between 1073 and 1180 (Paris, Bibliothèque Nationale, lat. 2287, fol. 169r) described the Lateran mosaic as 'exterius vero, super easdem fores ecclesiae est imago Salvatoris. Hinc et hinc imagines Gabrielis et Michael[is]'; first published by Müntz (1879), p. 116 n. 2; for the edited text, see Lauer (1911), p. 401.
63 There is still a tiny fragment of painted pattern visible on the edge of the original plaster, in the upper right corner of the façade. Smart (1971), p. 166, thought this might have been part of a painted windowframe. We believe it is more likely to have formed the upper curve of an archangel's wing.
64 '. . . illud altare ligneum stabilivit in formam et similitudinem altaris Abrahe quo iussus est a Domino filium immolare, cuius ligna crucem passionis Domini figurabant'. See de Blaauw (1990), pp. 136 n. 68.
65 This was mentioned in the account of Benjamin of Tudela, a Spanish Jew who visited the Basilica between 1165 and 1168; cited in de Blaauw (1990), pp. 134, 136.
66 John 10:9. Bede, *On the Temple*, 18:4; Bede (1995), p. 74.
67 Neff (2007), pp. 372–3.
68 Ruf (1974), p. 216; Ruf (2004), pp. 260–61.
69 For the identification of two of the clerics standing behind the bishop as cathedral canons, see Frugoni (2010b), p. 113.
70 Noted by, *inter alia*, Cook (1999), p. 58; Belting (1977), p. 83; Peters (1986), pp. 217–18; Romano (1998), p. 368.
71 Celano II, 204 (*FAED* II, pp. 377–8).
72 Peters (1986), p. 234. See also Finnegan (2008), pp. 18–20.
73 For the full inscription, see Chapter 1, pp. 26–7.
74 See Robson (2011).
75 English translation from Dozzini (2006), p. 32.
76 Scarpellini (1978), pp. 101–8.
77 Processo di canonizzazione di S. Chiara, IVe Testimonia, 16 (*FF*, p. 2478).
78 See Frugoni (2004b), p.100.
79 See Chapter 2, p. 37 and note 28.
80 For the papal connotations of Roman ciboria, see de Blaauw (2009), p. 139.
81 For the liturgy, see de Blaauw (1994), vol. I, pp. 430–34.
82 De Blaauw (1994), vol. I, p. 383; vol. II, p. 543.
83 De Blaauw (1994), vol. II, p. 544. The ciboria in Saint Peter's, San Paolo and the Lateran all seem to have had porphyry columns. The Lateran ciborium was destroyed by fire in 1308.
84 See Gardner (1970). A third ciborium, built to house an icon of the Virgin, is more difficult to date but its Gothic appearance probably places it *c.*1290–1300.
85 The Virgin and Child now displayed in the group is from the

sixteenth century. Arnolfo's was more likely a reclining Virgin of the Nativity, either holding the Christ Child or with him beside her in a manger. See Pomarici (2006).

86 Quoted by Biasiotti (1915), p. 28 n. 1. See also Romano (2006), p. 300. Panvinio was an Augustinian whose planned history of Roman churches was never completed owing to his untimely death, in 1568, at the age of thirty-nine.

87 Romano (2006), pp. 300–01. See also Pomarici (2006), pp. 113–14.

88 Scarpellini (1978), p. 106.

89 See Chapter 2, p. 42.

90 Unfortunately, Jerome's was the web of the vault that collapsed in the 1997 earthquake, and only fragments of the fresco were recovered from the rubble.

91 Biasiotti (1920), p. 239: 'in capella praedictae ecclesiae S. Mariae Majoris sub grata ferrea ante praesepe Domini requiescit'.

92 Biasiotti (1920), p. 238: RECUBO P[RAE]SEPIS AD ANTRU[M].

93 For details, see Chapter 1, note 92.

94 See Chapter 1, note 42.

95 NICOLAUS PAPA IIII FILIUS BEATI FRANCISCI. For the full inscription, see Chapter 1, p. 22 and note 53.

7 Ascending to God, Descending to Neighbour

1 Vasari (1966–87), vol. II: *Testo*, p. 100: 'E fra l'altre è bellissima una storia dove uno asetato, nel quale si vede vivo il desiderio dell'acque, bee stando chinato in terra a una fonte con grandissimo e veramente maraviglioso affetto, intantoché par quasi una persona viva che bea.' English translation from Vasari (1965), p. 41.

2 *LM* 7:12 (*FAED* II, p. 584; *FF*, pp. 841–2).

3 The scenes on the north nave wall come from Chapters 1–10 of the *Legenda maior*, in sequence, and the south wall continues from Chapter 11 onwards. The *Miracle of the Spring* is 7:12 and the *Preaching to the Birds* 12:3. The *Apparition at Arles* is the only other scene in the cycle that appears out of its Bonaventuran order; see Chapter 5.

4 Smart (1971), p. 191.

5 Cook (1999), p. 58.

6 Cook (1999), pp. 98–102 (cat. nr 68: Bardi dossal), pp. 165–8 (cat. nr 141: Pescia), pp. 209–11 (cat. nr 180: Siena).

7 See Chapter 4.

8 See notes 12 and 13 below.

9 For Moses, see Psalm 78:16 and Exodus 17:1–7. For the identification of Saint Francis with Moses, see Fleming (1982), Chapter 2; Clasen (1961).

10 See Chapter 6.

11 There is considerable disagreement among scholars about the relative importance of the Moses/Francis parallel. On the one hand, Fleming (1982), p. 64, argued that 'to write about Francis, or to paint about him, was also in some measure to write or paint about Moses. As Bonaventure says, almost brusquely, "he drew water from a rock in imitation of Moses".' On the other hand, Ratzinger (1971), p. 180 n. 36, said that Bonaventure made the Moses/Francis identification infrequently, and that it never acquired independent meaning. It is not often pointed out that, in his account of the miracle of the spring, Bonaventure compared Francis with Elisha as well as with Moses.

12 *Legenda maior*, Madrid, Biblioteca Cardenal Cisneros (also known as the Archivo Ibero-Americano), Cod. 768, fol. 39; see Einhorn (1992).

13 A second illumination, in a fifteenth-century *Legenda maior* (Rome, Museo Francescano, Cod. 1266, fol. 44), is a close copy of the Madrid manuscript. On a panel attributed to Taddeo di Bartolo (Landesmuseum, Hanover), the iconography is closer to that of Assisi, but Francis is still displaced from the centre. This panel was part of the predella of a double-sided altarpiece for the Franciscan church in Perugia, dated 1403. See Solberg (1992).

14 *LM* 13:1 (*FAED* II, p. 630; *FF*, p. 889).

15 This was perceptively observed by the editors of *FAED* (II, p. 705 note (a)): 'The resultant architectonic–artistic diptych serves as an arresting reminder, to those in the choir area as well as those departing the church, of the necessary synthesis of the contemplative–active dimensions of life.'

16 For the role of hermitages within the Franciscan Order, see Pellegrini (1984), Chapter 2; Merlo (1991).

17 *FAED* I, pp. 61–2.

18 Luke 10:38–42. Luke calls her Mary of Bethany, not Mary Magdalen. However, in the seventh century Pope Gregory the Great had declared the two Maries to be one and the same.

19 Quoted by Vauchez (1993), p. 41.

20 See Thomson (1975).

21 In the *Defense of the Mendicants*, the minister general warned that 'prelacy, because of the loftiness of its dignity and the number of its dangers, may be accepted only under compulsion, and with fear, by a man whose virtue has been proved'; Bonaventure (1966), p. 58.

22 Landini (1968), p. 119, hypothesized that clerics would have outnumbered lay friars by the time of the Constitutions of Narbonne in 1260. Şenocak (2012b), pp. 76–82, warns that it is impossible to know when (or if) this happened; however, from at least the 1240s the underlying mentality of the leadership favoured the educated friars, which implied clericalization, and recruitment of illiterate or 'useless' (*inutiles*) lay

brothers was heavily discouraged or even stopped. In *Exiit qui seminat*, his bull of 1279 clarifying the Franciscan Rule, Pope Nicholas III conceded that lay friars could be advanced in prayer and contemplation, but he conceived their role within the Order mainly as servants of their ordained brothers, who were engaged in study, divine services and pastoral ministry; see *FAED* III, pp. 757–8 and note (b). *BF* III, p. 413 (nr 127): 'Ad alios vero, qui se in praedictis spiritualibus operibus non exercent (nisi tales aliorum Fratrum licitis servitiis occupentur) ne otiose vivant, verba praedicta declaramus extendi; nisi et tales tam excellentis et notabilis contemplationis, et orationis existerent, quod merito propter hoc non essent a tanto bono et pio exercitio subtrahendi.'

23 Johnson (2007), pp. 100–01.

24 Field (1999), pp. 254–5.

25 See Emmen and Simoncioli (1963), pp. 389–400.

26 According to the fifteenth-century Spanish chronicler Sebastián de Olmedo, quoted by Mortier (1905), p. 98 n. 2: 'At vero in memorato Concilio Lugdunensi quia plures praelati et ecclesiarum Rectores apud Pontificem Senatumque Cardinalium aegre conqueri coeperunt quod Praedicatores scilicet et Minores omnia ad se traherent oporteretque ideo circa eorum statum aliquid immutari. Quibus tamen Papa primo quasi indignabundus simpliciter respondit dicens: Ite et vos bene vivite et studiis litterarum intendite si vultis quae petitis possidere. Hi enim cum Maria sedent secus pedes Domini et cum Martha satagunt circa frequens ministerium eius.' English translation by Moorman (1968), pp. 177–8.

27 Smart (1971) p. 188, perceptively pointed out the unity of design of the whole wall, but considered only the link between the Saint Francis scenes and the Virgin and Child over the central portal, and not that between the Saint Francis scenes and the biblical scenes above.

28 Although the *Crucifixion* in the Assisi New Testament cycle was no larger than any other scene on the south nave wall, we should not forget that the Upper Church was already adorned with Cimabue's two monumental *Crucifixion* frescoes in the transepts, as well as Giunta Pisano's panel crucifix (see Chapter 3).

29 ASC, Bollario, VII/220 and 220bis, VIII/225 and 225bis.

30 Hueck (2001), p. 46.

31 John of Caulibus (2000), p. 321. The date, authorship and genesis of the *Meditations* is still the subject of scholarly debate. The general consensus is that the oldest version is the so-called 'long Latin text' and that it was written between *c.*1336 and 1364 by John of Caulibus, a Tuscan Franciscan friar. The editors of the work believed there was 'a strong probability' that Caulibus was the author (John of Caulibus (2000), p. xiv). However, McNamer (2009) argued that the original version of the *Meditations* is preserved in Oxford, Bodleian Library, Ms Canon. Ital. 174. This much shorter Italian text could have been written in the early fourteenth century, almost certainly by a nun who was 'probably, but not necessarily, a Poor Clare' (p. 907).

32 The antiphon for Lauds on the feast of Saint Michael is 'Archangele Michael, constitui te principem super omnes animas suscipiendas' ('Archangel Michael, I have set you as prince over all the souls who are to be presented to me').

33 *LM* 9:3 (*FAED* II, p. 598; *FF*, p. 855); see also Celano II, 197 (*FAED* II, p. 374; *FF*, p. 616).

34 Acts 1:11.

35 Frankfurt, Städel Museum, *Sammlung von Umrissen und Durchzeichnungen dienend zur Geschichte der bildenden Künste des Mittelalters in Italien gezeichnet von Johann Anton Ramboux aus Trier in den Jahren 1818 bis 1822 und 1833–43*, vol. III: *Malereien aus der Zeit der Katakomben bis Cimabue*, p. 124 (nr 220).

36 Bonaventure (1994), p. 163.

37 Bonaventure (1994), p. 163 n. 50.

38 See Bonaventure (1963), p. 177, quoted in Johnson (2000), p. 78.

39 *Eximiae devotionis* (1 June 1291), *BF* IV, pp. 254–5 (nr 475).

40 '. . . pro representatione Spiritus Sancti in ecclesia superiori'; Hueck (2001), p. 46, citing Cenci (1974–6), vol. I, p. 218.

41 The thirteenth-century ordinal for Chartres cathedral contains instructions for Pentecostal doves to descend into the church, while at Rouen cathedral payments were made in 1379 for 'foliis, avibus et nebulis in festo Penthecostes'. The ordinal for the Benedictine nunnery at Barking Abbey, England, records that 'in die Pentecostes . . . et hac die dum "Veni creator Spiritus" canitur: descendet columba in medio chori . . . in signum spiritus sancti'. For these and other references, see Tripps (2000), pp. 192–4.

42 Hueck (2001), p. 46.

43 The full procedure for the general chapter is detailed in the Constitutions of Narbonne (1260), Rubric XI. For an English translation, see Bonaventure (1994), pp. 128–33.

44 Six general chapters were held at Assisi in the fourteenth century.

45 John 16:7.

46 *LM* 12:3 (*FAED* II, p. 624; *FF*, pp. 881–2).

47 *LM* 12:1–2 (*FAED* II, pp. 622–4; *FF*, pp. 879–81).

48 *Mira circa nos* (19 July 1228), *BF* I, pp. 42–4 (nr 25), at p. 44: 'Ne vero sibi soli proficeret in monte tantummodo Rachel amplexibus inhaerendo, contemplationi pulchrae quidem, sed sterili, ad Liae interdictum descendit cubiculum, minaturus gregem'; English translation in *FAED* I, p. 568.

49 The ascending Christ was more usually depicted in a central, frontal pose by this time.

50 This definition was popularized in the West through the Latin translation of *De fide orthodoxa*; John Damascene (1955), p. 267.
51 Bonaventure (1960), pp. 55–8.
52 The other four narrative scenes on the panel are all posthumous miracles.
53 Vatican City, Biblioteca Apostolica Vaticana, Archivio Capitolare di San Pietro, Ms B87, fol. 78r. Ciardi Dupré dal Poggetto (1991), pp. 199–200, placed the manuscript stylistically in the Rome–Assisi ambit, and suggested that it may have been a gift from Pope Nicholas IV to Saint Peter's.
54 The reverse chronology of the *Stigmatization* and the *Preaching to the Birds* is also found on the *vita* panel in Orte (near Rieti), where the two scenes are paired at the top of the gable, to either side of the central portrait of the saint; see Cook (1995b); Cook (1999), pp. 141–2 (cat. nr 115).
55 See Johnson (2000), p. 126, and, for a discussion of Bonaventure's use of the symbol of the mountain, pp. 125–7.
56 James of Milan (1949), Chapter 23; James of Milan (1999), trans. Murray at http://www.franciscans.org.au/spirituality/campion/Love's%20Prompting/Love's%20Prompting.pdf.
57 See above, p. 193.
58 It is so specified in the *Considerations of the Sacred Stigmata* (English translation in McKay, ed. (1963), p. 103), and in Bartholomew of Pisa's *De conformitate vitae beati Francisci ad vitam domini Iesu*, *AF* IV, p. 38; *AF* V, p. 12.
59 Graduale temporale, Cortona, Biblioteca del Comune e dell'Accademia Etrusca, Cod. 2A, fol. 1r; see Porzio, ed. (1982), pp. 360–61 (cat. nr 110); Degl'Innocenti Gambuti (1977), pp. 65–9, esp. p. 69.
60 Graduale temporale, Cortona, Biblioteca del Comune e dell'Accademia Etrusca, Cod. 1, fol. 2v; Porzio, ed. (1982), pp. 361–3 (cat. nr 111); Degl'Innocenti Gambuti (1977), pp. 75–94, esp. p. 86.
61 The antiphon for the first Sunday of Advent – that is, the first in the liturgical calendar. Two other Duecento miniatures are very similar to Cortona, Biblioteca del Comune e dell'Accademia Etrusca, Cod. 2A, fol. 1r: Cortona, Biblioteca del Comune e dell'Accademia Etrusca, Cod. 4c, fol. 2r, and Arezzo, Archivio Capitolare del Duomo, Cod. C, fol. 2r; see Porzio, ed. (1982), pp. 335–6, 370 (cat. nrs 87, 116); Degl'Innocenti Gambuti (1977), pp. 48–50, 65–7.
62 Psalm 83:6.
63 *De Ascensione Domini*, Sermo VIII, in Bonaventure (1882–1902), vol. IX, pp. 324–6.
64 Bonaventure (1970), Collation XXII, 20–23, pp. 350–52.
65 *FAED* II, p. 744.
66 Genesis 28:12.
67 Saint John Climacus, *The Ladder of Divine Ascent*, was one of the earliest and most influential texts, especially in the Byzantine Church. In the Latin Church, Chapter 7 of the Benedictine Rule references Jacob's ladder when it advises the monks to ascend to heaven via twelve steps of humility.
68 *FAED* II, p. 744.
69 *De Ascensione Domini*, Sermo IV, in Bonaventure (1882–1902), vol. IX, p. 320 (our translation).
70 Matthew of Acquasparta, Sermon 2, in *Sermons on Saint Francis*, http://www.franciscans.org.au/spirituality/campion/Aquasparta-3/St%20Francis.htm.
71 Moralia in Job, Liber IX, cap. 32; Gregory the Great (1874), col. 625.
72 Similarly, Dante's dream of the eagle in *Purgatorio*, Canto IX, 13–33, was interpreted as a *figura Christi* and associated with Jacob's ladder by Auerbach (1946), pp. 474–6; this idea was more fully developed by Ginsberg (1982). Both scholars quoted the passage from Gregory referred to in note 71.
73 Acts 2:3.
74 Acts 2:4–13.
75 'Spiritus Sanctus significatur per aquam.' See Cenci (1993), p. 511.
76 *In Pentecoste*, Sermo II, in Bonaventure (1882–1902), vol. IX, pp. 333–4, given to the friars in Paris, probably on the occasion of the general chapter of 1266. The biblical references are Genesis 2:10; Esther 10:6; Apocalypse (Revelation) 22:1; Genesis 16:14; Canticles (Song of Solomon) 4:15; 4 Kings (2 Kings) 3:16; and Judges 7:5.
77 This paragraph draws on Bonaventure, *In Pentecoste*, Sermo VIII, in Bonaventure (1882–1902), vol. IX, pp. 339–41.
78 See also Chapter 4:9 of Bonaventure's commentary on John's Gospel; Bonaventure (2007), pp. 221–2.
79 John 4:13.
80 For Bonaventure's exegesis on the story of the Samaritan woman in his commentary on John's Gospel, and other references to the Holy Spirit as water, see Johnson (2000), pp. 78–81.
81 In Bonaventure's text, Saint Francis tells the poor man to hurry to the rock where he will find 'aquam vivam' provided by Christ; *LM* 7:12 (*FAED*, II, p. 584; *FF*, p. 841).
82 See note 1.
83 See Johnson (2000), pp. 76–84.
84 Menestò (1993), p. 272, and see Chapter 2 above.
85 This is the text for two of Bonaventure's Pentecost sermons; see *In Pentecoste*, Sermo III and IV, in Bonaventure (1882–1902), vol. IX, p. 335.
86 Celano I, 89 (*FAED* I, p. 259; *FF*, p. 365); this text was noted in relation to the counter-façade images by Frugoni, in Zanardi, Frugoni and Zeri (1996), p. 206.
87 *Mira circa nos* (19 July 1228), *BF* I, p. 43 (nr 25): 'Spiritu fervoris concepto, asinique arrepta mandibula, praedicatione siquidem

simplici, nullis verborum persuasibilium humanae sapientiae coloribus adornata, sed tamen Dei virtute potenti . . . ex mandibula ipsa egressa copiosa est aqua, reficiens, abluens, et foecundans lapsos, sordidos, et arentes, quae in vitam aeternam saliens absque argento, et commutatione aliqua potest emi; cuius rivuli longe, lateque diffusi vineam irrigant usque ad mare palmites, et usque ad flumen propagines extendentem.' English translation in *FAED* I, pp. 566–7. The reference to the jawbone of an ass is an allusion to Samson (Judges 15:14–19); God made water flow from the jawbone to satiate Samson's thirst, after he had killed his enemies.

88 *LM*, Prologue 1 (*FAED* II, p. 527; *FF*, p. 778).

89 Apocalypse (Revelation) 7:2: 'Et vidi alterum angelum ascendentem ab ortu solis, habentem signum Dei vivi.'

90 The fact that the sign is a Tau comes from Ezekiel 9:4; Bonaventure connects Saint Francis with this text in *LM* 4:9 (*FAED* II, p. 556; *FF*, p. 810).

91 *LM*, Prologue 2 (*FAED* II, p. 527; *FF*, p. 779).

92 As well as in the Prologue, Bonaventure identified Francis as the 'alter angelus' of Apocalypse (Revelation) 7:2 in *LM* 13:10 (*FAED*, II, p. 638; *FF*, p. 898). John Pecham, in *A Canticle to Poverty* (*c.*1269–79), declared that he regarded Francis as the Angel of the Sixth Seal, along with many other typological identifications; see John Pecham (1999), trans. Murray at http://www.franciscans.org.au/spirituality/campion/Love's%20Prompting/A%20Canticle%20to%20Poverty.pdf.

93 The exception that proves the rule is Peter John Olivi's Apocalypse commentary, which was eventually condemned in 1326; see Burr (1989) and (1992), p. 97.

94 There is still no edition of Matthew's *Commentarium super Apocalypsim*, doubtless due to its challenging palaeography. The manuscript is Assisi, Biblioteca Comunale, Ms 51. The Apocalypse (Revelation) 7:2 passage at fol. 158r (old sequence fol. 336r) reads: '"Vidi alterum Angelum ascendentem ab ortu solis, habentem signum Dei vivi." Istud est optimum thema ad praedicandum de beato Francisco. Licet enim illud ex prima intentione intelligatur principaliter de Christo, potest tamen de ipso intelligi.' Quoted in Bihel (1927), pp. 69–70; Da Campagnola (1971), pp. 191–2.

95 This paragraph uses the translation by Murray; see Matthew of Acquasparta, *Sermons on Saint Francis*, at http://www.franciscans.org.au/spirituality/campion/Aquasparta-3/St%20Francis.htm.

96 The word 'sursumactio' is difficult to translate, but the editors of *FAED* pointed out that Bonaventure frequently used it in the context of the spiritual life to mean the continuing ascent into God. In the *Itinerarium*, for example, he described prayer as 'the mother and origin of the ascent [*sursumactio*]'; see *FAED* II, p. 544 note (b).

97 For the illumination, see note 53 above. For the La Verna relief, see Cook (1999), p. 120 (cat. nr 90).

98 Hills (1987), pp. 77–8, 115–16. For the importance of this text for the iconography of the *Stigmatization*, see Cooper (2009), pp. 292–5.

99 For a succinct discussion of the relationship between these three texts, and the dating arguments, see *FAED* III, pp. 429–34.

100 *The Deeds of Blessed Francis and his Companions* (2001), 9:69, pp. 457–8.

101 *AF* III, p. 643: 'Ad ipsius quoque Crucifixi praesentiam mons totus luce aurea refulgebat.' This was noted by Meiss (1964), p. 47 n. 85.

102 See Marrone (2001), vol. I.

103 Wisdom 7:26 and 7:29.

104 These ideas can be found very frequently in the writings of Bonaventure: see, *inter alia*, Bonaventure (2008), Conference XI, 5 and 17, pp. 186, 196–8; Bonaventure (1970), Collation I, esp. 10, pp. 5–6; *Sermones selecti de rebus theologicis*, Sermo IV: 'Christus unus omnium magister', in Bonaventure (1882–1902), vol. V, pp. 567–74, translated as 'Christ, the One Teacher of All', in Johnson, ed. (1999), pp. 152–66; *In Ascensione Domini*, Sermo I, in Bonaventure (1882–1902), vol. IX, pp. 314–18; *In Pentecoste*, Sermo VII, in Bonaventure (1882–1902), vol. IX, pp. 337–9.

105 Johnson, ed. (1999), p. 152.

106 It was published by Squadrani (1932).

107 Salimbene (1966), pp. 947–8, referred to him as 'frater Bartolomeus de Bononia magnus et cathedratus magister'. For Bartholomew's biography, see Longpré (1923).

108 Squadrani (1932), p. 231.

109 Bonaventure (2004), pp. 1780–88.

110 Marrone (2001), vol. I, pp. 221–2.

111 Bonaventure (2008), Collation XI, 4, pp. 185–6.

112 Bonaventure (1960), Chapter 7, 4, p. 57.

113 Johnson (2000), pp. 164–8.

114 *LM* 13:1 (*FAED* I, p. 631; *FF*, p. 890).

115 For the properties of the persons of the Trinity, see Bonaventure (1963), Part 1, Chapter 3, 6–9, pp. 39–40.

116 *LM* 11:1 (*FAED* II, p. 612; *FF*, p. 869).

117 Squadrani (1932), p. 363.

118 *LMin*, Chapter 6, Lesson 2 (*FAED* II, p. 710; *FF*, p. 1001).

119 Acts 2:3.

120 John of Caulibus (2000), p. 157.

121 Ibid. This analysis is based substantially on the writings of Saint Bernard. A very similar definition was made by Thomas Aquinas in the *Summa theologica*, where he ranked in increasing order of excellence the external works of the active life, then contemplation, and finally the active life of preaching

and teaching. 'For even as it is better to enlighten than merely to shine, so it is better to give to others the fruits of one's contemplation than simply to contemplate.' See Thomas Aquinas (1911/1981), p. 1993.

122 As remarked by Frugoni (2010b), p. 134.

123 For the remainder of this paragraph see Neff (2006), pp. 680, 683–5.

124 Neff (2006). For the attribution to John of Wales, see Flood (2002), pp. 93–4. The only extant copies of the *Meditatio pauperis in solitudine* are two manuscripts, probably from the early fourteenth century, both in the Biblioteca Comunale, Assisi (Ms 422 and Ms 439). We agree with Neff (2006), p. 681, that the presence of the *Meditatio pauperis* in Assisi in the late Duecento is plausible, although it cannot be proven. Swanson (1989), p. 214, noted that the friars of the Sacro Convento seem to have had a particular interest in John's writings and possessed virtually a complete library of his works.

125 See p. 193.

126 Genesis 32:24–30.

127 Bonaventure (1960), 7:3, p. 56.

128 In *LM* 6:6 the friar is not named. He is identified as Pacifico in *The Assisi Compilation* (2000), 65, pp. 167–8.

129 Neff (2006), p. 687.

130 *LM* 10:4 (*FAED* II, p. 607; *FF*, p. 864).

131 Luke 18:9–14.

132 Bonaventure (2004), p. 1729.

133 Jacobus de Voragine (1993), vol. I, p. 344.

134 Frugoni (2010b), pp. 125–6, citing Gieben (1996), argued that Sylvester's separate undergarment identifies him as a priest, according to the regulations on the habit in the Constitutions of Narbonne, 1260.

135 Discussing the significance of Saint Paul in Franciscan exegesis Neff (2006), pp. 699–700, pointed out that the only image of the apostle in the nave of the Upper Basilica is on the counter-façade, close to the Franciscan saints in the north side of the archivolt, and to Benjamin in the Genesis scene.

136 *LM* 10:4 (*FAED* II, p. 607; *FF*, p. 864). Other passages that connect rapture with light are *LM* 3:6 and *LM* 11:10 (*FAED* II, pp. 545, 618–19; *FF*, pp. 798, 877).

137 Marrone (2001), vol. I, p. 148.

138 *LM* 10:1 (*FAED* II, pp. 605; *FF*, p. 862).

139 2 Corinthians 12:2 and 12:4.

140 *LM* 13:4 (*FAED* II, p. 633; *FF*, pp. 893).

141 Matthew of Acquasparta, *Sermons on Saint Francis*, trans. Murray, at http://www.franciscans.org.au/spirituality/campion/Aquasparta–3/St%20Francis.htm.

142 Chapter 4, p. 105; and Neff (2006), p. 676.

143 This paragraph draws on Neff (2006), pp. 693–7.

144 Genesis 41:45.

145 Translated by Murray at http://www.franciscans.org.au/spirituality/campion/a%20meditation%20in%20solitude.pdf.

146 For a diagram of the *giornate*, see Zanardi, Frugoni and Zeri (1996), pp. 224–5.

147 All four of the Duecento *vita* panels that include this scene show the preaching Saint Francis holding a book: the Bardi dossal in Florence; the Pescia, Orte and Siena panels. See Cook (1999), pp. 98–102, 165–8, 141–2, 209–11 (cat. nrs 68, 141, 115, 180 respectively). The iconography seems to have been a little more varied in manuscripts: an important example to depict Saint Francis preaching to the birds without a book is the Vatican illumination (fig. 172 and p. 194).

148 Squadrani (1932), p. 363.

149 Squadrani (1932), p. 363 n. 2: 'Ut patet de apostolis quando caritate fuerunt inflammati in pentecoste, omnia sciebant ut legitur Actus apostolorum(?) et scientiam divinam habebant; sicut et Franciscus idiota magna sciebat ut mirarentur omnes.' The dating of the marginalia is uncertain, but given that such annotations were usually made by students or doctors using the book for study, it is likely to represent a reasonably learned Franciscan view; ibid., p. 223.

150 Acts 4:13.

151 *LM* 11:14 (*FAED* II, p. 620; *FF*, p. 879).

152 Zafarana (1981), p. 242, who quoted Matthew of Acquasparta's Sermon 1 on Saint Francis: 'et licet fuisset *illitteratus et simplex*, erant tamen verba eius non inania, nec risu digna, sed erant medullas cordis penetrantia'; Sermon 3 on the Translation, 'Nullus enim debet praesumere praedicare aut verbum Dei annuntiare, nisi Spiritus sanctus miserit eum, quoniam unctio eius docet de omnibus . . . Et inde est quod interdum *simpliciores* melius, utilius et efficacius praedicant quam magni clerici et litterati'; and Sermon 1 on the Purification of the Virgin, 'stultum est contemnere doctrinam sanctorum, quantumcumque fuerint *illitterati* . . . Exempla sunt infinita in Scriptura de prophetis, qui pro magna parte fuerunt *rusticani, idiotae et illitterati*; de apostolis, qui excepto Paulo omnes fuerunt similiter *illitterati, simplices*' [our emphases].

153 For the characteristic use of divisions and authorities in thirteenth-century mendicant sermons, see d'Avray (1985), pp. 172–7.

154 Roest (2000), pp. 276–81.

155 *Ad fructus uberes*, *BF* III, p. 480 (nr 16); see Moorman (1968), pp. 181–4.

156 See Little (1924). Ironically, it would be Caetani, after his elevation to the papal throne as Boniface VIII, who would in 1300 end the dispute with a more even-handed bull, *Super cathedram*.

157 *LM* 11:4 (*FAED* II, pp. 614–15; *FF*, pp. 871–2).

158 See Chapter 5.
159 For early Franciscan preaching and confession, see Zafarana (1981), pp. 212–13.
160 Frugoni (2010b), pp. 125–6, identified this friar as a priest from the undergarment visible beneath his habit; see note 134.
161 Roest (2000), p. 317 n. 163, citing Fussenegger, ed. (1960), pp. 237, 269–70.
162 Roest (2000), p. 317.
163 *LM* 12:7 (*FAED* II, pp. 625–6; *FF*, p. 884).
164 Celano I, 73 (*FAED* I, pp. 245–6; *FF*, pp. 348–9); Stephen of Bourbon, in Lemmens, ed. (1926), pp. 94–5; English translation in *FAED* II, pp. 789–90.
165 '. . . non in doctis humanae sapientiae verbis sed divino spiritu loqueretur'. This is based on 1 Corinthians 2:13: 'loquimur non in doctis humanae sapientiae verbis sed in doctrina spiritus'.
166 He must also have known the *Legenda maior* inside out: Bonaventure did not use the Pauline passage in this story, but in another, earlier passage on Saint Francis's preaching; see *LM* 4:5 (*FAED* II, p. 553; *FF*, pp. 806–7).
167 Bonaventure (1990), p. 28.
168 Brooke (2006), p. 400.
169 Frugoni (2010b), pp. 150–51.
170 Swanson found 144 surviving Latin manuscripts. Four of them are listed in the 1381 inventory of the Sacro Convento library at Assisi; see Swanson (1989), pp. 233–4, 257, 281–2.
171 John of Wales (1489/1964), Prologue (unpaginated): 'non solum in praedicatione declamatoria sed in collatione familiari et mutua'.
172 Luke 7:36–50.
173 'Set moderni, qui non sunt sancti nec sunt sic divina gratia illustrati, primo antequam predicent debent predicationis materiam ordinare, nec sic debent presumere de divino auxilio quin ad predicandum studeant, ne dicant que dicenda non sunt improvisi et ut eorum predicatio fiat populo fructuosa.' The Latin text was published, with a discussion of its authorship and an analysis of the surviving manuscripts, by Delorme (1944); here p. 185. For several examples of similar texts, see Zafarana (1981), pp. 230–31; Charland (1936), pp. 111–12.
174 Şenocak (2012b), p. 156.
175 Doyle (1983), p. 64. Bonaventure was not the first Franciscan to make the comparison between Saint Francis and Saint Paul in this context. It was also made in a Saint Francis sermon preached by a master called Guiard of Laon at the University of Paris in 1230. Şenocak (2012b), p. 107, believes this sermon to be the origin of the idea that Francis's learning was a divine gift: 'Sic beatus Franciscus doctus fuit a Domino solummodo et propter hoc coram Papa et cardinalibus ausus est praedicare'. See Davy (1931), p. 220.
176 Doyle (1983), p. 66.
177 Dalarun (2002), pp. 230, 254–5.
178 Frugoni (1998), p. 137.
179 Johnson (2000), p. 180.
180 Chapter 2, 13; Bonaventure (1966), pp. 31–2.
181 'The Rule and Life of the Lesser Brothers is this: to observe the Holy Gospel of Our Lord Jesus Christ by living in obedience, without anything of one's own, and in chastity.' English translation in *FAED* II, p. 100.
182 Although his argument was different from ours, Belting also noted that the papal saints in the roundels 'seem to serve as seals that authenticate a document' ('sembrano servire come dei sigilli che autenticano un documento'); Belting (1983), p. 95.
183 *LM* 13:9 (*FAED* II, p. 637; *FF*, p. 897). The stigmata were seen as the seal of Christ by Hugh of Digne and Dante as well as by Bonaventure; see Wolff (2008), pp. 94–5.
184 See Chapter 2, p. 49.
185 See Chapter 1, note 18.
186 *Exiit qui seminat* (14 August 1279), *BF* III, pp. 404–16 (nr 127), at p. 405: 'Hi sunt illius sanctae Regulae professores, quae evangelico fundatur eloquio, vitae Christi roboratur exemplo, fundatorum militantis Ecclesiae Apostolorum ejus sermonibus, actibusque firmatur. Haec est apud Deum et Patrem munda et immaculata Religio, quae descendens a Patre luminum per ejus Filium exemplariter, et verbaliter Apostolis tradita, et demum per Spiritum Sanctum Beato Francisco, et eum sequentibus inspirata totius in se quasi continet testimonium Trinitatis. Haec est, cui attestante Paulo nemo de cetero debet esse molestus, quam Christus passionis suae stigmatibus confirmavit volens institutorem ipsius passionis suae signis notabiliter insigniri.' English translation in *FAED* III, p. 740.

Conclusion

1 For the likely use of the Upper Church during Franciscan general chapters, see Hueck (2001), p. 46. The 1282 Strasbourg general chapter, which over 700 friars are known to have attended, gives some idea of the scale of the Assisi gathering. As Hueck observes, within the Basilica complex only the Upper Church could have accommodated such numbers.
2 Frugoni (2010a). For further discussion of the Pisa panel, see Cooper (forthcoming).
3 The bull *Ante thronum* granted an indulgence of one year and forty days for those visiting the Basilica on the feast of Saint Francis and its octave, while *Licet is* granted one of 100 days for visitors on any single day of the year. Both bulls are dated 21 January 1296; see *BF* IV, pp. 379–80 (nrs 49 and 50).

Bibliography

Abate, Giuseppe (1933). 'Memoriali, statuti ed atti di capitoli generali dei Frati Minori dei secoli XIII e XIV', *Miscellanea Francescana* 33, pp. 15–45, 320–36

—— (1935). 'Le "Constitutiones generales antique" dei Frati Minori nella redazione assisana del 1279', *Miscellanea Francescana* 35, pp. 58–106, 232–9

Alberzoni, Maria Pia (1999). 'L'*Approbatio*: Curia romana, Ordine Minoritico e *Liber*', in *Angèle de Foligno: Le dossier*, ed. Giulia Barone and Jacques Dalarun (Rome), pp. 293–318

Alessandri, Leto, and Francesco Pennacchi (1914). 'I più antichi inventari della sacristia del Sacro Convento di Assisi (1338–1473)', *Archivum Franciscanum Historicum* 7, pp. 66–107, 294–340

Allegrezza, Franca (2000). 'Niccolò III', in *Enciclopedia dei papi*, ed. Massimo Bray, vol. II (Rome), pp. 437–46

Analecta Franciscana (1885–), ed. Collegio San Bonaventura (Quaracchi)

Andaloro, Maria (1984a). 'Ancora una volta sull'*Ytalia* di Cimabue', *Arte Medievale* 2, pp. 143–81

—— (1984b). 'Il sogno di Innocenzo III all'Aracoeli, Niccolò IV e la basilica di S. Giovanni in Laterano', in *Studi in onore di Giulio Carlo Argan*, ed. Silvana Macchioni, vol. I (Rome), pp. 29–42

—— (2001). 'Tracce della prima decorazione pittorica nella Basilica di San Francesco ad Assisi', in *Il cantiere pittorico della Basilica Superiore di San Francesco in Assisi*, ed. Giuseppe Basile and Pasquale Magro (Assisi), pp. 71–100

——, ed. (2006a). *L'orizzonte tardoantico e le nuove immagini, 312–468*, vol. I of *La pittura medievale a Roma, 312–1431, corpus e atlante: Corpus*, ed. Maria Andaloro and Serena Romano (Rome)

——, ed. (2006b). *Suburbio, Vaticano, Rione Monti*, vol. I of *La pittura medievale a Roma 312–1431, corpus e atlante: Atlante percorsi visivi*, ed. Maria Andaloro and Serena Romano (Rome)

Angeli, Francesco Maria (1704). *Collis paradisi amoenitas, seu Sacri Conventus Assisiensis historiae* (Montefalco)

Arenberg, Carolus van (1666). *Icones antiquae quibus ostenditur Fratres Minores Capucinos eamdem gerere habitus formam* (Brussels)

Armstrong, Regis J., William J. Short and J. A. Wayne Hellman, eds (1999–2001). *Francis of Assisi: Early Documents*, 3 vols (New York)

The Assisi Compilation (2000), in *Francis of Assisi: Early Documents*, ed. Regis J. Armstrong, William J. Short and J. A. Wayne Hellman, vol. II (New York), pp. 118–230

Auerbach, Erich (1946). 'Figurative Texts Illustrating Certain Passages of Dante's *Commedia*', *Speculum* 21, pp. 474–89

Augustine of Hippo (1886). *Contra Maximinum haereticum Arianorum episcopum*, in *Patrologiae Latinae*, ed. J.-P. Migne, vol. XLII (Paris), cols 743–814

Banker, James R. (1991). 'The Program for the Sassetta Altarpiece in the Church of S. Francesco in Borgo S. Sepolcro', *I Tatti Studies* 4, pp. 11–58

Barone, Giulia (1983). 'Margherita Colonna e le Clarisse di S. Silvestro in Capite', in *Roma anno 1300*, ed. Angiola Maria Romanini (Rome), pp. 799–805

—— (2000). 'Niccolò IV', in *Enciclopedia dei papi*, ed. Massimo Bray, vol. II (Rome), pp. 455–9

Bartoli Langeli, Attilio, with Maria Immacolata Bossa and Lucia Fiumi (1997). *Le carte duecentesche del Sacro Convento di Assisi (Istrumenti, 1168–1300)* (Padua)

Bartolomasi, Bonaventura (1824). *Series chronologica historica ministrorum provincialium et commissariorum generalium qui Seraphicam S. P. N. Francisci provinciam dictam quoque de Umbria a primaeva institutione . . . usque ad praesens gubernarunt* (Rome)

—— (1932). 'Series chronologico-historica ministrorum provincialium et commissariorum generalium qui Seraphicam S. P. N. Francisci provinciam dictam quoque de Umbria a primaeva institutione Ordinis Minorum inde conventualium nuncupatorum', *Miscellanea Francescana* 32, pp. 201–26

Bede (1995). *On the Temple*, trans. Seán Connolly (Liverpool)

Bellosi, Luciano (1985). *La pecora di Giotto* (Turin)

—— (1998). *Cimabue* (Milan)

—— (2001). 'Un crocifisso di Giotto nella Basilica Superiore di Assisi?', in *Il cantiere pittorico della Basilica Superiore di San Francesco in Assisi*, ed. Giuseppe Basile and Pasquale Magro (Assisi), pp. 261–78

—— (2007). '"Nicolaus IV fieri precepit": Una testimonianza di valore inestimabile sulla decorazione murale della Basilica Superiore di San Francesco ad Assisi', *Prospettiva* 126–7, pp. 2–14

Belting, Hans (1977). *Die Oberkirche von San Francesco in Assisi: Ihre Dekoration als Aufgabe und die Genese einer neuen Wandmalerei* (Berlin)

—— (1981). *Das Bild und sein Publikum im Mittelalter: Form und Funktion früher Bildtafeln der Passion* (Berlin)

—— (1983). 'Assisi e Roma: Risultati, problemi, prospettive', in *Roma anno 1300*, ed. Angiola Maria Romanini (Rome), pp. 93–101

—— (1990). *The Image and its Public in the Middle Ages: Form and Function of Early Paintings of the Passion*, trans. Mark Bartusis and Raymond Meyer (New Rochelle, NY)

Berger, Élie, ed (1884–1920). *Les registres d'Innocent IV: Publiés ou analysés d'après les manuscrits originaux du Vatican et de la Bibliothèque Nationale*, 4 vols (Paris)

Bernard of Besse (1905–13). *Catalogus generalium ministrorum Ordinis Fratrum Minorum*, ed. Oswald Holder-Egger, Monumenta Germaniae Historica: *Scriptores*, vol. XXXII (Hanover and Leipzig), pp. 653–74

Biasiotti, Giovanni (1915). 'La basilica di S. Maria Maggiore di Roma prima delle innovazioni del secolo XVI', *Mélanges d'Archéologie et d'Histoire* 35, pp. 15–40

—— (1920). 'Le memorie di S. Girolamo in Santa Maria Maggiore di Roma', in *Miscellanea geronimiana: Scritti varii pubblicati nel XV centenario dalla morte di San Girolamo* (Rome), pp. 237–44

Biblia latina cum glossa ordinaria: Facsimile Reprint of the Editio Princeps Adolph Rusch of Strassburg 1480/81 (1992), introduction by Karlfried Froehlich and Margaret T. Gibson, 4 vols (Turnhout)

Bihel, Stephen (1927). 'S. Franciscus fuitne Angelus Sexti Sigilli?', *Antonianum* 2, pp. 59–90

Bihl, Michael (1911). 'De capitulo generali O. M. Metensi anno 1254 adsignando deque antiquo sigillo ministri generalis', *Archivum Franciscanum Historicum* 4, pp. 425–35

Binski, Paul (2001). 'How Northern was the Northern Master at Assisi?', *Proceedings of the British Academy* 117, pp. 73–138

—— (2009). 'The Patronage and Date of the Legend of St Francis in the Upper Church of S. Francesco at Assisi', *Burlington Magazine* 151, pp. 663–5

—— (2011). 'Art-Historical Reflections on the Fall of the Colonna, 1297', in *Rome across Time and Space: Cultural Transmission and the Exchange of Ideas, c.500–1400*, ed. Claudia Bolgia, Rosamond McKitterick and John Osborne (Cambridge), pp. 278–90

Blume, Dieter (1983). *Wandmalerei als Ordenspropaganda: Bildprogramme im Chorbereich franziskanischer Konvente Italiens bis zur Mitte des 14. Jahrhunderts* (Worms)

Boase, T. S. R. (1933). *Boniface VIII* (London)

Bolgia, Claudia (2003a). 'An Engraved Architectural Drawing at Santa Maria in Aracoeli, Rome', *Journal of the Society of Architectural Historians* 62, pp. 436–47

—— (2003b). 'The Church of S. Maria in Aracoeli, Rome: From the Earliest Times to *circa* 1400', unpublished PhD dissertation, University of Warwick

—— (2007). 'Ostentation, Power, and Family Competition in Late-Medieval Rome: The Earliest Chapels at S. Maria in Aracoeli', in *Aspects of Power and Authority in the Middle Ages*, ed. Brenda Bolton and Christine Meek (Turnhout), pp. 73–106

—— (2012) 'Mosaics and Gilded Glass in Franciscan Hands: "Professional" Friars in Thirteenth- and Fourteenth-Century Italy', in *Patrons and Professionals in the Middle Ages*, ed. Paul Binski and Elizabeth A. New (Donington), pp. 141–66

—— (forthcoming). *Santa Maria in Aracoeli and the Franciscans in Rome, c.1250–1400* (Aldershot)

Bonaventure of Bagnoregio (1882–1902). *Opera omnia*, ed. Collegio di San Bonaventura, 10 vols (Quaracchi)

—— (1960). *The Journey of the Mind to God*, in *Mystical Opuscula*, ed. and trans. José de Vinck, vol. I of *The Works of Bonaventure: Cardinal, Seraphic Doctor, and Saint* (Paterson, NJ), pp. 5–58

—— (1963). *The Breviloquium*, ed. and trans. José de Vinck, vol. II of *The Works of Bonaventure: Cardinal, Seraphic Doctor, and Saint* (Paterson, NJ)

—— (1966). *Defense of the Mendicants*, ed. and trans. José de Vinck, vol. IV of *The Works of Bonaventure, Cardinal, Seraphic Doctor, and Saint* (Paterson, NJ)

—— (1970). *Collations on the Six Days*, trans. José de Vinck, vol. V of *The Works of Bonaventure, Cardinal, Seraphic Doctor, and Saint* (Paterson, NJ)

—— (1990). *Sermons de tempore*, ed. Jacques-Guy Bougerol (Paris)

—— (1993). *Sermons de diversis*, ed. Jacques-Guy Bougerol, 2 vols (Paris)

—— (1994). *St. Bonaventure's Writings Concerning the Franciscan Order*, trans. Dominic Monti, vol. V of *Works of St. Bonaventure* (St. Bonaventure, NY)

—— (2004). *St. Bonaventure's Commentary on the Gospel of Luke, Chapters 17–24*, ed. and trans. Robert J. Karris, vol. VIII, part 3, of *Works of St. Bonaventure* (St. Bonaventure, NY)

—— (2007). *Commentary on the Gospel of John*, ed. and trans. Robert J. Karris, vol. XI of *Works of St. Bonaventure* (St. Bonaventure, NY)

—— (2008). *Collations on the Seven Gifts of the Holy Spirit*, ed. and trans. Zachary Hayes, with notes by Robert J. Karris, vol. XIV of *Works of St. Bonaventure* (St. Bonaventure, NY)

Bonito Fanelli, Rosalia (1980). 'Tessuti e ricami', in *Il tesoro della Basilica di San Francesco ad Assisi*, ed. Maria G. Ciardi Dupré dal Poggetto (Assisi), pp. 77–85

Bonsanti, Giorgio (1998). *The Basilica of St. Francis of Assisi: Glory and Destruction*, trans. Stephen Saltarelli (New York)

——, ed. (2002). *La Basilica di San Francesco ad Assisi*, 4 vols, Mirabilia Italiae 11 (Modena)

Bon Valsassina, Caterina, and Vittoria Garibaldi, eds (1994). *Dipinti, sculture e ceramiche della Galleria Nazionale dell'Umbria: Studi e restauri* (Florence)

Bortolan, Domenico (1887). 'Cronaca romana dall'anno 1288 al 1301', *Archivio Veneto* 33/2, pp. 425–33

Borzi, Attilio (1984). *Il duomo di Palestrina* (Palestrina)

—— (1997). *Sant'Agapito Martire* (Palestrina)

Boskovits, Miklós (2000a). 'Giotto: Un artista poco conosciuto?', in *Giotto: Bilancio critico di sessant'anni di studi e ricerche*, ed. Angelo Tartuferi (Florence), pp. 75–95

—— (2000b). 'Giotto di Bondone', in *DBI* 55 (Rome), pp. 401–23

Bougerol, Jacques-Guy (1982). 'Initia latinorum sermonum ad laudem Sancti Francisci', *Antonianum* 57, pp. 706–94

Bourdua, Louise (2004). *The Franciscans and Art Patronage in Late Medieval Italy* (Cambridge)

Boverio, Zaccaria (1632–9). *Annalium, seu Sacrarum historiarum Ordinis Minorum S. Francisci qui Capucini nuncupantur*, 2 vols (Lyon)

—— (1640). *De vero habitus forma a Seraphico B. P. Francisco instituta demonstrationes XI* (Cologne)

Bracaloni, Leone (1939). 'Il prodigioso crocifisso che parlò a S. Francesco', *Studi Francescani* 36, pp. 185–212

Brady, Ignatius (1976). 'St. Bonaventure's Sermons on Saint Francis', *Franziskanische Studien* 58, pp. 129–41

Brenk, Beat (2010). *The Apse, the Image and the Icon: An Historical Perspective of the Apse as a Space for Images* (Wiesbaden)

Brentano, Robert (1974). *Rome before Avignon: A Social History of Thirteenth-Century Rome* (New York)

Brooke, Rosalind B., ed. and trans. (1970). *Scripta Leonis, Rufini et Angeli sociorum S. Francisci: The Writings of Leo, Rufino and Angelo, Companions of St. Francis* (Oxford)

—— (2006). *The Image of St. Francis: Responses to Sainthood in the Thirteenth Century* (Cambridge)

Burr, David (1989). 'Franciscan Exegesis and Francis as Apocalyptic Figure', in *Monks, Nuns, and Friars in Mediaeval Society*, ed. Edward B. King, Jacqueline T. Schaefer and William B. Wadley (Sewanee, TN), pp. 51–62

—— (1992). 'Mendicant Readings of the Apocalypse', in *The Apocalypse in the Middle Ages*, ed. Richard K. Emmerson and Bernard McGinn (Ithaca, NY), pp. 89–102

—— (2001). *The Spiritual Franciscans: From Protest to Persecution in the Century after Saint Francis* (University Park, PA)

Cadei, Antonio (1978). 'La chiesa di S. Francesco a Cortona', *Storia della Città* 3/9, pp. 16–23

—— (1983). 'Assisi, S. Francesco: L'architettura e la prima fase della decorazione', in *Roma anno 1300*, ed. Angiola Maria Romanini (Rome), pp. 141–74

Callebaut, André (1914). 'Lettres franciscaines concernant la Belgique et la France aux XIIIe–XVe siècles', *Archivum Franciscanum Historicum* 7, pp. 247–63

—— (1917). 'Les provinciaux de la province de France au XIIIe siècle: Notes, documents et études', *Archivum Franciscanum Historicum* 10, pp. 289–356

Calpini, Luciana (1975). 'La guerra di Narni e Stroncone nel 1293', *Archivio della Società Romana di Storia Patria* 98, pp. 5–54

Cannon, Joanna (1982). 'Dating the Frescoes by the Maestro di S. Francesco at Assisi', *Burlington Magazine* 124, pp. 65–9

—— (2002). 'The Era of the Great Painted Crucifix: Giotto, Cimabue, Giunta Pisano, and their Anonymous Contemporaries', *Renaissance Studies* 16, pp. 571–81

Casagrande, Giovanna, Antonella d'Alessandro, and Silvia Gigante, eds (1988). *Assisi, Biblioteca del Convento di S. Francesco 'Fondo Moderno'*, vol. CIV of *Inventari dei manoscritti delle biblioteche d'Italia* (Florence)

Casimiro of Rome (1736). *Memorie istoriche della chiesa e convento di S. Maria in Araceli di Roma* (Rome)

Catalano, Niccolò (1652). *Fiume del terrestre paradiso diviso in quattro capi, o discorsi* (Florence)

Cellini, Pico (1955). 'Di Fra' Guglielmo e di Arnolfo', *Bollettino d'Arte*, 4th ser., 40, pp. 215–29

Cenci, Cesare (1974–6). *Documentazione di vita assisana, 1300–1530*, 3 vols (Assisi)

—— (1981). *Bibliotheca manuscripta ad Sacrum Conventum Assisiensem*, 2 vols (Assisi)

—— (1993). 'Le "Postillae dominicales" di Fr. Girolamo d'Ascoli', *Antonianum* 68, pp. 485–525

Chacón, Alfonso (1677). *Vitae et res gestae pontificum romanorum et S.R.E. cardinalium ab initio nascentis ecclesiae, usque ad Clementem IX. pont. max.*, 4 vols (Rome)

Charland, Thomas-Marie (1936). *Artes praedicandi: Contribution à l'histoire de la rhétorique au moyen âge* (Paris)

Christe, Yves (1970). 'À propos du décor absidal de Saint-Jean du Latran à Rome', *Cahiers Archéologiques* 20, pp. 197–206

Ciardi Dupré dal Poggetto, Maria Grazia (1991). 'La committenza e il mecenatismo artistico di Niccolò IV', in *Niccolò IV: Un pontificato tra oriente ed occidente*, ed. Enrico Menestò (Spoleto), pp. 193–222

Ciatti, Marco (2001). 'The Restoration and Study of the Crucifix', in *Giotto: The Santa Maria Novella Crucifix*, ed. Marco Ciatti and Max Seidel (Florence), pp. 25–64

Ciatti, Marco, and Max Seidel, eds (2001). *Giotto: The Santa Maria Novella Crucifix* (Florence)

Cioni Liserani, Elisabetta (1979). 'Alcune ipotesi per Guccio di Mannaia', *Prospettiva* 17, pp. 47–58

Clasen, Sophronius (1961). 'Franziskus, der neue Moses', *Wissenschaft und Weisheit* 24, pp. 200–08

Claussen, Peter Cornelius (2008). *Die Kirchen der Stadt Rom im Mittelalter, 1050–1300*, vol. II: *S. Giovanni in Laterano* (Stuttgart)

Coletti, Luigi (1949). *Gli affreschi della Basilica di Assisi* (Bergamo)

'Compendium chronicarum Fratrum Minorum scriptum a Patre Mariano de Florentia' (1908–11), *Archivum Franciscanum Historicum* 1 (1908), pp. 98–107; 2 (1909), pp. 92–107, 305–18, 457–72, 626–41; 3 (1910) 294–309, 700–15; 4 (1911), 122–37, 318–39, 559–87

Cook, William R. (1995a). 'The Cycle of the Life of Francis of Assisi in Rieti: The First "Copy" of the Assisi Frescoes', *Collectanea Franciscana* 65, pp. 115–47

—— (1995b). 'The Orte Dossal: A Traditional and Innovative Life of St. Francis of Assisi', *Arte Medievale* 9, pp. 41–7

—— (1996). 'New Sources, New Insights: The Bardi Dossal of the Life and Miracles of St. Francis of Assisi', *Studi Francescani* 93, pp. 325–46

—— (1999). *Images of St. Francis of Assisi in Painting, Stone and Glass, from the Earliest Images to ca.1320 in Italy: A Catalogue* (Florence)

Cooper, Donal (2000). '"In medio ecclesiae": Screens, Crucifixes and Shrines in the Franciscan Church Interior in Italy, *c.*1230–*c.*1400', unpublished PhD dissertation, University of London

—— (2001). 'Franciscan Choir Enclosures and the Function of Double-Sided Altarpieces in Pre-Tridentine Umbria', *Journal of the Warburg and Courtauld Institutes* 64, pp. 1–54

—— (2005). '"In loco tutissimo et firmissimo": The Tomb of St. Francis in History, Legend, and Art', in *The Art of the Franciscan Order in Italy*, ed. William R. Cook (Leiden), pp. 1–37

—— (2009). 'The Franciscan Genesis of Sassetta's Altarpiece', in *Sassetta: The Borgo San Sepolcro Altarpiece*, ed. Machtelt Israëls, 2 vols (Florence and Leiden), vol. I, pp. 285–303

—— (2011). 'Access All Areas? Spatial Divides in the Mendicant Churches of Late Medieval Tuscany', in *Ritual and Space in the Middle Ages*, ed. Frances Andrews (Donington), pp. 90–107

—— (forthcoming). 'Rethinking Early Italian Panel Painting and the Primacy of the Altarpiece: Giotto's *Stigmatization of Saint Francis* and its Pisan Context', *Art History*

Cooper, Donal, and Janet Robson (2003). 'Pope Nicholas IV and the Upper Church at Assisi', *Apollo* 157 (February), pp. 31–5

—— (2009). '"A great sumptuousness of paintings": Frescos and Franciscan Poverty at Assisi in 1288 and 1312', *Burlington Magazine* 151, pp. 656–62

—— (2011). 'Assisi e Padova, penitenza e taumaturgia: Due esperienze diverse di pellegrinaggio nel primo Trecento', *Il Santo* 51, pp. 475–89

Courtenay, William J. (2009). 'Franciscan Learning: University Education and Biblical Exegesis', in *Defenders and Critics of Franciscan Life: Essays in Honor of John V. Fleming*, ed. Michael F. Cusato and G. Geltner (Leiden), pp. 55–64

Crowe, Joseph A., and Giovanni Battista Cavalcaselle (1864). *A New History of Painting in Italy from the Second to the Sixteenth Century*, vol. I (London)
Curzi, Gaetano (2011). 'Giotto "finxit": Figurazione, rappresentazione degli edifici e illusionismo dei materiali nella pittura di Giotto', *Rivista d'Arte*, 5th ser., 1, pp. 3–38
Cutler, Anthony (1987). 'Under the Sign of the Deesis: On the Question of Representativeness in Medieval Art and Literature', *Dumbarton Oaks Papers* 41, pp. 145–54
Da Campagnola, Stanislao (1971). *L'Angelo del Sesto Sigillo e l''Alter Christus': genesi e sviluppo di due temi francescani nei secoli XIII–XIV* (Rome)
D'Acunto, Nicolangelo (2009). 'Le didascalie del ciclo francescano della Basilica Superiore di Assisi', in *Le immagini del francescanesimo* (Spoleto), pp. 169–93
Dalarun, Jacques (2002). *The Misadventure of Francis of Assisi: Towards a Historical Use of the Franciscan Legends*, trans. Edward Hagman (St. Bonaventure, NY)
D'Alatri, Mariano (1978). 'Panorama geografico, cronologico, e statistico sulla distribuzione degli *studia* degli ordini mendicanti: Italia', in *Le scuole degli ordini mendicanti (secoli XIII–XIV)* (Todi), pp. 49–72
Dante Alighieri (1971–5). *The Divine Comedy*, ed. and trans. Charles S. Singleton, 3 vols (London)
d'Avray, David (1985). *The Preaching of the Friars: Sermons diffused from Paris before 1300* (Oxford)
Davy, Marie-Madeleine (1931). *Les sermons universitaires parisiens de 1230–1231: Contribution à l'histoire de la prédication médiévale* (Paris)
De Angelis, Paolo (1621). *Basilicae S. Mariae Maioris de Urbe a Liberio Papa I usque ad Paulum V pont. max. descriptio et delineatio* (Rome)
de Blaauw, Sible (1986–7). 'Deambulatori e transetti: I casi di S. Maria Maggiore e del Laterano', *Rendiconti* 59, pp. 93–109
—— (1990). 'The Solitary Celebration of the Supreme Pontiff: The Lateran Basilica as the New Temple in the Medieval Liturgy of Maundy Thursday', in *Omnes circumadstantes: Contributions Towards a History of the Role of the People in the Liturgy, Presented to Herman Wegman*, ed. Charles Caspers and Marc Schneiders (Kampen), pp. 120–43
—— (1994). *Cultus et decor: Liturgia e architettura nella Roma tardoantica e medievale. Basilica Salvatoris, Sanctae Mariae, Sancti Petri*, 2 vols (Vatican City)
—— (2009). 'Arnolfo's High Altar Ciboria and Roman Liturgical Traditions', in *Arnolfo's Moment*, ed. David Friedman, Julian Gardner and Margaret Haines (Florence), pp. 123–40
—— (2011). 'Reception and Renovation of Early Christian Churches in Rome, c.1050–1300', in *Rome across Time and Space: Cultural Transmission and the Exchange of Ideas, c.500–1400*, ed. Claudia Bolgia, Rosamond McKitterick and John Osborne (Cambridge), pp. 151–66
The Deeds of Blessed Francis and his Companions (2001), in *Francis of Assisi: Early Documents*, ed. Regis J. Armstrong, William J. Short and J. A. Wayne Hellman, vol. III (New York), pp. 435–565
Degl'Innocenti Gambuti, Marcella (1977). *I codici miniati medievali della Biblioteca Comunale e dell'Accademia Etrusca di Cortona* (Florence)
De Kerval, Léon, ed. (1904). *Sancti Antonii de Padua vitae duae quarum altera hucusque inedita* (Paris)
Del Giudice, Giuseppe (1896). *La famiglia di Re Manfredi: Narrazione storica* (Naples)
Delorme, Ferdinand M. (1915). 'Un codex ignoré de la lettre de Philippe de Pérouse', *Archivum Franciscanum Historicum* 8, pp. 316–17
—— (1944). 'L'*Ars faciendi sermones* de Géraud du Pescher', *Antonianum* 19, pp. 169–98
—— (1945). 'Notice et extraits d'un manuscrit franciscain', *Collectanea Franciscana* 15, pp. 5–91
De Marchi, Andrea (2009). '*Cum dictum opus sit magnum*: Il documento pistoiese del 1274 e l'allestimento trionfale dei tramezzi in Umbria e Toscana fra Due e Trecento', in *Medioevo: Immagine e memoria*, ed. Arturo Carlo Quintavalle (Milan), pp. 603–21
Derbes, Anne (1996). *Picturing the Passion in Late Medieval Italy: Narrative Painting, Franciscan Ideologies, and the Levant* (Cambridge)
Derbes, Anne, and Mark Sandona (2008). *The Usurer's Heart: Giotto, Enrico Scrovegni, and the Arena Chapel in Padua* (University Park, PA)
De Wesselow, Thomas (2005). 'The Date of the St Francis Cycle in the Upper Church of San Francesco at Assisi: The Evidence of Copies and Considerations of Methods', in *The Art of the Franciscan Order in Italy*, ed. William R. Cook (Leiden), pp. 113–67
Digard, Georges, Maurice Faucon, Antoine Thomas and Robert Fawtier, eds (1884–1939). *Les registres de Boniface VIII: Recueil des bulles de ce pape*, 4 vols (Paris)
Dizionario biografico degli Italiani (1960–), ed. Istituto della Enciclopedia italiana (Rome)
Doucet, Victorin (1935). 'L'enseignement Parisien de Mathieu d'Aquasparta (1278–1279)', *Archivum Franciscanum Historicum* 28, pp. 568–70
Doyle, Eric, trans. and ed. (1983). *The Disciple and the Master: St. Bonaventure's Sermons on St. Francis of Assisi* (Chicago)

Dozzini, Bruno (2006). *Giotto: The 'Legend of St. Francis' in the Assisi Basilica* (Assisi)

Droandi, Isabella (2010). 'Per la pittura del Duecento nell'Aretino', in *Arte in terra d'Arezzo: Il medioevo*, ed. Marco Collareta and Paola Refice (Florence), pp. 181–206

Duffy, Eamon (1997). 'Finding St. Francis: Early Images, Early Lives', in *Medieval Theology and the Natural Body*, ed. Peter Biller and A. J. Minnis (York), pp. 193–236

Durliat, Marcel (1995). *Le parement d'autel brodé du Musée Paul-Dupuy*, Les Cahiers du Musée Paul-Dupuy, vol. I (Toulouse)

Ehrle, Franz (1892). 'Die ältesten Redactionen der Generalconstitutionen des Franziskanerordens', *Archiv für Literatur- und Kirchengeschichte des Mittelalters* 6, pp. 1–138

Einhorn, Jürgen W. (1992). 'Das große Franziskusleben des Hl. Bonaventura in zwei illuminierten Handschriften in Rom und Madrid', *Collectanea Franciscana* 62/1–2, pp. 5–61

Emmen, Aquilino and Feliciano Simoncioli (1963). 'La dottrina dell'Olivi sulla contemplazione, la vita attiva e mista', *Studi Francescani* 60, pp. 382–445

Eubel, Konrad (1913). *Hierarchia catholica medii aevi (medii et recentioris aevi)*, vol. I (1898); 2nd edn (Münster)

Faloci Pulignani, Michele (1886). 'Le sacre reliquie della Basilica di San Francesco in Assisi nel secolo XIV', *Miscellanea Francescana* 1, pp. 145–50

Fausti, Luigi (1917–19). 'Le pergamene dell'archivio del duomo di Spoleto', *Archivio per la Storia Ecclesiastica dell'Umbria* 4, pp. 287–416

Fea, Carlo (1820). *Descrizione ragionata della sagrosanta patriarcal basilica e cappella papale di S. Francesco d'Assisi, nella quale recentemente si è ritrovato il sepolcro e il corpo di sì gran santo e delle pitture e sculture di cui va ornato il medesimo tempio* (Rome)

Federici, Vincenzo (1899–1900). 'Regesto del Monastero di S. Silvestro de Capite', *Archivio della Reale Società Romana di Storia Patria* 22, pp. 213–300, 489–538; 23, pp. 67–128, 411–47

Field, Sean (1999). 'Annihilation and Perfection in Two Sermons by Gilbert of Tournai for the Translation of St. Francis', *Franciscana* 1, pp. 237–74

Finnegan, Suzanne M. (2008). '*The Lamentation of the Clares* in the Basilica of San Francesco at Assisi: Unveiling Meanings in a Forgotten Masterpiece', unpublished MA dissertation, Courtauld Institute of Art, London

Fisher, M. Roy (1956). 'Assisi, Padua and the Boy in the Tree', *Art Bulletin* 38, pp. 47–52

Fleming, John V. (1982). *From Bonaventure to Bellini: An Essay in Franciscan Exegesis* (Princeton, NJ)

Flood, David (2002). 'John of Wales' Commentary on the Franciscan Rule', *Franciscan Studies* 60, pp. 93–138

Forcella, Vincenzo (1869–84). *Iscrizioni delle chiese e d'altri edificii di Roma dal secolo XI fino ai giorni nostri*, 14 vols (Rome)

Franchi, Antonino (1990). *Nicolaus Papa IV, 1288–1292 (Girolamo d'Ascoli)* (Ascoli Piceno)

Frugoni, Chiara (1988). *Francesco: Un'altra storia* (Genoa)

—— (1993). *Francesco e l'invenzione delle stimmate: Una storia per parole e immagini fino a Bonaventura e Giotto* (Turin)

—— (1998). *Francis of Assisi: A Life*, trans. John Bowden (London)

—— (2001). 'L'ombra della Porziuncola nella Basilica Superiore di Assisi', *Mitteilungen des Kunsthistorischen Institutes in Florenz* 45, pp. 345–93

—— (2004a). 'Edifici e colonne nella Roma della "Liberazione di Pietro di Alife" ad Assisi', in *Domus et splendida palatia: Residenze papali e cardinalizie a Roma fra XII e XV secolo*, ed. Alessio Monciatti (Pisa), pp. 107–32

—— (2004b). 'Sui vari significati del Natale di Greccio, nei testi e nelle immagini', *Frate Francesco* 70, pp. 35–147

—— (2010a). 'La colonna spezzata', *Ricerche di Storia dell'Arte* 102, pp. 79–82

—— (2010b). *Le storie di San Francesco: Guida agli affreschi della Basilica Superiore di Assisi* (Turin)

—— (2011a). 'Gli affreschi della Basilica Superiore di Assisi: Una committenza di Papa Niccolò IV?', in *Arbor ramosa: Studi per Antonio Rigon da allievi, amici, colleghi*, ed. Luciano Bertazzo, Donato Gallo, Raimondo Michetti and Andrea Tilatti (Padua), pp. 215–23

—— (2011b). 'Playing with Clouds', *Burlington Magazine* 153, pp. 518–20

—— (2012a). 'Franciscan Iconographic Themes in the Altar Hanging of Toulouse: An overview', in *Le parement d'autel des Cordeliers de Toulouse. Anatomie d'un chef d'oeuvre du XIV siècle*, ed. Maria Alessandra Bilotta and Marie-Pierre Chaumet-Sarkissian (Toulouse), pp. 143–59

—— (2012b). 'Le ragione del diavolo nella nuvola nel ciclo francescano della Basilica Superiore di Assisi', *Frate Francescano* 78, pp. 371–86

Fussenegger, Geroldus, ed. (1960). 'Statuta provinciae Alemaniae Superioris annis 1303, 1309 et 1341 condita', *Archivum Franciscanum Historicum* 53, pp. 233–75

Gandolfo, Francesco (1983). 'Assisi e il Laterano', *Archivio della Società Romana di Storia Patria* 106, pp. 63–113

Garber, Josef (1918). *Wirkungen der Frühchristlichen Gemäldezyklen der alten Peters- und Pauls-Basiliken in Rom* (Berlin)

Gardner, Julian (1970). 'The Capocci Tabernacle in S. Maria Maggiore', *Papers of the British School at Rome* 38, pp. 220–30

—— (1971). 'S. Paolo fuori le Mura: Nicholas III and Pietro Cavallini', *Zeitschrift für Kunstgeschichte* 34, pp. 240–48
—— (1973a). 'Arnolfo di Cambio and Roman Tomb Design', *Burlington Magazine* 115, pp. 420–39
—— (1973b). 'Copies of Roman Mosaics in Edinburgh', *Burlington Magazine* 115, pp. 583–91
—— (1973c). 'Pope Nicholas IV and the Decoration of Santa Maria Maggiore', *Zeitschrift für Kunstgeschichte* 36, pp. 1–50
—— (1975). 'Some Cardinals' Seals of the Thirteenth Century', *Journal of the Warburg and Courtauld Institutes* 38, pp. 72–96
—— (1981). 'Some Franciscan Altars of the Thirteenth and Fourteenth Centuries', in *The Vanishing Past: Studies of Medieval Art, Liturgy and Metrology, Presented to Christopher Hohler*, ed. Alan Borg and Andrew Martindale (Oxford), pp. 29–38
—— (1982). 'The Louvre Stigmatization and the Problem of the Narrative Altarpiece', *Zeitschrift für Kunstgeschichte* 45, pp. 217–47
—— (1992). *The Tomb and the Tiara: Curial Tomb Sculpture in Rome and Avignon in the Later Middle Ages* (Oxford)
—— (1997). 'The Artistic Patronage of Pope Nicholas IV', *Annali della Scuola Normale Superiore di Pisa*, 4th ser., Quaderni 2, pp. 1–8
—— (2005). 'A Minor Episode of Public Disorder in Assisi: Francis Renounces his Inheritance', *Zeitschrift für Kunstgeschichte* 68, pp. 275–85
—— (2011). '"For whom the bell tolls": A Franciscan Bell-Founder, Franciscan Bells and a Franciscan Patron in Late Thirteenth-Century Rome', in *Medioevo: I committenti*, ed. Arturo Carlo Quintavalle (Milan), pp. 460–68
Garms, Jörg, Roswitha Juffinger and Bryan Ward-Perkins (1981). *Die mittelalterlichen Grabmäler in Rom und Latium vom 13. bis zum 15. Jahrhundert*, vol. I: *Die Grabplatten und Tafeln* (Rome and Vienna)
Gay, Jules, and Suzanne Vitte, eds (1938). *Les registres de Nicolas III (1277–1280): Recueil des bulles de ce pape* (Paris)
Gerson, Paula Lieber (1986). 'Suger as Iconographer: The Central Portal of the West Facade of Saint-Denis', in *Abbot Suger and Saint-Denis: A Symposium*, ed. Paula Lieber Gerson (New York), pp. 183–98
Gieben, Servus (1996). 'Per la storia dell'abito francescano', *Collectanea Franciscana* 66, pp. 431–78
—— (2001). 'La croce con frate Elia di Giunta Pisano', in *Il cantiere pittorico della Basilica Superiore di San Francesco in Assisi*, ed. Giuseppe Basile and Pasquale Magro (Assisi), pp. 101–10
Ginsberg, Warren (1982). 'Dante's Dream of the Eagle and Jacob's Ladder', *Dante Studies* 100, pp. 41–69
Giusto, Egidio (1911). *Le vetrate di S. Francesco in Assisi: studio storico iconografico* (Milan)
Goldschmidt, Adolph, and Kurt Weitzmann (1979). *Die byzantinischen Elfenbeinskulpturen des X.–XIII. Jahrhunderts*, 2 vols (Berlin)
Gordon, Dillian (1982). 'A Perugian Provenance for the Franciscan Double-Sided Altar-Piece by the Maestro di S. Francesco', *Burlington Magazine* 124, pp. 70–77
Gregorovius, Ferdinand (1859–72). *Geschichte der Stadt Rom im Mittelalter: Vom fünften Jahrhundert bis zum sechzehnten Jahrhundert*, 8 vols (Stuttgart)
Gregory the Great (1874). *Moralia in Job*, in *Patrologiae Latinae*, ed. J.-P. Migne, vol. LXXV (Paris), cols 509–1162
Grimaldi, Giacomo (1972). *Descrizione della basilica antica di S. Pietro in Vaticano: Codice Barberini latino 2733*, ed. Reto Niggl (Vatican City)
Guarino, Francesco (2007). 'Il fondo *diplomatico* dell'Archivio Storico Comunale di Bevagna: Inventario-regesto', *Archivi in Valle Umbra* 9, pp. 3–108
Guerrieri, Ruggero (1933). *Storia civile ed ecclesiastica del comune di Gualdo Tadino* (Gubbio)
Henri d'Avranches (1999). 'The Versified Life of St. Francis', in *Francis of Assisi: Early Documents*, ed. Regis J. Armstrong, William J. Short and J. A. Wayne Hellman, vol. I (New York), pp. 421–520
Herde, Peter (1993). 'Matteo d'Acquasparta cardinale', in *Matteo d'Acquasparta: Francescano, filosofo, politico*, ed. Enrico Menestò (Spoleto), pp. 79–108
Hertlein, Edgar (1964). *Die Basilika San Francesco in Assisi: Gestalt, Bedeutung, Herkunft* (Florence)
Hills, Paul (1987). *The Light of Early Italian Painting* (New Haven and London)
Hoffmann, Hartmut, ed. (1980). *Chronica monasterii Casinensis*, Monumenta Germaniae Historica: *Scriptores*, vol. XXXIV (Hanover)
Huber, Raphael M. (1948). *St. Anthony of Padua, Doctor of the Church Universal: A Critical Study of the Historical Sources of the Life, Sanctity, Learning, and Miracles of the Saint of Padua and Lisbon* (Milwaukee)
Hueck, Irene (1981a). 'La basilica francescana di Assisi nell'Ottocento: Alcuni documenti su restauri progettati ed interventi eseguiti', *Bollettino d'Arte*, 6th ser., 12, pp. 143–52
—— (1981b). 'Cimabue und das Bildprogramm der Oberkirche von San Francesco in Assisi', *Mitteilungen des Kunsthistorischen Institutes in Florenz* 25, pp. 279–324
—— (1982). 'L'oreficeria in Umbria dalla seconda metà del secolo XII alla fine del XIII', in *Francesco d'Assisi: Storia e arte*, ed. Francesco Porzio (Milan), pp. 168–87

—— (1983). 'Il cardinale Napoleone Orsini e la cappella di S. Nicola nella basilica francescana ad Assisi', in *Roma anno 1300*, ed. Angiola Maria Romanini (Rome), pp. 187–98

—— (1984). 'Der Lettner der Unterkirche von San Francesco in Assisi', *Mitteilungen des Kunsthistorischen Institutes in Florenz* 28, pp. 173–202

—— (1997). Review of Marino Bigaroni, Hans-Rudolf Meier and Elvio Lunghi, *La basilica di Santa Chiara in Assisi* (Perugia, 1994), in *Kunstchronik* 50, pp. 287–92

—— (2001). 'La Basilica Superiore come luogo liturgico: L'arredo e il programma della decorazione', in *Il cantiere pittorico della Basilica Superiore di San Francesco in Assisi*, ed. Giuseppe Basile and Pasquale Magro (Assisi), pp. 43–69

Iacovelli, Anacleto (1972). 'L'altare della Chiesa Superiore', *San Francesco Patrono d'Italia* 52, pp. 132–9

Inga, Giuseppina (1978). 'Gli insediamenti mendicanti a Cortona', *Storia della Città* 3/9, pp. 44–55

Inventaire Général des Monuments et Richesses Artistiques de la France (1986). *Les vitraux de Bourgogne, Franche-Comté et Rhône-Alpes*, Corpus Vitrearum: France, Série complémentaire: Recensement des vitraux anciens de la France, vol. III (Paris)

Israëls, Machtelt (2003). *Sassetta's Madonna della Neve: An Image of Patronage* (Leiden)

——, ed. (2009). *Sassetta: The Borgo San Sepolcro Altarpiece*, 2 vols (Florence and Leiden)

Jacobilli, Lodovico (1646). *Discorso della città di Foligno: Cronologia de' vescovi, governatori e podestà ch'hanno retta essa città* (Foligno)

Jacobus de Voragine (1993). *The Golden Legend: Readings on the Saints*, trans. and ed. William Granger Ryan, 2 vols (Princeton, NJ)

James of Milan (1949). *Stimulus amoris Fr. Iacobi Mediolanensis; Canticum pauperis Fr. Ioannis Peckam*, ed. Collegio San Bonaventura (Quaracchi)

—— (1999). *Love's Prompting by James of Milan and a Canticle to Poverty by John of Pecham*, trans. Campion Murray (Box Hill, Victoria), published online at http://www.franciscans.org.au/spirituality/campion/Love's%20Prompting/Love's%20Prompting.pdf

John Damascene (1955). *De fide orthodoxa: Versions of Burgundio and Cerbanus*, ed. Eligius M. Buytaert (St. Bonventure, NY)

John of Caulibus (2000). *Meditations on the Life of Christ*, trans. and ed. Francis X. Taney Sr., Anne Miller and C. Mary Stallings-Taney (Asheville, NC)

John of Wales (1489/1964). *Communiloquium, sive Summa collationum Johannis Gallensis* (Strasbourg); facsimile edn (Wakefield)

—— *A Meditation in Solitude*, trans. Campion Murray, published online at http://www.franciscans.org.au/spirituality/campion/a%20meditation%20in%20solitude.pdf

John Pecham (1999). *A Canticle to Poverty* in James of Milan, *Love's Prompting by James of Milan and a Canticle to Poverty by John of Pecham*, trans. Campion Murray (Box Hill, Victoria), published online at http://www.franciscans.org.au/spirituality/campion/Love's%20Prompting/A%20Canticle%20to%20Poverty.pdf

Johnson, Timothy J. (2000). *The Soul in Ascent: Bonaventure on Poverty, Prayer, and Union with God* (Quincy, IL)

—— (2007). 'The Prothemes of Bonaventure's *Sermones dominicales* and Minorite Prayer', in *Franciscans at Prayer*, ed. Timothy J. Johnson (Leiden), pp. 95–122

——, ed. (1999). *Bonaventure: Mystic of God's Word* (New York)

Kessler, Herbert L. (1989). '"Caput et speculum omnium ecclesiarum": Old St. Peter's and Church Decoration in Medieval Latium', in *Italian Church Decoration of the Middle Ages and Early Renaissance: Functions, Forms, and Regional Traditions*, ed. William Tronzo (Bologna), pp. 119–46; repr. in Kessler (2002b), pp. 45–74

—— (2002a). 'Corporeal Texts, Spiritual Paintings, and the Mind's Eye', in Kessler (2002b), pp. 159–78; repr. in *Reading Images and Texts: Medieval Images and Texts as Forms of Communication*, ed. Mariëlle Hageman and Marco Mostert (Turnhout, 2005), pp. 9–61

—— (2002b) *Old St. Peter's and Church Decoration in Medieval Italy* (Spoleto)

—— (2002c). 'Old St. Peter's as the Source and Inspiration of Medieval Church Decoration', in Kessler (2002b), pp. 75–96; first published in Italian as 'L'antica basilica di San Pietro come fonte e ispirazione per la decorazione delle chiese medievali', in *Fragmenta picta: Affreschi e mosaici staccati nel medioevo romano*, ed. Maria Andaloro (Rome, 1989), pp. 45–64

—— (2002d). 'St. Peter's Basilica at the Time of the First Jubilee', in Kessler (2002b), pp. 1–13; first published in Italian as 'La decorazione della basilica medievale di San Pietro', in *Romei e Giubilei: Il pellegrinaggio medievale a San Pietro (350–1350)*, ed. Mario D'Onofrio (Rome, 1999), pp. 263–70

Kleinschmidt, Beda (1915–28). *Die Basilika San Francesco in Assisi*, 3 vols (Berlin)

Krüger, Klaus (1992). *Der Frühe Bildkult des Franziskus in Italien: Gestalt- und Funktionswandel des Tafelbildes im 13. und 14. Jahrhundert* (Berlin)

La Malfa, Claudia (2003). 'Reassessing the Renaissance of the Palestrina Nile Mosaic', *Journal of the Warburg and Courtauld Institutes* 66, pp. 267–71

Landini, Lawrence C. (1968). *The Causes of the Clericalization of the Order of Friars Minor, 1209–1260, in the Light of Early Franciscan Sources* (Chicago)

Langlois, Ernest, ed. (1905). *Les registres de Nicolas IV: Recueil des bulles de ce pape* (Paris)

Lauer, Philippe (1911). *Le Palais de Latran: Étude historique et archéologique* (Paris)

Lavin, Marilyn Aronberg (1990). *The Place of Narrative: Mural Decoration in Italian Churches, 431–1600* (Chicago)

Lemmens, Leonardus, ed. (1926). *Testimonia minora saeculi XIII de S. Francisco Assisiensi* (Quaracchi)

Le Pogam, Pierre-Yves (2005). *De la 'Cité de Dieu' au 'Palais du Pape': Les résidences pontificales dans la seconde moitié du XIIIe siècle (1254–1304)* (Rome)

Lisner, Margrit (1990). 'Die Gewandfarben der Apostel in Giottos Arenafresken: Farbgebung und Farbikonographie', *Zeitschrift für Kunstgeschichte* 53, pp. 309–75

Little, A. G., ed. (1914). 'Definitiones capitulorum generalium Ordinis Fratrum Minorum, 1260–1282', *Archivum Franciscanum Historicum* 7, pp. 675–82

—— (1924). 'Measures Taken by the Prelates of France against the Friars (c.A.D. 1289–90)', in *Miscellanea Francesco Ehrle*, vol. III (Rome), pp. 49–66

Lloyd, Joan E. Barclay (2002). 'The River of Life in the Medieval Mosaics of S. Maria Maggiore in Rome', in *Reading Texts and Images: Essays on Medieval and Renaissance Art and Patronage in Honour of Margaret M. Manion*, ed. Bernard J. Muir (Exeter), pp. 35–55

Longpré, Efrem (1923). 'Bartolommeo di Bologna: Un maestro francescano del secolo XIII', *Studi Francescani* 9, pp. 365–84

—— (1928). 'Matthieu d'Aquasparta', *Dictionnaire de théologie catholique*, vol. X (Paris), cols 375–89

López, Athanasius (1908). 'Litterae ineditae Fr. Hieronymi ab Asculo Gen. Min. (1274–79): De additione facienda in Legenda Maj. S. Bonaventurae', *Archivum Franciscanum Historicum* 1, pp. 85–7

Luard, Henry Richards, ed. (1864–9), *Annales monastici*, 5 vols (London)

Ludovico of Pietralunga (1982). *Descrizione della Basilica di S. Francesco e di altri santuari di Assisi*, ed. Pietro Scarpellini (Treviso)

Lunardi, Roberto (2001). 'Santa Maria Novella and Giotto's Crucifix', in *Giotto: The Santa Maria Novella Crucifix*, ed. Marco Ciatti and Max Seidel (Florence), pp. 159–81

Lunghi, Elvio (1988). '"Come pintor che con essemplo pinga" (Purg., XXXII, 67)', in *Il tempio del santo patrono: Riflessi storico-artistici del culto di San Fortunato a Todi*, ed. Marcello Castrichini *et al.* (Todi), pp. 121–60

—— (1995a). *Il crocefisso di Giunta Pisano e l'icona del 'Maestro di San Francesco' alla Porziuncola* (Assisi)

—— (1995b). 'Presenza di Federico II nella chiesa di S. Francesco ad Assisi', in *Assisi al tempo di Federico II*, ed. Francesco Santucci (Assisi), pp. 213–42

—— (1997). 'Un "buon governo" nella leggenda francescana di Assisi?', in *In memoria di Salvatore Vivona: Saggi e studi*, ed. Giuseppe Catanzaro (Assisi), pp. 247–66

—— (2000). *La passione degli umbri: Crocifissi di legno in Valle Umbra tra medioevo e Rinascimento* (Foligno)

Maccarrone, Michele (1971). 'La storia della cattedra', in *La cattedra lignea di S. Pietro in Vaticano, Atti della Pontificia Accademia Romana di Archeologia: Memorie*, vol. X (Rome), pp. 3–70

—— (1983). 'Il sepolcro di Bonifacio VIII nella basilica vaticana', in *Roma anno 1300*, ed. Angiola Maria Romanini (Rome), pp. 753–71

McKay, Hugh, ed. (1963). *The Little Flowers of St. Francis. The Mirror of Perfection. St. Bonaventure's Life of St. Francis* (London and New York)

McNamer, Sarah (2009). 'The Origins of the *Meditationes vitae Christi*', *Speculum* 84, pp. 905–55

Maginnis, Hayden B. J. (1975). 'Assisi Revisited: Notes on Recent Observations', *Burlington Magazine* 117, pp. 511–17

—— (1980). 'A Lorenzettian Crucifix in Cortona', *Revue de l'Art Canadienne / Canadian Art Review* 7, pp. 59–61

Maines, Clark (1986). 'Good Works, Social Ties, and the Hope for Salvation: Abbot Suger and Saint-Denis', in *Abbot Suger and Saint-Denis: A Symposium*, ed. Paula Lieber Gerson (New York), pp. 77–94

Manacorda, Daniele (1982). *Archeologia urbana a Roma: Il progetto della Crypta Balbi* (Florence)

—— (2001). *Crypta Balbi: Archeologia e storia di un paesaggio urbano* (Milan)

Mann, H. K. (1928). *Tombs and Portraits of the Popes of the Middle Ages* (London)

Marinangeli, Bonaventura (1911). 'La serie di affreschi giotteschi rappresentanti la vita di S. Francesco nella Chiesa Superiore di Assisi', *Miscellanea Francescana* 13, pp. 97–112

Marrone, Steven (2001). *The Light of Thy Countenance: Science and Knowledge of God in the Thirteenth Century*, 2 vols (Leiden)

Martin, Frank (1993). *Die Apsisverglasung der Oberkirche von S. Francesco in Assisi: Ihre Entstehung und Stellung innerhalb der Oberkirchenausstattung* (Worms)

—— (1996). 'The St. Francis Master in the Upper Church of S. Francesco/Assisi: Some Considerations Regarding his Origins', *Gesta* 35, pp. 177–91

Martin, Frank, and Gerhard Ruf (1997). *Die Glasmalereien von San Francesco in Assisi: Entstehung und Entwicklung einer Gattung in Italien* (Regensburg)

Matthiae, Guglielmo (1967). *Mosaici medievali delle chiese di Roma* (Rome)

Matthew of Acquasparta (1962). *Matthaei ab Aquasparta O.F.M., S.R.E. Cardinalis, Sermones de S. Francisco, de S. Antonio et de S. Clara*, ed. Gedeon Gál (Quaracchi)

—— *Sermons on Saint Francis*, trans. Campion Murray, published online at http://www.franciscans.org.au/spirituality/campion/Aquasparta-3/St%20Francis.htm

Meiss, Millard (1964). *Giovanni Bellini's St. Francis in the Frick Collection* (Princeton, NJ)

Menestò, Enrico (1993). 'La biblioteca di Matteo d'Acquasparta', in *Matteo d'Acquasparta: Francescano, filosofo, politico*, ed. Enrico Menestò (Spoleto), pp. 257–89

Menestò, Enrico, Stefano Brufani and Giuseppe Cremascoli, eds (1995). *Fontes franciscani* (Assisi)

Merlo, Grado G. (1991). 'Eremitismo nel francescanesimo medievale', in *Eremitismo nel francescanesimo medievale* (Assisi), pp. 29–50

Meyer, Ann R. (2003). *Medieval Allegory and the Building of the New Jerusalem* (Cambridge)

Milizia, Umberto Maria (1994). *Il ciclo di Giotto ad Assisi: Struttura di una leggenda* (Rome)

Monacchia, Paola (1984). *Regesti delle pergamene di S. Francesco al Prato di Perugia (1245–1777)* (Assisi)

—— (2002). 'Archivi e conservazione della memoria', in *Assisi anno 1300*, ed. Stefano Brufani and Enrico Menestò (Assisi), pp. 377–404

Montgomery, James A., trans. and ed. (1927). *The History of Yaballaha III, Nestorian Patriarch and of his Vicar Bar Sauma* (New York)

Moorman, John (1968). *A History of the Franciscan Order from its Origins to the Year 1517* (Oxford)

Morello, Giovanni, and Laurence B. Kanter, eds (1999). *The Treasury of Saint Francis of Assisi* (Milan)

Mortier, Daniel Antonin (1905). *Histoire des maîtres généraux de l'Ordre des Frères Prêcheurs*, vol. II (Paris)

Mozzo, Marco (2003). 'Cavalcaselle e la Basilica Superiore di San Francesco ad Assisi: Documentazione, conservazione e restauro, 1860–1892', unpublished doctoral thesis, Scuola Normale Superiore di Pisa

Müntz, Eugène (1879). 'Notes sur les mosaïques chrétiennes de l'Italie, VI: Des éléments antiques dans les mosaïques romaines du moyen âge', *Revue Archéologique*, 38, pp. 109–17

Neff, Amy (2006). 'Lesser Brothers: Franciscan Mission and Identity at Assisi', *Art Bulletin* 88, pp. 676–706

—— (2007). 'Byzantine Icons, Franciscan Prayer: Images of Intercession and Ascent in the Upper Church of San Francesco, Assisi', in *Franciscans at Prayer*, ed. Timothy J. Johnson (Leiden), pp. 357–82

—— (2011). 'The Humble Man's Wedding: Two Late Thirteenth-Century Franciscan Images of the *Miracle at Cana*', in *Gothic Art and Thought in the Later Medieval Period: Essays in Honor of Willibald Sauerländer*, ed. Colum Hourihane (Princeton, NJ), pp. 292–323

Nessi, Silvestro (1980). 'Il tesoro di S. Francesco in Assisi: Formazione e dispersione', in *Il tesoro della Basilica di San Francesco ad Assisi*, ed. Maria G. Ciardi Dupré dal Poggetto (Assisi), pp. 13–23

—— (1994). *La Basilica di S. Francesco in Assisi e la sua documentazione storica* (1982); 2nd edn (Assisi)

—— (1995). 'La Chiesa Superiore di San Francesco in Assisi nel 1253', *Paragone (Arte)* 46, pp. 84–93

—— (2005). 'La grande croce dipinta da Giunta Pisano per la Basilica di San Francesco in Assisi', *Il Santo* 45, pp. 691–721

Nicolini, Ugolino (1982). 'I francescani tra scuole e università in Umbria', in *Francesco d'Assisi: Documenti e archivi, codici e biblioteche, miniature*, ed. Francesco Porzio (Milan), pp. 119–34

Odericus Canonicus (1766). *Ordo officiorum ecclesiae Senensis, ab Odorico, ejusdem ecclesiae canonico, anno MCCXIII compositus*, ed. Giovanni Crisostomo Trombelli (Bologna)

Oertel, Robert (1937). 'Giotto-Ausstellung in Florenz', *Zeitschrift für Kunstgeschichte* 6, pp. 219–38

Offner, Richard (1927). 'A Great "Madonna" by the St. Cecilia Master', *Burlington Magazine* 50, pp. 91–104

Oliger, Livario (1911). 'Due musaici con S. Francesco della chiesa di Aracoeli in Roma', *Archivum Franciscanum Historicum* 4, pp. 213–51

—— (1935). 'B. Margherita Colonna (†1280): Le due vite scritte dal fratello Giovanni Colonna senatore di Roma e da Stefania monaca di S. Silvestro in Capite, testi inediti del secolo XIII', *Lateranum*, new ser., 1/2, pp. 1–238

Osborne, John (2012). 'A Possible Colonna Family *stemma* in the Church of Santa Prassede, Rome', in *A Wider Trecento: Studies in 13th- and 14th-Century European Art Presented to Julian Gardner*, ed. Louise Bourdua and Robert Gibbs (Leiden and Boston), pp. 21–30

Pace, Valentino (1991). 'Committenza benedettina a Roma: Il caso di San Paolo fuori le mura nel XIII secolo: per Richard Krautheimer', *Zeitschrift für Kunstgeschichte* 54, pp. 181–9

—— (1993). 'La committenza artistica del cardinale Matteo d'Acquasparta nel quadro della cultura figurativa del suo tempo', in *Matteo d'Acquasparta: Francescano, filosofo, politico*, ed. Enrico Menestò (Spoleto), pp. 311–30

—— (1996). 'Per Iacopo Torriti, frate, architetto e "pictor"', *Mitteilungen des Kunsthistorischen Institutes in Florenz* 40, pp. 212–21

Pachymeres, George (1865). *De Michaele Palaeologo*, in *Patrologiae Graecae*, ed. J.-P. Migne, vol. CXLIII (Paris), cols 443–996

Pagnotti, Francesco (1898). 'Niccolò da Calvi e la sua vita d'Innocenzo IV con una breve introduzione sulla istoriografia pontificia dei secoli XIII e XIV', *Archivio della Reale Società Romana di Storia Patria* 21, pp. 7–120

Papini, Niccolò (1797). *L'Etruria francescana, o vero raccolta di notizie storiche interessanti l'Ordine de' Frati Minori conventuali di S. Francesco in Toscana*, vol. I (Siena)

Paravicini Bagliani, Agostino (1972). *Cardinali di curia e 'familiae' cardinalizie, dal 1227 al 1254*, 2 vols, Italia Sacra 18–19 (Padua)

Partner, Peter (1972). *The Lands of St. Peter: The Papal State in the Middle Ages and the Early Renaissance* (London)

Paschini, Pio (1955). *I Colonna* (Rome)

Pásztor, Edith (1993). 'L'età di Matteo d'Acquasparta', in *Matteo d'Acquasparta: Francescano, filosofo, politico*, ed. Enrico Menestò (Spoleto), pp. 19–50

Péano, Pierre (1983). 'Saint François au chapitre d'Arles', in *Francesco d'Assisi nella storia, secoli XIII–XV*, ed. Servus Gieben (Rome), pp. 239–49

Pellegrini, Luigi (1984). *Insediamenti francescani nell'Italia del Duecento* (Rome)

Pennacchi, Francesco (1919). 'Bullarium pontificium quod exstat in Archivio Sacri Conventus S. Francisci Assisiensis (nunc apud publicam Bibliothecam Assisii): Appendix', *Archivum Franciscanum Historicum* 12, pp. 471–543

Peters, Edward (1986). 'Restoring the Church and Restoring Churches: Event and Image in Franciscan Biography', *Franziskanische Studien* 68, pp. 213–36

Petrini, Pietrantonio (1793). *Di Sant'Agapito Prenestino, della basilica a lui eretta in Palestrina e delle sue reliquie ivi venerate* (Rome)

Piazza, Simone (2010). 'Mosaïques en façade des églises de Rome (XIIe–XIVe siècles): Renaissance et évolution d'un modèle paléochrétien', *Hortus Artium Medievalium* 16, pp. 125–38

Pietramellara, Carla, Alberto Arrighini, Claudio Batistini, and Massimo Lozza (1988). *Il Sacro Convento di Assisi* (Rome)

Pipino, Francesco (1726). *Chronicon Fratris Francisci Pipini Bononiensis Ordinis Praedicatorum*, ed. Luigi Antonio Muratori, Rerum Italicarum Scriptores, vol. IX (Milan), cols 583–748

Poeschke, Joachim (1983). 'Der "Franziskusmeister" und die Anfänge der Ausmalung von S. Francesco in Assisi', *Mitteilungen des Kunsthistorischen Institutes in Florenz* 27, pp. 125–70

Pomarici, Francesca (2006). 'Il presepe di Santa Maria Maggiore: Un riesame', in *Arnolfo di Cambio e la sua epoca: Costruire, scolpire, dipingere, decorare*, ed. Vittorio Franchetti Pardo (Rome), pp. 103–16

Porzio, Francesco, ed. (1982). *Francesco d'Assisi: Documenti e archivi, codici e biblioteche, miniature* (Milan)

Poulenc, Jérôme (1983). 'Saint François dans le "Vitrail des Anges" de l'Église Supérieure de la Basilique d'Assise', *Archivum Franciscanum Historicum* 76, pp. 701–13

Presutti, Giuseppe (1910). 'I Colonna di Riofreddo (sec. XIII e XIV)', *Archivio della Reale Società Romana di Storia Patria* 33, pp. 313–32

Ptolemy of Lucca (2009). *Historia ecclesiastica nova: nebst Fortsetzungen bis 1329*, ed. Ottavio Clavuot, Monumenta Germaniae Historica: *Scriptores*, vol. XXXIX (Hanover, 2009)

Ratzinger, Joseph (1971). *The Theology of History in St. Bonaventure* (Chicago)

Rehberg, Andreas (1999). *Kirche und Macht im römischen Trecento: Die Colonna und ihre Klientel auf dem kurialen Pfründenmarkt (1278–1378)* (Tübingen)

Robson, Janet (2004). 'Judas and the Franciscans: Perfidy Pictured in Lorenzetti's Passion Cycle at Assisi', *Art Bulletin* 86, pp. 31–57

—— (2005). 'The Pilgrim's Progress: Reinterpreting the Trecento Fresco Programme in the Lower Church at Assisi', in *The Art of the Franciscan Order in Italy*, ed. William R. Cook (Leiden), pp. 39–70

—— (2011). 'Assisi, Rome and the *Miracle of the Crib at Greccio*', in *Image, Memory and Devotion*, vol. II of *Liber amicorum Paul Crossley*, ed. Zoë Opačić and Achim Timmerman, Studies in Gothic Art (Leiden), pp. 145–56

Rocchi, Giuseppe (1982). *La Basilica di San Francesco ad Assisi: Interpretazione e rilievo* (Florence)

Rocchi Coopmans de Yoldi, Giuseppe (2002). 'L'architettura della Basilica di San Francesco di Assisi', in *La Basilica di San Francesco ad Assisi*, ed. Giorgio Bonsanti, 4 vols (Modena), vol. II/1: *Saggi*, pp. 17–111

Roest, Bert (2000). *A History of Franciscan Education (c.1210–1517)* (Leiden)

Romano, Serena (1998). 'La morte di San Francesco', *Zeitschrift für Kunstgeschichte* 61, pp. 339–68

—— (2001). *La Basilica di San Francesco ad Assisi: Pittori, botteghe, strategie narrative* (Rome)

—— (2006). 'I Colonna a Roma: 1288–1297', in *La nobiltà romana nel medioevo*, ed. Sandro Carocci (Rome), pp. 291–312
—— (2010). 'Le botteghe di Giotto: Qualche novità sulla cappella di San Nicola nella Basilica Inferiore di Assisi', in *Medioevo: Le officine*, ed. Arturo Carlo Quintavalle (Milan), pp. 584–96
Rosati, Fernando (1983). *La chiesa di San Francesco in Gubbio nella storia, nell'arte* (Città di Castello)
Rotondi, Giuseppe (1927). 'Una lettera al cardinale Federico Borromeo a proposito del crocifisso di Frate Elia', *Miscellanea Francescana* 27, pp. 189–97
Ruf, Gerhard (1974). *San Francesco e San Bonaventura: Un'interpretazione storico-salvifica degli affreschi della navata nella Chiesa Superiore di San Francesco in Assisi alla luce della teologia di San Bonaventura* (Assisi); rejacketed as *Giotto in Assisi: Nuova presentazione degli affreschi di Giotto nella Basilica Superiore*
—— (2004). *Die Fresken der Oberkirche San Francesco in Assisi: Ikonographie und Theologie* (Regensburg)
Sacchetti, Franco (1860–61). *Le novelle di Franco Sacchetti, pubblicate secondo la lezione del Codice Borghiniano, con note inedite di Vincenzio Borghini e Vincenzio Follini*, ed. Ottavio Gigli, 2 vols (Florence)
Salimbene of Parma (1905–13). *Cronica*, ed. Oswald Holder-Egger, Monumenta Germaniae Historica: *Scriptores*, vol. XXXII (Hanover and Leipzig)
—— (1966). *Cronica*, ed. Giuseppe Scalia, 2 vols (Bari)
Salter, E. Gurney, trans. (1926). *The Coming of the Friars to England and Germany, being the Chronicles of Brother Thomas of Eccleston and Brother Jordan of Giano* (London)
Salvi, Antonio (1990). 'Nicolai PP. IV musiva inscriptio in basilica lateranensi', *Collectanea Franciscana* 60, pp. 191–9
Sbaralea, G., *et al.*, eds (1759–68). *Bullarium franciscanum romanorum pontificum: Constitutiones, epistolas, ac diplomata continens tribus Ordinibus Minorum, Clarissarum, et Poenitentium a seraphico patriarcha Sancto Francisco institutis concessa ab illorum exordio ad nostra usque tempora*, 4 vols (Rome)
Scarpellini, Pietro (1978). 'Assisi e i suoi monumenti nella pittura dei secoli XIII–XIV', in *Assisi al tempo di San Francesco*, ed. Società Internazionale di Studi Francescani (Assisi), pp. 73–121
Scheeben, Heribert C., ed. (1935). 'Legenda Sancti Dominici', *Monumenta Ordinis Fratrum Praedicatorum Historica* 16, pp. 261–352
Schöne, Wolfgang (1957). 'Studien zur Oberkirche von Assisi', in *Festschrift Kurt Bauch*, ed. Berthold Hackelsberger, Georg Himmelheber and Michael Meier (Munich), pp. 50–116
Schuster, Ildefons (1912). 'Un protocollo di notar Pietro di Gregorio nell'archivio di Farfa', *Archivio della Reale Società Romana di Storia Patria* 35, pp. 541–82
Schwartz, Frithjof (2005). 'In medio ecclesiae: Giottos Tafelkreuz in Santa Maria Novella', *Wiener Jahrbuch für Kunstgeschichte* 54, pp. 95–114
Schwarz, Michael Viktor, with Michaela Zöschg (2008). *Giottus pictor*, vol. II: *Giottos Werke* (Vienna)
Sella, Pietro, ed. (1952). *Rationes decimarum Italiae nei secoli XIII e XIV: Umbria*, Studi e Testi, vol. CLXI (Vatican City)
Şenocak, Neslihan (2004). 'Circulation of Books in the Medieval Franciscan Order: Attitude, Methods, and Critics', *Journal of Religious History* 28/2, pp. 146–61
—— (2012a). 'The Franciscan *studium generale*: A New Interpretation', in *Philosophy and Theology in the 'studia' of the Religious Orders and at Papal and Royal Courts*, ed. Kent Emery Jr., William J. Courtenay and Stephen M. Metzger (Turnhout), pp. 221–36
—— (2012b) *The Poor and the Perfect: The Rise of Learning in the Franciscan Order, 1209–1310* (Ithaca and London)
Sensi, Mario (2002). *Il perdono di Assisi* (Assisi)
—— (2009). 'Gli spazi del *Liber*', in *Il 'Liber' di Angela da Foligno e la mistica dei secoli XIII–XIV in rapporto alle nuove culture*, ed. Enrico Menestò (Spoleto), pp. 257–312
Seppelt, Franz Xaver, ed. (1921). *Monumenta coelestiniana: Quellen zur Geschichte des Papstes Coelestin V* (Paderborn)
Smart, Alastair (1971). *The Assisi Problem and the Art of Giotto: A Study of the Legend of St. Francis in the Upper Church of San Francesco, Assisi* (Oxford); 2nd edn (1983)
—— (1978). *The Dawn of Italian Painting, 1250–1400* (Oxford)
Solberg, Gail E. (1992). 'A Reconstruction of Taddeo di Bartolo's Altar-Piece for S. Francesco a Prato, Perugia', *Burlington Magazine* 134, pp. 646–56
Sperandio, Bernardino (2001). 'Il restauro della santa cappella della Porziuncola in Santa Maria degli Angeli', *I Lunedì della Galleria* 6, pp. 59–110
Squadrani, Irenaeus (1932). 'Tractatus de luce Fr. Bartholomaei de Bononia', *Antonianum* 7, pp. 139–238, 337–76, 465–87
Stein, Judith E. (1976). 'Dating the Bardi St. Francis Master Dossal: Text and Image', *Franciscan Studies* 36, pp. 271–97
Stevenson, Joseph, ed. (1839). *Chronicon de Lanercost, 1201–1346: E codice Cottoniano nunc primum typis mandatum* (Edinburgh)
Supino, Igino Benvenuto (1924). *La Basilica di San Francesco d'Assisi* (Bologna)
—— (1926–7). 'La cappella di Gian Gaetano Orsini nella Basilica di S. Francesco d'Assisi', *Bollettino d'Arte*, 2nd ser., 6, pp. 131–5
Swanson, Jenny (1989). *John of Wales: A Study of the Works and Ideas of a Thirteenth-Century Friar* (Cambridge)
Tamanti, Giulia (2003). 'Il restauro degli affreschi di San Pietro in Valle: Aspetti tecnici e novità', in *Gli affreschi di San Pietro*

in Valle a Ferentillo: Le storie dell'Antico e del Nuovo Testamento, ed. Giulia Tamanti (Naples), pp. 11–40

Tenneroni, Annibale (1888). 'Inventario di sacri arredi appartenuti ai cardinali Bentivenga e Matteo Bentivenga d'Acquasparta', *Archivio Storico Italiano*, 5th ser., 2, pp. 260–66

Theis, Pia (2004). 'Die Oberkirche von S. Francesco in Assisi, oder *De missa pontificali*: Zur Ausstattung eines päpstlichen Sakralraumes', *Römische Historische Mitteilungen* 46, pp. 125–64

—— (2006). 'Visualisierung des Unsichtbaren: Päpstliche Liturgie in der Oberkirche von S. Francesco in Assisi', in *Architektur und Liturgie*, ed. Michael Altripp and Claudia Nauerth (Wiesbaden), pp. 53–61

Thier, Ludger, and Abele Calufetti, eds (1985). *Il libro della Beata Angela da Foligno: edizione critica* (Grottaferrata)

Thomas Aquinas (1911/1981). *Summa theologica*, vol. 4, trans. Fathers of the English Dominican Province (1911; repr. Allen, TX, 1981)

Thomas of Celano (1995), *Tractatus de miraculis Beati Francisci*, in *Fontes franciscani*, ed. Ernesto Menestò, Stefano Brufani and Giuseppe Cremascoli (Assisi), pp. 643–754; Eng. trans. as 'The Treatise on the Miracles of Saint Francis' in *Francis of Assisi: Early Documents*, ed. Regis J. Armstrong, William J. Short and J. A. Wayne Hellman, 3 vols (New York, 1999–2001), vol. II, pp. 399–468

—— (2011). *Memoriale: Editio critico-synoptica duarum redactionum ad fidem codicum manuscriptorum*, ed. Felice Accrocca and Aleksander Horowski (Rome)

Thomson, Williell R. (1975). *Friars in the Cathedral: The First Franciscan Bishops, 1226–1261* (Toronto)

Tomei, Alessandro (1987). 'Nuove acquisizioni per Jacopo Torriti a S. Giovanni in Laterano', *Arte Medievale*, pp. 183–203

—— (1990). *Iacobus Torriti pictor: Una vicenda figurativa del tardo Duecento romano* (Rome)

—— (2000). *Pietro Cavallini* (Milan)

Toubert, Hélène (1994). 'Desiderio da Montecassino', *Enciclopedia dell'arte medievale*, vol. V (Rome), pp. 640–43

Tripps, Johannes (2000). *Das handelnde Bildwerk in der Gotik: Forschungen zu den Bedeutungsschichten und der Funktion des Kirchengebäudes und seiner Ausstattung in der Hoch- und Spätgotik* (1998); 2nd edn (Berlin)

—— (2005). 'From Singing Saints to Descending Angels: Medieval Ceremonies and Cathedral Façades as Representations of the Heavenly Jerusalem', *Arte Cristiana* 93, pp. 1–13

Tronzo, William (1985). 'The Prestige of Saint Peter's: Observations on the Function of Monumental Narrative Cycles in Italy', in *Pictorial Narrative in Antiquity and the Middle Ages*, ed. Herbert L. Kessler and Marianna Shreve Simpson, Studies in the History of Art 16 (Washington, DC), pp. 93–112

Van Dijk, S. J. P. (1963). *Sources of the Modern Roman Liturgy: The Ordinals by Haymo of Faversham and Related Documents (1243–1307)*, 2 vols (Leiden)

Vasari, Giorgio (1965). *Lives of the Artists*, trans. George Bull, vol. I (London)

—— (1966–87). *Le vite de' più eccellenti pittori, scultori e architettori (nelle redazioni del 1550 e 1568)*, ed. Rosanna Bettarini and Paola Barocchi, 6 vols (Florence)

Vauchez, André (1968). 'Les stigmates de Saint François et leurs détracteurs dans les derniers siècles du moyen âge', *Mélanges d'Archéologie et d'Histoire* 80, pp. 595–625

—— (1993). *The Laity in the Middle Ages: Religious Beliefs and Devotional Practices*, ed. Daniel E. Bornstein, trans. Margery J. Schneider (Notre Dame, IN)

Vecchio, Silvana (1993). 'Elia d'Assisi', in *DBI* 42 (Rome), pp. 450–58

Venturi, Adolfo (1908). *La Basilica di Assisi* (Rome)

Venuti, Filippo (2004). *Notizie storiche e critiche sulla croce cortonese (De cruce cortonensi dissertatio)* (1751), ed. Edoardo Mori (Cortona)

Viscontini, Manuela (2006). 'I cicli vetero e neo testamentari nella navata di San Pietro in Vaticano', in *La pittura medievale a Roma, 312–1431*, vol. I: *Suburbio, Vaticano, Rione Monti*, ed. Maria Andaloro and Serena Romano (Milan), pp. 411–15

Wadding, Luke (1931). *Annales Minorum, seu Trium Ordinum a S. Francisco institutorum*, 8 vols (Lyon and Rome, 1625–54); rev. and expanded edn (Rome, 1731–1886); 3rd edn (Quaracchi)

Waetzoldt, Stephan (1964). *Die Kopien des 17. Jahrhunderts nach Mosaiken und Wandmalereien in Rom* (Vienna)

Waley, Daniel (1961). *The Papal State in the Thirteenth Century* (London)

—— (1982a). 'Agapito Colonna', in *DBI* 27 (Rome), pp. 253–4

—— (1982b). 'Giovanni Colonna', in *DBI* 27 (Rome), pp. 331–3

—— (1982c). 'Pietro Colonna', in *DBI* 27 (Rome), pp. 399–402

—— (1982d). 'Stefano Colonna, il Vecchio', in *DBI* 27 (Rome), pp. 433–7

—— (1983). 'Il Ducato di Spoleto dagli Svevi all'Albornez', in *Il Ducato di Spoleto*, vol. I (Spoleto), pp. 189–203

White, John (1956). 'Cavallini and the Lost Frescoes in S. Paolo', *Journal of the Warburg and Courtauld Institutes* 19, pp. 84–95

—— (1979). *Duccio: Tuscan Art and the Medieval Workshop* (London)

White, John, and Bruno Zanardi (1983). 'Cimabue and the Decorative Sequence in the Upper Church of S. Francesco,

Assisi', in *Roma anno 1300*, ed. Angiola Maria Romanini (Rome), pp. 103–17

Wiener, Jürgen (1991). *Die Bauskulptur von San Francesco in Assisi* (Werl/Westfalen)

Wolff, Ruth (1996). 'La "Liberazione dell'eretico Pietro": Considerazioni su un affresco nella Chiesa Superiore di San Francesco ad Assisi', *Arte Cristiana* 84, pp. 361–73

—— (2008). 'The Sealed Saint: Representations of Saint Francis of Assisi on Medieval Italian Seals', in *Good Impressions: Image and Authority in Medieval Seals*, ed. Noël Adams, John Cherry and James Robinson (London), pp. 91–9

Zaccaria, Giuseppe (1963). 'Diario storico della Basilica e Sacro Convento di S. Francesco in Assisi (1220–1927)', II: 'Trecento', *Miscellanea Francescana* 63, pp. 290–323

—— (1964). 'Diario storico della Basilica e Sacro Convento di S. Francesco in Assisi (1220–1927)', V: 'Seicento', *Miscellanea Francescana* 64, pp. 165–210

Zafarana, Zelina (1981). 'La predicazione francescana', in *Francescanesimo e vita religiosa dei laici nel '200* (Assisi), pp. 205–50

Zanardi, Bruno (2002). *Giotto e Pietro Cavallini: La questione di Assisi e il cantiere medievale della pittura a fresco* (Milan)

—— (2004). 'Giotto and the St. Francis Cycle at Assisi', in *The Cambridge Companion to Giotto*, ed. Anne Derbes and Mark Sandona (Cambridge), pp. 32–62

Zanardi, Bruno, Chiara Frugoni, and Federico Zeri (1996). *Il cantiere di Giotto: Le storie di San Francesco ad Assisi* (Milan)

Zazzera, Francesco (1628). *Della nobiltà dell'Italia*, vol. II (Naples)

Zucchetti, Giuseppe, ed. (1920). *Il Chronicon di Benedetto, monaco di S. Andrea del Soratte, e il Libellus de imperatoria potestate in urbe Roma* (Rome)

Illustration Credits

Alinari Archives, Florence: 1, 9, 42, 64, 145; Authors: 2, 3, 4, 16, 18, 32, 33, 35, 37, 38, 39, 40, 41, 43, 47, 54, 55, 72, 74, 77, 78, 84, 103, 130, 142, 156, 160, 161, 175, 178; Franco Cosimo Panini Editore © Management Fratelli Alinari: 5, 10, 48, 49, 57, 89, 165; Elvio Lunghi: 6, 60, 66, 67; Österreichische Nationalbibliothek, Vienna: 7; Stefan Diller www.assisi.de: 8, 12, 13, 28, 29, 31, 34, 36, 45, 46, 51, 53, 56, 58, 59, 65, 73, 75, 76, 79, 80, 81, 82, 83, 86, 87, 88, 91, 92, 93, 94, 95, 97, 98, 102, 104, 105, 106, 107, 108, 109, 110, 111, 112, 113, 114, 115, 116, 117, 119, 120, 121, 122, 123, 124, 125, 126, 127, 128, 131, 132, 133, 134, 135, 136, 137, 138, 139, 140, 141, 143, 144, 146, 147, 148, 149, 150, 151, 153, 154, 155, 157, 162, 163, 164, 166, 167, 168, 169, 176, 177, 179, 180, 181, 182, 183, 184, 185, 186, 187, 188, 189, 190, 191, 192, 193, 194, 195, 196, 197, 198, 199; © Photo SCALA, Florence: 11, 19, 24, 26, 129; Face2Face Studio Photographers, Rome: 14, 20, 21, 22, 25; Rijksarchief te Gent: 15; Galleria Colonna, Rome: 17; Biblioteca Hertziana, Rome: 23; National Gallery of Scotland, Edinburgh: 27; Elisabetta Cioni: 30; British School at Rome: 44; Dillian Gordon: 50; Ghigo Roli: 52; Istituto Storico dei Cappuccini, Rome: 61; Silvestro Nessi: 62; © Photo SCALA, Florence, courtesy of Ministero per i Beni e le Attività Culturali: 63, 118; Bruno Zanardi: 68; © Photo SCALA, Florence, courtesy of Fondo Edifici e Culto, Ministero dell'Interno: 69; © Photo SCALA, Florence, courtesy of White Images: 70; Paula Gerson and N. Geiger: 71; Kunsthistorisches Institut in Florenz: 85; Martin Brown: Map, 90, 96, 101; © 2013 Biblioteca Apostolica Vaticana: 99, 100, 152, 172; Réunion des Musée Nationaux (Musée du Louvre): 158; Sible de Blaauw/Machtelt Israëls: 159; Conway Library, Courtauld Institute of Art, courtesy of Evelyn Silber: 170; © Städel Museum, Frankfurt am Main: 171; Gaetano Poccetti/Biblioteca del Comune e dell'Accademia Etrusca di Cortona: 173, 174

Index

NOTE: Page numbers in italics refer to an illustration; page numbers followed by *n* and a number refer to information in a numbered note.